PENGUIN BOOKS

THE PENGUIN BOOK OF
TWENTIETH-CENTURY ESSAYS

Ian Hamilton has published two books of essays, *Walking Possessions* and *The Trouble with Money*, as well as biographies and poems. From 1974 to 1979 he edited the *New Review*.

D1330314

THE PENGUIN BOOK OF
Twentieth-Century Essays

Selected, with a Foreword and Notes by

IAN HAMILTON

PENGUIN BOOKS

PENGUIN BOOKS

Published by the Penguin Group
Penguin Books Ltd, 27 Wrights Lane, London w8 5TZ, England
Penguin Putnam Inc., 375 Hudson Street, New York, New York 10014, USA
Penguin Books Australia Ltd, Ringwood, Victoria, Australia
Penguin Books Canada Ltd, 10 Alcorn Avenue, Toronto, Ontario, Canada M4V 3B2
Penguin Books (NZ) Ltd, Private Bag 102902, NSMC, Auckland, New Zealand

Penguin Books Ltd, Registered Offices: Harmondsworth, Middlesex, England

First published by Allen Lane The Penguin Press 1999
Published in Penguin Books 2000
1 3 5 7 9 10 8 6 4 2

Printed in England by Clays Ltd, St Ives plc

Contents

CONTENTS

Acknowledgements

For permission to publish copyright material in this book grateful acknowledgement is made to the following:

A. Alvarez: 'Risk' from *GQ Magazine* (February 1991), © 1991 Al Alvarez, reprinted by permission of Gillon Aitken Associates; Kingsley Amis: 'Why Are You Telling Me All This?' from the *Spectator* (23 August 1986), © 1986 Kingsley Amis, reprinted by kind permission of Jonathan Clowes Ltd, London, on behalf of the Literary Estate of Sir Kingsley Amis; Martin Amis: 'Phantom of the Opera: the Republicans in 1988' from *Visiting Mrs Nabokov and Other Excursions* (Jonathan Cape, 1993), reprinted by permission of Random House UK Ltd and the Peters Fraser & Dunlop Group Ltd; Hannah Arendt: 'The Concentration Camps' from *Partisan Review*, Vol. XV, No. 7 (1948), reprinted by permission of Hannah Arendt Bluecher Literary Trust; W. H. Auden: 'The Guilty Vicarage' from *The Dyer's Hand* (Faber & Faber, 1963), reprinted by permission of the publisher; Maurice Baring: 'King Lear's Daughter' from *The Best of Modern Humour*, edited by Mordecai Richler (Allen Lane, 1983), reprinted by permission of A. P. Watt Ltd on behalf of The Trustees of Maurice Baring Will Trust; Julian Barnes: 'Mrs Thatcher Remembers' from *Letters from London* (Picador, 1995), reprinted by permission of Macmillan Ltd and The Peters Fraser & Dunlop Group Ltd; Max Beerbohm: 'Laughter' from *And Even Now* (Heinemann, 1920), reprinted by kind permission of Sir Rupert Hart-Davis; Edmund Blunden: 'The Somme Still Flows' from *Undertones of War* (Cobden-Sanderson, 1928), reprinted by permission of The Peters Fraser & Dunlop Group Ltd; John Carey: 'Down With Dons' from *Original Copy: Selected Reviews and Journalism* (Faber & Faber, 1987 originally published in *New Review*), reprinted by permission of the author; G. K. Chesterton: 'Woman' from *The Bodley Head G. K. Chesterton*, edited by P. J. Kavanagh (Bodley Head, 1985), reprinted by permission of A. P. Watt Ltd on behalf of The Royal Literary Fund; Joan Didion: 'Goodbye to All That' from *Slouching Towards Bethlehem*

(Andre Deutsch, 1968), reprinted by permission of the publisher; T. S. Eliot: 'Tradition and the Individual Talent' from *The Sacred Wood* (Methuen, 1920), reprinted by permission of Faber & Faber Ltd; F. Scott Fitzgerald: 'The Crack-Up' from *The Crack-Up and Other Stories* (Penguin Books, 1990), reprinted by permission of David Higham Associates; Paul Fussell: 'My War' from *The Boy Scout Handbook and Other Observations* (Oxford University Press, 1982), © 1982 by Oxford University Press Inc., reprinted by permission of the publisher; Martha Gellhorn: 'Memory' from *London Review of Books* (December 1996), reprinted by kind permission of the Martha Gellhorn estate; Graham Greene: 'The Lost Childhood' from *The Lost Childhood and Other Essays* (Eyre & Spottiswoode, 1951), reprinted by kind permission of David Higham Associates; Elizabeth Hardwick: 'The Oswald Family' from *Bartleby in Manhattan and Other Essays* (Random House, 1983), reprinted by kind permission of the author; A. P. Herbert: 'About Bathrooms' from *Light Articles Only* (Methuen, 1921), reprinted by permission of A. P. Watt Ltd on behalf of Crystal Hale and Jocelyn Herbert; Christopher Hitchens: 'On Not Knowing The Half Of It: Homage to Telegraphist Jacobs' from *Performance and Reality: Essays from Grand Street* (Hill & Wang, 1989), reprinted by permission of the author; Aldous Huxley: 'Sermons in Cats' from *Music at Night* (Fountain Press, 1931), reprinted by permission of Random House UK Ltd on behalf of Mrs Laura Huxley; Christopher Isherwood: 'The Head of a Leader' from *Exhumations* (Methuen, 1966), reprinted by permission of Random House UK Ltd; Dan Jacobson: 'Time of Arrival' from *Time of Arrival and Other Essays* (Weidenfeld & Nicolson, 1963), © Dan Jacobson, 1953, reprinted by permission of A. M. Heath & Co. Ltd on behalf of the author; Arthur Koestler: 'Return Trip to Nirvana' from *Essays, 1955–1967* (Hutchinson, 1968), reprinted by permission of The Peters Fraser & Dunlop Group Ltd; Philip Larkin: 'The Pleasure Principle' from *Required Writing: Miscellaneous Pieces, 1955–82* (Faber & Faber, 1983), reprinted by permission of the publisher; D. H. Lawrence: 'Why the Novel Matters' from *D. H. Lawrence: Selected Criticism* (Heinemann, 1956), reprinted by permission of Laurence Pollinger Ltd and the Estate of Frieda Lawrence Ravagli; F. R. Leavis: 'Mass Civilization and Minority Culture' from *Education and the University* (Chatto & Windus, 1943), reprinted by permission of Random House UK Ltd; Mary McCarthy: 'My Confession' from *Encounter* (February

1954), reprinted by permission of A. M. Heath & Company Ltd; Norman Mailer: 'The White Negro' from *Advertisements for Myself* (Flamingo, 1994), reprinted by permission of The Wylie Agency (UK) Ltd; Karl Miller: 'Are You Distraining Me?' from *New Review* (May 1976), reprinted by permission of the author; Nancy Mitford: 'The English Aristocracy' from *Encounter* (September 1955), reprinted by permission of The Peters Fraser & Dunlop Group Ltd on behalf of The Estate of Nancy Mitford; V. S. Naipaul: 'In the Middle of the Journey' from *The Overcrowded Barracoon* (Penguin Books, 1976), © 1972 V. S. Naipaul, reprinted by permission of Gillon Aitken Associates Ltd; George Orwell: 'England Your England' from *The Lion and the Unicorn: Socialism and the English Genius* (Penguin Twentieth Century Classics, 1990), © George Orwell, 1941, reprinted by permission of Martin Secker & Warburg Ltd and A. M. Heath & Co. Ltd on behalf of Mark Hamilton as the Literary Executor of the late Sonia Brownell Orwell; Jonathan Raban: 'Living on Capital' from *For Love and Money* (Collins Harvill, 1987), © 1987 Jonathan Raban, reprinted by permission of Gillon Aitken Associates Ltd; Philip Roth: 'My Baseball Years' from *Reading Myself and Others* (Jonathan Cape, 1975), reprinted by permission of Random House UK Ltd; Lytton Strachey: 'The Sad Story of Dr Colbatch' from *Portraits in Miniature* (Chatto & Windus, 1931), reprinted by permission of The Society of Authors as agents of the Strachey Trust; James Thurber: 'The Secret Life of James Thurber' from *The Thurber Carnival* (Penguin Books, 1971), © 1945 James Thurber, copyright renewed 1973 Helen Thurber and Rosemary A. Thurber, reprinted by arrangement with Rosemary A. Thurber and the Barbara Hogenson Agency; Gore Vidal: 'The Holy Family' from *Collected Essays, 1952–1972* (Heinemann, 1974), reprinted by permission of Curtis Brown Ltd; John Updike: 'The Bankrupt Man' from *Hugging the Shore* (Penguin Books, 1985; first published in Esquire), © John Updike, 1983, reprinted by permission of the publisher; Eudora Welty: 'The Little Store' from *The Eye of the Story: Selected Essays & Reviews* (Random House, 1979), © 1975 by Eudora Welty, reprinted by permission of Russell & Volkening as agents for the author; E. B. White: 'The Ring of Time' from *The Points of My Compass* (Hamish Hamilton, 1963), © 1956 by E. B. White, reprinted by permission of HarperCollins Publishers Inc; Edmund Wilson: 'Philocetes: The Wound and the Bow' from *The Wound and the Bow* (W. H. Allen, 1952), ©

1941, and copyright renewed © 1968 by Edmund Wilson, reprinted by permission of Farrar, Straus & Giroux, Inc; Tom Wolfe: 'These Radical Chic Evenings' from *Radical Chic and Mau-Mauing the Flak Catchers* (Farrar, Straus & Giroux, 1970), reprinted by permission of International Creative Management Inc; Virginia Woolf: 'How it Strikes a Contemporary' from *Collected Essays*, edited by A. McNeillie (Hogarth Press, 1994), reprinted by permission of Random House UK Ltd on behalf of the Estate of Virginia Woolf.

Foreword

'What are these essays but grotesque bodies pieced together of different members, without any definite shape, without any order, coherence or proportion, except they be accidental.' So said Michel Eyquem de Montaigne (1533–92), generally agreed to be the inventor of the essay-form. 'The essay', as a genre, has never been found easy to define. From Montaigne onwards, its best practitioners have usually shrunk from making high-flown or dogmatic claims for what they do. And this is hardly surprising, given its offhand beginnings. 'The freest form of literature', somebody else once called the essay-form and, sure enough, most attempted definitions tend to speak more of what an essay isn't than of what it is.

More often than not, the form's lawlessness is, recommendingly, insisted on. And so too, without fear of contradiction, is the low rank it tends to occupy in literary pantheons. As E. B. White once put it: 'The essayist, unlike the novelist, the poet and the playwright, must be content in his self-imposed role of second-class citizen. A writer who has his sights trained on the Nobel Prize or other earthly triumphs had best write a novel, a poem or a play, and leave the essayist to ramble about, content with living a free life and enjoying the satisfactions of a somewhat undisciplined existence.'

An essay is not poetry, an essay is not fiction, and yet now and then – as White himself has shown when he gets down to work – it can partake of both the fictional and the poetic. There are no set structures – although the best essays, examined closely enough, will turn out to have plenty of order, coherence and proportion. As with Montaigne, they may look accidental but they're not. An essay can be personal; it can be public. It can philosophize, it can polemicize, but it can also fail to look beyond its author's own backyard. It can be an extended book review, a piece of reportage, a travelogue, a revamped lecture, an amplified diary-jotting, a refurbished sermon. In other words, an essay can be just about anything it wants to be, anything its author chooses to 'essay'.

The only rule I can think of is that an essay must always be conscious of its wordage. It should never be long enough to be a book and never short enough to fit on, say, a single page. Where the upper word-limit falls I find it hard to judge – just as Macaulay and Carlyle did. In the Victorian age an essay's 'freedom' was often taken to mean the freedom to go on and on: in those days, immense length was seen as a sure sign that writers really meant what they were saying. On the matter of word-limits, though, a safe-ish guess might be that anything over 20,000 words stops being an essay and turns into something else, something that most of us will wish to call a book. And yet, at the same time, we can probably all think of books that are too short to warrant separate publication. And we can also think of non-fiction works which, if they weren't so long, would surely be called essays: I have in mind books like Mailer's *Armies of the Night* or Nicholson Baker's *U and I*.

In the end, no doubt, it's all to do with how the material gets marketed. If a piece of prose-writing is long enough to be bound between covers and sent out into the world, all by itself, we'll probably accept it as a book. If, on the other hand, it is too short for total independence and yet long enough to occupy two or three pages of a magazine, we won't argue if it's called an essay.

Of course, if an 'essay' is really, really short it runs the risk these days of being thought of as a 'column'. Is Russell Baker an essayist, or Art Buchwald? Well, almost but not quite, one is inclined to say – but not with much conviction. The current newspaper vogue for personalized diary-style opinion-bites can no doubt be traced back to the Edwardian (or neo-Augustan) style of essay-composition – the something-about-next-to-nothing school, as one might call it. 'About Bathrooms', the A. P. Herbert piece reprinted here as an example of that school, would nowadays be ten times shorter and might find a home at the rear end of a supplement on Lifestyles. Today the column rules, and brevity is all. After all, who is going to pay for a long essay about bathrooms, or – come to that – for a long anecdote by Russell Baker?

And this, you may contend, is to be welcomed. Do we really need more happy, stylish musings on 'Old China' or 'On Getting up on Cold Mornings', any more 'Adventures of a Shilling'? Probably not, although I sometimes miss such virtuoso feats of pointless eloquence. I still remember, with some fearful reverence, my Oxford entrance examination, in which I was required to write an essay 'On Pianos'. So this, I remember thinking at the time, is how they separate the dullards from the wits. There were perhaps a dozen ways of approaching such a subject, but which one was I meant to choose? What would Addison and Steele have done? Or Lamb? Or even Hazlitt? Or – to invoke figures from this century – Aldous Huxley and George Orwell? Huxley, we feel, would have known exactly how to treat a task like this; Orwell, on the other hand, would have considered it a waste of time.

Looking over the present selection, one can readily detect a drift away from the essay-as-performance. Twentieth-century essays – at any rate since the First World War and with one or two notable exceptions – tend to evince a sense of the momentous. They seem to say: don't think that I am writing this for fun. If there is eloquence, it's born – we are implicitly assured – of a necessity for eloquence. Even the most relaxed pieces in this book sound fairly urgent. Thus, Tom Wolfe on Radical Chic is more than just an entertainment, even though it is immensely entertaining. The underlying message is: these dreadful people must be skewered, *now*. The best twentieth-century essays tend to be *about* the twentieth century – a century seen, repeatedly, as repugnantly new-fangled, dangerous, perhaps apocalyptic. It is a century ruled by science and these writers, in the main, know little about science. A note of anxious, self-defensive ignorance is unavoidable – however witty and elegant the manner. Godless and scienceless, we humans still have plenty to defend.

In the eighteenth century essayists liked to present themselves as idlers, ramblers, tatlers and spectators. The suggestion was that they had time to spare; leisure in which to look at things intently, from curious new angles, and thus perhaps lighten the grave satisfactions of a stable universe. The twentieth-century essayist has tended to adopt an opposite approach, and to enjoy an opposite advantage. When time is running out, the need is to eliminate adornments.

With all this in mind, I have tried to organize the essays in this book so that, decade by decade, a portrayal of the century shows through: a portrayal with gaps, and of course a portrayal done from an Anglo–American perspective, but a passably compelling likeness, nonetheless. As everyone seems to agree: it's been the worst century so far, and most of the worst of it is covered here: Edmund Blunden on the First World War, Paul Fussell on the Second, Hannah Arendt on the concentration camps. I have also tried to set up a steady commentary on the century's political ideas and movements – 1930s' Leftism is ruefully explored by Mary McCarthy and Christopher Isherwood; the end of British imperialism by Dan Jacobson and Vidia Naipaul. I have also included some usefully revealing 'period-pieces', like Nancy Mitford's study of posh English manners (1950s-style) and James Baldwin's essay on American white power. These pieces may seem dated now but they were read avidly at the time of their publication, and perhaps even contributed to their own datedness.

This historical-documentary line has not, I hope, been strained for too eagerly. With the exception of two instances, which I won't name, my first consideration has been the quality of the writing. Now and then I've put in something because it touches me or makes me laugh, or because I remember the impact it had on me when I first read it in a magazine. It is of course magazines that keep the essay going and in many ways this book serves as a kind of tribute to those periodicals, now few and far between, which thought nothing of giving good writers five or ten thousand words in which to have their say. *Partisan Review*, *Encounter*, the *New Yorker*: this book would be much poorer without the impetus originally provided by these journals, and by others like them.

As what can now be called a matter of policy, I decided at the outset not to include strictly literary essays – writer A on writer B – largely because there were so many that I wanted to include. The rise of the literary 'profile', in newspapers and in glossy magazines, is usually deplored, but it has produced some good writing by good writers. The trouble is: it tends to get badly out of date – at least for the purposes of an anthology. Do we want to be told what writer X thought about his second book in 1986 when we know that since then he's produced three more? Also, the literary profile, without meaning to, tends to get sucked into the book-publicity machine: critical comment gets sacrificed to personality-portrayal. It is difficult to think of a magazine profile that has had, or could have had, the impact of, say, a Randall Jarrell essay in the 1940s.

It would have been easy, and a pleasure, to fill the present volume with literary-critical material but that would have been to turn it into a quite different book, a different project. Even so, I do regret the absence of R. P. Blackmur, Lionel Trilling, D. J. Enright, Christopher Ricks, Frank Kermode and several others. In the end, on the literary-critical front, I contented myself with two reputedly 'seminal' essays on what modern literature should be, or shouldn't be: Eliot's *Tradition and the Individual Talent* and F. R. Leavis's *Mass Civilization and Minority Culture*.

Leavis's essay is, of course, not just literary. It foreshadows what I take to be one of the key quarrels of the past four or five decades: between high culture and low culture (each of these, of course, 'so-called'). Norman Mailer on hipsterism and Arthur Koestler on hallucinations do seem to have a bearing on this great debate; so too Auden on detective novels, James Thurber on Dali and John Carey on elitist dons. George Orwell on seaside postcards or boys' comics would have been an obvious addition but I didn't want to sacrifice his excellent but lengthy England piece. As the century progresses, 'culture' gets harder to define, and maybe harder to defend. If only I could have chanced upon a lively and literate champion of the actively philistine position: C. P. Snow and his Two Cultures did come close, but not quite close enough.

This selection does, then, have a sort of plan, or pattern – and maybe the pattern could have been served by different essays. I tried hunting for better things but finally I came back – on the whole – to pieces I had known about for years, and had grown fond of. They may not all be seminal, or especially revealing of the *Zeitgeist*, but for me they've set a standard, and still do.

G. K. CHESTERTON

Woman

G. K. Chesterton was born in 1874 and was best known in his lifetime as a novelist and short-story writer. His several Father Brown detective stories were hugely popular in the twenties and thirties (see W. H. Auden's essay on p. 132) and in some circles are still much admired today. Chesterton was also a prolific journalist, versifier, literary critic, biographer and Roman Catholic moralist. His characteristically whimsical-provocative observations on the role of 'Woman' were first printed in 1906 and were collected in All Things Considered *(1908). Chesterton died in 1936.*

A correspondent has written me an able and interesting letter in the matter of some allusions of mine to the subject of communal kitchens. He defends communal kitchens. He defends communal kitchens very lucidly from the standpoint of the calculating collectivist; but, like many of his school, he cannot apparently grasp that there is another test of the whole matter, with which such calculation has nothing at all to do. He knows it would be cheaper if a number of us ate at the same time, so as to use the same table. So it would. It would also be cheaper if a number of us slept at different times, so as to use the same pair of trousers. But the question is not how cheap are we buying a thing, but what are we buying? It is cheap to own a slave. And it is cheaper still to be a slave.

My correspondent also says that the habit of dining out in restaurants, etc., is growing. So, I believe, is the habit of committing suicide. I do not desire to connect the two facts together. It seems fairly clear that a man could not dine at a restaurant because he had just committed suicide; and it would be extreme, perhaps, to suggest that he commits suicide because he has just dined at a restaurant. But the two cases when put side by side are enough to indicate the falsity and poltroonery of this eternal modern argument from what is in fashion. The question for brave men is not whether a certain thing is increasing; the question is whether we are increasing it. I dine very often in restaurants because the nature of my trade makes it convenient: but if I thought that by dining in restaurants I was working for the creation of communal meals, I would never enter a restaurant again; I would carry bread and cheese in my pocket or eat chocolate out of automatic machines. For the personal element in some things is sacred. I heard Mr Will Crooks put it perfectly the other day: 'The most sacred thing is to be able to shut your own door.'

My correspondent says, 'Would not our women be spared the drudgery of cooking and all its attendant worries, leaving them free for higher culture?' The first thing that occurs to me to say about this is very simple, and is, I imagine, a part of all our experience. If my correspondent can find any way of preventing women from worrying, he will indeed be a remarkable man. I think the matter is a much deeper one. First of all, my correspondent overlooks a distinction which is elementary in our human nature. Theoretically, I suppose, every one would like to be freed from worries. But nobody in the world would always like to be freed from worrying occupations. I should very much like (as far as my feelings at the moment go) to be free from the consuming nuisance of writing this article. But it does not follow that I should like to be free from the consuming nuisance of being a journalist. Because we are worried about a thing, it does not follow that we are not interested in it. The truth is the other way. If we are not interested, why on earth should we be worried? Women are worried about housekeeping, but those that are most interested are the most worried. Women are still more worried about their husbands and their children. And I suppose if we strangled the children and pole-axed the husbands it would leave women free for higher culture. That is, it would leave them free to begin to worry about that. For women would worry about higher culture as much as they worry about everything else.

I believe this way of talking about women and their higher culture is almost entirely a growth of the classes which (unlike the journalistic class to which I belong) have always a reasonable amount of money. One odd thing I specially notice. Those who write like this seem entirely to forget the existence of the working and wage-earning classes. They say eternally, like my correspondent, that the ordinary woman is always a drudge. And what, in the name of the Nine Gods, is the ordinary man? These people seem to think that the ordinary man is a Cabinet

Minister. They are always talking about man going forth to wield power, to carve his own way, to stamp his individuality on the world, to command and to be obeyed. This may be true of a certain class. Dukes, perhaps, are not drudges; but then, neither are Duchesses. The Ladies and Gentlemen of the Smart Set are quite free for the higher culture, which consists chiefly of motoring and Bridge. But the ordinary man who typifies and constitutes the millions that make up our civilization is no more free for the higher culture than his wife is.

Indeed, he is not so free. Of the two sexes the woman is in the more powerful position. For the average woman is at the head of something with which she can do as she likes; the average man has to obey orders and do nothing else. He has to put one dull brick on another dull brick, and do nothing else; he has to add one dull figure to another dull figure, and do nothing else. The woman's world is a small one, perhaps, but she can alter it. The woman can tell the tradesman with whom she deals some realistic things about himself. The clerk who does this to the manager generally gets the sack or shall we say (to avoid the vulgarism), finds himself free for higher culture. Above all . . . the woman does work which is in some small degree creative and individual. She can put the flowers or the furniture in fancy arrangements of her own. I fear the bricklayer cannot put the bricks in fancy arrangements of his own, without disaster to himself and others. If the woman is only putting a patch into a carpet, she can choose the thing with regard to colour. I fear it would not do for the office boy dispatching a parcel to choose his stamps with a view to colour; to prefer the tender mauve of the sixpenny to the crude scarlet of the penny stamp. A woman cooking may not always cook artistically; still she can cook artistically. She can introduce a personal and imperceptible alteration into the composition of a soup. The clerk is not encouraged to introduce a personal and imperceptible alteration into the figures in a ledger.

The trouble is that the real question I raised is not discussed. It is argued as a problem in pennies, not as a problem in people. It is not the proposals of these reformers that I feel to be false so much as their temper and their arguments. I am not nearly so certain that communal kitchens are wrong as I am that the defenders of communal kitchens are wrong. Of course, for one thing, there is a vast difference between the communal kitchens of which I spoke and the communal meal (*monstrum horrendum, informe*) which the darker and wilder mind of my correspondent diabolically calls up. But in both the trouble is that their defenders will not defend them humanly as human institutions. They will not interest themselves in the staring psychological fact that there are some things that a man or a woman, as the case may be, wishes to do for himself or herself. He or she must do it inventively, creatively, artistically, individually – in a word, badly. Choosing your wife (say) is one of these things. Is choosing your husband's dinner one of these things? That is the whole question: it is never asked.

And then the higher culture. I know that culture. I would not set any man free for it if I could help it. The effect of it on the rich men who are free for it is so horrible that it is worse than any of the other amusements of the millionaire – worse than gambling, worse even than philanthropy. It means thinking the smallest poet in Belgium greater than the greatest poet of England. It means losing every democratic sympathy. It means being unable to talk to a navvy about sport, or about beer, or about the Bible, or about the Derby, or about patriotism or about anything whatever that he, the navvy, wants to talk about. It means taking literature seriously, a very amateurish thing to do. It means pardoning indecency only when it is gloomy indecency. Its disciples will call a spade a spade: but only when it is a grave-digger's spade. The higher culture is sad, cheap, impudent, unkind, without honesty and without ease. In short, it is 'high'. That abominable word (also applied to game) admirably describes it.

No; if you were setting women free for something else I might be more melted. If you can assure me, privately and gravely, that you are setting women free to dance on the mountains like Maenads, or to worship some monstrous goddess, I will make a note of your request. If you are quite sure that the ladies in Brixton, the moment they give up cooking, will beat great gongs and blow horns to Mumbo-Jumbo, then I will agree that the occupation is at least human and is more or less entertaining. Women have been set free to be Bacchantes; they have been set free to be Virgin Martyrs; they have been set free to be Witches. Do not ask them now to sink so low as the higher culture.

I have my own little notions of the possible emancipation of women; but I suppose I should not be taken very seriously if I propounded them. I should favour anything that would increase the present enormous authority of women and their creative action in their own homes. The average woman, as I have said, is a despot; the average man is a serf.

I am for any scheme that any one can suggest that will make the average woman more of a despot. So far from wishing her to get her cooked meals from outside, I should like her to cook more wildly and at her own will than she does. So far from getting always the same meals from the same place, let her invent, if she likes, a new dish every day of her life. Let woman be more of a maker, not less. We are right to talk about 'Woman': only blackguards talk about women. Yet all men talk about men, and that is the whole difference. Men represent the deliberative and democratic element in life. Woman represents the despotic.

MAURICE BARING

King Lear's Daughter

Maurice Baring (1874–1945) was a member of the Baring banking family and worked for some years as a diplomat – mostly in Russia. A Catholic associate of Chesterton and Belloc, he wrote many now-forgotten novels, but his autobiography The Puppet Show of Memory *(1922) remains in print and is well thought of. As an essayist, Baring made a speciality of projecting himself into the characters of historical and literary figures. See* Dead Letter *(1910).*

LETTER FROM GONERIL, DAUGHTER OF KING LEAR, TO HER SISTER REGAN

I have writ my sister.
King Lear, Act I, Scene iv

THE PALACE, *November*

DEAREST REGAN,

I am sending you this letter by Oswald. We have been having the most trying time lately with Papa, and it ended today in one of those scenes which are so painful to people like you and me, who *hate* scenes. I am writing now to tell you all about it, so that you may be prepared. This is what has happened.

When Papa came here he brought a hundred knights with him, which is a great deal more than we could put up, and some of them had to live in the village. The first thing that happened was that they quarrelled with our people and refused to take orders from them, and whenever one told any one to do anything it was either – if it was one of Papa's men – 'not his place to do it'; or if it was one of our men, they said that Papa's people made work impossible. For instance, only the day before yesterday I found that blue vase which you brought back from Dover for me on my last birthday broken to bits. Of course I made a fuss, and Oswald declared that one of Papa's knights had knocked it

6

over in a drunken brawl. I complained to Papa, who flew into a passion and said that his knights, and in fact all his retainers, were the most peaceful and courteous people in the world, and that it was my fault, as I was not treating him or them with the respect which they deserved. He even said that I was lacking in filial duty. I was determined to keep my temper, so I said nothing.

The day after this the chief steward and the housekeeper and both my maids came to me and said that they wished to give notice. I asked them why. They said they couldn't possibly live in a house where there were such 'goings-on'. I asked them what they meant. They refused to say, but they hinted that Papa's men were behaving not only in an insolent but in a positively outrageous manner to them. The steward said that Papa's knights were never sober, that they had entirely demoralized the household, and that life was simply not worth living in the house; it was *impossible* to get anything done, and they couldn't sleep at night for the noise.

I went to Papa and talked to him about it quite quietly, but no sooner had I mentioned the subject than he lost all self-control, and began to abuse me. I kept my temper as long as I could, but of course one is only human, and after I had borne his revilings for some time, which were monstrously unfair and untrue, I at last turned and said something about people of his age being trying. Upon which he said that I was mocking him in his old age, that I was a monster of ingratitude – and he began to cry. I cannot tell you how painful all this was to me. I did everything I could to soothe him and quiet him, but the truth is, ever since Papa has been here he has lost control of his wits. He suffers from the oddest kind of delusions. He thinks that for some reason he is being treated like a beggar; and although he has a hundred knights – a hundred, mind you! (a great deal more than we have) – in the house, who do nothing but eat and drink all day long, he says he is not being treated like a King! I do hate unfairness.

When he gave up the crown he said he was tired of affairs, and meant to have a long rest; but from the very moment that he handed over the management of affairs to us he never stopped interfering, and was cross if he was not consulted about everything, and if his advice was not taken.

And what is still worse: ever since his last illness he has lost not only his memory but his control over language, so that often when he wants to say one thing he says just the opposite, and sometimes when he wishes to say some quite simple thing he uses *bad* language quite unconsciously. Of course we are used to this, and *we* don't mind, but I must say it is very awkward when strangers are here. For instance, the other day before quite a lot of people, quite unconsciously, he called me a dreadful name. Everybody was uncomfortable and tried not to laugh, but some people could not contain themselves. This sort of thing is constantly happening. So you will understand that Papa needs perpetual looking after and management. At the same time, the moment one suggests the slightest thing to him he boils over with rage.

But perhaps the most annoying thing which happened lately, or, at least, the thing which happens to annoy me most, is Papa's Fool. You know, darling, that I have always hated that kind of humour. He comes in just as one is sitting down to dinner, and beats one on the head with a hard, empty bladder, and sings utterly idiotic songs, which make me feel inclined to cry. The other day, when we had a lot of people here, just as we were sitting down in the banqueting-hall, Papa's Fool pulled my chair from behind me so that I fell sharply down on the floor. Papa shook with laughter, and said: 'Well done, little Fool,' and all the courtiers who were there, out of pure snobbishness, of course, laughed too. I call this not only very humiliating for me, but undignified in an old man and a king; of course Albany refused to interfere. Like all men and all husbands, he is an arrant coward.

However, the crisis came yesterday. I had got a bad headache, and was lying down in my room, when Papa came in from the hunt and sent Oswald to me, saying that he wished to speak to me. I said that I wasn't well, and that I was lying down – which was perfectly true – but that I would be down to dinner. When Oswald went to give my message Papa beat him, and one of his men threw him about the room and really hurt him, so that he has now got a large bruise on his forehead and a sprained ankle.

This was the climax. All our knights came to Albany and myself, and said that they would not stay with us a moment longer unless Papa exercised some sort of control over his men. I did not know what to do, but I knew the situation would have to be cleared up sooner or later. So I went to Papa and told him frankly that the situation was intolerable; that he must send away some of his people, and choose for the remainder men fitting to his age. The words were scarcely out of my mouth than he called me the most terrible names, ordered his horses to be saddled, and said that he would shake the dust from his feet and not stay a moment longer in this house. Albany tried to calm him, and begged him to stay, but he would not listen to a word, and said he would go and live with you.

So I am sending this by Oswald, that you may get it before Papa arrives and know how the matter stands. All I did was to suggest he should send away fifty of his men. Even fifty is a great deal, and puts us to any amount of inconvenience, and is a source of waste and extravagance – two things which I cannot bear. I am perfectly certain you will not be able to put up with his hundred knights any more than I was. And I beg you, my dearest Regan, to do your best to make Papa listen to sense. No one is fonder of him than I am. I think it would have been difficult to find a more dutiful daughter than I have always been. But there is a limit to all things, and one cannot have one's whole household turned into a pandemonium, and one's whole life into a series of wrangles, complaints, and brawls, simply because Papa in his old age is losing the control of his faculties. At the same time, I own that although I kept my temper for a long time, when it finally gave way I was perhaps a little sharp. I am not a saint, nor an angel, nor a lamb, but I do hate unfairness and injustice. It makes my blood boil. But I hope that you, with your angelic nature and your tact and your gentleness, will put everything right and make poor Papa listen to reason.

Let me hear at once what happens.

Your loving
GONERIL

PS – Another thing Papa does which is most exasperating is to quote Cordelia to one every moment. He keeps on saying: 'If only Cordelia were here,' or 'How unlike Cordelia!' And you will remember, darling, that when Cordelia was here Papa could not endure the sight of her. Her irritating trick of mumbling and never speaking up used to get terribly on his nerves. Of course, I thought he was even rather unfair on her, trying as she is. We had a letter from the French Court yesterday, saying that she is driving the poor King of France almost mad.

PPS – It is wretched weather. The poor little ponies on the heath will have to be brought in.

EDMUND BLUNDEN

The Somme Still Flows

Edmund Blunden (1896–1974) is best known as a poet but for fifty years he was a busily versatile figure on the English literary scene. He published several prose books and at various times worked in universities, as a teacher (for a time in the Far East) and on Fleet Street, as a literary journalist. Blunden served on the Western Front from 1915 until the end of the First World War, and recorded his experiences in Undertones of War *(1928). Shortly before his death, Blunden wrote: 'My experiences in the First World War have haunted me all my life and for many days I have, it seemed, lived in that world rather than this.'*

It was a sunny morning, that of July 1st 1916. The right notes for it would have been the singing of blackbirds and the ringing of the blacksmith's anvil. But, as the world soon knew, the music of that sunny morning was the guns. They had never spoken before with so huge a voice. Their sound crossed the sea. In Southdown villages the school-children sat wondering at that incessant drumming and the rattling of the windows. That night an even greater anxiety than usual forbade wives and mothers to sleep. The Battle of the Somme had begun.

This battle on the southern part of the British line overshadowed everything else. Even Ypres fell quiet. The three nations most prominently concerned on the Western Front concentrated their force in the once serene farmlands of Picardy. Their armies had arrived at a wonderful pitch of physical and spiritual strength. They were great organizations of athletes, willing to attempt any test that might be ordered. If the men of the Somme were probably unrivalled by any earlier armies, the materials and preparations of the battle were no less extraordinary. Railways, roads, motor transport, mules, water-supply, aircraft, guns, mortars, wire, grenades, timber, rations, camps, telegraphic systems – multiplied as in some absurd vision. Many of you who are reading now still feel the fever of that gathering typhoon.

Such monstrous accumulations, and transformations of a countryside which in the sleepier period of its war had been called 'The Garden of Eden', could not be concealed from the intended victims. Surprise on the large scale was impossible. But the British devised local surprises: rapidly dug jumping-off positions; field guns waiting to fire from the front trenches; the terrific mine ready to go up at La Boisselle. The defenders also had their secrets prepared for July 1st.

At last the moment came for mutual revelations. Villages, wiped out in a few hours, earned reputations for hopeless horror when our men rose in the daylight from their already destroyed positions and moved to capture them. Some of them they did capture. Few who survived long enough under German guns and machine-guns to enter the trenches opposite could have retained any illusions. They found themselves in a great trap of tunnels and concrete and steel rails and iron entanglements. From holes in the land they had crossed, from higher ground north and south, from untouched gunpits, these isolated men were also wiped out. I knew a colonel whose hair turned white in this experience. I knew Thiepval, in which battalions disappeared that day. I knew Thiepval Wood, before which in the mud of November were withering bodies of the British and German combatants of July 1st.

The outbreak of the Somme battle may be described as a tremendous question-mark. By the end of the day both sides had seen, in a sad scrawl of broken earth and murdered men, the answer to that question. No road. No thoroughfare. Neither race had won, nor could win, the War. The War had won, and would go on winning. But, after all the preparation, the ambition, the ideals and the rhythms of these contending armies, there could not be any stopping. Tomorrow is always another day, and hope springs eternal. The battle of the Somme would continue from summer to winter. The experiment of the century must be repeated, varied, newly equipped. Perhaps luck would play a part. Perhaps external conditions would affect these machine-gun emplacements, and the lucky lads from Adelaide or Sunderland walking onward through the explosions.

Accordingly, what had been begun on July 1st became a slow slaugh-tering process; the Somme might have been a fatal quicksand into which division after division was drawn down. In order to illustrate that remark, I am going to sketch the history of the division in which I served during the offensive. Though we were far north of the battle-field in June 1916, we nevertheless came under its fiery influence; for, on the last day of June, we were sent into a 'minor operation' as they called it, with the object of keeping back German troops and artillery from the real affair. Our brigade assaulted; crossed a flat water-meadow, full of deep dykes and thick barbed wire, under every kind of fire; and a great many of us were dead or wounded within a couple of hours. 'Like a butcher's shop,' said a plain-spoken private to the general next day. When we had to some extent recovered from this minor operation, the powerful and ominous words came round, 'We're going South.'

War is not all war, and there lies the heart of the monster. 'Going South' was at first more like a holiday adventure than the descent to the valley of the shadow. I still make myself pictures of that march, and could not guess at any summer days more enchanting. The very fact that, after ceaseless rumours and contradictions, we were now certainly destined for the Somme battle made us shut our minds to the future and embrace the present. We marched with liberal halts through wooded uplands, under arcades of elms, past mill-streams and red and white farms; and, as we marched, we sang. Not even the indifferent map-reading of the boyish officer at the head of the battalion could damp our spirits. What were kilometres? At twilight we took over our billets in clay-walled barns, or farm-houses with vineleaves at the windows and 'café, monsieur' at any moment. Every man knew his neighbour. Never was such candour or such confidence.

We stayed longer at the hamlet which provided our training-ground. Indeed, its chalky hill-sides were said to be precisely similar to our future share of the Somme battlefield. In an interval of our successful attacks on the dummy trenches of our ghostly enemy, we lay down by companies while some particularly well-nourished experts from General Headquarters eulogized the beauty of the bayonet. We went to sleep. Presently rainy weather set in, but when we continued our journey to the battle the sun burned and the dust rose along the road. It was towards the end of August.

After several postponements we made our first appearance in the fighting. We did not know, most of us, that the lines which we had dreams of capturing had been attacked on July 1st. But, as I stared across a valley at the German positions, a day or two before our action, I was puzzled by a small heap of what was clearly British barbed wire, on its original reels, a long way behind the enemy's front trench. In the cold early mist of September 3rd our division went over. A few astonishing officers and men fought their way to those coils of wire. One or two returned from them in the evening, by which time history had repeated itself. The shattered battalions withdrew from the valleys and ridges still echoing with bombardment and the pounding of machine-guns. The Somme had pulled us under once, and we emerged just gasping. Somewhere to the south there had been a success.

We did not withdraw far. We quickly returned to the line and remained in the trenches, from which two mighty attacks had been launched, week upon week. South, there was still a vague hope. Trenches were said to be changing hands beyond Thiepval Hill, which still frowned upon our ragged remains of trenches. We witnessed and heard furious attacks in that direction, rolling smoke, bursts of flame, soaring signal-lights; but these closed in autumn darkness. One day a sensation was caused. Down there in the south the British had made an attack with Tanks, which we understood to be as big as houses and capable of pushing houses down. Then the Somme was still a promising experiment!

For our own next attack we had no assistance of tanks. It was now a long age since July 1st and its blue skies. Yet October 21st was a still, frosty day. A surprise was reserved for our opponents: we were to attack a few minutes after noon. We did. Some of us had now seen three attacks, others had just arrived from the barrack-squares, where sacks of straw are nimbly transfixed by unshelled and unbombed soldiers. We took our trench, and were then submitted to artillery concentration, which went on two days. There were enough of us left to hand over the conquered ground to the 'next for the barber', and to crawl back through endless shell-holes and dead. The captured trench was partly floored with bodies.

Almost at once we were in the line again, and after some days of curious peace we moved to a desperate mud-field east of Thiepval – one of the classic terrors of the Western Front. The year was breaking up now. The craters were swimming with foul water. What was left of the trenches became lanes of yellow and blood-brown slime, deeper than our average height. The tracks beside them were usually smoking with accurate gunfire. The alternative was, generally, to be blown to pieces or to be drowned. After several days of the Schwaben Redoubt, with the corpses choking the dug-out entrances, we were informed of another surprise arranged for the enemy. Our division was to take part in a large attack. This occurred on November 13th. The division surpassed itself, capturing ground and one labyrinth of dug-outs with many hundreds of Germans in them. Still, there was no sign yet of the fabled green country beyond the Somme battle. That evening I was sent forward with a runner on a reconnaissance. It was growing dark, a drizzling rain was steadily increasing, and on every side was the glare and wailing and crashing of bombardment. We passed through the new posts of the British advance, shivering in water-holes, and then we went blindly astray. After our painful wandering through the barrages of two artilleries and the crazy ruins of trench and battery systems, we were lucky enough to find a way back. That night, retracing our adventure with the colonel and his maps, we found that we had been in the outskirts of a village named Grandcourt. Grandcourt! We felt a little proud. But it came out that some British soldiers had made their miraculous way to that village through the German forts and fire on that remote summer's morning, July 1st.

After this winter battle we left the Somme – but who were 'we'? Not those who had marched south in the time of ripening orchards; a very different body of men. We had been passed through the furnace and the quicksand. What had happened to this division was typical of the experience of all divisions in all the armies. There is no escape from the answer given on July 1st to the question of the human race. War had been 'found out', overwhelmingly found out. War is an ancient impostor, but none of his masks and smiles and gallant trumpets can any longer delude us; he leads the way through the cornfields to the cemetery of all that is best. The best is, indeed, his special prey. What men did in the battle of the Somme, day after day, and month after month, will never be excelled in honour, unselfishness, and love; except by those who come after and resolve that their experience shall never again fall to the lot of human beings.

VIRGINIA WOOLF

How it Strikes a Contemporary

Virginia Woolf was born in 1882, the daughter of a celebrated essayist, Sir Leslie Stephen. Although Woolf's novels speak of solitude and introversion, she herself – in the 1910s and 1920s – was a formidably visible figure on the literary landscape: as a reviewer and publisher, and as an acerbic salon-socialite. Woolf's Collected Essays *now occupy four volumes and cover an impressive range – it would have been easy, and a pleasure, to have represented her more fully here, but space forbids. 'How it Strikes a Contemporary' was first collected in* The Common Reader *(1925). Woolf died, by suicide, in 1941.*

In the first place a contemporary can scarcely fail to be struck by the fact that two critics at the same table at the same moment will pronounce completely different opinions about the same book. Here, on the right, it is declared a masterpiece of English prose; on the left, simultaneously, a mere mass of waste-paper which, if the fire could survive it, should be thrown upon the flames. Yet both critics are in agreement about Milton and about Keats. They display an exquisite sensibility and have undoubtedly a genuine enthusiasm. It is only when they discuss the work of contemporary writers that they inevitably come to blows. The book in question, which is at once a lasting contribution to English literature and a mere farrago of pretentious mediocrity, was published about two months ago. That is the explanation; that is why they differ.

The explanation is a strange one. It is equally disconcerting to the reader who wishes to take his bearings in the chaos of contemporary literature and to the writer who has a natural desire to know whether his own work, produced with infinite pains and in almost utter darkness, is likely to burn for ever among the fixed luminaries of English letters or, on the contrary, to put out the fire. But if we identify ourselves with the reader and explore his dilemma first, our bewilderment is short-lived enough. The same thing has happened so often before. We have heard the doctors disagreeing about the new and agreeing about the old twice a year on the average, in spring and autumn, ever since Robert Elsmere, or was it Stephen Phillips, somehow pervaded the atmosphere, and there was the same disagreement among grown-up people about these books too. It would be much more marvellous, and indeed much more upsetting, if, for a wonder, both gentlemen agreed, pronounced Blank's book an undoubted masterpiece, and thus faced us with the necessity of deciding whether we should back their judgement to the extent of ten and sixpence. Both are critics of reputation; the opinions tumbled out so spontaneously here will be starched and stiffened into columns of sober prose which will uphold the dignity of letters in England and America.

It must be some innate cynicism, then, some ungenerous distrust of contemporary genius, which determines us automatically as the talk goes on that, were they to agree – which they show no signs of doing – half a guinea is altogether too large a sum to squander upon contemporary enthusiasms, and the case will be met quite adequately by a card to the library. Still the question remains, and let us put it boldly to the critics themselves. Is there no guidance nowadays for a reader who yields to none in reverence for the dead, but is tormented by the suspicion that reverence for the dead is vitally connected with understanding of the living? After a rapid survey both critics are agreed that there is unfortunately no such person. For what is their own judgement worth where new books are concerned? Certainly not ten and sixpence. And from the stores of their experience they proceed to bring forth terrible examples of past blunders; crimes of criticism which, if they had been committed against the dead and not against the living, would have lost them their jobs and imperilled their reputations. The only advice they can offer is to respect one's own instincts, to follow them fearlessly and, rather than submit them to the control of any critic or reviewer alive, to check them by reading and reading again the masterpieces of the past.

Thanking them humbly, we cannot help reflecting that it was not always so. Once upon a time, we must believe, there was a rule, a discipline, which controlled the great republic of readers in a way which is now unknown. That is not to say that the great critic – the Dryden, the Johnson, the Coleridge, the Arnold – was an impeccable judge of contemporary work, whose verdicts stamped the book indelibly and saved the reader the trouble of reckoning the value for himself. The mistakes of these great men about their own contemporaries are too notorious to be worth recording. But the mere fact of their existence had a centralising influence. That alone, it is not fantastic to suppose, would have controlled the disagreements of the dinner-table and given to random chatter about some book just out an authority now entirely to seek. The diverse schools would have debated as hotly as ever, but at the back of every reader's mind would have been the consciousness that there was at least one man who kept the main principles of literature closely in view: who, if you had taken to him some eccentricity of the moment, would have brought it into touch with permanence and tethered it by his own authority in the contrary blasts of praise and blame.* But when it comes to the making of a critic, nature must be generous and society ripe. The scattered dinner-tables of the modern world, the chase and eddy of the various currents which compose the society of our time, could only be dominated by a giant of fabulous dimensions. And where is even the very tall man whom we have the right to expect? Reviewers we have but no critic; a million competent and incorruptible policemen but no judge. Men of taste and learning and ability are for ever lecturing the young and celebrating the dead. But the too frequent result of their able and industrious pens is a desiccation of the living tissues of literature into a network of little bones. Nowhere shall we find the downright vigour of a Dryden, or Keats with his fine and natural bearing, his profound insight and sanity, or Flaubert and the tremendous power of his fanaticism, or Coleridge, above all, brewing in his head the whole of poetry and letting issue now and then one of those profound general statements which are caught up by the mind when hot with the friction of reading as if they were of the soul of the book itself.

And to all this, too, the critics generously agree. A great critic, they say, is the rarest of beings. But should one miraculously appear, how

---

* How violent these are two quotations will show. 'It [*Told by an Idiot*] should be read as the *Tempest* should be read, and as *Gulliver's Travels* should be read, for if Miss Macaulay's poetic gift happens to be less sublime than those of the author of the *Tempest*, and if her irony happens to be less tremendous than that of the author of *Gulliver's Travels*, her justice and wisdom are no less noble than theirs.' – *The Daily News*.

The next day we read: 'For the rest one can only say that if Mr Eliot had been pleased to write in demotic English *The Waste Land* might not have been, as it just is to all but anthropologists, and literati, so much waste-paper.' – *The Manchester Guardian*.

should we maintain him, on what should we feed him? Great critics, if they are not themselves great poets, are bred from the profusion of the age. There is some great man to be vindicated, some school to be founded or destroyed. But our age is meagre to the verge of destitution. There is no name which dominates the rest. There is no master in whose workshop the young are proud to serve apprenticeship. Mr Hardy has long since withdrawn from the arena, and there is something exotic about the genius of Mr Conrad which makes him not so much an influence as an idol, honoured and admired, but aloof and apart. As for the rest, though they are many and vigorous and in the full flood of creative activity, there is none whose influence can seriously affect his contemporaries, or penetrate beyond our day to that not very distant future which it pleases us to call immortality. If we make a century our test, and ask how much of the work produced in these days in England will be in existence then, we shall have to answer not merely that we cannot agree upon the same book, but that we are more than doubtful whether such a book there is. It is an age of fragments. A few stanzas, a few pages, a chapter here and there, the beginning of this novel, the end of that, are equal to the best of any age or author. But can we go to posterity with a sheaf of loose pages, or ask the readers of those days, with the whole of literature before them, to sift our enormous rubbish heaps for our tiny pearls? Such are the questions which the critics might lawfully put to their companions at table, the novelists and poets.

At first the weight of pessimism seems sufficient to bear down all opposition. Yes, it is a lean age, we repeat, with much to justify its poverty; but, frankly, if we pit one century against another the comparison seems overwhelmingly against us. *Waverley, The Excursion, Kubla Khan, Don Juan, Hazlitt's Essays, Pride and Prejudice, Hyperion,* and *Prometheus Unbound* were all published between 1800 and 1821. Our century has not lacked industry; but if we ask for masterpieces it appears on the face of it that the pessimists are right. It seems as if an age of genius must be succeeded by an age of endeavour; riot and extravagance by cleanliness and hard work. All honour, of course, to those who have sacrificed their immortality to set the house in order. But if we ask for masterpieces, where are we to look? A little poetry, we may feel sure, will survive; a few poems by Mr Yeats, by Mr Davies, by Mr De la Mare. Mr Lawrence, of course, has moments of greatness, but hours of something very different. Mr Beerbohm, in his way, is perfect, but it is not a big way. Passages in *Far Away and Long Ago* will undoubtedly go to posterity entire. *Ulysses* was a memorable catastrophe – immense in daring, terrific in disaster. And so, picking and choosing, we select now this, now that, hold it up for display, hear it defended or derided, and finally have to meet the objection that even so we are only agreeing with the critics that it is an age incapable of sustained effort, littered with fragments, and not seriously to be compared with the age that went before.

But it is just when opinions universally prevail and we have added lip service to their authority that we become sometimes most keenly conscious that we do not believe a word that we are saying. It is a barren and exhausted age, we repeat; we must look back with envy to the past. Meanwhile it is one of the first fine days of spring. Life is not altogether lacking in colour. The telephone, which interrupts the most serious conversations and cuts short the most weighty observations, has a romance of its own. And the random talk of people who have no chance of immortality and thus can speak their minds out has a setting, often, of lights, streets, houses, human beings, beautiful or grotesque, which will weave itself into the moment for ever. But this is life; the talk is about literature. We must try to disentangle the two, and justify the rash revolt of optimism against the superior plausibility, the finer distinction, of pessimism.

Our optimism, then, is largely instinctive. It springs from the fine day and the wine and the talk; it springs from the fact that when life throws up such treasures daily, daily suggests more than the most voluble can express, much though we admire the dead, we prefer life as it is. There is something about the present which we would not exchange, though we were offered a choice of all past ages to live in. And modern literature, with all its imperfections, has the same hold on us and the same fascination. It is like a relation whom we snub and scarify daily, but, after all, cannot do without. It has the same endearing quality of being that which we are, that which we have made, that in which we live, instead of being something, however august, alien to ourselves and beheld from the outside. Nor has any generation more need than ours to cherish its contemporaries. We are sharply cut off from our predecessors. A shift in the scale – the war, the sudden slip of masses held in position for ages – has shaken the fabric from top to bottom, alienated us from the past and made us perhaps too vividly conscious of the present. Every day we find ourselves doing, saying, or thinking things that would have been impossible to our fathers. And we feel the differences which have not been noted far more keenly than the resemblances which have been very perfectly expressed. New books lure us to read them partly in the hope that they will reflect this re-arrangement of our attitude – these scenes, thoughts, and apparently fortuitous groupings of incongruous things which impinge upon us with so keen a sense of novelty – and, as literature does, give it back into our keeping, whole and comprehended. Here indeed there is every reason for optimism. No age can have been more rich than ours in writers determined to give expression to the differences which separate them from the past and not to the resemblances which connect them with it. It would be invidious to mention names, but the most casual reader dipping into poetry, into fiction, into biography can hardly fail to be impressed by the courage, the sincerity, in a word, by the widespread originality of our time. But our exhilaration is strangely curtailed. Book after book leaves us with the same sense of promise unachieved, of intellectual poverty, of brilliance which has been snatched from life but not transmuted into literature. Much of what is best in contemporary work has the appearance of being noted under pressure, taken down in a bleak shorthand which preserves with astonishing brilliance the movements and expressions of the figures as they pass across the screen. But the flash is soon over, and there remains with us a profound dissatisfaction. The irritation is as acute as the pleasure was intense.

After all, then, we are back at the beginning, vacillating from extreme to extreme, at one moment enthusiastic, at the next pessimistic, unable to come to any conclusion about our contemporaries. We have asked the critics to help us, but they have deprecated the task. Now, then, is the time to accept their advice and correct these extremes by consulting the masterpieces of the past. We feel ourselves indeed driven to them, impelled not by calm judgement but by some imperious need to anchor our instability upon their security. But, honestly, the shock of the comparison between past and present is at first disconcerting. Undoubtedly there is a dullness in great books. There is an unabashed tranquillity in page after page of Wordsworth and Scott and Miss Austen which is sedative to the verge of somnolence. Opportunities occur and they neglect them. Shades and subtleties accumulate and they ignore them. They seem deliberately to refuse to gratify those senses which are stimulated so briskly by the moderns; the senses of sight, of sound, of touch – above all, the sense of the human being, his depth and the variety of his perceptions, his complexity, his confusion, his self, in short. There is little of all this in the works of Wordsworth and Scott and Jane Austen. From what, then, arises that sense of security which gradually, delightfully, and completely overcomes us? It is the power of their belief – their conviction, that imposes itself upon us. In Wordsworth, the philosophic poet, this is obvious enough. But it is equally true of the careless Scott, who scribbled masterpieces to build castles before breakfast, and of the modest maiden lady who wrote furtively and quietly simply to give pleasure. In both there is the same natural conviction that life is of a certain quality. They have their judgement of conduct. They know the relations of human beings towards each other and towards the universe. Neither of them probably has a word to say about the matter outright, but everything depends on it. Only believe, we find ourselves saying, and all the rest will come of itself. Only believe, to take a very simple instance which the recent publication of *The Watsons* brings to mind, that a nice girl will instinctively try to soothe the feelings of a boy who has been snubbed at a dance, and then, if you believe it implicitly and unquestioningly, you will not only make people a hundred years later feel the same thing, but you will make them feel it as literature. For certainty of that kind is the condition which makes it possible to write. To believe that your impressions hold good for others is to be released from the cramp and confinement of personality. It is to be free, as Scott was free, to explore with a vigour which still holds us spell-bound the whole world of adventure and romance. It is also the first step in that mysterious process in which Jane Austen was so great an adept. The little grain of experience once selected, believed in, and set outside herself, could be put precisely in its place, and she was then free to make of it, by a process which never yields its secrets to the analyst, into that complete statement which is literature.

So then our contemporaries afflict us because they have ceased to believe. The most sincere of them will only tell us what it is that happens to himself. They cannot make a world, because they are not free of other human beings. They cannot tell stories because they do not believe that stories are true. They cannot generalise. They depend on their senses and emotions, whose testimony is trustworthy, rather than on their intellects, whose message is obscure. And they have perforce to deny themselves the use of some of the most powerful and some of the most exquisite of the weapons of their craft. With the whole wealth of the English language at the back of them, they timidly pass about from hand to hand and book to book only the meanest copper coins. Set down at a fresh angle of the eternal prospect they can only whip out their notebooks and record with agonised intensity the flying gleams, which light on what? and the transitory splendours, which may, perhaps, compose nothing whatever. But here the critics interpose, and with some show of justice.

If this description holds good, they say, and is not, as it may well be, entirely dependent upon our position at the table and certain purely personal relationships to mustard pots and flower vases, then the risks of judging contemporary work are greater than ever before. There is every excuse for them if they are wide of the mark; and no doubt it would be better to retreat, as Matthew Arnold advised, from the burning ground of the present to the safe tranquillity of the past. 'We enter on burning ground,' wrote Matthew Arnold, 'as we approach the poetry of times so near to us, poetry like that of Byron, Shelley, and Words-worth, of which the estimates are so often not only personal, but personal with passion,' and this, they remind us, was written in the year 1880. Beware, they say, of putting under the microscope one inch of a ribbon which runs many miles; things sort themselves out if you wait; moderation, and a study of the classics are to be recommended. Moreover, life is short; the Byron centenary is at hand; and the burning question of the moment is, did he, or did he not, marry his sister? To sum up, then – if indeed any conclusion is possible when everybody is talking at once and it is time to be going – it seems that it would be wise for the writers of the present to renounce the hope of creating masterpieces. Their poems, plays, biographies, novels are not books but notebooks, and Time, like a good schoolmaster, will take them in his hands, point to their blots and scrawls and erasions, and tear them across; but he will not throw them into the waste-paper basket. He will keep them because other students will find them very useful. It is from notebooks of the present that the masterpieces of the future are made. Literature, as the critics were saying just now, has lasted long, has undergone many changes, and it is only a short sight and a parochial mind that will exaggerate the importance of these squalls, however they may agitate the little boats now tossing out at sea. The storm and the drenching are on the surface; continuity and calm are in the depths.

As for the critics whose task it is to pass judgement upon the books of the moment, whose work, let us admit, is difficult, dangerous, and often distasteful, let us ask them to be generous of encouragement, but sparing of those wreaths and coronets which are so apt to get awry, and fade, and make the wearers, in six months' time, look a little ridiculous. Let them take a wider, a less personal view of modern literature, and look indeed upon the writers as if they were engaged upon some vast building, which being built by common effort, the separate workmen may well remain anonymous. Let them slam the door upon the cosy company where sugar is cheap and butter plentiful, give over, for a time at least, the discussion of that fascinating topic – whether Byron married his sister – and, withdrawing, perhaps, a handsbreadth from the table where we sit chattering, say something interesting about literature. Let us buttonhole them as they leave, and recall to their memory that gaunt aristocrat, Lady Hester Stanhope, who kept a milk-white horse in her stable in readiness for the Messiah and was for ever scanning the mountain tops, impatiently but with confidence, for signs of his approach, and ask them to follow her example; scan the horizon; see the past in relation to the future; and so prepare the way for masterpieces to come.

T. S. ELIOT

Tradition and the Individual Talent

T. S. Eliot (1888–1965) is nowadays, by general consent, seen as the most important poet of the century, and at least part of that importance derives from his performance as a prose-writer. 'Tradition and the Individual Talent' was first published in 1920 – two years before The Waste Land *– and is still viewed as a key text by critics of the 'conservative–modernist' persuasion.*

I

In English writing we seldom speak of tradition, though we occasionally apply its name in deploring its absence. We cannot refer to 'the tradition' or to 'a tradition'; at most, we employ the adjective in saying that the poetry of So-and-so is 'traditional' or even 'too traditional'. Seldom, perhaps, does the word appear except in a phrase of censure. If otherwise, it is vaguely approbative, with the implication, as to the work approved, of some pleasing archæological reconstruction. You can hardly make the word agreeable to English ears without this comfortable reference to the reassuring science of archæology.

Certainly the word is not likely to appear in our appreciations of living or dead writers. Every nation, every race, has not only its own creative, but its own critical turn of mind; and is even more oblivious of the shortcomings and limitations of its critical habits than of those of its creative genius. We know, or think we know, from the enormous mass of critical writing that has appeared in the French language the critical method or habit of the French; we only conclude (we are such unconscious people) that the French are 'more critical' than we, and sometimes even plume ourselves a little with the fact, as if the French were the less spontaneous. Perhaps they are; but we might remind ourselves that criticism is as inevitable as breathing, and that we should be none the worse for articulating what passes in our minds when we read a book and feel an emotion about it, for criticizing our own minds in their work of criticism. One of the facts that might come to light in this process is our tendency to insist, when we praise a poet, upon those aspects of his work in which he least resembles anyone else. In these aspects or parts of his work we pretend to find what is individual, what is the peculiar essence of the man. We dwell with satisfaction upon the poet's difference from his predecessors, especially his immediate predecessors; we endeavour to find something that can be isolated in order to be enjoyed. Whereas if we approach a poet without this prejudice we shall often find that not only the best, but the most individual parts of his work may be those in which the dead poets, his ancestors, assert their immortality most vigorously. And I do not mean the impressionable period of adolescence, but the period of full maturity.

Yet if the only form of tradition, of handing down, consisted in following the ways of the immediate generation before us in a blind or timid adherence to its successes, 'tradition' should positively be discouraged. We have seen many such simple currents soon lost in the sand; and novelty is better than repetition. Tradition is a matter of much wider significance. It cannot be inherited, and if you want it you must obtain it by great labour. It involves, in the first place, the historical sense, which we may call nearly indispensable to anyone who would continue to be a poet beyond his twenty-fifth year; and the historical sense involves a perception, not only of the pastness of the past, but of its presence; the historical sense compels a man to write not merely with his own generation in his bones, but with a feeling that the whole of the literature of Europe from Homer and within it the whole of the literature of his own country has a simultaneous existence and composes a simultaneous order. This historical sense, which is a sense of the timeless as well as of the temporal and of the timeless and of the temporal together, is what makes a writer traditional. And it is at the same time what makes a writer most acutely conscious of his place in time, of his contemporaneity.

No poet, no artist of any art, has his complete meaning alone. His significance, his appreciation is the appreciation of his relation to the dead poets and artists. You cannot value him alone; you must set him, for contrast and comparison, among the dead. I mean this as a principle of æsthetic, not merely historical, criticism. The necessity that he shall conform, that he shall cohere, is not one-sided; what happens when a new work of art is created is something that happens simultaneously to all the works of art which preceded it. The existing monuments form an ideal order among themselves, which is modified by the introduction of the new (the really new) work of art among them. The existing order is complete before the new work arrives; for order to persist after the supervention of novelty, the *whole* existing order must be, if ever so slightly, altered; and so the relations, proportions, values of each work of art toward the whole are readjusted; and this is conformity between the old and the new. Whoever has approved this idea of order, of the form of European, of English literature, will not find it preposterous that the past should be altered by the present as much as the present is directed by the past. And the poet who is aware of this will be aware of great difficulties and responsibilities.

In a peculiar sense he will be aware also that he must inevitably be judged by the standards of the past. I say judged, not amputated, by them; not judged to be as good as, or worse or better than, the dead; and certainly not judged by the canons of dead critics. It is a judgment, a comparison, in which two things are measured by each other. To conform merely would be for the new work not really to conform at all; it would not be new, and would therefore not be a work of art. And we do not quite say that the new is more valuable because it fits in; but its fitting in is a test of its value – a test, it is true, which can only be slowly and cautiously applied, for we are none of us infallible judges of conformity. We say: it appears to conform, and is perhaps individual, or it appears individual, and may conform; but we are hardly likely to find that it is one and not the other.

To proceed to a more intelligible exposition of the relation of the poet to the past: he can neither take the past as a lump, an indiscriminate bolus, nor can he form himself wholly on one or two private admirations, nor can he form himself wholly upon one preferred period. The first course is inadmissible, the second is an important experience of youth, and the third is a pleasant and highly desirable supplement. The poet must be very conscious of the main current, which does not at all flow invariably through the most distinguished reputations. He must be quite aware of the obvious fact that art never improves, but that the material of art is never quite the same. He must be aware that the mind of Europe – the mind of his own country – a mind which he learns in time to be much more important than his own private mind – is a mind which changes, and that this change is a development which abandons nothing *en route*, which does not superannuate either Shakespeare, or Homer, or the rock drawing of the Magdalenian draughtsmen. That this development, refinement perhaps, complication certainly, is not, from the point of view of the artist, any improvement. Perhaps not even an improvement from the point of view of the psychologist or not to the extent which we imagine; perhaps only in the end based upon a complication in economics and machinery. But the difference between the present and the past is that the conscious present is an awareness of the past in a way and to an extent which the past's awareness of itself cannot show.

Some one said: 'The dead writers are remote from us because we *know* so much more than they did.' Precisely, and they are that which we know.

I am alive to a usual objection to what is clearly part of my programme for the *métier* of poetry. The objection is that the doctrine requires a ridiculous amount of erudition (pedantry), a claim which can be rejected by appeal to the lives of poets in any pantheon. It will even be affirmed that much learning deadens or perverts poetic sensibility. While, however, we persist in believing that a poet ought to know as much as will not encroach upon his necessary receptivity and necessary laziness, it is not desirable to confine knowledge to whatever can be put into a useful shape for examinations, drawing-rooms, or the still more pretentious modes of publicity. Some can absorb knowledge, the more tardy must sweat for it. Shakespeare acquired more essential history from Plutarch than most men could from the whole British Museum. What is to be insisted upon is that the poet must develop or procure the consciousness of the past and that he should continue to develop this consciousness throughout his career.

What happens is a continual surrender of himself as he is at the moment to something which is more valuable. The progress of an artist is a continual self-sacrifice, a continual extinction of personality.

There remains to define this process of depersonalization and its relation to the sense of tradition. It is in this depersonalization that art may be said to approach the condition of science. I shall, therefore, invite you to consider, as a suggestive analogy, the action which takes place when a bit of finely filiated platinum is introduced into a chamber containing oxygen and sulphur dioxide.

II

Honest criticism and sensitive appreciation is directed not upon the poet but upon the poetry. If we attend to the confused cries of the newspaper critics and the susurrus of popular repetition that follows, we shall hear the names of poets in great numbers; if we seek not Blue-book knowledge but the enjoyment of poetry, and ask for a poem, we shall seldom find it. In the last article I tried to point out the importance of the relation of the poem to other poems by other authors, and suggested the conception of poetry as a living whole of all the poetry that has ever been written. The other aspect of this Impersonal theory of poetry is the relation of the poem to its author. And I hinted, by an analogy, that the mind of the mature poet differs from that of the immature one not precisely in any valuation of 'personality', not being necessarily more interesting, or having 'more to say', but rather by being a more finely perfected medium in which special, or very varied, feelings are at liberty to enter into new combinations.

The analogy was that of the catalyst. When the two gases previously mentioned are mixed in the presence of a filament of platinum, they form sulphurous acid. This combination takes place only if the platinum is present; nevertheless the newly formed acid contains no trace of platinum, and the platinum itself is apparently unaffected; has remained inert, neutral, and unchanged. The mind of the poet is the shred of platinum. It may partly or exclusively operate upon the experience of the man himself; but, the more perfect the artist, the more completely separate in him will be the man who suffers and the mind which creates; the more perfectly will the mind digest and transmute the passions which are its material.

The experience, you will notice, the elements which enter the presence of the transforming catalyst, are of two kinds: emotions and feelings. The effect of a work of art upon the person who enjoys it is an experience different in kind from any experience not of art. It may be formed out of one emotion, or may be a combination of several; and various feelings, inhering for the writer in particular words or phrases or images, may be added to compose the final result. Or great poetry may be made without the direct use of any emotion whatever: composed out of feelings solely. Canto XV of the *Inferno* (Brunetto Latini) is a working up of the emotion evident in the situation; but the effect, though single as that of any work of art, is obtained by considerable complexity of detail. The last quatrain gives an image, a feeling attaching to an image, which 'came', which did not develop simply out of what precedes, but which was probably in suspension in the poet's mind until the proper combination arrived for it to add itself to. The poet's mind is in fact a receptacle for seizing and storing up numberless feelings, phrases, images, which remain there until all the particles which can unite to form a new compound are present together.

If you compare several representative passages of the greatest poetry you see how great is the variety of types of combination, and also how completely any semi-ethical criterion of 'sublimity' misses the mark. For it is not the 'greatness', the intensity, of the emotions, the components, but the intensity of the artistic process, the pressure, so to speak, under which the fusion takes place, that counts. The episode of Paolo and Francesca employs a definite emotion, but the intensity of the poetry is something quite different from whatever intensity in the supposed experience it may give the impression of. It is no more intense, furthermore, than Canto XXVI, the voyage of Ulysses, which has not the direct dependence upon an emotion. Great variety is possible in the process of transmutation of emotion: the murder of Agamemnon, or the agony of Othello, gives an artistic effect apparently closer to a possible original than the scenes from Dante. In the *Agamemnon*, the artistic emotion approximates to the emotion of an actual spectator; in *Othello* to the emotion of the protagonist himself. But the difference between art and the event is always absolute; the combination which is the murder of Agamemnon is probably as complex as that which is the voyage of Ulysses. In either case there has been a fusion of elements. The ode of Keats contains a number of feelings which have nothing particular to do with the nightingale, but which the nightingale, partly, perhaps, because of its attractive name, and partly because of its reputation, served to bring together.

The point of view which I am struggling to attack is perhaps related to the metaphysical theory of the substantial unity of the soul: for my meaning is, that the poet has, not a 'personality' to express, but a particular medium, which is only a medium and not a personality, in which impressions and experiences combine in peculiar and unexpected ways. Impressions and experiences which are important for the man may take no place in the poetry, and those which become important in the poetry may play quite a negligible part in the man, the personality.

I will quote a passage which is unfamiliar enough to be regarded with fresh attention in the light – or darkness – of these observations:

> And now methinks I could e'en chide myself
> For doating on her beauty, though her death
> Shall be revenged after no common action.
> Does the silkworm expend her yellow labours
> For thee? For thee does she undo herself?
> Are lordships sold to maintain ladyships
> For the poor benefit of a bewildering minute?
> Why does yon fellow falsify highways,
> And put his life between the judge's lips,
> To refine such a thing – keeps horse and men
> To beat their valours for her? . . .

In this passage (as is evident if it is taken in its context) there is a combination of positive and negative emotions: an intensely strong attraction toward beauty and an equally intense fascination by the ugliness which is contrasted with it and which destroys it. This balance of contrasted emotion is in the dramatic situation to which the speech is pertinent, but that situation alone is inadequate to it. This is, so to speak, the structural emotion, provided by the drama. But the whole effect, the dominant tone, is due to the fact that a number of floating feelings, having an affinity to this emotion by no means superficially evident, have combined with it to give us a new art emotion.

It is not in his personal emotions, the emotions provoked by particular events in his life, that the poet is in any way remarkable or interesting. His particular emotions may be simple, or crude, or flat. The emotion in his poetry will be a very complex thing, but not with the complexity of the emotions of people who have very complex or unusual emotions in life. One error, in fact, of eccentricity in poetry is to seek for new human emotions to express; and in this search for novelty in the wrong place it discovers the perverse. The business of the poet is not to find new emotions, but to use the ordinary ones and, in working them up into poetry, to express feelings which are not in actual emotions at all. And emotions which he has never experienced will serve his turn as well as those familiar to him. Consequently, we must believe that 'emotion recollected in tranquillity' is an inexact formula. For it is neither emotion, nor recollection, nor, without distortion of meaning, tranquillity. It is a concentration, and a new thing resulting from the concentration, of a very great number of experiences which to the practical and active person would not seem to be experiences at all; it is a concentration which does not happen consciously or of deliberation. These experiences are not 'recollected', and they finally unite in an atmosphere which is 'tranquil' only in that it is a passive attending upon the event. Of course this is not quite the whole story. There is a great deal, in the writing of poetry, which must be conscious and deliberate. In fact, the bad poet is usually unconscious where he ought to be conscious, and conscious where he ought to be unconscious. Both errors tend to make him 'personal'. Poetry is not a turning loose of emotion, but an escape from emotion; it is not the expression of personality, but an escape from personality. But, of course, only those who have personality and emotions know what it means to want to escape from these things.

III

ὁ δὲ νοῦς ἴσως θειοτέρον τι χαὶ ἀπαθές ἔστιν

This essay proposes to halt at the frontier of metaphysics or mysticism, and confine itself to such practical conclusions as can be applied by the responsible person interested in poetry. To divert interest from the poet to the poetry is a laudable aim: for it would conduce to a juster estimation of actual poetry, good and bad. There are many people who appreciate the expression of sincere emotion in verse, and there is a smaller number of people who can appreciate technical excellence. But very few know when there is expression of *significant* emotion, emotion which has its life in the poem and not in the history of the poet. The emotion of art is impersonal. And the poet cannot reach this impersonality without surrendering himself wholly to the work to be done. And he is not likely to know what is to be done unless he lives in what is not merely the present, but the present moment of the past, unless he is conscious, not of what is dead, but of what is already living.

MAX BEERBOHM

Laughter

Max Beerbohm was born in 1872 and from the age of twenty was well known in London literary circles as an elegantly mordant caricaturist and essayist. He also had a reputation as a drama critic and as an expert parodist. Although Beerbohm's Oxford fantasy, Zuleika Dobson, *is now probably his best-known work, he has always been something of a connoisseur's delight. For a satirist, he had remarkably few enemies. The 'incomparable Max', as Shaw called him, never seemed to be axe-grinding or malicious. Perhaps Beerbohm's modesty was genuine. His essay 'Laughter' was first collected in* And Even Now *(1920). Beerbohm died in 1956.*

M. Bergson, in his well-known essay on this theme, says – well, he says many things; but none of these, though I have just read them, do I clearly remember, nor am I sure that in the act of reading I understood any of them. That is the worst of these fashionable philosophers – or rather, the worst of me. Somehow I never manage to read them till they are just going out of fashion, and even then I don't seem able to cope with them. About twelve years ago, when everyone suddenly talked to me about Pragmatism and William James, I found myself moved by a dull but irresistible impulse to try Schopenhauer, of whom, years before that, I had heard that he was the easiest reading in the world, and the most exciting and amusing. I wrestled with Schopenhauer for a day or so, in vain. Time passed; M. Bergson appeared 'and for his hour was lord of the ascendant'; I tardily tackled William James. I bore in mind, as I approached him, the testimonials that had been lavished on him by all my friends. Alas, I was insensible to his thrillingness. His gaiety did not make me gay. His crystal clarity confused me dreadfully. I could make nothing of William James. And now, in the fullness of time, I have been floored by M. Bergson.

It distresses me, this failure to keep pace with the leaders of thought as they pass into oblivion. It makes me wonder whether I am, after all, an absolute fool. Yet surely I am not that. Tell me of a man or a woman, a place or an event, real or fictitious: surely you will find me a fairly intelligent listener. Any such narrative will present to me some image, and will stir me to not altogether fatuous thoughts. Come to me in some grievous difficulty: I will talk to you like a father, even like a lawyer. I'll be hanged if I haven't a certain mellow wisdom. But if you are by way of weaving theories as to the nature of things in general, and if you want to try those theories on someone who will luminously confirm them or powerfully rend them, I must, with a hang-dog air, warn you that I am not your man. I suffer from a strong suspicion that things in general cannot be accounted for through any formula or set of formulæ, and that any one philosophy, howsoever new, is no better than another. That is in itself a sort of philosophy, and I suspect it accordingly; but it has for me the merit of being the only one I can make head or tail of. If you try to expound any other philosophic system to me, you will find not merely that I can detect no flaw in it (except the one great flaw just suggested), but also that I haven't, after a minute or two, the vaguest notion of what you are driving at. 'Very well,' you say, 'instead of trying to explain all things all at once, I will explain some little, simple, single thing.' It was for sake of such shorn lambs as myself, doubtless, that M. Bergson sat down and wrote about – Laughter. But I have profited by his kindness no more than if he had been treating of the Cosmos. I cannot tread even a limited space of air. I have a gross satisfaction in the crude fact of being on hard ground again, and I utter a coarse peal of – Laughter.

At least, I say I do so. In point of fact, I have merely smiled. Twenty years ago, ten years ago, I should have laughed, and have professed to you that I had merely smiled. A very young man is not content to be very young, nor even a young man to be young: he wants to share the dignity of his elders. There is no dignity in laughter, there is much of it in smiles. Laughter is but a joyous surrender, smiles give token of mature criticism. It may be that in the early ages of this world there was far more laughter than is to be heard now, and that æons hence laughter will be obsolete, and smiles universal – everyone, always, mildly, slightly, smiling. But it is less useful to speculate as to mankind's past and future than to observe men. And you will have observed with me in the club-room that young men at most times look solemn, whereas old men or men of middle age mostly smile; and also that those young men do often laugh loud and long among themselves, while we others – the gayest and best of us in the most favourable circumstances – seldom achieve more than our habitual act of smiling. Does the sound of that laughter jar on us? Do we liken it to the crackling of thorns under a pot? Let us do so. There is no cheerier sound. But let us not assume it to be the laughter of fools because we sit quiet. It is absurd to disapprove of what one envies, or to wish a good thing were no more because it has passed out of our possession.

But (it seems that I must begin every paragraph by questioning the sincerity of what I have just said) *has* the gift of laughter been withdrawn from me? I protest that I do still, at the age of forty-seven, laugh often and loud and long. But not, I believe, so long and loud and often as in my less smiling youth. And I am proud, nowadays, of laughing, and grateful to anyone who makes me laugh. That is a bad sign. I no longer take laughter as a matter of course. I realise, even after reading M. Bergson on it, how good a thing it is. I am qualified to praise it.

As to what is most precious among the accessories to the world we live in, different men hold different opinions. There are people whom the sea depresses, whom mountains exhilarate. Personally, I want the sea always – some not populous edge of it for choice; and with it sunshine, and wine, and a little music. My friend on the mountain yonder is of tougher fibre and sterner outlook, disapproves of the sea's laxity and instability, has no ear for music and no palate for the grape, and regards the sun as a rather enervating institution, like central heating in a house. What he likes is a grey day and the wind in his face; crags at a great altitude; and a flask of whisky. Yet I think that even he, if we were trying to determine from what inner sources mankind derives the greatest pleasure in life, would agree with me that only the emotion of love takes higher rank than the emotion of laughter. Both these emotions are partly mental, partly physical. It is said that the mental symptoms of love are wholly physical in origin. They are not the less ethereal for that. The physical sensations of laughter, on the other hand, are reached by a process whose starting-point is in the mind. They are not the less 'gloriously of our clay'. There is laughter that goes so far as to lose all touch with its motive, and to exist only, grossly, in itself. This is laughter at its best. A man to whom such laughter has often been granted may happen to die in a workhouse. No matter. I will not admit that he has failed in life. Another man, who has never laughed thus, may be buried in Westminster Abbey, leaving more than a million pounds overhead. What then? I regard him as a failure.

Nor does it seem to me to matter one jot how such laughter is achieved. Humour may rollick on high planes of fantasy or in depths of silliness. To many people it appeals only from those depths. If it appeal to them irresistibly, they are more enviable than those who are sensitive only to the finer kind of joke and not so sensitive as to be mastered and dissolved by it. Laughter is a thing to be rated according to its own intensity.

Many years ago I wrote an essay in which I poured scorn on the fun purveyed by the music halls, and on the great public for which that fun was quite good enough. I take that callow scorn back. I fancy that the fun itself was better than it seemed to me, and might not have displeased me if it had been wafted to me in private, in presence of a few friends. A public crowd, because of a lack of broad impersonal humanity in me, rather insulates than absorbs me. Amidst the guffaws of a thousand strangers I become unnaturally grave. If these people were the entertainment, and I the audience, I should be sympathetic enough. But to be one of them is a position that drives me spiritually aloof. Also, there is to me something rather dreary in the notion of going anywhere for the specific purpose of being amused. I prefer that laughter shall take me unawares. Only so can it master and dissolve me. And in this respect, at any rate, I am not peculiar. In music halls and such places, you may hear loud laughter, but – not see silent laughter, not see strong men weak, helpless, suffering, gradually convalescent, dangerously relapsing. Laughter at its greatest and best is not there.

To such laughter nothing is more propitious than an occasion that demands gravity. To have good reason for not laughing is one of the surest aids. Laughter rejoices in bonds. If music halls were schoolrooms for us, and the comedians were our schoolmasters, how much less talent would be needed for giving us how much more joy! Even in private and accidental intercourse, few are the men whose humour can reduce us, be we never so susceptible, to paroxysms of mirth. I will wager that nine-tenths of the world's best laughter is laughter *at*, not *with*. And it is the people set in authority over us that touch most surely our sense of the ridiculous. Freedom is a good thing, but we lose through it golden moments. The schoolmaster to his pupils, the monarch to his courtiers, the editor to his staff – how priceless they are! Reverence is a good thing, and part of its value is that the more we revere a man, the more sharply are we struck by anything in him (and there is always much) that is incongruous with his greatness. And herein lies one of the reasons why as we grow older we laugh less. The men we esteemed so great are gathered to their fathers. Some of our coevals may, for aught we know, be very great, but good heavens! we can't esteem *them* so.

Of extreme laughter I know not in any annals a more satisfying example than one that is to be found in Moore's *Life of Byron*. Both Byron and Moore were already in high spirits when, on an evening in the spring of 1813, they went 'from some early assembly' to Mr Rogers' house in St James's Place and were regaled there with an impromptu meal. But not high spirits alone would have led the two young poets to such excess of laughter as made the evening so very memorable. Luckily they both venerated Rogers (strange as it may seem to us) as the greatest of living poets. Luckily, too, Mr Rogers was ever the kind of man, the coldly and quietly suave kind of man, with whom you don't take liberties, if you can help it – with whom, if you *can't* help it, to take liberties is in itself a most exhilarating act. And he had just received a presentation copy of Lord Thurloe's latest book, *Poems on Several Occasions*. The two young poets found in this elder's Muse much that was so execrable as to be delightful. They were soon, as they turned the pages, held in throes of laughter, laughter that was but intensified by the endeavours of their correct and nettled host to point out the genuine merits of his friend's work. And then suddenly – oh, joy – 'we lighted,' Moore records, 'on the discovery that our host, in addition to his sincere approbation of some of this book's contents, had also the motive of gratitude for standing by its author, as one of the poems was a warm and, I need not add, well-deserved panegyric on himself. We were, however' – the narrative has an added charm from Tom Moore's demure care not to offend or compromise the still-surviving Rogers – 'too far gone in nonsense for even this eulogy, in which we both so heartily agreed, to stop us. The opening line of the poem was, as well as I can recollect, "When Rogers o'er this labour bent"; and Lord Byron undertook to read it aloud – but he found it impossible to get beyond the first two words. Our laughter had now increased to such a pitch that nothing could restrain it. Two or three times he began; but no sooner had the words "When Rogers" passed his lips, than our fit burst out afresh – till even Mr Rogers himself, with all his feeling of our injustice, found it impossible not to join us; and we were, at last, all three in such a state of inextinguishable laughter, that, had the author himself been of our party, I question much whether he could have resisted the infection.' The final fall and dissolution of Rogers, Rogers behaving as badly as either of them, is all that was needed to give perfection to this heart-warming scene. I like to think that on a certain night in spring, year after year, three ghosts revisit that old room and (without, I hope, inconvenience to Lord Northcliffe, who may happen to be there) sit rocking and writhing in the grip of that old shared rapture. Uncanny! Well, not more so than would have seemed to Byron and Moore and Rogers the notion that more than a hundred years away from them was someone joining in their laughter – as *I* do.

Alas, I cannot join in it more than gently. To imagine a scene, however vividly, does not give us the sense of being, or even of having been, present at it. Indeed, the greater the glow of the scene reflected, the sharper is the pang of our realisation that we were *not* there, and of our annoyance that we weren't. Such a pang comes to me with special force whenever my fancy posts itself outside the Temple's gate in Fleet Street, and there, at a late hour of the night of May 10th 1773, observes a gigantic old man laughing wildly, but having no one with him to share and aggrandise his emotion. Not that he is alone; but the young man beside him laughs only in politeness and is inwardly puzzled, even shocked. Boswell has a keen, an exquisitely keen, scent for comedy, for the fun that is latent in fine shades of character; but imaginative burlesque, anything that borders on lovely nonsense, he was not formed to savour. All the more does one revel in his account of what led up to the moment when Johnson, 'to support himself, laid hold of one of the posts at the side of the foot pavement, and sent forth peals so loud that in the silence of the night his voice seemed to resound from Temple Bar to Fleet Ditch'.

No evening ever had an unlikelier ending. The omens were all for gloom. Johnson had gone to dine at General Paoli's, but was so ill that he had to leave before the meal was over. Later he managed to go to Mr Chambers' rooms in the Temple. 'He continued to be very ill' there, but gradually felt better, and 'talked with a noble enthusiasm of keeping up the representation of respectable families', and was great on 'the dignity and propriety of male succession'. Among his listeners, as it happened, was a gentleman for whom Mr Chambers had that day drawn up a will devising his estate to his three sisters. The news of this might have been expected to make Johnson violent in wrath. But no, for some reason he grew violent only in laughter, and insisted thenceforth on calling that gentleman The Testator and chaffing him without mercy. 'I daresay he thinks he has done a mighty thing. He won't stay till he gets home to his seat in the country, to produce this wonderful deed: he'll call up the landlord of the first inn on the road; and after a suitable preface upon mortality and the uncertainty of life, will tell him that he should not delay in making his will; and Here, Sir, will he say, is *my* will, which I have just made, with the assistance of one of the ablest lawyers in the kingdom; and he will read it to him. He believes he has made this will; but he did not make it; you, Chambers, made it for him. I hope you have had more conscience than to make him say "being of sound understanding!" ha, ha, ha! I hope he has left me a legacy. I'd have his will turned into verse, like a ballad.' These flights annoyed Mr Chambers, and are recorded by Boswell with the apology that he wishes his readers to be 'acquainted with the slightest occasional characteristics of so eminent a man'. Certainly, there is nothing ridiculous in the fact of a man making a will. But this is the measure of Johnson's achievement. He had created gloriously much out of nothing at all. There he sat, old and ailing and unencouraged by the company, but soaring higher and higher in absurdity, more and more rejoicing, and still soaring and rejoicing after he had gone out into the night with Boswell, till at last in Fleet Street his paroxysms were too much for him and he could no more. Echoes of that huge laughter come ringing down the ages. But is there also perhaps a note of sadness for us in them? Johnson's endless sociability came of his inherent melancholy: he could not bear to be alone; and his very mirth was but a mode of escape from the dark thoughts within him. Of these the thought of death was the most dreadful to him, and the most insistent. He was for ever wondering how death would come to him, and how he would acquit himself in the extreme moment. A later but not less devoted Anglican, meditating on his own end, wrote in his diary that 'to die in church appears to be a great euthanasia, but not,' he quaintly and touchingly added, 'at a time to disturb worshippers'. Both the sentiment here expressed and the reservation drawn would have been as characteristic of Johnson as they were of Gladstone. But to die of laughter – this, too, seems to me a great euthanasia; and I think that for Johnson to have died thus, that night in Fleet Street, would have been a grand ending to 'a life radically wretched'. Well, he was destined to outlive another decade; and, selfishly, who can wish such a life as his, or such a Life as Boswell's, one jot shorter!

Strange, when you come to think of it, that of all the countless folk who have lived before our time on this planet not one is known in history or in legend as having died of laughter. Strange, too, that not to one of all the characters in romance has such an end been allotted. Has it ever struck you what a chance Shakespeare missed when he was finishing the Second Part of *King Henry the Fourth*? Falstaff was not the man to stand cowed and bowed while the new young king lectured him and cast him off. Little by little, as Hal proceeded in that portentous allocution, the humour of the situation would have mastered old Sir John. His face, blank with surprise at first, would presently have glowed and widened, and his whole bulk have begun to quiver. Lest he should miss one word, he would have mastered himself. But the final words would have been the signal for release of all the roars pent up in him; the welkin would have rung; the roars, belike, would have gradually subsided in dreadful rumblings of more than utterable or conquerable mirth. Thus and thus only might his life have been rounded off with dramatic fitness, *secundum ipsius naturam*. He never should have been left to babble of green fields and die 'an it had been any christom child'.

Falstaff is a triumph of comedic creation because we are kept laughing equally at and with him. Nevertheless, if I had the choice of sitting with him at the Boar's Head or with Johnson at the Turk's, I shouldn't hesitate for an instant. The agility of Falstaff's mind gains much of its effect by contrast with the massiveness of his body; but in contrast with Johnson's equal agility is Johnson's moral as well as physical bulk. His sallies 'tell' the more startlingly because of the noble weight of character behind them: they are the better because *he* makes them. In Falstaff there isn't this final incongruity and element of surprise. Falstaff is but a sublimated sample of 'the funny man'. We cannot, therefore, laugh so greatly with him as with Johnson. (Nor even *at* him; because we are not tickled so much by the weak points of a character whose points are all weak ones; also because we have no reverence trying to impose restraint upon us.) Still, Falstaff has indubitably the power to convulse us. I don't mean we ever are convulsed in reading *Henry the Fourth*. No printed page, alas, can thrill us to extremities of laughter. These are ours only if the mirthmaker be a living man whose jests we hear as they come fresh from his own lips. All I claim for Falstaff is that he would be able to convulse us if he were alive and accessible. Few, as I have said, are the humorists who can induce this state. To master and dissolve us, to give us the joy of being worn down and tired out with laughter, is a success to be won by no man save in virtue of a rare staying-power. Laughter becomes extreme only if it be consecutive. There must be no pauses for recovery. Touch-and-go humour, however happy, is not enough. The jester must be able to grapple his theme and hang on to it, twisting it this way and that, and making it yield magically all manner of strange and precious things, one after another, without pause. He must have invention keeping pace with utterance. He must be inexhaustible. Only so can he exhaust us.

I have a friend whom I would praise. There are many other of my friends to whom I am indebted for much laughter; but I do believe that if all of them sent in their bills tomorrow and all of them overcharged me not a little, the total of all those totals would be less appalling than that which looms in my own vague estimate of what I owe to Comus. Comus I call him here in observance of the line drawn between public and private virtue, and in full knowledge that he would of all men be the least glad to be quite personally thanked and laurelled in the market-place for the hours he has made memorable among his cronies. No one is so diffident as he, no one so self-postponing. Many people have met him again and again without faintly suspecting 'anything much' in him. Many of his acquaintances – friends, too – relatives, even – have lived and died in the belief that he was quite ordinary. Thus is he the more greatly valued by his cronies. Thus do we pride ourselves on possessing some curious right quality to which alone he is responsive. But it would seem that either this asset of ours or its effect on him is intermittent. He can be dull and null enough with us sometimes – a mere asker of questions, or drawer of comparisons between this and that brand of cigarettes, or full expatiator on the merits of some new patent razor. A whole hour and more may be wasted in such humdrum and darkness. And then – something will have happened. There has come a spark in the murk; a flame now, presage of a radiance: Comus has begun. His face is a great part of his equipment. A cast of it might be somewhat akin to the comic mask of the ancients; but no cast could be worthy of it; mobility is the essence of it. It flickers and shifts in accord to the matter of his discourse; it contracts and it expands; is there anything its elastic can't express? Comus would be eloquent even were he dumb. And he is mellifluous. His voice, while he develops an idea or conjures up a scene, takes on a peculiar richness and unction. If he be describing an actual scene, voice and face are adaptable to those of the actual persons therein. But it is not in such mimicry that he excels. As a reporter he has rivals. For the most part, he moves on a higher plane than that of mere fact: he imagines, he creates, giving you not a person, but a type, a synthesis, and not what anywhere has been, but what anywhere might be – what, as one feels, for all the absurdity of it, just would be. He knows his world well, and nothing human is alien to him, but certain skeins of life have a special hold on him, and he on them. In his youth he wished to be a clergyman; and over the clergy of all grades and denominations his genius hovers and swoops and ranges with a special mastery. Lawyers he loves less; yet the legal mind seems to lie almost as wide-open to him as the sacerdotal; and the legal manner in all its phases he can unerringly burlesque. In the minds of journalists, diverse journalists, he is not less thoroughly at home, so that of the wild contingencies imagined by him there is none about which he cannot reel off an oral 'leader' or 'middle' in the likeliest style, and with as much ease as he can preach a High Church or Low Church sermon on it. Nor are his improvisations limited by prose. If a theme call for nobler treatment, he becomes an unflagging fountain of ludicrously adequate blank-verse. Or again, he may deliver himself in rhyme. There is no form of utterance that comes amiss to him for interpreting the human comedy, or for broadening the farce into which that comedy is turned by him. Nothing can stop him when once he is in the vein. No appeals move him. He goes from strength to strength while his audience is more and more piteously debilitated.

What a gift to have been endowed with! What a power to wield! And how often I have envied Comus! But this envy of him has never taken root in me. His mind laughs, doubtless, at his own conceptions; but not his body. And if you tell him something that you have been sure will convulse him you are likely to be rewarded with no more than a smile betokening that he sees the point. Incomparable laughter-giver, he is not much a laugher. He is vintner, not toper. I would therefore not change places with him. I am well content to have been his beneficiary during thirty years, and to be so for as many more as may be given us.

D. H. LAWRENCE

Why the Novel Matters

D. H. Lawrence (1885–1930) was a prolific writer in genres other than the novel – the form, of course, on which his reputation rests. He was a poet, a playwright, a travel writer and – from time to time – an essayist. He wrote books on psycho-analysis and on the Bible. Altogether, he gave the impression that there was no subject on which he did not have decided views. Lawrence's essays tended to be as aggressively dogmatic as everything else he wrote, and 'Why the Novel Matters' was one topic on which he could claim special expertise. See D. H. Lawrence: Selected Criticism *(Heinemann, 1956) for other literary pieces.*

We have curious ideas of ourselves. We think of ourselves as a body with a spirit in it, or a body with a soul in it, or a body with a mind in it. *Mens sana in corpore sano.* The years drink up the wine, and at last throw the bottle away, the body, of course, being the bottle.

It is a funny sort of superstition. Why should I look at my hand, as it so cleverly writes these words, and decide that it is a mere nothing compared to the mind that directs it? Is there really any huge difference between my hand and my brain? Or my mind? My hand is alive, it flickers with a life of its own. It meets all the strange universe in touch, and learns a vast number of things, and knows a vast number of things. My hand, as it writes these words, slips gaily along, jumps like a grasshopper to dot an *i*, feels the table rather cold, gets a little bored if I write too long, has its own rudiments of thought, and is just as much *me* as is my brain, my mind, or my soul. Why should I imagine that there is a *me* which is more *me* than my hand is? Since my hand is absolutely alive, me alive.

Whereas, of course, as far as I am concerned, my pen isn't alive at all. My pen *isn't me* alive. Me alive ends at my finger-tips.

Whatever is me alive is me. Every tiny bit of my hands is alive, every little freckle and hair and fold of skin. And whatever is me alive is me. Only my finger-nails, those ten little weapons between me and an inanimate universe, they cross the mysterious Rubicon between me alive and things like my pen, which are not alive, in my own sense.

So, seeing my hand is all alive, and me alive, wherein is it just a bottle, or a jug, or a tin can, or a vessel of clay, or any of the rest of that nonsense? True, if I cut it it will bleed, like a can of cherries. But then the skin that is cut, and the veins that bleed, and the bones that should never be seen, they are all just as alive as the blood that flows. So the tin can business, or vessel of clay, is just bunk.

And that's what you learn, when you're a novelist. And that's what you are very liable *not* to know, if you're a parson, or a philosopher, or a scientist, or a stupid person. If you're a parson, you talk about souls in heaven. If you're a novelist, you know that paradise is in the palm of your hand, and on the end of your nose, because both are alive; and alive, and man alive, which is more than you can say, for certain, of paradise. Paradise is after life, and I for one am not keen on anything that is *after* life. If you are a philosopher, you talk about infinity, and the pure spirit which knows all things. But if you pick up a novel, you realise immediately that infinity is just a handle to this self-same jug of a body of mine; while as for knowing, if I find my finger in the fire, I know that fire burns, with a knowledge so emphatic and vital, it leaves Nirvana merely a conjecture. Oh, yes, my body, me alive, *knows*, and knows intensely. And as for the sum of all knowledge, it can't be anything more than an accumulation of all the things I know in the body, and you, dear reader, know in the body.

These damned philosophers, they talk as if they suddenly went off in steam, and were then much more important than they are when they're in their shirts. It is nonsense. Every man, philosopher included, ends in his own finger-tips. That's the end of his man alive. As for the words and thoughts and sighs and aspirations that fly from him, they are so many tremulations in the ether, and not alive at all. But if the tremulations reach another man alive, he may receive them into his life, and his life may take on a new colour, like a chameleon creeping from a brown rock on to a green leaf. All very well and good. It still doesn't alter the fact that the so-called spirit, the message or teaching of the philosopher or the saint, isn't alive at all, but just a tremulation upon the ether, like a radio message. All this spirit stuff is just tremulations upon the ether. If you, as man alive, quiver from the tremulation of the ether into new life, that is because you are man alive, and you take sustenance and stimulation into your alive man in a myriad ways. But to say that the message, or the spirit which is communicated to you, is more important than your living body, is nonsense. You might as well say that the potato at dinner was more important.

Nothing is important but life. And for myself, I can absolutely see life nowhere but in the living. Life with a capital L is only man alive. Even a cabbage in the rain is cabbage alive. All things that are alive are amazing. And all things that are dead are subsidiary to the living. Better a live dog than a dead lion. But better a live lion than a live dog. *C'est la vie!*

It seems impossible to get a saint, or a philosopher, or a scientist, to stick to this simple truth. They are all, in a sense, renegades. The saint wishes to offer himself up as spiritual food for the multitude. Even Francis of Assisi turns himself into a sort of angel-cake, of which anyone may take a slice. But an angel-cake is rather less than man alive. And poor St Francis might well apologise to his body, when he is dying: 'Oh, pardon me, my body, the wrong I did you through the years!' It was no wafer, for others to eat.

The philosopher, on the other hand, because he can think, decides that nothing but thoughts matter. It is as if a rabbit, because he can make little pills, should decide that nothing but little pills matter. As for the scientist, he has absolutely no use for me so long as I am man alive. To the scientist, I am dead. He puts under the microscope a bit of dead me, and calls it me. He takes me to pieces, and says first one piece, and then another piece, is me. My heart, my liver, my stomach have all been scientifically me, according to the scientist; and nowadays I am either a brain, or nerves, or glands, or something more up-to-date in the tissue line.

Now I absolutely flatly deny that I am a soul, or a body, or a mind, or an intelligence, or a brain, or a nervous system, or a bunch of glands, or any of the rest of these bits of me. The whole is greater than the part. And therefore, I, who am man alive, am greater than my soul, or spirit, or body, or mind, or consciousness, or anything else that is merely a part of me. I am a man, and alive. I am man alive, and as long as I can, I intend to go on being man alive.

For this reason I am a novelist. And being a novelist, I consider myself superior to the saint, the scientist, the philosopher, and the poet, who are all great masters of different bits of man alive, but never get the whole hog.

The novel is the one bright book of life. Books are not life. They are only tremulations on the ether. But the novel as a tremulation can make the whole man alive tremble. Which is more than poetry, philosophy, science, or any other book-tremulation can do.

The novel is the book of life. In this sense, the Bible is a great confused novel. You may say, it is about God. But it is really about man alive. Adam, Eve, Sarai, Abraham, Isaac, Jacob, Samuel, David, Bath-sheba, Ruth, Esther, Solomon, Job, Isaiah, Jesus, Mark, Judas, Paul, Peter: what is it but man alive, from start to finish? Man alive, not mere bits. Even the Lord is another man alive, in a burning bush, throwing the tablets of stone at Moses's head.

I do hope you begin to get my idea, why the novel is supremely important, as a tremulation on the ether. Plato makes the perfect ideal being tremble in me. But that's only a bit of me. Perfection is only a bit, in the strange make-up of man alive. The Sermon on the Mount makes the selfless spirit of me quiver. But that, too, is only a bit of me. The Ten Commandments set the old Adam shivering in me, warning me that I am a thief and a murderer, unless I watch it. But even the old Adam is only a bit of me.

I very much like all these bits of me to be set trembling with life and the wisdom of life. But I do ask that the whole of me shall tremble in its wholeness, some time or other.

And this, of course, must happen in me, living.

But as far as it can happen from a communication, it can only happen when a whole novel communicates itself to me. The Bible – but *all* the Bible – and Homer, and Shakespeare: these are the supreme old novels. These are all things to all men. Which means that in their wholeness they affect the whole man alive, which is the man himself, beyond any part of him. They set the whole tree trembling with a new access of life, they do not just stimulate growth in one direction.

I don't want to grow in any one direction any more. And, if I can help it, I don't want to stimulate anybody else into some particular direction. A particular direction ends in a *cul-de-sac*. We're in a *cul-de-sac* at present.

I don't believe in any dazzling revelation, or in any supreme Word.

'The grass withereth, the flower fadeth, but the Word of the Lord shall stand for ever.' That's the kind of stuff we've drugged ourselves with. As a matter of fact, the grass withereth, but comes up all the greener for that reason, after the rains. The flower fadeth, and therefore the bud opens. But the Word of the Lord, being man-uttered and a mere vibration on the ether, becomes staler and staler, more and more boring, till at last we turn a deaf ear and it ceases to exist, far more finally than any withered grass. It is grass that renews its youth like the eagle, not any Word.

We should ask for no absolutes, or absolute. Once and for all and for ever, let us have done with the ugly imperialism of any absolute. There is no absolute good, there is nothing absolutely right. All things flow and change, and even change is not absolute. The whole is a strange assembly of apparently incongruous parts, slipping past one another.

Me, man alive, I am a very curious assembly of incongruous parts. My yea! of today is oddly different from my yea! of yesterday. My tears of tomorrow will have nothing to do with my tears of a year ago. If the one I love remains unchanged and unchanging, I shall cease to love her. It is only because she changes and startles me into change and defies my inertia, and is herself staggered in her inertia by my changing, that I can continue to love her. If she stayed put, I might as well love the pepper-pot.

In all this change, I maintain a certain integrity. But woe betide me if I try to put my finger on it. If I say of myself, I am this, I am that! – then, if I stick to it, I turn into a stupid fixed thing like a lamp-post. I shall never know wherein lies my integrity, my individuality, my me. I *can* never know it. It is useless to talk about my ego. That only means that I have made up an *idea* of myself, and that I am trying to cut myself out to pattern. Which is no good. You can cut your cloth to fit your coat, but you can't clip bits off your living body, to trim it down to your idea. True, you can put yourself into ideal corsets. But even in ideal corsets, fashions change.

Let us learn from the novel. In the novel, the characters can do nothing but *live*. If they keep on being good, according to pattern, or bad, according to pattern, or even volatile, according to pattern, they cease to live, and the novel falls dead. A character in a novel has got to live, or it is nothing.

We, likewise, in life have got to live, or we are nothing.

What we mean by living is, of course, just as indescribable as what we mean by *being*. Men get ideas into their heads, of what they mean by Life, and they proceed to cut life out to pattern. Sometimes they go into the desert to seek God, sometimes they go into the desert to seek cash, sometimes it is wine, woman, and song, and again it is water, political reform, and votes. You never know what it will be next: from killing your neighbour with hideous bombs and gas that tears the lungs, to supporting a Foundlings' Home and preaching infinite Love, and being co-respondent in a divorce.

In all this wild welter, we need some sort of guide. It's no good inventing Thou Shalt Nots!

What then? Turn truly, honourably to the novel, and see wherein you are man alive, and wherein you are dead man in life. You may love a woman as man alive, and you may be making love to a woman as sheer dead man in life. You may eat your dinner as man alive, or as a mere masticating corpse. As man alive you may have a shot at your enemy. But as a ghastly simulacrum of life you may be firing bombs into men who are neither your enemies nor your friends, but just things you are dead to. Which is criminal, when the things happen to be alive.

To be alive, to be man alive, to be whole man alive: that is the point. And at its best, the novel, and the novel supremely, can help you. It can help you not to be dead man in life. So much of a man walks about dead and a carcass in the street and house, today: so much of women is merely dead. Like a pianoforte with half the notes mute.

But in the novel you can see, plainly, when the man goes dead, the woman goes inert. You can develop an instinct for life, if you will, instead of a theory of right and wrong, good and bad.

In life, there is right and wrong, good and bad, all the time. But what is right in one case is wrong in another. And in the novel you see one man becoming a corpse, because of his so-called goodness, another going dead, because of his so-called wickedness. Right and wrong is an instinct: but an instinct of the whole consciousness in a man, bodily, mental, spiritual at once. And only in the novel are *all* things given full play, or at least, they may be given full play, when we realise that life itself, and not inert safety, is the reason for living. For out of the full play of all things emerges the only thing that is anything, the wholeness of a man, the wholeness of a woman, man alive, and live woman.

DESMOND MACCARTHY

Literary Booms

Desmond MacCarthy (1877–1952) started out as a fringe member of the Bloomsbury Group and was at first seen as a coming novelist. His expected fiction masterpiece did not come to pass, and MacCarthy spent most of his career as a literary essayist and book reviewer, writing for the New Statesman *(where he signed himself 'Affable Hawk') and, in his later years, the* Sunday Times. *In 1952 he was knighted for his 'services to literature'. 'Literary Booms' appeared in* Criticism *(1932), one of several collections of MacCarthy's prose.*

The other day I was walking down the Strand with a friend. He has written many books and some are very good indeed. Even those which died a natural death in infancy contained pages which showed what he could do, and an individuality of phrase which makes those who love his best books like even his worst. In short, he has a solid reputation.

We passed a poster; his name was on it in large black letters. He made a grimace. 'Angels and ministers of grace defend us!' he exclaimed, 'I hope I am not going to have a Boom.'

'What! don't you want to make money?' I said. 'Why, only half an hour ago, while we were sitting over lunch, didn't you say that you wished that a little man, bent double under a sack of gold, would come in and dump it at your feet? And there is,' I said, pointing to the vendor of papers, who was holding the poster like an apron in front of him, 'There is the little old man, and you won't look at him!'

'A Boom,' he replied, 'is fatal to a man like me. Only the greatest can survive a Boom. When Goethe wrote *The Sorrows of Werther* all Europe wept and went into ecstasies, and Napoleon took it with him on campaigns. Goethe survived his Boom, I admit. *Pickwick* had a prodigious Boom, and Dickens towered till he died. But they were men of the first magnitude, and notice this, they were young, very young, when it happened. Goethe was twenty-one; Dickens twenty-three. Byron was a youth when *Childe Harold* made him a popular idol – "O the ivy and myrtle of sweet two and twenty!" The richest mines in them were unworked; they had immense surprises in them still, and how rich those treasure were!

'But a Boom for a middle-aged man like me, who has already expressed himself, is simply fatal. It may mean a year or so of big cheques and gratifying fuss, but afterwards heart-breaking, draggle-tailed disappointment. It means people will soon be sick of me; that they will take up my newest book with an unconscious prejudice against it. Everything that can be said in praise of my work having been said again and again, the intelligent will set to work to interest the public in their own cleverness by displaying my faults. I shall become a mark for detraction. If I repeat myself (and we are all musical boxes with a set of tunes), even with improvement, the public will still be told that my latest book is not a patch on my early ones. And the young (one minds this) will begin to hate the very sight of my name. They will chuck me with joy into the limbo of overrated reputations. No, thank you, no Boom, please, for me. It wouldn't, in the long run, even pay me in money. A hit to the boundary is all very well, but a Boom is "lost ball", six and out – I believe that's how the little boys score in Battersea Park cricket.'

I was impressed by the energy of his protest, and when we parted I reflected on literary Booms. How brief they were! That was the first thing that struck me; next, that they were getting briefer and briefer as the *machine à la gloire* became more resonant and effective. I had already seen the reputations of many novelists and poets, splendid spreading growths like Jonah's gourd, wither away. How unnecessarily cruel it was! I remembered how Stephen Phillips had once been hailed as the greatest of modern poets. The elderly pundits, whom the quality of his verse had reminded of the poetry which had thrilled them in their youth (it is horribly true, we only really understand the poetry we loved before we were twenty-five), had acclaimed him. I recalled, too, the silence which followed their fanfaronades upon Fame's trumpet, and the contempt of the young generation for poor Phillips. I thought of X and Y and Z, of A and B. There was a whole alphabet of them! I remembered how hard it had been to get the generation which followed that which adulated Tennyson to recognize even his most indubitable beauties. I marked in myself a tendency to curl my mind into a prickly ball like a hedgehog when a work of some incessantly belauded contemporary came into my hands.

Then I thought of Martin Tupper. Byron said he awoke one morning to find himself famous; Martin Tupper awoke one morning to find himself a laughing-stock. And what a Boom he had had! He had sold many more thousands of the *Proverbial Philosophy* than ever Byron sold of *Childe Harold*. *The Spectator*, in reviewing it, said: 'Martin Tupper has won for himself the vacant throne waiting for him amidst the immortals, and, after a long and glorious term of popularity among those who know when their hearts are touched, has been adopted by the suffrage of mankind and the final decree of publishers into the same rank with Wordsworth, and Tennyson, and Browning.' The *Court Journal* declared it to be 'a book as full of sweetness as a honeycomb, of gentleness as a woman's heart; in its wisdom worthy of the disciple of Solomon, in its genius the child of Milton'.

'If men delight to read Tupper both in England and America, why,' asked the *Saturday Review*, 'should they not study him both in the nineteenth and twentieth centuries?' The *Daily News* wrote: 'The imagination staggers in attempting to realize the number of copies of his works which have been published abroad . . . he may now disregard criticism.'

Alas, in his later years, this must have been hard to do. Lord Melbourne had made him an FRS; the Court had patronized him; Society had idolized him; the Press had eulogized him; wherever he went he had received what he calls himself 'palatial welcomes'. 'I have experienced almost annually', he writes in his Autobiography, 'the splendid hospitalities of the Mansion House and most of the City Companies.' The Prince Consort invited him to Buckingham Palace. 'Ladies,' he tells us, 'claimed him as an unseen friend.' He was so nearly being made a peer that with prudent foresight he had coronets painted on his dinner service.

Suddenly the bubble of reputation burst. Obscurity descended on him like an extinguisher. Years afterwards, writing in 1886 (he lived to be nearly as old as Queen Victoria), he mentions as a curious fact that 'it is taken for granted that the author of *Proverbial Philosophy* has been dead for generations'. He tells us how he and his daughter were at a party where someone, on hearing her name, had asked her if she were descended from the famous Martin Tupper, and how, on her pointing to her father, the inquirer had started as though he had seen a ghost. He had seen a ghost. For years Tupper had been leading a posthumous existence, and a posthumous existence of the most unpleasant kind. He had become an emblem of the fatuous-sublime, of early-Victorian absurdity; he was referred to as unconsciously, cruelly, and cursorily as if he had been a character in a book. Poor old man! Boom! There is something ominous in the very word. Boom! Boom! Boom! Listen, it is the sound of a cannon shattering reputations!

ALDOUS HUXLEY

Sermons in Cats

Aldous Huxley was born in 1894 and died in 1963. The 1920s' vogue for Huxley's novels now seems puzzling, although the somewhat later Brave New World *(1932) continues to be valued. In his early fictions like* Antic Hay *(1922) and* Those Barren Leaves *(1925), it now seems clear that most of the leading characters were* essayistes manqués, *and that Huxley's true gifts as a writer had more to do with ideas than with imagination. As he once said: 'The essay is a literary device for saying almost everything about almost anything' – a device for which his fictional characters do somewhat seem to yearn. 'Sermons in Cats' first appeared in* Music at Night *(1931).*

I met, not long ago, a young man who aspired to become a novelist. Knowing that I was in the profession, he asked me to tell him how he should set to work to realize his ambition. I did my best to explain. 'The first thing,' I said, 'is to buy quite a lot of paper, a bottle of ink, and a pen. After that you merely have to write.' But this was not enough for my young friend. He seemed to have a notion that there was some sort of esoteric cookery book, full of literary recipes, which you had only to follow attentively to become a Dickens, a Henry James, a Flaubert – 'according to taste', as the authors of recipes say, when they come to the question of seasoning and sweetening. Wouldn't I let him have a glimpse of this cookery book? I said that I was sorry, but that (unhappily – for what an endless amount of time and trouble it would save!) I had never even seen such a work. He seemed sadly disappointed; so, to console the poor lad, I advised him to apply to the professors of dramaturgy and short-story writing at some reputable university; if any one possessed a trustworthy cookery book of literature, it should surely be they. But even this was not enough to satisfy the young man. Disappointed in his hope that I would give him the fictional equivalent of *One Hundred Ways of Cooking Eggs* or the *Carnet de la Ménagère*, he began to cross-examine me about my methods of 'collecting material'.

Did I keep a notebook or a daily journal? Did I jot down thoughts and phrases in a card index? Did I systematically frequent the drawing-rooms of the rich and fashionable? Or did I, on the contrary, inhabit the Sussex downs? or spend my evenings looking for 'copy' in East End gin-palaces? Did I think it was wise to frequent the company of intellectuals? Was it a good thing for a writer of novels to try to be well educated, or should he confine his reading exclusively to other novels? And so on. I did my best to reply to these questions – as non-committally, of course, as I could. And as the young man still looked rather disappointed, I volunteered a final piece of advice, gratuitously. 'My young friend,' I said, 'if you want to be a psychological novelist and write about human beings, the best thing you can do is to keep a pair of cats.' And with that I left him.

I hope, for his own sake, that he took my advice. For it was good advice – the fruit of much experience and many meditations. But I am afraid that, being a rather foolish young man, he merely laughed at what he must have supposed was only a silly joke: laughed, as I myself foolishly laughed when, years ago, that charming and talented and extraordinary man, Ronald Firbank, once told me that he wanted to write a novel about life in Mayfair and so was just off to the West Indies to look for copy among the Negroes. I laughed at the time; but I see now that he was quite right. Primitive people, like children and animals, are simply civilized people with the lid off, so to speak – the heavy elaborate lid of manners, conventions, traditions of thought and feeling beneath which each one of us passes his or her existence. This lid can be very conveniently studied in Mayfair, shall we say, or Passy, or Park Avenue. But what goes on underneath the lid in these polished and elegant districts? Direct observation (unless we happen to be endowed with a very penetrating intuition) tells us but little; and, if we cannot infer what is going on under other lids from what we see, introspectively, by peeping under our own, then the best thing we can do is to take the next boat for the West Indies, or else, less expensively, pass a few mornings in the nursery, or alternatively, as I suggested to my literary young friend, buy a pair of cats.

Yes, a pair of cats. Siamese by preference; for they are certainly the most 'human' of all the race of cats. Also the strangest, and, if not the most beautiful, certainly the most striking and fantastic. For what disquieting pale blue eyes stare out from the black velvet mask of their faces! Snow-white at birth, their bodies gradually darken to a rich mulatto color. Their forepaws are gloved almost to the shoulder like the long black kid arms of Yvette Guilbert; over their hind legs are tightly drawn the black silk stockings with which Félicien Rops so perversely and indecently clothed his pearly nudes. Their tails, when they have tails – and I would always recommend the budding novelist to buy the tailed variety; for the tail, in cats, is the principal organ of emotional expression and a Manx cat is the equivalent of a dumb man – their tails are tapering black serpents endowed, even when the body lies in Sphinx-like repose, with a spasmodic and uneasy life of their own. And what strange voices they have! Sometimes like the complaining of small children; sometimes like the noise of lambs; sometimes like the agonized and furious howling of lost souls. Compared with these fantastic creatures, other cats, however beautiful and engaging, are apt to seem a little insipid.

Well, having bought his cats, nothing remains for the would-be novelist but to watch them living from day to day; to mark, learn, and inwardly digest the lessons about human nature which they teach; and finally – for, alas, this arduous and unpleasant necessity always arises – finally write his book about Mayfair, Passy, or Park Avenue, whichever the case may be.

Let us consider some of these instructive sermons in cats, from which the student of human psychology can learn so much. We will begin – as every good novel should begin, instead of absurdly ending – with marriage. The marriage of Siamese cats, at any rate as I have observed it, is an extraordinarily dramatic event. To begin with, the introduction of the bridegroom to his bride (I am assuming that, as usually happens in the world of cats, they have not met before their wedding day) is the signal for a battle of unparalleled ferocity. The young wife's first reaction to the advances of her would-be husband is to fly at his throat. One is thankful, as one watches the fur flying and listens to the piercing yells of rage and hatred, that a kindly providence has not allowed these devils to grow any larger. Waged between creatures as big as men, such battles would bring death and destruction to everything within a radius of hundreds of yards. As things are, one is able, at the risk of a few scratches, to grab the combatants by the scruffs of their necks and drag them, still writhing and spitting, apart. What would happen if the newly-wedded pair were allowed to go on fighting to the bitter end I do not know, and have never had the scientific curiosity or the strength of mind to try to find out. I suspect that, contrary to what happened in Hamlet's family, the wedding baked meats would soon be serving for a funeral. I have always prevented this tragical consummation by simply shutting up the bride in a room by herself and leaving the bridegroom for a few hours to languish outside the door. He does not languish dumbly; but for a long time there is no answer, save an occasional hiss or growl, to his melancholy cries of love. When, finally, the bride begins replying in tones as soft and yearning as his own, the door may be opened. The bridegroom darts in and is received, not with tooth and claw as on the former occasion, but with every demonstration of affection.

At first sight there would seem, in this specimen of feline behaviour, no special 'message' for humanity. But appearances are deceptive; the lids under which civilized people live are so thick and so profusely sculptured with mythological ornaments, that it is difficult to recognize the fact, so much insisted upon by D. H. Lawrence in his novels and stories, that there is almost always a mingling of hate with the passion of love and that young girls very often feel (in spite of their sentiments and even their desires) a real abhorrence of the fact of physical love. Unlidded, the cats make manifest this ordinarily obscure mystery of human nature. After witnessing a cats' wedding no young novelist can rest content with the falsehood and banalities which pass, in current fiction, for descriptions of love.

Time passes and, their honeymoon over, the cats begin to tell us things about humanity which even the lid of civilization cannot conceal in the world of men. They tell us – what, alas, we already know – that husbands soon tire of their wives, particularly when they are expecting or nursing families; that the essence of maleness is the love of adventure and infidelity; that guilty consciences and good resolutions are the psychological symptoms of that disease which spasmodically affects practically every male between the ages of eighteen and sixty – the disease called 'the morning after', and that with the disappearance of the disease the psychological symptoms also disappear, so that when temptation comes again, conscience is dumb and good resolutions count for nothing. All these unhappily too familiar truths are illustrated by the cats with a most comical absence of disguise. No man has ever dared to manifest his boredom so insolently as does a Siamese tomcat, when he yawns in the face of his amorously importunate wife. No man has ever dared to proclaim his illicit amours so frankly as this same tom caterwauling on the tiles. And how slinkingly – no man was ever so abject – he returns next day to the conjugal basket by the fire! You can measure the guiltiness of his conscience by the angle of his back-pressed ears, the droop of his tail. And when, having sniffed him and so discovered his infidelity, his wife, as she always does on these occasions, begins to scratch his face (already scarred, like a German student's, with the traces of a hundred duels), he makes no attempt to resist; for, self-convicted of sin, he knows that he deserves all he is getting.

It is impossible for me in the space at my disposal to enumerate all the human truths which a pair of cats can reveal or confirm. I will cite only one more of the innumerable sermons in cats which my memory holds – an acted sermon which, by its ludicrous pantomime, vividly brought home to me the most saddening peculiarity of our human nature, its irreducible solitariness. The circumstances were these. My she-cat, by now a wife of long standing and several times a mother, was passing through one of her occasional phases of amorousness. Her husband, now in the prime of life and parading that sleepy arrogance which is the characteristic of the mature and conquering male (he was now the feline equivalent of some herculean young Alcibiades of the Guards), refused to have anything to do with her. It was in vain that she uttered her love-sick mewing, in vain that she walked up and down in front of him rubbing herself voluptuously against doors and chairlegs as she passed, it was in vain that she came and licked his face. He shut his eyes, he yawned, he averted his head, or, if she became too importunate, got up and slowly, with an insulting air of dignity and detachment, stalked away. When the opportunity presented itself, he escaped and spent the next twenty-four hours upon the tiles. Left to herself, the wife went wandering disconsolately about the house, as though in search of a vanished happiness, faintly and plaintively mewing to herself in a voice and with a manner that reminded one irresistibly of Mélisande in Debussy's opera. '*Je ne suis pas heureuse ici*,' she seemed to be saying. And, poor little beast, she wasn't. But, like her big sisters and brothers of the human world, she had to bear her unhappiness in solitude, uncomprehended, unconsoled. For in spite of language, in spite of intelligence and intuition and sympathy, one can never really communicate anything to anybody. The essential substance of every thought and feeling remains incommunicable, locked up in the impenetrable strong-room of the individual soul and body. Our life is a sentence of perpetual solitary confinement. This mournful truth was overwhelmingly borne in on me as I watched the abandoned and love-sick cat as she walked unhappily round my room. '*Je ne suis pas heureuse ici*,' she kept mewing, '*Je ne suis pas heureuse ici*.' And her expressive black tail would lash the air in a tragical gesture of despair. But each time it twitched, hop-la! from under the armchair, from behind the book-case, wherever he happened to be hiding at the moment, out jumped her only son (the only one, that is, we had not given away), jumped like a ludicrous toy tiger, all claws out, on to the moving tail. Sometimes he would miss, sometimes he caught it, and getting the tip between his teeth would pretend to worry it, absurdly ferocious. His mother would have to jerk it violently to get it out of his mouth. Then, he would go back under his armchair again and, crouching down, his hindquarters trembling, would prepare once more to spring. The tail, the tragical, despairingly gesticulating tail, was for him the most irresistible of playthings. The patience of the mother was angelical. There was never a rebuke or a punitive reprisal; when the child became too intolerable, she just moved away; that was all. And meanwhile, all the time, she went on mewing, plaintively, despairingly. '*Je ne suis pas heureuse ici, je ne suis pas heureuse ici*.' It was heartbreaking. The more so as the antics of the kitten were so extraordinarily ludicrous. It was as though a slap-stick comedian had broken in on the lamentations of Mélisande – not mischievously, not wittingly, for there was not the smallest intention to hurt in the little cat's performance, but simply from lack of comprehension. Each was alone serving his life-sentence of solitary confinement. There was no communication from cell to cell. Absolutely no communication. These sermons in cats can be exceedingly depressing.

A. P. HERBERT

About Bathrooms

A. P. Herbert (1890–1971) was a popular writer for Punch *during the 1930s but he also wrote on legal matters (especially on divorce law and writers' rights) and for fifteen years sat as Independent MP for Oxford University. In addition, Herbert was well known as a librettist, light versifier and none-too-heavy novelist. The* Water Gypsies *is probably his best-known work, although in 1950 he scored a conspicuous popular success with* Bless the Bride, *a musical. Altogether, Herbert published eighty books, and his autobiography* APH: His Life and Times *appeared in 1970.*

Of all the beautiful things which are to be seen in shop windows perhaps the most beautiful are those luxurious baths in white enamel, hedged round with attachments and conveniences in burnished metal. Whenever I see one of them I stand and covet it for a long time. Yet even these super-baths fall far short of what a bath should be; and as for the perfect bathroom I question if any one has even imagined it.

The whole attitude of modern civilization to the bathroom is wrong. Why, for one thing, is it always the smallest and barest room in the house? The Romans understood these things; we don't. I have never yet been in a bathroom which was big enough to do my exercises in without either breaking the light or barking my knuckles against a wall. It ought to be a *big* room and opulently furnished. There ought to be pictures in it, so that one could lie back and contemplate them – a picture of troops going up to the trenches, and another picture of a bus-queue standing in the rain, and another picture of a windy day with some snow in it. Then one would really enjoy one's baths.

And there ought to be rich rugs in it and profound chairs; one would walk about in bare feet on the rich rugs while the bath was running; and one would sit in the profound chairs while drying the ears.

The fact is, a bathroom ought to be equipped for comfort, like a drawing-room, a good, full, velvety room; and as things are it is solely equipped for singing. In the drawing-room, where we want to sing, we put so many curtains and carpets and things that most of us can't sing at all; and then we wonder that there is no music in England. Nothing is more maddening than to hear several men refusing to join in a simple chorus after dinner, when you know perfectly well that every one of them has been singing in a high tenor in his bath before dinner. We all know the reason, but we don't take the obvious remedy. The only thing to do is to take all the furniture out of the drawing-room and put it in the bathroom – all except the piano and a few cane chairs. Then we shouldn't have those terrible noises in the early morning, and in the evening everybody would be a singer. I suppose that is what they do in Wales.

But if we cannot make the bathroom what it ought to be, the supreme and perfect shrine of the supreme moment of the day, the one spot in the house on which no expense or trouble is spared, we can at least bring the bath itself up to date. I don't now, as I did, lay much stress on having a bath with fifteen different taps. I once stayed in a house with a bath like that. There was a hot tap and a cold tap, and hot sea-water and cold sea-water, and PLUNGE and SPRAY and SHOWER and WAVE and FLOOD, and one or two more. To turn on the top tap you had to stand on a step-ladder, and they were all very highly polished. I was naturally excited by this, and an hour before it was time to dress for dinner I slunk upstairs and hurried into the bathroom and locked myself in and turned on all the taps at once. It was strangely disappointing. The sea-water was mythical. Many of the taps refused to function at the same time as any other, and the only two which were really effective were WAVE and FLOOD. WAVE shot out a thin jet of boiling water which caught me in the chest, and FLOOD filled the bath with cold water long before it could be identified and turned off.

No, taps are not of the first importance, though, properly polished, they look well. But no bath is complete without one of those attractive bridges or trays where one puts the sponges and the soap. Conveniences like that are a direct stimulus to washing. The first time I met one I washed myself all over two or three times simply to make the most of knowing where the soap was. Now and then, in fact, in a sort of bravado I deliberately lost it, so as to be able to catch it again and put it back in full view on the tray. You can also rest your feet on the tray when you are washing them, and so avoid cramp.

Again, I like a bathroom where there is an electric bell just above the bath, which you can ring with the big toe. This is for use when one has gone to sleep in the bath and the water has frozen, or when one has begun to commit suicide and thought better of it. Apart from these two occasions it can be used for Morsing instructions about breakfast to the cook – supposing you have a cook. And if you haven't a cook a little bell-ringing in the basement does no harm.

But the most extraordinary thing about the modern bath is that there is no provision for shaving in it. Shaving in the bath I regard as the last word in systematic luxury. But in the ordinary bath it is very difficult. There is nowhere to put anything. There ought to be a kind of shaving tray attached to every bath, which you could swing in on a flexible arm, complete with mirror and soap and strop, new blades and shaving-papers and all the other confounded paraphernalia. Then, I think, shaving would be almost tolerable, and there wouldn't be so many of these horrible beards about.

The same applies to smoking. It is incredible that today in the twentieth century there should be no recognized way of disposing of a cigarette-end in the bath. Personally, I only smoke pipes in the bath, but it is impossible to find a place in which to deposit even a pipe so that it will not roll off into the water. But I have a brother-in-law who smokes cigars in the bath, a disgusting habit. I have often wondered where he hid the ends, and I find now that he has made a *cache* of them in the gas-ring of the geyser. One day the ash will get into the burners and then the geyser will explode.

Next door to the shaving and smoking tray should be the book-rest. I don't myself do much reading in the bath, but I have several sisters-in-law who keep on coming to stay, and they all do it. Few things make the leaves of a book stick together so easily as being dropped in a hot bath, so they had better have a book-rest; and if they go to sleep I shall set in motion my emergency waste mechanism, by which the bath can be emptied in malice from outside.

Another of my inventions is the Progress Indicator. It works like the indicators outside lifts, which show where the lift is and what it is doing. My machine shows what stage the man inside has reached – the washing stage or the merely wallowing stage, or the drying stage, or the exercises stage. It shows you at a glance whether it is worth while to go back to bed or whether it is time to dig yourself in on the mat.

The machine is specially suitable for hotels and large country houses where you can't find out by hammering on the door and asking, because nobody takes any notice.

When you have properly fitted out the bathroom on these lines all that remains is to put the telephone in and have your meals there; or rather to have your meals there and not put the telephone in. It must still remain the one room where a man is safe from that.

LYTTON STRACHEY

The Sad Story of Dr Colbatch

Lytton Strachey was born in 1880 and was a leading figure in the so-called Bloomsbury Group. He began his writing life as a poet but nowadays his chief fame rests on his prose output – and in particular on the iconoclastic historical studies collected in Eminent Victorians *(1918). Admired as an influential figure in the history of biography, Strachey was never one for impartiality or meticulous research. His gift was for the swift, brilliantly prejudiced character-sketch, and in this vein he has indeed had many imitators – not all of whom, alas, have shared his brilliance. The essay reprinted here is taken from his* Portraits in Miniature *(1931). Strachey died in 1932.*

The Rev. Dr Colbatch could not put up with it any more. Animated by the highest motives, he felt that he must intervene. The task was arduous, odious, dangerous; his antagonist most redoubtable; but Dr Colbatch was a Doctor of Divinity, Professor of Casuistry in the University of Cambridge, a Senior Fellow of Trinity College, and his duty was plain; the conduct of the Master could be tolerated no longer; Dr Bentley must go.

In the early years of the eighteenth century the life of learning was agitated, violent, and full of extremes. Everything about it was on the grand scale. Erudition was gigantic, controversies were frenzied, careers were punctuated by brutal triumphs, wild temerities, and dreadful mortifications. One sat, bent nearly double, surrounded by four circles of folios, living to edit Hesychius and confound Dr Hody, and dying at last with a stomach half-full of sand. The very names of the scholars of those days had something about them at once terrifying and preposterous: there was Graevius, there was Wolfius, there was Cruquius; there were Torrentius and Rutgersius; there was the gloomy Baron de Stosch, and there was the deplorable De Pauw. But Richard Bentley was greater than all these. Combining extraordinary knowledge and almost infinite memory with an acumen hardly to be distinguished from inspiration, and a command of logical precision which might have been envied by mathematicians or generals in the field, he revivified with his daemonic energy the whole domain of classical scholarship. The peer of the mightiest of his predecessors – of Scaliger, of Casaubon – turning, in skilful strength, the magic glass of science, he brought into focus the world's comprehension of ancient literature with a luminous exactitude of which they had never dreamed. His prowess had first declared itself in his *Dissertation upon the Epistles of Phalaris*, in which he had obliterated under cartloads of erudition and ridicule the miserable Mr Boyle. He had been rewarded, in the year 1700, when he was not yet forty, with the Mastership of Trinity; and then another side of his genius had appeared. It became evident that he was not merely a scholar, that he was a man of action and affairs, and that he intended to dominate over the magnificent foundation of Trinity with a command as absolute as that which he exercised over questions in Greek grammar. He had immediately gathered into his own hands the entire control of the College; he had manipulated the statutes, rearranged the finances, packed the Council; he had compelled the Society to rebuild and redecorate, at great expense, his own Lodge; he had brought every kind of appointment – scholarships, fellowships, livings – to depend simply upon his will. The Fellows murmured and protested in vain; their terrible tyrant treated them with scant ceremony. 'You will die in your shoes!' he had shouted at one tottering Senior who had ventured to oppose him; and another fat and angry old gentleman he had named 'The College Dog'. In fact, he treated his opponents as if they had been corrupt readings in an old manuscript. At last there was open war. The leading Fellows had appealed to the Visitor of the College, the Bishop of Ely, to remove the Master; and the Master had replied by denying the Bishop's competence and declaring that the visitatorial power lay with the Crown. His subtle mind had detected an ambiguity in the Charter; the legal position was, indeed, highly dubious; and for five years, amid indescribable animosities, he was able to hold his enemies at bay. In the meantime, he had not been idle in other directions: he had annihilated Le Clerc, who, ignorant of Greek, was rash enough to publish a Menander; he had produced a monumental edition of Horace; and he had pulverized Free thinking in the person of Anthony Collins. But his foes had pressed upon him; and eventually it had seemed that his hour was come. In 1714 he had been forced to appear before the Bishop's court; his defence had been weak; the Bishop had drawn up a judgment of deprivation. Then there had been a *coup de théâtre*. The Bishop had suddenly died before delivering judgment. All the previous proceedings lapsed, and Bentley ruled once more supreme in Trinity.

It was at this point that the Rev. Dr Colbatch, animated by the highest motives, felt that he must intervene. Hitherto he had filled the rôle of a peacemaker; but now the outrageous proceedings of the triumphant Master – who, in the flush of victory, was beginning to expel hostile Fellows by force from the College, and had even refused to appoint Dr Colbatch himself to the Vice-Mastership – called aloud for the resistance of every right-thinking man. And Dr Colbatch flattered himself that he could resist to some purpose. He had devoted his life to the study of the law; he was a man of the world; he was acquainted with Lord Carteret; and he had written a book on Portugal. Accordingly, he hurried to London and interviewed great personages, who were all of them extremely sympathetic and polite; then he returned to Trinity, and, after delivering a fulminating sermon in the chapel, he bearded the Master at a College meeting, and actually had the nerve to answer him back. Just then, moreover, the tide seemed to be turning against the tyrant. Bentley, not content with the battle in his own College, had begun a campaign against the University. There was a hectic struggle, and then the Vice-Chancellor, by an unparalleled exercise of power, deprived Bentley of his degrees: the Master of Trinity College and the Regius Professor of Divinity was reduced to the status of an under-graduate. This delighted the heart of Dr Colbatch. He flew to London, where Lord Carteret, as usual, was all smiles and agreement. When, a little later, the College living of Orewell fell vacant, Dr Colbatch gave a signal proof of his power; for Bentley, after refusing to appoint him to the living, at last found himself obliged to give way. Dr Colbatch entered the rectory in triumph; was it not clear that that villain at the Lodge was a sinking man? But, whether sinking or no, the villain could still use a pen to some purpose. In a pamphlet on a proposed edition of the New Testament, Bentley took occasion to fall upon Dr Colbatch tooth and nail. The rector of Orewell was 'a casuistic drudge', a 'plodding pupil of Escobar', an insect, a snarling dog, a gnawing rat, a maggot, and a cabbage-head. His intellect was as dark as his countenance; his 'eyes, muscles, and shoulders were wrought up into the most solemn posture of gravity'; he grinned horribly; he was probably mad; and his brother's beard was ludicrously long.

On this Dr Colbatch, chattering with rage, brought an action against the Master for libel in the Court of the Vice-Chancellor. By a cunning legal device Bentley arranged that the action should be stopped by the Court of King's Bench. Was it possible that Dr Colbatch's knowledge of the law was not impeccable? He could not believe it, and forthwith composed a pamphlet entitled *Jus Academicum*, in which the whole case, in all its bearings, was laid before the public. The language of the pamphlet was temperate, the references to Bentley were not indecently severe; but, unfortunately, in one or two passages some expressions seemed to reflect upon the competence of the Court of King's Bench. The terrible Master saw his opportunity. He moved the Court of King's Bench to take cognizance of the *Jus Academicum* as a contempt of their jurisdiction. A cold shiver ran down Dr Colbatch's spine. Was it conceivable? . . . But no! He had friends in London, powerful friends, who would never desert him. He rushed to Downing Street; Lord Townshend was reassuring; so was the Lord Chief Justice; and so was the Lord Chancellor. 'Here', said Lord Carteret, waving a pen, 'is the magician's wand that will always come to the rescue of Dr Colbatch.' Surely all was well. Nevertheless, he was summoned to appear before the Court of King's Bench in order to explain his pamphlet. The judge was old and testy; he misquoted Horace – 'Jura negat sibi nata, nihil non abrogat'; '*Arrogat*, my lord!' said Dr Colbatch. A little later the judge once more returned to the question, making the same error. '*Arrogat*, my lord!' cried Dr Colbatch for the second time. Yet once again, in the course of his summing-up, the judge pronounced the word 'abrogat'; '*Arrogat*, my lord!' screamed Dr Colbatch for the third time. The interruption was fatal. The unhappy man was fined £50 and imprisoned for a week.

A less pertinacious spirit would have collapsed under such a dire misadventure; but Dr Colbatch fought on. For ten years more, still animated by the highest motives, he struggled to dispossess the Master. Something was gained when yet another Bishop was appointed to the See of Ely – a Bishop who disapproved of Bentley's proceedings. With indefatigable zeal Dr Colbatch laid the case before the Bishop of London, implored the Dean and Chapter of Westminster to interfere, and petitioned the Privy Council. In 1729 the Bishop of Ely summoned Bentley to appear before him; whereupon Bentley appealed to the Crown to decide who was the Visitor of Trinity College. For a moment Dr Colbatch dreamed of obtaining a special Act of Parliament to deal with his enemy; but even he shrank from such a desperate expedient; and at length, in 1732, the whole case came up for decision before the House of Lords. At that very moment Bentley published his edition of *Paradise Lost*, in which all the best passages were emended and rewritten – a book remarkable as a wild aberration of genius, and no less remarkable as containing, for the first time in print, 'tow'ring o'er the alphabet like Saul', the great Digamma. If Bentley's object had been to impress his judges in his favour, he failed; for the House of Lords decided that the Bishop of Ely was the Visitor. Once more Bentley was summoned to Ely House. Dr Colbatch was on tenterhooks; the blow was about to fall; nothing could avert it now, unless – he trembled – if the Bishop were to die again? But the Bishop did not die; in 1734 he pronounced judgement; he deposed Bentley.

So, after thirty years, a righteous doom had fallen upon that proud and wicked man. Dr Colbatch's exultation was inordinate: it was only equalled, in fact, by his subsequent horror, indignation, and fury. For Bentley had discovered in the Statutes of the College a clause which laid it down that, when the Master was to be removed, the necessary steps were to be taken by the Vice-Master. Now the Vice-Master was Bentley's creature; he never took the necessary steps; and Bentley never ceased, so long as he lived, to be Master of Trinity. Dr Colbatch petitioned the House of Lords, he applied to the Court of King's Bench, he beseeched Lord Carteret – all in vain. His head turned; he was old, haggard, dying. Tossing on his bed at Orewell, he fell into a delirium; at first his mutterings were inarticulate; but suddenly, starting up, a glare in his eye, he exclaimed, with a strange emphasis, to the utter bewilderment of the bystanders, '*Arrogat*, my lord!' and immediately expired.

H. L. MENCKEN

Reflections on Journalism

H. L. Mencken (1880–1956) began his writing career, as he relates here, in newspaper journalism but later became famous as the pugnacious editor of the American Mercury, *and for* The American Language *(1919–48), a continuing 'enquiry into the development of English in the United States', in which Mencken predicted that English would eventually become 'a kind of dialect of American just as the language spoken by the Americans was once a dialect of English'.*

REMINISCENCE

I

Looking back over a dull life, mainly devoted to futilities, I can discern three gaudy and gorgeous years. They were my first three years as a newspaper reporter in Baltimore, and when they closed I was still short of twenty-two. I recall them more and more brightly as I grow older, and take greater delight in the recalling. Perhaps the imagination of a decaying man has begun to gild them. But gilded or not, they remain superb, and it is inconceivable that I'll ever see their like again. It is the fate of man, I believe, to be wholly happy only once in his life. Well, I had my turn while I was still fully alive, and could enjoy every moment.

It seems to me that the newspaper reporters of today know very little of the high adventure that bathed the reporters of my time, now nearly thirty years ago. The journalism of that era was still somewhat wild-cattish: all sorts of mushroom papers sprang up; any man with a second-hand press and a few thousand dollars could start one. Thus there was a steady shifting of men from paper to paper, and even the most sober journals got infected with the general antinomianism of the craft. Salaries were low, but nobody seemed to care. A reporter who showed any sign of opulence was a sort of marvel, and got under suspicion. The theory was that journalism was an art, and that to artists money was somehow offensive.

Now all that is past. A good reporter used to make as much as a bartender or a police sergeant; he now makes as much as the average doctor or lawyer, and probably a great deal more. His view of the world he lives in has thus changed. He is no longer a free-lance in human society, thumbing his nose at its dignitaries, he has got a secure lodgment in a definite stratum, and his wife, if he has one, maybe has social ambitions. The highest sordid aspiration that any reporter had, in my time, was to own two complete suits of clothes. Today they have dinner coats, and some of them even own plug hats.

II

This general poverty, I suspect, bore down harshly upon some of my contemporaries, especially older ones, but as for me, I never felt it as oppressive, for no one was dependent on me, and I could always make extra money by writing bad fiction and worse verse. I had enough in Summer to take a holiday. In Winter, concerts and the theaters were free to me. Did I dine in a restaurant? Then I know very well that opinion in the craft frowned upon any bill beyond 50 cents. I remember clearly, and with a shudder still, how Frank Kent once proposed to me that we debauch ourselves at a place where the dinner was $1. I succumbed, but with an evil conscience. And Frank, too, looked over his shoulder when we sneaked in.

The charm of the life, in those remote days, lay in the reporter's freedom. Today he is at the end of a telephone wire, and his city editor can reach him and annoy him in ten minutes. There were very few telephones in 1899, and it was seldom that even the few were used. When a reporter was sent out on a story, the whole operation was in his hands. He was expected to get it without waiting for further orders. If he did so, he was rewarded with what, in newspaper offices, passed for applause. If he failed, he stood convicted of incompetence or worse. There was no passing of the buck. Every man faced a clear and undivided responsibility.

That responsibility was not oppressive to an active young man: it was flattering to him. He felt himself a part of important events, with no string tied to him. Through his eyes thousands of people would see what was happening in this most surprising and fascinating of worlds. If he made a good job of it, the fact would be noticed by the elders he respected. If he fell down, then those same elders would not hesitate to mark the fact profanely. In either case, he was almost completely his own man. There was no rewrite-man at the other end of a telephone wire to corrupt his facts and spoil his fine ideas. Until he got back with his story there was no city editor's roar in his ear, and even after he had got back that roar tended to be discreetly faint until he had got his noble observations on paper. There was, of course, such a thing then as rattling a reporter, but it was viewed as evil. Today the problem is to derattle him.

III

I believe that a young journalist, turned loose in a large city, had more fun a quarter of a century ago than any other man. The Mauve Decade was just ending, and the new era of standardization and efficiency had not come in. Here in Baltimore life was unutterably charming. The town was still a series of detached neighborhoods, many of them ancient and with lives all their own. Marsh Market was as distinct an entity as Cairo or Samarkand. The water-front was immensely romantic. The whole downtown region was full of sinister alleys, and in every alley there were mysterious saloons. One went out with the cops to fires, murders, and burglaries, riding in their clumsy wagon. Any reporter under twenty-five, if not too far gone in liquor, could overtake the fire-horses.

I do not recall that crime was common in Baltimore in those days, but certainly the town was not as mercilessly policed as it is today. Now the cops are instantly alert to every departure, however slight, from the YMCA's principles of decorum, but in that era they were very tolerant to eccentricity. The dance-halls that then flourished in the regions along the harbor would shock them to death today, and they'd be horrified by some of the old-time saloons. In such places rough-houses were common, and where a rough-house began the cops flocked, and where the cops flocked young reporters followed. It was, to any young-ster with humor in him, a constant picnic. Odd fish were washed up by the hundred. Strange marvels unrolled continuously. And out of marvels copy was made, for the newspapers were not yet crowded with comic strips and sporting pages. What was on the police blotter was only the half of it. The energetic young reporter was supposed to go out and see for himself. In particular, he was supposed to see what the older and duller men failed to see. If it was news, well and good. But if it was not news, then it was better than news.

IV

The charm of journalism, to many of its practitioners, lies in the contacts it gives them with the powerful and eminent. They enjoy communion with men of wealth, high officers of state, and other such magnificoes. The delights of that privilege are surely not to be cried down, but it seems to me that I got a great deal more fun, in my days on the street, out of the lesser personages who made up the gaudy life of the city. A mayor was thrilling once or twice, but after that he tended to become a stuffed shirt, speaking platitudes out of a tin throat. But a bartender was different every day, and so was a police sergeant, and so were the young doctors at the hospital, and so were the catchpolls in the courts, and so were the poor wretches who passed before the brass rail in the police station.

There was no affectation about these lesser players in the endless melodrama. They were not out to make impressions even upon newspaper reporters; their aim, in the phrase of Greenwich Village, was to lead their own lives. I recall some astounding manifestations of that yearning. There was the lady who celebrated her one-hundredth arrest for drunkenness by stripping off all her clothes and throwing them at the police lieutenant booking her. There was the policeman who, on a bet, ate fifty fried hard crabs. There was the morgue-keeper who locked himself in his morgue, drunk and howling, and had to be clawed out by firemen. There was the detective who spent his Sundays exhorting in Methodist churches. There was the Irish lad who lived by smuggling bottles of beer to prisoners in the old Central Police Station. There was the saloon-keeper who so greatly venerated journalists that he set them a favored rate of three drinks for the price of two. Above all, there was the pervasive rowdiness and bawdiness of the town – the general air of devil-may-care freedom – the infinite oddity and extravagance of its daily, and especially nightly, life.

It passed with the fire of 1904. I was a city editor by that time and the show had begun to lose its savor. But I was still sufficiently interested in it to mourn the change. The old Baltimore had a saucy and picturesque personality; it was unlike any other American city. The new Baltimore that emerged from the ashes was simply a virtuoso piece of Babbitts. It put in all the modern improvements, especially the bad ones. Its cops climbed out of the alleys behind the old gin-mills and began harassing decent people on the main streets. I began to lose interest in active journalism in 1905. Since 1906, save as an occasional sentimental luxury, I have never written a news story or a headline.

F. SCOTT FITZGERALD

The Crack-Up

F. Scott Fitzgerald (1896–1940) was, as the world knows, a glittering Jazz Age success when very young. His masterpiece, The Great Gatsby, *was published in 1925, when he was not yet thirty. Alcoholism, poverty and general dissipation followed and in the mid-1930s Fitzgerald endured the nervous breakdown so candidly recorded here. 'The Crack-Up' was published in four parts in the magazine* Esquire, *and these parts were brought together as one essay by Edmund Wilson, shortly after his friend Fitzgerald's death.*

I

Of course all life is a process of breaking down, but the blows that do the dramatic side of the work – the big sudden blows that come, or seem to come, from outside – the ones you remember and blame things on and, in moments of weakness, tell your friends about, don't show their effect all at once. There is another sort of blow that comes from within – that you don't feel until it's too late to do anything about it, until you realize with finality that in some regard you will never be as good a man again. The first sort of breakage seems to happen quick – the second kind happens almost without your knowing it but is realized suddenly indeed.

Before I go on with this short history, let me make a general observation – the test of a first-rate intelligence is the ability to hold two opposed ideas in the mind at the same time, and still retain the ability to function. One should, for example, be able to see that things are hopeless and yet be determined to make them otherwise. This philosophy fitted on to my early adult life, when I saw the improbable, the implausible, often the 'impossible', come true. Life was something you dominated if you were any good. Life yielded easily to intelligence and effort, or to what proportion could be mustered of both. It seemed a romantic business to be a successful literary man – you were not ever going to be as famous as a movie star but what note you had was probably longer-lived – you were never going to have the power of a man of strong political or religious convictions but you were certainly more independent. Of course within the practice of your trade you were forever unsatisfied – but I, for one, would not have chosen any other.

As the twenties passed, with my own twenties marching a little ahead of them, my two juvenile regrets – at not being big enough (or good enough) to play football in college, and at not getting overseas during the war – resolved themselves into childish waking dreams of imaginary heroism that were good enough to go to sleep on in restless nights. The big problems of life seemed to solve themselves, and if the business of fixing them was difficult, it made one too tired to think of more general problems.

Life, ten years ago, was largely a personal matter. I must hold in balance the sense of the futility of effort and the sense of the necessity to struggle; the conviction of the inevitability of failure and still the determination to 'succeed' – and, more than these, the contradiction between the dead hand of the past and the high intentions of the future. If I could do this through the common ills – domestic, professional and personal – then the ego would continue as an arrow shot from nothingness to nothingness with such force that only gravity would bring it to earth at last.

For seventeen years, with a year of deliberate loafing and resting out in the center – things went on like that, with a new chore only a nice prospect for the next day. I was living hard, too, but: 'Up to forty-nine it'll be all right,' I said. 'I can count on that. For a man who's lived as I have, that's all you could ask.'

—And then, ten years this side of forty-nine, I suddenly realized that I had prematurely cracked.

II

Now a man can crack in many ways – can crack in the head – in which case the power of decision is taken from you by others! or in the body, when one can but submit to the white hospital world; or in the nerves. William Seabrook in an unsympathetic book tells, with some pride and a movie ending, of how he became a public charge. What led to his alcoholism or was bound up with it, was a collapse of his nervous system. Though the present writer was not so entangled – having at the time not tasted so much as a glass of beer for six months – it was his nervous reflexes that were giving way – too much anger and too many tears.

Moreover, to go back to my thesis that life has a varying offensive, the realization of having cracked was not simultaneous with a blow, but with a reprieve.

Not long before, I had sat in the office of a great doctor and listened to a grave sentence. With what, in retrospect, seems some equanimity, I had gone on about my affairs in the city where I was then living, not caring much, not thinking how much had been left undone, or what would become of this and that responsibility, like people do in books; I was well insured and anyhow I had been only a mediocre caretaker of most of the things left in my hands, even of my talent.

But I had a strong sudden instinct that I must be alone. I didn't want to see any people at all. I had seen so many people all my life – I was an average mixer, but more than average in a tendency to identify myself, my ideas, my destiny, with those of all classes that I came in contact with. I was always saving or being saved – in a single morning I would go through the emotions ascribable to Wellington at Waterloo. I lived in a world of inscrutable hostiles and inalienable friends and supporters.

But now I wanted to be absolutely alone and so arranged a certain insulation from ordinary cares.

It was not an unhappy time. I went away and there were fewer people. I found I was good-and-tired. I could lie around and was glad to, sleeping or dozing sometimes twenty hours a day and in the intervals trying resolutely not to think – instead I made lists – made lists and tore them up, hundreds of lists: of cavalry leaders and football players and cities, and popular tunes and pitchers, and happy times, and hobbies and houses lived in and how many suits since I left the army and how many pairs of shoes (I didn't count the suit I bought in Sorrento that shrunk, nor the pumps and dress shirt and collar that I carried around for years and never wore, because the pumps got damp and grainy and the shirt and collar got yellow and starch-rotted). And lists of women I'd liked, and of the times I had let myself be snubbed by people who had not been my betters in character or ability.

—And then suddenly, surprisingly, I got better.

—And cracked like an old plate as soon as I heard the news.

That is the real end of this story. What was to be done about it will have to rest in what used to be called the 'womb of time'. Suffice it to say that after about an hour of solitary pillow-hugging, I began to realize that for two years my life had been a drawing on resources that I did not possess, that I had been mortgaging myself physically and spiritually up to the hilt. What was the small gift of life given back in comparison to that? – when there had once been a pride of direction and a confidence in enduring independence.

I realized that in those two years, in order to preserve something – an inner hush maybe, maybe not – I had weaned myself from all the things I used to love – that every act of life from the morning tooth-brush to the friend at dinner had become an effort. I saw that for a long time I had not liked people and things, but only followed the rickety old pretense of liking. I saw that even my love for those closest to me was become only an attempt to love, that my casual relations – with an editor, a tobacco seller, the child of a friend, were only what I remembered I *should* do, from other days. All in the same month I became bitter about such things as the sound of the radio, the advertisements in the magazines, the screech of tracks, the dead silence of the country – contemptuous at human softness, immediately (if secretively) quarrelsome toward hardness – hating the night when I couldn't sleep and hating the day because it went toward night. I slept on the heart side now because I knew that the sooner I could tire that out, even a little, the sooner would come that blessed hour of nightmare which, like a catharsis, would enable me to better meet the new day.

There were certain spots, certain faces I could look at. Like most Middle Westerners, I have never had any but the vaguest race prejudices – I always had a secret yen for the lovely Scandinavian blondes who sat on porches in St Paul but hadn't emerged enough economically to be part of what was then society. They were too nice to be 'chicken' and too quickly off the farmlands to seize a place in the sun, but I remember going round blocks to catch a single glimpse of shining hair – the bright shock of a girl I'd never know. This is urban, unpopular talk. It strays afield from the fact that in these latter days I couldn't stand the sight of Celts, English, Politicians, Strangers, Virginians, Negroes (light or dark), Hunting People, or retail clerks, and middlemen in general, all writers (I avoided writers very carefully because they can perpetuate trouble as no one else can) – and all the classes as classes and most of them as members of their class . . .

Trying to cling to something, I liked doctors and girl children up to the age of about thirteen and well-brought-up boy children from about eight years old on. I could have peace and happiness with these few categories of people. I forgot to add that I liked old men – men over seventy, sometimes over sixty if their faces looked seasoned. I liked Katharine Hepburn's face on the screen, no matter what was said about her pretentiousness, and Miriam Hopkins' face, and old friends if I only saw them once a year and could remember their ghosts.

All rather inhuman and undernourished, isn't it? Well, that, children, is the true sign of cracking up.

It is not a pretty picture. Inevitably it was carted here and there within its frame and exposed to various critics. One of them can only be described as a person whose life makes other people's lives seem like death – even this time when she was cast in the usually unappealing role of Job's comforter. In spite of the fact that this story is over, let me append our conversation as a sort of postscript:

'Instead of being so sorry for yourself, listen –' she said. (She always says 'Listen', because she thinks while she talks – *really* thinks.) So she said: 'Listen. Suppose this wasn't a crack in you – suppose it was a crack in the Grand Canyon.'

'The crack's in me,' I said heroically.

'Listen! The world only exists in your eyes – your conception of it. You can make it as big or as small as you want to. And you're trying to be a little puny individual. By God, if I ever cracked, I'd try to make the world crack with me. Listen! The world only exists through your apprehension of it, and so it's much better to say that it's not you that's cracked – it's the Grand Canyon.'

'Baby et up all her Spinoza?'

'I don't know anything about Spinoza. I know –' She spoke, then, of old woes of her own, that seemed, in the telling, to have been more dolorous than mine, and how she had met them, over-ridden them, beaten them.

I felt a certain reaction to what she said, but I am a slow-thinking man, and it occurred to me simultaneously that of all natural forces, vitality is the incommunicable one. In days when juice came into one as an article without duty, one tried to distribute it – but always without success; to further mix metaphors, vitality never 'takes'. You have it or you haven't it, like health or brown eyes or honor or a baritone voice. I might have asked some of it from her, neatly wrapped and ready for home cooking and digestion, but I could never have got it – not if I'd waited around for a thousand hours with the tin cup of self-pity. I could walk from her door, holding myself very carefully like cracked crockery, and go away into the world of bitterness, where I was making a home with such materials as are found there – and quote to myself after I left her door:

'Ye are the salt of the earth. But if the salt hath lost its savour, wherewith shall it be salted?'

Matthew 5:13.

III HANDLE WITH CARE

In a previous article this writer told about his realization that what he had before him was not the dish that he had ordered for his forties. In fact – since he and the dish were one, he described himself as a cracked plate, the kind that one wonders whether it is worth preserving. Your editor thought that the article suggested too many aspects without regarding them closely, and probably many readers felt the same way – and there are always those to whom all self-revelation is contemptible, unless it ends with a noble thanks to the gods for the Unconquerable Soul.

But I had been thanking the gods too long, and thanking them for nothing. I wanted to put a lament into my record, without even the background of the Euganean Hills to give it color. There weren't any Euganean hills that I could see.

Sometimes, though, the cracked plate has to be retained in the pantry, has to be kept in service as a household necessity. It can never again be warmed on the stove nor shuffled with the other plates in the dishpan; it will not be brought out for company, but it will do to hold crackers late at night or to go into the ice box under left-overs . . .

Hence this sequel – a cracked plate's further history.

Now the standard cure for one who is sunk is to consider those in actual destitution or physical suffering – this is an all-weather beatitude for gloom in general and fairly salutory day-time advice for everyone. But at three o'clock in the morning, a forgotten package has the same tragic importance as a death sentence, and the cure doesn't work – and in a real dark night of the soul it is always three o'clock in the morning, day after day. At that hour the tendency is to refuse to face things as long as possible by retiring into an infantile dream – but one is continually startled out of this by various contacts with the world. One meets these occasions as quickly and carelessly as possible and retires once more back into the dream, hoping that things will adjust themselves by some great material or spiritual bonanza. But as the withdrawal persists there is less and less chance of the bonanza – one is not waiting for the fade-out of a single sorrow, but rather being an unwilling witness of an execution, the disintegration of one's own personality . . .

Unless madness or drugs or drink come into it, this phase comes to a dead-end, eventually, and is succeeded by a vacuous quiet. In this you can try to estimate what has been sheared away and what is left. Only when this quiet came to me, did I realize that I had gone through two parallel experiences.

The first time was twenty years ago, when I left Princeton in junior year with a complaint diagnosed as malaria. It transpired, through an X-ray taken a dozen years later, that it had been tuberculosis – a mild case, and after a few months of rest I went back to college. But I had lost certain offices, the chief one was the presidency of the Triangle Club, a musical comedy idea, and also I dropped back a class. To me college would never be the same. There were to be no badges of pride, no medals, after all. It seemed on one March afternoon that I had lost every single thing I wanted – and that night was the first time that I hunted down the spectre of womanhood that, for a little while, makes everything else seem unimportant.

Years later I realized that my failure as a big shot in college was all right – instead of serving on committees, I took a bearing on English poetry; when I got the idea of what it was all about, I set about learning how to write. On Shaw's principle that 'If you don't get what you like, you better like what you get,' it was a lucky break – at the moment it was a harsh and bitter business to know that my career as a leader of men was over.

Since that day I have not been able to fire a bad servant, and I am astonished and impressed by people who can. Some old desire for personal dominance was broken and gone. Life around me was a solemn dream, and I lived on the letters I wrote to a girl in another city. A man does not recover from such jolts – he becomes a different person and, eventually, the new person finds new things to care about.

The other episode parallel to my current situation took place after the war, when I had again over-extended my flank. It was one of those tragic loves doomed for lack of money, and one day the girl closed it out on the basis of common sense. During a long summer of despair I wrote a novel instead of letters, so it came out all right, but it came out all right for a different person. The man with the jingle of money in his pocket who married the girl a year later would always cherish an abiding distrust, an animosity, toward the leisure class – not the conviction of a revolutionist but the smouldering hatred of a peasant. In the years since then I have never been able to stop wondering where my friends' money came from, nor to stop thinking that at one time a sort of *droit de seigneur* might have been exercised to give one of them my girl.

For sixteen years I lived pretty much as this latter person, distrusting the rich, yet working for money with which to share their mobility and the grace that some of them brought into their lives. During this time I had plenty of the usual horses shot from under me – I remember some of their names – *Punctured Pride, Thwarted Expectation, Faithless, Show-off, Hard Hit, Never Again*. And after awhile I wasn't twenty-five, then not even thirty-five, and nothing was quite as good. But in all these years I don't remember a moment of discouragement. I saw honest men through moods of suicidal gloom – some of them gave up and died; others adjusted themselves and went on to a larger success than mine; but my morale never sank below the level of self-disgust when I had put on some unsightly personal show. Trouble has no necessary connection with discouragement – discouragement has a germ of its own, as different from trouble as arthritis is different from a stiff joint.

When a new sky cut off the sun last spring, I didn't at first relate it to what had happened fifteen or twenty years ago. Only gradually did a certain family resemblance come through – an over-extension of the flank, a burning of the candle at both ends; a call upon physical resources that I did not command, like a man over-drawing at his bank. In its impact this blow was more violent than the other two but it was the same in kind – a feeling that I was standing at twilight on a deserted range, with an empty rifle in my hands and the targets down.

No problem set – simply a silence with only the sound of my own breathing.

In this silence there was a vast irresponsibility toward every obligation, a deflation of all my values. A passionate belief in order, a disregard of motives or consequences in favor of guess work and prophecy, a feeling that craft and industry would have a place in any world – one by one, these and other convictions were swept away. I saw that the novel, which at my maturity was the strongest and supplest medium for conveying thought and emotion from one human being to another, was becoming subordinated to a mechanical and communal art that, whether in the hands of Hollywood merchants or Russian idealists, was capable of reflecting only the tritest thought, the most obvious emotion. It was an art in which words were subordinate to images, where personality was worn down to the inevitable low gear of collaboration. As long past as 1930, I had a hunch that the talkies would make even the best selling novelist as archaic as silent pictures. People still read, if only Professor Candy's book of the month – curious children nosed at the slime of Mr Tiffany Thayer in the drugstore libraries – but there was a rankling indignity, that to me had become almost an obsession, in seeing the power of the written word subordinated to another power, a more glittering, a grosser power . . .

I set that down as an example of what haunted me during the long night – this was something I could neither accept nor struggle against, something which tended to make my efforts obsolescent, as the chain stores have crippled the small merchant, an exterior force, unbeatable – (I have the sense of lecturing now, looking at a watch on the desk before me and seeing how many more minutes –).

Well, when I had reached this period of silence, I was forced into a measure that no one ever adopts voluntarily: I was impelled to think. God, was it difficult! The moving about of great secret trunks. In the first exhausted halt, I wondered whether I had ever thought. After a long time I came to these conclusions, just as I write them here:

1. That I had done very little thinking, save within the problems of my craft. For twenty years a certain man had been my intellectual conscience. That was Edmund Wilson.
2. That another man represented my sense of the 'good life', though I saw

him once in a decade, and since then he might have been hung. He is in the fur business in the Northwest and wouldn't like his name set down here. But in difficult situations I had tried to think what *he* would have thought, how *he* would have acted.

3. That a third contemporary had been an artistic conscience to me – I had not imitated his infectious style, because my own style, such as it is, was formed before he published anything, but there was an awful pull toward him when I was on a spot.

4. That a fourth man had come to dictate my relations with other people when these relations were successful: how to do, what to say. How to make people at least momentarily happy (in opposition to Mrs Post's theories of how to make everyone thoroughly uncomfortable with a sort of systematized vulgarity). This always confused me and made me want to go out and get drunk, but this man had seen the game, analyzed it and beaten it, and his word was good enough for me.

5. That my political conscience had scarcely existed for ten years save as an element of irony in my stuff. When I became again concerned with the system I should function under, it was a man much younger than myself who brought it to me, with a mixture of passion and fresh air.

So there was not an 'I' any more – not a basis on which I could organize my self-respect – save my limitless capacity for toil that it seemed I possessed no more. It was strange to have no self – to be like a little boy left alone in a big house, who knew that now he could do anything he wanted to do, but found that there was nothing that he wanted to do –

(The watch is past the hour and I have barely reached my thesis. I have some doubts as to whether this is of general interest, but if anyone wants more, there is plenty left, and your editor will tell me. If you've had enough, say so – but not too loud, because I have the feeling that someone, I'm not sure who, is sound asleep – someone who could have helped me to keep my shop open. It wasn't Lenin, and it wasn't God.)

IV PASTING IT TOGETHER

I have spoken in these pages of how an exceptionally optimistic young man experienced a crack-up of all values, a crack-up that he scarcely knew of until long after it occurred. I told of the succeeding period of desolation and of the necessity of going on, but without benefit of Henley's familiar heroics, 'my head is bloody but unbowed'. For a check-up of my spiritual liabilities indicated that I had no particular head to be bowed or unbowed. Once I had had a heart but this was about all I was sure of.

This was at least a starting place out of the morass in which I floundered: 'I felt – therefore I was.' At one time or another there had been many people who had leaned on me, come to me in difficulties or written me from afar, believed implicitly in my advice and my attitude toward life. The dullest platitude monger or the most unscrupulous Rasputin who can influence the destinies of many people must have some individuality, so the question became one of finding why and where I had changed, where was the leak through which, unknown to myself, my enthusiasm and my vitality had been steadily and prematurely trickling away.

One harassed and despairing night I packed a brief case and went off a thousand miles to think it over. I took a dollar room in a drab little town where I knew no one and sunk all the money I had with me in a stock of potted meat, crackers and apples. But don't let me suggest that the change from a rather overstuffed world to a comparative asceticism was any Research Magnificent – I only wanted absolute quiet to think out why I had developed a sad attitude toward sadness, a melancholy attitude toward melancholy and a tragic attitude toward tragedy – *why I had become identified with the objects of my horror or compassion.*

Does this seem a fine distinction? It isn't: identification such as this spells the death of accomplishment. It is something like this that keeps insane people from working. Lenin did not willingly endure the sufferings of his proletariat, nor Washington of his troops, nor Dickens of his London poor. And when Tolstoy tried some such merging of himself with the objects of his attention, it was a fake and a failure. I mention these because they are the men best known to us all.

It was dangerous mist. When Wordsworth decided that 'there had passed away a glory from the earth', he felt no compulsion to pass away with it, and the Fiery Particle Keats never ceased his struggle against TB nor in his last moments relinquished his hope of being among the English poets.

My self-immolation was something sodden-dark. It was very distinctly not modern – yet I saw it in others, saw it in a dozen men of honor and industry since the war. (I heard you, but that's too easy – there were Marxians among these men.) I had stood by while one famous contemporary of mine played with the idea of the Big Out for half a year; I had watched when another, equally eminent, spent months in an asylum unable to endure any contact with his fellow men. And of those who had given up and passed on I could list a score.

This led me to the idea that the ones who had survived had made some sort of clean break. This is a big word and is no parallel to a jail-break when one is probably headed for a new jail or will be forced back to the old one. The famous 'Escape' or 'run away from it all' is an excursion in a trap even if the trap includes the south seas, which are only for those who want to paint them or sail them. A clean break is something you cannot come back from; that is irretrievable because it makes the past cease to exist. So, since I could no longer fulfill the obligations that life had set for me or that I had set for myself, why not slay the empty shell who had been posturing at it for four years? I must continue to be a writer because that was my only way of life, but I would cease any attempts to be a person – to be kind, just or generous. There were plenty of counterfeit coins around that would pass instead of these and I knew where I could get them at a nickel on the dollar. In thirty-nine years an observant eye has learned to detect where the milk is watered and the sugar is sanded, the rhinestone passed for diamond and the stucco for stone. There was to be no more giving of myself – all giving was to be outlawed henceforth under a new name, and that name was Waste.

The decision made me rather exuberant, like anything that is both real and new. As a sort of beginning there was a whole shaft of letters to be tipped into the waste basket when I went home, letters that wanted something for nothing – to read this man's manuscript, market this man's poem, speak free on the radio, indite notes of introduction, give this interview, help with the plot of this play, with this domestic situation, perform this act of thoughtfulness or charity.

The conjuror's hat was empty. To draw things out of it had long been a sort of sleight of hand, and now, to change the metaphor, I was off the dispensing end of the relief roll forever.

The heady villainous feeling continued.

I felt like the beady-eyed men I used to see on the commuting train from Great Neck fifteen years back – men who didn't care whether the world tumbled into chaos tomorrow if it spared their houses. I was one with them now, one with the smooth articles who said:

'I'm sorry but business is business.' Or:

'You ought to have thought of that before you got into this trouble.' Or

'I'm not the person to see about that.'

And a smile – ah, I would get me a smile. I'm still working on that smile. It is to combine the best qualities of a hotel manager, an experienced old social weasel, a headmaster on visitors' day, a colored elevator man, a pansy pulling a profile, a producer getting stuff at half its market value, a trained nurse coming on a new job, a body-vender in her first rotogravure, a hopeful extra swept near the camera, a ballet dancer with an infected toe, and of course the great beam of loving kindness common to all those from Washington to Beverly Hills who must exist by virtue of the contorted pan.

The voice too – I am working with a teacher on the voice. When I have perfected it the larynx will show no ring of conviction except the conviction of the person I am talking to. Since it will be largely called upon for the elicitation of the word 'Yes', my teacher (a lawyer) and I are concentrating on that, but in extra hours. I am learning to bring into it that polite acerbity that makes people feel that far from being welcome they are not even tolerated and are under continual and scathing analysis at every moment. These times will of course not coincide with the smile. This will be reserved exclusively for those from whom I have nothing to gain, old worn-out people or young struggling people. They won't mind – what the hell, they get it most of the time anyhow.

But enough. It is not a matter of levity. If you are young and you should write asking to see me and learn how to be a sombre literary man writing pieces upon the state of emotional exhaustion that often overtakes writers in their prime – if you should be so young and so fatuous as to do this, I would not do so much as acknowledge your letter, unless you were related to someone very rich and important indeed. And if you were dying of starvation outside my window, I would go out quickly and give you the smile and the voice (if no longer the hand) and stick around till somebody raised a nickel to phone for the ambulance, that is if I thought there would be any copy in it for me.

I have now at last become a writer only. The man I had persistently tried to be became such a burden that I have 'cut him loose' with as little compunction as a Negro lady cuts loose a rival on Saturday night. Let the good people function as such – let the overworked doctors die in harness, with one week's 'vacation' a year that they can devote to straightening out their family affairs, and let the underworked doctors scramble for cases at one dollar a throw; let the soldiers be killed and enter immediately into the Valhalla of their profession. That is their contract with the gods. A writer need have no such ideals unless he makes them for himself, and this one has quit. The old dream of being an entire man in the Goethe–Byron–Shaw tradition, with an opulent American touch, a sort of combination of J. P. Morgan, Topham Beauclerk and St Francis of Assisi, has been relegated to the junk heap of the shoulder pads worn for one day on the Princeton freshman football field and the overseas cap never worn overseas.

So what? This is what I think now: that the natural state of the sentient adult is a qualified unhappiness. I think also that in an adult the desire to be finer in grain than you are, 'a constant striving' (as those people say who gain their bread by saying it) only adds to this unhappiness in the end – that end that comes to our youth and hope. My own happiness in the past often approached such an ecstasy that I could not share it even with the person dearest to me but had to walk it away in quiet streets and lanes with only fragments of it to distil into little lines in books – and I think that my happiness, or talent for self-delusion or what you will, was an exception. It was not the natural thing but the unnatural – unnatural as the Boom; and my recent experience parallels the wave of despair that swept the nation when the Boom was over.

I shall manage to live with the new dispensation, though it has taken some months to be certain of the fact. And just as the laughing stoicism which has enabled the American Negro to endure the intolerable conditions of his existence has cost him his sense of the truth – so in my case there is a price to pay. I do not any longer like the postman, nor the grocer, nor the editor, nor the cousin's husband, and he in turn will come to dislike me, so that life will never be very pleasant again, and the sign *Cave Canem* is hung permanently just above my door. I will try to be a correct animal though, and if you throw me a bone with enough meat on it I may even lick your hand.

JAMES THURBER

The Secret Life of James Thurber

James Thurber (1894–1961) was for many years, and for many readers, the quintessential New Yorker *humorist, known for his cartoons as well as for his writings. Along with E. B. White, Thurber helped to shape the magazine's distinctive tone, although – vide My Years With Ross (1958) – the effort did not always seem worthwhile. Thurber's 'The Secret Life of Walter Mitty' (1942) is probably his best-known story. Salvador Dali's* Secret Life, *which Thurber lampoons here, was published in 1944, and was also the subject of an amusing essay by George Orwell.*

I have only dipped here and there into Salvador Dali's *The Secret Life of Salvador Dali* (with paintings by Salvador Dali and photographs of Salvador Dali), because anyone afflicted with what my grandmother's sister Abigail called 'the permanent jump' should do no more than skitter through such an autobiography, particularly in these melancholy times.

One does not have to skitter far before one comes upon some vignette which gives the full shape and flavor of the book: the youthful dreamer of dreams biting a sick bat or kissing a dead horse, the slender stripling going into man's estate with the high hope and fond desire of one day eating a live but roasted turkey, the sighing lover covering himself with goat dung and aspic that he might give off the true and noble odor of the ram. In my flying trip through Dali I caught other glimpses of the great man: Salvador adoring a seed ball fallen from a plane tree, Salvador kicking a tiny playmate off a bridge, Salvador caressing a crutch, Salvador breaking the old family doctor's glasses with a leather-thonged mattress-beater. There would appear to be only two things in the world that revolt him (and I don't mean a long-dead hedgehog). He is squeamish about skeletons and grasshoppers. Oh, well, we all have our idiosyncrasies.

Señor Dali's memoirs have set me to thinking. I find myself muttering as I shave, and on two occasions I have swung my crutch at a little neighbor girl on my way to the post office. Señor Dali's book sells for six dollars. My own published personal history (Harper & Brothers, 1933) sold for $1.75. At the time I complained briefly about this unusual figure, principally on the ground that it represented only fifty cents more than the price asked for a book called *The Adventures of Horace the Hedgehog*, published the same month. The publishers explained that the price was a closely approximated vertical, prefigured on the basis of profitable ceiling, which in turn was arrived at by taking into consideration the effect on diminishing returns of the horizontal factor.

In those days all heads of business firms adopted a guarded kind of double talk, commonly expressed in low, muffled tones, because nobody knew what was going to happen and nobody understood what had. Big business had been frightened by a sequence of economic phenomena which had clearly demonstrated that our civilization was in greater danger of being turned off than of gradually crumbling away. The upshot of it all was that I accepted the price of $1.75. In so doing, I accepted the state of the world as a proper standard by which the price of books should be fixed. And now, with the world in ten times as serious a condition as it was in 1933, Dali's publishers set a price of six dollars on his life story. This brings me to the inescapable conclusion that the price-fixing principle, in the field of literature, is not global but personal. The trouble, quite simply, is that I told too much about what went on in the house I lived in and not enough about what went on inside myself.

Let me be the first to admit that the naked truth about me is to the naked truth about Salvador Dali as an old ukulele in the attic is to a piano in a tree, and I mean a piano with breasts. Señor Dali has the jump on me from the beginning. He remembers and describes in detail what it was like in the womb. My own earliest memory is of accompanying my father to a polling booth in Columbus, Ohio, where he voted for William McKinley.

It was a drab and somewhat battered tin shed set on wheels, and it was filled with guffawing men and cigar smoke; all in all, as far removed from the paradisiacal placenta of Salvador Dali's first recollection as could well be imagined. A fat, jolly man dandled me on his knee and said that I would soon be old enough to vote against William Jennings

Bryan. I thought he meant that I could push a folded piece of paper into the slot of the padlocked box as soon as my father was finished. When this turned out not to be true, I had to be carried out of the place kicking and screaming. In my struggles I knocked my father's derby off several times. The derby was not a monstrously exciting love object to me, as practically everything Salvador encountered was to him, and I doubt, if I had that day to live over again, that I could bring myself, even in the light of exotic dedication as I now know it, to conceive an intense and perverse affection for the derby. It remains obstinately in my memory as a rather funny hat, a little too large in the crown, which gave my father the appearance of a tired, sensitive gentleman who had been persuaded against his will to take part in a game of charades.

We lived on Champion Avenue at the time, and the voting booth was on Mound Street. As I set down these names, I begin to perceive an essential and important difference between the infant Salvador and the infant me. This difference can be stated in terms of environment. Salvador was brought up in Spain, a country colored by the legends of Hannibal, El Greco, and Cervantes. I was brought up in Ohio, a region steeped in the tradition of Coxey's Army, the Anti-Saloon League, and William Howard Taft. It is only natural that the weather in little Salvador's soul should have been stirred by stranger winds and enveloped in more fantastic mists than the weather in my own soul. But enough of mewling apology for my lack-lustre early years. Let us get back to my secret life, such as it was, stopping just long enough to have another brief look at Señor Dali on our way.

Salvador Dali's mind goes back to a childhood half imagined and half real, in which the edges of actuality were sometimes less sharp than the edges of dream. He seems somehow to have got the idea that this sets him off from Harry Spencer, Charlie Doakes, I. Feinberg, J. J. McNaboe, Willie Faulkner, Herbie Hoover, and me. What Salvie had that the rest of us kids didn't was the perfect scenery, characters, and costumes for his desperate little rebellion against the clean, the conventional, and the comfortable. He put perfume on his hair (which would have cost him his life in, say, Bayonne, N. J., or Youngstown, Ohio), he owned a lizard with two tails, he wore silver buttons on his shoes, and he knew, or imagined he knew, little girls named Galuchka and Dullita. Thus he was born halfway along the road to paranoia, the soft Poictesme of his prayers, the melting Oz of his oblations, the capital, to put it so that you can see what I am trying to say, of his heart's desire. Or so, anyway, it must seem to a native of Columbus, Ohio, who, as a youngster, bought his twelve-dollar suits at the F. & R. Lazarus Co., had his hair washed out with Ivory soap, owned a bull terrier with only one tail, and played (nicely and a bit diffidently) with little girls named Irma and Betty and Ruby.

Another advantage that the young Dali had over me, from the standpoint of impetus toward paranoia, lay in the nature of the adults who peopled his real world. There was, in Dali's home town of Figueras, a family of artists named Pitchot (musicians, painters, and poets), all of whom adored the ground that the *enfant terrible* walked on. If one of them came upon him throwing himself from a high rock – a favorite relaxation of our hero – or hanging by his feet with his head immersed in a pail of water, the wild news was spread about the town that greatness and genius had come to Figueras. There was a woman who put on a look of maternal interest when Salvador threw rocks at her. The mayor of the town fell dead one day at the boy's feet. A doctor in the community (not the one he had horsewhipped) was seized of a fit and attempted to beat him up. (The contention that the doctor was out of his senses at the time of the assault is Dali's, not mine.)

The adults around me when I was in short pants were neither so glamorous nor so attentive. They consisted mainly of eleven maternal great-aunts, all Methodists, who were staunch believers in physic, mustard plasters, and Scripture, and it was part of their dogma that artistic tendencies should be treated in the same way as hiccups or hysterics. None of them was an artist, unless you can count Aunt Lou, who wrote sixteen-stress verse, with hit-and-miss rhymes, in celebration of people's birthdays or on the occasion of great national disaster. It never occurred to me to bite a bat in my aunts' presence or to throw stones at them. There was one escape, though: my secret world of idiom.

Two years ago my wife and I, looking for a house to buy, called on a firm of real-estate agents in New Milford. One of the members of the firm, scrabbling through a metal box containing many keys, looked up to say, 'The key to the Roxbury house isn't here.' His partner replied, 'It's a common lock. A skeleton will let you in.' I was suddenly once again five years old, with wide eyes and open mouth. I pictured the

Roxbury house as I would have pictured it as a small boy, a house of such dark and nameless horrors as have never crossed the mind of our little bat-biter.

It was of sentences like that, nonchalantly tossed off by real-estate dealers, great-aunts, clergymen, and other such prosaic persons, that the enchanted private world of my early boyhood was made. In this world, businessmen who phoned their wives to say that they were tied up at the office sat roped to their swivel chairs, and probably gagged, unable to move or speak, except somehow, miraculously, to telephone; hundreds of thousands of businessmen tied to their chairs in hundreds of thousands of offices in every city of my fantastic cosmos. An especially fine note about the binding of all the businessmen in all the cities was that whoever did it always did it around five o'clock in the afternoon.

Then there was the man who left town under a cloud. Sometimes I saw him all wrapped up in the cloud, and invisible, like a cat in a burlap sack. At other times it floated, about the size of a sofa, three or four feet above his head, following him wherever he went. One could think about the man under the cloud before going to sleep; the image of him wandering around from town to town was a sure soporific.

Not so the mental picture of a certain Mrs Huston, who had been terribly cut up when her daughter died on the operating table. I could see the doctors too vividly, just before they set upon Mrs Huston with their knives, and I could hear them. 'Now, Mrs Huston, will we get up on the table like a good girl, or will we have to be put there?' I could usually fight off Mrs Huston before I went to sleep, but she frequently got into my dreams, and sometimes she still does.

I remember the grotesque creature that came to haunt my meditations when one evening my father said to my mother, 'What did Mrs Johnson say when you told her about Betty?' and my mother replied, 'Oh, she was all ears.' There were many other wonderful figures in the secret, surrealist landscapes of my youth: the old lady who was always up in the air, the husband who did not seem to be able to put his foot down, the man who lost his head during a fire but was still able to run out of the house yelling, the young lady who was, in reality, a soiled dove. It was a world that, of necessity, one had to keep to oneself and brood over in silence, because it would fall to pieces at the touch of words. If you brought it out into the light of actual day and put it to the test of questions, your parents would try to laugh the miracles away, or they would take your temperature and put you to bed. (Since I always ran a temperature, whenever it was taken, I was put to bed and left there all alone with Mrs Huston.)

Such a world as the world of my childhood is, alas, not year-proof. It is a ghost that, to use Henley's words, gleams, flickers, vanishes away. I think it must have been the time my little Cousin Frances came to visit us that it began surely and forever to dissolve. I came into the house one rainy dusk and asked where Frances was. 'She is,' said our cook, 'up in the front room crying her heart out.' The fact that a person could cry so hard that his heart would come out of his body, as perfectly shaped and glossy as a red velvet pincushion, was news to me. For some reason I had never heard the expression, so common in American families whose hopes and dreams run so often counter to attainment. I went upstairs and opened the door of the front room. Frances, who was three years older than I, jumped up off the bed and ran past me, sobbing, and down the stairs.

My search for her heart took some fifteen minutes. I tore the bed apart and kicked up the rugs and even looked in the bureau drawers. It was no good. I looked out the window at the rain and the darkening sky. My cherished mental image of the man under the cloud began to grow dim and fade away. I discovered that, all alone in a room, I could face the thought of Mrs Huston with cold equanimity. Downstairs, in the living room, Frances was still crying. I began to laugh.

Ah there, Salvador!

MARTHA GELLHORN

Memory

Martha Gellhorn (1908–98) was one of the century's most celebrated war reporters, but she also wrote novels and short stories. The Short Novels of Martha Gellhorn *was published in 1991. As a war reporter, Gellhorn was particularly valued for her despatches from the Spanish Civil War, which she covered for* Collier's *magazine. It was in Spain that she met Ernest Hemingway, to whom she was married for a time, but of whom she wrote later with some coldness. Gellhorn's autobiography* Travels With Myself and Another *was published in 1979. Her essay, 'Memory', appeared in* London Review of Books *in December 1996.*

This is how my memory works.

I was sitting in the big inner courtyard of the New Tiran Hotel, Naama Bay, south Sinai, drinking duty-free whisky and watching the new moon. The sky was dark blue with light behind it, not yet the real desert blackness. I had the place to myself, silence made the evening faultless. I was not thinking, I was basking in sensations of my skin. I could still feel the cool smooth water of the Red Sea from that late afternoon's snorkelling. The warm air now was soft on my arms and legs, the tiles of the paving hot under my bare feet. It is wonderful to know exactly when you are happy.

Without warning or reason, I was in a room in Gaylords Hotel in Madrid. It was winter, late 1937 at a guess. I don't know where Gaylords is; we walked there and back to the Florida Hotel in the dark. E. had been invited to have drinks with Koltzov and I was included in my tag-along role. E. was excited about this rare occasion. No one in our little buddy circle of correspondents had been inside Gaylords or met Koltzov. Gaylords was known to be the Russians' hotel. Koltzov, E. said, was officially the *Pravda* correspondent in Madrid but really he was Stalin's man, Stalin's eyes and ears on the spot.

Koltzov's sitting-room was well and expensively furnished like any sitting-room in a first-class hotel in peacetime. It was lit by table lamps and warm. It did not look or feel like any other place I had been in Spain. Koltzov was a small thin man, with thick, well-cut, grey hair. He wore a dark, excellent suit. He had the kind of face that makes an immediate impression of brilliance, of wit, and the quiet manners of complete confidence. I thought he was forty or so, and more French than Russian. There were a few other people. I noticed only a plump, motherly middle-aged woman, probably the real *Pravda* correspondent, who did the hostess's job, seeing that the vodka glasses were filled and, more important, passing things to eat, tidbits, I seem to see dabs of caviar on real bread. I cared much more about food but E. must have been overjoyed by the supply of vodka.

And there was Modesto. We were introduced when we arrived, and he had moved across the room, leaving E. to talk with Koltzov. One sentence hit me hard, though I was not listening carefully. Koltzov said: 'We take Villanueva de la Mierda and they take Córdoba.' Maybe it wasn't Córdoba but it was definitely Villanueva de la Mierda. How dare he, living in such singular luxury, speak with cynicism or disdain about the brave, poorly armed men fighting this war. For I believed in the cause of the Spanish Republic as I believed in nothing before or since. I did not like Koltzov, I did not listen any more and I walked away to a table which held a tray of the invaluable tidbits.

Modesto joined me. Press opinion agreed that Modesto was the most talented general in the Republican Army. He looked to be in his early thirties, tall for a Spaniard who is born poor, lean, at ease in his good body. He wore an inconspicuous, unadorned khaki uniform. He had fine dark eyes, very bright, and amused now. He was an intensely attractive man and I was pleased that he had come to talk to me, though I knew that in Spain being blonde was considered a sort of accomplishment. Seeing me wolf the little dabs of caviar he asked if I were hungry. I said: 'Like everyone else in Madrid.' He smiled, which changed his face from its serious, aloof expression. We were getting on happily but with no personal undertones or overtones.

E. suddenly appeared beside us wearing an ugly, shark smile, the first time I had seen it. He addressed Modesto as 'Mi General', already offensive, the style in the old monarchist army. He suggested that they hold in their teeth the opposite ends of his bandana handkerchief, now pulled from his pocket, and settle this matter by playing Russian roulette since they were now among Russians, two revolvers, one bullet in each chamber. It was an amusing game, either two men died, or one, or neither. As a boor's joke it was outstanding; it managed a double insult, to me as a piece of female property, to Modesto as a thief on the prowl. My heart's desire was to kick E. powerfully, but I do not know how to kick people. Modesto did not see it as a joke, boorish or otherwise. His eyes went cold. He said: 'Vamos.'

As they could hardly shoot each other among the lamps and tables and sofas, Modesto headed for the outer door, E. following. Supposedly they would pick up revolvers along the way. It was too idiotic and shaming, a fine example of E.'s gift for making scenes. Koltzov must have sensed a quarrel because he took Modesto's arm, talking fast with irritation. The words 'tontería', 'absurdo', 'niños', 'borracho' flicked about. He led Modesto, still talking, to a far corner of the room. E. had spoiled this party, which promised to be so agreeable, so comfortable in a warm room, and with plenty of delicious food for me. The motherly woman ushered us politely but firmly to our coats and through the entry passage into the hotel corridor. We were not invited again. We walked back to the Florida along the dark cold streets in hostile silence.

We met Modesto once more, at his front wherever that was. By the men's clothing, I know it was no longer winter. It was unheard of to visit a general, uninvited, at his command post during an action. The form during any action was to be as unobtrusive as possible, and avoid all officers who, rightly, thought reporters a nuisance until the situation calmed down. I have no idea how we came to be there with Modesto.

His command post at the moment was a stone wall, the kind peasants build to mark out their land. It stretched along a low hill. The action was going on below. In my mind, it is only a blur of dust. We sat in a row on the wall. First there was a big, overweight, very white-skinned, balding man, in a grubby civilian shirt and trousers. He was not introduced. He could have been German or Russian, but Franco had the Germans. He was presumably a military adviser attached to Modesto's staff. Then there was Modesto, bareheaded and neat in an open-necked khaki shirt with sleeves rolled up, khaki trousers and espadrilles. He had been civil and cool to us. He was perfectly relaxed, his eyes fixed on whatever lay below us. E. sat next to him, seriously unkempt as usual. He favoured lumberjack shirts and shapeless duck trousers, with a dirty tennis visor to shade his eyes. I was last, but my memory never includes a picture of me, I am simply there.

E. was asking Modesto technical tactical questions, as of one general to another. The answers were brief. Leaning forward, I could see Modesto's face. He did not turn his head to answer E., his face impassive. I could not tell by his voice whether he was annoyed or bored. This conversation was punctuated by loud explosions. It had to be a mortar attack. I was knowledgeable about artillery, from living in Madrid, and I would have known what was happening if it were shell fire. But who knows about mortars? They give no preliminary information. They just land and explode. I assumed the men knew what these explosions, growing louder, meant and would take suitable steps.

It was creeping fire, that much I understood, as each sudden explosion came nearer. After the last, very loud, very close, the balding civilian said something harsh to Modesto; I caught, 'por una mujer'. Modesto laughed and lazily stood up. In fact, E. and Modesto were playing Russian roulette with mortar bombs. Neither man would lose face by moving first. Stuff the little lady and the stout civilian type, the boys had important business to attend to: their vanity. I'm sure that E. was jealous of Modesto's reputation for bravery, of his commanding an army, not merely reporting this war. But why did Modesto let himself get sucked into such nonsense? Perhaps the old Spanish obsession with honour. He had been insulted, he would now humiliate the insulter. Something like that. After more than half a century, these submerged and dotty incidents are as clear as if I were seeing them on TV. They had nothing to do with me, mine was a walk-on part.

From Madrid, my memory took me without pause to Prague. It was right after Munich, after Chamberlain waved his piece of paper and said 'peace for our time', and was cheered for his evil stupidity.

A long, dark corridor in the Hradcany Palace was lined with wood benches. I suppose anyone could walk there for I had no special pass and I must have been wandering around trying to get the feel of things, smell the atmosphere. I found Koltzov sitting on a bench, the only person in that corridor. He looked shrunken, all his brilliance gone. I sat beside him. He had no energy for talking and I could not stop.

I babbled the nightmare news of Barcelona, a whole city starving to death. In the children's wing of the big general hospital the wards were filled with beautiful small children wounded in the daily air-raids.

Languid, silver Italian planes flew very high and casually dumped their bombs anywhere, everywhere. The children were silent, none cried or complained. There were also the children wounded by hunger. Four-year-old tuberculars. An adorable little girl, maybe two years old. She laughed when the nurse picked her up, laughed with joy at the game when the nurse held her up high. Her legs were limp as rope, this pinkish rope dangling below a swollen belly. I tried to talk about their eyes, huge and dark, and how they followed the clanking trolley that brought their food. Twice a day, always the same. Soup that was only hot water with a few green leaves and a few slivers of grey meat floating in it, and a small piece of bread, war bread, made of sawdust or sand.

The roads along the coast from Tarragona had become a sluggish human mire, carts, bicycles, prams, but mainly people trudging with heavy bundles. The smallest child who could walk also carried some family possessions. The old walked, too. The Moors were advancing and the soldiers of the Republic were fighting in retreat. These refugees were a new sight of war. No one had yet seen such a thing, thousands, tens of thousands of peasants, moving away from what they had always known to nowhere. They were exhausted and must have been deeply afraid but they were silent, too. No one talked, wept, screamed, cursed God and man. They were machine-gunned if the Germans felt like it, the Germans had the fighter planes, but this beaten army of refugees was hardly worth the trouble, the bullets. Too much pain, I said, nameless, helpless millions. Who cares about their pain?

Then my editor sent me from Barcelona to Czechoslovakia when the Czech Army mobilised. I told Koltzov it had been like a fiesta. The fine army in high spirits, with their splendid equipment, rolled along the roads to take up position in their fortifications on the border. The people lined the roads and cheered them and threw flowers, and the soldiers sang and waved. In Prague the mood was sober and determined. The nation was united, ready to defend their admirable state, no matter what it cost. The marvellous feeling of will; no panic about Hitler. They counted on themselves, their armaments factories, their iron and coal, their wheat. They were practical, steady people and they did not believe that Hitler was some kind of invincible superman. Now the awful silence was beginning here, the silence that was the sound of doom, and fear where there had been none.

I was talking fast in French, our only common language, and I don't know whether Koltzov was listening. He sat hunched over, staring at the floor. He said it was pointless to stay here longer. He took me to dinner in a small, bleak, workers' restaurant, not his sort of place. When the heavy bowls of soup were served, he began to talk. He had been waiting in that corridor in the Hradcany for four days. He came with a message from Stalin for President Beneš of Czechoslovakia. The message was that if the Czechs would fight, the Soviet Army and Air Force would join them at once and until the end. Troops, tanks, artillery, planes, everything. It was the third and last chance to stop Hitler. The Rhineland, Spain and now here. The last chance; they could do it if the Czechs would fight.

Beneš would not receive Koltzov. He would not send a deputy to relay the message. He ignored Koltzov, he left him sitting in that public corridor without even the courtesy of a spoken or written rejection. The Czechs should have fought. Beneš was a decent man but fatally wrong for that time and place. He failed his people.

Koltzov was tired and hopeless. He foresaw everything exactly as it happened. We despaired further over thick, greasy food. Then we shook hands on a dark street corner and said goodbye.

I don't know when I heard that Koltzov had been shot, the bad news messenger. It was not a rumour, it was reported by a friend of Koltzov's mistress, Maria Osten, a German with long, almond-shaped green eyes. She had gone to Moscow to try to save him or bury him.

Here my memory cut off, closed down, blanked out. I was back watching the brilliant new moon. Memory must be structured on dates. There can be no coherence or sequence to it unless it is anchored in time. But I have no grasp of time and no control over my memory. I cannot order it to deliver. Unexpectedly, it flings up pictures, disconnected with no before or after. It makes me feel a fool. What is the use in having lived so long, travelled so widely, listened and looked so hard if at the end you could know what you know?

CHRISTOPHER ISHERWOOD

The Head of a Leader

*Christopher Isherwood (1904–87) was a close friend of W. H. Auden
and Stephen Spender in the 1930s and collaborated with Auden on
travel books and verse dramas. His memoir,* Lions and Shadows, *and
the short stories collected in* Goodbye to Berlin, *provide important
source-material for literary historians and each is cast in Isherwood's
familiar half true/half invented method of narration. This is the manner
too of 'The Head of a Leader', which began life as a semi-fictional
portrait of Ernst Toller, the German dramatist, poet and revolutionary,
who committed suicide in 1939 – about six weeks after the last meeting
recounted here.*

'Comme il est beau!' someone murmured in my ear, at the moment of
our first meeting – and I agreed without hesitation. He *was* beautiful,
with the immediately striking, undeniable beauty of a peacock, or a
great lady of the theatre. But, as he advanced to greet us from the hotel
doorway – the smallest central figure of a little group – I could not help
noticing that the square vigorous body was a trifle too short for his
splendid silver head – the head which a dictator had valued at five
thousand dollars.

A girl introduced us, and I found myself looking into those famous,
burning dark eyes, which every photograph had failed to reproduce:
'Ah . . . Mr Isherwood. This is a great pleasure.' His lips parted, in the
most flattering, the most imperious of smiles. Then the glance hardened,
became penetrating, commanding. Still grasping my hand, steering me
by the elbow, he led me a little aside from the others. They drew back
respectfully to let us pass, like the staff officers of a general who wishes
to confer with an important messenger. 'Tell me, first – what do you
think of Portugal? Ah, we shall have much to talk about!'

But through supper it was he who did most of the talking – and I
was glad, like the others, merely to sit and listen; to follow, with amused,
willing admiration, his every gesture and word. He was all that I had

hoped for – more brilliant, more convincing than his books, more daring than his most epic deeds. It was easy enough to see him on that cinema platform, fifteen years ago, when he told the workers: 'You must occupy the factories. You must resist.' I could picture him at the magnificent moment of defeat, crying out to his judges: 'You can silence me. You can never silence History.' I watched him pace his cell, five years long, in the mountain fortress, aloof and dangerous as the untamed tiger. Yes, he had done all that. And he could do it again – tomorrow, if need be. The years, which had cloaked him with authority, had left the vital spark untouched. The man of forty was as undaunted as the boy of twenty-five.

We spoke of Portugal. 'A great change is coming soon to this country,' he told us. 'The peasants live like the humblest animals. Feudalism is still a reality. But there is much discontentment. The forces of Progress are working underground. The masses are learning to read, and their primer is the Communist Manifesto. It is passed from hand to hand, secretly, like a precious diamond, or a bomb.'

'But, Ernst, how can you possibly *know* that?' one of the boldest members of the party, a beautiful young girl, interrupted. 'Why, you've only been here forty-eight hours. And you don't even speak the language!'

Not the smallest trace of displeasure, or impatience, was visible. With perfect good humour, the lordly, flattering eyes paid tribute to her youth, her charm; pardoned her inexperience: 'My dear Mary,' his voice was very gentle, 'I do not know these things. I feel them. Why should I wish to deceive you? You can trust me.'

We could trust him, as thousands had trusted him, unreservedly, absolutely. Somebody proposed his health, and we drank it, in the local red wine of Cascaes, which is sour as the blood of the exploited peasants. Slightly blood-drunk, I looked down from a vast height at our party, sitting there in the garden, under the vine-leaves and stars, and saw this evening as a sentence in a great book, a classic, which would one day be written – probably by Ernst himself. Later, he told funny stories, and began to sing, in a fine tenor, the songs of his own ungrateful country. He was in excellent spirits. He made us all laugh. Yet even this moment was somehow solemn, and epic. The general was entertaining his troops; building up their morale on the night before a desperate battle.

*

It was two years before I saw him again, in London, at a time when the newspapers were full of his activities. Single-handed, he was conducting a propaganda campaign on behalf of his compatriots, the starving refugees who were now scattered over half Europe. His success was sensational. He had contrived, somehow, to reach audiences outside the circles of the Left. He had touched the heart of the huge, apathetic Public. He had caught the ears of the right people, the Powers, and the powers behind the Powers. They invited him to their houses, as an honoured guest. Even the conservative press spoke well of him. He was in the process of becoming a respectable institution.

At last, one evening, I ran into him, in the middle of Regent Street. It was shortly before midnight, and I had just come out of the Café Royal. Hardly to my surprise, he recognized me at once – it was only natural, I felt, that his memory for faces, like everything else about him, should be regal: 'Ah, Isherwood! Good that we meet! And now we shall be together for a few hours, I hope? Tell me, where can we talk?'

I was feeling dreadfully tired; and I had to get up early in the morning to leave London on a long journey. But such was the epic quality of his presence that I felt childishly ashamed to have to admit that I was on my way home to bed. Revolutionaries never sleep. So I muttered something about an important engagement – some kind of meeting, I hinted – and added, with cowardly cunning: 'But Stephen's in there. I've just left him. I'm sure he'd be delighted to see you.' Stephen was a mutual friend.

He accepted my excuses benevolently, with a little pat on the shoulder. He seemed amused and touched by my slight embarrassment. 'Stephen is in there? Good. I shall surprise him.' And turning to a charming girl who, as I now became aware for the first time, had been accompanying him, he commanded, with the most regally natural simplicity: 'Please get me a flower.'

The girl showed no surprise. She must have been accustomed to this sort of thing. She turned back at once, in the direction of Piccadilly Circus, leaving us together on the pavement, dividing the slowly-moving current of the passers-by.

'You have heard about my work?' he asked, immediately.

'Yes, indeed,' I said.

'It is tremendous, Isherwood. Tremendous. I tell you, this has been a revelation to me – of what can be done with these people. In all my experience, I should not have believed it possible. You know my secret? I have discovered how to treat them!'

'And how do you treat them?'

'You see, these men are accustomed to rule an empire. To be obeyed. They are educated to believe in discipline. They do not understand a mere request. They ignore it. They despise it. But they can understand an order!'

'An order?' I laughed. 'That doesn't sound very easy.'

'It *is* easy!' His dark eyes flashed superbly. 'At first, I made many mistakes. I wrote letters, very polite: "Could you please spare me one hundred pounds?" No answer. Then I got impatient, angry. I telegraphed: "Send me one thousand." And I received it immediately. Immediately! By return of post!'

He was as delighted as a child. I nodded encouragingly, being careful not to smile.

'Yes, it is easy ... But when one sees what could be done in this country – what one man with the absolute determination could achieve ... I think to myself: Suppose this power were to be used for evil? For destruction? Seriously, Isherwood, there are moments when I feel frightened!'

But he did not look frightened. Standing there, under the street lamp, he seemed positively drunk with triumph – the fine nostrils were dilated, the lips curved in an imperial smile. His vanity was not ridiculous. He wore it superbly. It became him, like a brilliant jewel.

We were interrupted by the girl's return. I had expected her to come back empty-handed; but, to my astonishment, she was carrying a large white chrysanthemum. Goodness knows where, at that late hour, she had found, stolen or bought it. He accepted it as a matter of course, thanking her merely with a small, gracious nod. Then, clasping my hand, he told me: 'It was a great pleasure, Isherwood. We shall meet again soon. I have something I wish to discuss with you – you will be able to help me, I think. Good-bye.'

Holding the flower like a sceptre, attended by the dark-haired girl, he turned and entered the Café.

I must confess that, after this, I began to avoid him. During the weeks which followed I heard several complaints from my friends of the tasks he had contrived to set them – one was ordered to produce letters of introduction, another to use his influence with an important uncle, a third had to translate an entire blank-verse play. He found uses for everybody, even the humblest. And no one had ventured to refuse. I knew, only too well, that I should not have the moral courage to refuse him myself – and I was extremely busy just then. So I kept away from parties at which I knew he would be present. When, two or three times, he rang me up, he was always told that I was out.

But there was no escaping him for long. One afternoon he caught me, drinking coffee with a publisher, amidst the biscuit-coloured columns and immemorially ancient leather sofas of a Pall Mall club. He sat down at once, uninvited, at our table, and mildly scandalized the waiter by asking for a cream bun: 'My task here is almost finished,' he told us. 'Next week I shall sail for the United States.'

In his hand was an oddly-shaped brown paper parcel. He unwrapped it slowly, with great deliberation, glancing up at our faces to enjoy the suspense he was dramatically creating: 'The man who gave me this has a little shop in the Tottenham Court Road. I have been in to see him once or twice. Today, he said to me: "I have read about your work in the newspapers. I wish you to take this as a present from me." Wasn't it a charming thought?'

The paper fell back. Before us stood a small bronze bust of Goethe. Neither the publisher nor myself found any suitable comment.

'Was it not charming?' he insisted delightedly. 'This poor shopkeeper – he wished to give me some token of his appreciation for what I had done. And, mind you, he was not a foreigner, like myself. He was an Englishman. Just an ordinary Englishman.'

His mood changed. He became thoughtful, preoccupied. He turned the bust slowly, with his long, delicately moulded fingers:

'Goethe . . .' he mused, 'if he had lived today – would he have been on our side? Would he have been reliable?' He looked up at us suddenly, shook his head: 'I am afraid not.'

After a suitable pause, the publisher asked him if he would have some more coffee.

'No thank you. No.' He rose at once to his feet, cramming the bust and its paper into his pocket. 'I am late already.' He bowed hastily, and strode down the corridor. At the corner, he stopped – stationing himself in the shadows of the Library entrance, like an assassin. From this position he called to us, with mock-conspiratorial gaiety: 'I am waiting for the Archbishop!'

I thought I could slip away quietly, but I was wrong. Just as I had reached the foot of the staircase he called after me: 'Isherwood! One moment!' I started guiltily at the sound of my name.

'Isherwood, you must do me a great kindness. Next Tuesday I embark on the *Normandie*. While I am on board, I wish to receive a cablegram, signed by six famous writers, appealing to President Roosevelt to use his influence to help me on my mission . . . There must be at least six names – all world-famous. You understand?'

Yes, I understood. As I left the Club, I sighed deeply.

It was in New York that we met again – for the fourth and last time. Six months had passed. The Spanish Civil War was over. The dictators, in the hour of their triumph, were uttering new threats. On a beautiful cold spring afternoon I crossed Central Park to the hotel at which he was staying.

He opened the door to me himself. To my surprise, I found him quite alone:

'You must please excuse all this untidiness,' he told me. 'If I had known that you were coming I would have made some preparations.'

Even as we sat down, I was struck by the change in his appearance, and in his manner. He looked older, yellower, thinner. The black eyes were sombre, and almost gentle. And his pleasure at my visit was quite touching:

'How are you, my friend? What have you been doing? Please tell me some news of England.'

I told him everything I could think of. I did all the talking. He listened attentively, smoking one cigarette after another. I noticed that his hands trembled a little, as he lit them. At length, I asked:

'But what about your work?'

The eyes did not brighten, as I had expected. Instead, he shrugged his shoulders slightly:

'It is accomplished. The funds have been raised. We were success-ful.'

'I'm very glad.'

'There were difficulties, of course . . . When I landed in New York I had hoped to make great publicity for the scheme, to give interviews to the Press . . . But I was unlucky. Not one single journalist came to my cabin. Not one. And do you know why? They were all crowding around a foreign film actress, and a dwarf!'

'A dwarf?'

'Yes. This dwarf, it seems, was particularly important, because of his extremely small size. He was more interesting to the reporters than all the thousands of my unhappy countrymen.'

His disdainful smile, as he said this, had something of its old magnificence. But only for an instant. His face darkened again, into moody silence.

'And what are you doing now?' I asked him.

Once more, he shrugged his shoulders.

'I am here. As you see.'

'Shall you stay long?'

'Who knows?' he sighed. 'At the present, my plans are very uncertain.' Glancing round the hotel bedroom, so large and luxurious and unfriendly, and at his three scarred, shabby suitcases standing in the corner, I realized, with a slight shock, that he, who had successfully demanded so many thousands of dollars, was probably short of money. Perhaps he could not even pay his bill. He seemed to know what I was thinking, for he smiled, sadly and gently, as he walked across to the window.

'You know,' he told me, 'I long very greatly to return to Europe.'

'You don't like it here?'

'I hate it.' He said this quietly, quite without passion, stating a simple fact.

'Look,' he pointed. 'Over there is the Zoological Garden. You have seen the sea-lions?'

'Yes. I've seen them.'

'When I am lying in bed at night, I can hear them. And sometimes it seems to me that they are angry, that they are crying aloud to demand the destruction of this city.'

I laughed. We both looked out, at the white shafts of the skyscrapers, splendid in the pale sunshine, along the edge of the park.

I told him: 'A friend of mine calls them The Fallen Angels.'

'The Fallen Angels? Good. Very good . . .' I could watch his mind playing with the idea. 'One might write something . . .' he began. Then he checked himself, paused; said, with sudden decision: 'Isherwood, you must write about this town. You must write a great drama, or a novel.'

It was a command – one of his many commands. But I could not accept it meekly: 'Why don't you', I suggested, 'write that novel yourself?'

He shook his head – and the finality of this refusal was the last memory of him which I was to carry away with me. 'No, Isherwood. No. I shall never write about this country. I have come here too late.'

GEORGE ORWELL

England Your England

George Orwell (1903–50) wrote two famous novels, Animal Farm *and* 1984, *but each of these appeared towards the end of his life. For most of his literary career, Orwell was admired for his non-fiction prose – and in particular for his first-person sociological investigations,* Down and Out in Paris and London *and* The Road to Wigan Pier. *As an essayist, Orwell broke new ground with his splendidly non-snooty studies of popular culture – 'Boys' Weeklies', 'The Art of Donald McGill'. He was also a skilful and candid autobiographer: his pieces on public-school life and on his experience as an imperialist in Burma are now read as classics of left-wing polemic. 'England Your England' was written in 1941.*

As I write, highly civilized human beings are flying overhead, trying to kill me.

They do not feel any enmity against me as an individual, nor I against them. They are 'only doing their duty', as the saying goes. Most of them, I have no doubt, are kind-hearted law-abiding men who would never dream of committing murder in private life. On the other hand, if one of them succeeds in blowing me to pieces with a well-placed bomb, he will never sleep any the worse for it. He is serving his country, which has the power to absolve him from evil.

One cannot see the modern world as it is unless one recognizes the overwhelming strength of patriotism, national loyalty. In certain circumstances it can break down, at certain levels of civilization it does not exist, but as a *positive* force there is nothing to set beside it. Christianity and international Socialism are as weak as straw in comparison with it. Hitler and Mussolini rose to power in their own countries very largely because they could grasp this fact and their opponents could not.

Also, one must admit that the divisions between nation and nation are founded on real differences of outlook. Till recently it was thought proper to pretend that all human beings are very much alike, but in fact anyone able to use his eyes knows that the average of human behaviour differs enormously from country to country. Things that could happen in one country could not happen in another. Hitler's June Purge, for instance, could not have happened in England. And, as western peoples go, the English are very highly differentiated. There is a sort of backhanded admission of this in the dislike which nearly all foreigners feel for our national way of life. Few Europeans can endure living in England, and even Americans often feel more at home in Europe.

When you come back to England from any foreign country, you have immediately the sensation of breathing a different air. Even in the first few minutes dozens of small things conspire to give you this feeling. The beer is bitter, the coins are heavier, the grass is greener, the advertisements are more blatant. The crowds in the big towns, with their mild knobbly faces, their bad teeth and gentle manners, are different from a European crowd. Then the vastness of England swallows you up, and you lose for a while your feeling that the whole nation has a single identifiable character. Are there really such things as nations? Are we not 46 million individuals, all different? And the diversity of it, the chaos! The clatter of clogs in the Lancashire mill towns, the to-and-fro of the lorries on the Great North Road, the queues outside the Labour Exchanges, the rattle of pin-tables in the Soho pubs, the old maids biking to Holy Communion through the mists of the autumn mornings – all these are not only fragments, but *characteristic* fragments, of the English scene. How can one make a pattern out of this muddle?

But talk to foreigners, read foreign books or newspapers, and you are brought back to the same thought. Yes, there *is* something distinctive and recognizable in English civilization. It is a culture as individual as that of Spain. It is somehow bound up with solid breakfasts and gloomy Sundays, smoky towns and winding roads, green fields and red pillar-boxes. It has a flavour of its own. Moreover it is continuous, it stretches into the future and the past, there is something in it that persists, as in a living creature. What can the England of 1940 have in common with the England of 1840? But then, what have you in common with the child of five whose photograph your mother keeps on the mantelpiece? Nothing, except that you happen to be the same person.

And above all, it is *your* civilization, it is *you*. However much you hate it or laugh at it, you will never be happy away from it for any length of time. The suet puddings and the red pillar-boxes have entered into your soul. Good or evil, it is yours, you belong to it, and this side the grave you will never get away from the marks that it has given you.

Meanwhile England, together with the rest of the world, is changing. And like everything else it can change only in certain directions, which up to a point can be foreseen. That is not to say that the future is fixed, merely that certain alternatives are possible and others not. A seed may grow or not grow, but at any rate a turnip seed never grows into a parsnip. It is therefore of the deepest importance to try and determine what England *is*, before guessing what part England *can play* in the huge events that are happening.

II

National characteristics are not easy to pin down, and when pinned down they often turn out to be trivialities or seem to have no connexion with one another. Spaniards are cruel to animals, Italians can do nothing without making a deafening noise, the Chinese are addicted to gambling. Obviously such things don't matter in themselves. Nevertheless, nothing is causeless, and even the fact that Englishmen have bad teeth can tell one something about the realities of English life.

Here are a couple of generalizations about England that would be accepted by almost all observers. One is that the English are not gifted artistically. They are not as musical as the Germans or Italians, painting and sculpture have never flourished in England as they have in France. Another is that, as Europeans go, the English are not intellectual. They have a horror of abstract thought, they feel no need for any philosophy or systematic 'world-view'. Nor is this because they are 'practical', as they are so fond of claiming for themselves. One has only to look at their methods of town-planning and water-supply, their obstinate clinging to everything that is out of date and a nuisance, a spelling system that defies analysis and a system of weights and measures that is intelligible only to the compilers of arithmetic books, to see how little they care about mere efficiency. But they have a certain power of acting without taking thought. Their world-famed hypocrisy – their double-faced attitude towards the Empire, for instance – is bound up with this. Also, in moments of supreme crisis the whole nation can suddenly draw together and act upon a species of instinct, really a code of conduct which is understood by almost everyone, though never formulated. The phrase that Hitler coined for the Germans, 'a sleep-walking people', would have been better applied to the English. Not that there is anything to be proud of in being a sleep-walker.

But here it is worth noticing a minor English trait which is extremely well marked though not often commented on, and that is a love of flowers. This is one of the first things that one notices when one reaches England from abroad, especially if one is coming from southern Europe. Does it not contradict the English indifference to the arts? Not really, because it is found in people who have no aesthetic feelings whatever. What it does link up with, however, is another English characteristic which is so much a part of us that we barely notice it, and that is the addiction to hobbies and spare-time occupations, the *privateness* of English life. We are a nation of flower-lovers, but also a nation of stamp-collectors, pigeon-fanciers, amateur carpenters, coupon-snippers, darts-players, crossword-puzzle fans. All the culture that is most truly native centres round things which even when they are communal are not official – the pub, the football match, the back garden, the fireside and the 'nice cup of tea'. The liberty of the individual is still believed in, almost as in the nineteenth century. But this has nothing to do with economic liberty, the right to exploit others for profit. It is the liberty to have a home of your own, to do what you like in your spare time, to choose your own amusements instead of having them chosen for you from above. The most hateful of all names in an English ear is Nosey Parker. It is obvious, of course, that even this purely private liberty is a lost cause. Like all other modern peoples, the English are in process of being numbered, labelled, conscripted, 'co-ordinated'. But the pull of their impulses is in the other direction, and the kind of regimentation that can be imposed on them will be modified in consequence. No party rallies, no Youth Movements, no coloured shirts, no Jew-baiting or 'spontaneous' demonstrations. No Gestapo either, in all probability.

But in all societies the common people must live to some extent *against* the existing order. The genuinely popular culture of England is something that goes on beneath the surface, unofficially and more or less frowned on by the authorities. One thing one notices if one looks directly at the common people, especially in the big towns, is that they are not puritanical. They are inveterate gamblers, drink as much beer as their wages will permit, are devoted to bawdy jokes, and use probably the foulest language in the world. They have to satisfy these tastes in the face of astonishing, hypocritical laws (licensing laws, lottery acts, etc., etc.) which are designed to interfere with everybody but in practice allow everything to happen. Also, the common people are without definite religious belief, and have been so for centuries. The Anglican Church never had a real hold on them, it was simply a preserve of the landed gentry, and the Nonconformist sects only influenced minorities. And yet they have retained a deep tinge of Christian feeling, while almost forgetting the name of Christ. The power-worship which is the new religion of Europe, and which has infected the English intelligentsia, has never touched the common people. They have never caught up with power politics. The 'realism' which is preached in Japanese and Italian newspapers would horrify them. One can learn a good deal about the spirit of England from the comic coloured postcards that you see in the windows of cheap stationers' shops. These things are a sort of diary upon which the English people have unconsciously recorded themselves. Their old-fashioned outlook, their graded snobberies, their mixture of bawdiness and hypocrisy, their extreme gentleness, their deeply moral attitude to life, are all mirrored there.

The gentleness of the English civilization is perhaps its most marked characteristic. You notice it the instant you set foot on English soil. It is a land where the bus conductors are good-tempered and the policemen carry no revolvers. In no country inhabited by white men is it easier to shove people off the pavement. And with this goes something that is always written off by European observers as 'decadence' or hypocrisy, the English hatred of war and militarism. It is rooted deep in history, and it is strong in the lower-middle class as well as the working class. Successive wars have shaken it but not destroyed it. Well within living memory it was common for 'the redcoats' to be booed at in the street and for the landlords of respectable public-houses to refuse to allow soldiers on the premises. In peace-time, even when there are two million unemployed, it is difficult to fill the ranks of the tiny standing Army, which is officered by the county gentry and a specialized stratum of the middle class, and manned by farm labourers and slum proletarians. The mass of the people are without military knowledge or tradition, and their attitude towards war is invariably defensive. No politician could rise to power by promising them conquests or military 'glory', no Hymn of Hate has ever made any appeal to them. In the last war the songs which the soldiers made up and sang of their own accord were not vengeful but humorous and mock-defeatist.* The only enemy they ever named was the sergeant-major.

In England all the boasting and flag-wagging, the 'Rule Britannia' stuff, is done by small minorities. The patriotism of the common people is not vocal or even conscious. They do not retain among their historical memories the name of a single military victory. English literature, like other literatures, is full of battle-poems, but it is worth noticing that the ones that have won for themselves a kind of popularity are always a tale of disasters and retreats. There is no popular poem about Trafalgar or Waterloo, for instance. Sir John Moore's army at Corunna, fighting a desperate rearguard action before escaping overseas (just like Dunkirk!), has more appeal than a brilliant victory. The most stirring battle-poem in English is about a brigade of cavalry which charged in the wrong direction. And of the last war, the four names which have really engraved themselves on the popular memory are Mons, Ypres, Gallipoli and Passchendaele, every time a disaster. The names of the great battles that finally broke the German armies are simply unknown to the general public.

The reason why the English anti-militarism disgusts foreign observers is that it ignores the existence of the British Empire. It looks like sheer hypocrisy. After all, the English have absorbed a quarter of the earth and held on to it by means of a huge navy. How dare they then turn round and say that war is wicked?

It is quite true that the English are hypocritical about their Empire. In the working class this hypocrisy takes the form of not knowing that the Empire exists. But their dislike of standing armies is a perfectly sound instinct. A navy employs comparatively few people, and it is an external weapon which cannot affect home politics directly. Military

---

* For example:

> I don't want to join the bloody Army,
> I don't want to go unto the war;
> I want no more to roam,
> I'd rather stay at home
> Living on the earnings of a whore.

But it was not in that spirit that they fought.

dictatorships exist everywhere, but there is no such thing as a naval dictatorship. What English people of nearly all classes loathe from the bottom of their hearts is the swaggering officer type, the jingle of spurs and the crash of boots. Decades before Hitler was ever heard of, the word 'Prussian' had much the same significance in England as 'Nazi' has today. So deep does this feeling go that for a hundred years past the officers of the British Army, in peace-time, have always worn civilian clothes when off duty.

One rapid but fairly sure guide to the social atmosphere of a country is the parade-step of its army. A military parade is really a kind of ritual dance, something like ballet, expressing a certain philosophy of life. The goose-step, for instance, is one of the most horrible sights in the world, far more terrifying than a dive-bomber. It is simply an affirmation of naked power; contained in it, quite consciously and intentionally, is the vision of a boot crashing down on a face. Its ugliness is part of its essence, for what it is saying is 'Yes, I *am* ugly, and you daren't laugh at me', like the bully who makes faces at his victim. Why is the goose-step not used in England? There are, heaven knows, plenty of army officers who would be only too glad to introduce some such thing. It is not used because the people in the street would laugh. Beyond a certain point, military display is only possible in countries where the common people dare not laugh at the army. The Italians adopted the goose-step at about the time when Italy passed definitely under German control, and, as one would expect, they do it less well than the Germans. The Vichy government, if it survives, is bound to introduce a stiffer parade-ground discipline into what is left of the French army. In the British army the drill is rigid and complicated, full of memories of the eighteenth century, but without definite swagger; the march is merely a formalized walk. It belongs to a society which is ruled by the sword, no doubt, but a sword which must never be taken out of the scabbard.

And yet the gentleness of English civilization is mixed up with barbarities and anachronisms. Our criminal law is as out of date as the muskets in the Tower. Over against the Nazi Storm Trooper you have got to set that typically English figure, the hanging judge, some gouty old bully with his mind rooted in the nineteenth century, handing out savage sentences. In England people are still hanged by the neck and flogged with the cat-o'-nine-tails. Both of these punishments are obscene as well as cruel, but there has never been any genuinely popular outcry against them. People accept them (and Dartmoor, and Borstal) almost as they accept the weather. They are part of 'the law', which is assumed to be unalterable.

Here one comes upon an all-important English trait: the respect for constitutionalism and legality, the belief in 'the law' as something above the State and above the individual, something which is cruel and stupid, of course, but at any rate *incorruptible*.

It is not that anyone imagines the law to be just. Everyone knows that there is one law for the rich and another for the poor. But no one accepts the implications of this, everyone takes it for granted that the law, such as it is, will be respected, and feels a sense of outrage when it is not. Remarks like 'They can't run me in; I haven't done anything wrong', or 'They can't do that; it's against the law', are part of the atmosphere of England. The professed enemies of society have this feeling as strongly as anyone else. One sees it in prison-books like Wilfred Macartney's *Walls Have Mouths* or Jim Phelan's *Jail Journey*, in the solemn idiocies that take place at the trials of conscientious objectors, in letters to the papers from eminent Marxist professors, pointing out that this or that is a 'miscarriage of British justice'. Everyone believes in his heart that the law can be, ought to be and, on the whole, will be impartially administered. The totalitarian idea that there is no such thing as law, there is only power, has never taken root. Even the intelligentsia have only accepted it in theory.

An illusion can become a half-truth, a mask can alter the expression of a face. The familiar arguments to the effect that democracy is 'just the same as' or 'just as bad as' totalitarianism never take account of this fact. All such arguments boil down to saying that half a loaf is the same as no bread. In England such concepts as justice, liberty and objective truth are still believed in. They may be illusions, but they are very powerful illusions. The belief in them influences conduct, national life is different because of them. In proof of which, look about you. Where are the rubber truncheons, where is the castor oil? The sword is still in the scabbard, and while it stays there corruption cannot go beyond a certain point. The English electoral system, for instance, is an all-but open fraud. In a dozen obvious ways it is gerrymandered in the interest of the moneyed class. But until some deep change has occurred in the public mind, it cannot become *completely* corrupt. You do not arrive at the polling booth to find men with revolvers telling you which way to vote, nor are the votes miscounted, nor is there any direct bribery. Even hypocrisy is a powerful safeguard. The hanging judge, that evil old man in scarlet robe and horsehair wig, whom nothing short of dynamite will ever teach what century he is living in, but who will at any rate interpret the law according to the books and will in no circumstances take a money bribe, is one of the symbolic figures of England. He is a symbol of the strange mixture of reality and illusion, democracy and privilege, humbug and decency, the subtle network of compromise by which the nation keeps itself in its familiar shape.

III

I have spoken all the while of 'the nation', 'England', 'Britain', as though 45 million souls could somehow be treated as a unit. But is not England notoriously two nations, the rich and the poor? Dare one pretend that there is anything in common between people with £100,000 a year and people with £1 a week? And even Welsh and Scottish readers are likely to have been offended because I have used the word 'England' oftener than 'Britain', as though the whole population dwelt in London and the Home Counties and neither north nor west possessed a culture of its own.

One gets a better view of this question if one considers the minor point first. It is quite true that the so-called races of Britain feel themselves to be very different from one another. A Scotsman, for instance, does not thank you if you call him an Englishman. You can see the hesitation we feel on this point by the fact that we call our islands by no less than six different names, England, Britain, Great Britain, the British Isles, the United Kingdom and, in very exalted moments, Albion. Even the differences between north and south England loom large in our own eyes. But somehow these differences fade away the moment that any two Britons are confronted by a European. It is very rare to meet a foreigner, other than an American, who can distinguish between English and Scots or even English and Irish. To a Frenchman, the Breton and the Auvergnat seem very different beings, and the accent of Marseilles is a stock joke in Paris. Yet we speak of 'France' and 'the French', recognizing France as an entity, a single civilization, which in fact it is. So also with ourselves. Looked at from the outside, even the Cockney and the Yorkshireman have a strong family resemblance.

And even the distinction between rich and poor dwindles somewhat when one regards the nation from the outside. There is no question about the inequality of wealth in England. It is grosser than in any European country, and you have only to look down the nearest street to see it. Economically, England is certainly two nations, if not three or four. But at the same time the vast majority of the people *feel* themselves to be a single nation and are conscious of resembling one another more than they resemble foreigners. Patriotism is usually stronger than class-hatred, and always stronger than any kind of internationalism. Except for a brief moment in 1920 (the 'Hands off Russia' movement) the British working class have never thought or acted internationally. For two and a half years they watched their comrades in Spain slowly strangled, and never aided them by even a single strike.* But when their own country (the country of Lord Nuffield and Mr Montagu Norman) was in danger, their attitude was very different. At the moment when it seemed likely that England might be invaded, Anthony Eden appealed over the radio for Local Defence Volunteers. He got a quarter of a million men in the first twenty-four hours, and another million in the subsequent month. One has only to compare these figures with, for instance, the number of conscientious objectors to see how vast is the strength of traditional loyalties compared with new ones.

In England patriotism takes different forms in different classes, but it runs like a connecting thread through nearly all of them. Only the Europeanized intelligentsia are really immune to it. As a positive emotion it is stronger in the middle class than in the upper class – the cheap public schools, for instance, are more given to patriotic demonstrations than the expensive ones – but the number of definitely treacherous rich men, the Laval–Quisling type, is probably very small. In the working class patriotism is profound, but it is unconscious. The working man's heart does not leap when he sees a Union Jack. But the famous 'insularity' and 'xenophobia' of the English is far stronger in the working class than in the bourgeoisie. In all countries the poor are more national than the rich, but the English working class are outstanding in their abhorrence of foreign habits. Even when they are obliged to live abroad

---

* It is true that they aided them to a certain extent with money. Still, the sums raised for the various aid-Spain funds would not equal five per cent of the turnover of the football pools during the same period.

for years they refuse either to accustom themselves to foreign food or to learn foreign languages. Nearly every Englishman of working-class origin considers it effeminate to pronounce a foreign word correctly. During the war of 1914–18 the English working class were in contact with foreigners to an extent that is rarely possible. The sole result was that they brought back a hatred of all Europeans, except the Germans, whose courage they admired. In four years on French soil they did not even acquire a liking for wine. The insularity of the English, their refusal to take foreigners seriously, is a folly that has to be paid for very heavily from time to time. But it plays its part in the English *mystique*, and the intellectuals who have tried to break it down have generally done more harm than good. At bottom it is the same quality in the English character that repels the tourist and keeps out the invader.

Here one comes back to two English characteristics that I pointed out, seemingly rather at random, at the beginning of the last chapter. One is the lack of artistic ability. This is perhaps another way of saying that the English are outside the European culture. For there is one art in which they have shown plenty of talent, namely literature. But this is also the only art that cannot cross frontiers. Literature, especially poetry, and lyric poetry most of all, is a kind of family joke, with little or no value outside its own language-group. Except for Shakespeare, the best English poets are barely known in Europe, even as names. The only poets who are widely read are Byron, who is admired for the wrong reasons, and Oscar Wilde, who is pitied as a victim of English hypocrisy. And linked up with this, though not very obviously, is the lack of philosophical faculty, the absence in nearly all Englishmen of any need for an ordered system of thought or even for the use of logic.

Up to a point, the sense of national unity is a substitute for a 'world-view'. Just because patriotism is all but universal and not even the rich are uninfluenced by it, there can come moments when the whole nation suddenly swings together and does the same thing, like a herd of cattle facing a wolf. There was such a moment unmistakably, at the time of the disaster in France. After eight months of vaguely wondering what the war was about, the people suddenly knew what they had got to do: first, to get the army away from Dunkirk, and secondly to prevent invasion. It was like the awakening of a giant. Quick! Danger! The Philistines be upon thee, Samson! And then the swift unanimous action

– and then, alas, the prompt relapse into sleep. In a divided nation that would have been exactly the moment for a big peace movement to arise. But does this mean that the instinct of the English will always tell them to do the right thing? Not at all; merely that it will tell them to do the same thing. In the 1931 General Election, for instance, we all did the wrong thing in perfect unison. We were as single-minded as the Gadarene swine. But I honestly doubt whether we can say that we were shoved down the slope against our will.

It follows that British democracy is less of a fraud than it sometimes appears. A foreign observer sees only the huge inequality of wealth, the unfair electoral system, the governing-class control over the press, the radio and education, and concludes that democracy is simply a polite name for dictatorship. But this ignores the considerable agreement that does unfortunately exist between the leaders and the led. However much one may hate to admit it, it is almost certain that between 1931 and 1940 the National Government represented the will of the mass of the people. It tolerated slums, unemployment and a cowardly foreign policy. Yes, but so did public opinion. It was a stagnant period, and its natural leaders were mediocrities.

In spite of the campaigns of a few thousand left-wingers it is fairly certain that the bulk of the English people were behind Chamberlain's foreign policy. More, it is fairly certain that the same struggle was going on in Chamberlain's mind as in the minds of ordinary people. His opponents professed to see in him a dark and wily schemer, plotting to sell England to Hitler, but it is far likelier that he was merely a stupid old man doing his best according to his very dim lights. It is difficult otherwise to explain the contradictions of his policy, his failure to grasp any of the courses that were open to him. Like the mass of the people he did not want to pay the price either of peace or of war. And public opinion was behind him all the while, in policies that were completely incompatible with one another. It was behind him when he went to Munich, when he tried to come to an understanding with Russia, when he gave the guarantee to Poland, when he honoured it, and when he prosecuted the war half-heartedly. Only when the results of his policy became apparent did it turn against him; which is to say that it turned against its own lethargy of the past seven years. Thereupon the people picked a leader nearer to their mood, Churchill, who was at any rate able to grasp that wars are not won without fighting. Later, perhaps, they will pick another leader who can grasp that only Socialist nations can fight effectively.

Do I mean by all this that England is a genuine democracy? No, not even a reader of the *Daily Telegraph* could quite swallow that.

England is the most class-ridden country under the sun. It is a land of snobbery and privilege, ruled largely by the old and silly. But in any calculation about it one has got to take into account its emotional unity, the tendency of nearly all its inhabitants to feel alike and act together in moments of supreme crisis. It is the only great country in Europe that is not obliged to drive hundreds of thousands of its nationals into exile or the concentration camp. At this moment, after a year of war, newspapers and pamphlets abusing the Government, praising the enemy and clamouring for surrender are being sold on the streets, almost without interference. And this is less from a respect for freedom of speech than from a simple perception that these things don't matter. It is safe to let a paper like *Peace News* be sold, because it is certain that 95 per cent of the population will never want to read it. The nation is bound together by an invisible chain. At any normal time the ruling class will rob, mismanage, sabotage, lead us into the muck; but let popular opinion really make itself heard, let them get a tug from below that they cannot avoid feeling, and it is difficult for them not to respond. The left-wing writers who denounce the whole of the ruling class as 'pro-Fascist' are grossly over-simplifying. Even among the inner clique of politicians who brought us to our present pass, it is doubtful whether there were any *conscious* traitors. The corruption that happens in England is seldom of that kind. Nearly always it is more in the nature of self-deception, of the right hand not knowing what the left hand doeth. And being unconscious, it is limited. One sees this at its most obvious in the English press. Is the English press honest or dishonest? At normal times it is deeply dishonest. All the papers that matter live off their advertisements, and the advertisers exercise an indirect censorship over news. Yet I do not suppose there is one paper in England that can be straightforwardly bribed with hard cash. In the France of the Third Republic all but a very few of the newspapers could notoriously be bought over the counter like so many pounds of cheese. Public life in England has never been *openly* scandalous. It has not reached the pitch of disintegration at which humbug can be dropped.

England is not the jewelled isle of Shakespeare's much-quoted passage, nor is it the inferno depicted by Dr Goebbels. More than either it resembles a family, a rather stuffy Victorian family, with not many black sheep in it but with all its cupboards bursting with skeletons. It has rich relations who have to be kowtowed to and poor relations who are horribly sat upon, and there is a deep conspiracy of silence about the source of the family income. It is a family in which the young are generally thwarted and most of the power is in the hands of irresponsible uncles and bedridden aunts. Still, it is a family. It has its private language and its common memories, and at the approach of an enemy it closes its ranks. A family with the wrong members in control – that, perhaps, is as near as one can come to describing England in a phrase.

IV

Probably the Battle of Waterloo *was* won on the playing-fields of Eton, but the opening battles of all subsequent wars have been lost there. One of the dominant facts in English life during the past three-quarters of a century has been the decay of ability in the ruling class.

In the years between 1920 and 1940 it was happening with the speed of a chemical reaction. Yet at the moment of writing it is still possible to speak of a ruling class. Like the knife which has had two new blades and three new handles, the upper fringe of English society is still almost what it was in the mid nineteenth century. After 1832 the old landowning aristocracy steadily lost power, but instead of disappearing or becoming a fossil they simply intermarried with the merchants, manufacturers and financiers who had replaced them, and soon turned them into accurate copies of themselves. The wealthy ship-owner or cotton-miller set up for himself an alibi as a country gentleman, while his sons learned the right mannerisms at public schools which had been designed for just that purpose. England was ruled by an aristocracy constantly recruited from parvenus. And considering what energy the self-made men possessed, and considering that they were buying their way into a class which at any rate had a tradition of public service, one might have expected that able rulers could be produced in some such way.

And yet somehow the ruling class decayed, lost its ability, its daring, finally even its ruthlessness, until a time came when stuffed shirts like Eden or Halifax could stand out as men of exceptional talent. As for

Baldwin, one could not even dignify him with the name of stuffed shirt. He was simply a hole in the air. The mishandling of England's domestic problems during the nineteen-twenties had been bad enough, but British foreign policy between 1931 and 1939 is one of the wonders of the world. Why? What had happened? What was it that at every decisive moment made every British statesman do the wrong thing with so unerring an instinct?

The underlying fact was that the whole position of the moneyed class had long ceased to be justifiable. There they sat, at the centre of a vast empire and a world-wide financial network, drawing interest and profits and spending them – on what? It was fair to say that life within the British Empire was in many ways better than life outside it. Still, the Empire was undeveloped, India slept in the Middle Ages, the Dominions lay empty, with foreigners jealously barred out, and even England was full of slums and unemployment. Only half a million people, the people in the country houses, definitely benefited from the existing system. Moreover, the tendency of small businesses to merge together into large ones robbed more and more of the moneyed class of their function and turned them into mere *owners*, their work being done for them by salaried managers and technicians. For long past there had been in England an entirely functionless class, living on money that was vested they hardly knew where, the 'idle rich', the people whose photographs you can look at in the *Tatler* and the *Bystander*, always supposing that you want to. The existence of these people was by any standard unjustifiable. They were simply parasites, less useful to society than his fleas are to a dog.

By 1920 there were many people who were aware of all this. By 1930 millions were aware of it. But the British ruling class obviously could not admit to themselves that their usefulness was at an end. Had they done that they would have had to abdicate. For it was not possible for them to turn themselves into mere bandits, like the American millionaires, consciously clinging to unjust privileges and beating down opposition by bribery and tear-gas bombs. After all, they belonged to a class with a certain tradition, they had been to public schools where the duty of dying for your country, if necessary, is laid down as the first and greatest of the Commandments. They had to *feel* themselves true patriots, even while they plundered their countrymen. Clearly there was only one escape for them – into stupidity. They could keep society in its existing shape only by being *unable* to grasp that any improvement was possible. Difficult though this was, they achieved it, largely by fixing their eyes on the past and refusing to notice the changes that were going on round them.

There is much in England that this explains. It explains the decay of country life, due to the keeping-up of a sham feudalism which drives the more spirited workers off the land. It explains the immobility of the public schools, which have barely altered since the eighties of the last century. It explains the military incompetence which has again and again startled the world. Since the fifties every war in which England has engaged has started off with a series of disasters, after which the situation has been saved by people comparatively low in the social scale. The higher commanders, drawn from the aristocracy, could never prepare for modern war, because in order to do so they would have had to admit to themselves that the world was changing. They have always clung to obsolete methods and weapons, because they inevitably saw each war as a repetition of the last. Before the Boer War they prepared for the Zulu War, before 1914 for the Boer War, and before the present war for 1914. Even at this moment hundreds of thousands of men in England are being trained with the bayonet, a weapon entirely useless except for opening tins. It is worth noticing that the Navy and, latterly, the Air Force, have always been more efficient than the regular Army. But the Navy is only partially, and the Air Force hardly at all, within the ruling-class orbit.

It must be admitted that so long as things were peaceful the methods of the British ruling class served them well enough. Their own people manifestly tolerated them. However unjustly England might be organized, it was at any rate not torn by class warfare or haunted by secret police. The Empire was peaceful as no area of comparable size has ever been. Throughout its vast extent, nearly a quarter of the earth, there were fewer armed men than would be found necessary by a minor Balkan State. As people to live under, and looking at them merely from a liberal, *negative* standpoint, the British ruling class had their points. They were preferable to the truly modern men, the Nazis and Fascists. But it had long been obvious that they would be helpless against any serious attack from the outside.

They could not struggle against Nazism or Fascism, because they could not understand them. Neither could they have struggled against

Communism, if Communism had been a serious force in western Europe. To understand Fascism they would have had to study the theory of Socialism, which would have forced them to realize that the economic system by which they lived was unjust, inefficient and out of date. But it was exactly this fact that they had trained themselves never to face. They dealt with Fascism as the cavalry generals of 1914 dealt with the machine gun – by ignoring it. After years of aggression and massacres, they had grasped only one fact, that Hitler and Mussolini were hostile to Communism. Therefore, it was argued, they *must* be friendly to the British dividend-drawer. Hence the truly frightening spectacle of Conservative MPs wildly cheering the news that British ships, bringing food to the Spanish Republican government, had been bombed by Italian aeroplanes. Even when they had begun to grasp that Fascism was dangerous, its essentially revolutionary nature, the huge military effort it was capable of making, the sort of tactics it would use, were quite beyond their comprehension. At the time of the Spanish civil war, anyone with as much political knowledge as can be acquired from a sixpenny pamphlet on Socialism knew that if Franco won, the result would be strategically disastrous for England; and yet generals and admirals who had given their lives to the study of war were unable to grasp this fact. This vein of political ignorance runs right through English official life, through Cabinet ministers, ambassadors, consuls, judges, magistrates, policemen. The policeman who arrests the 'Red' does not understand the theories the 'Red' is preaching; if he did, his own position as bodyguard of the moneyed class might seem less pleasant to him. There is reason to think that even military espionage is hopelessly hampered by ignorance of the new economic doctrines and the ramifications of the underground parties.

The British ruling class were not altogether wrong in thinking that Fascism was on their side. It is a fact that any rich man, unless he is a Jew, has less to fear from Fascism than from either Communism or democratic Socialism. One ought never to forget this, for nearly the whole of German and Italian propaganda is designed to cover it up. The natural instinct of men like Simon, Hoare, Chamberlain, etc., was to come to an agreement with Hitler. But – and here the peculiar feature of English life that I have spoken of, the deep sense of national solidarity, comes in – they could only do so by breaking up the Empire and selling their own people into semi-slavery. A truly corrupt class would have done this without hesitation, as in France. But things had not gone that distance in England. Politicians who would make cringing speeches about 'the duty of loyalty to our conquerors' are hardly to be found in English public life. Tossed to and fro between their incomes and their principles, it was impossible that men like Chamberlain should do anything but make the worst of both worlds.

One thing that has always shown that the English ruling class are *morally* fairly sound, is that in time of war they are ready enough to get themselves killed. Several dukes, earls and what-not were killed in the recent campaign in Flanders. That could not happen if these people were the cynical scoundrels that they are sometimes declared to be. It is important not to misunderstand their motives, or one cannot predict their actions. What is to be expected of them is not treachery or physical cowardice, but stupidity, unconscious sabotage, an infallible instinct for doing the wrong thing. They are not wicked, or not altogether wicked; they are merely unteachable. Only when their money and power are gone will the younger among them begin to grasp what century they are living in.

V

The stagnation of the Empire in the between-war years affected everyone in England, but it had an especially direct effect upon two important sub-sections of the middle class. One was the military and imperialist middle class, generally nicknamed the Blimps, and the other the left-wing intelligentsia. These two seemingly hostile types, symbolic opposites – the half-pay colonel with his bull neck and diminutive brain, like a dinosaur, the highbrow with his domed forehead and stalk-like neck – are mentally linked together and constantly interact upon one another; in any case they are born to a considerable extent into the same families.

Thirty years ago the Blimp class was already losing its vitality. The middle-class families celebrated by Kipling, the prolific lowbrow families whose sons officered the Army and Navy and swarmed over all the waste places of the earth from the Yukon to the Irrawaddy, were dwindling before 1914. The thing that had killed them was the telegraph. In a narrowing world, more and more governed from Whitehall, there was every year less room for individual initiative. Men like Clive, Nelson, Nicholson, Gordon would find no place for themselves in the modern British Empire. By 1920 nearly every inch of the colonial empire was in the grip of Whitehall. Well-meaning, over- civilized men, in dark suits and black felt hats, with neatly rolled umbrellas crooked over the left forearm, were imposing their constipated view of life on Malaya and Nigeria, Mombasa and Mandalay. The one-time empire builders were reduced to the status of clerks, buried deeper and deeper under mounds of paper and red tape. In the early twenties one could see, all over the Empire, the older officials, who had known more spacious days, writhing impotently under the changes that were happening. From that time onwards it has been next door to impossible to induce young men of spirit to take any part in imperial administration. And what was true of the official world was true also of the commercial. The great monopoly companies swallowed up hosts of petty traders. Instead of going out to trade adventurously in the Indies, one went to an office stool in Bombay or Singapore. And life in Bombay or Singapore was actually duller and safer than life in London. Imperialist sentiment remained strong in the middle class, chiefly owing to family tradition, but the job of administering the Empire had ceased to appeal. Few able men went east of Suez if there was any way of avoiding it.

But the general weakening of imperialism, and to some extent of the whole British morale, that took place during the nineteen-thirties, was partly the work of the left-wing intelligentsia, itself a kind of growth that had sprouted from the stagnation of the Empire.

It should be noted that there is now no intelligentsia that is not in some sense 'Left'. Perhaps the last right-wing intellectual was T. E. Lawrence. Since about 1930 everyone describable as an 'intellectual' has lived in a state of chronic discontent with the existing order. Necessarily so, because society as it was constituted had no room for him. In an Empire that was simply stagnant, neither being developed nor falling to pieces, and in an England ruled by people whose chief asset was their stupidity, to be 'clever' was to be suspect. If you had the kind of brain that could understand the poems of T. S. Eliot or the theories of Karl Marx, the higher-ups would see to it that you were kept out of any important job. The intellectuals could find a function for themselves only in the literary reviews and the left-wing political parties.

The mentality of the English left-wing intelligentsia can be studied in half a dozen weekly and monthly papers. The immediately striking thing about all these papers is their generally negative, querulous attitude, their complete lack at all times of any constructive suggestion. There is little in them except the irresponsible carping of people who have never been and never expect to be in a position of power. Another marked characteristic is the emotional shallowness of people who live in a world of ideas and have little contact with physical reality. Many intellectuals of the Left were flabbily pacifist up to 1935, shrieked for war against Germany in the years 1935–9, and then promptly cooled off when the war started. It is broadly though not precisely true that the people who were most 'Anti-Fascist' during the Spanish civil war are most defeatist now. And underlying this is the really important fact about so many of the English intelligentsia – their severance from the common culture of the country.

In intention, at any rate, the English intelligentsia are Europeanized. They take their cookery from Paris and their opinions from Moscow. In the general patriotism of the country they form a sort of island of dissident thought. England is perhaps the only great country whose intellectuals are ashamed of their own nationality. In left-wing circles it is always felt that there is something slightly disgraceful in being an Englishman and that it is a duty to snigger at every English institution, from horse-racing to suet puddings. It is a strange fact, but it is unquestionably true, that almost any English intellectual would feel more ashamed of standing to attention during 'God save the King' than of stealing from a poor-box. All through the critical years many left-wingers were chipping away at English morale, trying to spread an outlook that was sometimes squashily pacifist, sometimes violently pro-Russian, but always anti-British. It is questionable how much effect this had, but it certainly had some. If the English people suffered for several years a real weakening of morale, so that the Fascist nations judged that they were 'decadent' and that it was safe to plunge into war, the intellectual sabotage from the Left was partly responsible. Both the *New Statesman* and the *News Chronicle* cried out against the Munich settlement, but even they had done something to make it possible. Ten years of systematic Blimp-baiting affected even the Blimps themselves and made it harder than it had been before to get intelligent young men to enter the armed forces. Given the stagnation of the Empire the military middle class must have decayed in any case, but the spread of a shallow Leftism hastened the process.

It is clear that the special position of the English intellectuals during the past ten years, as purely *negative* creatures, mere anti-Blimps, was a by-product of ruling-class stupidity. Society could not use them, and they had not got it in them to see that devotion to one's country implies 'for better, for worse'. Both Blimps and highbrows took for granted, as though it were a law of nature, the divorce between patriotism and intelligence. If you were a patriot you read *Blackwood's Magazine* and publicly thanked God that you were 'not brainy'. If you were an intellectual you sniggered at the Union Jack and regarded physical courage as barbarous. It is obvious that this preposterous convention cannot continue. The Bloomsbury highbrow, with his mechanical snigger, is as out of date as the cavalry colonel. A modern nation cannot afford either of them. Patriotism and intelligence will have to come together again. It is the fact that we are fighting a war, and a very peculiar kind of war, that may make this possible.

VI

One of the most important developments in England during the past twenty years has been the upward and downward extension of the middle class. It has happened on such a scale as to make the old classification of society into capitalists, proletarians and petit-bourgeois (small property-owners) almost obsolete.

England is a country in which property and financial power are concentrated in very few hands. Few people in modern England *own* anything at all, except clothes, furniture and possibly a house. The peasantry have long since disappeared, the independent shopkeeper is being destroyed, the small business-man is diminishing in numbers. But at the same time modern industry is so complicated that it cannot get along without great numbers of managers, salesmen, engineers, chemists and technicians of all kinds, drawing fairly large salaries. And these in turn call into being a professional class of doctors, lawyers, teachers, artists, etc., etc. The tendency of advanced capitalism has therefore been to enlarge the middle class and not to wipe it out, as it once seemed likely to do.

But much more important than this is the spread of middle-class ideas and habits among the working class. The British working class are now better off in almost all ways than they were thirty years ago. This is partly due to the efforts of the trade unions, but partly to the mere advance of physical science. It is not always realized that within rather narrow limits the standard of life of a country can rise without a corresponding rise in real wages. Up to a point civilization can lift itself up by its boot-tags. However unjustly society is organized, certain technical advances are bound to benefit the whole community, because certain kinds of goods are necessarily held in common. A millionaire cannot, for example, light the streets for himself while darkening then for other people. Nearly all citizens of civilized countries now enjoy the use of good roads, germ-free water, police protection, free libraries and probably free education of a kind. Public education in England has been meanly starved of money, but it has nevertheless improved, largely owing to the devoted efforts of the teachers, and the habit of reading has become enormously more widespread. To an increasing extent the rich and the poor read the same books, and they also see the same films and listen to the same radio programmes. And the differences in their way of life have been diminished by the mass production of cheap clothes and improvements in housing. So far as outward appearance goes, the clothes of rich and poor, especially in the case of women, differ far less than they did thirty or even fifteen years ago. As to housing, England still has slums which are a blot on civilization, but much building has been done during the past ten years, largely by the local authorities. The modern council house, with its bathroom and electric light, is smaller than the stockbroker's villa, but it is recognizably the same kind of house, which the farm labourer's cottage is not. A person who has grown up in a council housing estate is likely to be – indeed, visibly *is* – more middle-class in outlook than a person who has grown up in a slum.

The effect of all this is a general softening of manners. It is enhanced by the fact that modern industrial methods tend always to demand less muscular effort and therefore to leave people with more energy when their day's work is done. Many workers in the light industries are less truly manual labourers than is a doctor or a grocer. In tastes, habits, manners and outlook the working class and the middle class are drawing together. The unjust distinctions remain, but the real differences diminish. The old-style 'proletarian' – collarless, unshaven and with muscles warped by heavy labour – still exists, but he is constantly decreasing in numbers; he only predominates in the heavy-industry areas of the north of England.

After 1918 there began to appear something that had never existed in England before: people of indeterminate social class. In 1910 every human being in these islands could be 'placed' in an instant by his clothes, manners and accent. That is no longer the case. Above all, it is not the case in the new townships that have developed as a result of cheap motor cars and the southward shift of industry. The place to look for the germs of the future England is in the light-industry areas and along the arterial roads. In Slough, Dagenham, Barnet, Letchworth, Hayes – everywhere, indeed, on the outskirts of great towns – the old pattern is gradually changing into something new. In those vast new wildernesses of glass and brick the sharp distinctions of the older kind of town, with its slums and mansions, or of the country, with its manor houses and squalid cottages, no longer exist. There are wide gradations of income but it is the same kind of life that is being lived at different levels, in labour-saving flats or council houses, along the concrete roads and in the naked democracy of the swimming-pools. It is a rather restless, cultureless life, centring round tinned food, *Picture Post*, the radio and the internal combustion engine. It is a civilization in which children grow up with an intimate knowledge of magnetos and in complete ignorance of the Bible. To that civilization belong the people who are most at home in and most definitely *of* the modern world, the technicians and the higher-paid skilled workers, the airmen and their mechanics, the radio experts, film producers, popular journalists and industrial chemists. They are the indeterminate stratum at which the older class distinctions are beginning to break down.

This war, unless we are defeated, will wipe out most of the existing class privileges. There are every day fewer people who wish them to continue. Nor need we fear that as the pattern changes life in England will lose its peculiar flavour. The new red cities of Greater London are crude enough, but these things are only the rash that accompanies a change. In whatever shape England emerges from the war, it will be deeply tinged with the characteristics that I have spoken of earlier. The intellectuals who hope to see it Russianized or Germanized will be disappointed. The gentleness, the hypocrisy, the thoughtlessness, the reverence for law and the hatred of uniforms will remain, along with the suet puddings and the misty skies. It needs some very great disaster, such as prolonged subjugation by a foreign enemy, to destroy a national culture. The Stock Exchange will be pulled down, the horse plough will give way to the tractor, the country houses will be turned into children's holiday camps, the Eton and Harrow match will be forgotten, but England will still be England, an everlasting animal stretching into the future and the past, and like all living things, having the power to change out of recognition and yet remain the same.

W · H · AUDEN

The Guilty Vicarage

W. H. Auden (1907–73) is best known as a poet, but he published three books of critical prose and performed also as a librettist and verse-dramatist. Auden was a deeply erudite literary figure, but his interests extended far beyond the literary – religion, geology, psychology, linguistics, general science and so on, were for him not merely hobbies. He had, as an envious contemporary remarked, a good deal of exciting lumber in his mental attic. He also had a taste for the low-brow, the risqué, the beneath-contempt. 'The Guilty Vicarage' was first collected in The Dyer's Hand (1963).

> I had not known sin, but by law.
>
> ROMANS 7

A CONFESSION

For me, as for many others, the reading of detective stories is an addiction like tobacco or alcohol. The symptoms of this are: firstly, the intensity of the craving – if I have any work to do, I must be careful not to get hold of a detective story for, once I begin one, I cannot work or sleep till I have finished it. Secondly, its specificity – the story must conform to certain formulas (I find it very difficult, for example, to read one that is not set in rural England). And, thirdly, its immediacy. I forget the story as soon as I have finished it, and have no wish to read it again. If, as sometimes happens, I start reading one and find after a few pages that I have read it before, I cannot go on. Such reactions convince me that, in my case at least, detective stories have nothing to do with works of art. It is possible, however, that an analysis of the detective story, i.e. of the kind of detective story I enjoy, may throw light, not only on its magical function, but also, by contrast, on the function of art.

DEFINITION

The vulgar definition, 'a Whodunit', is correct. The basic formula is this: a murder occurs; many are suspected; all but one suspect, who is the murderer, are eliminated; the murderer is arrested or dies.

This definition excludes:

1. Studies of murderers whose guilt is known, e.g. *Malice Afore-thought*. There are borderline cases in which the murderer is known and there are no false suspects, but the proof is lacking, e.g. many of the stories of Freeman Wills Crofts. Most of these are permissible.

2. Thrillers, spy stories, stories of master crooks, etc., when the identification of the criminal is subordinate to the defeat of his criminal designs.

The interest in the thriller is the ethical and characteristic conflict between good and evil, between Us and Them. The interest in the study of a murderer is the observation, by the innocent many, of the sufferings of the guilty one. The interest in the detective story is the dialectic of innocence and guilt.

As in the Aristotelian description of tragedy, there is Concealment (the innocent seem guilty and the guilty seem innocent) and Manifestation (the real guilt is brought to consciousness). There is also peripeteia, in this case not a reversal of fortune but a double reversal from apparent guilt to innocence and from apparent innocence to guilt. The formula may be diagrammed as follows:

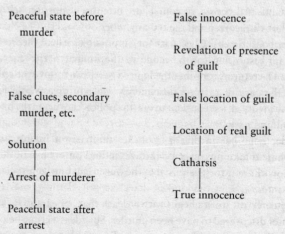

Peaceful state before murder	False innocence
	Revelation of presence of guilt
False clues, secondary murder, etc.	False location of guilt
	Location of real guilt
Solution	Catharsis
Arrest of murderer	True innocence
Peaceful state after arrest	

In Greek tragedy the audience knows the truth; the actors do not, but discover or bring to pass the inevitable. In modern, e.g. Elizabethan, tragedy the audience knows neither less nor more than the most knowing of the actors. In the detective story the audience does not know the truth at all; one of the actors – the murderer – does; and the detective, of his own free will, discovers and reveals what the murderer, of his own free will, tries to conceal.

Greek tragedy and the detective story have one characteristic in common in which they both differ from modern tragedy; namely, the characters are not changed in or by their actions: in Greek tragedy because their actions are fated, in the detective story because the decisive event, the murder, has already occurred. Time and space therefore are simply the when and where of revealing either what has to happen or what has actually happened. In consequence, the detective story probably should, and usually does, obey the classical unities, whereas modern tragedy, in which the characters develop with time, can only do so by a technical tour de force; and the thriller, like the picaresque novel, even demands frequent changes of time and place.

WHY MURDER?

There are three classes of crime: A. offenses against God and one's neighbor or neighbors; B. offenses against God and society; C. offenses against God. (All crimes, of course, are offenses against oneself.)

Murder is a member and the only member of Class B. The character common to all crimes in Class A is that it is possible, at least theoretically, either that restitution can be made to the injured party (e.g. stolen goods can be returned), or that the injured party can forgive the criminal (e.g. in the case of rape). Consequently, society as a whole is only indirectly involved; its representatives (the police, etc.) act in the interests of the injured party.

Murder is unique in that it abolishes the party it injures, so that society has to take the place of the victim and on his behalf demand restitution or grant forgiveness; it is the one crime in which society has a direct interest.

Many detective stories begin with a death that appears to be suicide and is later discovered to have been murder. Suicide is a crime belonging to Class C in which neither the criminal's neighbors nor society has any interest, direct or indirect. As long as a death is believed to be suicide, even private curiosity is improper; as soon as it is proved to be murder, public inquiry becomes a duty.

The detective story has five elements – the milieu, the victim, the murderer, the suspects, the detective.

THE MILIEU (HUMAN)

The detective story requires:

1. A closed society so that the possibility of an outside murderer (and hence of the society being totally innocent) is excluded; and a closely related society so that all its members are potentially suspect (cf. the thriller, which requires an open society in which any stranger may be a friend or enemy in disguise).

Such conditions are met by: a) the group of blood relatives (the Christmas dinner in the country house); b) the closely knit geographical group (the old world village); c) the occupational group (the theatrical company); d) the group isolated by the neutral place (the Pullman car).

In this last type the concealment–manifestation formula applies not only to the murder but also to the relations between the members of the group who first appear to be strangers to each other, but are later found to be related.

2. It must appear to be an innocent society in a state of grace, i.e. a society where there is no need of the law, no contradiction between the aesthetic individual and the ethical universal, and where murder, therefore, is the unheard-of act which precipitates a crisis (for it reveals that some member has fallen and is no longer in a state of grace). The law becomes a reality and for a time all must live in its shadow, till the fallen one is identified. With his arrest, innocence is restored, and the law retires forever.

The characters in a detective story should, therefore, be eccentric (aesthetically interesting individuals) and good (instinctively ethical) – good, that is, either in appearance, later shown to be false, or in reality, first concealed by an appearance of bad.

It is a sound instinct that has made so many detective story writers choose a college as a setting. The ruling passion of the ideal professor is the pursuit of knowledge for its own sake so that he is related to other human beings only indirectly through their common relation to the truth; and those passions, like lust and avarice and envy, which relate individuals directly and may lead to murder are, in his case, ideally excluded. If a murder occurs in a college, therefore, it is a sign that some colleague is not only a bad man but also a bad professor. Further, as the basic premise of academic life is that truth is universal and to be shared with all, the *gnosis* of a concrete crime and the *gnosis* of abstract ideas nicely parallel and parody each other.

(The even more ideal contradiction of a murder in a monastery is excluded by the fact that monks go regularly to confession and, while the murderer might well not confess his crime, the suspects who are innocent of murder but guilty of lesser sins cannot be supposed to conceal them without making the monastery absurd. Incidentally, is it an accident that the detective story has flourished most in predominantly Protestant countries?)

The detective story writer is also wise to choose a society with an elaborate ritual and to describe this in detail. A ritual is a sign of harmony between the aesthetic and the ethical in which body and mind, individual will and general laws, are not in conflict. The murderer uses his knowledge of the ritual to commit the crime and can be caught only by someone who acquires an equal or superior familiarity with it.

THE MILIEU (NATURAL)

In the detective story, as in its mirror image, the Quest for the Grail, maps (the ritual of space) and timetables (the ritual of time) are desirable. Nature should reflect its human inhabitants, i.e. it should be the Great Good Place; for the more Eden-like it is, the greater the contradiction of murder. The country is preferable to the town, a well-to-do neighborhood (but not too well-to-do – or there will be a suspicion of ill-gotten gains) better than a slum. The corpse must shock not only because it is a corpse but also because, even for a corpse, it is shockingly out of place, as when a dog makes a mess on a drawing-room carpet.

Mr Raymond Chandler has written that he intends to take the body out of the vicarage garden and give the murder back to those who are good at it. If he wishes to write detective stories, i.e. stories where the reader's principal interest is to learn who did it, he could not be more mistaken, for in a society of professional criminals, the only possible motives for desiring to identify the murderer are blackmail or revenge, which both apply to individuals, not to the group as a whole, and can equally well inspire murder. Actually, whatever he may say, I think Mr Chandler is interested in writing, not detective stories, but serious studies of a criminal milieu, the Great Wrong Place, and his powerful but extremely depressing books should be read and judged, not as escape literature, but as works of art.

THE VICTIM

The victim has to try to satisfy two contradictory requirements. He has to involve everyone in suspicion, which requires that he be a bad character; and he has to make everyone feel guilty, which requires that he be a good character. He cannot be a criminal because he could then be dealt with by the law and murder would be unnecessary. (Blackmail is the only exception.) The more general the temptation to murder he arouses, the better; e.g. the desire for freedom is a better motive than money alone or sex alone. On the whole, the best victim is the negative Father or Mother Image.

If there is more than one murder, the subsequent victims should be more innocent than the initial victim, i.e. the murderer should start with a real grievance and, as a consequence of righting it by illegitimate means, be forced to murder against his will where he has no grievances but his own guilt.

THE MURDERER

Murder is negative creation, and every murderer is therefore the rebel who claims the right to be omnipotent. His pathos is his refusal to suffer. The problem for the writer is to conceal his demonic pride from the other characters and from the reader, since, if a person has this pride, it tends to appear in everything he says and does. To surprise the reader when the identity of the murderer is revealed, yet at the same time to convince him that everything he has previously been told about the murderer is consistent with his being a murderer, is the test of a good detective story.

As to the murderer's end, of the three alternatives – execution, suicide, and madness – the first is preferable; for if he commits suicide he refuses to repent, and if he goes mad he cannot repent, but if he does not repent society cannot forgive. Execution, on the other hand, is the act of atonement by which the murderer is forgiven by society. In real life I disapprove of capital punishment, but in a detective story the murderer must have no future.

(*A Suggestion for Mr Chandler:* Among a group of efficient professional killers who murder for strictly professional reasons, there is one to whom, like Leopold and Loeb, murder is an *acte gratuit*. Presently murders begin to occur which have not been commissioned. The group is morally outraged and bewildered; it has to call in the police to detect the amateur murderer, rescue the professionals from a mutual suspicion which threatens to disrupt their organization, and restore their capacity to murder.)

THE SUSPECTS

The detective-story society is a society consisting of apparently innocent individuals, i.e. their aesthetic interest as individuals does not conflict with their ethical obligations to the universal. The murder is the act of disruption by which innocence is lost, and the individual and the law become opposed to each other. In the case of the murderer this opposition is completely real (till he is arrested and consents to be punished); in the case of the suspects it is mostly apparent.

But in order for the appearance to exist, there must be some element of reality; e.g. it is unsatisfactory if the suspicion is caused by chance or the murderer's malice alone. The suspects must be guilty of something, because, now that the aesthetic and the ethical are in opposition, if they are completely innocent (obedient to the ethical) they lose their aesthetic interest and the reader will ignore them.

For suspects, the principal causes of guilt are:

1. the wish or even the intention to murder
2. crimes of Class A or vices of Class C (e.g. illicit amours) which the suspect is afraid or ashamed to reveal
3. a *hubris* of intellect which tries to solve the crime itself and despises the official police (assertion of the supremacy of the aesthetic over the ethical). If great enough, this *hubris* leads to its subject getting murdered
4. a *hubris* of innocence which refuses to cooperate with the investigation
5. a lack of faith in another loved suspect, which leads its subject to hide or confuse clues

THE DETECTIVE

Completely satisfactory detectives are extremely rare. Indeed, I only know of three: Sherlock Holmes (Conan Doyle), Inspector French (Freeman Wills Crofts), and Father Brown (Chesterton).

The job of detective is to restore the state of grace in which the aesthetic and the ethical are as one. Since the murderer who caused their disjunction is the aesthetically defiant individual, his opponent, the detective, must be either the official representative of the ethical or the exceptional individual who is himself in a state of grace. If he is the former, he is a professional; if he is the latter, he is an amateur. In either case, the detective must be the total stranger who cannot possibly be involved in the crime; this excludes the local police and should, I think, exclude the detective who is a friend of one of the suspects. The professional detective has the advantage that, since he is not an individual but a representative of the ethical, he does not need a motive for investigating the crime; but for the same reason he has the disadvantage of being unable to overlook the minor ethical violations of the suspects, and therefore it is harder for him to gain their confidence.

Most amateur detectives, on the other hand, are unsatisfactory either because they are priggish supermen, like Lord Peter Wimsey and Philo Vance, who have no motive for being detectives except caprice, or because, like the detectives of the hard-boiled school, they are motivated by avarice or ambition and might just as well be murderers.

The amateur detective genius may have weaknesses to give him aesthetic interest, but they must not be of a kind which outrage ethics. The most satisfactory weaknesses are the solitary oral vices of eating and drinking or childish boasting. In his sexual life, the detective must be either celibate or happily married.

Between the amateur detective and the professional policeman stands the criminal lawyer whose *telos* is, not to discover who is guilty, but to prove that his client is innocent. His ethical justification is that human law is ethically imperfect, i.e not an absolute manifestation of the universal and divine, and subject to chance aesthetic limitations, e.g. the intelligence or stupidity of individual policemen and juries (in consequence of which an innocent man may sometimes be judged guilty).

To correct this imperfection, the decision is arrived at through an aesthetic combat, i.e. the intellectual gifts of the defense versus those of the prosecution, just as in earlier days doubtful cases were solved by physical combat between the accused and the accuser.

The lawyer-detective (e.g. Joshua Clunk) is never quite satisfactory, therefore, because of his commitment to his client, whom he cannot desert, even if he should really be the guilty party, without ceasing to be a lawyer.

SHERLOCK HOLMES

Holmes is the exceptional individual who is in a state of grace because he is a genius in whom scientific curiosity is raised to the status of a heroic passion. He is erudite but his knowledge is absolutely specialized (e.g. his ignorance of the Copernican system), he is in all matters outside his field as helpless as a child (e.g. his untidiness), and he pays the price for his scientific detachment (his neglect of feeling) by being the victim of melancholia which attacks him whenever he is unoccupied with a case (e.g. his violin playing and cocaine taking).

His motive for being a detective is, positively, a love of the neutral truth (he has no interest in the feelings of the guilty or the innocent), and negatively, a need to escape from his own feelings of melancholy. His attitude towards people and his technique of observation and deduction are those of the chemist or physicist. If he chooses human beings rather than inanimate matter as his material, it is because investigating the inanimate is unheroically easy since it cannot tell lies, which human beings can and do, so that in dealing with them, observation must be twice as sharp and logic twice as rigorous.

INSPECTOR FRENCH

His class and culture are those natural to a Scotland Yard inspector. (The old Oxonian Inspector is insufferable.) His motive is love of duty. Holmes detects for his own sake and shows the maximum indifference to all feelings except a negative fear of his own. French detects for the sake of the innocent members of society, and is indifferent only to his own feelings and those of the murderer. (He would much rather stay at home with his wife.) He is exceptional only in his exceptional love of duty which makes him take exceptional pains; he does only what all could do as well if they had the same patient industry (his checking of alibis for tiny flaws which careless hurry had missed). He outwits the murderer, partly because the latter is not quite so painstaking as he, and partly because the murderer must act alone, while he has the help of all the innocent people in the world who are doing their duty, e.g. the postmen, railway clerks, milkmen, etc., who become, accidentally, witnesses to the truth.

FATHER BROWN

Like Holmes, an amateur; yet, like French, not an individual genius. His activities as a detective are an incidental part of his activities as a priest who cares for souls. His prime motive is compassion, of which the guilty are in greater need than the innocent, and he investigates murders, not for his own sake, nor even for the sake of the innocent, but for the sake of the murderer who can save his soul if he will confess and repent. He solves his cases, not by approaching them objectively like a scientist or a policeman, but by subjectively imagining himself to be the murderer, a process which is good not only for the murderer but for Father Brown himself because, as he says, 'it gives a man his remorse beforehand'.

Holmes and French can only help the murderer as teachers, i.e they can teach him that murder will out and does not pay. More they cannot do since neither is tempted to murder; Holmes is too gifted, French too well trained in the habit of virtue. Father Brown can go further and help the murderer as an example, i.e. as a man who is also tempted to murder, but is able by faith to resist temptation.

THE READER

The most curious fact about the detective story is that it makes its greatest appeal precisely to those classes of people who are most immune to other forms of daydream literature. The typical detective story addict is a doctor or clergyman or scientist or artist, i.e. a fairly successful professional man with intellectual interests and well-read in his own field, who could never stomach the *Saturday Evening Post* or *True Confessions* or movie magazines or comics. If I ask myself why I cannot enjoy stories about strong silent men and lovely girls who make love in a beautiful landscape and come into millions of dollars, I cannot answer that I have no fantasies of being handsome and loved and rich, because of course I have (though my life is, perhaps, sufficiently fortunate to make me less envious in a naïve way than some). No, I can only say that I am too conscious of the absurdity of such wishes to enjoy seeing them reflected in print.

I can, to some degree, resist yielding to these or similar desires which tempt me, but I cannot prevent myself from having them to resist; and it is the fact that I have them which makes me feel guilty, so that instead of dreaming about indulging my desires, I dream about the removal of the guilt which I feel at their existence. This I still do, and must do, because guilt is a subjective feeling where any further step is only a reduplication – feeling guilty about guilt. I suspect that the typical reader of detective stories is, like myself, a person who suffers from a sense of sin. From the point of view of ethics, desires and acts are good and bad, and I must choose the good and reject the bad, but the I which makes this choice is ethically neutral; it only becomes good or bad in its choice. To have a sense of sin means to feel guilty at there being an ethical choice to make, a guilt which, however 'good' I may become, remains unchanged. It is sometimes said that detective stories are read by respectable law-abiding citizens in order to gratify in fantasy the violent or murderous wishes they dare not, or are ashamed to, translate into action. This may be true for the reader of thrillers (which I rarely enjoy), but it is quite false for the reader of detective stories. On the contrary, the magical satisfaction the latter provide (which makes them escape literature, not works of art) is the illusion of being dissociated from the murderer.

The magic formula is an innocence which is discovered to contain guilt; then a suspicion of being the guilty one; and finally a real innocence from which the guilty other has been expelled, a cure effected, not by me or my neighbors, but by the miraculous intervention of a genius from outside who removes guilt by giving knowledge of guilt. (The detective story subscribes, in fact, to the Socratic daydream: 'Sin is ignorance.')

If one thinks of a work of art which deals with murder, *Crime and Punishment* for example, its effect on the reader is to compel an identification with the murderer which he would prefer not to recognize. The identification of fantasy is always an attempt to avoid one's own suffering: the identification of art is a sharing in the suffering of another. Kafka's *The Trial* is another instructive example of the difference between a work of art and the detective story. In the latter it is certain that a crime has been committed and, temporarily, uncertain to whom the guilt should be attached; as soon as this is known, the innocence of everyone else is certain. (Should it turn out that after all no crime has been committed, then all would be innocent.) In *The Trial*, on the other hand, it is the guilt that is certain and the crime that is uncertain; the aim of the hero's investigation is not to prove his innocence (which would be impossible for he knows he is guilty), but to discover what, if anything, he has done to make himself guilty. K, the hero, is, in fact, a portrait of the kind of person who reads detective stories for escape.

The fantasy, then, which the detective story addict indulges is the fantasy of being restored to the Garden of Eden, to a state of innocence, where he may know love as love and not as the law. The driving force behind this daydream is the feeling of guilt, the cause of which is unknown to the dreamer. The fantasy of escape is the same, whether one explains the guilt in Christian, Freudian, or any other terms. One's way of trying to face the reality, on the other hand, will, of course, depend very much on one's creed.

MARY MCCARTHY

My Confession

Mary McCarthy (1912–89) is now best known as a novelist and autobiographer, author of The Group *(1963) and* Memoirs of a Catholic Girlhood *(1957). She began her writing life, though, as a literary journalist. During the 1930s, as she records here, she was associated with the New York intellectuals who brought out* Partisan Review *(for which McCarthy worked, as theatre critic, for a time). During the 1940s and 1950s she tended to concentrate on fiction but in the mid-1960s she re-emerged as a political essayist, writing prolifically against the Vietnam War. 'My Confession' first appeared in* Partisan Review *in 1954.*

Every age has a keyhole to which its eye is pasted. Spicy court-memoirs, the lives of gallant ladies, recollections of an ex-nun, a monk's confession, an atheist's repentance, true-to-life accounts of prostitution and bastardy gave our ancestors a penny peep into the forbidden room. In our own day, this type of sensational fact–fiction is being produced largely by ex-Communists. Public curiosity shows an almost prurient avidity for the details of political defloration, and the memoirs of ex-Communists have an odd resemblance to the confessions of a white slave. Two shuddering climaxes, two rendezvous with destiny, form the poles between which these narratives vibrate: the first describes the occasion when the subject was seduced by Communism; the second shows him wrestling himself from the demon embrace. Variations on the form are possible. Senator McCarthy, for example, in his book, *McCarthyism, the Fight for America*, uses a tense series of flashbacks to dramatize his encounter with Communism: the country lies passive in Communism's clasp; he is given a tryst with destiny in the lonely Arizona hills, where, surrounded by 'real Americans without any synthetic sheen', he attains the decision that will send him down the long marble corridors to the Senate Caucus Room to bare the shameful commerce.

The diapason of choice plays, like movie music, round today's apostle to the Gentiles: Whittaker Chambers on a bench and, in a reprise, awake all night, at a dark window, facing the void. These people, unlike ordinary beings, are shown the true course during a lightning storm of revelation, on the road to Damascus. And their decisions are lonely decisions, silhouetted against a background of public incomprehension and hostility.

I object. I have read the reminiscences of Mr Chambers and Miss Bentley. I too have had a share in the political movements of our day, and my experience cries out against their experience. It is not the facts I balk at – I have never been an espionage agent – but the studio atmosphere of sublimity and purpose that enfolds the facts and the chief actor. Where Whittaker Chambers is mounted on his tractor, or Elizabeth Bentley, alone, is meditating her decision in a white New England church, I have the sense that they are on location and that, at any moment, the director will call 'Cut'. It has never been like that for me; events have never waited, like extras, while I toiled to make up my mind between good and evil. In fact, I have never known these mental convulsions, which appear quite strange to me when I read about them, even when I do not question the author's sincerity.

Is it really so difficult to tell a good action from a bad one? I think one usually knows right away or a moment afterwards, in a horrid flash of regret. And when one genuinely hesitates – or at least it is so in my case – it is never about anything of importance, but about perplexing trivial things, such as whether to have fish or meat for dinner, or whether to take the bus or subway to reach a certain destination, or whether to wear the beige or the green. The 'great' decisions – those I can look back on pensively and say, 'That was a turning-point' – have been made without my awareness. Too late to do anything about it, I discover that I have chosen. And this is particularly striking when the choice has been political or historic. For me, in fact, the mark of the historic is the nonchalance with which it picks up an individual and deposits him in a trend, like a house playfully moved by a tornado. My own experience with Communism prompts me to relate it, just because it had this inadvertence that seems to me lacking in the true confessions of reformed Communists. Like Stendhal's hero, who took part in something confused and disarrayed and insignificant that he later learned was the Battle of Waterloo, I joined the anti-Communist move-ment without meaning to and only found out afterwards, through others, the meaning or 'name' assigned to what I had done. This occurred in the late fall of 1936.

Three years before, I had graduated from college – Vassar, the same college Elizabeth Bentley had gone to – without having suffered any fracture of my political beliefs or moral frame. All through college, my official political philosophy was royalism; though I was not much interested in politics, it irritated me to be told that 'you could not turn the clock back'. But I did not see much prospect for kingship in the United States (unless you imported one, like the Swedes), and, *faute de mieux*, I awarded my sympathies to the Democratic Party, which I tried to look on as the party of the Southern patriciate. At the same time, I had an aversion to Republicans – an instinctive feeling that had been with me since I was a child of eight pedalling my wagon up and down our cement driveway and howling, 'Hurray for Cox', at the Republican neighbours who passed by. I disliked business men and business attitudes partly, I think, because I came from a professional (though Republican) family and had picked up a disdain for business men as being beneath us, in education and general culture. And the anti-Catholic prejudice against Al Smith during the 1928 election, the tinkling amusement at Mrs Smith's vulgarity, democratized me a little in spite of myself: I was won by Smith's plebeian charm, the big coarse nose, and rubbery politician's smile.

But this same distrust of uniformity made me shrink, in 1932, from the sloppily dressed socialist girls at college who paraded for Norman Thomas and tirelessly argued over 'cokes'; their eager fellowship and scrawled placards and heavy personalities bored me – there was something, to my mind, deeply athletic about this socialism. It was a kind of political hockey played by big, gaunt, dyspeptic girls in pants. It startled me a little, therefore, to learn that in an election poll taken of the faculty, several of my favourite teachers had voted for Thomas; in them, the socialist faith appeared rather charming, I decided – a gracious and attractive oddity, like the English Ovals they gave you when you came for tea. That was the winter Hitler was coming to power and, hearing of the anti-Jewish atrocities, I had a flurry of political indignation. I wrote a prose-poem that dealt, in a mixed-up way, with the Polish Corridor and the Jews. This poem was so unlike me that I did not know whether to be proud of it or ashamed of it when I saw it in a college magazine. At this period, we were interested in surrealism and automatic writing, and the poem had a certain renown because it had come out of my interior without much sense or order, just the way automatic writing was supposed to do. But there my political development stopped.

The depression was closer to home; in New York I used to see apple-sellers on the street corners, and, now and then, a bread-line, but I had a very thin awareness of mass poverty. The depression was too close to home to awaken anything but curiosity and wonder – the feelings of a child confronted with a death in the family. I was conscious of the suicides of stock-brokers and business men, and of the fact that some of my friends had to go on scholarships and had their dress allowances curtailed, while their mothers gaily turned to doing their own cooking. To most of us at Vassar, I think, the depression was chiefly an upper-class phenomenon.

My real interests were literary. In a paper for my English Renaissance seminar, I noted a resemblance between the Elizabethan puritan pundits and the school of Marxist criticism that was beginning to pontificate about proletarian literature in the *New Masses*. I disliked the modern fanatics, cold, envious little clerics, equally with the insufferable and ridiculous Gabriel Harvey – Cambridge pedant and friend of Spenser – who tried to introduce the rules of Latin quantity into English verse and vilified a true poet who had died young, in squalor and misery. I really hated absolutism and officiousness of any kind (I preferred my kings martyred) and was pleased to be able to recognize a Zeal-of-the-Land Busy in proletarian dress. And it was through a novel that I first learned, in my senior year, about the Sacco–Vanzetti case. The discovery that two innocent men had been executed only a few years back while I, oblivious, was in boarding school, gave me a disturbing shock. The case was still so near that I was tantalized by a feeling that it was not too late to do something – try still another avenue, if Governor Fuller and the Supreme Court obdurately would not be moved. An unrectified case of injustice has a terrible way of lingering, restlessly, in the social atmosphere like an unfinished equation. I went on to the Mooney case, which vexed not only my sense of equity but my sense of plausibility – how was it possible for the prosecution to lie so, in broad daylight, with the whole world watching?

When in May 1933, however, before graduation, I went down to apply for a job at the old *New Republic* offices, I was not drawn there by the magazine's editorial policy – I hardly knew what it was – but because the book-review section seemed to me to possess a certain elegance and independence of thought that would be hospitable to a critical spirit like me. And I was badly taken aback when the book-review editor, to whom I had been shunted – there was no job – puffed his pipe and remarked that he would give me a review if I could show him that I was either a genius or starving. 'I'm not starving,' I said quickly; I knew I was not a genius and I was not pleased by the suggestion that I would be taking bread from other people's mouths. I did not think this a fair criterion and in a moment I said so. In reply, he put down his pipe, shrugged, reached out for the material I had brought with me, and half-promised, after an assaying glance, to send me a book. My notice finally appeared; it was not very good, but I did not know that and was elated. Soon I was reviewing novels and biographies for both the *New Republic* and the *Nation* and preening myself on the connection. Yet, whenever I entered the *New Republic*'s waiting-room, I was seized with a feeling of nervous guilt towards the shirt-sleeved editors upstairs and their busy social conscience, and, above all, towards the shabby young men who were waiting too and who had, my bones told me, a better claim than I to the book I hoped to take away with me. They looked poor, pinched, scholarly, and supercilious, and I did not know which of these qualities made me, with my clicking high heels and fall 'ensemble', seem more out of place.

I cannot remember the moment when I ceased to air my old royalist convictions and stuffed them away in an inner closet as you do a dress or an ornament that you perceive strikes the wrong note. It was probably at the time when I first became aware of Communists as a distinct entity. I had known about them, certainly, in college, but it was not until I came to New York that I began to have certain people, celebrities, pointed out to me as Communists and to turn my head to look at them, wonderingly. I had no wish to be one of them, but the fact that they were there – an unreckoned factor – made my own political opinions take on a protective coloration. This process was accelerated by my marriage – a week after graduation – to an actor and playwright who was in some ways very much like me. He was the son of a Minnesota normal school administrator who had been the scapegoat in an academic scandal that had turned him out of his job and reduced him, for a time, when my husband was nine or ten, to selling artificial limbs and encyclopædia sets from door to door. My husband still brooded over his father's misfortune, like Hamlet or a character in Ibsen, and this had given his nature a sardonic twist that inclined him to behave like a paradox – to follow the mode and despise it, live in a Beekman Place apartment while lacking the money to buy groceries, play bridge with society couples and poker with the stage electricians, dress in the English style and carry a walking-stick while wearing a red necktie.

He was an odd-looking man, prematurely bald, with a tense, arresting figure, a broken nose, a Standard English accent, and wry, circumflexed eyebrows. There was something about him both baleful and quizzical; whenever he stepped on to the stage he had the ironic air of a symbol. This curious appearance of his disqualified him for most Broadway roles; he was too young for character parts and too bald for juveniles. Yet just this disturbing ambiguity – a Communist painter friend did a drawing of him that brought out a resemblance to Lenin – suited the portentous and equivocal atmosphere of left-wing drama. He smiled dryly at Marxist terminology, but there was social anger in him. During the years we were married, the only work he found was in productions of 'social' significance. He played for the Theatre Union in *The Sailors of Cattaro*, about a mutiny in the Austrian fleet, and in *Black Pit*, about coal-miners; the following year, he was in *Winterset* and Archibald MacLeish's *Panic* – the part of a blind man in both cases. He wrote revue sketches and unproduced plays, in a mocking, despairing, but none the less radical vein; he directed the book of a musical called *Americana* that featured the song, 'Brother, Can You Spare a Dime?' I suppose there was something in him of both the victim and the leader, an undertone of totalitarianism; he was very much interested in the mythic qualities of leadership and talked briskly about a Farmer–Labour party in his stage English accent. Notions of the superman and the genius flickered across his thoughts. But this led him, as it happened, away from politics, into sheer personal vitalism, and it was only in plays that he entered 'at the head of a mob'. In personal life he was very winning, but that is beside the point here.

The point is that we both, through our professional connections, began to take part in a left-wing life, to which we felt superior, which we laughed at, but which nevertheless was influencing us without our being aware of it. If the composition of the body changes every seven years, the composition of our minds during the seven years of our engagement and marriage had slowly changed, so that though our thoughts looked the same to us, inside we had been altered, like an old car which has had part after part replaced in it under the hood.

We wore our rue with a difference; we should never have considered joining the Communist Party. We were not even fellow-travellers; we did not sign petitions or join 'front' groups. We were not fools, after all, and were no more deceived by the League against War and Fascism, say, than by a Chinatown bus with a carload of shills aboard. It was part of our metropolitan sophistication to know the truth about Communist fronts. We accepted the need for social reform, but we declined to draw the 'logical' inference that the Communists wanted us to draw from this. We argued with the comrades backstage in the dressing-rooms and at literary cocktail parties; I was attacked by a writer in the *New Masses*. We knew about Lovestoneites and Trotskyites, even while we were ignorant of the labour theory of value, the law of uneven development, the theory of permanent revolution v socialism in one country, and so on. 'Lovestone is a Lovestoneite!' John wrote in wax on his dressing-room mirror, and on his door in the old Civic Repertory he put up a sign: 'Through these portals pass some of the most beautiful tractors in the Ukraine.'

The comrades shrugged and laughed, a little unwillingly. They knew we were not hostile but merely unserious, politically. The comrades who knew us best used to assure us that our sophistication was just an armour; underneath, we must care for the same things they did. They were mistaken, I am afraid. Speaking for myself, I cannot remember a single broad altruistic emotion visiting me during that period – the kind of emotion the simpler comrades, with their shining eyes and exalted faces, seemed to have in copious secretion. And yet it was true: we were not hostile. We marched in May Day parades, just for the fun of it, and sang, 'Hold the Fort, for We are Coming', and '*Bandiera Rossa*', and 'The International', though we always bellowed 'The *Socialist* International shall be the human race', instead of 'The International Soviet', to pique the Communists in our squad. We took part in evening clothes in a consumers' walkout at the Waldorf to support a waiters' strike; the Communists had nothing to do with this and we grew very excited (we did have negative feelings) when another young literary independent was arrested and booked. During a strike at a department store, John joined the sympathetic picketing and saw two of his fellow-actors carried off in the Black Maria; they missed a matinée and set off a controversy about what was the *first* responsibility of a Communist playing in a proletarian drama. We went once or twice to a class for actors in Marxism, just to see what was up; we went to a debate on Freud and/or Marx, to a debate on the execution of the hundred and four White Guards following Kirov's assassination.

Most ex-Communists nowadays, when they write their autobiographies or testify before congressional committees, are at pains to point out that their actions were very, very bad and their motives very, very good. I would say the reverse of myself, though without the intensives. I see no reason to disavow my actions, which were perfectly all right, but my motives give me a little embarrassment, and just because I cannot disavow them: that fevered, contentious, trivial show-off in the May Day parade is still recognizably me.

We went to dances at Webster Hall and took our uptown friends. We went to parties to raise money for the sharecroppers, for the Theatre Union, for the *New Masses*. These parties generally took place in a borrowed apartment, often a sculptor's or commercial artist's studio; you paid for your drinks, which were dispensed at a long, wet table; the liquor was dreadful; the glasses were small, and there was never enough ice. Long-haired men in turtle-necked sweaters marched into the room in processions and threw their overcoats on the floor, against the wall, and sat on them; they were only artists and bit-actors, but they gave these affairs a look of gangsterish menace, as if the room were guarded by the goons of the future. On couches with wrinkled slipcovers, little spiky-haired girls, like spiders, dressed in peasant blouses and carapaced with Mexican jewellery, made voracious passes at baby-faced juveniles; it was said that they 'did it for the Party', as a recruiting effort. Vague, soft-faced old women with dust mops of whitish hair wandered benevolently about seeking a listener; on a sofa against a wall, like a deity, sat a bearded scion of an old Boston family, stiff as a post. All of us, generally, became very drunk; the atmosphere was horribly sordid, with cigarette burns on tables, spilled drinks, ashes everywhere, people passed out on the bed with the coats or necking, you could not be sure which. Nobody cared what happened because there was no host or hostess. The fact that a moneyed person had been simple enough to lend the apartment seemed to make the guests want to desecrate it, to show that they were exercising not a privilege but a right.

Obviously, I must have hated these parties, but I went to them, partly because I was ashamed of my own squeamishness, and partly because I had a curiosity about the Communist men I used to see there, not the actors or writers, but the higher-ups, impresarios and theoreticians – dark, smooth-haired owls with large white lugubrious faces and glasses. These were the spiritual directors of the Communist cultural celebrities and they moved about at these parties like so many monks or abbés in a worldly salon. I had always liked to argue with the clergy, and I used to argue with these men, who always had the air, as they stood with folded arms, of listening not to a disagreement but to a confession. Whenever I became tight, I would bring up (oh, *vino veritas*) the Tsar and his family. I did not see why they all had had to be killed – the Tsar himself, yes, perhaps, and the Tsarina, but not the young girls and the children. I knew the answer, of course (the young Tsarevitch or one of his sisters might have served as a rallying point for the counter-revolutionary forces), but still I gazed hopefully into these docents' faces, seeking a trace of scruple or compassion. But I saw only a marmoreal astuteness. The question was of bourgeois origin, they said with finality.

The next morning I was always bitterly ashamed. I had let these omniscient men see the real me underneath, and the other me squirmed and gritted her teeth and muttered, Never, never, *never* again. And yet they had not convinced me – there was the paradox. The superiority I felt to the Communists I knew had, for me at any rate, good grounding; it was based on their lack of humour, their fanaticism, and the slow drip of cant that thickened their utterance like a nasal catarrh. *And yet* I was tremendously impressed by them. They made me feel pretty shallow; they had, shall I say, a daily ugliness in their life that made my pretty life tawdry. I think all of us who moved in that ambience must have felt something of the kind, even while we laughed at them. When John and I, for instance, would say of a certain actor, 'He is a Party member', our voices always contained a note of respect. This respect might be mixed with pity, as when we saw some blue-eyed young profile, fresh from his fraternity and his C average, join up because a sleazy girl had persuaded him. The literary Communists I sincerely despised because I was able to judge the quality of the work they published and see their dishonesty and contradictions; even so, when I beheld them in person, at a Webster Hall dance, I was troubled and felt perhaps I had wronged them – perhaps there was something in them that my vision could not perceive, as some eyes cannot perceive colour.

People sometimes say that they envied the Communists because they were so 'sure'. In my case, this was not exactly it; I was sure, too, intellectually speaking, as far as I went. That is, I had a clear mind and was reasonably honest, while many of the Communists I knew were pathetically fogged up. In any case, my soul was not particularly hot for certainties.

And yet in another way I did envy the Communists, or, to be more accurate, wonder whether I ought to envy them. I could not, I saw, be a Communist because I was not 'made that way'. Hence, to be a Communist was to possess a sort of privilege. And this privilege, like all privileges, appeared to be a sort of power. Any form of idiocy or aberration can confer this distinction on its owner, at least in our age, which aspires to a 'total' experience; in the thirties it was the Communists who seemed fearsomely to be the happy few, not because they had peace or certitude but because they were a mutation – a mutation that threatened, in the words of their own anthem, to become the human race.

There was something arcane in every Communist, and the larger this area was the more we respected him. That was why the literary Communists, who operated in the open, doing the hatchet work on artists' reputations, were held in such relatively low esteem. An underground worker rated highest with us; next were the theoreticians and oracles; next were the activists, who mostly worked, we heard, on the waterfront. Last came the rank and file, whose work consisted of making speeches, distributing leaflets, attending party and faction meetings, joining front organizations, marching in parades and demonstrations. These people we dismissed as uninteresting not so much because their work was routine but because the greater part of it was visible. In the same way, among individual comrades, we looked up to those who were close-lipped and stern about their beliefs and we disparaged the more voluble members – the forensic little actors who tried to harangue us in the dressing-rooms. The idea of a double life was what impressed us: the more talkative comrades seemed to have only one life, like us; but even they, we had to remind ourselves, had a secret annex to their personality, which was signified by their Party name. It is hard not to respect somebody who has an alias.

Of fellow-travellers, we had a very low opinion. People who were not willing to 'go the whole way' filled us with impatient disdain. The only fellow-travellers who merited our notice were those of whom it was said: the Party prefers that they remain on the outside. I think some fellow-travellers circulated such stories about themselves deliberately, in order to appear more interesting. There was another type of fellow-traveller who let it be known that they stayed out of the Party because of some tiny doctrinal difference with Marxism. This tiny difference magnified them enormously in their own eyes and allowed them to bear gladly the accusation of cowardice. I knew one such person very well – a spruce, ingratiating swain, the heir to a large fortune – and I think it was not cowardice but a kind of pietistic vanity. He felt he cut more of a figure if he seemed to be doing the Party's dirty work gratuitously, without compulsion, like an oblate.

In making these distinctions (which were the very distinctions the Party made), I had no idea, of course, that I was allowing myself to be influenced by the Party in the field where I was most open to suspicion – the field of social snobbery. Yet in fact I was being deterred from forming any political opinions of my own, lest I find I was that despised article, a 'mere' socialist or watery liberal, in the same way that a young snob coming to college and seeing who the 'right' people are will strive to make no friends rather than be caught with the wrong ones.

For me, the Communist Party was *the* party, and even though I did not join it, I prided myself on knowing that it was the pinnacle. It is only now that I see the social component in my attitude. At the time, I simply supposed that I was being clear-sighted and logical. I used to do research and typing for a disgruntled middle-aged man who was a freak for that day – an anti-Communist Marxist – and I was bewildered by his anti-Party bias. While we were drinking hot tea, Russian style, from glasses during the intervals of our work, I would try to show him his mistake. 'Don't you think it's rather futile,' I expostulated, 'to criticize the Party the way you do, from the outside? After all, it's the *only* working-class Party, and if *I* were a Marxist I would join it and try to reform it.' Snorting, he would raise his small deep-set blue eyes and stare at me and then try patiently to show me that there was no democracy in the Party. I listened disbelievingly. It seemed to me that it would just be a question of converting first one comrade and then another to your point of view till gradually you had achieved a majority. And when my employer assured me that they would throw you out if you tried that, my twenty-three-year-old wisdom cocked an eyebrow. I thought I knew what was the trouble: he was a pathologically lazy man and his growling criticisms of the Party were simply a form of malingering, like the aches and pains he used to manufacture to avoid working on an article. A real revolutionary who was not afraid of exertion would get into the Party and fight.

The curious idea that being critical of the Party was a compelling reason for joining it must have been in the air, for the same argument was brought to bear on me in the summer of 1936 – the summer my husband and I separated and that I came closest to the gravitational pull of the Communist world. Just before I went off to Reno, there was a week in June when I stayed in Southampton with the young man I was planning to marry and a little Communist organizer in an old summer house furnished with rattan and wicker and Chinese matting and mother-of-pearl and paper fans. We had come there for a purpose. The little organizer had just been assigned a car – a battered old Ford roadster that had been turned over to the Party for the use of some poor organizer; it may have been the very car that figured in the Hiss case. My fiancé, who had known him for years, perhaps from the peace movement, was going to teach him to drive. We were all at a pause in our lives. The following week our friend was supposed to take the car to California and do propaganda work among the migrant fruit-pickers; I was to go to Reno; my fiancé, a vivacious young bachelor, was to conquer his habits of idleness and buckle down to a serious job. Those seven days, therefore, had a special, still quality, like the days of a novena you make in your childhood; a part of each of them was set aside for the Party's task. It was early in June; the musty house that belonged to my fiancé's parents still had the winter-smell of mice and old wood and rust and mildew. The summer colony had not yet arrived; the red flag, meaning that it was dangerous to swim, flew daily on the beach; the roads were nearly empty. Every afternoon we would take the old car, canvas flapping, to a deserted stretch of straight road in the dunes, where the neophyte could take the wheel.

He was a large-browed, dwarfish man in his late thirties, with a deep widow's peak, a bristly short moustache, and a furry western accent – rather simple, open-natured, and cheerful, the sort of person who might have been a small-town salesman or itinerant newspaperman. There was an energetic, hopeful innocence about him that was not confined to his political convictions – he could *not* learn to drive. Every day the same thing happened; he would settle his frail yet stocky figure trustingly in the driver's seat, grip the wheel, step on the starter, and lose control of the car, which would shoot ahead in first or backward in reverse for a few perilous feet till my fiancé turned off the ignition; Ansel always mistook the gas for the brake and forgot to steer while he was shifting gears.

It was clear that he would never be able to pass the driver's test at the county seat. In the evenings, to make up to him for his oncoming disappointment (we smiled when he said he could start without a licence), we encouraged him to talk about the Party and tried to take an intelligent interest. We would sit by the lamp and drink and ask questions, while he smoked his short pipe and from time to time took a long draught from his highball, like a man alone musing in a chair.

And finally one night, in the semi-dark, he knocked out his pipe and said to me: 'You're very critical of the Party. Why don't you join it?' A thrill went through me, but I laughed, as when somebody has proposed to you and you are not sure whether they are serious. 'I don't think I'd make very good material.' 'You're wrong,' he said gravely. 'You're just the kind of person the Party needs. You're young and idealistic and independent.' I broke in: 'I thought independence was just what the Party didn't want.' 'The Party needs criticism,' he said. 'But it needs it from the inside. If people like you who agree with its main objectives would come in and criticize, we wouldn't be so narrow and sectarian.' 'You admit the Party is narrow?' exclaimed my fiancé. 'Sure, I admit it,' said Ansel, grinning. 'But it's partly the fault of people like Mary who won't come in and broaden us.' And he confided that he himself made many of the same criticisms I did, but he made them from within the Party, and so could get himself listened to. 'The big problem of the American Party,' said Ansel, puffing at his pipe, 'is the smallness of the membership. People say we're ruled from Moscow; I've never seen any sign of it. But let's suppose it's true, for the sake of argument. This just means that the American Party isn't big enough yet to stand on its own feet. A big, indigenous party couldn't be ruled from Moscow. The will of the members would have to rule it, just as their dues and contributions would support it.' 'That's where I come in, I suppose?' I said, teasing. 'That's where you come in,' he calmly agreed. He turned to my fiancé. 'Not you,' he said. 'You won't have the time to give to it. But for Mary I think it would be an interesting experiment.'

An interesting experiment . . . I let the thought wander through my mind. The subject recurred several times, by the lamplight, though with no particular urgency. Ansel, I thought (and still think), was speaking sincerely and partly in my own interest, almost as a spectator, as if he would be diverted to see how I worked out in the Party. All this gave me quite a new sense of Communism and of myself too; I had never looked upon my character in such a favourable light. And as a beneficiary of Ansel's charity, I felt somewhat ashamed of the very doubt it raised: the suspicion that he might be blind to the real facts of inner Party life. I could admire where I could not follow, and, studying Ansel, I decided that I admired the Communists and would probably be one, if I were the person he thought me. Which I was afraid I was not. For me, such a wry conclusion is always uplifting, and I had the feeling that I mounted in understanding when Sunday morning came and I watched Ansel pack his sturdy suitcase and his briefcase full of leaflets into the old roadster. He had never yet driven more than a few yards by himself, and we stood on the front steps to await what was going to happen: he would not be able to get out of the driveway, and we would have to put him on the train and return the car to the Party when we came back to New York. As we watched, the car began to move; it picked up speed and grated into second, holding to the middle of the road as it turned out of the driveway. It hesitated and went into third: Ansel was driving! Through the back window we saw his figure hunched over the wheel; the road dipped and he vanished. We had witnessed a miracle, and we turned back into the house, frightened. All day we sat waiting for the call that would tell us there had been an accident, but the day passed without a sound, and by nightfall we accepted the phenomenon and pictured the little car on the highway, travelling steadily west in one indefatigable thrust, not daring to stop for petrol or refreshment, lest the will of the driver falter.

This parting glimpse of Ansel through the car's back window was, as it turned out, ultimate. Politically speaking, we reached a watershed that summer. The first Moscow trial took place in August. I knew nothing of this event because I was in Reno and did not see the New York papers. Nor did I know that the Party line had veered to the right and that all the fellow-travellers would be voting, not for Browder as I was now prepared to do (if only I remembered to register), but for Roosevelt. Isolated from these developments in the mountain altitudes, I was blossoming, like a lone winter rose overlooked by the frost, into a revolutionary thinker of the pure, uncompromising strain. The detached particles of the past three years' experience suddenly 'made sense', and I saw myself as a radical.

'Book Bites Mary,' wrote back a surprised literary editor when I sent him, from Reno, a radiant review of a novel about the Paris Commune that ended with the heroine sitting down to read the Communist Manifesto. In Seattle, when I came to stay with my grandparents, I found a strike on and instantly wired the *Nation* to ask if I could cover it. Every night I was off to the Labor Temple or a longshoremen's hall while my grandparents took comfort from the fact that I seemed to be against Roosevelt, the Democrats, and the tsars of the A. F. of L. – they did not quite grasp my explanation, that I was criticizing 'from the left'.

Right here, I come up against a puzzle: why didn't I take the *next step*? But it is only a puzzle if one thinks of me not as a concrete entity but as a term in a logical operation: you agree with the Communist Party; *ergo*, you join it. I reasoned that way but I did not behave so. There was something in me that capriciously resisted being a term in logic, and the very fact that I cannot elicit any specific reason why I did not join the Party shows that I was never really contemplating it, though I can still hear my own voice, raised very authoritatively at a cafeteria-table at the Central Park Zoo, pointing out to a group of young intellectuals that if we were serious we would join the Communists.

This was in September and I was back in New York. The Spanish Civil War had begun. The pay-as-you-go parties were now all for the Loyalists, and young men were volunteering to go and fight in Spain. I read the paper every morning with tears of exaltation in my eyes, and my sympathies rained equally on Communists, Socialists, Anarchists, and the brave Catholic Basques. My heart was tense and swollen with Popular Front solidarity. I applauded the Lincoln Battalion, protested non-intervention, hurried into Wanamaker's to look for cotton-lace stockings: I was boycotting silk on account of Japan in China. I was careful to smoke only union-made cigarettes; the white package with Sir Walter Raleigh's portrait came proudly out of my pocketbook to rebuke Chesterfields and Luckies.

It was a period of intense happiness; the news from the battlefront was often encouraging and the practice of virtue was surprisingly easy. I moved into a one-room apartment on a crooked street in Greenwich Village and exulted in being poor and alone. I had a part-time job and read manuscripts for a publisher; the very riskiness of my situation was zestful – I had decided not to get married. The first month or so was scarifyingly lonely, but I survived this, and, starting early in November, I began to feel the first stirrings of popularity. A new set of people, rather smart and moneyed, young Communists with a little 'name', progressive hosts and modernist hostesses, had discovered me. The fact that I was poor and lived in such a funny little apartment increased the interest felt: I was passed from hand to hand, as a novelty, like Gulliver among the Brobdingnagians. During those first days in November, I was chiefly conscious of what a wonderful time I was starting to have. All this while, I had remained ignorant of the fissure that was opening. Nobody had told me of the trial of Zinoviev and Kamenev – the trial of the sixteen – or of the new trial that was being prepared in Moscow, the trial of Pyatakov and Radek.

Then, one afternoon in November, I was taken to a cocktail party, in honour of Art Young, the old *Masses* cartoonist, whose book, *The Best of Art Young*, was being published that day. It was the first publisher's party I had ever been to, and my immediate sensation was one of disappointment: nearly all these people were strangers and, to me, quite unattractive. Art Young, a white-haired little kewpie, sitting in a corner, was pointed out to me, and I turned a respectful gaze on him, though I had no clear idea who he was or how he had distinguished himself. I presumed he was a veteran Communist, like a number of the stalwarts in the room, survivors of the old *Masses* and the *Liberator*. Their names were whispered to me and I nodded; this seemed to be a commemorative occasion, and the young men hovered in groups around the old men, as if to catch a word for posterity. On the outskirts of certain groups I noticed a few poorly dressed young men, bolder spirits, nervously flexing their lips, framing sentences that would propel them into the conversational centre, like actors with a single line to speak.

The solemnity of these proceedings made me feel terribly ill-at-ease. It was some time before I became aware that it was not just me who was nervous: the whole room was under a constraint. Some groups were avoiding other groups, and now and then an arrow of sarcasm would wing like a sniper's bullet from one conversation to another.

I was standing, rather bleakly, by the refreshment table, when a question was thrust at me: Did I think Trotsky was entitled to a hearing? It was a novelist friend of mine, dimple-faced, shaggy-headed, earnest, with a whole train of people, like a deputation, behind him. Trotsky? I glanced for help at a sour little man I had been talking with, but he merely shrugged. My friend made a beckoning gesture and a circle closed in. What had Trotsky done? Alas, I had to ask. A tumult of voices proffered explanations. My friend raised a hand for silence. Leaning on the table, he supplied the background, speaking very slowly, in his dragging, disconsolate voice, like a school-teacher wearied of his subject. Trotsky, it appeared, had been accused of fostering a counter-revolutionary plot in the Soviet Union – organizing terrorist centres and conspiring with the Gestapo to murder the Soviet leaders. Sixteen old Bolsheviks had confessed and implicated him. It had been in the press since August.

I blushed; everybody seemed to be looking at me strangely. 'Where has she *been*?' said a voice. I made a violent effort to take in what had been said. The enormity of the charge dazed me, and I supposed that some sort of poll was being taken and that I was being asked to pronounce on whether Trotsky was guilty or innocent. I could tell from my friend's low, even, melancholy tone that he regarded the charges as derisory. 'What do you want me to say?' I protested. 'I don't know anything about it.' 'Trotsky denies the charges,' patiently intoned my friend. 'He declares it's a GPU fabrication. Do you think he's entitled to a hearing?' My mind cleared. 'Why, of course.' I laughed – were there people who would say that Trotsky was *not* entitled to a hearing? But my friend's voice tolled a rebuke to this levity. 'She says Trotsky is entitled to his day in court.'

The sour little man beside me made a peculiar sucking noise. 'You disagree?' I demanded, wonderingly. 'I'm smart,' he retorted. 'I don't let anybody ask me. You notice, he doesn't ask me?' 'Shut up, George,' said my novelist friend impatiently. 'I'm asking *her*. One thing more, Mary,' he continued gravely. 'Do you believe that Trotsky should have the right of asylum?' The right of asylum! I looked for someone to share my amusement – were we in ancient Greece or the Middle Ages? I was sure the US Government would be delighted to harbour such a distinguished foreigner. But nobody smiled back. Everybody watched dispassionately, as for form's sake I assented to the phrasing: yes, Trotsky, in my opinion, was entitled to the right of asylum.

I went home with the serene feeling that all these people were slightly crazy. *Right of asylum, his day in court* – in a few hours I had forgotten the whole thing.

Four days later I tore open an envelope addressed to me by something that called itself 'Committee for the Defence of Leon Trotsky', and idly scanned the contents. 'We demand for Leon Trotsky the right of a fair hearing and the right of asylum.' Who were these demanders, I wondered, and, glancing down the letterhead, I discovered my own name. I sat down on my unmade studio couch, shaking. How dared they help themselves to my signature? This was the kind of thing the Communists were always being accused of pulling; apparently, Trotsky's admirers had gone to the same school. I had paid so little heed to the incident at the party that a connection was slow to establish itself. Reading over the list of signers, I recognized 'names' that had been present there and remembered my novelist-friend going from person to person, methodically polling . . .

How were they feeling, I wondered, when they opened their mail this morning? My own feelings were crisp. In two minutes I had decided to withdraw my name and write a note of protest. Trotsky had a right to a hearing, but I had a right to my signature. For even if there had been a legitimate misunderstanding (it occurred to me that perhaps I had been the only person there not to see the import of my answers), nothing I had said committed me to Trotsky's *defence*.

The 'decision' was made, but according to my habit I procrastinated. The severe letter I proposed to write got put off till the next day and then the next. Probably I was not eager to offend somebody who had been a good friend to me. Nevertheless, the letter would undoubtedly have been written, had I been left to myself. But within the next

forty-eight hours the phone calls began. People whom I had not seen
for months or whom I knew very slightly telephoned to advise me to
get off the newly formed Committee. These calls were not precisely
threatening. Indeed, the caller often sounded terribly weak and awkward, as if he did not like the mission he had been assigned. But they
were peculiar. For one thing, they always came after nightfall and
sometimes quite late, when I was already in bed. Another thing, there was
no real effort at persuasion: the caller stated his purpose in standardized
phrases, usually plaintive in tone (the Committee was the tool of
reaction, and all liberal people should dissociate themselves from its
activities, which were an unwarranted intervention in the domestic
affairs of the Soviet Union), and then hung up, almost immediately,
before I had a proper chance to answer. Odd too – the voices were not
those of my Communist friends but of virtual strangers. These people
who admonished me to 'think about it' were not people whose individual
opinions could have had any weight with me. And when I did think
about it, this very fact took on an ominous character: I was not being
appealed to personally but impersonally warned.

Behind these phone calls there was a sense of massed power, as if
all over the city the Party were wheeling its forces into disciplined
formations, like a fleet or an army manœuvring. This, I later found,
was true: a systematic telephone campaign was going on to dislodge
members from the Committee. The phone calls generally came after
dark and sometimes (especially when the recipient was elderly) in the
small hours of the morning. The more prominent signers got anonymous
messages and threats.

And in the morning papers and the columns of the liberal magazines
I saw the results. During the first week, name after name fell off the
Committee's letterhead. Prominent liberals and literary figures issued
statements deploring their mistake. And a number of people protested
that their names had been used without permission.

There, but for the grace of God, went I, I whispered, awestruck, to
myself, hugging my guilty knowledge. Only Heaven – I plainly saw –
by making me dilatory had preserved me from joining this sorry band.
Here was the occasion when I should have been wrestling with my
conscience or standing, floodlit, at the crossroads of choice. But in fact
I was only aware that I had had a providential escape. I had been saved
from having to decide about the Committee; *I* did not decide it – the

Communists with their pressure tactics took the matter out of my hands. We all have an instinct that makes us side with the weak, if we do not stop to reason about it, the instinct that makes a householder shield a wounded fugitive without first conducting an inquiry into the rights and wrongs of his case. Such 'decisions' are simple reflexes; they do not require courage; if they did, there would be fewer of them. When I saw what was happening, I rebounded to the defence of the Committee without a single hesitation – it was nobody's business, I felt, how I happened to be on it, and if anybody had asked me, I should have lied without a scruple.

Of course, I did not foresee the far-reaching consequences of my act – how it would change my life. I had no notion that I was now an anti-Communist, where before I had been either indifferent or pro-Communist. I did, however, soon recognize that I was in a rather awkward predicament – not a moral quandary but a social one. I knew nothing about the cause I had espoused; I had never read a word of Lenin or Trotsky, nothing of Marx but the Communist Manifesto, nothing of Soviet history; the very names of the old Bolsheviks who had confessed were strange and almost barbarous in my ears. As for Trotsky, the only thing that made me think that he might be innocent was the odd behaviour of the Communists and the fellow-travelling liberals, who seemed to be infuriated at the idea of a free inquiry. All around me, in the fashionable Stalinist circles I was now frequenting, I began to meet with suppressed excitement and just-withheld disapproval. Jewelled lady-authors turned white and shook their bracelets angrily when I came into a soirée; rising young men in publishing or advertising tightened their neckties dubiously when I urged them to examine the case for themselves; out dancing in a night-club, tall, collegiate young Party members would press me to their shirt-bosoms and tell me not to be silly, honey.

And since I seemed to meet more Stalinists every day, I saw that I was going to have to get some arguments with which to defend myself. It was not enough, apparently, to say you were for a fair hearing; you had to rebut the entire case of the prosecution to get anybody to incline an ear in your direction. I began to read, headlong, the literature on the case – the pamphlets issued by Trotsky's adherents, the Verbatim Report of the second trial published by the Soviet Union, the 'bourgeois' press, the Communist press, the radical press. To my astonishment (for I had scarcely dared think it), the trials did indeed seem to be a monstrous frame-up. The defendant, Pyatakov, flew to Oslo to 'conspire' with Trotsky during a winter when, according to the authorities, no planes landed at the Oslo airfield; the defendant, Holtzmann, met Trotsky's son, Sedov, in 1936, at the Hotel Bristol in Copenhagen, which had burned down in 1912; the witness, Romm, met Trotsky in Paris at a time when numerous depositions testified that he had been in Royan, among clouds of witnesses, or on the way there from the south of France.

These were only the most glaring discrepancies – the ones that got in the newspapers. Everywhere you touched the case something crumbled. The carelessness of the case's manufacture was to me its most terrifying aspect; the slovenly disregard for credibility defied the credence, in its turn. How did they dare? I think I was more shaken by finding that I was on the right side than I would have been the other way round. And yet, except for a very few people, nobody seemed to mind whether the Hotel Bristol had burned down or not, whether a real plane had landed, whether Trotsky's life and writings were congruent with the picture given of him in the trials. When confronted with the facts of the case, people's minds sheered off from it like jelly from a spoon.

Anybody who has ever tried to rectify an injustice or set a record straight comes to feel that he is going mad. And from a social point of view, he *is* crazy, for he is trying to undo something that is finished, to unravel the social fabric. That is why my liberal friends looked so grave and solemn when I would press them to come along to a meeting and listen to a presentation of the facts – for them this was a Decision, too awful to be considered lightly. The Moscow trials were an historical fact and those of us who tried to undo them were uneasily felt to be crackpots, who were trying to turn the clock back. And of course the less we were listened to, the more insistent and earnest we became, even while we realized we were doing our cause harm. It is impossible to take a moderate tone under such conditions. If I admitted, though, to being a little bit hipped on the subject of Trotsky, I could sometimes gain an indulgent if flickering attention – the kind of attention that stipulates, 'She's a bit off but let's hear her story.' And now and then, by sheer chance, one of my hearers would be arrested by some stray point in my narrative; the disparaging smile would slowly fade from his features, leaving a look of blank consternation. He would go off and investigate for himself, and in a few days, when we met again, he would be a crackpot too.

Most of us who became anti-Communists at the time of the trials were drawn in, like me, by accident and almost unwillingly. Looking back, as on a love-affair, a man could say that if he had not had lunch in a certain restaurant on a certain day, he might not have been led to ponder the facts of the Moscow trials. Or not then at any rate. And had he pondered them at a later date, other considerations would have entered and his conversations would have had a different style. On the whole, those of us who became anti-Communists during that year, 1936–7, have remained liberals – a thing that is less true of people of our generation who were converted earlier or later. A certain doubt of orthodoxy and independence of mass opinion was riveted into our anti-Communism by the heat of that period. As soon as I make this statement, exceptions leap into my mind, but I think as a generalization it will stand. Those who became anti-Communist earlier fell into two classes: the experts and those to whom any socialist ideal was repugnant. Those whose eyes were opened later, by the Nazi–Soviet pact, or still later, by God knows what, were left bruised and full of self-hatred or self-commiseration, because they had palliated so much and truckled to a power-centre; to them, Communism's chief sin seems to be that it deceived *them*, and their public atonement takes on both a vindicating and a vindicative character.

We were luckier. Our anti-Communism came to us neither as the fruit of a special wisdom nor as a humiliating awakening from a prolonged deception, but as a natural event, the product of chance and propinquity. One thing followed another, and the will had little to say about it. For my part, during that year, I realized, with a certain wistfulness, that it was too late for me to become any kind of Marxist. Marxism, I saw, from the learned young man I listened to at Committee meetings, was something you had to take up young, like ballet dancing.

So, I did not try to be a Marxist or a Trotskyite, though for the first time I read a little in the Marxist canon. But I got the name of being a Trotskyite, which meant, in the end, that I saw less of the conventional Stalinists I had been mingling with and less of conventional people generally. (My definition of a conventional person was quite broad: it included anyone who could hear of the Moscow trials and maintain an unruffled serenity.) This, then, was a break or a rupture, not very noticeable at first, that gradually widened and widened, without any conscious effort on my part, sometimes to my regret. This estrangement was not marked by any definite stages; it was a matter of tiny choices. Shortly after the Moscow trials, for instance, I changed from the *Herald-Tribune* to the *Times*; soon I had stopped doing crossword puzzles, playing bridge, reading detective stories and popular novels. I did not 'give up' these things, they departed from me, as it were, on tiptoe, seeing that my thoughts were elsewhere.

To change from the *Herald-Tribune* to the *Times*, is not, I am aware, as serious a step as breaking with international Communism when you have been its agent; and it occurs to me that Mr Chambers and Miss Bentley might well protest the comparison, pointing out that they were profoundly dedicated people, while I was a mere trifler, that their decisions partook of the sublime, where mine descended to the ridiculous – as Mr Chambers says, he was ready to give his life for his beliefs. Fortunately (though I could argue the point, for we all give our lives for our beliefs, piecemeal or whole), I have a surprise witness to call for my side, who did literally die for his political views.

I am referring to Trotsky, the small, frail, pertinacious old man who wore whiskers, wrinkles, glasses, shock of grizzled hair, like a gleeful disguise for the erect young student, the dangerous revolutionary within him. Nothing could be more alien to the convulsed and tormented moonscapes of the true confessions of ex-Communists than Trotsky's populous, matter-of-fact recollections set out in *My Life*. I have just been re-reading this volume, and though I no longer subscribe to its views, which have certainly an authoritarian and doctrinaire cast that troubles me today, nevertheless, I experience a sense of recognition here that I cannot find in the pages of our own repentant 'revolutionaries'. The old man remained unregenerate; he never admitted that he had sinned. That is probably why nobody seems to care for, or feel apologetic to, his memory. It is an interesting point – and relevant, I think, to my story – that many people today actually have the impression that Trotsky died a natural death.

In a certain sense, this is perfectly true. I do not mean that he lived by violence and therefore might reasonably be expected to die by violence. He was a man of words primarily, a pamphleteer and orator. He was armed, as he said, with a pen and peppered his enemies with a fusillade of articles. Hear the concluding passages of his autobiography: 'Since my exile, I have more than once read musings in the newspapers on the subject of the "tragedy" that has befallen me. I know no *personal* tragedy. I know the change of two chapters of revolution. One American paper which published an article of mine accompanied it with a profound note to the effect that in spite of the blows the author had suffered, he had, as evidenced by his article, preserved his clarity of reason. I can only express my astonishment at the philistine attempt to establish a connection between the power of reasoning and a government post, between mental balance and the present situation. I do not know, and I never have known, of any such connection. In prison, with a book or pen in my hand, I experienced the same sense of deep satisfaction that I did at mass-meetings of the revolution. I felt the mechanics of power as an inescapable burden, rather than as a spiritual satisfaction.'

This was not a man of violence. Nevertheless, one can say that he died a natural death – a death that was in keeping with the open manner of his life. There was nothing arcane in Trotsky; that was his charm. Like an ordinary person, he was hospitably open to hazard and accident. In his autobiography, he cannot date the moment when he became a socialist.

One factor in his losing out in the power-struggle at the time of Lenin's death was his delay in getting the telegram that should have called him home from the Caucasus, where he was convalescing, to appear at Lenin's funeral – *had* he got the telegram, perhaps the outcome would have been different. Or again, perhaps not. It may be that the whims of chance are really the importunities of design. But if there is a Design, it aims, in real lives, like the reader's or mine or Trotsky's, to look natural and fortuitous; that is how it gets us into its web.

Trotsky himself, looking at his life in retrospect, was struck, as most of us are on such occasions, by the role chance had played in it. He tells how one day, during Lenin's last illness, he went duck-shooting with an old hunter in a canoe on the River Dubna, walked through a bog in felt boots – only a hundred steps – and contracted influenza. This was the reason he was ordered to Sukhu for the cure, missed Lenin's funeral, and had to stay in bed during the struggle for primacy that raged that autumn and winter. 'I cannot help noting', he says, 'how obligingly the accidental helps the historical law. Broadly speaking, the entire historical process is a refraction of historical law through the accidental. In the language of biology, one might say that the historical law is realized through the natural selection of accidents.' And with a faint touch of quizzical gaiety he sums up the problem as a Marxian: 'One can foresee the consequences of a revolution or a war, but it is impossible to foresee the consequences of an autumn shooting-trip for wild ducks.' This shrug before the unforeseen implies an acceptance of consequences that is a far cry from penance and prophecy. Such, it concedes, is life. *Bravo*, old sport, I say, even though the hall is empty.

F. R. LEAVIS

Mass Civilization and Minority Culture

F. R. Leavis (1895–1978) was best known in his lifetime as an embattled literary academic. Based at Downing College, Cambridge, Leavis – together with his combative wife, Queenie – was regularly involved in university in-fighting, most of it to do with his campaign to reform the university's otiose English Department (as he saw it). Outside the university, though, he was an influential figure: his magazine Scrutiny *and his* New Bearings in English Poetry *(1932) had much to do with the advancement of modernist techniques in verse, and with the undermining of metropolitan literary chic. Early on, Leavis expressed alarm at the growing influence of mass-culture but he also saw that a good deal of so-called 'minority culture' was scarcely worth defending. The survival of a serious literature, he contended, would ultimately depend on an elite trained in the universities – and trained, preferably, by Queenie and himself.*

And this function is particularly important in our modern world, of which the whole civilization is, to a much greater degree than the civilization of Greece and Rome, mechanical and external, and tends constantly to become more so.

Culture and Anarchy, 1869

For Matthew Arnold it was in some ways less difficult. I am not thinking of the so much more desperate plight of culture today,* but (it is not, at bottom, an unrelated consideration) of the freedom with which he could use such phrases as 'the will of God' and 'our true selves'. Today one must face problems of definition and formulation where Arnold could pass lightly on. When, for example, having started by saying that

---

* 'The word, again, which we children of God speak, the voice which most hits our collective thought, the newspaper with the largest circulation in England, nay with the largest circulation in the whole world, is the *Daily Telegraph*!' – *Culture and Anarchy*.
  It is the *News of the World* that has the largest circulation today.

culture has always been in minority keeping, I am asked what I mean by 'culture', I might (and do) refer the reader to *Culture and Anarchy*; but I know that something more is required.

In any period it is upon a very small minority that the discerning appreciation of art and literature depends: it is (apart from cases of the simple and familiar) only a few who are capable of unprompted, first-hand judgment. They are still a small minority, though a larger one, who are capable of endorsing such first-hand judgment by genuine personal response. The accepted valuations are a kind of paper currency based upon a very small proportion of gold. To the state of such a currency the possibilities of fine living at any time bear a close relation. There is no need to elaborate the metaphor: the nature of the relation is suggested well enough by this passage from Mr I. A. Richards, which should by now be a *locus classicus*:

But it is not true that criticism is a luxury trade. The rearguard of Society cannot be extricated until the vanguard has gone further. Goodwill and intelligence are still too little available. The critic, we have said, is as much concerned with the health of the mind as any doctor with the health of the body. To set up as a critic is to set up as a judge of values . . . For the arts are inevitably and quite apart from any intentions of the artist an appraisal of existence. Matthew Arnold, when he said that poetry is a criticism of life, was saying something so obvious that it is constantly overlooked. The artist is concerned with the record and perpetuation of the experiences which seem to him most worth having. For reasons which we shall consider . . . he is also the man who is most likely to have experiences of value to record. He is the point at which the growth of the mind shows itself.*

This last sentence gives the hint for another metaphor. The minority capable not only of appreciating Dante, Shakespeare, Donne, Baude-laire, Conrad (to take major instances) but of recognizing their latest successors constitute the consciousness of the race (or of a branch of it) at a given time. For such capacity does not belong merely to an isolated aesthetic realm: it implies responsiveness to theory as well as to art, to science and philosophy in so far as these may affect the sense of the human situation and of the nature of life. Upon this minority depends our power of profiting by the finest human experience of the

* *The Principles of Literary Criticism*, p. 61.

past; they keep alive the subtlest and most perishable parts of tradition. Upon them depend the implicit standards that order the finer living of an age, the sense that this is worth more than that, this rather than that is the direction in which to go, that the centre* is here rather than there. In their keeping, to use a metaphor that is metonymy also and will bear a good deal of pondering, is the language, the changing idiom, upon which fine living depends, and without which distinction of spirit is thwarted and incoherent. By 'culture' I mean the use of such a language. I do not suppose myself to have produced a tight definition, but the account, I think, will be recognized as adequate by anyone who is likely to read this essay.

It is a commonplace today that culture is at a crisis. It is a commonplace more widely accepted than understood: at any rate, realization of what the crisis portends does not seem to be common. I am, for instance, sometimes answered that it has all happened before, during the Alexandrian period, or under the Roman Empire. Even if this were true it would hardly be reassuring, and I note the contention mainly in order to record my suspicion that it comes from Spengler,† where, of course, authority may also be found for an attitude of proud philosophic indifference. For Spengler, the inexorable cycle moves once more to its inevitable end. But the common absence of concern for what is happening is not to be explained by erudition or philosophy. It is itself a symptom, and a phrase for it comes aptly to hand in Mr H. G. Wells' new book, *The Autocracy of Mr Parham*: 'Essentially it was a vast and increasing inattention.'

It seems, then, not unnecessary to restate the obvious. In support of the belief that the modern phase of human history is unprecedented it is enough to point to the machine. The machine, in the first place, has brought about change in habit and the circumstances of life at a rate for which we have no parallel. The effects of such change may be studied in *Middletown*, a remarkable work of anthropology, dealing (I am afraid it is not superfluous to say) with a typical community of the Middle West. There we see in detail how the automobile (to take one

---

* '. . . the mass of the public is without any suspicion that the value of these organs is relative to their being nearer a certain ideal centre of correct information, taste and intelligence, or farther away from it.' – *Culture and Anarchy*.

† A good account of some aspects of the modern phase may be found in *The Decline of the West*, Vol. II, chapter IV.

instance) has, in a few years, radically affected religion,* broken up the family, and revolutionized social custom. Change has been so catastrophic that the generations find it hard to adjust themselves to each other, and parents are helpless to deal with their children. It seems unlikely that the conditions of life can be transformed in this way without some injury to the standard of living (to wrest the phrase from the economist): improvisation can hardly replace the delicate traditional adjustments, the mature, inherited codes of habit and valuation, without severe loss, and loss that may be more than temporary. It is a breach in continuity that threatens: what has been inadvertently dropped may be irrecoverable or forgotten.

To this someone will reply that Middletown is America and not England. And it is true that in America change has been more rapid, and its effects have been intensified by the fusion of peoples. But the same processes are at work in England and the western world generally, and at an acceleration. It is a commonplace that we are being Americanized, but again a commonplace that seems, as a rule, to carry little understanding with it. Americanization is often spoken of as if it were something of which the United States are guilty. But it is something from which Lord Melchett, our 'British-speaking'† champion, will not save us even if he succeeds in rallying us to meet that American enterprise which he fears 'may cause us to lose a great structure of self-governing brotherhoods whose common existence is of infinite importance to the future continuance of the Anglo-Saxon race, and of the gravest import to the development of all that seems best in our modern civilization'.‡ For those who are most defiant of America do not propose to reverse the processes consequent upon the machine. We are to have greater efficiency, better salesmanship, and more mass-production and standardization. Now, if the worst effects of mass-production and standardization were represented by Woolworth's there would be no need

* 'One gains a distinct impression that the religious basis of all education was more taken for granted if less talked about thirty-five years ago, when high school "chapel" was a religio–inspirational service with a "choir" instead of the "pep session" which it tends to become today.' – *Middletown*, by R. S. and H. M. Lynd, p. 204. This kind of change, of course, is not due to the automobile alone.
† 'That would be one of the greatest disasters of the British-speaking people, and one of the greatest disasters to civilization.' – Lord Melchett, *Industry and Politics*, p. 278.
‡ Ibid., p. 281.

to despair. But there are effects that touch the life of the community more seriously. When we consider, for instance, the processes of mass-production and standardization in the form represented by the Press, it becomes obviously of sinister significance that they should be accompanied by a process of levelling-down.

Of Lord Northcliffe, Mr Hamilton Fyfe, his admiring biographer, tells us (*Northcliffe: an Intimate Biography*, p. 270):

He knew what the mass of newspaper-readers wanted, and he gave it to them. He broke down the dignified idea that the conductors of newspapers should appeal to the intelligent few. He frankly appealed to the unintelligent many. Not in a cynical spirit, not with any feeling of contempt for their tastes; but because on the whole he had more sympathy with them than with the others, and because they were as the sands of the sea in numbers. He did not aim at making opinion less stable, emotion more superficial. He did this, without knowing he did it, because it increased circulation.

Two pages later we are told:

The Best People did read the *Daily Mail*. It was now seen in first-class railway compartments as much as in third-class. It had made its way from the kitchen and the butler's pantry of the big country house up to the hall table.

'Giving the public what it wants,' is, clearly, a modest way of putting it. Lord Northcliffe showed people what they wanted, and showed the Best People that they wanted the same as the rest. It is enough by way of commentary on the phrase to refer to the history of the newspaper press during the last half-century: a history of which the last notable event is the surrender of the *Daily Herald* to the operation of that 'psychological Gresham's Law' which Mr Norman Angell notes:

... the operation of a psychological Gresham's Law; just as in commerce debased coin, if there be enough of it, must drive out the sterling, so in the contest of motives, action which corresponds to the more primitive feelings and impulses, to first thoughts and established prejudices, can be stimulated by the modern newspaper far more easily than that prompted by rationalized second thought.*

Let us face the truth [says Mr Norman Angell further on]: the conditions of the modern Press cause the Bottomleys more and more and the Russells

* *The Press and the Organisation of Society*, p. 33.

and Dickinsons less and less to form the national character. The forces under review are not merely concerned with the mechanical control of ideas. They transform the national temperament.*

All this, again, is commonplace, but commonplace, again, on which it seems necessary to insist. For the same 'psychological Gresham's Law' has a much wider application than the newspaper press. It applies even more disastrously to the films: more disastrously, because the films have a so much more potent influence.† They provide now the main form of recreation in the civilized world; and they involve surrender, under conditions of hypnotic receptivity, to the cheapest emotional appeals, appeals the more insidious because they are associated with a compellingly vivid illusion of actual life. It would be difficult to dispute that the result must be serious damage to the 'standard of living' (to use the phrase as before). All this seems so obvious that one is diffident about insisting on it. And yet people will reply by adducing the attempts that have been made to use the film as a serious medium of art. Just as, when broadcasting is in question, they will point out that they have heard good music broadcast and intelligent lectures. The standardizing influence of broadcasting hardly admits of doubt, but since there is here no Hollywood engaged in purely commercial exploitation the

* Ibid., p. 43.
Vide also p. 35: 'When Swift wrote certain of his pamphlets, he presented a point of view contrary to the accepted one, and profoundly affected his country's opinion and policy. Yet at most he circulated a few thousand copies. One of the most important was printed at his own expense. Any printer in a back street could have furnished all the material capital necessary for reaching effectively the whole reading public of the nation. Today, for an unfamiliar opinion to gain headway against accepted opinion, the mere mechanical equipment of propaganda would be beyond the resources of any ordinary individual.'

† 'The motion picture, by virtue of its intrinsic nature, is a species of amusing and informational Esperanto, and, potentially at least, a species of aesthetic Esperanto of all the arts; if it may be classified as one, the motion picture has in it, perhaps more than any other, the resources of universality ... The motion picture tells its stories directly, simply, quickly and elementally, not in words but in pictorial pantomime. To see is not only to believe; it is also in a measure to understand. In theatrical drama, seeing is closely allied with hearing, and hearing, in turn, with mental effort. In the motion picture, seeing is all – or at least nine-tenths of all.' – *Encyclopædia Britannica*, 14th Ed.: 'Motion Pictures: A Universal Language.'

The *Encyclopædia Britannica*, fourteenth edition, is itself evidence of what is happening: 'humanized, modernized, pictorialized', as the editors announce.

levelling-down is not so obvious. But perhaps it will not be disputed that broadcasting, like the films, is in practice mainly a means of passive diversion, and that it tends to make active recreation, especially active use of the mind, more difficult.* And such agencies are only a beginning. The near future holds rapid developments in store.

Contemplating that deliberate exploitation of the cheap response which characterizes our civilization, we may say that a new factor in history is an unprecedented use of applied psychology. This might be thought to flatter Hollywood, but, even so, there can be no room for doubt when we consider advertising, and the progress it has made in two or three decades. (And 'advertising' may be taken to cover a great deal more than comes formally under that head.) 'It ought to be plain even to the inexperienced,' writes an authority, Mr Gilbert Russell (in *Advertisement Writing*), 'that successful copywriting depends upon insight into people's minds: not into individual minds, mark, but into the way average people think and act, and the way they react to suggestions of various kinds.' And again: 'Advertising is becoming increasingly exact every day. Where instinct used to be enough, it is being replaced by inquiry. Advertising men nowadays don't say, "The public will buy this article from such and such a motive": they employ what is called market research to find out the buying motives, as exactly as time and money and opportunity permit, from the public itself.'

So, as another authority, Mr Harold Herd, Principal of the Regent Institute, says (*Bigger Results from Advertising*): 'Now that advertising is more and more recruiting the best brains of the country we may look forward to increasingly scientific direction of this great public force.'

---

* Mr Edgar Rice Burroughs (creator of Tarzan), in a letter that I have been privileged to see, writes: 'It has been discovered through repeated experiments that pictures that require thought for appreciation have invariably been box-office failures. The general public does not wish to think. This fact, probably more than any other, accounts for the success of my stories, for without this specific idea in mind I have, nevertheless, endeavoured to make all of my descriptions so clear that each situation could be visualized readily by any reader precisely as I saw it. My reason for doing this was not based upon a low estimate of general intelligence, but upon the realization that in improbable situations, such as abound in my work, the greatest pains must be taken to make them appear plausible. I have evolved, therefore, a type of fiction that may be read with the minimum of mental effort.' The significance of this for my argument does not need comment. Mr Burroughs adds that his books sell at over a million copies a year. There is not room here to make the comparisons suggested by such documents as the *Life of James Lackington* (1791).

Mr Gilbert Russell, who includes in his list of books for 'A Copy Writer's Bookshelf' the works of Shakespeare, the Bible, *The Forsyte Saga*, *The Oxford Book of English Verse*, *Fiery Particles* by C. E. Montague, and Sir Arthur Quiller-Couch's *The Art of Writing*, tells us that:

Competent copy cannot be written except by men who have read lovingly, who have a sense of the romance of words, and of the picturesque and the dramatic phrase; who have versatility enough and judgment enough to know how to write plainly and pungently, or with a certain affectation. Briefly, competent copy is a matter not only of literary skill of a rather high order, but also skill of a particular specialized kind.

The influence of such skill is to be seen in contemporary fiction. For if, as Mr Thomas Russell (author of *What did you do in the Great War, daddy?*), tells us, 'English is the best language in the world for advertising', advertising is doing a great deal for English. It is carrying on the work begun by Mr Rudyard Kipling, and, where certain important parts of the vocabulary are concerned, making things more difficult for the fastidious. For what is taking place is not something that affects only the environment of culture, stops short, as it were, at the periphery. This should be obvious, but it does not appear to be so to many who would recognize the account I have given above as matter of commonplace. Even those who would agree that there has been an overthrow of standards, that authority has disappeared, and that the currency has been debased and inflated, do not often seem to realize what the catastrophe portends. My aim is to bring this home, if possible, by means of a little concrete evidence. I hope, at any rate, to avert the charge of extravagant pessimism.

For consider, to begin with, Mr Arnold Bennett. The history of how the author of *The Old Wives' Tale* has since used his creative talents I will not dwell upon further than to suggest that such a history would have been impossible in any other age. It is Mr Arnold Bennett, the arbiter of taste, that I have chiefly in mind. In this capacity too he has a history. If one reads the articles which he contributed to the *New Age* twenty years ago (they are reprinted in *Books and Authors*) it is to break into admiring comment again and again. It is, for instance, impossible not to applaud when he is impudent about the Professors:

I never heard him lecture, but I should imagine that he was an ideal University Extension lecturer. I do not mean this to be in the least complimentary to him as a critic. His book, *Illustrations of Tennyson*, was an entirely sterile exercise, proving on every page that the author had no real perceptions about literature. It simply made creative artists laugh. They knew. His more recent book on modern tendencies displayed in an acute degree the characteristic inability of the typical professor to toddle alone when released from the leading strings of tradition.

I fear that most of our professors are in a similar fix. There is Professor George Saintsbury, a regular Albert Memorial of learning.

*   *   *

It may not be generally known (and I do not state it as a truth) that Professor Raleigh is a distant connection of the celebrated family of Pains, pyrotechnicians.

Yes, it is impossible not to applaud. And yet there is something in the manner – well, twenty years later we find it more pronounced:

Nevertheless, though performances of Greek plays usually send me to sleep – so far off and incredible is the motivation of them, I murmur about the original author on reading some of the dialogues of Plato: 'This fellow knew exactly how to do it.' And of Homer: 'This fellow knew the whole job.' And of Aristotle: 'This is the only fellow who ever really could do it.' And when I first set eyes on the Acropolis at Athens I said out loud – no mere murmuring: 'These fellows could do it.' (*Evening Standard*, 19 Jan. 1928.)

When I try to comment on the manner of this I can only murmur: 'Matthew Arnold could have done it.' It is, of course, not merely manner: the Man from the North brought something more fundamental with him. There is an ominous note in the first passage I quoted: 'It simply made creative artists laugh. They knew.' Mr Bennett is a creative artist, and Mr Bennett knows. And for some years now Mr Bennett has been the most powerful maker of literary reputations in England. To compute how many bad books a year, on the average, Mr Bennett has turned into literature would hardly be worth the labour. It is enough to instance some of his achievements and to quote some of his pontifical utterances from the *Evening Standard*. Here is the typical achievement:

Mr Arnold Bennett's reputation as a maker of 'best sellers' has been heightened by the addition of one more to the list of other people's books which the public has clamoured for on his word.

Last week *Vivandière* meant nothing to most people, and the name of Miss Phoebe Fenwick Gaye conveyed no more.

Then Mr Arnold Bennett, in his weekly article on books in the *Evening Standard*, mentioned that *Vivandière* was this young woman's first novel, and that it was very good.

The demand for the book which has suddenly arisen has cleared the first edition right out of existence, and still the clamour goes on. Martin Secker, the publishers, told the *Evening Standard* of the sudden overwhelming demand which followed Mr Arnold Bennett's praise.

A member of the firm said:

'The demand was so great that the first edition was completely sold out and we have had to get busy with a second edition, which will be ready tomorrow.'

Mr Arnold Bennett made in this way *Jew Süss*. He also made, I understand, *The Bridge of San Luis Rey*; for, though he saw through the academic critics, he takes readily to Academy art. But his critical prowess is best exhibited by quotation from the *Evening Standard*:

22 Nov. 1928: '*The Golden Age* is a destructive master-piece.'

13 Dec. 1928: 'Mr Eliot is a fine poet – sometimes, if not in that celebrated piece of verse, *The Waste Land*, at the mention of which the very young bow the head in adoration.'

3 May 1928: 'Mr Stanley Baldwin made no mistake about Mary Webb.'

3 Jan 1929: 'The novel is making progress. It has been galvanized by the very important experiments of James Joyce, D. H. Lawrence, R. H. Mottram, and Aldous Huxley: all of whom have brought something new into it. The biggest of these is, or was, James Joyce . . . R. H. Mottram is a genius. He writes like a genius,' etc.

8 Nov. 1928: '. . . In particular I have failed to perceive any genuine originality in the method of *Mrs Dalloway*. If originality there is, it fails of its object of presenting a character, . . . Here is Mr Muir discussing the modern novel, and he makes but passing reference to D. H. Lawrence, and no reference at all to R. H. Mottram, the two novelists who more than any other of their contemporaries, continually disclose genuine originality, the two real British geniuses of the new age!'

24 Jan. 1929: 'I have just read Edith Sitwell's new poem, *Gold Coast Customs*. In its intense individuality, its frightening freshness of vision, its verbal difficulties, it stands by itself.'

Mr Bennett, we perceive, is a judge of poetry as well as of the novel: he can distinguish. He is adequate to the subtle complexities of Miss Sitwell, but he will stand no nonsense from Mr Eliot. And he has no misconception about the kind of success that alone can justify a poet:

These parasites on society cannot, or apparently will not, understand that the first duty of, for instance, a poet is not to write poetry, but to keep himself in decency, and his wife and children if he has them, to discharge his current obligations, and to provide for old age. (*Evening Standard*, 9 June 1927.)

No, it was not merely a manner that Mr Bennett brought with him from the Five Towns. And it is not merely expression that one finds so gross in his critical vocabulary: 'Value for money'; 'let there be no mistake about it, this is a big book'; 'a high-class poet'; '. . . I enjoyed reading *Creative Writing*. It is full of chunks of horse-sense about writing.' But Mr Bennett is capable of modesty: it has occurred to him, for instance, to be modest about his qualifications for judging poetry. And his modesty is, if possible, even more damning than his assurance. He writes in *Journal, 1929*:

I met a poet there; he was modest; he remarked in a somewhat sad tone that I rarely mentioned poetry in my articles on new books. I told him that I gave poetry a miss for the good reason that I had no technical knowledge of prosody. (True, you can have a knowledge of prosody without having a feeling for poetry, but you cannot properly assess poetry without knowing a lot about prosody.)

Mr Bennett will not understand what is meant by saying that this would-be confession is, instead, self-betrayal: so complete is his ignorance about poetry.

How is it that he can go on exposing himself in this way without becoming a byword and a laughing-stock? (For the author of *The Old Wives' Tale* is a public figure, and differs in this from the minor pontiffs who compete with him in the Sunday papers and elsewhere.) It is that there is no longer an informed and cultivated public. If there is no public to break into a roar of laughter when Mr Bennett tells us that R. H. Mottram, like James Joyce, is a genius, or that D. H. Lawrence and R. H. Mottram (poor Mr Mottram!) are the two real British geniuses of the new age, how should there be a public to appreciate Mr Bennett's modesty about poetry? (For fiction, as we all know, is read and enjoyed.) Why should Mr Bennett's pontifications make a stir when Mr J. C. Squire, specialist in poetry and 'himself a poet', can, in prefacing one of the best-known anthologies of modern verse (*Selections from Modern Poets*), write:

Should our age be remembered by posterity solely as an age during which fifty men had written lyrics of some durability for their truth and beauty, it would not be remembered with contempt. It is in that conviction that I have compiled this anthology;

and Mr Harold Monro, even more a specialist in poetry and also 'himself a poet', in the *Introduction* to *Twentieth Century Poetry*:

Is it a great big period, or a minutely small? Reply who can? Somebody with whom I was talking cried: 'They are all only poetical persons – *not* poets. Who will be reading them a century hence?' To which I answered: 'There are so many of them that, a century hence, they may appear a kind of Composite Poet; there may be 500 excellent poems proceeding from 100 poets mostly not so great, but well worth remembering a century hence.'

Such pronouncements could be made only in an age in which there were no standards, no living tradition of poetry spread abroad, and no discriminating public. It is the plight of culture generally that is exemplified here.* In the *Advertisement* to the first edition of *Lyrical Ballads* I light on this:

An accurate taste in poetry, as in all other arts, Sir Joshua Reynolds has

---

* 'For there is no such gulf between poetry and life as over-literary persons sometimes suppose. There is no gap between our everyday emotional life and the material of poetry. The verbal expression of this life, at its finest, is forced to use the technique of poetry; that is the only essential difference. We cannot avoid the material of poetry. If we do not live in consonance with good poetry, we must live in consonance with bad poetry. And, in fact, the idle hours of most lives are filled with reveries that are simply bad private poetry. On the whole evidence, I do not see how we can avoid the conclusion that a general insensitivity to poetry does witness a low level of general imaginative life.' – I. A. Richards, *Practical Criticism*, pp. 319–20.

observed, is an acquired talent, which can only be produced by severe thought, and a long continued intercourse with the best models of composition.

When Wordsworth wrote that, severe thought and long-continued intercourse with the best models were more widely possible than now. What distractions have come to beset the life of the mind since then! There seems every reason to believe that the average cultivated person of a century ago was a very much more competent reader than his modern representative. Not only does the modern dissipate himself upon so much more reading of all kinds: the task of acquiring discrimination is much more difficult. A reader who grew up with Wordsworth moved among a limited set of signals (so to speak): the variety was not overwhelming. So he was able to acquire discrimination as he went along. But the modern is exposed to a concourse of signals so bewildering in their variety and number that, unless he is especially gifted or especially favoured, he can hardly begin to discriminate. Here we have the plight of culture in general. The landmarks have shifted, multiplied and crowded upon one another, the distinctions and dividing lines have blurred away, the boundaries are gone, and the arts and literatures of different countries and periods have flowed together, so that, if we revert to the metaphor of 'language' for culture, we may, to describe it, adapt the sentence in which Mr T. S. Eliot describes the intellectual situation: 'When there is so much to be known, when there are so many fields of knowledge in which the same words are used with different meanings, when every one knows a little about a great many things, it becomes increasingly difficult for anyone to know whether he knows what he is talking about or not.'

We ought not, then, to be surprised that now, when a strong current of criticism is needed as never before, there should hardly be in England a cultivated public large enough to support a serious critical organ. The *Criterion* carries on almost alone. It is accused of being solemn, and seems to owe its new-found security to a specific ecclesiastical interest. For the short-lived *Calendar of Modern Letters*, as intelligent and lively a review as ever appeared in English, died for lack of support. Whatever support the *Dial* may have enjoyed on this side the Atlantic, it now comes no longer, and only the *New Adelphi* is left to carry on with the *Criterion*. There is, of course, the *Times Literary Supplement*, but it would be a misnomer to call it a critical organ. For the hope of intelligent reviewing we are left (apart from the *Criterion* and the *New Adelphi*) to the *Nation and Athenaeum* and the *New Statesman*, and they, of course, have no room for any but short articles.

The critically adult public, then, is very small indeed: they are a very small minority who are capable of fending for themselves amid the smother of new books. But there is a relatively large public that goes for guidance to the *Observer* and the *Sunday Times*, and a still larger one that goes to weeklies like *John o' London's* (which have surprising circulations). Now it would take greater enterprise and vigour than are common in these publics to make much use of the kind of help to be found in such quarters. The reader must have a great deal more done for him. Again we have to learn from America: the problem has been solved there by the Book of the Month Club and similar organizations. The problem is now rapidly being solved here, where The Book Society has already been followed by The Book Guild.

Out of the thousands of books published every year [writes Miss Ethel Mannin for the Book Guild] – there are between 12,000 and 14,000 – how on earth is the ordinary person to sift the sheep from the goats? Distinguished critics attempt to guide the public, but they are often so hopelessly 'high-brow' and 'precious', and simply add to the general confusion and bewilderment.

When the aims of The Book Guild were explained to me, therefore, it seemed too good to be true – an organization which would cater *for the ordinary intelligent reader*, not for the highbrows – an organization which would realize that *a book can have a good story and a popular appeal and yet be good literature* – be good literature and yet be absorbingly interesting, of the kind you can't put down once you've started, an organization which would not recommend a book as a work of genius simply because it had been eulogized by some pedantic critic or other, but which would conscientiously sift really good stuff out of the mass of the affected and pretentious which is just as tiresome as the blatantly third rate.

There are so many really good books written nowadays that it is utterly impossible for the ordinary person to keep track of them all – even the critics don't succeed in doing so. The Book Guild by means of its Recommended List of Alternative Titles is able, as it were, to keep its finger on the pulse of the best of contemporary work, whilst at the same time providing something for everybody and that something the best of its kind – etc.

As for the method, we may turn to the official account of 'How the Book Society operates':

Publishers throughout the country are submitting their most important works in advance of publication to the selection committees. From these the Committee select their 'books of the month', and in addition compile a supplementary list of others they can thoroughly recommend.

On the morning of publication every member of the Book Society receives a first edition of the book the committee have chosen. Enclosed in this book is a copy of the *Book Society News* which contains reviews by members of the committee both of the selected book and of those on the supplementary list. If any members feel that the book chosen is not *their* book, they may return it within five days and will receive by return whatever book they select in exchange from the supplementary list.

Mr Hugh Walpole, Miss Clemence Dane (author of *Tradition and Hugh Walpole*), Mrs Sylvia Lynd, Mr J. B. Priestley (who wrote of a book of Mr Walpole's: '*Rogue Herries* is a grand tale, a real full-time man's job in fiction, and everybody should read it'), and the President of Magdalen College, Oxford, then, have, with their compeers of The Book Guild, taken into their keeping the future of English taste, and they will undoubtedly have a very great influence.* The average member of their flocks will probably get through a greater amount of respectable reading than before. But the most important way in which their influence will work is suggested by this passage from a book I have already referred to, *Advertisement Writing*, by Mr Gilbert Russell:

Some years ago a manufacturer was making some hundred of different patterns of the same article. His factory was therefore constantly concerned with small runs, necessitating frequent setting-up of machines. This was

---

* A member is reported as writing: 'No man likes to be told what is good for him, it is an affront to his intelligence. Neither will he allow Mr Walpole nor Mr Priestley nor John Milton to tell him what to read. But he is simply a fool if he is not impressed by their decisions in matters of literary taste. And that is where the Book Society comes in.'

'The speaker had evidently no notion that there was a scale of value for judgments on these topics, and that the judgments of the *Saturday Review* ranked high on this scale, and those of the *British Banner* low; the taste of the bathos implanted by nature in the literary judgments of man had never, in my friend's case, encountered any let or hindrance.' – *Culture and Anarchy*.

expensive, and the manufacturing economies of large-scale production were out of reach. It was seen that if the number of patterns could be reduced from hundreds to scores, factory economies could be effected. This course was beset with difficulties, however. The retail trade was accustomed to order individual patterns to suit individual shopkeepers, and the travellers were afraid of losing orders if they told their shopkeeper friends that individual preferences and fads could no longer be provided for, and orders must be booked from a score of standard patterns. Nevertheless the manufacturer was determined. What he did was to reduce his hundreds of patterns to the score that were most often ordered. The whole of his marketing policy became one of concentrating selling effort upon this score of patterns. The thing had to be done gradually. But this was the settled purpose which he had in mind, and his advertising policy had to conform to his marketing policy. For instance, in catalogues to the retail trade nearly all the former hundred patterns were mentioned, and most of them illustrated as they had always been, but the score or so of patterns that he was concentrating upon were illustrated in *colour*. And, exactly as expected, the vast bulk of the orders came in for these. Similarly, advertisements emphasized the standard lines, the object of the advertising policy being to educate the public into demanding what the manufacturer wanted to sell, so that the retail trade should order what the public actually demanded. In time, of course, all the patterns were dropped except the standard ones.

This saves a great deal of comment. Standardization advances to fresh triumphs.

The Book Society has at its command the psychological resources of modern advertising:

How often, sitting in some strange house, have your eyes wandered to the bookshelves in an effort to get some idea of the character of its owner? The books you read are often a guide to your character. The Book Society will help you to get those books you most want to have on your bookshelf.*

We are reminded of the way in which the compatriots of George F. Babbitt are persuaded to express their personalities in 'interior decoration'. There is, in fact, a strong American flavour about the 'literature' of both concerns. Both, for example, make great play with the American adjective 'worth-while': 'Build a worth-while library!'; 'a

---

* *The Books you Read*. Published by the Book Society.

worth-while book': 'I believe that the Book Society will prove to many people that a few pounds spent on new books in the year is a happy and worth-while experience' (Mr Hugh Walpole). The significance of this use, of course, lies in the atmosphere of uplift and hearty mass sentiment that the word brings with it. An appreciative member writes: 'Finally, as a member of the Book Society, I am conscious of a pleasant feeling of comradeship, it is something of a great adventure, original, happily conceived, well carried out, with friendly methods of working.' – Innocent enough, in all conscience. But there is, belonging to the same vocabulary as 'worth-while', another word that the sovereign powers of both organizations use even more – 'high-brow'. And the attitude behind the word 'high-brow' is exhibited with commendable guile-lessness by Mr George A. Birmingham (Canon Hannay) of The Book Guild. This reverend gentleman writes in *The Book Guild Bulletin* for 14 July 1930:

The detective novel writers have their own clientele, though they make no appeal to the young ladies who throng the counters of Boot's libraries and but little to the sheep-like crowd who follow the dictates of high-brow literary critics.

Lest the point should be missed he repeats it:

. . . not food for the Messrs Boot's young ladies or for the literary sheep whom I have already mentioned.

If the independent and intelligent critics who unpack the books chosen for them by Mr George A. Birmingham, Miss Ethel Mannin,* Mr Walpole, and Miss Clemence Dane† do not know now how they should

---

* The *Nation and Athenaeum* reviewer of Miss Mannin's recent book, *Confessions and Impressions*, says: '. . . I confess that the impression her book makes upon me is that it is cheap, crude, vulgar and uneducated.' – *Nation and Athenaeum*, 9 August 1930.

† 'And it is easy to believe that the modern English novel, which is suffering so severely nowadays from specialists, high-brows, and cranks, will benefit as thoroughly from its course of Edgar Wallace and Sax Rohmer as it did a century ago from its dose of Monk Lewis, Maturin and Mrs Radcliffe.' – *Tradition and Hugh Walpole*, by Clemence Dane, p. 27.

There is nothing more discussible than this in the windy, pretentious, eloquent vacuity of Miss Dane's book, which received respectful attention on the front page of the *Times Literary Supplement*, 31 July 1930.

feel towards the snobs who question the taste of these authorities – then they are not the independent and intelligent critics they are taken for.

'High-brow' is an ominous addition to the English language. I have said earlier that culture has always been in minority keeping. But the minority now is made conscious, not merely of an uncongenial, but of a hostile environment. 'Shakespeare', I once heard Mr Dover Wilson say, 'was not a high-brow.' True: there were no 'high-brows' in Shakespeare's time. It was possible for Shakespeare to write plays that were at once popular drama and poetry that could be appreciated only by an educated minority. *Hamlet* appealed at a number of levels of response, from the highest downwards. The same is true of *Paradise Lost, Clarissa, Tom Jones, Don Juan, The Return of the Native*. The same is not true, Mr George A. Birmingham might point out, of *The Waste Land, Hugh Selwyn Mauberley, Ulysses* or *To the Lighthouse*. These works are read only by a very small specialized public and are beyond the reach of the vast majority of those who consider themselves educated. The age in which the finest creative talent tends to be employed in works of this kind is the age that has given currency to the term 'high-brow'. But it would be as true to say that the attitude implicit in 'high-brow' causes this use of talent as the converse. The minority is being cut off as never before from the powers that rule the world; and as Mr George A. Birmingham and his friends succeed in refining and standardizing and conferring authority upon 'the taste of the bathos implanted by nature in the literary judgments of man' (to use Matthew Arnold's phrase), they will make it more and more inevitable that work expressing the finest consciousness of the age should be so specialized as to be accessible only to the minority.

'Civilization' and 'culture' are coming to be antithetical terms. It is not merely that the power and the sense of authority are now divorced from culture, but that some of the most disinterested solicitude for civilization is apt to be, consciously or unconsciously, inimical to culture. Mr H. G. Wells, for example, belongs, for the minority, to the past, but it is probable that he represents a good deal of the future. And he returns the compliment paid him by the minority. In his last book, *The Autocracy of Mr Parham*, he makes his butt, a wax-work grotesque labelled 'Oxford Don', representative not only of tribal nationalism, imperialism, and The Old Diplomacy, but also of culture. There is, one gathers, nothing more to be said for art than Mr Parham, in the National Gallery, says to Sir Bussy Woodcock. And the book ends with Sir Bussy (representative and defence-mechanism of Mr Wells) declaring of a proposed newspaper propaganda to Mr Parham: 'It would be up against everything you are.' 'History is bunk!' said Mr Henry Ford. Mr Wells, who is an authority, endorses.

Sir Bussy's is not the only scheme for using a civilized technique on behalf of a civilizing education. Dr John B. Watson (who is vice-president of an advertising concern) writes:*

We hear of no technique for learning how to behave emotionally or unemotionally. Anybody can teach you to play tennis, drive a motor-car, set type, to paint or to draw. We have schools and instructors for all this, but who has set up a school for teaching us to be afraid and not afraid, to fall in love and to fall out of love, to be jealous or not jealous, to be slow to anger and quick to forget, not to let the sun go down on our wrath, to forgive freely, not to give way to angry passions? And yet some of these modes of behaviour make up the essence of the Christian religion, as a matter of fact, they are part of every civilized code.

So Dr Watson explains the technique that is to replace the unscientific traditional ways. As for standards of moral and other value, he is modest: he does not dictate:

It is not the behaviourist's business to say what is good for society. Society must make up its mind what it wants its members to be and to do; then it is up to the behaviourist to find the methods and technique that will bring the child up in the way it should grow.†

He has misgivings, it is true:

The behaviourist, then, has given society the rough pattern of a new weapon for controlling the individual. Will it use this weapon when perfected as a steam roller to flatten out all that is different in human personalities (which it can do, in spite of 'heredity', producing thereby a race of conformists)? Or will it use this method wisely?‡

But even if Dr Watson were in charge it would go ill with culture:

* *The Ways of Behaviourism*, p. 48.
† *The Ways of Behaviourism*, p. 60–1.
‡ Ibid., p. 86.

The new things in the universe come from the doers – the chemist, the physicist, the engineer, the biologist, the business man. With them doing leads to thinking, and thinking in turn leads to doing. With the poet, the day-dreamer, thinking leads not to doing but *merely to other words* either spoken or thought; the endless chain of words is never broken.*

We have too many philosophic verbal speculators, rhetoricians, poets and dreamers now.†

Dr Watson, of course, is an American and in England regarded as a crank. But there is reason to suppose that Behaviourism has already had a good deal of practical effect in America. And, in any case, Dr Watson only exhibits in an extreme form traits commonly to be observed in highly intelligent and disinterested persons of scientific training who devote themselves to the future of humanity. Anyone who has met a Eugenist will recognize these traits. Major Leonard Darwin, President of the Eugenics Education Society, for instance, thinks that human excellence may, for practical Eugenic purposes, be measured by earning capacity.‡ Then there is Sir Richard Paget, author of the recent important book, *Human Speech*. In a little book called *Babel*, published in the *To-day and To-morrow* series, Sir Richard argues, cogently, that it is time English was deliberately and scientifically improved and standardized as a language of thought. 'Broadcasting, long-distance telephony, the talking film, and the gramophone', he says truly, 'will make such standardization possible, and even comparatively easy to establish.' Anything else a language may be besides a 'method of symbolizing human thought' he considers as so little important that he can say:

If the keepers of our language maintain a die-hard attitude and succeed in preventing reasoned improvement, the result will, I suggest, be that language will be less and less used for intellectual and rational purposes, and relegated to an altogether inferior status as the symbolism of sentiment and small talk.

This is the only recognition Sir Richard gives to English Literature. He, too, proposes to use compulsion: he would suppress Mr James Joyce, or, rather, the future die-hard of Mr Joyce's kind:

I can see no alternative but that there should, eventually, be a censorship of

* Ibid., p. 63.
† Ibid., p. iii.
‡ *The Need for Eugenic Reform*, Major Leonard Darwin.

words, and that the printing or use in public of such improper words should be forbidden.

It is no laughing matter: Sir Richard Paget does in some way represent enlightenment as against conservative inertia. On the one hand, the academic custodians of tradition are what they are. On the other, there is so strong a case to be made out for some such reform as Sir Richard Paget advocates. No one aware of the situation and concerned about the future of Shakespeare's language can view quite happily the interest taken by some of the most alert minds of our day in such a scheme as 'Basic English'.* This instrument, embodying the extreme of analytical economy, is, of course, intended for a limited use. But what hope is there that the limits will be kept? If 'Basic English' proves as efficacious as it promises it will not remain a mere transition language for the Chinese. What an excellent instrument of education it would make, for instance, in the English-speaking countries! And, if hopes are fulfilled, the demand for literature in 'Basic English' will grow to vast dimensions as Asia learns how to use this means of access to the West. It seems incredible that the English language as used in the West should not be affected, especially in America, where it is so often written as if it were not native to the writer, and where the general use of it is so little subject to control by sentimental conservatism. Mass-production and standardization have not achieved their supreme triumph yet:

Meanwhile the president of the Radio Corporation of America proclaims an era at hand when 'the oldest and the newest civilization will throb together at the same intellectual appeal, and to the same artistic emotions.'†

We cannot be indifferent in the face of such possibilities. For, as we noted above, when we used the metaphor of 'language' in defining culture we were using more than a metaphor. The most important part of this 'language' is actually a matter of the use of words. Without the living subtlety of the finest idiom (which is dependent upon use) the heritage dies.‡ It is a measure of the desperateness of the situation that

---

* *Vide Basic English*, C. K. Ogden, and *Carl and Anna in Basic English* (Psyche Miniatures Series).

† *Middletown*, p. 268.

‡ 'From the beginning civilization has been dependent upon speech, for words are our chief link with the past and with one another and the channel of our spiritual inheritance. As the other vehicles of tradition, the family and the community, for example, are

intelligent people, when this is put to them, should be able to reply: 'Oh, but you can go on using *your* language: what does it matter what the rest of the world does?' So difficult can it be for really alert and unprejudiced minds today to understand what it is that is being discussed: things have gone so far already.

The prospects of culture, then, are very dark. There is the less room for hope in that a standardized civilization is rapidly enveloping the whole world. The glimpse of Russia that is permitted us does not afford the comfort that we are sometimes invited to find there. Anyone who has seen Eisenstein's film, *The General Line*, will appreciate the comment made by a writer in the *New Republic* (4 June 1930), comparing it with an American film:

One fancies, thinking about these things, that America might well send *The Silent Enemy* to Russia and say, 'This is what living too long with too much machinery does to people. Think twice, before you commit yourselves irrevocably to the same course.'

But it is vain to resist the triumph of the machine. It is equally vain to console us with the promise of a 'mass culture' that shall be utterly new. It would, no doubt, be possible to argue that such a 'mass culture' might be better than the culture we are losing, but it would be futile: the 'utterly new' surrenders everything that can interest us.*

What hope, then, is there left to offer? The vague hope that recovery *must* come, somehow, in spite of all? Mr I. A. Richards seems to authorize hope: he speaks of 'reasons for thinking that this century is in a cultural trough rather than upon a crest'; and says that 'the situation is likely to get worse before it is better.'† 'Once the basic level has been reached,' he suggests, 'a slow climb back may be possible. That at least is a hope that may be reasonably entertained.'‡ But it is a hope that looks very desperate in face of the downward acceleration described

---

dissolved, we are forced more and more to reply upon language.' – *Practical Criticism*, pp. 320–1.

* '... indeed, this gentleman, taking the bull by the horns, proposes that we should for the future call industrialism culture, and then of course there can be no longer any misapprehension of their true character; and besides the pleasure of being wealthy and comfortable, they will have authentic recognition as vessels of sweetness and light.' – *Culture and Anarchy*.

† *Practical Criticism*, p. 320.

‡ Ibid., p. 249.

above, and it does not seem to point to any factor that might be counted upon to reverse the process.

Are we then to listen to Spengler's* (and Mr Henry Ford's†) admonition to cease bothering about the inevitable future? That is impossible. Ridiculous, priggish and presumptuous as it may be, if we care at all about the issues we cannot help believing that, for the immediate future, at any rate, we have some responsibility. We cannot help clinging to some such hope as Mr Richards offers; to the belief (unwarranted, possibly) that what we value most matters too much to the race to be finally abandoned, and that the machine will yet be made a tool.

It is for us to be as aware as possible of what is happening, and, if we can, to 'keep open our communications with the future'.

* 'Up to now everyone has been at liberty to hope what he pleased about the future. Where there are no facts, sentiment rules. But henceforward it will be every man's business to inform himself of what *can* happen and therefore of what with the unalterable necessity of destiny and irrespective of personal ideals, hopes or desires, *will* happen.' – *The Decline of the West*, Vol. I, p. 39.

† 'But what of the future? Shall we not have over-production? Shall we not some day reach a point where the machine becomes all powerful, and the man of no consequence?

'No man can say anything of the future. We need not bother about it. The future has always cared for itself in spite of our well-meant efforts to hamper it. If today we do the task we can best do, then we are doing all that we can do.

'Perhaps we may over-produce, but that is impossible until the whole world has all its desires. And if that should happen, then surely we ought to be content.' – Henry Ford, *To-day and To-morrow*, pp. 272–3.

EUDORA WELTY

The Little Store

Eudora Welty was born in Jackson, Mississippi in 1909 and most of her writing is rooted in the region of her birth. During the 1930s Welty travelled throughout the South for the Works Progress Administration, working as a photographer, and it was not until the 1940s that she made her mark as a short-story writer. She also wrote novels, including The Robber Bridegroom *(1942),* The Ponder Heart *(1954) and* The Optimist's Daughter *(1972), for which she won a Pulitzer Prize. In 1984 her autobiographical memoir,* One Writer's Beginnings, *was a surprise bestseller in the United States. Welty's essays are collected in* The Eye of the Story *(1987), a volume which includes 'The Little Store'—an essay first published in 1975.*

Two blocks away from the Mississippi State Capitol, and on the same street with it, where our house was when I was a child growing up in Jackson, it was possible to have a little pasture behind your backyard where you could keep a Jersey cow, which we did. My mother herself milked her. A thrifty homemaker, wife, mother of three, she also did all her own cooking. And as far as I can recall, she never set foot inside a grocery store. It wasn't necessary.

For her regular needs, she stood at the telephone in our front hall and consulted with Mr Lemly, of Lemly's Market and Grocery downtown, who took her order and sent it out on his next delivery. And since Jackson at the heart of it was still within very near reach of the open country, the blackberry lady clanged on her bucket with a quart measure at your front door in June without fail, the watermelon man rolled up to your house exactly on time for the Fourth of July, and down through the summer, the quiet of the early-morning streets was pierced by the calls of farmers driving in with their plenty. One brought his with a song, so plaintive we would sing it with him:

> Milk, milk,
> Buttermilk,
> Snap beans – butterbeans –
> Tender okra – fresh greens . . .
> And buttermilk.

My mother considered herself pretty well prepared in her kitchen and pantry for any emergency that, in her words, might choose to present itself. But if she should, all of a sudden, need another lemon or find she was out of bread, all she had to do was call out, 'Quick! Who'd like to run to the Little Store for me?'

I would.

She'd count out the change into my hand, and I was away. I'll bet the nickel that would be left over that all over the country, for those of my day, the neighbourhood grocery played a similar part in our growing up.

Our store had its name – it was that of the grocer who owned it, whom I'll call Mr Sessions – but 'the Little Store' is what we called it at home. It was a block down our street toward the capitol and half a block further, around the corner, toward the cemetery. I knew even the sidewalk to it as well as I knew my own skin. I'd skipped my jumping-rope up and down it, hopped its length through mazes of hopscotch, played jacks in its islands of shade, serpentined along it on my Princess bicycle, skated it backward and forward. In the twilight I had dragged my steamboat by its string (this was homemade out of every new shoebox, with candle in the bottom lighted and shining through colored tissue paper pasted over windows scissored out in the shapes of the sun, moon and stars) across every crack of the walk without letting it bump or catch fire. I'd 'played out' on that street after supper with my brothers and friends as long as 'first-dark' lasted; I'd caught its lightning bugs. On the first Armistice Day (and this will set the time I'm speaking of) we made our own parade down that walk on a single velocipede – my brother pedaling, our little brother riding the handlebars, and myself standing on the back, all with arms wide, flying flags in each hand. (My father snapped that picture as we raced by. It came out blurred.)

As I set forth for the Little Store, a tune would float toward me from the house where there lived three sisters, girls in their teens, who ratted their hair over their ears, wore headbands like gladiators, and were considered to be very popular. They practiced for this in the daytime; they'd wind up the Victrola, leave the same record on they'd played before, and you'd see them bobbing past their dining-room windows while they danced with each other. Being three, they could go all day, cutting in:

> Everybody ought to know-oh
> How to do the Tickle-Toe
> (how to do the Tickle-Toe) –

they sang it and danced to it, and as I went by to the same song, I believed it.

A little further on, across the street, was the house where the principal of our grade school lived – lived on, even while we were having vacation. What if she would come out? She would halt me in my tracks – she had a very carrying and well-known voice in Jackson, where she'd taught almost everybody – saying, 'Eudora Alice Welty, spell OBLIGE.' OBLIGE was the word that she of course knew had kept me from making 100 on my spelling exam. She'd make me miss it again now, by boring her eyes through me from across the street. This was my vacation fantasy, one good way to scare myself on the way to the store.

Down near the corner waited the house of a little boy named Lindsey. The sidewalk here was old brick, which the roots of a giant chinaberry tree had humped up and tilted this way and that. On skates, you took it fast, in a series of skittering hops, trying not to touch ground anywhere. If the chinaberries had fallen and rolled in the cracks, it was like skating through a whole shooting match of marbles. I crossed my fingers that Lindsey wouldn't be looking.

During the big flu epidemic he and I, as it happened, were being nursed through our sieges at the same time. I'd hear my father and mother murmuring to each other, at the end of a long day, 'And I wonder how poor little *Lindsey* got along today?' Just as, down the street, he no doubt would have to hear his family saying, 'And I wonder how is poor *Eudora* by now?' I got the idea that a choice was going to be made soon between poor little Lindsey and poor Eudora, and I came up with a funny poem. I wasn't prepared for it when my father told me it wasn't funny and my mother cried that if I couldn't be ashamed for myself, she'd have to be ashamed for me:

> There was a little boy and his name was Lindsey.
> He went to heaven with the influinzy.

He didn't, he survived it, poem and all, the same as I did. But his chinaberries could have brought me down in my skates in a flying act of contrition before his eyes, looking pretty funny myself, right in front of his house.

Setting out in this world, a child feels so indelible. He only comes to find out later that it's all the others along his way who are making themselves indelible to him.

Our Little Store rose right up from the sidewalk; standing in a street of family houses, it alone hadn't any yard in front, any tree or flowerbed. It was a plain frame building covered over with brick. Above the door, a little railed porch ran across on an upstairs level and four windows with shades were looking out. But I didn't catch on to those.

Running in out of the sun, you met what seemed total obscurity inside. There were almost tangible smells – licorice recently sucked in a child's cheek, dill-pickle brine that had leaked through a paper sack in a fresh trail across the wooden floor, ammonia-loaded ice that had been hoisted from wet croker sacks and slammed into the icebox with its sweet butter at the door, and perhaps the smell of still-untrapped mice.

Then through the motes of cracker dust, cornmeal dust, the Gold Dust of the Gold Dust Twins that the floor had been swept out with, the realities emerged. Shelves climbed to high reach all the way around, set out with not too much of any one thing but a lot of things – lard, molasses, vinegar, starch, matches, kerosene, Octagon soap (about a year's worth of octagon-shaped coupons cut out and saved brought a signet ring addressed to you in the mail. Furthermore, when the postman arrived at your door, he blew a whistle). It was up to you to remember what you came for, while your eye traveled from cans of sardines to ice cream salt to harmonicas to fly paper (over your head, batting around on a thread beneath the blades of the ceiling fan, stuck with its testimonial catch).

Its confusion may have been in the eye of its beholder. Enchantment is cast upon you by all those things you weren't supposed to have need for, it lures you close to wooden tops you'd outgrown, boy's marbles and agates in little net pouches, small rubber balls that wouldn't bounce straight, frazzly kitestring, clay bubble-pipes that would snap off in your teeth, the stiffest scissors. You could contemplate those long narrow boxes of sparklers gathering dust while you waited for it to be the Fourth of July or Christmas, and noisemakers in the shape of tin frogs for somebody's birthday party you hadn't been invited to yet, and see that they were all marvelous.

You might not have even looked for Mr Sessions when he came around his store cheese (as big as a doll's house) and in front of the counter looking for you. When you'd finally asked him for, and received from him in its paper bag, whatever single thing it was that you had been sent for, the nickel that was left over was yours to spend.

Down at a child's eye level, inside those glass jars with mouths in their sides through which the grocer could run his scoop or a child's hand might be invited to reach for a choice, were wineballs, all-day suckers, gumdrops, peppermints. Making a row under the glass of a counter were the Tootsie Rolls, Hershey Bars, Goo-Goo Clusters, Baby Ruths. And whatever was the name of those pastilles that came stacked in a cardboard cylinder with a cardboard lid? They were thin and dry, about the size of tiddlywinks, and in the shape of twisted rosettes. A kind of chocolate dust came out with them when you shook them out in your hand. Were they chocolate? I'd say rather they were brown. They didn't taste of anything at all, unless it was wood. Their attraction was the number you got for a nickel.

Making up your mind, you circled the store around and around, around the pickle barrel, around the tower of Cracker Jack boxes; Mr Sessions had built it for us himself on top of a packing case, like a house of cards.

If it seemed too hot for Cracker Jacks, I might get a cold drink. Mr Sessions might have already stationed himself by the cold-drinks barrel, like a mind reader. Deep in ice water that looked black as ink, murky shapes that would come up as Coca-Colas, Orange Crushes, and various flavors of pop, were all swimming around together. When you gave the word, Mr Sessions plunged his bare arm in to the elbow and fished out your choice, first try. I favored a locally bottled concoction called Lake's Celery. (What else could it be called? It was made by a Mr Lake out of celery. It was a popular drink here for years but was not known universally, as I found out when I arrived in New York and ordered one in the Astor bar.) You drank on the premises, with feet set wide apart to miss the drip, and gave him back his bottle.

But he didn't hurry you off. A standing scales was by the door, with a stack of iron weights and a brass slide on the balance arm, that would weigh you up to three hundred pounds. Mr Sessions, whose hands were gentle and smelled of carbolic, would lift you up and set your feet on the platform, hold your loaf of bread for you, and taking his time while — you stood still for him, he would make certain of what you weighed today. He could even remember what you weighed the last time, so you could subtract and announce how much you'd gained. That was goodbye.

Is there always a hard way to go home? From the Little Store, you could go partway through the sewer. If your brothers had called you a scarecat, then across the next street beyond the Little Store, it was possible to enter this sewer by passing through a privet hedge, climbing down into the bed of a creek, and going into its mouth on your knees. The sewer – it might have been no more than a 'storm sewer' – came out and emptied here, where Town Creek, a sandy, most often shallow little stream that ambled through Jackson on its way to the Pearl River, ran along the edge of the cemetery. You could go in darkness through this tunnel to where you next saw light (if you ever did) and climb out through the culvert at your own street corner.

I was a scarecat, all right, but I was a reader with my own refuge in storybooks. Making my way under the sidewalk, under the street and the streetcar track, under the Little Store, down there in the wet dark by myself, I could be Persephone entering into my six-month sojourn underground – though I didn't suppose Persephone had to crawl, hanging onto a loaf of bread, and come out through the teeth of an iron grating. Mother Ceres would indeed be wondering where she could find me, and mad when she knew. 'Now am I going to have to start marching to the Little Store for *myself*?'

I couldn't picture it. Indeed, I'm unable today to picture the Little Store with a grown person in it, except for Mr Sessions and the lady who helped him, who belonged there. We children thought it was ours. The happiness of errands was in part that of running for the moment away from home, a free spirit. I believed the Little Store to be a center of the outside world, and hence of happiness – as I believed what I found in the Cracker Jack box to be a genuine prize, which was as simply as I believed in the Golden Fleece.

But a day came when I ran to the store to discover, sitting on the front step, a grown person, after all – more than a grown person. It was the Monkey Man, together with his monkey. His grinding-organ was lowered to the step beside him. In my whole life so far, I must have laid eyes on the Monkey Man no more than five or six times. An itinerant of rare and wayward appearances, he was not punctual like the Gipsies, who every year with the first cool days of fall showed up in the aisles of Woolworth's. You never knew when the Monkey Man might decide to favor Jackson, or which way he'd go. Sometimes you heard him as close as the next street, and then he didn't come up yours.

But now I saw the Monkey Man at the Little Store, where I'd never seen him before. I'd never seen him sitting down. Low on that familiar doorstep, he was not the same any longer, and neither was his monkey. They looked just like an old man and an old friend of his that wore a fez, meeting quietly together, tired, and resting with their eyes fixed on some place far away, and not the same place. Yet their romance for me didn't have it in its power to waver. I wavered. I simply didn't know how to step around them, to proceed on into the Little Store for my mother's emergency as if nothing had happened. If I could have gone in there after it, whatever it was, I would have given it to them – putting it into the monkey's cool little fingers. I would have given them the Little Store itself.

In my memory they are still attached to the store – so are all the others. Everyone I saw on my way seemed to me then part of my errand, and in a way they were. As I myself, the free spirit, was part of it too.

All the years we lived in that house where we children were born, the same people lived in the other houses on our street too. People changed through the arithmetic of birth, marriage and death, but not by going away. So families just accrued stories, which through the fullness of time, in those times, their own lives made. And I grew up in those.

But I didn't know there'd ever been a story at the Little Store, one that was going on while I was there. Of course, all the time the Sessions family had been living right overhead there, in the upstairs rooms behind the little railed porch and the shaded windows; but I think we children never thought of that. Did I fail to see them as a family because they weren't living in an ordinary house? Because I so seldom saw them close together, or having anything to say to each other? She sat in the back of the store, her pencil over a ledger, while he stood and waited on children to make up their minds. They worked in twin black eye-shades, held on their gray heads by elastic bands. It may be harder to recognize kindness – or unkindness, either – in a face whose eyes are in shadow. His face underneath his shade was as round as the little wooden wheels in the Tinker Toy box. So was her face. I didn't know, perhaps didn't even wonder: were they husband and wife or brother and sister? Were they father and mother? There were a few other persons, of various ages, wandering singly in by the back door and out. But none of their relationships could I imagine, when I'd never seen them sitting down together around their own table.

The possibility that they had any other life at all, anything beyond what we could see within the four walls of the Little Store, occurred to me only when tragedy struck their family. There was some act of violence. The shock to the neighborhood traveled to the children, of course; but I couldn't find out from my parents what had happened. They held it back from me, as they'd already held back many things, 'until the time comes for you to know.'

You could find out some of these things by looking in the unabridged dictionary and the encyclopedia – kept to hand in our dining room – but you couldn't find out there what had happened to the family who for all the years of your life had lived upstairs over the Little Store, who had never been anything but patient and kind to you, who never once had sent you away. All I ever knew was its aftermath: they were the only people ever known to me who simply vanished. At the point where their life overlapped into ours, the story broke off.

We weren't being sent to the neighbourhood grocery for facts of life, or death. But of course those are what we were on the track of, anyway. With the loaf of bread and the Cracker Jack prize, I was bringing home the intimations of pride and disgrace, and rumors and early news of people coming to hurt one another, while others practiced for joy – storing up a portion for myself of the human mystery.

GRAHAM GREENE

The Lost Childhood

Graham Greene was born in 1904, and died in 1991. In addition to the novels for which he is best known, Greene wrote extensively in other fields: film criticism, plays, screenplays, travelogues and autobiography. 'The Lost Childhood' is a literary reminiscence which first appeared in The Lost Childhood and Other Essays *in 1951. Almost fifty years later, the essay can now be read alongside the various biographies of Greene that have come out since his death. We learn from these that Greene, as a schoolboy, tried to kill himself and that in 1920 he reputedly became 'one of the first schoolboys in England to be psycho-analysed'.*

Perhaps it is only in childhood that books have any deep influence on our lives. In later life we admire, we are entertained, we may modify some views we already hold, but we are more likely to find in books merely a confirmation of what is in our mind already: as in a love affair it is our own features that we see reflected flatteringly back.

But in childhood all books are books of divination, telling us about the future, and like the fortune-teller who sees a long journey in the cards or death by water they influence the future. I suppose that is why books excited us so much. What do we ever get nowadays from reading to equal the excitement and the revelation in those first fourteen years? Of course I should be interested to hear that a new novel by Mr E. M. Forster was going to appear this spring, but I could never compare that mild expectation of civilized pleasure with the missed heartbeat, the appalled glee I felt when I found on a library shelf a novel by Rider Haggard, Percy Westerman, Captain Brereton or Stanley Weyman which I had not read before. It is in those early years that I would look for the crisis, the moment when life took a new slant in its journey towards death.

I remember distinctly the suddenness with which a key turned in a lock and I found I could read – not just the sentences in a reading book with the syllables coupled like railway carriages, but a real book. It was paper-covered with the picture of a boy, bound and gagged, dangling at the end of a rope inside a well with the water rising above his waist – an adventure of Dixon Brett, detective. All a long summer holiday I kept my secret, as I believed: I did not want anybody to know that I could read. I suppose I half consciously realized even then that this was the dangerous moment. I was safe so long as I could not read – the wheels had not begun to turn, but now the future stood around on bookshelves everywhere waiting for the child to choose – the life of a chartered accountant perhaps, a colonial civil servant, a planter in China, a steady job in a bank, happiness and misery, eventually one particular form of death, for surely we choose our death much as we choose our job. It grows out of our acts and our evasions, out of our fears and out of our moments of courage. I suppose my mother must have discovered my secret, for on the journey home I was presented for the train with another real book, a copy of Ballantyne's *Coral Island* with only a single picture to look at, a coloured frontispiece. But I would admit nothing. All the long journey I stared at the one picture and never opened the book.

But there on the shelves at home (so many shelves for we were a large family) the books waited – one book in particular, but before I reach that one down let me take a few others at random from the shelf. Each was a crystal in which the child dreamed that he saw life moving. Here in a cover stamped dramatically in several colours was Captain Gilson's *The Pirate Aeroplane*. I must have read that book six times at least – the story of a lost civilization in the Sahara and of a villainous Yankee pirate with an aeroplane like a box kite and bombs the size of tennis balls who held the golden city to ransom. It was saved by the hero, a young subaltern who crept up to the pirate camp to put the aeroplane out of action. He was captured and watched his enemies dig his grave. He was to be shot at dawn, and to pass the time and keep his mind from uncomfortable thoughts the amiable Yankee pirate played cards with him – the mild nursery game of Kuhn Kan. The memory of that nocturnal game on the edge of life haunted me for years, until I set it to rest at last in one of my own novels with a game of poker played in remotely similar circumstances.

And here is *Sophy of Kravonia* by Anthony Hope – the story of a kitchen-maid who became a queen. One of the first films I ever saw, about 1911, was made from that book, and I can hear still the rumble of the Queen's guns crossing the high Kravonian pass beaten hollowly out on a single piano. Then there was Stanley Weyman's *The Story of Francis Cludde*, and above all other books at that time of my life *King Solomon's Mines*.

This book did not perhaps provide the crisis, but it certainly influenced the future. If it had not been for that romantic tale of Allan Quatermain, Sir Henry Curtis, Captain Good, and, above all, the ancient witch Gagool, would I at nineteen have studied the appointments list of the Colonial Office and very nearly picked on the Nigerian Navy for a career? And later, when surely I ought to have known better, the odd African fixation remained. In 1935 I found myself sick with fever on a camp bed in a Liberian native's hut with a candle going out in an empty whisky bottle and a rat moving in the shadows. Wasn't it the incurable fascination of Gagool with her bare yellow skull, the wrinkled scalp that moved and contracted like the hood of a cobra, that led me to work all through 1942 in a little stuffy office in Freetown, Sierra Leone? There is not much in common between the land of the Kukuanas, behind the desert and the mountain range of Sheba's Breast, and a tin-roofed house on a bit of swamp where the vultures moved like domestic turkeys and the pi-dogs kept me awake on moonlit nights with their wailing, and the white women yellowed by atebrin drove by to the club; but the two belonged at any rate to the same continent, and, however distantly, to the same region of the imagination – the region of uncertainty, of not knowing the way about. Once I came a little nearer to Gagool and her witch-hunters, one night in Zigita on the Liberian side of the French Guinea border, when my servants sat in their shuttered hut with their hands over their eyes and someone beat a drum and a whole town stayed behind closed doors while the big bush devil – whom it would mean blindness to see – moved between the huts.

But *King Solomon's Mines* could not finally satisfy. It was not the right answer. The key did not quite fit. Gagool I could recognize – didn't she wait for me in dreams every night, in the passage by the linen cupboard, near the nursery door? and she continues to wait, when the mind is sick or tired, though now she is dressed in the theological garments of Despair and speaks in Spenser's accents:

The longer life, I wote the greater sin,
The greater sin, the greater punishment.

Gagool has remained a permanent part of the imagination, but Quatermain and Curtis – weren't they, even when I was only ten years old, a little too good to be true? They were men of such unyielding integrity (they would only admit to a fault in order to show how it might be overcome) that the wavering personality of a child could not rest for long against those monumental shoulders. A child, after all, knows most of the game – it is only an attitude to it that he lacks. He is quite well aware of cowardice, shame, deception, disappointment. Sir Henry Curtis perched upon a rock bleeding from a dozen wounds but fighting on with the remnant of the Greys against the hordes of Twala was too heroic. These men were like Platonic ideas: they were not life as one had already begun to know it.

But when – perhaps I was fourteen by that time – I took Miss Marjorie Bowen's *The Viper of Milan* from the library shelf, the future for better or worse really struck. From that moment I began to write. All the other possible futures slid away: the potential civil servant, the don, the clerk had to look for other incarnations. Imitation after imitation of Miss Bowen's magnificent novel went into exercise-books – stories of sixteenth-century Italy or twelfth-century England marked with enormous brutality and a despairing romanticism. It was as if I had been supplied once and for all with a subject.

Why? On the surface *The Viper of Milan* is only the story of a war between Gian Galeazzo Visconti, Duke of Milan, and Mastino della Scala, Duke of Verona, told with zest and cunning and an amazing pictorial sense. Why did it creep in and colour and explain the terrible living world of the stone stairs and the never quiet dormitory? It was no good in that real world to dream that one would ever be a Sir Henry Curtis, but della Scala, who at last turned from an honesty that never paid and betrayed his friends and died dishonoured and a failure even at treachery – it was easier for a child to escape behind his mask. As for Visconti, with his beauty, his patience, and his genius for evil, I had watched him pass by many a time in his black Sunday suit smelling of mothballs. His name was Carter. He exercised terror from a distance like a snowcloud over the young fields. Goodness has only once found a perfect incarnation in a human body and never will again, but evil can always find a home there. Human nature is not black and white but black and grey. I read all that in *The Viper of Milan* and I looked round and I saw that it was so.

There was another theme I found there. At the end of *The Viper of Milan* – you will remember if you have once read it – comes the great scene of complete success – della Scala is dead, Ferrara, Verona, Novara, Mantua have all fallen, the messengers pour in with news of fresh victories, the whole world outside is cracking up, and Visconti sits and jokes in the wine-light. I was not on the classical side or I would have discovered, I suppose, in Greek literature instead of in Miss Bowen's novel the sense of doom that lies over success – the feeling that the pendulum is about to swing. That too made sense; one looked around and saw the doomed everywhere – the champion runner who one day would sag over the tape; the head of the school who would atone, poor devil, during forty dreary undistinguished years; the scholar ... and when success began to touch oneself too, however mildly, one could only pray that failure would not be held off for too long.

One had lived for fourteen years in a wild jungle country without a map, but now the paths had been traced and naturally one had to follow them. But I think it was Miss Bowen's apparent zest that made me want to write. One could not read her without believing that to write was to live and to enjoy, and before one had discovered one's mistake it was too late – the first book one does enjoy. Anyway she had given me my pattern – religion might later explain it to me in other terms, but the pattern was already there – perfect evil walking the world where perfect good can never walk again, and only the pendulum ensures that after all in the end justice is done. Man is never satisfied, and often I have wished that my hand had not moved further than *King Solomon's Mines*, and that the future I had taken down from the nursery shelf had been a district office in Sierra Leone and twelve tours of malarial duty and a finishing dose of blackwater fever when the danger of retirement approached. What is the good of wishing? The books are always there, the moment of crisis waits, and now our children in their turn are taking down the future and opening the pages. In his poem 'Germinal' A. E. wrote:

In ancient shadows and twilights
Where childhood had strayed,
The world's great sorrows were born
And its heroes were made.
In the lost boyhood of Judas
Christ was betrayed.

PAUL FUSSELL

My War

Paul Fussell (1924–) is a Californian literary academic who, early on in his university career, wrote distinguished books on Samuel Johnson and on poetic metre. At the age of 19, though, Fussell had been called up for military service. He became an infantry lieutenant and in 1945 he was severely wounded. This war experience was to mark his later writing: most impressively, perhaps, in The Great War and Modern Memory *(1975) and* Wartime *(1989). His essay 'My War' appears in* The Boy Scout Handbook *(1982).*

My war is virtually synonymous with my life. I entered the war when I was nineteen, and I have been in it ever since. Melville's Ishmael says that a whale-ship was his Yale College and his Harvard. An infantry division was mine, the 103rd, whose dispirited personnel wore a colorful green and yellow cactus on their left shoulders. These hillbillies and Okies, drop-outs and used-car salesmen and petty criminals were my teachers and friends.

How did an upper-middle-class young gentleman find himself in so unseemly a place? Why wasn't he in the Navy, at least, or in the OSS or Air Corps administration or editing the *Stars and Stripes* or being a general's aide? The answer is comic: at the age of twenty I found myself leading forty riflemen over the Vosges Mountains and watching them torn apart by German artillery and machine-guns because when I was sixteen, in junior college, I was fat and flabby, with feminine tits and a big behind. For years the thing I'd hated most about school was gym, for there I was obliged to strip and shower communally. Thus I chose to join the ROTC (infantry, as it happened) because that was a way to get out of gym, which meant you never had to take off your clothes and invite – indeed, compel – ridicule. You rationalized by noting that this was 1939 and that a little 'military training' might not, in the long run, be wasted. Besides, if you worked up to be a cadet officer, you got to wear a Sam Browne belt, from which depended a nifty saber.

When I went on to college, it was natural to continue my technique for not exposing my naked person, and luckily my college had an infantry ROTC unit, where I was welcomed as something of an experienced hand. This was in 1941. When the war began for the United States, college students were solicited by various 'programs' of the navy and marine corps and coast guard with plans for transforming them into officers. But people enrolled in the ROTC unit were felt to have committed themselves already. They had opted for the infantry, most of them all unaware, and that's where they were going to stay. Thus while shrewder friends were enrolling in Navy V-1 or signing up for the pacific exercises of the Naval Japanese Language Program or the Air Corps Meteorological Program, I signed up for the Infantry Enlisted Reserve Corps, an act guaranteeing me one extra semester in college before I was called. After basic training, advancement to officer training was promised, and that seemed a desirable thing, even if the crossed rifles on the collar did seem to betoken some hard physical exertion and discomfort – marching, sleeping outdoors, that sort of thing. But it would help 'build you up', and besides officers, even in the Infantry, got to wear those wonderful pink trousers and receive constant salutes.

It was such imagery of future grandeur that in spring 1943 sustained me through eighteen weeks of basic training in 100-degree heat at dreary Camp Roberts, California, where to toughen us, it was said, water was forbidden from 8 am to 5 pm ('water discipline', this was called). Within a few weeks I'd lost all my flab and with it the whole ironic 'reason' I found myself there at all. It was abundantly clear already that 'infantry' had been a big mistake: it was not just stupid and boring and bloody, it was athletic, and thus not at all for me. But supported by vanity and pride I somehow managed to march thirty-five miles and tumble through the obstacle course, and a few months later I found myself at the Infantry School, Fort Benning, Georgia, where, training to become an officer, I went through virtually the same thing over again. As a Second Lieutenant of Infantry I 'graduated' in the spring of 1944 and was assigned to the 103rd Division at Camp Howze, Texas, the local equivalent of Camp Roberts, only worse: Roberts had white-painted two-storey clapboard barracks, Howze one-storey tar-paper shacks. But the heat was the same, and the boredom, and the local whore-culture, and the hillbilly songs:

> Who's that gal with the red dress on?
> Some folks call her Dinah.
> She stole my heart away,
> Down in Carolina.

The 103rd Division had never been overseas, and all the time I was putting my rifle platoon through its futile exercises we were being prepared for the invasion of southern France, which followed the landings in Normandy. Of course we didn't know this, and assumed from the training ('water discipline' again) that we were destined for the South Pacific. There were some exercises involving towed gliders that seemed to portend nothing at all but self-immolation, we were so inept with these devices. In October 1944 we were all conveyed by troop transports to Marseilles.

It was my first experience of abroad, and my life-long affair with France dates from the moment I first experienced such un-American phenomena as: formal manners and a respect for the language; a well-founded skepticism; the pollarded plane trees on the Avenue R. Schuman; the red wine and real bread; the *pissoirs* in the streets; the international traffic signs and the visual public language hinting a special French understanding of things: *Hôtel de Ville, Défense d'afficher*; the smell of aromatic tobacco when one has been brought up on Virginia and Burley. An intimation of what we might be opposing was supplied by the aluminum Vichy coinage. On one side, the fasces and *Etat Français*. No more Republic. On the other, *Liberté, Egalité, Fraternité* replaced by *Travail* (as in *Arbeit Macht Frei*), *Famille*, and *Patrie* (as in *Vaterland*). But before we had time to contemplate all this, we were moving rapidly northeast. After a truck ride up the Rhône Valley, still pleasant with girls and flowers and wine, our civilized period came to an abrupt end. On the night of November 11 (nice irony there) we were introduced into the line at Saint-Dié, in Alsace.

We were in 'combat'. I find the word embarrassing, carrying as it does false chivalric overtones (as in 'single combat'). But synonyms are worse: *fighting* is not accurate, because much of the time you are being shelled, which is not fighting but suffering; *battle* is too high and remote; *in action* is a euphemism suited more to dire telegrams than description.

'Combat' will have to do, and my first hours of it I recall daily, even now. They fueled, and they still fuel, my view of things.

Everyone knows that a night relief is among the most difficult of infantry maneuvers. But we didn't know it, and in our innocence we expected it to go according to plan. We and the company we were replacing were cleverly and severely shelled: it was as if the Germans a few hundred feet away could see us in the dark and through the thick pine growth. When the shelling finally stopped, at about midnight, we realized that, although near the place we were supposed to be, until daylight we would remain hopelessly lost. The order came down to stop where we were, lie down among the trees, and get some sleep. We would finish the relief at first light. Scattered over several hundred yards, the two hundred and fifty of us in F Company lay down in a darkness so thick we could see nothing at all. Despite the terror of our first shelling (and several people had been hit), we slept as soundly as babes. At dawn I awoke, and what I saw all around were numerous objects I'd miraculously not tripped over in the dark. These objects were dozens of dead German boys in greenish-gray uniforms, killed a day or two before by the company we were relieving. If darkness had hidden them from us, dawn disclosed them with open eyes and greenish-white faces like marble, still clutching their rifles and machine-pistols in their seventeen-year-old hands, fixed where they had fallen. (For the first time I understood the German phrase for the war-dead: *die Gefallenen*.) Michelangelo could have made something beautiful out of these forms, in the *Dying Gaul* tradition, and I was startled to find that in a way I couldn't understand, at first they struck me as beautiful. But after a moment, no feeling but shock and horror. My adolescent illusions, largely intact to that moment, fell away all at once, and I suddenly knew I was not and never would be in a world that was reasonable or just. The scene was less apocalyptic than shabbily ironic: it sorted so ill with modern popular assumptions about the idea of progress and attendant improvements in public health, social welfare, and social justice. To transform guiltless boys into cold marble after passing them through unbearable fear and humiliation and pain and contempt seemed to do them an interesting injustice. I decided to ponder these things. In 1917, shocked by the Battle of the Somme and recovering from neurasthenia, Wilfred Owen was reading a life of Tennyson. He wrote his mother: 'Tennyson, it seems, was always a great child. So should I have been but for Beaumont Hamel.' So should I have been but for Saint-Dié.

After that, one day was much like another: attack at dawn, run and fall and crawl and sweat and worry and shoot and be shot at and cower from mortar shells, always keeping up a jaunty carriage in front of one's platoon; and at night, 'consolidate' the objective, usually another hill, sometimes a small town, and plan the attack for the next morning. Before we knew it we'd lost half the company, and we all realized then that for us there would be no way out until the war ended but sickness, wounds, or oblivion. And the war would end only as we pressed our painful daily advance. Getting it over was our sole motive. Yes, we knew about the Jews. But our skins seemed to us more valuable at the time.

The word for the German defense all along was clever, a word that never could have been applied to our procedures. It was my first experience, to be repeated many times in later years, of the cunning ways of Europe versus the blunter ways of the New World. Although manned largely by tired thirty-year-old veterans (but sharp enough to have got out of Normandy alive), old men, and crazy youths, the German infantry was officered superbly, and their defense, which we experienced for many months, was disciplined and orderly. My people would have run, or at least 'snaked off'. But the Germans didn't, until the very end. Their uniforms were a scandal – rags and beat-up boots and unauthorized articles – but somehow they held together. Nazis or not, they did themselves credit. Lacking our lavish means, they compensated by patience and shrewdness. Not until well after the war did I discover that many times when they unaccountably located us hidden in deep woods and shelled us accurately, they had done so by inferring electronically the precise positions of the radios over which we innocently conversed.

As the war went on, the destruction of people became its sole means. I felt sorry for the Germans I saw killed in quantity everywhere – along the roads, in cellars, on roof-tops – for many reasons. They were losing, for one thing, and their deaths meant nothing, though they had been persuaded that resistance might 'win the war'. And they were so pitifully dressed and accoutered: that was touching. Boys with raggedy ad hoc uniforms and *Panzerfausts* and too few comrades. What were they doing? They were killing themselves; and for me, who couldn't imagine being killed, for people my age voluntarily to get themselves killed caused my mouth to drop open.

Irony describes the emotion, whatever it is, occasioned by perceiving some great gulf, half-comic, half-tragic, between what one expects and what one finds. It's not quite 'disillusion', but it's adjacent to it. My experience in the war was ironic because my innocence before had prepared me to encounter in it something like the same reasonableness that governed prewar life. This, after all, was the tone dominating the American relation to the war: talk of 'the future', allotments and bond purchases carefully sent home, hopeful fantasies of 'the postwar world'. I assumed, in short, that everyone would behave according to the clear advantages offered by reason. I had assumed that in war, like chess, when you were beaten you 'resigned', that when outnumbered and outgunned you retreated; that when you were surrounded you surrendered. I found out differently, and with a vengeance. What I found was people obeying fatuous and murderous 'orders' for no reason I could understand, killing themselves because someone 'told them to', prolonging the war when it was hopelessly lost because – because it was unreasonable to do so. It was my introduction to the shakiness of civilization. It was my first experience of the profoundly irrational element, and it made ridiculous all talk of plans and preparations for the future and goodwill and intelligent arrangements. Why did the red-haired young German machine-gunner firing at us in the woods not go on living – marrying, going to university, going to the beach, laughing, smiling – but keep firing long after he had made his point, and require us to kill him with a grenade?

Before we knew it it was winter, and the winter in 1944–45 was the coldest in Europe for twenty-five years. For the ground troops conditions were unspeakable, and even the official history admits the disaster, imputing the failure to provide adequate winter clothing – analogous to the similar German oversight when the Russian winter of 1941/42 surprised the planners – to optimism, innocence, and 'confidence':

Confidence born of the rapid sweep across Europe in the summer of 1944 and the conviction on the part of many that the successes of Allied arms would be rewarded by victory before the onset of winter contributed to the unpreparedness for winter combat.

The result of thus ignoring the injunction 'Be Prepared' was 64,008 casualties from 'cold injury' – not wounds but pneumonia and trench-foot. The official history sums up: 'This constitutes more than four 15,000-man divisions. Approximately 90 per cent of cold casualties involved riflemen and there were about 4000 riflemen per infantry division. Thus closer to 13 divisions were critically disabled for combat.' We can appreciate those figures by recalling that the invasion of Normany was initially accomplished by only six divisions (nine if we add the airborne). Thus crucial were little things like decent mittens and gloves, fur-lined parkas, thermal underwear – all of which any normal peacetime hiker or skier would demand as protection against prolonged exposure. But 'the winter campaign in Europe was fought by most combat personnel in a uniform that did not give proper protection': we wore silly long overcoats, right out of the nineteenth century; thin field jackets, designed to convey an image of manliness at Fort Bragg; and dress wool trousers. We wore the same shirts and huddled under the same blankets as Pershing's troops in the expedition against Pancho Villa in 1916. Of the 64,008 who suffered 'cold injury' I was one. During February 1945 I was back in various hospitals for a month with pneumonia. I told my parents it was flu.

That month away from the line helped me survive for four weeks more but it broke the rhythm and, never badly scared before, when I returned to the line early in March I found for the first time that I was terrified, unwilling to take the chances which before had seemed rather sporting. My month of safety had renewed my interest in survival, and I was psychologically and morally ill-prepared to lead my platoon in the great Seventh Army attack of March 15 1945. But lead it I did, or rather push it, staying as far in the rear as was barely decent. And before the day was over I had been severely rebuked by a sharp-eyed lieutenant-colonel who threatened court martial if I didn't pull myself together. Before that day was over I was sprayed with the contents of a soldier's torso when I was lying behind him and he knelt to fire at a machine-gun holding us up: he was struck in the heart, and out of the holes in the back of his field jacket flew little clouds of tissue, blood, and powdered cloth. Near him another man raised himself to fire, but the machine-gun caught him in the mouth, and as he fell he looked back at me with surprise, blood and teeth dribbling out onto the leaves. He was one to whom early on I had given the Silver Star for heroism, and he didn't want to let me down.

As if in retribution for my cowardice, in the late afternoon, near Engwiller, Alsace, clearing a wood full of Germans cleverly dug in, my platoon was raked by shells from an 88, and I was hit in the back and leg by shell fragments. They felt like red-hot knives going in, but I was as interested in the few quiet moans, like those of a hurt child drifting off to sleep, of my thirty-seven-year-old platoon sergeant – we'd been together since Camp Howze – killed instantly by the same shell. We were lying together, and his immediate neighbor on the other side, a lieutenant in charge of a section of heavy machine-guns, was killed instantly too. And my platoon was virtually wiped away. I was in disgrace, I was hurt, I was clearly expendable – while I lay there the supply sergeant removed my issue wristwatch to pass on to my replacement – and I was twenty years old.

I bore up all right while being removed from 'the field' and passed back through the first-aid stations where I was known. I was deeply on morphine, and managed brave smiles as called for. But when I got to the evacuation hospital thirty miles behind the lines and was coming out from the anesthetic of my first operation, all my affectations of control collapsed, and I did what I'd wanted to do for months. I cried, noisily and publicly, and for hours. I was the scandal of the ward. There were lots of tears back there: in the operating room I saw a nurse dissolve in shoulder-shaking sobs when a boy died with great stertorous gasps on the operating table she was attending. That was the first time I'd seen anyone cry in the whole European Theater of Operations, and I must have cried because I felt that there, out of 'combat', tears were licensed. I was crying because I was ashamed and because I'd let my men be killed and because my sergeant had been killed and because I recognized as never before that he might have been me and that statistically if in no other way he was me, and that I had been killed too. But ironically I had saved my life by almost losing it, for my leg wound providentially became infected, and by the time it was healed and I was ready for duty again, the European war was over, and I journeyed back up through a silent Germany to re-join my reconstituted platoon 'occupying' a lovely Tyrolean valley near Innsbruck. For the infantry there was still the Japanese war to sweat out, and I was destined for it, despite the dramatic gash in my leg. But thank God the Bomb was dropped while I was on my way there, with the result that I can write this.

That day in mid-March that ended me was the worst of all for F Company. We knew it was going to be bad when it began at dawn, just like an episode from the First World War, with an hour-long artillery preparation and a smoke-screen for us to attack through. What got us going and carried us through was the conviction that, suffer as we might, we were at least 'making history'. But we didn't even do that. Liddell Hart's 766-page *History of the Second World War* never heard of us. It mentions neither March 15th nor the 103rd Infantry Division. The only satisfaction history has offered is the evidence that we caused Josef Goebbels some extra anxiety. The day after our attack he entered in his log under 'Military Situation':

In the West the enemy has now gone over to the attack in the sector between Saarbrücken and Hagenau in addition to the previous flashpoints . . . His objective is undoubtedly to drive in our front on the Saar and capture the entire region south of the Moselle and west of the Rhine.

And he goes on satisfyingly: 'Mail received testifies to a deep-seated lethargy throughout the German people degenerating almost into hopelessness. There is very sharp criticism of the . . . entire national leadership.' One reason: 'The Moselle front is giving way.' But a person my age I met thirty years later couldn't believe that there was still any infantry fighting in France in the spring of 1945 and, puzzled by my dedicating a book of mine to my dead platoon sergeant with the date March 15 1945, confessed that he couldn't figure out what had happened to him.

To become disillusioned you must earlier have been illusioned. Evidence of the illusions suffered by the youth I was is sadly available in the letters he sent, in unbelievable profusion, to his parents. They radiate a terrible naïveté, together with a pathetic disposition to be pleased in the face of boredom and, finally, horror. The young man had heard a lot about the importance of 'morale' and ceaselessly labored to sustain his own by sustaining his addressees'. Thus: 'We spent all of Saturday on motor maintenance,' he writes from Fort Benning; 'a very interesting subject.' At Benning he believes all he's told and fails to perceive that he's being prepared for one thing only, and that a nasty, hazardous job, whose performers on the line have a life expectancy of six weeks. He assures his parents: 'I can get all sorts of assignments from here: . . .

Battalion staff officer, mess officer, rifle platoon leader, weapons platoon leader, company executive officer, communications officer, motor officer, etc.' (Was it an instinct for protecting himself from a truth half-sensed that made him bury *rifle platoon leader* in the middle of this list?) Like a bright schoolboy, he is pleased when grown-ups tell him he's done well. 'I got a compliment on my clean rifle tonight. The lieutenant said, "Very good." I said, "Thank you, sir." ' His satisfaction in making Expert Rifleman is touching; it is 'the highest possible rating,' he announces. And although he is constantly jokey, always on the lookout for what he terms 'laffs', he seems to have no sense of humor:

We're having a very interesting week . . . , taking up the carbine, automatic rifle, rifle grenade, and the famous 'bazooka'. We had the bazooka today, and it was very enjoyable, although we could not fire it because of lack of ammunition.

He has the most impossible standards of military excellence, and he enlists his critical impulse in the service of optimistic self-deception. Appalled by the ineptitude of the 103rd Division in training, he writes home: 'As I told you last time, this is a very messed up division. It will never go overseas as a unit, and is now serving mainly as a replacement training center, disguised as a combat division.'

Because the image of himself actually leading troops through bullets and shellfire is secretly unthinkable, fatuous hope easily comes to his assistance. In August 1944, with his division preparing to ship abroad, he asserts that the Germans seem to be 'on their last legs'. Indeed, he reports, 'bets are being made . . . that the European war will be over in six weeks.' But October finds him on the transport heading for the incredible, and now he 'expects', he says, that 'this war will end some time in November or December,' adding, 'I feel very confident and safe.' After the epiphanies of the line in November and December, he still entertains hopes for an early end, for the Germans are rational people, and what rational people would persist in immolating themselves once it's clear that they've lost the war? 'This *can't* last much longer,' he finds.

The letters written during combat are full of requests for food packages from home, and interpretation of this obsession is not quite as simple as it seems. The C and K rations were tedious, to be sure, and as readers of *All Quiet on the Western Front* and *The Middle Parts of Fortune* know, soldiers of all times and places are fixated on food. But how explain this young man's requests for 'fantastic items' like gherkins, olives, candy-coated peanuts (the kind 'we used to get out of slot-machines at the beach'), cans of chili and tamales, cashew nuts, devilled ham, and fig pudding? The lust for a little swank is the explanation, I think, the need for some exotic counterweight to the uniformity, the dullness, the lack of point and distinction he sensed everywhere. These items also asserted an unbroken contact with home, and a home defined as the sort of place fertile not in corned-beef hash and meat-and-vegetable stew but gum drops and canned chicken. In short, an upper-middle-class venue.

Upper-middle-class too, I suspect, is the unimaginative cruelty of some of these letters, clear evidence of arrested emotional development. 'Period' anti-Semitic remarks are not infrequent, and they remain unrebuked by any of his addressees. His understanding of the American South (he's writing from Georgia) can be gauged from his remark, 'Everybody down here is illiterate.' In combat some of his bravado is a device necessary to his emotional survival, but some bespeaks a genuine insensitivity:

Feb. 1 1945

Dear Mother and Dad:

Today is the division's 84th consecutive day on line. The average is 90–100 days, although one division went 136 without being relieved . . .

This house we're staying in used to be the headquarters of a local German Motor Corps unit, and it's full of printed matter, uniforms, propaganda, and pictures of Der Führer. I am not collecting any souveniers [*sic*], although I have had ample opportunity to pick up helmets, flags, weapons, etc. The only thing I have kept is a Belgian pistol, which one German was carrying who was unfortunate enough to walk right into my platoon. That is the first one I had the job of shooting. I have kept the pistol as a souvenier of my first Kraut.

It is odd how hard one becomes after a little bit of this stuff, but it gets to be more like killing mad dogs than people . . .

Love to all,
Paul

The only comfort I can take today in contemplating these letters is the ease with which their author can be rationalized as a stranger. Even the handwriting is not now my own. There are constant shows of dutifulness to parents, and even grandparents, and mentions of church-going, surely anomalous in a leader of assault troops. Parental approval is indispensable: 'This week I was "Class A Agent Officer" for Co. F, paying a $6000 payroll without losing a cent! I felt very proud of myself!' And the complacency! The twittiness! From hospital, where for a time he's been in an enlisted men's ward: 'Sometimes I enjoy being with the men just as much as associating with the officers.' (*Associating* is good.) The letter-writer is more pretentious than literate ('Alright', 'thank's', 'curiousity'), and his taste is terrible. He is thrilled to read Bruce Barton's *The Man Nobody Knows* ('It presents Christ in a very human light'), Maugham's *The Summing Up*, and the short stories of Erskine Caldwell. Even his often-sketched fantasies of the postwar heaven are grimly conventional: he will get married (to whom?); he will buy a thirty-five-foot sloop and live on it; he will take a year of non-serious literary graduate study at Columbia; he will edit a magazine for yachtsmen. He seems unable to perceive what is happening, constantly telling his addressee what will please rather than what he feels. He was never more mistaken than when he assured his parents while recovering from his wounds, 'Please try not to worry, as no permanent damage has been done.'

But the shock of these wounds and the long period recovering from them seem to have matured him a tiny bit, and some of his last letters from the hospital suggest that one or two scales are beginning to fall from his eyes:

One of the most amazing things about this war is the way the bizarre and unnatural become the normal after a short time. Take this hospital and its atmosphere: after a long talk with him, an eighteen-year-old boy without legs seems like the *normal* eighteen-year-old. You might even be surprised if a boy of the same age should walk in on both his legs. He would seem the freak and the object of pity. It is easy to imagine, after seeing some of these men, that *all* young men are arriving on this planet with stumps instead of limbs.

The same holds true with life at the front. The same horrible unrealness that is so hard to describe . . . I think I'll have to write a book about all this some time.

But even here, he can't conclude without reverting to cliché and twirpy optimism:

Enough for this morning. I'm feeling well and I'm very comfortable, and the food is improving. We had chicken and ice cream yesterday!

He has not read Swift yet, but in the vision of the young men with their stumps there's perhaps a hint that he's going to. And indeed, when he enrolled in graduate school later, the first course he was attracted to was 'Swift and Pope'. And ever since he's been trying to understand satire, and even to experiment with it himself.

It was in the army that I discovered my calling. I hadn't known that I was a teacher, but I found I could explain things: the operation of flamethrowers, map-reading, small-arms firing, 'field sanitation'. I found I could 'lecture' and organize and make things clear. I could start at the beginning of a topic and lead an audience to the end. When the war was over, being trained for nothing useful, I naturally fell into the course which would require largely a mere continuation of this act. In becoming a college teacher of literature I was aware of lots of company: thousands of veterans swarmed to graduate schools to study literature, persuaded that poetry and prose could save the world, or at least help wash away some of the intellectual shame of the years we'd been through. From this generation came John Berryman and Randall Jarrell and Delmore Schwartz and Saul Bellow and Louis Simpson and Richard Wilbur and John Ciardi and William Meredith and all the others who, afire with the precepts of the New Criticism, embraced literature, and the teaching of it, as a quasi-religious obligation.

To this day I tend to think of all hierarchies, especially the academic one, as military. The undergraduate students, at the 'bottom', are the recruits and draftees, privates all. Teaching assistants and graduate students are the non-coms, with grades (only officers have 'ranks') varying according to seniority: a G-4 is more important than a G-1, etc. Instructors, where they still exist, are the Second and First Lieutenants, and together with the Assistant Professors (Captains) comprise the company-grade officers. When we move up to the tenured ranks, Associate Professors answer to field-grade officers, Majors and Colonels. Professors are Generals, beginning with Brigadier – that's a newly promoted one. Most are Major Generals, and upon retirement they will be advanced to Lieutenant-General ('Professor Emeritus'). The main academic administration is less like a higher authority in the same structure than an adjacent echelon, like a group of powerful congressmen, for example, or people from the Judge Advocate's or Inspector General's departments. The Board of Trustees, empowered to make professorial appointments and thus confer academic ranks and privileges, is the equivalent of the President of the United States, who signs commissions very like Letters of Academic Appointment: 'Reposing special trust and confidence in the . . . abilities of—, I do appoint him,' etc. It is not hard to see also that the military principle crudely registered in the axiom Rank Has Its Privileges operates in academic life, where there are plums to be plucked like frequent leaves of absence, single-occupant offices, light teaching loads, and convenient, all-weather parking spaces.

I think this generally unconscious way of conceiving of the academic hierarchy is common among people who went to graduate school immediately after the war, and who went on the GI Bill. Perhaps many were attracted to university teaching as a postwar profession because in part they felt they understood its mechanisms already. Thus their ambitiousness, their sense that if to be a First Lieutenant is fine, to work up to Lieutenant-General is wonderful. And I suspect that their conception of instruction is still, like mine, tinged with Army. I think all of us of that vintage feel uneasy with forms of teaching which don't recognize a clear hierarchy – team-teaching, for example, or even the seminar, which assumes the fiction that leader and participants possess roughly equal knowledge and authority. For students (that is, enlisted men) to prosecute a rebellion, as in the 1960s and early 70s, is tantamount to mutiny, an offense, as the Articles of War indicate, 'to be punished by death, or such other punishment as a court-martial shall direct'. I have never been an enthusiast for The Movement.

In addition to remaining rank-conscious, I persist in the army habit of exact personnel classification. For me, everyone still has an invisible 'spec number' indicating what his job is or what he's supposed to be doing. Thus a certain impatience with people of ambiguous identity, or worse, people who don't seem to do anything, like self-proclaimed novelists and poets who generate no apprehensible product. These seem to me the T-5s of the postwar world, mere Technicians Fifth Grade, parasites, drones, non-combatants.

Twenty years after the First World War Siegfried Sassoon reports that he was still having dreams about it, dreams less of terror than of obligation. He dreams that the War is still going on and I have got to return to the Front. I complain bitterly to myself because it hasn't stopped yet. I am worried because I can't find my active-service kit. I am worried because I have forgotten how to be an officer. I feel that I can't face it again, and sometimes I burst into tears and say, 'It's no good, I can't do it.' But I know that I can't escape going back, and search frantically for my lost equipment.

That's uniquely the dream of a junior officer. I had such dreams too, and mine persisted until about 1960, when I was thirty-six, past re-call age.

Those who actually fought on the line in the war, especially if they were wounded, constitute an in-group forever separate from those who did not. Praise or blame does not attach: rather, there is the accidental possession of a special empirical knowledge, a feeling of a mysterious shared ironic awareness manifesting itself in an instinctive skepticism about pretension, publicly enunciated truths, the vanities of learning, and the pomp of authority. Those who fought know a secret about themselves, and it's not very nice. As Frederic Manning said in 1929, remembering 1914–18: 'War is waged by men; not by beasts, or by gods. It is a peculiarly human activity. To call it a crime against mankind is to miss at least half its significance; it is also the punishment of a crime.'

And now that those who fought have grown much older, we must wonder at the frantic avidity with which we struggled then to avoid death, digging our foxholes like madmen, running from danger with burning lungs and pounding hearts. What, really, were we so frightened of? Sometimes now the feeling comes over us that Housman's lines which in our boyhood we thought attractively cynical are really just:

> Life, to be sure, is nothing much to lose;
> But young men think it is, and we were young.

EDMUND WILSON

Philoctetes: The Wound and the Bow

Edmund Wilson (1895–1972) is commonly regarded as America's most eminent twentieth-century man of letters. He worked as a journalist for most of his career – he edited Vanity Fair *in the 1920s and later had posts with the* New Republic *and the* New Yorker. *In spite of his vast learning, he held himself aloof from academe: his real ambition was to make a living from his poetry, plays and fiction. In spite of the success of one novel,* Memoirs of Hecate County *(1946), his reputation today rests mainly on his achievements as a critic. 'Philoctetes: The Wound and the Bow' is the title-essay of a collection published in 1941.*

The *Philoctetes* of Sophocles is far from being his most popular play. The myth itself has not been one of those which have excited the modern imagination. The idea of Philoctetes' long illness and his banishment to the bleak island is dreary or distasteful to the young, who like to identify themselves with men of action – with Heracles or Perseus or Achilles; and for adults the story told by Sophocles fails to set off such emotional charges as are liberated by the crimes of the Atreidai and the tragedies of the siege of Troy. Whatever may have been dashing in the legend has been lost with the other plays and poems that dealt with it. Philoctetes is hardly mentioned in Homer; and we have only an incomplete account of the plays by Aeschylus and Euripides, which hinged on a critical moment of the campaign of the Greeks at Troy and which seem to have exploited the emotions of Greek patriotism. We have only a few scattered lines and phrases from that other play by Sophocles on the subject, the *Philoctetes at Troy*, in which the humiliated hero was presumably to be cured of his ulcer and to proceed to his victory over Paris.

There survives only this one curious drama which presents Philoctetes in exile – a drama which does not supply us at all with what we ordinarily expect of Greek tragedy, since it culminates in no catastrophe, and which indeed resembles rather our modern idea of a comedy (though the record of the lost plays of Sophocles shows that there must have been others like it). Its interest depends almost as much on the latent interplay of character, on a gradual psychological conflict, as that of *Le Misanthrope*. And it assigns itself, also, to a category even more special and less generally appealing through the fact (though this, again, was a feature not uncommon with Sophocles) that the conflict is not even allowed to take place between a man and a woman. Nor does it even put before us the spectacle – which may be made exceedingly thrilling – of the individual in conflict with his social group, which we get in such plays devoid of feminine interest as *Coriolanus* and *An Enemy of the People*. Nor is the conflict even a dual one, as most dramatic conflicts are – so that our emotions seesaw up and down between two opposed persons or groups: though Philoctetes and Odysseus struggle for the loyalty of Neoptolemus, he himself emerges more and more distinctly as representing an independent point of view, so that the contrast becomes a triple affair which makes more complicated demands on our sympathies.

A French dramatist of the seventeenth century, Chateaubrun, found the subject so inconceivable that, in trying to concoct an adaptation which would be acceptable to the taste of his time, he provided Philoctetes with a daughter named Sophie with whom Neoptolemus was to fall in love and thus bring the drama back to the reliable and eternal formula of Romeo and Juliet and the organizer who loves the factory-owner's daughter. And if we look for the imprint of the play on literature since the Renaissance, we shall find a very meagre record: a chapter of Fénelon's *Télémaque*, a discussion in Lessing's *Laocoön*, a sonnet of Wordsworth's, a little play by André Gide, an adaptation by John Jay Chapman – this is all, so far as I know, that has any claim to interest.

And yet the play itself *is* most interesting, as some of these writers have felt; and it is certainly one of Sophocles' masterpieces. If we come upon it in the course of reading him, without having heard it praised, we are surprised to be so charmed, so moved – to find ourselves in the presence of something that is so much less crude in its subtlety than either a three-cornered modern comedy like *Candida* or *La Parisienne* or an underplayed affair of male loyalty in a story by Ernest Hemingway, to both of which it has some similarity. It is as if having the three men on the lonely island has enabled the highly sophisticated Sophocles to get further away from the framework of the old myths on which he has to depend and whose barbarities, anomalies and absurdities, tactfully and realistically though he handles them, seem sometimes almost as much out of place as they would in a dialogue by Plato. The people of the *Philoctetes* seem to us more familiar than they do in most of the other Greek tragedies,* and they take on for us a more intimate meaning. Philoctetes remains in our mind, and his incurable wound and his invincible bow recur to us with a special insistence. But what is it they mean? How is it possible for Sophocles to make us accept them so naturally? Why do we enter with scarcely a stumble into the situation of people who are preoccupied with a snakebite that lasts for ever and a weapon that cannot fail?

Let us first take account of the peculiar twist which Sophocles seems to have given the legend, as it had come to him from the old epics and the dramatists who had used it before him.

The main outline of the story ran as follows: The demigod Heracles had been given by Apollo a bow that never missed its mark. When, poisoned by Deianeira's robe, he had had himself burned on Mount Oeta, he had persuaded Philoctetes to light the pyre and had rewarded him by bequeathing to him this weapon. Philoctetes had thus been formidably equipped when he had later set forth against Troy with Agamemnon and Menelaus. But on the way they had to stop off at the tiny island of Chrysè to sacrifice to the local deity. Philoctetes approached the shrine first, and he was bitten in the foot by a snake. The infection became peculiarly virulent; and the groans of Philoctetes made it impossible to perform the sacrifice, which would be spoiled by ill-omened sounds; the bite began to suppurate with so horrible a smell that his companions could not bear to have him near them. They removed him to Lemnos, a neighbouring island which was much larger than Chrysè and inhabited, and sailed away to Troy without him.

Philoctetes remained there ten years. The mysterious wound never healed. In the meantime, the Greeks, hard put to it at Troy after the deaths of Achilles and Ajax and baffled by the confession of their

---

* 'Apropos of the rare occasions when the ancients seem just like us, it always has seemed to me that a wonderful example was the repentance of the lad in the (*Philoctetes?*) play of Sophocles over his deceit, and the restoration of the bow.' – Mr Justice Holmes to Sir Frederick Pollock, 2 October 1921.

soothsayer that he was unable to advise them further, had kidnapped the soothsayer of the Trojans and had forced him to reveal to them that they could never win till they had sent for Neoptolemus, the son of Achilles, and given him his father's armour, and till they had brought Philoctetes and his bow.

Both these things were done. Philoctetes was healed at Troy by the son of the physician Asclepius; and he fought Paris in single combat and killed him. Philoctetes and Neoptolemus became the heroes of the taking of Troy.

Both Aeschylus and Euripides wrote plays on this subject long before Sophocles did; and we know something about them from a comparison of the treatments by the three different dramatists which was written by Dion Chrysostom, a rhetorician of the first century AD. Both these versions would seem to have been mainly concerned with the relation of Philoctetes to the success of the Greek campaign. All three of the plays dealt with the same episode: the visit of Odysseus to Lemnos for the purpose of getting the bow; and all represented Odysseus as particularly hateful to Philoctetes (because he had been one of those responsible for abandoning him on the island), and obliged to resort to cunning. But the emphasis of Sophocles' treatment appears fundamentally to have differed from that of the other two. In the drama of Aeschylus, we are told, Odysseus was not recognized by Philoctetes, and he seems simply to have stolen the bow. In Euripides, he was disguised by Athena in the likeness of another person, and he pretended that he had been wronged by the Greeks as Philoctetes had been. He had to compete with a delegation of Trojans, who had been sent to get the bow for their side and who arrived at the same time as he; and we do not know precisely what happened. But Dion Chrysostom regarded the play as 'a masterpiece of declamation' and 'a model of ingenious debate', and Jebb thinks it probable that Odysseus won the contest by an appeal to Philoctetes' patriotism. Since Odysseus was pretending to have been wronged by the Greeks, he could point to his own behaviour in suppressing his personal resentments in the interests of saving Greek honour. The moral theme thus established by Aeschylus and Euripides both would have been simply, like the theme of the wrath of Achilles, the conflict between the passions of an individual – in this case, an individual suffering from a genuine wrong – and the demands of duty to a common cause.

This conflict appears also in Sophocles; but it takes on a peculiar aspect. Sophocles, in the plays of his we have, shows himself particularly successful with people whose natures have been poisoned by narrow fanatical hatreds. Even allowing for the tendency of Greek heroes, in legend and history both, to fly into rather childish rages, we still feel on Sophocles' part some sort of special point of view, some sort of special sympathy, for these cases. Such people – Electra and the embittered old Oedipus – suffer as much as they hate: it is because they suffer they hate. They horrify, but they waken pity. Philoctetes is such another: a man obsessed by a grievance, which in his case he is to be kept from forgetting by an agonizing physical ailment; and for Sophocles his pain and hatred have a dignity and an interest. Just as it is by no means plain to Sophocles that in the affair of Antigone *versus* Creon it is the official point of view of Creon, representing the interests of his victorious faction, which should have the last word against Antigone, infuriated by a personal wrong; so it is by no means plain to him that the morality of Odysseus, who is lying and stealing for the fatherland, necessarily deserves to prevail over the animus of the stricken Philoctetes.

The contribution of Sophocles to the story is a third person who will sympathize with Philoctetes. This new character is Neoptolemus, the young son of Achilles, who, along with Philoctetes, is indispensable to the victory of the Greeks and who has just been summoned to Troy. Odysseus is made to bring him to Lemnos for the purpose of deceiving Philoctetes and shanghai-ing him aboard the ship.

The play opens with a scene between Odysseus and the boy, in which the former explains the purpose of their trip. Odysseus will remain in hiding in order not to be recognized by Philoctetes, and Neoptolemus will go up to the cave in which Philoctetes lives and win his confidence by pretending that the Greeks have robbed him of his father's armour, so that he, too, has a grievance against them. The youth in his innocence and candour objects when he is told what his rôle is to be, but Odysseus persuades him by reminding him that they can only take Troy through his obedience and that once they have taken Troy, he will be glorified for his bravery and wisdom. 'As soon as we have won,' Odysseus assures him, 'we shall conduct ourselves with perfect honesty. But for one short day of dishonesty, allow me to direct you what to do – and then for ever after you will be known as the most righteous of men.' The line of argument adopted by Odysseus is one with which the politics of our time have made us very familiar. 'Isn't it base, then, to tell falsehoods?' Neoptolemus asks. 'Not', Odysseus replies, 'when a falsehood will bring our salvation.'

Neoptolemus goes to talk to Philoctetes. He finds him in the wretched cave – described by Sophocles with characteristic realism: the bed of leaves, the crude wooden bowl, the filthy bandages drying in the sun – where he has been living in rags for ten years, limping out from time to time to shoot wild birds or to get himself wood and water. The boy hears the harrowing story of Philoctetes' desertion by the Greeks and listens to his indignation. The ruined captain begs Neoptolemus to take him back to his native land, and the young man pretends to consent. (Here and elsewhere I am telescoping the scenes and simplifying a more complex development.) But just as they are leaving for the ship, the ulcer on Philoctetes' foot sets up an ominous throbbing in preparation for one of its periodical burstings: 'She returns from time to time,' says the invalid, 'as if she were sated with her wanderings.' In a moment he is stretched on the ground, writhing in abject anguish and begging the young man to cut off his foot. He gives Neoptolemus the bow, telling him to take care of it till the seizure is over. A second spasm, worse than the first, reduces him to imploring the boy to throw him into the crater of the Lemnian volcano: so he himself, he says, had lit the fire which consumed the tormented Heracles and had got in return these arms, which he is now handing on to Neoptolemus. The pain abates a little; 'It comes and goes,' says Philoctetes; and he entreats the young man not to leave him. 'Don't worry about that. We'll stay.' 'I shan't even make you swear it, my son.' 'It would not be right to leave you' (it would not be right, of course, even from the Greeks' point of view). They shake hands on it. A third paroxysm twists the cripple; now he asks Neoptolemus to carry him to the cave, but shrinks from his grasp and struggles. At last the abscess bursts, the dark blood begins to flow, Philoctetes, faint and sweating, falls asleep.

The sailors who have come with Neoptolemus urge him to make off with the bow. 'No,' the young man replies. 'He cannot hear us; but I am sure that it will not be enough for us to recapture the bow without him. It is he who is to have the glory – it was he the god told us to bring.'

While they are arguing, Philoctetes awakes and thanks the young man with emotion: 'Agamemnon and Menelaus were not so patient and loyal.' But now they must get him to the ship, and the boy will have to see him undeceived and endure his bitter reproaches. 'The men will carry you down,' says Neoptolemus. 'Don't trouble them: just help me up,' Philoctetes replies. 'It would be too disagreeable for them to take me all the way to the ship.' The smell of the suppuration has been sickening. The young man begins to hesitate. The other sees that he is in doubt about something: 'You're not so overcome with disgust at my disease that you don't think you can have me on the ship with you?' –

> οὐ δή σε δυσχέρεια τοῦ νοσήματος
> ἔπεισεν ὥστε μή μ' ἄγειν ναύτην ἔτι;

The answer is one of the most effective of those swift and brief speeches of Sophocles which for the first time make a situation explicit (my attempts to render this dialogue colloquially do no justice to the feeling and point of the verse):

> ἅπαντα δυσχέρεια, τὴν αὑτοῦ φύσιν
> ὅταν λιπών τις δρᾷ τὰ μὴ προσεικότα.

'Everything becomes disgusting when you are false to your own nature and behave in an unbecoming way.'

He confesses his real intentions; and a painful scene occurs. Philoctetes denounces the boy in terms that would be appropriate for Odysseus; he sees himself robbed of his bow and left to starve on the island. The young man is deeply worried: 'Why did I ever leave Scyros?' he asks himself. 'Comrades, what shall I do?'

At this moment, Odysseus, who has been listening, pops out from his hiding place. With a lash of abuse at Neoptolemus, he orders him to hand over the arms. The young man's spirit flares up: when Odysseus invokes the will of Zeus, he tells him that he is degrading the gods by lending them his own lies. Philoctetes turns on Odysseus with an invective which cannot fail to impress the generous Neoptolemus: Why have they come for him now? he demands. Is he not still just as ill-omened and loathsome as he had been when they made him an outcast? They have only come back to get him because the gods have told them they must.

The young man now defies his mentor and takes his stand with Philoctetes. Odysseus threatens him: if he persists, he will have the whole Greek army against him, and they will see to it that he is punished for his treason. Neoptolemus declares his intention of taking Philoctetes home; he gives him back his bow. Odysseus tries to intervene; but Philoctetes has got the bow and aims an arrow at him. Neoptolemus seizes his hand and restrains him. Odysseus, always prudent, beats a quiet retreat.

Now the boy tries to persuade the angry man that he should, nevertheless, rescue the Greeks. 'I have proved my good faith,' says Neoptolemus; 'you know that I am not going to coerce you. Why be so wrong-headed? When the gods afflict us, we are obliged to bear our misfortunes; but must people pity a man who suffers through his own choice? The snake that bit you was an agent of the gods, it was the guardian of the goddess's shrine, and I swear to you by Zeus that the sons of Asclepius will cure you if you let us take you to Troy.' Philoctetes is incredulous, refuses. 'Since you gave me your word,' he says, 'take me home again.' 'The Greeks will attack me and ruin me.' 'I'll defend you.' 'How can you?' 'With my bow.' Neoptolemus is forced to consent.

But now Heracles suddenly appears from the skies and declares to Philoctetes that what the young man says is true, and that it is right for him to go to Troy. He and the son of Achilles shall stand together like lions and shall gloriously carry the day. – The *deus ex machina* here may of course figure a change of heart which has taken place in Philoctetes as the result of his having found a man who recognizes the wrong that has been done him and who is willing to champion his cause in defiance of all the Greek forces. His patron, the chivalrous Heracles, who had himself performed so many generous exploits, asserts his influence over his heir. The long hatred is finally exorcized.

In a fine lyric utterance which ends the play, Philoctetes says farewell to the cavern, where he has lain through so many nights listening to the deep-voiced waves as they crashed against the headland, and wetted by the rain and the spray blown in by the winter gales. A favourable wind has sprung up; and he sails away to Troy.

It is possible to guess at several motivations behind the writing of the *Philoctetes*. The play was produced in 409, when – if the tradition of his longevity be true – Sophocles would have been eighty-seven; and it is supposed to have been followed by the *Oedipus Coloneus*, which is assigned to 405 or 406. The latter deals directly with old age; but it would appear that the *Philoctetes* anticipates this theme in another form. Philoctetes, like the outlawed Oedipus, is impoverished, humbled, abandoned by his people, exacerbated by hardship and chagrin. He is accursed: Philoctetes' ulcer is an equivalent for the abhorrent sins of Oedipus, parricide and incest together, which have made of the ruler a pariah. And yet somehow both are sacred persons who have acquired superhuman powers, and who are destined to be purged of their guilt. One passage from the earlier play is even strikingly repeated in the later. The conception of the wave-beaten promontory and the sick man lying in his cave assailed by the wind and rain turns up in the *Oedipus Coloneus* (Colonus was Sophocles' native deme) with a figurative moral value. So the ills of old age assail Oedipus. Here are the lines, in A. E. Housman's translation:

> This man, as me, even so,
> Have the evil days overtaken;
> And like as a cape sea-shaken
> With tempest at earth's last verges
> And shock of all winds that blow,
> His head the seas of woe,
> The thunders of awful surges
> Ruining overflow:
> Blown from the fall of even,
> Blown from the dayspring forth,
> Blown from the noon in heaven,
> Blown from night and the North.

But Oedipus has endured as Philoctetes has endured in the teeth of all the cold and the darkness, the screaming winds and the bellowing breakers: the blind old man is here in his own person the headland that stands against the storm.

We may remember a widely current story about the creator of these two figures. It is said that one of Sophocles' sons brought him into court in his advanced old age on the complaint that he was no longer competent to manage his property. The old poet is supposed to have recited a passage from the play which he had been writing: the chorus in praise of Colonus, with its clear song of nightingales, its wine-dark ivy, its crocus glowing golden and its narcissus moist with dew, where the stainless stream of the Cephisus wanders through the broad-swelling plain and where the grey-leaved olive grows of itself beneath the gaze of the grey-eyed Athena – shining Colonus, breeder of horses and of oarsmen whom the Nereids lead. The scene had been represented on the stage and Sophocles had been made to declare: 'If I am Sophocles, I am not mentally incapable; if I am mentally incapable, I am not Sophocles.' In any case, the story was that the tribunal, composed of his fellow clansmen, applauded and acquitted the poet and censored the litigating son. The ruined and humiliated heroes of Sophocles' later plays are still persons of mysterious virtue, whom their fellows are forced to respect.

There is also a possibility, even a strong probability, that Sophocles intended Philoctetes to be identified with Alcibiades. This brilliant and unique individual, one of the great military leaders of the Athenians, had been accused by political opponents of damaging the sacred statues of Hermes and burlesquing the Eleusinian mysteries, and had been summoned to stand trial at Athens while he was away on his campaign against Sicily. He had at once gone over to the Spartans, commencing that insolent career of shifting allegiances which ended with his returning to the Athenian side. At a moment of extreme danger, he had taken over a part of the Athenian fleet and had defeated the Spartans in two sensational battles in 411 and 410, thus sweeping them out of the Eastern Aegean and enabling the Athenians to dominate the Hellespont. The *Philoctetes* was produced in 409, when the Athenians already wanted him back and were ready to cancel the charges against him and to restore him to citizenship. Alcibiades was a startling example of a bad character who was indispensable. Plutarch says that Aristophanes well describes the Athenian feeling about Alcibiades when he writes: 'They miss him and hate him and long to have him back.' And the malady of Philoctetes may have figured his moral defects: the unruly and unscrupulous nature which, even though he seems to have been innocent of the charges brought against him, had given them a certain plausibility. It must have looked to the Athenians, too, after the victories of Abydos and Cyzicus, as if he possessed an invincible bow. Plutarch says that the men who had served under him at the taking of Cyzicus did actually come to regard themselves as undefeatable and refused to share quarters with other soldiers who had fought in less successful engagements.

Yet behind both the picture of old age and the line in regard to Alcibiades, one feels in the *Philoctetes* a more general and fundamental idea: the conception of superior strength as inseparable from disability.

For the superiority of Philoctetes does not reside merely in the enchanted bow. When Lessing replied to Winckelmann, who had referred to Sophocles' cripple as if he were an example of the conventional idea of impassive classical fortitude, he pointed out that, far from exemplifying impassivity, Philoctetes becomes completely demoralized every time he has one of his seizures, and yet that this only heightens our admiration for the pride which prevents him from escaping at the expense of helping those who have deserted him. 'We despise', say the objectors, 'any man from whom bodily pain extorts a shriek. Ay, but not always; not for the first time, nor if we see that the sufferer strains every nerve to stifle the expression of his pain; not if we know him otherwise to be a man of firmness; still less if we witness evidences of his firmness in the very midst of his sufferings, and observe that, although pain may have extorted a shriek, it has extorted nothing else from him, but that on the contrary he submits to the prolongation of his pain rather than renounce one iota of his resolutions, even where such a concession would promise him the termination of his misery.'

For André Gide, in his *Philoctète*, the obstinacy of the invalid hermit takes on a character almost mystical. By persisting in his bleak and lonely life, the Philoctetes of Gide wins the love of a more childlike Neoptolemus and even compels the respect of a less hard-boiled Odysseus. He is practising a kind of virtue superior not only to the virtue of the latter, with his code of obedience to the demands of the group, but also to that of the former, who forgets his patriotic obligations for those of a personal attachment. There is something above the gods, says the Philoctetes of Gide; and it is a virtue to devote oneself to this. But what is it? asks Neoptolemus. I do not know, he answers; oneself! The misfortune of his exile on the island has enabled him to perfect himself: 'I have learned to express myself better,' he tells them, 'now that I am no longer with men. Between hunting and sleeping, I occupy myself with thinking. My ideas, since I have been alone so that nothing, not even suffering, disturbs them, have taken a subtle course which sometimes I can hardly follow. I have come to know more of the secrets of life than my masters had ever revealed to me. And I took to telling the story of my sufferings, and if the phrase was very beautiful, I was by so much consoled; I even sometimes forgot my sadness by uttering it. I came to understand that words inevitably become more beautiful from the moment they are no longer put together in response to the demands of others . . .' The Philoctetes of Gide is, in fact, a literary man: at once a moralist and an artist, whose genius becomes purer and deeper in ratio to his isolation and outlawry. In the end, he lets the intruders steal the bow after satisfying himself that Neoptolemus can handle it, and subsides into a blissful tranquillity, much relieved that there is no longer any reason for people to seek him out.

With Gide we come close to a further implication, which even Gide does not fully develop but which must occur to the modern reader: the idea that genius and disease, like strength and mutilation, may be inextricably bound up together. It is significant that the only two writers of our time who have especially interested themselves in Philoctetes – André Gide and John Jay Chapman – should both be persons who have not only, like the hero of the play, stood at an angle to the morality of society and defended their position with stubbornness, but who have suffered from psychological disorders which have made them, in Gide's case, ill-regarded by his fellows; in Chapman's case, excessively difficult. Nor is it perhaps accidental that Charles Lamb, with his experience of his sister's insanity, should in his essay on *The Convalescent* choose the figure of Philoctetes as a symbol for his own 'nervous fever'.

And we must even, I believe, grant Sophocles some special insight into morbid psychology. The tragic themes of all three of the great dramatists – the madnesses, the murders and the incests – may seem to us sufficiently morbid. The hero with an incurable wound was even a stock subject of myth not confined to the Philoctetes legend: there was also the story of Telephus, also wounded and also indispensable, about which both Sophocles and Euripides wrote plays. But there is a difference between the treatment that Sophocles gives to these conventional epic subjects and the treatments of the other writers. Aeschylus is more religious and philosophical; Euripides more romantic and sentimental. Sophocles by comparison is clinical. Arthur Platt, who had a special interest in the scientific aspect of the classics, says that Sophocles was scrupulously up to date in the physical science of his time. He was himself closely associated by tradition with the cult of the healer Asclepius, whose son is to cure Philoctetes: Lucian had read a poem which he had dedicated to the doctor-god; and Plutarch reports that Asclepius was supposed to have visited his hearth. He is said also to have been actually a priest of another of the medical cults. Platt speaks particularly of his medical knowledge – which is illustrated by the naturalism and precision of his description of Philoctetes' infected bite.

But there is also in Sophocles a cool observation of the behaviour of psychological derangements. The madness of Ajax is a genuine madness, from which he recovers to be horrified at the realization of what he has done. And it was not without good reason that Freud laid Sophocles under contribution for the naming of the Oedipus complex – since Sophocles had not only dramatized the myth that dwelt with the violation of the incest taboo, but had exhibited the suppressed impulse behind it in the speech in which he makes Jocasta attempt to reassure Oedipus by reminding him that it was not uncommon for men to dream about sleeping with their mothers – 'and he who thinks nothing of this gets through his life most easily'. Those who do not get through life so easily are presented by Sophocles with a very firm grasp on the springs of their abnormal conduct. Electra is what we should call nowadays schizophrenic: the woman who weeps over the urn which is supposed to contain her brother's ashes is not 'integrated', as we say, with the Fury who prepares her mother's murder. And certainly the fanaticism of Antigone – 'fixated', like Electra, on her brother – is intended to be abnormal, too. The banishment by Jebb from Sophocles' text of the passage in which Antigone explains the unique importance of a brother and his juggling of the dialogue in the scene in which she betrays her indifference to the feelings of the man she is supposed to marry are certainly among the curiosities of Victorian scholarship – though he was taking his cue from the complaint of Goethe that Antigone had been shown by Sophocles as acting from trivial motives and Goethe's hope that her speech about her brother might some day be shown to be spurious. Aristotle had cited this speech of Antigone's as an outstanding example of the principle that if anything peculiar occurs in a play the cause must be shown by the dramatist. It was admitted by Jebb that his rewriting of these passages had no real textual justification; and in one case he violates glaringly the convention of the one-line dialogue. To accept his emendation would involve the assumption that Aristotle did not know what the original text had been and was incapable of criticizing the corrupted version. No: Antigone forgets her fiancé and kills herself for her brother. Her timid sister (like Electra's timid sister) represents the normal feminine point of view. Antigone's point of view is peculiar, as Aristotle says. (The real motivation of Antigone has been retraced with unmistakable accuracy by Professor Walter R. Agard in *Classical Philology* of July 1937.)

These insane or obsessed people of Sophocles all display a perverse kind of nobility. I have spoken of the authority of expiation which emanates from the blasted Oedipus. Even the virulence of Electra's revenge conditions the intensity of her tenderness for Orestes. And so the maniacal fury which makes Ajax run amok, the frenzy of Heracles in the Nessus robe, terribly though they transform their victims, can never destroy their virtue of heroes. The poor disgraced Ajax will receive his due of honour after his suicide and will come to stand higher in our sympathies than Menelaus and Agamemnon, those obtuse and brutal captains, who here as in the *Philoctetes* are obviously no favourites of Sophocles'. Heracles in his final moments bids his spirit curb his lips with steel to keep him from crying out, and carry him through his self-destructive duty as a thing that is to be desired.

Some of these maladies are physical in origin, others are psychological; but they link themselves with one another. The case of Ajax connects psychological disorder as we get it in Electra, for example, with the access of pain and rage that causes Heracles to kill the herald Lichas; the case of Heracles connects a poisoning that produces a murderous fury with an infection that, though it distorts the personality, does not actually render the victim demented: the wound of Philoctetes, whose agony comes in spasms like that of Heracles. All these cases seem intimately related.

It has been the misfortune of Sophocles to figure in academic tradition as the model of those qualities of coolness and restraint which that tradition regards as classical. Those who have never read him – remembering the familiar statue – are likely to conceive something hollow and marmoreal. Actually, as C. M. Bowra says, Sophocles is 'passionate and profound'. Almost everything that we are told about him by the tradition of the ancient world suggests equanimity and amiability and the enjoyment of unusual good fortune. But there is one important exception: the anecdote in Plato's *Republic* in which Sophocles is represented as saying that the release from amorous desire which had come to him in his old age had been like a liberation from an insane and cruel master. He *has* balance and logic, of course: those qualities that the classicists admire; but these qualities only count because they master so much savagery and madness. Somewhere even in the fortunate Sophocles there had been a sick and raving Philoctetes.

And now let us go back to the *Philoctetes* as a parable of human character. I should interpret the fable as follows. The victim of a malodorous disease which renders him abhorrent to society and periodically degrades him and makes him helpless is also the master of a superhuman art which everybody has to respect and which the normal man finds he needs. A practical man like Odysseus, at the same time coarse-grained and clever, imagines that he can somehow get the bow without having Philoctetes on his hands or that he can kidnap Philoctetes the bowman without regard for Philoctetes the invalid. But the young son of Achilles knows better. It is at the moment when his sympathy for Philoctetes would naturally inhibit his cheating him – so the supernatural influences in Sophocles are often made with infinite delicacy to shade into subjective motivations – it is at this moment of his natural shrinking that it becomes clear to him that the words of the seer had meant that the bow would be useless without Philoctetes himself. It is in the nature of things – of this world where the divine and the human fuse – that they cannot have the irresistible weapon without its loathsome owner, who upsets the processes of normal life by his curses and his cries, and who in any case refuses to work for men who have exiled him from their fellowship.

It is quite right that Philoctetes should refuse to come to Troy. Yet it is also decreed that he shall be cured when he shall have been able to forget his grievance and to devote his divine gifts to the service of his own people. It is right that he should refuse to submit to the purposes of Odysseus, whose only idea is to exploit him. How then is the gulf to be got over between the ineffective plight of the bowman and his proper use of his bow, between his ignominy and his destined glory? Only by the intervention of one who is guileless enough and human enough to treat him, not as a monster, nor yet as a mere magical property which is wanted for accomplishing some end, but simply as another man, whose sufferings elicit his sympathy and whose courage and pride he admires. When this human relation has been realized, it seems at first that it is to have the consequence of frustrating the purpose of the expedition and ruining the Greek campaign. Instead of winning over the outlaw, Neoptolemus has outlawed himself as well, at a time when both the boy and the cripple are desperately needed by the Greeks.

Yet in taking the risk to his cause which is involved in the recognition of his common humanity with the sick man, in refusing to break his word, he dissolves Philoctetes' stubbornness, and thus cures him and sets him free, and saves the campaign as well.

HANNAH ARENDT

The Concentration Camps

Hannah Arendt (1906–75) was born in Germany and emigrated to the United States in 1941. In the 1950s she established herself as one of America's most forceful political philosophers. Her books included The Origins of Totalitarianism *(1951) and* The Human Condition *(1958). Her essay 'The Concentration Camps' appeared in* Partisan Review *in 1948. In the 1960s, it should perhaps be added, Arendt caused a controversy with her book* Eichmann in Jerusalem *in which she accused the Jews of complicity in their own destruction and – in the view of angered Jewish intellectuals – seemed also to mitigate the evil of Nazism by speaking of Adolf Eichmann's 'banality'.*

The SS has made the camp the most totalitarian society in existence up to now.

DAVID ROUSSET

There are three possible approaches to the reality of the concentration camp: the inmate's experience of immediate suffering, the recollection of the survivor, and the fearful anticipation of those who dread the concentration camp as a possibility for the future.

Immediate experience is expressed in the reports which 'record but do not communicate' things that evade human understanding and human experience; things therefore that, when suffered by men, transform them into 'uncomplaining animals' (*The Dark Side of the Moon*, New York, 1947). There are numerous such reports by survivors; only a few have been published, partly because, quite understandably, the world wants to hear no more of these things, but also because they all leave the reader cold, that is, as apathetic and baffled as the writer himself, and fail to inspire those passions of outrage and sympathy through which men have always been mobilized for justice, for 'Misery that goes too deep arouses not compassion but repugnance and hatred' (Rousset).

Der SS-Staat by Eugen Kogon and *Les Jours de notre mort* by David Rousset are products of assimilated recollection. Both authors have consciously written for the world of the living, both wish to make themselves understood at any cost, and both have cast off the insane contempt for those 'who never went through it', that in the direct reports so often substitutes for communication. This conscious good will is the only guaranty that those who return will not, after a brief period of sullen resentment against humanity in general, adapt themselves to the real world and become once more the exact same unsuspecting fools that they were when they entered the camps. Both books are indispensable for an understanding not only of the concentration camps, but of the totalitarian regime as a whole. They become useless and even dangerous as soon as they attempt a positive interpretation – Kogon because he cites apparent historical precedents and believes that the camps can be understood psychologically, Rousset because he seeks the consolation of an 'extreme experience' in a kind of suffering which, strictly speaking, no longer permits of experience, and thus arrives at a meaningless affirmation of life that is extremely dangerous because it romanticizes and transfigures what must never under any circumstances be repeated on this earth.[1] What is really true, on the contrary, was recently remarked by Isaac Rosenfeld in *The New Leader* (14 February 1948): 'We still don't understand what happened to the Jews of Europe, and perhaps we never will . . . By now we know all there is to know. But it hasn't helped . . . as there is no response great enough to equal the facts that provoked it. There is nothing but numbness, and in the respect of numbness we . . . are no different from the murderers who went ahead and did their business and paid no attention to the screams.'

Fearful anticipation is the most widespread and perhaps the only fitting approach to the reality of the concentration camp. It certainly has a great deal to do with the attitudes of men under the totalitarian terror, although it always seems to go hand in hand with a remarkable and very characteristic uncertainty which impedes both rebellion and any clear, articulated understanding of the thing feared. Kogon reports: 'Only a very, very few of those who entered a concentration camp for the first time had the slightest idea . . . of what awaited them. [Some] were prepared for the worst. But these ideas were always nebulous; the reality far exceeded them.' The reason for the uncertainty was precisely that this reality was utterly incredible and inconceivable. In totalitarian regimes, uncertainty as well as fear is manufactured and fostered by the propagandistic treatment of the institution of terror. 'There was hardly anything connected with the SS that was not kept secret. The biggest secret of all was the routine of the concentration camps ... whose only purpose was to spread an anonymous terror of a general political character' (Kogon). Concentration camps and everything connected with them are systematically publicized and at the same time kept absolutely secret. They are used as a threat, but all actual reports about them are suppressed or denounced as fantastic.

It is not surprising that those who made terror the actual foundation of their power should know how to exploit it through publicity and propaganda. The surprising thing is that the psychological and political effects of this propaganda could survive the collapse of the Nazi regime and the opening up of the concentration camps. One would think that the eye-witness reports and, to an even greater degree, the works of ordered recollection which substantiate one another and speak directly to the reader, in Rousset's case most persuasively, should have punctured the propagandist claim that such things were absurd horror stories. This, as we all know, is not the case. Despite overwhelming proofs, anyone speaking or writing about concentration camps is still regarded as suspect; and if the speaker has resolutely returned to the world of the living, he himself is often assailed by doubts with regard to his own truthfulness, as though he had mistaken a nightmare for reality.

This doubt of people concerning themselves and the reality of their own experience only reveals what the Nazis have always known: that men determined to commit crimes will find it expedient to organize them on the vastest, most improbable scale. Not only because this renders all punishments provided by the legal system inadequate and absurd; but because the very immensity of the crimes guarantees that the murderers who proclaim their innocence with all manner of lies will be more readily believed than the victims who tell the truth. The Nazis did not even consider it necessary to keep this discovery to themselves. Hitler circulated millions of copies of his book in which he stated that to be successful, a lie must be enormous – which did not prevent people from believing him as, similarly, the Nazis' proclamations, repeated *ad nauseam*, that the Jews would be exterminated like bedbugs (i.e. with poison gas), prevented anybody from *not* believing them.

There is a great temptation to explain away the intrinsically incredible by means of liberal rationalizations. In each one of us, there lurks such a liberal, wheedling us with the voice of common sense. We attempt to understand elements in present or recollected experience that simply surpass our powers of understanding. We attempt to classify as criminal a thing which, as we all feel, no such category was ever intended to cover. What meaning has the concept of murder when we are confronted with the mass production of corpses? We attempt to understand the behavior of concentration camp inmates and SS men psychologically, when the very thing that must be realized is that the psyche (or character) *can* be destroyed even without the destruction of the physical man; that, indeed, as Rousset convincingly shows, psyche, character, or individuality seem under certain circumstances to express themselves only through the rapidity or slowness with which they disintegrate. The end result in any case is inanimate men, i.e. men who can no longer be psychologically understood, whose return to the psychologically or otherwise intelligibly human world closely resembles the resurrection of Lazarus – as Rousset indicates in the title of his book. All statements of common sense, whether of a psychological or sociological nature, serve only to encourage those who think it 'superficial' to 'dwell on horrors' (Georges Bataille, in *Critique*, January 1948).

If it is true that the concentration camps are the most consequential institution of totalitarian rule, 'dwelling on horrors' would seem to be indispensable for the understanding of totalitarianism. But recollection can no more do this than can the uncommunicative eye-witness report. In both these genres there is an inherent tendency to run away from the experience; instinctively or rationally, both types of writer are so much aware of the terrible abyss that separates the world of the living from that of the living dead, that they cannot supply anything more than a series of remembered occurrences that must seem just as incredible to those who relate them as to their audience. Only the fearful imagination of those who have been aroused by such reports but have not actually been smitten in their own flesh, of those who are consequently free from the bestial, desperate terror which, when confronted by real, present horror, inexorably paralyzes everything that is not mere reaction, can afford to keep thinking about horrors. Such thoughts are useful only for the perception of political contexts and the mobilization of political passions. A change of personality of any sort whatever can no more be induced by thinking about horrors than by the real experience of horror. The reduction of a man to a bundle of reactions separates him as radically as mental disease from everything within him that is personality or character. When, like Lazarus, he rises from the dead, he finds his personality or character unchanged, just as he had left it.

Nor can horror or thinking about horrors become a basis for a political community or a party in the narrower sense. Attempts have failed to create a European elite with a program of inter-European understanding on the basis of the common experience of the concentration camp, much in the same way that similar attempts after the First World War failed to draw political consequences from the experience of the front-line soldier. In both cases it developed that the experiences themselves could impart only nihilistic platitudes, such as: 'Victim and executioner are alike ignoble; the lesson of the camps is the brotherhood of abjection; if you haven't acted with the same degree of ignominy, it's only because you didn't have time . . . but the underlying rot that rises, rises, rises, is absolutely, terrifyingly the same' (Rousset). Political consequences like postwar pacifism followed from the universal fear of war, not from experience of the war. An insight, led and mobilized by fear, into the structure of modern war would have led not to a pacifism without reality, but to the view that the only acceptable ground for modern war is to fight against conditions under which we no longer wish to live – and our knowledge of the camps and torture chambers of totalitarian regimes has convinced us only too well that such conditions are possible. An insight into the nature of totalitarian rule, directed by our fear of the concentration camp, might serve to devaluate all outmoded political shadings from right to left and, beside and above them, to introduce the most essential political criterion for judging the events of our time: Will it lead to totalitarian rule or will it not?

In any case fearful anticipation has the great advantage that it dispels the sophistical–dialectical interpretations of politics, which all rest on the superstition that some good can come out of evil. Such dialectical acrobatics retained at least an appearance of justification as long as the worst evil that man could inflict on man was murder. But murder, as we know today, is still a limited evil. The murderer who kills a man who must die in any event, moves within the familiar realm of life and death, between which there is a necessary relation that is the basis of dialectics, although dialecticians are not always aware of it. The murderer leaves a corpse and does not claim that his victim never existed; he may obscure the traces of his own identity, but he does not efface the memory and grief of those who loved his victim; he destroys a life, but he does not destroy the very fact of its ever having existed.

The horror of the concentration and extermination camps can never be fully embraced by the imagination for the very reason that it stands outside of life and death. The inmates are more effectively cut off from the world of the living than if they were dead, because terror compels oblivion among those who know them or love them. 'What extraordinary women you are here,' exclaimed the Soviet police when Polish women insisted on knowing the whereabouts of their husbands who had disappeared. 'In our country, when the husband is arrested, the wife sues for divorce and looks for another man' (*The Dark Side of the Moon*). Murder in the camps is as impersonal as the squashing of a gnat, a mere technique of management, as when a camp is overcrowded and is liquidated – or an accidental by-product, as when a prisoner succumbs to torture. Systematic torture and systematic starvation create an atmosphere of permanent dying, in which death as well as life is effectively obstructed.

The fear of the absolute Evil which permits of no escape knows that this is the end of dialectical evolutions and developments. It knows that modern politics revolves around a question which, strictly speaking, should never enter into politics, the question of all or nothing: of all, that is, a human society rich with infinite possibilities; or exactly nothing, that is, the end of mankind.

II

There are no parallels to the life of the concentration camps. All seeming parallels create confusion and distract attention from what is essential. Forced labor in prisons and penal colonies, banishment, slavery, all seem for a moment to offer helpful comparisons, but on closer examination lead nowhere.

Forced labor as a punishment is limited as to time and intensity. The convict retains his rights over his body; he is not absolutely tortured and he is not absolutely dominated. Banishment banishes only from one part of the world to another part of the world, also inhabited by human beings; it does not exclude from the human world altogether. Throughout history slavery has been an institution within a social order; slaves were not, like concentration camp inmates, withdrawn from the sight and hence the protection of their fellow men; as instruments of labor they had a definite price and as property a definite value. The concentration camp inmate has no price, because he can always be replaced and he belongs to no one. From the point of view of normal society he is absolutely superfluous, although in times of acute labor shortage, as in Russia and in Germany during the war, he is used for work.

The concentration camp as an institution was not established for the sake of any possible labor yield; the only permanent economic function of the camps has been the financing of their own supervisory apparatus; thus from the economic point of view the concentration camps exist mostly for their own sake. Any work that has been performed could have been done much better and more cheaply under different conditions.[2] The example of Russia, whose concentration camps are usually referred to as forced labor camps, because the Soviet bureaucracy has given them this flattering title, shows most clearly that the main point is not forced labor; forced labor is the normal condition of the whole Russian proletariat which has been deprived of freedom of movement and can be mobilized anywhere at any time.

The incredibility of the horrors is closely bound up with their economic uselessness. The Nazis carried this uselessness to the point of open anti-utility when in the midst of the war, despite the shortage of rolling stock, they transported millions of Jews to the east and set up enormous, costly extermination factories. In the midst of a strictly utilitarian world the obvious contradiction between these acts and military expediency gave the whole enterprise an air of mad unreality.

However, such unreality, created by an apparent lack of purpose, is the very basis of all forms of concentration camp. Seen from outside, they and the things that happen in them can be described only in images drawn from a life after death, that is, a life removed from earthly purposes. Concentration camps can very aptly be divided into three types corresponding to three basic Western conceptions of a life after death: Hades, purgatory, and hell. To Hades correspond those relatively mild forms, once popular even in nontotalitarian countries, for getting undesirable elements of all sorts – refugees, stateless persons, the asocial and the unemployed – out of the way; as DP camps, which are nothing other than camps for persons who have become superfluous and bothersome, they have survived the war. Purgatory is represented by the Soviet Union's labor camps, where neglect is combined with chaotic forced labor. Hell in the most literal sense was embodied by those types of camp perfected by the Nazis, in which the whole of life was thoroughly and systematically organized with a view to the greatest possible torment.

All three types have one thing in common: the human masses sealed off in them are treated as if they no longer existed, as if what happened to them were no longer of any interest to anybody, as if they were already dead and some evil spirit gone mad were amusing himself by stopping them for a while between life and death before admitting them to eternal peace.

It is not so much the barbed wire as the skillfully manufactured unreality of those whom it fences in that provokes such enormous cruelties and ultimately makes extermination look like a perfectly normal measure. Everything that was done in the camps is known to us from the world of perverse, malignant fantasies. The difficult thing to understand is that, like such fantasies, these gruesome crimes took place in a phantom world, in a world in which there were neither consequences nor responsibilities; and finally neither the tormentors nor the tormented, and least of all the outsider, could be aware that what was happening was anything more than a cruel game or an absurd dream.

The films which the Allies circulated in Germany and elsewhere after the war showed clearly that this atmosphere of insanity and unreality is not dispelled by pure reportage. To the unprejudiced observer they are just about as convincing as the pictures of mysterious substances taken at spiritualist seances. Common sense reacted to the horrors of Buchenwald and Auschwitz with the plausible argument: 'What crime must these people have committed that such things were done to them!'; or, in Germany and Austria, in the midst of starvation, overpopulation, and general hatred: 'Too bad that they've stopped gassing the Jews'; and everywhere with the skeptical shrug that greets ineffectual propaganda.

If the propaganda of truth fails to convince the average Philistine precisely because it is too monstrous, it is positively dangerous to those who know from their own imaginings that they themselves are capable of doing such things and are therefore perfectly willing to believe in the reality of what they have seen. Suddenly it becomes evident that things which for thousands of years the human imagination had banished to a realm beyond human competence, can be manufactured right here on earth. Hell and purgatory, and even a shadow of their perpetual duration, can be established by the most modern methods of destruction and therapy. When people of this sort, who are far more numerous in any large city than we like to think, see these films, or read reports of the same things, the thought that comes to their minds is that the power of man is far greater than they ever dared to think and that men can realize hellish fantasies without making the sky fall or the earth open.

The one thing that cannot be reproduced is what made the traditional conceptions of hell tolerable to man: the Last Judgment, the idea of an absolute standard of justice combined with the infinite possibility of grace. For in the human estimation there is no crime and no sin commensurable with the everlasting torments of hell. Hence the discomfiture of common sense, which asks: What crime must these people have committed in order to suffer so inhumanly? Hence also the absolute innocence of the victims: no man ever deserved this. Hence finally the grotesque haphazardness with which concentration camp victims were chosen in the perfected terror state: such 'punishment' can, with equal justice and injustice, be inflicted on anyone.

III

In comparison with the insane end-result – concentration camp society – the process by which men are prepared for this end, and the methods by which individuals are adapted to these conditions, are transparent and logical. The insane mass manufacture of corpses is preceded by the historically and politically intelligible preparation of living corpses.

In another connection it might be possible, indeed it would be necessary, to describe this preparatory process as a consequence of the political upheavals of our century. The impetus and, what is more important, the silent consent to such unprecedented conditions in the heart of Europe are the products of those events which in a period of political disintegration suddenly and unexpectedly made hundreds of thousands of human beings homeless, stateless, outlawed and unwanted, while millions of human beings were made economically superfluous and socially burdensome by unemployment. This in turn could only happen because the rights of man, which had never been philosophically established but merely formulated, which had never been politically secured but merely proclaimed, have, in their traditional form, lost all validity.

Meanwhile, however, totalitarian regimes exploited these developments for their own purposes. In order to understand these purposes, we must examine the process of preparing living corpses in its entirety. After all, loss of passport, residence, and the right to work, was only a very provisional, summary preparation, which could hardly have produced adequate results.

The first essential step was to kill the juridical person in man; this was done by placing the concentration camp outside the normal penal system, and by selecting its inmates outside the normal judicial procedure in which a definite crime entails a predictable penalty. Thus criminals, who for other reasons are an essential element in concentration camp society, are ordinarily sent to a camp only on completion of their prison sentence. Deviations from this rule in Russia must be attributed to the catastrophic shortage of prisons and to a desire, so far unrealized, to transform the whole penal system into a system of concentration camps.

The inclusion of criminals is necessary in order to make plausible the propagandistic claim that the institution exists for asocial elements. It is equally essential, as long as there is a penal system in the country, that they should be sent to the camps only on completion of their sentence, that is, when they are actually entitled to their freedom. It is, paradoxically, harder to kill the juridical person in a man who is guilty of some crime than in a totally innocent man. The stateless persons who in all European countries have lost their civil rights along with their nationality have learned this only too well; their legal position improved automatically as soon as they committed a theft: then they were no longer without rights but had the same rights as all other thieves. In order to kill the juridical person in man, the concentration camp must under no circumstances become a calculable punishment for definite offenses. Criminals do not properly belong in the concentration camps; if nevertheless they constitute the sole permanent category among the inmates, it is a concession of the totalitarian state to the prejudices of society which can in this way most readily be accustomed to the existence of the camps. The amalgamation of criminals with all other categories has moreover the advantage of making it shockingly evident to all other arrivals that they have landed in the lowest level of society. It soon turns out, to be sure, that they have every reason to envy the lowest thief and murderer; but meanwhile the lowest level is a good beginning. Moreover it is an effective means of camouflage: this happens only to criminals and nothing worse is happening than what deservedly happens to criminals.[3]

The criminals everywhere constitute the aristocracy of the camps. (In Germany, during the war, they were replaced in the leadership by the Communists, because not even a minimum of rational work could be performed under the chaotic conditions created by a criminal administration. This was merely a temporary transformation of concentration camps into forced labor camps, a thoroughly atypical phenomenon of limited duration. With his limited, wartime experience of Nazi concentration camps, Rousset overestimates the influence and power of the Communists.) What places the criminals in the leadership is not so much the affinity between supervisory personnel and criminal elements – in the Soviet Union apparently the supervisors are not, like the SS, a special elite of criminals – as the fact that only criminals have been sent to the camp in connection with some definite activity and that in them consequently the destruction of the juridical person cannot be fully successful, since they at least know why they are in a concentration camp. For the politicals this is only subjectively true; their actions, in so far as they were actions and not mere opinions or someone else's vague suspicions, or accidental membership in a politically disapproved group, are as a rule not covered by the normal legal system of the country and not juridically defined.

To the amalgam of politicals and criminals, with which concentration camps in Russia and Germany started out, was added at an early date a third element which was soon to constitute the majority of all concentration camp inmates. This largest group has consisted ever since of people who had done nothing whatsoever that, either in their own consciousness or the consciousness of their tormentors, had any rational connection with their arrest. In Germany, after 1938, this element was represented by masses of Jews, in Russia by any groups which, for any reason having nothing to do with their actions, had incurred the disfavor of the authorities. These groups, innocent in every sense, are the most suitable for thorough experimentation in disfranchisement and destruction of the juridical person, and therefore they are both qualitatively and quantitatively the most essential category of the camp population. This principle was most fully realized in the gas chambers which, if only because of their enormous capacity, could not be intended for individual cases but only for people in general. In this connection, the following dialogue sums up the situation of the individual: 'For what purpose, may I ask, do the gas chambers exist?' – 'For what purpose were you born?' (Rousset). It is this third group of the totally innocent who in every case fare the worst in the camps. Criminals and politicals are assimilated to this category; thus deprived of the protective distinction that comes of their having done something, they are utterly exposed to the arbitrary.

Contrasting with the complete haphazardness with which the inmates are selected are the categories, meaningless in themselves but useful from the standpoint of organization, into which they are usually divided on their arrival. In the German camps there were criminals, politicals, asocial elements, religious offenders, and Jews, all distinguished by insignia. When the French set up concentration camps after the Spanish civil war, they immediately introduced the typical totalitarian amalgam of politicals with criminals and the innocent (in this case the stateless), and despite their inexperience proved remarkably inventive in devising meaningless categories of inmates. Originally devised in order to prevent any growth of solidarity among the inmates, this technique proved particularly valuable because no one could know whether his own category was better or worse than someone else's. In Germany this eternally shifting though pedantically organized edifice was given an appearance of solidity by the fact that under any and all circumstances the Jews were the lowest category. The gruesome and grotesque part of it was that the inmates identified themselves with these categories, as though they represented a last authentic remnant of their juridical person. It is no wonder that a Communist of 1933 should have come out of the camps more Communistic than he went in, a Jew more Jewish.

While the classification of inmates by categories is only a tactical, organizational measure, the arbitrary selection of victims indicates the essential principle of the institution. If the concentration camps had been dependent on the existence of political adversaries, they would scarcely have survived the first years of the totalitarian regimes. 'The camps would have died out if in making its arrests the Gestapo had considered only the principle of opposition' (Kogon). But the existence of a political opposition is for a concentration camp system only a pretext, and the purpose of the system is not achieved even when, under the most monstrous terror, the population becomes more or less voluntarily coordinated, i.e. relinquishes its political rights. The aim of an arbitrary system is to destroy the civil rights of the whole population, who ultimately become just as outlawed in their own country as the stateless and homeless. The destruction of a man's rights, the killing of the juridical person in him, is a prerequisite for dominating him entirely. For even free consent is an obstacle; and this applies not only to special categories such as criminals, political opponents, Jews, but to every inhabitant of a totalitarian state.

Any, even the most tyrannical, restriction of this arbitrary persecution to certain opinions of a religious or political nature, to certain modes of intellectual or erotic social behavior, to certain freshly invented 'crimes', would render the camps superfluous, because in the long run no attitude and no opinion can withstand the threat of so much horror; and above all it would make for a new system of justice, which, given any stability at all, could not fail to produce a new juridical person in man, that would elude the totalitarian domination. The so-called 'Volksnutzen' of the Nazis, constantly fluctuating (because what is useful today can be injurious tomorrow) and the eternally shifting party line of the Soviet Union which, being retroactive, almost daily makes new groups of people available for the concentration camps, are the only guaranty for the continued existence of the concentration camps and hence for the continued total disfranchisement of man.

IV

The next decisive step in the preparation of living corpses is the murder of the moral person in man. This is done in the main by making martyrdom, for the first time in history, impossible. Rousset writes:

How many people here still believe that a protest has even historic importance? This skepticism is the real masterpiece of the SS. Their great accomplishment. They have corrupted all human solidarity. Here the night has fallen on the future. When no witnesses are left, there can be no testimony. To demonstrate when death can no longer be postponed is an attempt to give death a meaning, to act beyond one's own death. In order to be successful, a gesture must have social meaning. There are hundreds of thousands of us here, all living in absolute solitude. That is why we are subdued no matter what happens.

The camps and the murder of political adversaries are only part of organized oblivion that not only embraces carriers of public opinion such as the spoken and the written word, but extends even to the families and friends of the victim. Grief and remembrance are forbidden. In the Soviet Union a woman will sue for divorce immediately after her husband's arrest in order to save the lives of her children; if her husband chances to come back, she will indignantly turn him out of the house. The Western world has hitherto, even in its darkest periods, granted the slain enemy the right to be remembered as a self-evident acknowledgment of the fact that we are all men (and *only* men). It is only because even Achilles set out for Hector's funeral, only because the most despotic governments honored the slain enemy, only because the Romans allowed the Christians to write their martyrologies, only because the Church kept its heretics alive in the memory of men, that all was not lost and never could be lost. The concentration camps, by making death itself anonymous – in the Soviet Union it is almost impossible even to find out whether a prisoner is dead or alive – robbed death of the meaning which it had always been possible for it to have. In a sense they took away the individual's own death, proving that henceforth nothing belonged to him and he belonged to no one. His death merely set a seal on the fact that he had never really existed.

This attack on the moral person might still have been opposed by man's conscience which tells him that it is better to die a victim than to live as a bureaucrat of murder. The totalitarian governments have cut the moral person off from this individualist escape by making the decisions of conscience absolutely questionable and equivocal.

When a man is faced with the alternative of betraying and thus murdering his friends or of sending his wife and children, for whom he is in every sense responsible, to their death; when even suicide would mean the immediate murder of his own family – how is he to decide? The alternative is no longer between good and evil, but between murder and murder. In perhaps the only article which really gets to the core of this matter, Camus (in *Twice a Year*, 1947) tells of a woman in Greece, who was allowed by the Nazis to choose which among her three children should be killed.

Through the creation of conditions under which conscience ceases to be adequate and to do good becomes utterly impossible, the consciously organized complicity of all men in the crimes of totalitarian regimes is extended to the victims and thus made really total. The SS implicated concentration camp inmates – criminals, politicals, Jews – in their crimes by making them responsible for a large part of the administration, thus confronting them with the hopeless dilemma whether to send their friends to their death, or to help murder other men who happened to be strangers.

Once the moral person has been killed, the one thing that still prevents men from being made into living corpses is the differentiation of the individual, his unique identity. In a sterile form such individuality can be preserved through a persistent stoicism, and it is certain that many men under totalitarian rule have taken and are each day still taking refuge in this absolute isolation of a personality without rights or conscience. There is no doubt that this part of the human person, precisely because it depends so essentially on nature and on forces that cannot be controlled by the will, is the hardest to destroy (and when destroyed is most easily repaired).

The methods of dealing with this uniqueness of the human person are numerous and we shall not attempt to list them all. They begin with the monstrous conditions in the transports to the camps, when hundreds of human beings are packed into a cattle car stark naked, glued to each other, and shunted back and forth over the countryside for days on end; they continue upon arrival at the camp, the well-organized shock of the first hours, the shaving of the head, the grotesque camp clothing; and they end in the utterly unimaginable tortures so gauged as not to kill the body, at any event not quickly. The aim of all these methods, in any case, is to manipulate the human body – with its infinite possibilities of suffering – in such a way as to make it destroy the human person as inexorably as certain mental diseases of organic origin.

It is here that the utter lunacy of the entire process becomes most apparent. Torture, to be sure, is an essential feature of the whole totalitarian police and judiciary apparatus; it is used every day to make people talk. This type of torture, since it pursues a definite rational aim, has certain limitations: either the prisoner talks within a certain time, or he is killed. But to this rationally conducted torture another, irrational, sadistic type was added in the first Nazi concentration camps and in the cellars of the Gestapo. Carried on for the most part by the SA, it pursued no aims and was not systematic, but depended on the initiative of largely abnormal elements. The mortality was so high that only a few concentration camp inmates of 1933 survived these first years. This type of torture seemed to be not so much a calculated political institution as a concession of the regime to its criminal and abnormal elements, who were thus rewarded for services rendered. Behind the blind bestiality of the SA, there often lay a deep hatred and resentment against all those who were socially, intellectually, or physically better off than themselves, and who now, as if in fulfillment of their wildest dreams, were in their power. This resentment, which never died out entirely in the camps, strikes us as a last remnant of humanly understandable feeling.

The real horror began, however, when the SS took over the administration of the camps. The old spontaneous bestiality gave way to an absolutely cold and systematic destruction of human bodies, calculated to destroy human dignity; death was avoided or postponed indefinitely. The camps were no longer amusement parks for beasts in human form, that is, for men who really belonged in mental institutions and prisons; the reverse became true: they were turned into 'drill grounds' (Kogon), on which perfectly normal men were trained to be full-fledged members of the SS.

The killing of man's individuality, of the uniqueness shaped in equal parts by nature, will, and destiny, which has become so self-evident a premise for all human relations that even identical twins inspire a certain uneasiness, creates a horror that vastly overshadows the outrage of a juridical–political person and the despair of the moral person. It is this horror that gives rise to the nihilistic generalizations which maintain plausibly enough that essentially all men alike are beasts. Actually the experience of the concentration camps does show that human beings can be transformed into specimens of the human beast, and that man's 'nature' is only 'human' in so far as it opens up to man the possibility of becoming something highly unnatural, that is, a man.

After murder of the moral person and annihilation of the juridical person, the destruction of the individuality is almost always successful. Conceivably some laws of mass psychology may be found to explain why millions of human beings allowed themselves to be marched unresistingly into the gas chambers, although these laws would explain nothing else but the destruction of individuality. It is more significant that those individually condemned to death very seldom attempted to take one of their executioners with them, that there were scarcely any serious revolts, and that even in the moment of liberation there were very few spontaneous massacres of the SS men. For to destroy individuality is to destroy spontaneity, man's power to begin something new out of his own resources, something new that cannot be explained on the basis of reactions to environment and events. Nothing then remains but ghastly marionettes with human faces, which all behave like the dog in Pavlov's experiments, which all react with perfect reliability even when going to their own death, and which do nothing but react. This is the real triumph of the system:

The triumph of the SS demands that the tortured victim allow himself to be led to the noose without protesting, that he renounce and abandon himself to the point of ceasing to affirm his identity. And it is not for nothing. It is not gratuitously, out of sheer sadism, that the SS men desire this defeat. They know that the system which succeeds in destroying its victim before he mounts the scaffold . . . is incomparably the best for keeping a whole people in slavery. In submission. Nothing is more terrible than these processions of human beings going like dummies to their death. The man who sees this says to himself: 'For them to be thus reduced, what power must be concealed in the hands of the masters,' and he turns away, full of bitterness but defeated (Rousset).

V

It is characteristic of totalitarian terror that it increases as the regime becomes more secured, and accordingly concentration camps are expanded as political opposition decreases.[4] Totalitarian demands do not seem to be satisfied by political success in establishing a one-party state, and it seems as though political opposition were by no means the cause of terror but rather a barrier to its full development. This seems absurd only if we apply to modern totalitarian movements those standards of utility which they themselves expressly reject as obsolete, sentimental, and bourgeois.

If on the contrary we take totalitarian aspirations seriously and refuse to be misled by the common-sense assertion that they are utopian and unrealizable, it develops that the society of the dying established in the camps is the only form of society in which it is possible to dominate man entirely. Those who aspire to total domination must liquidate all spontaneity, such as the mere existence of individuality will always engender, and track it down in its most private forms, regardless of how unpolitical and harmless these may seem. Pavlov's dog, the human specimen reduced to the most elementary reactions, the bundle of reactions that can always be liquidated and replaced by other bundles of reactions that behave in exactly the same way, is the model 'citizen' of a totalitarian state; and such a citizen can be produced only imperfectly outside of the camps.

The uselessness of the camps, their cynically admitted anti-utility, is only apparent. In reality they are more essential to the preservation of the regime's power than any of its other institutions. Without concentration camps, without the undefined fear they inspire and the very well-defined training they offer in totalitarian domination, which has nowhere else been fully tested with all of its most radical possibilities, a totalitarian state can neither inspire its nuclear troops with fanaticism nor maintain a whole people in complete apathy. The dominating and the dominated would only too quickly sink back into the 'old bourgeois routine'; after early 'excesses', they would succumb to everyday life with its human laws; in short, they would develop in the direction which all observers counseled by common sense were so prone to predict. The tragic fallacy of all these prophecies originating in a world that was still safe, was to suppose that there was such a thing as one human nature established for all time, to identify this human nature with history and thus declare that the idea of total domination was not only inhuman but also unrealistic. Meanwhile we have learned that the power of man is so great that he really can be what he wishes to be.

It is in the very nature of totalitarian regimes to demand unlimited power. Such power can only be secured if literally all men, without a single exception, are reliably dominated in every aspect of their life. In the realm of foreign affairs new neutral territories must constantly be subjugated, while at home ever-new human groups must be mastered in expanding concentration camps, or, when circumstances require, liquidated to make room for others. Here the question of opposition is unimportant both in foreign and domestic affairs. Any neutrality, indeed any spontaneously given friendship is from the standpoint of totalitarian domination just as dangerous as open hostility, precisely because spontaneity as such, with its incalculability, is the greatest of all obstacles to total domination over man. The Communists of non-Communist countries, who fled or were called to Moscow, learned by bitter experience that they constituted a menace to the Soviet Union. Convinced Communists are in this sense, which alone has any reality today, just as ridiculous and just as menacing to the regime in Russia as for example the convinced Nazis of the Roehm faction were to the Nazis.

What makes conviction and opinion of any sort so ridiculous and dangerous under totalitarian conditions is that totalitarian regimes take the greatest pride in having no need of them, or of any human help of any kind. Men insofar as they are more than animal reaction and fulfillment of functions are entirely superfluous to totalitarian regimes. Totalitarianism strives not toward despotic rule over men, but toward a system in which men are superfluous. Total power can be achieved and safeguarded only in a world of conditioned reflexes, of marionettes without the slightest trace of spontaneity. Precisely because man's resources are so great, he can be fully dominated only when he becomes a specimen of the animal-species man.

Therefore character is a threat and even the most unjust legal rules are an obstacle; but individuality, anything indeed that distinguishes one man from another, is intolerable. As long as all men have not been made equally superfluous – and this has been accomplished only in concentration camps – the ideal of totalitarian domination has not been achieved. Totalitarian states strive constantly, though never with complete success, to establish the superfluity of man – by the arbitrary selection of various groups for concentration camps, by constant purges of the ruling apparatus, by mass liquidations. Common sense protests desperately that the masses are submissive and that all this gigantic apparatus of terror is therefore superfluous; if they were capable of telling the truth, the totalitarian rulers would reply: The apparatus seems superfluous to you only because it serves to make men superfluous.

They will not speak so frankly. But the concentration camps, and even more so the corpse factories invented by the Nazis speak only too clearly. Today, with population almost everywhere on the increase, masses of people are continuously being rendered superfluous by political, social, and economic events. At such a time the instruments devised for making human beings superfluous are bound to offer a great temptation: why not use these same instruments to liquidate human beings who have already become superfluous?

This side of the matter is only too well understood by the common sense of the mob which in most countries is too desperate to retain much fear of death. The Nazis, who were well aware that their defeat would not solve the problems of Europe, knew exactly what they were doing when, toward the end of the war – which by then they knew they had lost – they set up those factories of annihilation which demonstrated the swiftest possible solution to the problem of superfluous human masses. There is no doubt that this solution will from now on occur to millions of people whenever it seems impossible to alleviate political, or social, or economic misery in a manner worthy of man.

1 That Rousset's purely literary vitalism could survive the years in Buchenwald would seem to be striking proof of Kogon's thesis that 'most of the prisoners [left] the concentration camps with exactly the same convictions that they had before; if anything, these convictions became more accentuated' (p. 302). David Rousset concludes 702 pages of horror, which prove many times over that it is possible to kill man's humanity without killing his body, with a short paragraph of 'triumph', that sounds as if it had been written by a literary hack who had never set foot outside of Paris. 'We never blasphemed against life. Our systems of the world were not alike, but more profoundly, more remotely, our affirmation of the power and creative grandeur of life, our absolute faith in its triumph remained intact. We never believed in the final disaster of humanity. For collectively it is the highest, strongest expression of the vital gesture in the history of the universe.' It is not surprising that this 'vital gesture' should have appealed to Georges Bataille with his theory of 'extreme experience' – yet it is somehow surprising that the proponents of extremity and meaninglessness should not have changed their mind in the face of a reality that surpassed all their dreams. Bataille (*Critique*, October 1947) writes: 'One of Rousset's most unexpected reactions is his exultation, almost to the point of euphoria, before the idea of participating in an experience that made no sense. Nothing could be more virile, more *healthy*.' The translation is quoted from *Instead* (No. 1, 1948); it would seem to be no accident that this pseudo-profound reflection was the first break in the silence that the intellectuals have maintained on this whole matter.

2 Kogon has the following to say of working conditions in the Nazi camps, which

presumably were better organized from this point of view than those of the Soviet Union: 'A large part of the work exacted in the concentration camps was useless; either it was superfluous or it was so miserably planned that it had to be done over two or three times. Buildings often had to be begun several times because the foundations kept caving in' (p. 58). As for Russian conditions, even Dallin (*Forced Labor in Soviet Russia*, p. 105), who has built his whole book on the thesis that the purpose of the Russian camps was to provide cheap labor, is forced to admit: 'Actually, the efficiency of forced labor, despite incentives and compulsion, was and is on an extremely low level. The average efficiency of a slave laborer has certainly been below 50 per cent of that of a free Russian worker, whose productivity in turn has never been high.'

3 'Gestapo and SS have always attached great importance to mixing the categories of inmates in the camps. In no camp have the inmates belonged exclusively to one category' (Kogon, p. 19). In Russia it has also been customary from the first to mix political prisoners and criminals. During the first ten years of Soviet power, the leftist political groups enjoyed certain privileges as compared with counter-revolutionaries and criminals. But 'after the end of the twenties, the politicals were even officially treated as inferior to the common criminals' (Dallin, pp. 177 ff).

4 This is evident in Russia as well as in Germany. In Russia, the concentration camps, which were originally intended for enemies of the regime, began to swell enormously after 1930, i.e. at a time when not only all armed resistance had been quelled, but when all opposition to Stalin within the Party had been liquidated. In the first years there were in Germany at most ten camps with a total of no more than ten thousand inmates. All effective resistance against the Nazis ceased by the end of 1936. But at the outbreak of the war there were more than a hundred concentration camps, which after 1940 seem to have maintained an average population of one million.

CYRIL CONNOLLY

An American in London

Cyril Connolly (1903–74) is best known for his war-time editorship of the magazine, Horizon. *Early on in his career, Connolly wrote novels – The* Rock Pool *(1936) and* The Unquiet Grave *(1944) – but in later years his reputation as an artist was chiefly built on his capacity for lordly non-production. See* Enemies of Promise *(1938). In the 1950s Connolly took over from Desmond MacCarthy as chief book reviewer for the* Sunday Times *and his writing thereafter was mostly confined to commissioned non-fiction: essays, travel-pieces, parodies and so on. 'An American in London' first appeared in* Partisan Review *in 1949.*

The first warm Sunday at the end of March is the unofficial beginning of spring. The park smells of new grass, the noise of the mower is heard, the crocus carpets are on display, the boats are set free on the lake, huge crowds saunter up and down in the sunshine, as night falls other cries mingle with those of the waterfowl, contraceptives reappear in the gutters, a body (making the third unsolved murder of Regent's Park) is found in the thirteen-acre garden of Barbara Hutton's featureless house where once the dresses of the ballerinas invited by Lord Hertford, the 'Pasha' of the region, moving among the trees all night would be glimpsed by the respectable guests arriving for breakfast. Soon the leaves will be on the trees and the first American writers, on their way to Paris and a summer in Italy, will settle here for a day or two. These early migrants play an important role, for they reawaken the comatose winterbound group of hibernators who have not been able to get away to the sunshine by reminding them that they still have reputations, that although their corporeal selves are bound by drudgery and currency restrictions to their native soil, their books are free to wander where they will. Let us suppose that a young novelist, we will call him Harold Bisbee, whose first novel so perfectly shaded off the social boundary between the Far and the Middle West, has collected enough prize money to visit his London and Paris publishers on his way to the island of

Procida, goal of so many Near-Far Western friends. What is he going to find here?

His first disappointment will be his hotel, for there no longer exists in London a single hotel in which it is a pleasure for an artist to stay. That particular vision of the literary life which was conjured up by Garland's Hotel in Suffolk Place (till a bomb removed it), by the old Royal York at Brighton, or by the Royal Bath at Bournemouth with its memories of Henry James and Gosse, the hotel with its aroma of the 90s, its gilt and plush, its red or green flock walls and mahoganied private sitting rooms where discreet and elderly waiters serve pints of claret to literary gentlemen, the hotel we have imagined from so many memoirs, where Thackeray called on Turgenev or Conrad on Hardy or Maugham on Max, whose letter-heading plucks our heart in James's letters: Hôtel de Russie, Rome; Grand Hôtel, Pau; Hôtel de l'Europe, Avignon; Hôtel de l'Ecu, Genève; when we come to London – ah, Bisbee – it doesn't exist. The best hotels of London are large and anonymous, the smaller ones have all been renovated. The Russell in Russell Square is central for visits to publishers and the place has some Pompeian Art Nouveau and a period flavour, but it is essentially the hotel for Midland businessmen. The other hotels round the British Museum have had to be completely done over since the Gibraltar refugees or Ministry of Information were there. Of the fashionable hotels, the Connaught has the most atmosphere, but it is rather too chic for a serious young writer. If Bisbee stays at too expensive a hotel he will frighten off the elusive men of letters whom he is here to study, and only the publishers will call. The southern rooms of the Savoy and the northern rooms of the Hyde Park are the nicest rooms in London in summer, or else high up in the Dorchester, but all are expensive and somehow unsuitable. I think that the only place where Bisbee could stay without being disillusioned on his first day would be in one of those bachelor chambers round Clarges or Half Moon Street or Curzon Street, kept by retired butlers. James, I see, lived at 3 Bolton Street when he first came to London in the 80s. I expect Bisbee could live there too. Having arrived and unpacked, laid out the cartons of 'Luckies' which are to cut his swathe through European society and, alas, taken a pull at the bottle of Bourbon he is bringing over to his publisher, London loneliness will descend on poor Harold. He looks up at the waving plane-trees, the long sad spring sunset, he rings up one or two people who are out and sallies forth to dine alone and collect first impressions. Critical moment. Where will he eat? I can't say I envy him. He should, of course, for that first evening, go to an oyster bar: Cunningham's in Curzon Street (round the corner from his rooms), Wilson's in King Street, St James's, Driver's or Bentley's or Wheelers, and then look in at some pub – such as the Red Lion in Duke of York Street – whose interior is a delight. Then it is time to wander sadly home through the asphalt evening, looking at St James's, the Park, the buses, the prostitutes with their fur scarves and little dogs and back to the inevitable Henry James companion-volume ('When the warm weather comes I find London evenings very detestable') and so to bed. In the morning the telephone at 3 Bolton Street gets busy, his publisher takes him out to luncheon at the Etoile, literary London is at his feet.

What will be his impressions? As he looks round the crowded cocktail party, hugging a thimble of something warm and sweet with a recoil like nail-polish remover, he will certainly observe four facts about English writers. They are not young, they are not rich, they are even positively shabby; on the other hand they seem kind and they look distinguished and their publishers look hardly more prosperous and hardly less distinguished than they do. No one, certainly, can be in this for the money. Of the people he most wants to meet there will be a fair sprinkling, for private individuals can no longer afford to give cocktail parties and most writers will not miss this chance of a pleasurable spring reunion. The Sitwells are generally in the country but Mr Eliot will probably be there accompanied by Mr John Hayward (Dr Johnson disguised as Boswell) and they already convey an atmosphere particularly English to the gathering (not angels but Anglicans, as Gregory said). Towering over the rest are Mr Stephen Spender and Mr John Lehmann, two eagle heads in whose expressions amiability struggles with discrimination (Bisbee's European visit will largely depend on their summing up). About nine inches below them come the rank and file, Mr Roger Senhouse, Mr Raymond Mortimer, Mr V. S. Pritchett, Miss Rose Macaulay, Miss Elizabeth Bowen, Quennell, Pryce-Jones, Connolly, we all are there. But where is Bisbee's opposite number? Why is Mr Dylan Thomas still the youngest person present? Where are the under-thirties? If Bisbee is observant he will have remarked on the two outstanding peculiarities of English literary life: the absence of young writers at the bottom, the fusion of author with publisher at the top.

In such a gathering nearly everyone will have two or three jobs. Authors are either publishers or editors; if they do not edit or publish they will be on the British Council or the BBC. Culture is made and diffused by the same people. The cow serves in the milk bar. This explains the amazing coherence of English literary life, which often surprises visitors. It is easy to get 90 per cent of English writers happily into the same room because nearly all work in the same business. Editor–author, publisher–author, BBC–author, in turn the hunters and the hunted, they are in constant communication. Then again, they are nearly all of an age, which is now from about forty to fifty. But the remunerative pressure of culture-diffusion tends gradually to extinguish the creative spark and Bisbee would do well to make a point of never asking these charming, friendly and distinguished people what they are writing now, or what they plan to write in the future. Make clear that you have read our books, at least one of them, that you regard us as authors first and publishers, editors, broadcasters, or village explainers afterward, and then try to understand the endless struggle with unfeeling demands for income tax, with rising costs and standards of living, the impossibility, for English writers, of living cheaply in a sun-warmed cottage by the Pacific, the fatal English mixture of intelligence, administrative ability, humour and good sense with imagination which makes it so hard for us to exist only as artists, to suffer only as artists, to be deprived as artists of the human right to bring up and educate a family. We live here in a time when only successful novelists can make a living by their pens. Poets are doomed; essayists, critics fare little better; biographers may just survive. These mellow, sensitive, elderly and so individual faces who surround young Bisbee are perhaps the last known herd in existence of that mysterious animal, 'the English man of letters' – if there are no young people in the group, is it entirely due to the retardation of war, or is it not, perhaps, that there is so little to tempt them?

One might continue the daydream further. Let us picture Harold Bisbee with his clear eyes, charming mouth, slow western accent, his anecdotes of Cody, Nebraska, his passion for the 1920s, his success story ties, his Bebop records, his wonderful *'trouvaille'*, James's butler's granddaughter his cook in Bolton Street! Let us picture him really endearing himself to all our tired literary business men and women, who fling open their doors with a welcome they have long ceased to keep for each other, as he in turn slowly falls under the spell of their charm and taste and conversation – that wonderful conversation which uncovers as it proceeds the skeletons of the books they have not written. Might he not find in us the ideal subject – always such a problem – for a second novel? What could be a better field for his energy and powers of analysis than to consider this trusting group of middle-aged friends and discover, quite ruthlessly, what has gone wrong? Was it our schools? Was it our families? Was it the war? Is it taxation? Is it the Socialist Government? Is the Government not socialist enough? Or is it the next war? The uncertainty of living '*entre trois guerres*'? I see summer coming; Bisbee's ticket to Paris expires; now he's too late for the Pont Royal, now the season at Procida's over; and, lo, the squares and parks of London are thick with golden plane-tree leaves, autumn mists curl through Bolton Street, in leafy Kensington or river-scented Chelsea all doors open to Bisbee. 'Yes, I knew Lytton well.' 'I once met David Garnett.' One night an English girl, struck by something poetical in his fading youth, takes him to her bed '*sauter pour mieux reculer*', as is the English way, and after talking about frigidity there for an hour and a half she tells him about her former lovers, and bursts into tears. November is here, and all the other prize-winning novelists have returned home. Haggard, unshaven, a fugitive now from his account at Bolton Street, Bisbee walks the streets. He has discovered George Moore. It is by a busman's café in Ebury Street that a good grey head, a hawk-like glance bends over him, one night. 'You're Harold Bisbee, aren't you? I used to know your stuff. Been with us a long time now, son, haven't you? Almost one of us. How would you like a job? Publishing – but there's a bit of editing to do as well. Fine. My office, tomorrow, at nine!'

RANDALL JARRELL

The Obscurity of the Poet

Randall Jarrell (1914–65) is revered nowadays as an acute and entertaining critic of modern poetry – chiefly American poetry, on which he wrote with regularity during the 1940s and 1950s. Jarrell was himself a poet of some merit and he also wrote stories for children, and one novel – Pictures from an Institution (1954) – which is still admired as an amusing anti-academic satire. Jarrell's Poetry and the Age (1953) brings together some of his best poetry criticism and it includes the piece reprinted here – an essay which, as the text shows, began life as a lecture (given by Jarrell at a Harvard Summer School conference in 1950).

When I was asked to talk about the Obscurity of the Modern Poet I was delighted, for I have suffered from this obscurity all my life. But then I realized that I was being asked to talk not about the fact that people don't read poetry, but about the fact that most of them wouldn't understand it if they did: about the difficulty, not the neglect, of contemporary poetry. And yet it is not just modern poetry, but poetry, that is today obscure. *Paradise Lost* is what it was; but the ordinary reader no longer makes the mistake of trying to read it – instead he glances at it, weighs it in his hand, shudders, and suddenly, his eyes shining, puts it on his list of the ten dullest books he has ever read, along with *Moby Dick, War and Peace, Faust*, and Boswell's *Life of Johnson*. But I am doing this ordinary reader an injustice: it was not the Public, nodding over its lunch-pail, but the educated reader, the reader the universities have trained, who a few weeks ago, to the Public's sympathetic delight, put together this list of the world's dullest books.

Since most people know about the modern poet only that he is *obscure* – i.e. that he is *difficult*, i.e. that he is *neglected* – they naturally make a causal connection between the two meanings of the word, and decide that he is unread because he is difficult. Some of the time this is true; some of the time the reverse is true: the poet seems difficult *because* he is not read, *because* the reader is not accustomed to reading his or any other poetry. But most of the time neither is a cause – both are no more than effects of that long-continued, world-overturning cultural and social revolution (seen at its most advanced stage here in the United States) which has made the poet difficult and the public unused to any poetry exactly as it has made poet and public divorce their wives, stay away from church, dislike bull-baiting, free the slaves, get insulin shots for diabetes, or do a hundred thousand other things, some bad, some good, and some indifferent. It is superficial to extract two parts from this world-high whole, and to say of them: 'This one, here, is the cause of that one, there; and that's all there is to it.'

If we were in the habit of reading poets their obscurity would not matter; and, once we are out of the habit, their clarity does not help. Matthew Arnold said, with plaintive respect, that there was hardly a sentence in *Lear* that he hadn't needed to read two or three times; and three other appreciable Victorian minds, Beetle, Stalky, and McTurk, were even harder on it. They are in their study; Stalky reads:

> Never any.
> It pleased the king his master, very late,
> To strike at me, upon his misconstruction,
> When he, conjunct, and flattering in his displeasure,
> Tripped me behind: being down, insulted, railed,
> And put upon him such a deal of man
> That worthy'd him, got praises of the King
> For him attempting who was self-subdued;
> And, in the fleshment of this dread exploit,
> Drew me on here.

Stalky says: 'Now, then, my impassioned bard, *construez*! That's Shakespeare'; and Beetle answers, 'at the end of a blank half minute': 'Give it up! He's drunk.' If schoolboys were forced to read 'The Phoenix and the Turtle', what *would* Beetle have said of these two stanzas?

> Property was thus appalled
> That the self was not the same;
> Single nature's double name
> Neither two nor one was called,

Reason, in itself confounded,
Saw division grow together;
To themselves yet either-neither,
Simple were so well compounded . . .

You and I can afford to look at Stalky and Company, at Arnold, with dignified superiority: we know what those passages mean; we know that Shakespeare is never *obscure*, as if he were some modernist poet gleefully pasting puzzles together in his garret. Yet when we look at a variorum Shakespeare – with its line or two of text at the top of the page, its forty or fifty lines of wild surmise and quarrelsome conjecture at the bottom – we are troubled. When the Alexandrian poet Lycophron refers – and he is rarely so simple – to the *centipede, fair-faced, stork-hued daughters of Phalacra*, and they turn out to be boats, one ascribes this to Alexandrian decadence; but then one remembers that Welsh and Irish and Norse poets, the poets of a hundred barbarous cultures, loved nothing so much as referring to the very dishes on the table by elaborate descriptive epithets – periphrases, kennings – which their hearers had to be specially educated to understand. (Loved nothing so much, that is, except riddles.) And just consider the amount of classical allusions that those polite readers, our ancestors, were expected to recognize – and did recognize. If I recite to you, *The brotherless Heliades* | *Melt in such amber tears as these*, many of you will think, *Beautiful*; a good many will think, *Marvell*; but how many of you will know to whom Marvell is referring?

Yet the people of the past were not repelled by this obscurity (seemed, often, foolishly to treasure it); nor are those peoples of the present who are not so far removed from the past as we: who have preserved, along with the castles, the injustice, and the social discrimination of the past, a remnant of its passion for reading poetry. It is hard to be much more difficult than Mallarmé; yet when I went from bookstore to bookstore in Paris, hunting for one copy of Corbière, I began to feel a sort of mocking frustration at the poems by Mallarmé, letters by Mallarmé, letters to Mallarmé, biographies of, essays on, and homage to Mallarmé with which the shelves of those bookstores tantalized me. For how long now the French poet has been writing as if the French public did not exist – as if it were, at best, a swineherd dreaming of that far-away princess the poet; yet it looks at him with traditional awe, and reads in dozens of literary newspapers, scores of literary magazines, the details of his life, opinions, temperament, and appearance. And in the Germanic countries people still glance at one with attentive respect, as if they thought that one might at any moment be about to write a poem; I shall never forget hearing a German say, in an objective, considering tone, as if I were an illustration in a book called *Silver Poets of the Americas*: 'You know, he looks a little like Rilke.' In several South American countries poetry has kept most of the popularity and respect it formerly enjoyed; in one country, I believe Venezuela, the president, the ambassador whom he is sending to Paris, and the waiter who serves their coffee will four out of five times be poets. 'What sort of poetry do *these* poets write?' is a question of frightening moment for us poor Northern poets; if the answer is, 'Nice simple stuff', we shall need to question half our ways. But these poets, these truly popular poets, seem to have taken as models for their verse neither the poems of Homer, of Shakespeare, nor of Racine, but those of Pablo Picasso: they are all surrealists.

Is Clarity the handmaiden of Popularity, as everybody automatically assumes? how much does it help to be immediately plain? In England today few poets are as popular as Dylan Thomas – his magical poems have corrupted a whole generation of English poets; yet he is surely one of the most obscure poets who ever lived. Or to take an opposite example: the poems of the students of Yvor Winters are quite as easy to understand as those which Longfellow used to read during the Children's Hour; yet they are about as popular as those other poems (of their own composition) which *grave Alice, and laughing Allegra, and Edith with golden hair* used to read to Longfellow during the Poet's Hour. If Dylan Thomas is obscurely famous, such poets as these are clearly unknown.

When someone says to me something I am not accustomed to hearing, or do not wish to hear, I say to him: *I do not understand you*; and we respond in just this way to poets. When critics first read Wordsworth's poetry they felt that it was silly, but many of them *said*, with Byron, that 'he who understands it would be able | To add a story to the Tower of Babel'. A few years before, a great critic praising the work of that plainest of poets, John Dryden, had remarked that he 'delighted to tread on the brink where sense and nonsense mingle'. Dryden himself had found Shakespeare's phrases 'scarcely intelligible; and of those which we understand some are ungrammatical, others coarse; and his whole style is so pestered with figurative expressions that it is as affected as it is coarse'. The reviewers of 'The Love Song of J. Alfred Prufrock', even those who admired it most, found it almost impossible to understand; that it was hopelessly obscure seemed to them self-evident. Today, when college girls find it exactly as easy, exactly as hard, as 'The Bishop Orders his Tomb at St Praxed's', one is able to understand these critics' despairing or denunciatory misunderstanding only by remembering that the first generation of critics spoke of Browning's poem in just the terms that were later applied to Eliot's. How long it takes the world to catch up! Yet it really never 'catches up', but is simply replaced by another world that does not need to catch up; so that when the old say to us, 'What shall I do to understand Auden (or Dylan Thomas, or whoever the latest poet is)?' we can only reply: 'You must be born again.' An old gentleman at a party, talking to me about a poem we both admired, the *Rubaiyat*, was delighted to find that our tastes agreed so well, and asked me what modern poet I like best. Rather cutting my coat to his cloth, I answered: 'Robert Frost.' He looked at me with surprise, and said with gentle but undisguised finality: 'I'm afraid he is a little after my time.' This happened in 1950; yet surely in 1850 some old gentleman, fond of Gray and Cowper and Crabbe, must have uttered to the young Matthew Arnold the same words . . . but this time with reference to the poetry of William Wordsworth.

We cannot even be sure what people will find obscure; when I taught at Salzburg I found that my European students did not find 'The Waste Land' half as hard as Frost's poetry, since one went with, and the other against, all their own cultural presuppositions; I had not simply to explain 'Home-Burial' to them, I had to persuade them that it was a poem. And another example occurs to me: that of Robert Hillyer. In a review of *The Death of Captain Nemo* that I read, the reviewer's first complaint was that the poem is obscure. I felt as if I had seen Senator McCarthy denounced as an agent of the Kremlin; for how could Mr Hillyer be obscure?

That the poet, the modern poet is, understandably enough, for all sorts of good reasons, more obscure than even he has any imaginable right to be – this is one of those great elementary (or, as people say nowadays, *elemental*) attitudes about which it is hard to write anything that is not sensible and gloomily commonplace; one might as well talk on faith and works, on heredity and environment, or on that old question: why give the poor bath-tubs when they only use them to put coal in? Anyone knows enough to reply to this question: 'They don't; and, even if they did, *that*'s not the reason you don't want to help pay for the tubs.' Similarly, when someone says, 'I don't read modern poetry because it's all stuff that nobody on earth can understand,' I know enough to be able to answer, though not aloud: 'It isn't; and, even if it were, *that*'s not the reason you don't read it.' Any American poet under a certain age, a fairly advanced age – the age, one is tempted to say, of Bernard Shaw – has inherited a situation in which no one looks at him and in which, consequently, everyone complains that he is invisible: for that corner into which no one looks is always dark. And people who have inherited the custom of not reading poets justify it by referring to the obscurity of the poems they have never read – since most people decide that poets are obscure very much as legislators decide that books are pornographic: by glancing at a few fragments someone has strung together to disgust them. When a person says accusingly that he can't understand Eliot, his tone implies that most of his happiest hours are spent at the fireside among worn copies of the *Agamemnon*, *Phèdre*, and the Symbolic Books of William Blake; and it is melancholy to find, as one commonly will, that for months at a time he can be found pushing eagerly through the pages of *Gone with the Wind* or *Forever Amber*, where *with head, hands, wings, or feet* this poor fiend *pursues his way, and swims, or sinks, or wades, or creeps, or flies*; that all his happiest memories of Shakespeare seem to come from a high school production of *As You Like It* in which he played the wrestler Charles; and that he has, by some obscure process of free association, combined James Russell, Amy, and Robert Lowell into one majestic whole: a bearded cigar-smoking ambassador to the Vatican who, after accompanying Theodore Roosevelt on his first African expedition, came home to dictate on his deathbed the 'Concord Hymn'. Many a man, because Ezra Pound is too obscure for him, has shut for ever the pages of *Paradise Lost*; or so one would gather, from the theory and practice such people combine.

The general public [in this lecture I hardly speak of the happy few, who grow fewer and unhappier day by day] has set up a criterion of its own, one by which every form of contemporary art is condemned.

This criterion is, in the case of music, melody; in the case of painting, representation; in the case of poetry, clarity. In each case one simple aspect is made the test of a complicated whole, becomes a sort of loyalty oath for the work of art. Although judging by this method is almost as irrelevant as having the artist pronounce *shibboleth*, or swear that he is not a Know-Nothing, a Locofocoist, or a Bull Moose, it is as attractive, in exactly the same way, to the public that judges: instead of having to perceive, to enter, and to interpret those new worlds which new works of art are, the public can notice at a glance whether or not these pay lip-service to its own 'principles', and can then praise or blame them accordingly. Most of the music of earlier centuries, of other continents, has nothing the public can consider a satisfactory melody; the tourist looking through the galleries of Europe very soon discovers that most of the Old Masters were not, representationally speaking, half so good as the painters who illustrate *Collier's Magazine*; how difficult and dull the inexperienced reader would find most of the great poetry of the past, if he could ever be induced to read it! Yet it is always in the name of the easy past that he condemns the difficult present.

Anyone who has spent much time finding out what people do when they read a poem, what poems actually mean for them, will have discovered that a surprising part of the difficulty they have comes from their almost systematic unreceptiveness, their queer unwillingness to pay attention even to the reference of pronouns, the meaning of the punctuation, which subject goes with which verb, and so on; 'after all,' they seem to feel, 'I'm not reading *prose*.' You need to read good poetry with an attitude that is a mixture of sharp intelligence and of willing emotional empathy, at once penetrating and generous: as if you were listening to *The Marriage of Figaro*, not as if you were listening to *Tristan* or to Samuel Butler's Handelian oratorios; to read poetry – as so many readers do – like Mortimer Snerd pretending to be Dr Johnson, or like Uncle Tom recollecting Eva, is hardly to read poetry at all. When you begin to read a poem you are entering a foreign country whose laws and language and life are a kind of translation of your own; but to accept it because its stews taste exactly like your old mother's hash, or to reject it because the owl-headed goddess of wisdom in its temple is fatter than the Statue of Liberty, is an equal mark of that want of imagination, that inaccessibility to experience, of which each of us who dies a natural death will die.

That the poetry of the first half of this century often *was* too difficult – just as the poetry of the eighteenth century *was* full of antitheses, that of the metaphysicals full of conceits, that of the Elizabethan dramatists full of rant and quibbles – is a truism that it would be absurd to deny. How our poetry got this way – how romanticism was purified and exaggerated and 'corrected' into modernism; how poets carried all possible tendencies to their limits, with more than scientific zeal; how the dramatic monologue, which once had depended for its effect upon being a departure from the norm of poetry, now became in one form or another the norm; how poet and public stared at each other with righteous indignation, till the poet said, 'Since you won't read me, I'll make sure you can't' – is one of the most complicated and interesting of stories. But Modernism was not 'that lion's den from which no tracks return', but only a sort of canvas whale from which Jonah after Jonah, throughout the late 20s and early 30s, made a penitent return, back to rhyme and metre and plain broad Statement; how many young poets today are, if nothing else, plain! Yet how little posterity – if I may speak of that imaginary point where the poet and the public intersect – will care about all the tendencies of our age, all those good or bad intentions with which ordinary books are paved; and how much it will care for those few poems which, regardless of intention, manage at once to sum up, to repudiate, and to transcend both the age they appear in and the minds they are produced by. One judges an age, just as one judges a poet, by its best poems – after all, most of the others have disappeared; when posterity hears that our poems are obscure, it will smile indifferently – just as we do when we are told that the Victorians were sentimental, the Romantics extravagant, the Augustans conventional, the metaphysicals conceited, and the Elizabethans bombastic – and go back to its (and our) reading: to Hardy's 'During Wind and Rain', to Wordsworth's story of the woman Margaret, to Pope's 'Epistle to Dr Arbuthnot', to Marvell's 'Horatian Ode', to Shakespeare's *Antony and Cleopatra*, to Eliot's *Four Quartets*, and to all the rest of those ageless products of an age.

In this age, certainly, poetry persists under many disadvantages. Just as it has been cut off from most of the people who in another age would have read it, so it has been cut off from most of the people who in another age would have written it. Today poems, good poems, are written almost exclusively by 'born poets'. We have lost for good the poems that would have been written by the modern equivalents of Henry VIII or Bishop King or Samuel Johnson; born novelists, born theologians, born princes; minds with less of an innate interest in words and more of one in the world which produces words. We are accustomed to think of the poet, when we think of him at all, as someone Apart; yet was there – as so many poets and readers of poetry seem to think – *was* there in the Garden of Eden, along with Adam and Eve and the animals, a Poet, the ultimate ancestor of Robert P. Tristram Coffin? . . . When I last read poems in New York City, a lady who, except for bangs, a magenta jersey blouse, and the expression of Palamède de Charlus, was indistinguishable from any other New Yorker, exclaimed to me about a poet whom the years have fattened for the slaughter: 'He read like a young god.' I felt that the next poet was going to be told that I read like the young Joaquin Miller; for this lady was less interested in those wonderful things, poems, than in those other things, poets – not realizing that it is their subordination to the poems they write that makes them admirable. She seemed to me someone who, because he has inherited a pearl necklace, can never again look at an oyster without a shudder of awe. And this reminds one that, today, many of the readers a poet would value most have hardly learned to read any poetry; and many of those who regularly read his poems have values so different from his that he is troubled by their praise, and vexed but reassured by their blame.

Tomorrow morning some poet may, like Byron, wake up to find himself famous – for having written a novel, for having killed his wife; it will not be for having written a poem. That is still logically, but no longer socially, possible. Let me illustrate with a story. I once met on a boat, travelling to Europe with his wife and daughter, a man with whom I played ping-pong. Having learned from a friend that I wrote poetry, he asked one day with uninterested politeness, 'Who are the American poets you like best?' I said, 'Oh, T. S. Eliot, Robert Frost.' Then this man – this father who every night danced with his daughter with the well-taught, dated, decorous attractiveness of the hero of an old *Saturday Evening Post* serial by E. Phillips Oppenheim; who had had the best professional in Los Angeles teach his wife and daughter the tennis strokes he himself talked of with wearying authority; who never in his life had gone through a doorway before anyone over the age of seven – this well-dressed, well-mannered, travelled, urbane, educated gentleman said placidly: 'I don't believe I've heard of them.' For so far as literature, the arts, philosophy, and science were concerned, he might better have been the policeman on the corner. But he was perfectly correct in thinking – not that he had ever thought about it – that a knowledge of these things is not an essential requirement of the society of which he is a part. We belong to a culture whose old hierarchy of values – which demanded that a girl read Pope just as it demanded that she go to church and play the pianoforte – has virtually disappeared; a culture in which the great artist or scientist, in the relatively infrequent cases in which he has become widely known, has the status of Betty Grable or of the columnist who writes that, the night before, he met both these 'celebrities' at the Stork Club.

When, a hundred and fifty years ago, a man had made his fortune, he found it necessary to provide himself with lace, carriages, servants, a wife of good family, a ballerina, a fencing master, a dancing master, a chaplain, a teacher of French, a string quartet perhaps, the editions of Pope and Steele and Addison through which he worked a laborious way on unoccupied evenings: there was so much for him to learn to *do*, there in his new station in life, that he must often have thought with nostalgia of the days in which all that he had to do was make his fortune. We have changed most of that: in our day the rich are expected not to do but to be; and those ties, tenuous, ambiguous, and immemorial, which bound to the Power of a state its Wisdom and its Grace, have at last been severed.

When Mill and Marx looked at a handful of working-men making their slow firm way through the pages of Shelley or Herbert Spencer or *The Origin of Species*, they thought with confident longing, just as Jefferson and Lincoln had, of the days when every man would be literate, when an actual democracy would make its choices with as much wisdom as any imaginary state where the philosopher is king; and no gleam of prophetic insight came to show them those working-men, two million strong, making their easy and pleasant way through the pages of the New York *Daily News*. The very speeches in which Jefferson and Lincoln spoke of their hope for the future are incomprehensible to most of the voters of that future, since the vocabulary and syntax of the speeches are more difficult – more obscure – than anything the voters have read or heard. For when you defeat me in an election simply because you were, as I was not, born and bred in a log cabin, it is only a question of time until you are beaten by someone whom the pigs brought up out in the yard. The truth that all men are politically equal, the recognition of the injustice of fictitious differences, becomes a belief in the fictitiousness of differences, a conviction that it is reaction or snobbishness or Fascism to believe that any individual differences of real importance can exist. We dislike having to believe in what Goethe called inborn or innate merits; yet – as a later writer more or less says – many waiters are born with the taste of duchesses, and most duchesses are born (and die) with the tastes of waiters: we can escape from the level of society, but not from the level of intelligence, to which we were born.

One of our universities recently made a survey of the reading habits of the American public; it decided that forty-eight per cent of all Americans read, during a year, no book at all. I picture to myself that reader – non-reader, rather; one man out of every two – and I reflect, with shame: 'Our poems are too hard for him.' But so, too, are *Treasure Island, Peter Rabbit*, pornographic novels – any book whatsoever. The authors of the world have been engaged in a sort of conspiracy to drive this American away from books; have, in 77 million out of 160 million cases, succeeded. A sort of dream-situation often occurs to me in which I call to this imaginary figure, 'Why don't you read books?' – and he always answers, after looking at me steadily for a long time: 'Huh?'

If my tone is mocking, the tone of someone accustomed to helplessness, this is natural: the poet is a condemned man for whom the State will not even buy breakfast – and as someone said, 'If you're going to hang me, you mustn't expect to be able to intimidate me into sparing your feelings during the execution.' The poet lives in a world whose newspapers and magazines and books and motion pictures and radio stations and television stations have destroyed, in a great many people, even the capacity for understanding real poetry, real art of any kind. The man who monthly reads, with vacant relish, the carefully predigested sentences which the *Reader's Digest* feeds to him as a mother pigeon feeds her squabs – this man *cannot* read the *Divine Comedy*, even if it should ever occur to him to try: it is too obscure. Yet one sort of clearness shows a complete contempt for the reader, just as one sort of obscurity shows a complete respect. Which patronizes and degrades the reader, the *Divine Comedy* with its four levels of meaning, or the

Reader's Digest with its one level so low that it seems not a level but an abyss into which the reader consents to sink? The writer's real dishonesty is to give an easy paraphrase of the hard truth. Yet the average article in our magazines gives any subject whatsoever the same coat of easy, automatic, 'human' interest; every year *Harper's Magazine* sounds more like *Life* and the *Saturday Evening Post*. Goethe said, 'The author whom a lexicon can keep up with is worth nothing'; Somerset Maugham says that the finest compliment he ever received was a letter in which one of his readers said: 'I read your novel without having to look up a single word in the dictionary.' These writers, plainly, lived in different worlds.

Since the animal organism thinks, truly reasons, only when it is required to, thoughtfulness is gradually disappearing among readers; and popular writing has left nothing to the imagination for so long now that imagination too has begun to atrophy. Almost all the works of the past are beginning to seem to the ordinary reader flat and dull, because they do not supply the reader's response along with that to which he responds. Boys who have read only a few books in their lives, but a great many comic books, will tell one, so vividly that it is easy to sympathize: 'I don't like books because they don't really show you things; they're too slow; you have to do all the work yourself.' When, in a few years, one talks to boys who have read only a few comic books, but have looked at a great many television programmes – what will *they* say?

On this subject of the obscurity of the poet, of the new world that is taking the place of the old, I have written you a poem—an obscure one. I once encountered, in a book, a house that had a formal garden, an English garden, a kitchen garden, and a cutting garden; through these gardens gentlemen walked in silk stockings, their calves padded like those of Mephistopheles; and I made that cutting garden, those padded calves, my symbols for the past. For the present and the future I had so many symbols I didn't know what to do: they came into the poem without knocking, judged it, and did not leave when they had judged; but the one that summed them all up – that had, for me, the sound of the Last Morning of Judgment – was a slogan from a wine-advertisement, one that I used to see every day in the New York subways. My poem is called 'The Times Worsen':

If sixteen shadows flapping on the line
All sleek with bluing – a Last Morning's wash –
Whistle, 'Now that was thoughty, Mrs Bean,'
I tell myself, I try: *A dream, a dream.*
But my plaid spectacles are matt as gouache;
When, Sundays, I have finished all the funnies,
I have not finished all the funnies. Men
Walk in all day (to try me) without knocking –
My jurors: these just, vulgar, friendly shades.
The cutting garden of my grandmama,
My great-great-great-grandfather's padded calves
(Greeted, at cockcrow, with the soft small smile
Of Lilith, his first morganatic wife)
Are only a tale from E. T. W. Hoffmann.
When Art goes, what remains is Life.
The World of the Future does not work by halves:
Life is that 'wine like Mother used to make –
So rich you can almost cut it with a knife.'

The World of the Future! That world where vegetables are either frozen, canned, or growing in the fields; where little children, as they gaze into the television viewplate at the Babes dead under the heaped-up leaves of the Wood, ask pleadingly: 'But where was their electric blanket?'; where old books, hollowed-out to hold fudge, grace every coffee-table; where cavemen in grammar school pageants, clad in pelts of raw cotton, are watched by families dressed entirely – except for the Neolite of their shoe-soles – in rayon, cellulose, and spun nylon; where, among the related radiances of a kitchen's white-enamelled electric stove, electric dish-washer, electric refrigerator, electric washing-machine, electric dryer, electric ironer, disposal unit, air conditioner, and Waring Blendor, the home-maker sits in the trim coveralls of her profession; where, above the concrete cavern that holds a General Staff, the rockets are invisible in the sky . . . Of this world I often think.

I do not know whether, at this point, any of my hearers will feel like saying to me, 'But all this is Negative. What do you want us to *do* about all this?' If I have sounded certain about 'all this', let me apologize: these are conclusions which I have come to slowly and reluctantly, as the world forced them on me. Would that I were one of those happy reactionaries, born with a Greek vocabulary as other children are born with birthmarks or incomes, who at the age of four refuse indignantly to waste on that 'humanitarian phantasy of a sentimental liberalism, the Kindergarten', the hours they instead devote to memorizing their catechism! But I had a scientific education and a radical youth; am old-fashioned enough to believe, like Goethe, in Progress – the progress I see and the progress I wish for and do not see. So I say what I have said about the poet, the public, and their world angrily and unwillingly. If my hearers say, 'But what should we do?' what else can I answer but 'Nothing'? There is nothing to do different from what we already do: if poets write poems and readers read them, each as best they can – if they try to live not as soldiers or voters or intellectuals or economic men, but as human beings – they are doing all that can be done. But to expect them (by, say, reciting one-syllable poems over the radio) to bring back that Yesterday in which people stood on chairs to look at Lord Tennyson, is to believe that General Motors can bring back 'the tradition of craftsmanship' by giving, as it does, prizes to Boy Scouts for their scale-models of Napoleonic coaches; to believe that the manners of the past can be restored by encouraging country-people to say *Grüss Gott* or *Howdy, stranger* to the tourists they meet along summer lanes.

Art matters not merely because it is the most magnificent ornament and the most nearly unfailing occupation of our lives, but because it is life itself. From Christ to Freud we have believed that, if we know the truth, the truth will set us free: art is indispensable because so much of this truth can be learned through works of art and through works of art alone – or which of us could have learned for himself what Proust and Chekhov, Hardy and Yeats and Rilke, Shakespeare and Homer learned for us? and in what other way could they have made us see the truths which they themselves saw, those differing and contradictory truths which seem nevertheless, to the mind which contains them, in some sense a single truth? And all these things, by their very nature, demand to be shared; if we are satisfied to know these things ourselves, and to look with superiority or indifference at those who do not have that knowledge, we have made a refusal that corrupts us as surely as anything can. If while most of our people (the descendants of those who, ordinarily, listened to Grimm's Tales and the ballads and the Bible; who, exceptionally, listened to Aeschylus and Shakespeare) listen not to simple or naïve art, but to an elaborate and sophisticated substitute for art, an immediate and infallible synthetic as effective and terrifying as advertisements or the speeches of Hitler – if, knowing all this, we say: *Art has always been a matter of a few*, we are using a truism to hide a disaster. One of the oldest, deepest, and most nearly conclusive attractions of democracy is manifested in our feeling that through it not only material but also spiritual goods can be shared: that in a democracy bread and justice, education and art, will be accessible to everybody. If a democracy should offer its citizens a show of education, a sham art, a literacy more dangerous than their old illiteracy, then we should have to say that it is not a democracy at all, but one more variant of those 'People's Democracies' which share with any true democracy little more than the name. Goethe said: The only way in which we can come to terms with the great superiority of another person is love. But we can also come to terms with superiority, with true Excellence, by denying that such a thing as Excellence can exist; and, in doing so, we help to destroy it and ourselves.

I was sorry to see this conference given its (quite traditional) name of The Defence of Poetry. Poetry does not need to be defended, any more than air or food needs to be defended; poetry – using the word in its widest sense, the only sense in which it is important – has been an indispensable part of any culture we know anything about. Human life without some form of poetry is not human life but animal existence. Our world today is not an impossible one for poets and poetry: poets can endure its disadvantages, and good poetry is still being written – Yeats, for instance, thought the first half of this century the greatest age of lyric poetry since the Elizabethan. But what will happen to the public – to that portion of it divorced from any real art even of the simplest kind – I do not know. Yet an analogy occurs to me.

One sees, in the shops of certain mountainous regions of Austria, bands of silver links, clasped like necklaces, which have at the front jewelled or enamelled silver plates, sometimes quite large ones. These pieces of jewelry are called *goitre-bands*: they are ornaments which in the past were used to adorn a woman's diseased, enormously swollen neck. If the women who wore them could have been told that they had been made hideous by the lack of an infinitesimal proportion of iodine in the water of the mountain valley in which they lived, they would have laughed at the notion. They would have laughed even more heartily at the notion that their necks *were* hideous – and their lovers would have asked, as they looked greedily at the round flesh under the flaxen pigtails, how anyone could bear to caress the poor, thin, scrawny, chickenish necks of those other women they now and then saw, foreigners from that flatland which travellers call the world.

I have talked about the poet and his public; but who is his public, really? In a story by E. M. Forster called *The Machine Stops*, there is a conversation between a mother and her son. They are separated by half the circumference of the earth; they sit under the surface of the earth in rooms supplied with air, with food, and with warmth as automatically as everything else is supplied to these people of the far future. 'Imagine', as Forster says, 'a swaddled lump of flesh – a woman, about five feet high, with a face as white as a fungus.' She has just refused to go to visit her son; she has no time. Her son replies:

'The airship barely takes two days to fly between me and you.'

'I dislike airships.'

'Why?'

'I dislike seeing the horrible brown earth, and the sea, and the stars when it is dark. I get no ideas in an airship.'

'I do not get them anywhere else.'

'What kind of ideas can the air give you?'

He paused for an instant.

'Do you not know four big stars that form an oblong, and three stars close together in the middle of the oblong, and hanging from these stars, three other stars?'

'No, I do not. I dislike the stars. But did they give you an idea? How interesting; tell me.'

'I had an idea that they were like a man.'

'I do not understand.'

'The four big stars are the man's shoulders and his knees. The three stars in the middle are like the belts that men wore once, and the three stars hanging are like a sword.'

'A sword?'

'Men carried swords about with them, to kill animals and other men.'

'It does not strike me as a very good idea, but it is certainly original.'

As long as those stars remain in this shape; as long as there is a man left to look at them and to discover that they are the being Orion: for at least this long the poet will have his public. And when this man too is gone, and neither the poems, the poet, nor the public exist any longer – and this possibility can no longer seem to us as strange as it would once have seemed – there is surely some order of the world, some level of being, at which they still subsist: an order in which the lost plays of Aeschylus are no different from those that have been preserved, an order in which the past, the present, and the future have in some sense the same reality. Or so – whether we think so or not – so we all feel. People always ask: *For whom does the poet write?* He needs only to answer, *For whom do you do good? Are you kind to your daughter because in the end someone will pay you for being?. . .* The poet writes his poem for its own sake, for the sake of that order of things in which the poem takes the place that has awaited it.

But this has been said, better than it is ever again likely to be said, by the greatest of the writers of this century, Marcel Proust; and I should like to finish this lecture by quoting his sentences:

All that we can say is that everything is arranged in this life as though we entered it carrying the burden of obligations contracted in a former life; there is no reason inherent in the conditions of life on this earth that can make us consider ourselves obliged to do good, to be fastidious, to be polite even, nor make the talented artist consider himself obliged to begin over again a score of times a piece of work the admiration aroused by which will matter little to his body devoured by worms, like the patch of yellow wall painted with so much knowledge and skill by an artist who must for ever remain unknown and is barely identified under the name Vermeer. All these obligations which have not their sanction in our present life seem to belong to a different world, founded upon kindness, scrupulosity, self-sacrifice, a world entirely different from this, which we leave in order to be born into this world, before perhaps returning to the other to live once again beneath the sway of those unknown laws which we have obeyed because we bore their precepts in our hearts, knowing not whose hand had traced them there – those laws to which every profound work of the intellect brings us nearer and which are invisible only – and still! – to fools.

V. S. NAIPAUL

In the Middle of the Journey

V. S. Naipaul (1932–) was born in Trinidad and educated at University College, Oxford. After graduation, Naipaul settled in England, but his subsequent fiction and travel-writing rarely strayed from themes of post-colonial bemusement and disorder. This preoccupation, over the years, has won him few friends in the so-called Third World: Naipaul's lofty and fastidious manner reminds some Third World intellectuals of their erstwhile colonial masters. Naipaul has published several books on India (he is, as he has often stressed, of Indian descent). 'In the Middle of the Journey' was first collected in The Overcrowded Barracoon *(1972).*

Coming from a small island – Trinidad is no bigger than Goa – I had always been fascinated by size. To see the wide river, the high mountain, to take the twenty-four-hour train journey: these were some of the delights the outside world offered. But now after six months in India my fascination with the big is tinged with disquiet. For here is a vastness beyond imagination, a sky so wide and deep that sunsets cannot be taken in at a glance but have to be studied section by section, a landscape made monotonous by its size and frightening by its very simplicity and its special quality of exhaustion: poor choked crops in small crooked fields, undersized people, undernourished animals, crumbling villages and towns which, even while they develop, have an air of decay. Dawn comes, night falls; railway stations, undistinguishable one from the other, their name-boards cunningly concealed, are arrived at and departed from, abrupt and puzzling interludes of populousness and noise; and still the journey goes on, until the vastness, ceasing to have a meaning, becomes insupportable, and from this endless repetition of exhaustion and decay one wishes to escape.

To state this is to state the obvious. But in India the obvious is overwhelming, and often during these past six months I have known moments of near-hysteria, when I have wished to forget India, when I have escaped to the first-class waiting room or sleeper not so much for privacy and comfort as for protection, to shut out the sight of the thin bodies prostrate on railway platforms, the starved dogs licking the food-leaves clean, and to shut out the whine of the playfully assaulted dog. Such a moment I knew in Bombay, on the day of my arrival, when I felt India only as an assault on the senses. Such a moment I knew five months later, at Jammu, where the simple, frightening geography of the country becomes plain – to the north the hills, rising in range after ascending range; to the south, beyond the temple spires, the plains whose vastness, already experienced, excited only unease.

Yet between these recurring moments there have been so many others, when fear and impatience have been replaced by enthusiasm and delight, when the town, explored beyond what one sees from the train, reveals that the air of exhaustion is only apparent, that in India, more than in any other country I have visited, things are happening. To hear the sounds of hammer on metal in a small Punjab town, to visit a chemical plant in Hyderabad where much of the equipment is Indian-designed and manufactured, is to realize that one is in the middle of an industrial revolution, in which, perhaps because of faulty publicity, one had never really seriously believed. To see the new housing colonies in towns all over India is to realize that, separate from the talk of India's ancient culture (which invariably has me reaching for my *lathi*), the Indian aesthetic sense has revived and is now capable of creating, out of materials which are international, something which is essentially Indian. (India's ancient culture, defiantly paraded, has made the Ashoka Hotel one of New Delhi's most ridiculous buildings, outmatched in absurdity only by the Pakistan High Commission, which defiantly asserts the Faith.)

I have been to unpublicized villages, semi-developed and undeveloped. And where before I would have sensed only despair, now I feel that the despair lies more with the observer than the people. I have learned to see beyond the dirt and the recumbent figures on string beds, and to look for the signs of improvement and hope, however faint: the brick-topped road, covered though it might be with filth; the rice planted in rows and not scattered broadcast; the degree of ease with which the villager faces the official or the visitor. For such small things I have learned to look: over the months my eye has been adjusted.

Yet always the obvious is overwhelming. One is a traveller and as soon as the dread of a particular district has been lessened by familiarity, it is time to move on again, through vast tracts which will never become familiar, which will sadden; and the urge to escape will return.

Yet in so many ways the size of the country is only a physical fact. For, perhaps because of the very size, Indians appear to feel the need to categorize minutely, delimit, to reduce to manageable proportions.

'Where do you come from?' It is the Indian question, and to people who think in terms of the village, the district, the province, the community, the caste, my answer that I am a Trinidadian is only puzzling.

'But you look Indian.'

'Well, I am Indian. But we have been living for several generations in Trinidad.'

'But you look Indian.'

Three or four times a day the dialogue occurs, and now I often abandon explanation. 'I am a Mexican, really.'

'Ah.' Great satisfaction. Pause. 'What do you do?'

'I write.'

'Journalism or books?'

'Books.'

'Westerns, crime, romance? How many books do you write a year? How much do you make?'

So now I invent: 'I am a teacher.'

'What are your qualifications?'

'I am a BA.'

'Only a BA? What do you teach?'

'Chemistry. And a little history.'

'How interesting!' said the man on the Pathankot–Srinagar bus. 'I am a teacher of chemistry too.'

He was sitting across the aisle from me, and several hours remained of our journey.

In this vast land of India it is necessary to explain yourself, to define your function and status in the universe. It is very difficult.

If I thought in terms of race or community, this experience of India would surely have dispelled it. An Indian, I have never before been in streets where everyone is Indian, where I blend unremarkably into the crowd. This has been curiously deflating, for all my life I have expected some recognition of my difference; and it is only in India that I have recognized how necessary this stimulus is to me, how conditioned I have been by the multiracial society of Trinidad and then by my life as an outsider in England. To be a member of a minority community has always seemed to me attractive. To be one of four hundred and thirty-nine million Indians is terrifying.

A colonial, in the double sense of one who had grown up in a Crown colony and one who had been cut off from the metropolis, be it either England or India, I came to India expecting to find metropolitan attitudes. I had imagined that in some ways the largeness of the land would be reflected in the attitudes of the people. I have found, as I have said, the psychology of the cell and the hive. And I have been surprised by similarities. In India, as in tiny Trinidad, I have found the feeling that the metropolis is elsewhere, in Europe or America. Where I had expected largeness, rootedness and confidence, I have found all the colonial attitudes of self-distrust.

'I am craze phor phoreign,' the wife of a too-successful contractor said. And this craze extended from foreign food to German sanitary fittings to a possible European wife for her son, who sought to establish his claim further by announcing at the lunch table, 'Oh, by the way, did I tell you we spend three thousand rupees a month?'

'You are a tourist, you don't know,' the chemistry teacher on the Srinagar bus said. 'But this is a terrible country. Give me a chance and I leave it tomorrow.'

For among a certain class of Indians, usually more prosperous than their fellows, there is a passionate urge to explain to the visitor that they must not be considered part of poor, dirty India, that their values and standards are higher, and they live perpetually outraged by the country which gives them their livelihood. For them the second-rate foreign product, either people or manufactures, is preferable to the Indian. They suggest that for them, as much as for the European 'technician', India is only a country to be temporarily exploited. How strange to find, in free India, this attitude of the conqueror, this attitude of plundering – a frenzied attitude, as though the opportunity might at any moment be withdrawn – in those very people to whom the developing society has given so many opportunities.

This attitude of plundering is that of the immigrant colonial society. It has bred, as in Trinidad, the pathetic philistinism of the *renonçant* (an excellent French word that describes the native who renounces his own culture and strives towards the French). And in India this philistinism, a blending of the vulgarity of East and West – those sad dance floors, those sad 'western' cabarets, those transistor radios tuned to Radio Ceylon, those Don Juans with leather jackets or check tweed jackets – is peculiarly frightening. A certain glamour attaches to this philistinism, as glamour attaches to those Indians who, after two or three years in a foreign country, proclaim that they are neither of the East nor of the West.

The observer, it must be confessed, seldom sees the difficulty. The contractor's wife, so anxious to demonstrate her Westernness, regularly consulted her astrologer and made daily trips to the temple to ensure the continuance of her good fortune. The schoolteacher, who complained with feeling about the indiscipline and crudity of Indians, proceeded, as soon as we got to the bus station at Srinagar, to change his clothes in public.

The Trinidadian, whatever his race, is a genuine colonial. The Indian, whatever his claim, is rooted in India. But while the Trinidadian, a colonial, strives towards the metropolitan, the Indian of whom I have been speaking, metropolitan by virtue of the uniqueness of his country, its achievements in the past and its manifold achievements in the last decade or so, is striving towards the colonial.

Where one had expected pride, then, one finds the spirit of plunder. Where one had expected the metropolitan one finds the colonial. Where one had expected largeness one finds narrowness. Goa, scarcely liberated, is the subject of an unseemly inter-State squabble. Fifteen years after Independence the politician as national leader appears to have been replaced by the politician as village headman (a type I had thought peculiar to the colonial Indian community of Trinidad, for whom politics was a game where little more than PWD contracts was at stake). To the village headman India is only a multiplicity of villages. So that the vision of India as a great country appears to be something imposed from without and the vastness of the country turns out to be oddly fraudulent.

Yet there remains a concept of India – as what? Something more than the urban middle class, the politicians, the industrialists, the separate villages. Neither this nor that, we are so often told, is the 'real' India. And how well one begins to understand why this word is used! Perhaps India is only a word, a mystical idea that embraces all those vast plains and rivers through which the train moves, all those anonymous figures asleep on railway platforms and the footpaths of Bombay, all those poor fields and stunted animals, all this exhausted, plundered land. Perhaps it is this, this vastness which no one can ever get to know: India as an ache, for which one has a great tenderness, but from which at length one always wishes to separate oneself.

E. B. WHITE

The Ring of Time

E. B. White (1898–1985) has claims to be thought of as the inventor of New Yorkerese: his prose was always cordial, superior, relaxed, urbane, but with a sharply teasing edge, and this distinctive style of his was certainly perfected in the New Yorker *of the 1920s, when White was responsible for the magazine's 'Talk of the Town' section. Most of White's numerous books of essays were collections of work from the* New Yorker, *or from* Harper's, *to which he defected in the late 1930s (for* Harper's *he wrote a column called 'One Man's Meat'). Between columns, White also penned the children's classic,* Charlotte's Web.

Fiddler Bayou, March 22 1956

After the lions had returned to their cages, creeping angrily through the chutes, a little bunch of us drifted away and into an open doorway nearby, where we stood for a while in semidarkness, watching a big brown circus horse go harumphing around the practice ring. His trainer was a woman of about forty, and the two of them, horse and woman, seemed caught up in one of those desultory treadmills of afternoon from which there is no apparent escape. The day was hot, and we kibitzers were grateful to be briefly out of the sun's glare. The long rein, or tape, by which the woman guided her charge counterclockwise in his dull career formed the radius of their private circle, of which she was the revolving center; and she, too, stepped a tiny circumference of her own, in order to accommodate the horse and allow him his maximum scope. She had on a short-skirted costume and a conical straw hat. Her legs were bare and she wore high heels, which probed deep into the loose tanbark and kept her ankles in a state of constant turmoil. The great size and meekness of the horse, the repetitious exercise, the heat of the afternoon, all exerted a hypnotic charm that invited boredom; we spectators were experiencing a languor – we neither expected relief nor felt entitled to any. We had paid a dollar to get into the grounds, to be sure, but we had got our dollar's worth a few minutes before, when the lion trainer's whiplash had got caught around a toe of one of the lions. What more did we want for a dollar?

Behind me I heard someone say, 'Excuse me, please,' in a low voice. She was halfway into the building when I turned and saw her – a girl of sixteen or seventeen, politely threading her way through us onlookers who blocked the entrance. As she emerged in front of us, I saw that she was barefoot, her dirty little feet fighting the uneven ground. In most respects she was like any of two or three dozen showgirls you encounter if you wander about the winter quarters of Mr John Ringling North's circus, in Sarasota – cleverly proportioned, deeply browned by the sun, dusty, eager, and almost naked. But her grave face and the naturalness of her manner gave her a sort of quick distinction and brought a new note into the gloomy octagonal building where we had all cast our lot for a few moments. As soon as she had squeezed through the crowd, she spoke a word or two to the older woman, whom I took to be her mother, stepped to the ring, and waited while the horse coasted to a stop in front of her. She gave the animal a couple of affectionate swipes on his enormous neck and then swung herself aboard. The horse immediately resumed his rocking canter, the woman goading him on, chanting something that sounded like 'Hop! Hop!'

In attempting to recapture this mild spectacle, I am merely acting as recording secretary for one of the oldest of societies – the society of those who, at one time or another, have surrendered, without even a show of resistance, to the bedazzlement of a circus rider. As a writing man, or secretary, I have always felt charged with the safekeeping of all unexpected items of worldly or unworldly enchantment, as though I might be held personally responsible if even a small one were to be lost. But it is not easy to communicate anything of this nature. The circus comes as close to being the world in microcosm as anything I know; in a way, it puts all the rest of show business in the shade. Its magic is universal and complex. Out of its wild disorder comes order; from its rank smell rises the good aroma of courage and daring; out of its preliminary shabbiness comes the final splendor. And buried in the familiar boasts of its advance agents lies the modesty of most of its people. For me the circus is at its best before it has been put together. It is at its best at certain moments when it comes to a point, as through a burning glass, in the activity and destiny of a single performer out of so many. One ring is always bigger than three. One rider, one aerialist, is always greater than six. In short, a man has to catch the circus unawares to experience its full impact and share its gaudy dream.

The ten-minute ride the girl took achieved – as far as I was concerned, who wasn't looking for it, and quite unbeknownst to her, who wasn't even striving for it – the thing that is sought by performers everywhere, on whatever stage, whether struggling in the tidal currents of Shakespeare or bucking the difficult motion of a horse. I somehow got the idea she was just cadging a ride, improving a shining ten minutes in the diligent way all serious artists seize free moments to hone the blade of their talent and keep themselves in trim. Her brief tour included only elementary postures and tricks, perhaps because they were all she was capable of, perhaps because her warmup at this hour was unscheduled and the ring was not rigged for a real practice session. She swung herself off and on the horse several times, gripping his mane. She did a few knee-stands – or whatever they are called – dropping to her knees and quickly bouncing back up on her feet again. Most of the time she simply rode in a standing position, well aft on the beast, her hands hanging easily at her sides, her head erect, her straw-colored ponytail lightly brushing her shoulders, the blood of exertion showing faintly through the tan of her skin. Twice she managed a one-foot stance – a sort of ballet pose, with arms outstretched. At one point the neck strap of her bathing suit broke and she went twice around the ring in the classic attitude of a woman making minor repairs to a garment. The fact that she was standing on the back of a moving horse while doing this invested the matter with a clownish significance that perfectly fitted the spirit of the circus – jocund, yet charming. She just rolled the strap into a neat ball and stowed it inside her bodice while the horse rocked and rolled beneath her in dutiful innocence. The bathing suit proved as self-reliant as its owner and stood up well enough without benefit of strap.

The richness of the scene was in its plainness, its natural condition – of horse, of ring, of girl, even to the girl's bare feet that gripped the bare back of her proud and ridiculous mount. The enchantment grew not out of anything that happened or was performed but out of something that seemed to go round and around and around with the girl, attending her, a steady gleam in the shape of a circle – a ring of ambition, of happiness, of youth. (And the positive pleasures of equilibrium under difficulties.) In a week or two, all would be changed, all (or almost all) lost: the girl would wear makeup, the horse would wear gold, the ring would be painted, the bark would be clean for the feet of the horse, the girl's feet would be clean for the slippers that she'd wear. All, all would be lost.

As I watched with the others, our jaws adroop, our eyes alight, I became painfully conscious of the element of time. Everything in the hideous old building seemed to take the shape of a circle, conforming to the course of the horse. The rider's gaze, as she peered straight ahead, seemed to be circular, as though bent by force of circumstance; then time itself began running in circles, and so the beginning was where the end was, and the two were the same, and one thing ran into the next and time went round and around and got nowhere. The girl wasn't so young that she did not know the delicious satisfaction of having a perfectly behaved body and the fun of using it to do a trick most people can't do, but she was too young to know that time does not really move in a circle at all. I thought: 'She will never be as beautiful as this again –' a thought that made me acutely unhappy – and in a flash my mind (which is too much of a busy-body to suit me) had projected her twenty-five years ahead, and she was now in the center of the ring, on foot, wearing a conical hat and high-heeled shoes, the image of the older woman, holding the long rein, caught in the treadmill of an afternoon long in the future. 'She is at that enviable moment in life [I thought] when she believes she can go once around the ring, make one complete circuit, and at the end be exactly the same age as at the start.' Everything in her movements, her expression, told you that for her the ring of time was perfectly formed, changeless, predictable, without beginning or end, like the ring in which she was traveling at this moment with the horse that wallowed under her. And then I slipped back into my trance, and time was circular again – time, pausing quietly with the rest of us, so as not to disturb the balance of a performer.

Her ride ended as casually as it had begun. The older woman stopped the horse, and the girl slid to the ground. As she walked toward us to leave, there was a quick, small burst of applause. She smiled broadly, in surprise and pleasure; then her face suddenly regained its gravity and she disappeared through the door.

It has been ambitious and plucky of me to attempt to describe what is indescribable, and I have failed, as I knew I would. But I have discharged my duty to my society; and besides, a writer, like an acrobat, must occasionally try a stunt that is too much for him. At any rate, it is worth reporting that long before the circus comes to town, its most notable performances have already been given. Under the bright lights of the finished show, a performer need only reflect the electric candle power that is directed upon him; but in the dark and dirty old training rings and in the makeshift cages, whatever light is generated, whatever excitement, whatever beauty, must come from original sources – from internal fires of professional hunger and delight, from the exuberance and gravity of youth. It is the difference between planetary light and the combustion of stars.

The South is the land of the sustained sibilant. Everywhere, for the appreciative visitor, the letter 's' insinuates itself in the scene: in the sound of sea and sand, in the singing shell, in the heat of sun and sky, in the sultriness of the gentle hours, in the siesta, in the stir of birds and insects. In contrast to the softness of its music, the South is also cruel and hard and prickly. A little striped lizard, flattened along the sharp green bayonet of a yucca, wears in its tiny face and watchful eye the pure look of death and violence. And all over the place, hidden at the bottom of their small sandy craters, the ant lions lie in wait for the ant that will stumble into their trap. (There are three kinds of lions in this region: the lions of the circus, the ant lions, and the Lions of the Tampa Lions Club, who roared their approval of segregation at a meeting the other day – all except one, a Lion named Monty Gurwit, who declined to roar and thereby got his picture in the paper.)

The day starts on a note of despair: the sorrowing dove, alone on its telephone wire, mourns the loss of night, weeps at the bright perils of the unfolding day. But soon the mockingbird wakes and begins an early rehearsal, setting the dove down by force of character, running through a few slick imitations, and trying a couple of original numbers into the bargain. The redbird takes it from there. Despair gives way to good humor. The Southern dawn is a pale affair, usually, quite different from our northern daybreak. It is a triumph of gradualism; night turns to day imperceptibly, softly, with no theatrics. It is subtle and undisturbing. As the first light seeps in through the blinds I lie in bed half awake, despairing with the dove, sounding the A for the brothers Alsop. All seems lost, all seems sorrowful. Then a mullet jumps in the bayou outside the bedroom window. It falls back into the water with a smart smack. I have asked several people why the mullet incessantly jump and I have received a variety of answers. Some say the mullet jump to shake off a parasite that annoys them. Some say they jump for the love of jumping – as the girl on the horse seemed to ride for the love of riding (although she, too, like all artists, may have been shaking off some parasite that fastens itself to the creative spirit and can be got rid of only by fifty turns around a ring while standing on a horse).

In Florida at this time of year, the sun does not take command of the day until a couple of hours after it has appeared in the east. It seems to carry no authority at first. The sun and the lizard keep the same schedule; they bide their time until the morning has advanced a good long way before they come fully forth and strike. The cold lizard waits astride his warming leaf for the perfect moment; the cold sun waits in his nest of clouds for the crucial time.

On many days, the dampness of the air pervades all life, all living. Matches refuse to strike. The towel, hung to dry, grows wetter by the hour. The newspaper, with its headlines about integration, wilts in your hand and falls limply into the coffee and the egg. Envelopes seal themselves. Postage stamps mate with one another as shamelessly as grasshoppers. But most of the time the days are models of beauty and wonder and comfort, with the kind sea stroking the back of the warm sand. At evening there are great flights of birds over the sea, where the light lingers; the gulls, the pelicans, the terns, the herons stay aloft for half an hour after land birds have gone to roost. They hold their ancient formations, wheel and fish over the Pass, enjoying the last of day like children playing outdoors after suppertime.

To a beachcomber from the North, which is my present status, the race problem has no pertinence, no immediacy. Here in Florida I am a guest in two houses – the house of the sun, the house of the State of Florida. As a guest, I mind my manners and do not criticize the customs of my hosts. It gives me a queer feeling, though, to be at the center of the greatest social crisis of my time and see hardly a sign of it. Yet the very absence of signs seems to increase one's awareness. Colored people do not come to the public beach to bathe, because they would not be made welcome there; and they don't fritter away their time visiting the circus, because they have other things to do. A few of them turn up at the ballpark, where they occupy a separate but equal section of the left-field bleachers and watch Negro players on the visiting Braves team using the same bases as the white players, instead of separate (but equal) bases. I have had only two small encounters with 'color'. A colored woman named Viola, who had been a friend of my wife's sister years ago, showed up one day with some laundry of ours that she had consented to do for us, and with the bundle she brought a bunch of nasturtiums, as a sort of natural accompaniment to the delivery of clean clothes. The flowers seemed a very acceptable thing and I was touched by them. We asked Viola about her daughter, and she said she was at Kentucky State College, studying voice.

The other encounter was when I was explaining to our cook, who is from Finland, the mysteries of bus travel in the American Southland. I showed her the bus stop, armed her with a timetable, and then, as a matter of duty, mentioned the customs of the Romans. 'When you get on the bus,' I said, 'I think you'd better sit in one of the front seats – the seats in back are for colored people.' A look of great weariness came into her face, as it does when we use too many dishes, and she replied, 'Oh, I know – isn't it silly!'

Her remark, coming as it did all the way from Finland and landing on this sandbar with a plunk, impressed me. The Supreme Court said nothing about silliness, but I suspect it may play more of a role than one might suppose. People are, if anything, more touchy about being thought silly than they are about being thought unjust. I note that one of the arguments in the recent manifesto of Southern Congressmen in support of the doctrine of 'separate but equal' was that it had been founded on 'common sense'. The sense that is common to one generation is uncommon to the next. Probably the first slave ship, with Negroes lying in chains on its decks, seemed commonsensical to the owners who operated it and to the planters who patronized it. But such a vessel would not be in the realm of common sense today. The only sense that is common, in the long run, is the sense of change – and we all instinctively avoid it, and object to the passage of time, and would rather have none of it.

The Supreme Court decision is like the Southern sun, laggard in its early stages, biding its time. It has been the law in Florida for two years now, and the years have been like the hours of the morning before the sun has gathered its strength. I think the decision is as incontrovertible and warming as the sun, and, like the sun, will eventually take charge.

But there is certainly a great temptation in Florida to duck the passage of time. Lying in warm comfort by the sea, you receive gratefully the gift of the sun, the gift of the South. This is true seduction. The day is a circle – morning, afternoon, and night. After a few days I was clearly enjoying the same delusion as the girl on the horse – that I could ride clear around the ring of day, guarded by wind and sun and sea and sand, and be not a moment older.

DAN JACOBSON

Time of Arrival

Dan Jacobson was born in Johannesburg in 1929 and has lived in London since the 1950s. His several distinguished novels include The Evidence of Love *(1960),* The Beginners *(1966),* The Rape of Tamar *(1970) and* Hidden in the Heart *(1998). For many years Jacobson was a Professor of English Literature at University College London. Recently he has tended to concentrate on non-fiction:* Time and Time Again, *an autobiographical memoir, appeared in 1985 and was followed by* The Electronic Elephant *(1994) and* Heshel's Kingdom *(1998). An earlier version of 'Time of Arrival' is collected in* Time of Arrival and Other Essays *(1962).*

It was just after midday that the boat docked at Dover. We went through the Customs shed and on to the pallid grey platform of the railway station. With all the anxieties of arrival upon me, in England for the first time, a few days after my twenty-first birthday, I nevertheless felt at peace. One could not help feeling at peace, the station was so quiet, the officials were so homely in appearance, the voices of the passengers were raised in such a clear, almost bird-like way. I bought *The Times* and the *New Statesman*, and felt with gratification, after years of handling only the overseas editions, the thickness of the paper between my fingers; with the same gratification I saw the dateline on the papers to be the actual date, not that of two or three weeks before. So I was in England, truly in England at last. I had not known how much I had wanted to be in England until then; until, on that platform, an anxiety came to rest, and something else within me – an ambition perhaps, or a hope – began to stir.

I remember vividly those casual yet oddly decisive moments on Dover station, and the very different moment of arrival at Victoria, but nothing of the journey between. Victoria seemed huge to me, echoing, dark; black-clothed people scurried bewilderingly under the vault, in all directions. Fortunately, I was travelling with my brother, who had been in London before, and knew his way about the city a little. As it was still early in the afternoon we decided we would not bother for the moment about finding accommodation, but would simply leave our luggage in the station cloakroom and go out for a look around.

The pavements outside were a little paler than the overcast sky; the cobbled space in front of the station seemed overcrowded with lumbering red buses. We did not go far on that first exploration; we merely caught one of the buses to Hyde Park Corner, crossed into the park, and walked up towards Marble Arch. Already, on that walk, I was struck by what was for me to be one of London's most surprising features: its spaciousness, the size of its streets, squares and public places. (The size of the city itself was another matter, and quite distinct from what I am speaking of here: in a way, the area the city as a whole covered did not come as such a surprise to me, partly because I could not, and still cannot, grasp it: it is beyond reckoning, beyond the widest span of one's imagination.) I suppose I had heard so much about the 'tight little island', about England being 'cramped', 'crowded', and 'pinched' – and had also heard so much about the 'wide open spaces' of South Africa, about the 'vastness' of the veld – that somehow in my mind there was an expectation that everything in England would really be small, reduced in scale, somehow toylike. And it was true that many of the individual buildings were small, and did seem to have been rammed against one another, in a frozen jostle for space. Nevertheless, again and again, on other walks, I was to be surprised by such random things as the sheer mass of the piers and arches of bridges; the width of the steps leading up to monuments; the striving, swaying height of the trees in the parks, and the breadth of the expanses of grass around them; the acres upon acres of the city given over to railways gleaming in parallel lines; the stretches of terraced houses which seemed to wear their encrusted ornamentation like a frown, and which stood in endless repetition down wide, windblown streets.

On that first walk it was Hyde Park itself which was imposing, and the lumps of statuary just inside and outside the park, and the glimpses of streets and buildings beyond. It was mid-afternoon, in late March, and bitterly cold; there seemed to be nothing spring-like in the air, though I was surprised to see how green was the grass in the park. From nowhere, it seemed, a gust of rain was suddenly dashed into our faces as we walked; it did not seem at all to have come from the sky. The gust ceased as abruptly as it had begun. But the sun did not come out; it looked as though the sun never had come out, and never would. Through the streets, between the trees, over the grass, the light *moved*. That is the only way I can describe the thickness of the light; the swiftness with which it changed; the slightness of the individual changes; the way it could change at a distance and yet remain unchanged nearby. It was as if between ourselves and the source of light there had been put an infinite number of filters, which were constantly being removed and replaced, nearer and farther, in a perpetual alternation.

Within this shifting light, colours had a strange intensity; they seemed to well up continuously within each object, instead of being a static, hard, settled dye or tone. Because of this suffusion or seepage of colour, one almost expected the objects themselves to be vague in outline, to run together, so their precision and firmness of line came invariably as a surprise. This was true even of the faces of people, which were either vague or suddenly vivid, featureless or disconcertingly quick in expression. Even on that first walk I saw how fine, how subtle, how eccentric the faces of the English were. Each face seemed to carry within it the shadows, the suggestions, of innumerable others which had neither come to the surface nor been entirely lost.

Unexpectedly, it began to grow dark, really dark, though it was not yet five o'clock. So we had to think of finding an hotel, and went back from Marble Arch to Victoria to collect our luggage. My brother knew that there were many cheap hotels in Bloomsbury. We told a taxi-driver simply to take us there; he drove to Tavistock Square, and we stopped him at the first hotel we saw. It was a narrow converted house. Everything inside it was narrow too: the entrance-hall, the manager's cubicle, the manager's face, the staircase, the room into which we were eventually shown. The room smelled heavily of damp; it had a single large window, overlooking a fire-escape and a brick wall; right against the sky, above everything else, a battery of chimney-pots stood poised. An Irish maid came in to make up the beds; an elderly woman, with eyes that seemed to move about too much, under a tired, deeply lined brow. She was silent throughout, until my brother went out of the room; then she came up to me, took my arm with her hand in a fierce grip, brought her face close to mine and said passionately, 'You're lucky there's the two of you. It gets too queer when you're alone!' A moment later she was gone.

*

Quite by chance I had been reading on my way to England a miscellany which contained, among other things, a collection of letters written by Virginia Woolf to Logan Pearsall Smith. The letters had been addressed, I remembered, from Tavistock Square. The first thing I did was to get the book from my suitcase and look up the number of the house she had lived in. When we came out of the hotel we walked around the square, looking for the house among the black, flat-fronted dwellings which remained on two sides of it. The house itself, however, no longer existed. In its place was a bomb-site. We leaned over a low brick wall, looking into the hole in the ground where the house should have been. Down below were stumps of walls, some of them overgrown, others showing bits of coloured plaster and tile. Great wooden beams rose out of the hole to buttress the building from which the one on this site had been severed.

I must have spent hours, during my first few weeks in London, looking into such bomb-sites, wondering about them, searching in myself for a response to them which seemed adequate, and never finding it. Many of the ruins were dramatic, even melodramatic, to look at, with bare walls as flat as shadows, and the sky showing through gaps which had once been doors and windows; others were merely quiet, wasted, charred spaces, where only a few ledges and bits of brick revealed the basements of what had once been houses, churches, office-blocks, blocks of flats. How could such weights of masonry have been brought down by flame and explosion into heaps of rubble? How had the rubble been carted away, leaving the streets trim, though gaping? In the end one had to look at the ruins as one looked at everything else: as part of the spectacle of London, as another sign of the things that people had done over the hundreds of years they had been in London, just another evidence of their having lived and died in the place.

Anyway, the house Virginia Woolf had written those letters from was no longer there, and I was disappointed to see this. But the rest of the square was presumably much as it had been when she had been alive and had written her letters to Logan Pearsall Smith. He and she had exchanged elaborate, self-conscious mock-insults about 'Chelsea', which he was supposed to represent, and 'Bloomsbury', which of course had been hers. Part of what they had meant by Bloomsbury I saw to be these trees and houses, the glimpses above them of some of the buildings of London University, the traffic in Southampton Row. Was there nothing else? Within the disappointment that the house should have been scooped out of the square another began to grow. So this was it. I had seen it. True, I had not seen, and thought it unlikely I would ever see, any of the people who had made up the Bloomsbury society; but the physical Bloomsbury was about me. The disappointment was not with its appearance, which was black enough, and severe enough, and imposing enough; it arose from the very fact of my having seen it. The half-conscious, always-unfinished guesswork which had been so inextricably an aspect of my reading, throughout my childhood and adolescence in South Africa, the dreamlike otherness or remoteness in the books I had read, which I had valued more than I had supposed, were being taken from me, bit by bit. Here was one bit of it gone. I would never again be able to visit a Bloomsbury of my own imagination – a district vaguer and therefore more glamorous than the reality; one less hard and angular and self-defining. I would not have exchanged my glimpse of the Bloomsbury of brick and tar, of tree-trunk and iron railing, for anything I might have been able to imagine; but still, there was a loss.

Another loss I knew was my own imagination of myself in Blooms-bury, or anywhere else in London. Coming to London had not – not yet, at any rate – changed me, transformed me, made a new man of me. Bloomsbury was what it had been before I had seen it. So was I.

Breakfasts in the hotel were gloomy meals, taken in a small dining room where everybody spoke in subdued tones, but for one man in a checked suit who rustled his *Daily Telegraph* loudly and demanded almost every morning, in a voice that carried across the room, that they give the 'cat' to the 'hooligans' whose doings he read about in the papers. He was strong on 'niggers' too. He was like a caricature of the hanging, flogging Englishman of the most benighted kind: seething with grievances and rages which reddened his round face, thickened his voice, and made his small blond moustache bristle. Did he have any suspicion of the social changes to come over the next few decades? I think not. He was my first living exemplar of the English flair for self-imitation; the zeal, the whole-heartedness with which many English-men conform to certain ideal types of such familiarity, not to say staleness, that the outsider positively expects some 'real' man buried within the type to give him a secret wink of irony, a little gesture or nod of complicity. But the outsider waits in vain. The man (or woman) is absorbed completely in his role. Don or dustman, *New Statesman* intellectual or flogging Tory, débutante or char: it is impossible to say which came first, the type or the individual. So it was with this man; and so too, in a different way, it was with the other guests in the hotel, who appeared to be either students or a few elderly ladies who lived there permanently. (There were no foreigners among them, apart from ourselves.) None of the other guests ever argued with or even commented upon the remarks of the hanger and flogger. Instead, in a curious, dismal, English fashion they managed wordlessly to dissociate themselves from him without putting forward any views of their own. Indeed, still wordlessly, they even managed to suggest that it wasn't so much the man's views they disapproved of, as the vehemence with which he put them forward. The hotel, incidentally, unlike others in the neighbourhood, did not have a single African or Indian guest.

Breakfast was the only meal we took in the hotel: most of the time, by day and in the evenings too, we were out sightseeing. We went to Westminster Abbey; we wandered about the Strand, and St Paul's and the City; we stood in Piccadilly and Parliament Square; we went to Downing Street and across St James's Park and into Mayfair. As we went about I hardly knew whether I was actually seeing the streets and buildings in front of me or merely confirming that they were there, as the pictures and books had told me they would be. There was deep satisfaction in this confirmation: so deep I cannot easily describe it, for it was not just the reality of the buildings that was confirmed, but also, in an odd, unexpected way, my own reality too. So place ran into place into place in a progression that seemed endless in length and breadth, and was limited in other dimensions, aesthetically or historically, only by my own ignorance. At every point the progression yielded some interest; it could not help doing so, for the pleasure of confirmation did not wait upon the famous buildings or vistas, but could be roused by any ordinary street or sign, both for what it was and for being where it was. However, one great fact about London was so overwhelming that I couldn't possibly think of it as a recollection or a reminder of what I had already been told. That was the shabbiness of the city.

I think I would have found London shabby under any circumstances, during the first few weeks after my arrival, because of the sky above it: everything, I felt, must look its worst under a sky that continually trailed clouds and smoke low over the buildings, and sometimes thinned a little to reveal a sun coloured like the blood-spot in an egg. However, I had come there a few years after a war which had halted the erection of new buildings, and the repair of old ones, which had destroyed or partially destroyed thousands of others; and which had then left the country to endure a kind of siege of rationing and austerity, and their accompanying gloom. There were times when I felt that an inward dissolution would do as effectively over a wider area what the bombs had done where they had fallen, and that the blackened, gutted hulks of houses one saw everywhere were the condition towards which the whole city was slowly, inevitably sinking. The public buildings were filthy, pitted with shrapnel-scars, running with pigeon dung from every coign and eave; eminent statesmen and dead kings of stone looked out upon the world with soot-blackened faces, like coons in a grotesque carnival; bus tickets and torn newspapers blew down the streets or lay in white heaps in the parks; cats bred in the bomb-sites, where people flung old shoes, tin cans, and cardboard boxes; whole suburbs of private houses were peeling, cracking, crazing, their windows unwashed, their steps unswept, their gardens untended; innumerable little cafés reeked of chips frying in stale fat; in the streets that descended the slope from Bloomsbury to King's Cross old men with beards and old women in canvas shoes wandered about, talking to themselves and warding off imaginary enemies with ragged arms. As for the rest of the people – how pale they were, what dark clothes they wore, what black homes they came from, how many of them there were swarming in the streets, queueing on the pavements, standing packed on underground escalators. You saw crowds when you left the hotel, you travelled a mile and saw crowds, another mile and more crowds, another mile the same; and around them always the same run-down, decaying, decrepit, sagging, rotten city.

One night I walked about in an area which I now suspect must have been Paddington, on my way to an address I have forgotten and so cannot return to. I remember crossing a bridge over some railway lines, and looking across the parapet to a desolation of lines, shunting and stationary trains, red and green winking lights, floodlights on tall towers, iron and brick sheds from which flames occasionally broke. It was early evening, but the sun had been gone for hours, if it had ever shown itself at all during the day, and white smoke rose in plumes from the railyard and drifted across and between the lights. It seemed as though a town, a whole country, lay beneath me, and as though the bridge I stood on spanned it all. Farther along, on the other side of the bridge, was a terrace, with a little private road running the length of the row. The houses were four or five storeys tall, and were in darkness; each had its portico in front of it, with gaunt fluted pillars holding it up. Even in the half-light one could see how dilapidated they all were; ruined, cavernous, peeling. Sheets of corrugated iron were nailed over the ground-floor windows. I knocked on the door and no one answered; by then I did not expect anyone to answer; it was obvious that I had come to the wrong place. But I did not move away immediately. Standing on that abandoned doorstep, with the hoarse sound of the railyard in my ears and the darkness of the portico over me, I felt a perverse pleasure in the fact that I did not know where I was and that the people I was looking for were no longer there. I wanted to be lonely and anonymous and to feel within myself the dissolution of all that I had been by name and background.

Yet, confusingly, this city offered me a continuity between past and present, between words and things, which I had hardly known I was seeking until it was offered to me. And past and present pointed to the future. How could I avoid dreaming of the friends I might make in London, the fame I might win there, the houses I might one day be able to enter?

I had the addresses of just two people in London, neither of whom was a friend of mine, and with whom I was unable, as it turned out, to establish any kind of friendship. I had hoped that these people would help me to find a room; in the end I found one simply by catching a train to the Finchley Road Tube Station, and then walking up the road until I came to one of those glassed-in little notice-boards, advertising rooms to let and 'light removals' and vacancies for charwomen. (I went to Finchley Road because my brother had advised me to try the Hampstead area; he had never been out to Hampstead, but had heard that it was a pleasant area to live in.) Many of the notices for rooms carried discouraging messages like 'Gentiles Only' or 'British and Gentile Only' or 'No Coloureds' or even, testifying to some obscure convulsion of the English conscience, 'Regret No Coloureds'. I went to the nearest address which seemed as though it might be prepared to take me, in a street that ran directly off the Finchley Road. The house was a three-storeyed Victorian giant of a place; the housekeeper lived in the basement, a school of dancing occupied the ground floor, and the rest of it was let in single and double rooms.

The housekeeper was a woman with dyed blonde hair and a mouth painted in the shape of a Cupid's bow, even though her upper lip did not in the least have a suitable shape for one. So the bow was simply drawn on, heavily, the peak of it coming just under her nose, where a man might have worn a moustache, and the tips of it reaching into her cheeks on both sides. She looked drunken or clown-like in that paint. I never saw her without it. I never saw her drunk either. In fact, she was a quiet, artless woman who slept with one of the lodgers on the top floor, and perhaps for that reason was not given to prying into the affairs of the others in the house. And she kept the place clean. The room I was offered was small, sparsely furnished, and fitted with the inevitable, ancient gas-fire and gas-ring. But the view out of the window was a wide one; it looked over the Ministry of Food offices in the Finchley Road to the vague dark spread of South Hampstead, Kilburn, Willesden, Paddington, places whose names I did not even know.

I took my luggage into the room, and then I went to see off my brother at Waterloo Station. He was returning to South Africa. Once he had gone, I had absolutely nothing to do. I decided to go to Regent's Park. The last time I had visited it I had entered it from Baker Street; this time I got off the train at Regent's Park Station, and found myself in a place that looked nothing like the park I was slightly familiar with. Flat green plains of grass stretched away to black trees on the horizon; there was hardly a soul about, for it was mid-morning on a weekday. I began walking. The silence and emptiness round me made me feel nervous; even the pallor of my shadow on the grass was strange. Eventually in the distance I saw what looked like the crumbling battlements of a castle: there seemed to be a central circular keep, and crenellated walls going down on both sides of it. It looked ruinous, historic, ominous, lifted up against the horizon. It was part of the zoo, I found out, when I came closer. There were bears on the battlements. The thought of going in to stare at the animals seemed even more desperate than the thought of going back to my room. I continued walking pretty much in a circle – I had no alternative really, given the shape of the park – and at last came out at Baker Street. From there I did what I had been flinching from doing since I had left my brother: I went back to my room.

The house was quiet; it was only in the afternoon that the dancing-classes began, when the piano jangled and the floors shook with the combined thumping of all the little girls who came to the house carrying their dancing shoes in small cloth bags. I looked out of the window, over the glitter of the traffic in the Finchley Road, towards the vague blue and black spread which was only a part of the city, and which yet stretched to the very limit of my sight. Now that I was on my own I knew that I had really come to London. Evidently London did not care.

Shortly after I had moved into my room, a friend in South Africa wrote that I should look up G; I would get on well with him, my friend promised me. This, I found out, was true enough: it would have been true of practically anybody, for G was indiscriminately affable and garrulous. He was a slight, stoop-shouldered man in his middle twenties, who appeared much older than he was, because of the prominence of his pale, bald, soft-looking scalp. G was living with a Cockney woman, an ex-prostitute (or so G claimed), whose previous lover was in jail, from where he wrote letters describing how he was going to 'cut up' G when he got out. G told me all this within a few minutes of our meeting. He told me about it not only because he was garrulous, but because he was so proud of his girl-friend, her criminal admirer, and his own association with them both – all of it being so far removed from the Johannesburg, Jewish, middle-class respectability in which he had been brought up. He lived in a basement flat in Belsize Park: an ill-lit subterranean place with huge rooms, rubbish bins at its entrance, and Picasso prints on its walls. Gas-fires and electric lights seemed always to be burning in the flat, and the smell of damp was driven out at intervals only by the smell of bacon and eggs.

Maisie (or was her name Milly?) listened complacently to G's account of their situation; she was slight and fair-haired, and seemed demure enough, until she spoke. When she spoke, she swore: at the weather, at a pot she might be trying to clean, at the landlord, at G. He used to call Maisie 'my love' and 'my sweetheart', exaggeratedly, on every possible occasion; but no endearment ever crossed her lips. G had a theory, I remember, that a man who thinks a thought or visualises a scene is as much an artist as the man who writes down his thought or puts the scene on canvas; and no matter what we used to begin talking about, we would sooner or later find ourselves discussing this theory. He himself was writing a novel which would, he said, demonstrate the theory: when I asked him why, in view of the nature of the theory, he bothered to write the novel, he answered with several other theories which I have altogether forgotten. But quite another answer was given by Maisie: 'Him! Write a book? That'll be the fucking day!'

Through G I met Naomi K and her husband. Like G, Naomi was South African, Jewish, and from a well-to-do home; like G again, she was in flight from all these things. She was married to a tall, bearded, pipe-smoking, more-than-faintly anti-Semitic Gentile, who used to torment her by imitating her parents' accents. ('Dey vanted Naomi to marry a nize bizhnezh boy,' he would say, charmingly.) Both Naomi and he were artists; he could afford to be more flamboyantly artistic in manner than she, since they lived off what she earned as a teacher in the nursery department of a small orthodox Jewish school. Naomi was a tiny, jumpy, black-haired woman, who was continually expressing girl-like enthusiasms over cats, or dogs, or children, or budding trees. Derek, her husband, was enthusiastic about nothing, except perhaps puncturing Naomi's enthusiasms, which he did with an air of great fatigue, made all the more disdainful by the smoke that dribbled from his lips when he spoke. She would falter and apologize; he would dribble more smoke. On the whole it was more painful to be with them than with G and Maisie.

These were my only friends in London at that time. I feel guilty in writing disparagingly of them now – just as I used to feel guilty, then, in visiting them. The guilt arose from my knowing I would hardly have sought their company if I had had other people to visit. But I simply knew nobody else. I used solemnly to ration myself to seeing each couple on alternate Sundays only, I remember. At their flats, on these odd Sundays, I met a few other people – most of them South Africans, a few of them Americans or Australians – but I became friendly with none among them. In all, the first months of my stay in London were as lonely as any I have ever experienced. Even after I had got a job as a teacher at a small private school I was as lonely after school-hours and on weekends, as I had been before.

This loneliness I felt to be really disturbing or frightening, however, only when it was brought home to me as something else – as a kind of inward dislodgement or displacement of my own senses. There were two recurring, almost hallucinatory experiences which had this effect on me. Sometimes, in the crowded streets I used to see approaching me a man or a woman whom I had known in Johannesburg, where I had been a student at the university. I would feel no especial surprise at this, until, as I drew nearer, the resemblance between the person approaching and my acquaintance would suddenly and totally disappear. Then I would realise that I had felt no surprise at 'seeing' X or Y or Z because I had imagined myself to be *in* Johannesburg. The shock was always a double one: I was shocked that I should have fallen into the fantasy, and I was shocked on coming out of it to see around me once again the streets of a colder, darker and infinitely bigger city. The other experience was very similar, and usually occurred when I came out of a cinema or theatre. Being disorientated, I would look around to find the way I should go, and a few times I found myself walking perhaps half a block under the impression that in this direction lay the Melville tram terminus, or Eloff Street, or Park Station – all of which were in Johannesburg, not London. A further complication of these experiences was the fact that Johannesburg was not my home-town; merely the other big city in which I had once lived, and in which I had at times been lonely too.

I was so much the more grateful, therefore, that almost all of London, though new to me, was yet familiar in a ghostly way; and that the familiarity should have been so sustaining, even exhilarating. Everywhere I went I saw the visible, external frame or setting of much that had hitherto seemed to exist only as an abstraction within me, and that I had never truly believed could exist in any other way. Now I saw the sky under which so many imagined actions had taken place, and the streets where they had been enacted: these were the faces the protagonists had worn and these the accents in which they had spoken. It was as though some part of my imagination had been dry before, deprived of the nourishment it did not even know it needed; now, immersed in the English medium, it slowly filled itself and expanded. The medium was thicker and heavier than I could ever have anticipated; ultimately it was more burdensome too. There was so much I did not know and never would know; there was so little I could ever do, in comparison with what had been done and done and done and done a hundred thousand times, and more. Yet better that burden, I was sure, than none at all.

In the Charing Cross Road, one night, I saw the performance of an escape-artist and his assistant. By the time I joined the crowd, the artist had already been completely covered in a kind of canvas shroud, which the assistant was knotting with ropes in front and behind. The assistant was stripped to the waist, the artist was a bundle without face or limbs, and the arena on which they performed was marked out on the pavement by a long leather whip which the audience was not supposed to cross. These trappings were obviously intended to give the show a spicy or gamy quality. The assistant pitched the bundle on to the ground, and then chained it up, jocularly pushing it about, hectoring it, tugging hard at the ropes and chains, and eventually leaving it lying on the pavement while he went around demanding money from the crowd. The skin of his shoulders was goose-pimpled with cold. On the pavement the bundle breathed, but was otherwise quite still. When the collection was over, the assistant picked up the whip, trailed it over the ground, and suddenly lifted it as if to strike at the creature under him. But he just cracked the whip in the air, once, and a second time, and the bundle began writhing and squirming, its chains rattling and tinkling against the cement slabs, grunts and heavy breathing coming from within it. It rolled over and over, towards the audience and back again; occasionally it lay still before contracting and expanding in a spasm.

The man succeeded in freeing himself in the end: a wizened, gingerish face peered morosely out of the shroud, and the audience immediately began to disperse, as if everyone in it was ashamed of himself. There was no applause, and the man obviously expected none. He had escaped too many times before; and had seen too many crowds edge guiltily away from him.

Summer came: or rather, summer slowly diffused itself. The weather was not hot, merely warm; but the warmth was like heat in comparison with the cold that had persisted for so long before. I remember looking out of the window of my classroom, one afternoon, while the boys were busy with their exercise books, and being surprised at the sight of the sun shining directly upon the street outside: I had never before seen it so strong and clear, in England. Yet behind its rays there was still a blue or grey vibration in the light, a hint of darkness. On another afternoon I took the boys of my class on an outing to Epping Forest. The day was overcast, but warm and windless; the brown and grey leaves of the previous autumn lay in drifts underfoot; the leaves overhead were the softest green, so soft that they seemed more an exhalation than a growth. The woods were silent, except for our own shouting and crashing through the leaves and undergrowth. When we came to an open space we played rounders, and then had lunch, the boys sharing with me the sandwiches their mothers had packed for them. After lunch it grew steadily warmer; the clouds seemed to move lower, the air to become heavier. The shouts of the boys no longer carried as they had done before, among the trees, and I brought them together and made for the road and the bus-stop, anxious lest we should be caught by the rain. But it held off until we were back among the lights and traffic and cinema posters just outside the school; then it came down briefly and boisterously; no sooner was the downpour over than the air was clear and bright again.

London in summer was very different to what it had been in the bleak, dark spring: in some ways a more relaxed city; in others, an even shabbier one, for the sun exposed much that was better concealed. The intensity of the difference was unexpected to me, for in South Africa – or at least in the part of South Africa from which I came – summer and winter look much alike. Here the days lengthened extravagantly; the trees continued to thicken and darken with foliage; people, wearing a kind of clothing they had not worn before, thronged together in the parks; whole suburbs which had previously been hidden by smoke and mist as I went on the bus to school now revealed their black and red roofs, their roads, their football fields. It seemed that in England even the calendar had visible external meanings that I had not fully understood before. And the chief of these meanings was movement; the passage of time made manifest.

II

Until I came to England it had never really occurred to me that the successive ages and periods of the history text-books could be something other than a sequence of names and numbers which you carried about in your head, like the multiplication tables; I did not know that historical periods could present themselves directly to your vision as you walked about the streets. Now, as I went around London, or made my first solitary forays in the countryside, it seemed to me that the past was something that could actually be seen tapering away from the present, or rather within the present, like a perspective within a picture.

It was self-evident that there should be more Norman than Roman or Anglo-Saxon buildings to be seen; more Gothic than Norman; more Renaissance than Gothic . . . and so on, for century after century, up to the present day. But there they all were, buildings or the ruins of buildings from each of these periods, and the relation they had to one another, in number as well as in appearance, was in itself an historical narrative of a kind, a collective manifestation of the ways in which people had worked and what they had worked at; what they had produced, preserved, inherited; how they had boasted, aspired to excellence, chosen to recognise themselves and compelled others to recognise them. The narrative, in short, was also a style; and the style a tradition. (I could not have imagined then, no one could have imagined, the changes in cityscape and landscape that were to take place over the following decades, and which were to make the perspective I am speaking of seem far more tenuous or dubious than it already was.)

Everything that could be said about the buildings applied also, of course, to the institutions housed in them or around them. But then, the British appeared to have the knack not just of closely fitting together their lives and their institutions, but even of turning each into the other. Clubs, pubs, colleges, civil service, schools, trade unions, games, churches, television programmes, the class system, the very characters that individual people had or felt they should have: all provided evidence, one way or another, of this kind of interchangeability. Even the huge green trees in the parks, standing at conversable distances from one another, freighted with leafage and buoyant with the shifting airs of summer, while lovers lay beneath them in motionless disarray – those too looked like more than trees in their places; to my eye they were positively institutional as well.

The country seemed so full, so packed with life, that again and again I couldn't help feeling that if I were merely to close my hand in the air, I would grasp more than air: I would find between my fingers a texture, a colour, a weight.

*

Once I had settled into my job at the school I used to go much less often to the West End; usually I went in only on Friday evenings, after I'd been paid for my work. When I had been delayed at school I would arrive at Piccadilly Circus or Leicester Square just as the rush-hour began. It used to be part of my Friday evening's entertainment to stand at the foot of the packed escalators of these stations, looking at the crowds descending. Always it seemed as though they were about to topple and fall of their own weight down the steep incline; one felt dizzy standing beneath them, watching the endless chain as it wheeled over with its upright human freight and began its descent. No matter how quickly people stepped from the stairs and hurried away once they had reached the bottom, the wedge on the escalator remained solid, unbroken, it filled entirely the space that was given to it.

Altogether, the London underground was one of the great sights of the city for me. I had never imagined that it would be so complex; that I would spend as much of my time in it as I did; that it would dispose of such huge numbers of people; that it would have its own architecture, its own light, air, smells and noises, and would impose upon the people who travelled in it a characteristic expression of the face; that the stations would be so much alike and yet differ so much from one another, and from themselves at different times of the day. In fact, while I was still unfamiliar with it – before it became merely commonplace, an indifferent and occasionally uncomfortable passage through which I had to make my way so many times a week – the underground seemed to me a symbol or image of a kind that was all the more portentous for being so obscure. It was impossible for me to keep out of my mind all sorts of half-ideas about purgatory and the after-life, as I bewilderedly made my way through one subterranean tunnel to the next, among the hurrying crowds, bent on their own destinations. At the same time, the underground appeared to be the true centre or source of the city's life, rather than an image of its death. One felt inside it, more so than anywhere else, as though London were nothing but a great machine, contracting and expanding to its own deep, mechanical rhythms; a machine which the people who lived in London did not control but merely had to obey. So they were brought together and hurled apart again, as the machine dictated.

But even to think of the machine 'dictating' to the anonymous crowds made it seem too personal. The machine itself did not know what it was doing: it merely flashed its lights, moved its stairs, sent its trains hurtling along grey, ribbed tunnels, festooned with cables; its servants cried out 'Mind the gap' above the sigh of closing doors and the shuffling sound of the passengers' feet, above the thunderous fading roar of other trains in other tunnels. Sometimes the machine breathed in gales that cut through one's clothing, at other times the air hung still and oppressively warm; there were trains that stopped in mid-tunnel and waited, in a humming and shivering silence, before they moved again; at times the platforms and escalators were deserted, yet the trains still emerged and departed, the stairs continued to rattle and fold in and out of each other. All this vast activity and movement seemed to serve no purpose but that of its own continuation, could not serve any other purpose, for there appeared to be no consciousness that guided or directed it.

I used to wonder, at first, why there were so few literary references to the underground; before I learned to take it for granted, I wondered why everyone else did. In fact, there was one writer I knew of who had used it in his work, and it is partly for this reason, and not only because of what he wrote about the City and its river, about its churches and canals, that T. S. Eliot has remained for me pre-eminently the poet of London; as much London's poet as Dickens is still its novelist.

On these Friday evenings, I would emerge from the underground station and make straight for the theatre of my choice. I would book a stool in the gallery queue, and then try to fill in the time that remained until the theatre opened. Usually, I just walked around the West End and Soho, and looked at shop windows and people, or grubbed among the second-hand books which were then still to be found in the Charing Cross Road, or went a few times to the National Gallery; I ate some kind of a meal and returned to the theatre always in good time. Often enough I was glad to get into it simply to rest my feet.

The cocooned, cosy plush and gilt of the theatres, their ornate chandeliers and braided, pink light-shades in clusters here and there on the walls, were novelties and yet familiar from the descriptions I had read of them; they were 'sights' in much the same way as the faces of the actors and actresses I had seen previously only on the cinema screen. As much as when I walked in the streets, I was sightseeing at the theatre. But this was not the only reason why I went so regularly. I hoped earnestly to discover in myself a passion for the theatre of the kind I had so often read about. It goes almost without saying that I can now hardly remember a single one of the plays I saw; hardly a title, a plot, a joke, a stage-setting. All I can remember are my own efforts to persuade myself into an enthusiasm I was never really able to feel.

Of course, I hoped also that up there in the gallery I would meet some beautiful, young, sincere, lonely, ardent, female theatre-lover, and that a friendship, and more than a friendship, would develop between us. The closest I came to it, however, was to see several times at various theatres a quite pretty girl, who grew to recognise me, and who I think would have welcomed an approach from me. What held me back was that this girl was always accompanied by her youthful and goodlooking mother – which was something my fantasies had never bargained for. I couldn't possibly tackle them both, of that I was sure; so the girl and I never did more than exchange a few uncertain smiles.

In the novels I read, young men in the position I was in were continually picking up attractive girls in streets and parks and book-shops; I had no such luck. As a matter of fact, of the loners I have since met in London, only one man has seemed able to do it again and again. He found his girls for the most part in coffee-bars, which weren't in existence my first year in London, and in museums, which at that time I did not much frequent. But I doubt if I'd have been much more successful even if coffee-bars had been in existence and had I made a habit of visiting museums more often. I hadn't the knack. All I did have was a host of images of the girl I would eventually meet. Sometimes she was English, sometimes South African; sometimes she was tall, sometimes slight; sometimes she was dark, sometimes fair; sometimes she was sophisticated, sometimes naive; invariably, she was generous, high-spirited, and compliant. But because I was without friends, visited no homes, went to no parties, it seemed that I had no chance of meeting her – though all too often I would catch a glimpse of her, in a crowd of other girls, or on the arm of another man.

Always, everywhere, I felt myself to be touched, nudged, pulled by the sexual underworld of London; an underworld much wider than that of the whores who then used to stand on every West End corner after nightfall, or of the homosexuals hanging about outside the men's lavatories in Leicester Square and Trafalgar Square tube-stations. These the newspapers wrote about every other weekend; but they never said a word about the furtive encounters and withdrawals that took place in darkened, half-empty cinemas; about the rubber-shops with their dangling trusses, books on flagellation, and their offers to send you 'further literature' in 'plain wrappers'; about the wild, imploring graffiti scribbled upon the doors and walls of practically every public lavatory; about the packed tube-trains, where the crowds swayed promiscuously against one another, heads respectably averted, bodies rammed together. Or, for that matter, about the sedate, secluded middle-class house in which I lodged, and in which almost every room seemed filled with whispers that sometimes rose to cries, behind the closed doors, sniggers, sobs, expostulations.

I knew none of the people who lodged in the house; we passed each other on the stairs, and greeted one another, and that was all. Yet it surprises me now to realise just how much I did learn about them; at least about those who lived on my landing. There was, for example, the Danish student (so-called: he was much older in appearance than any student had the right to be) in the room next door to mine. His girl spent one week in his room crying almost continuously, and then left for Australia: that I guessed from the silence which descended upon his room when the week was over, and from the Australian air-letters addressed to him, in a feminine hand, which shortly afterwards began to appear on the window-ledge where the housekeeper left all our letters. Had she always planned to go to Australia? Had she threatened to go to Australia unless he married her? Or was she Australian, and had she wept simply because she had to go home and he wouldn't follow? In any case, the Scandinavian did not pine for her. The last girl had cried; his new one laughed. I would hear the deep, gurgling sound of her laughter at all hours of the night – above the sound of Radio Luxembourg, to which the radio in that room seemed to be permanently tuned.

The room next to mine on the other side was occupied by an elderly German Jewish widow, whose daughter, I gathered from overheard snatches of conversation in German and English, was unhappily married. The daughter complained to her mother about her husband's stinginess with money, his angry moods, his absences; the mother counselled patience. I saw the husband a few times on the stairs: a tall, fair, high-coloured man, with the face of a disgruntled boy. To judge from his accent, he too was a German Jew, but he always spoke in

English. He had almost as many complaints against his wife as she had against him; what was very odd about his way of delivering these complaints was that he seemed to take it for granted that his mother-in-law would agree with him. 'She's impossible, isn't she?' he would say to his mother-in-law at the end of some story about her daughter, or, 'What can you do with someone like that, tell me, please.' These familial confrontations took place about once a week (the daughter came three or four times a week), and usually ended up with the three of them going, at the mother's suggestion, to the pictures.

Across the landing there lived the quietest of the couples on my floor: a tall, well-spoken Englishman in his middle thirties, who went off every morning in a dark suit and bowler hat to the bank or insurance office in which he worked, and his small, curly-headed, youthful Cypriot boy-friend. The youngster was apparently supported by his friend and seldom went out. He used to potter about the house, and have long conversations with the housekeeper, and listen to the soap-operas on the radio. When he did go out he wore clothes of a very different kind from those of his friend; striped shirts, black jeans, belts with big silver buckles. The two of them seemed staid and settled, and I shall never know why the Englishman suddenly left; certainly, there had been no loud rows before his departure.

It must have been just two or three days after the Englishman had left that the young man knocked on my door. He had come with a suggestion, or an invitation. Wouldn't I move in with him? We had never done more than greet one another, as I have said, or exchange a few remarks about the weather. Now he stood with his back against the wall, a pace away from the door, and smiled at me guilelessly. 'It's a fine room,' he said. 'It's too dear for me. But with you – with the two of us – it'd be easy.' And he made a gesture with his hand, twisting the palm of it open, towards me. The invitation, and the gesture which accompanied it, seemed somehow both obscene and touching. Still he smiled; he was a round-cheeked, brown-eyed boy, with white teeth and dark curls that fell all over his forehead. I wondered what it was about me that had made him think I might be a suitable successor to his English friend. 'No, thank you,' I said. 'It's kind of you to ask me, but –'

Nevertheless he persisted. He invited me to come and look at the room, which was much bigger than the one I had. He would keep it clean, cook, look after everything. So I told him (untruthfully) that I was preparing for an examination, I studied in the evenings, and couldn't possibly consider sharing with anyone. 'Oh,' he assured me, his smile even more artless than before, 'I can be very quiet.'

This time I simply shook my head in silence. My gaze, I'm sure, was far more embarrassed than the one with which he met it. But he was very polite; almost condescending. He shrugged, said he hoped I didn't mind that he'd asked me, and slid out of the room. A few days later he was gone. His room was then occupied by a couple of girl students, one of whom I thought attractive in a soft, eager, earnest, innocent way. Even when you know nothing about them or their circumstances, girls like that somehow make you feel that you should sympathise with their views and admire their pluck. I looked forward to meeting her on the stairs; when we did meet I tried to make our conversation last as long as possible. The development of our friendship was cut short by an unfortunate accident, however. All the people on my landing shared a single, huge bathroom-cum-lavatory. One afternoon I opened the door of this room, and there, on the lavatory seat, sat this girl, with her pants around her ankles. She had forgotten to lock the door behind her. For the briefest and most protracted of seconds we stared at one another; then she gave a kind of moan, and reached down towards her ankles, while I retreated, muttering apologies and banging the door closed behind me.

From then on the poor girl couldn't say a word to me. When she saw me she blushed, she ducked, she scurried away down the passage or up the stairs. As long as I lived in the house she never forgave me, or herself, for what had happened.

The story I had told the Cypriot about working for an examination had been untrue. But it was true that I was working almost every evening, at this time. I had begun writing, in earnest – or so I thought. At any rate, what drove me to start working seemed to me earnest enough.

I was still seeing the Ks and G and his girl-friend, on alternate weeks; in addition there was a girl I had known at university in Johannesburg whom I saw even more infrequently. Generally, this meant that in every week I was in the company of others one evening or perhaps one weekend afternoon; the other six nights, the rest of the weekends, I was on my own. I was no longer able to fill them, as I had been able to at first, simply by being on the move.

Loneliness had had its pleasures; there had been something extraordinarily satisfying, at times, in the thought that none of the people who ever saw me knew who I was; conversely, there was a kind of exhilaration in the thought that at any given moment none of the people who did know me could guess just where I was, what I was doing, where I would go next. But I found that these moments of excitement or self-satisfaction were recurring less and less frequently. Also, I had begun to have fears that were worse than the mild hallucinations or displacements that I had been afflicted with in my first few weeks in the city, when again and again, in broad daylight, I had found myself thinking I was back in Johannesburg, or had made a habit of 'recognising' people who in fact were complete strangers to me. Chiefly, I was afraid now of falling ill or having an accident. 'It could be weeks before anyone would even know!'—that seemed to be the real horror of the situation.

Actually, I was exaggerating the forlornness of my own position. Now that I was working, any absence of mine would certainly have been noticed after a very few days. But it is always easy to be superior to one's own anxieties when one no longer feels them; the truth is that if I had fallen ill I would probably have had a thoroughly miserable time of it. In the best of health, I was finding my loneliness quite heavy enough a burden, anyway. It was at this time, I remember, that the notices which used to be posted up outside Tottenham Court Road police station began to have a macabre fascination for me. 'Found: in Thames, near Greenwich, body of man, aged 20–23, wearing brown sports jacket and grey flannels, height 5' 7", scar on right cheek . . .' 'Found: 63 – Crescent, N. W., body of woman, aged 50 years approx . . .' To prevent such a notice ever being posted up about me, I wrote my name and parents' address in South Africa on a piece of paper, and put it in my wallet. It embarrassed me to do this, I remember; but I did it, nevertheless.

So I stayed in my room more than ever before; I felt safer there than anywhere else. Because I had to do something to fill in these phobic hours, I began to write a novel. However, if I began work on it as a means of self-defence, it was not long before I thought of the book as a means of attack; as the instrument through which I might be able to subdue the city beyond the walls of the room. I had no precise idea of what London would look like to me once it was subdued; but I was sure, at least, that it would seem a very different place from what it had been hitherto. Months later I finished the novel, and was glad to put it quietly out of sight.

One afternoon I came home early from school – I forget why – and found a little girl waiting on the doorstep. She had come for her dancing lesson (the ground floor of the house was still occupied by the school of dancing). While I looked through my pockets for my key she told me that her daddy had brought her in his car, and that he was going to fetch her when the lesson was over. She said she'd been ringing at the door-bell but no one had answered it.

At the time I wasn't struck by the oddity of this. Usually, on afternoons when lessons were held in the house, the front door was simply left wide open. I cannot remember what the little girl looked like, except that she had freckles on her face, and that like all the little girls who came for their classes she carried her dancing-shoes in a small cloth bag. What I do recall was that her voice was sweet and clear, and that I was touched by the volubility with which she chattered to me during the minute or two we stood together on the step. As it happened, I really had to hunt for my key, in every pocket, before I finally found it. Then I opened the door. As I did it, I felt rather pleased with myself for having been able to help her. Once we were inside I simply went straight up the stairs, and she very politely called after me, from the big, gloomy lobby of the house, 'Good-bye. Thank you.' I replied to her without looking back.

How long it was before she called to me again, I cannot now say. Indeed, in many ways the whole incident has the quality of a bad dream; except that I know, to my regret, that it wasn't a dream, that it actually happened. I think that I settled down to read, once I was in my room, or perhaps I just lay on my bed; in any case, I remained awake. It seems almost unbelievable to me now that I could have sat or lain there, in that dead-silent house, without thinking that something was amiss. But I know quite well how I was able to do it. I had simply forgotten about the little girl; I had smiled at her, and listened to her chatter, and opened the door for her, and then she had just gone out of my mind, as though I had never seen her. So much so that I did not even think of her when I heard a child's voice calling out, of all things, 'I'm only seven.'

I thought the call came from somewhere outside in the street; it struck me as rather a strange thing for a child to shout out, but I assumed it was some part of a game or an argument. Afterwards, that first call struck me as being as pitiful as anything that followed; it showed so clearly how the girl's own puniness, in that enormous, silent house, must have been borne in upon her. But I wasn't thinking of her, then. That first call was followed by a long silence, and then by a shriek as terrified, and therefore as terrifying, as any I have ever heard. 'Mister man! Help me! I don't know my way home! You're my friend!' A moment later the front door shut with a bang that shook the entire house.

Only then, when it was too late, I realized that the voice was that of the little girl that I had let into the house; that it was to me she had been calling. I knew at once what had happened; I should have known before I had opened the door, which should not have been closed; I should certainly have known when I had left her in that still, empty lobby. There was no dancing lesson that afternoon; it had been cancelled for some reason, and her parents had either not been told or had forgotten, and had dropped her at the gate as usual. Then I had let her in. There was not a soul in the house apart from myself; by some mischance everyone was out – the housekeeper, the widow, the girl students, everyone. The little girl had sat alone in the half-darkness, and waited, and waited, until terror had overwhelmed her. But she had not forgotten me as I had forgotten her; she had cried out to me, telling me that she was only seven; again she had waited, until there had come that shriek, that appeal to me as her friend; then, before I could do anything, she had fled from the house.

Her friend! The one who had brought her into the house, and had ignored her first cry for help! I was down the stairs in an instant, and out in the street. I looked up the slope of the hill; there was no one to be seen that way. The distance the other way, down to the Finchley Road, was only about fifty yards; I was sure she must have made for it, though I could not see her. I ran down to the corner. It was hopeless. The pavements of Finchley Road were crowded with people, throngs of them, advancing and retreating, pausing, hurrying forward, turning aside; in the road itself trucks ground their gears, moved forward, stood idle, their exhaust fumes rising in the air. There wasn't a sign of the little girl. I ran half a block in one direction, turned and ran back in the other. She was gone, lost in the crowd. In the months that followed I looked for her many times, when the children gathered in groups outside the house before or after their lessons, but she was never among them.

III

Not long after that episode, the circumstances in which I was living in London changed greatly. For a variety of reasons unconnected with one another, the isolation I had been living in came suddenly to an end. Yet the experience of coming to London and living alone in it for those months had left me with a series of questions which were to become as intimately a part of me as my memories. When I looked back at South Africa, the country of my birth, it seemed to me not only flat and bare, not only given over to the political and social torments peculiar to it, but also haphazard, unformed, flat; the very faces of the people, I now thought, were lacking in depth and subtlety, their voices empty of resonance. English society, in all its embodiments and manifestations, was incomparably more elaborate than anything I had dreamed of before. Space itself seemed denser in England, used more intensively to a greater variety of purposes; the same was true of time, even in its passage from season to season, not to speak of the freight from the past it carried with it.

Well, what difference did this make? Or rather: why did it make such a difference to me? To the east there were countries as ancient, as dense socially, as England, where a few years before people were murdered in their millions simply because they came of the same stock as myself. My grandparents and parents had literally saved their lives by migrating from Europe to South Africa. Where, then, did that leave the advantages supposedly to be derived from living among ancient buildings and great works of art and other such residues of the past? How could I reconcile my own family history with the delight I took in that congruence between the written word and the visible world which Europe had always taken for granted, and which unadorned, undescribed South Africa lacked?

History and art both pretended to be so much more than spectacles or diversions; they hinted at meanings, purposes, revelations, conclusions. But the one stumbled blindly from event to event; the other proffered us modes of self-comprehension which appeared to have no discernible effect on the way we actually behaved to one another or how we felt about ourselves. Then what was the good of them? Of having their accumulations around us? What help did they give us? And if these were inappropriate questions to ask, what would be the right ones?

Looking back, it seems easy to say that even in asking such questions I was irrevocably committing myself to living in England. It did not feel like that then. Everything then was provisional, doubtful, tentative, and was felt all the more intensely for being so. I had ambitions but no plans; yearnings but no object for them. The amplitude and the opacity of the future were one.

NANCY MITFORD

The English Aristocracy

Nancy Mitford (1904–73) was well known as a novelist in the immediate post-war years – with The Pursuit of Love *(1945) and* Love in a Cold Climate *(1949) – but in the 1950s she achieved instant notoriety with her studies of upper-class British manners and usages: studies in which she promoted the U/non-U distinctions which, in some circles, are still deployed today. The U/non-U formulation was in fact invented by a Professor Alan Ross in a 1954 paper on 'Upper-Class English Usage'. It was on this paper that Mitford based her famous essay in* Encounter *in 1955. Her book,* Noblesse Oblige: An Enquiry into the Identifiable Characteristics of the English Aristocracy, *followed in 1956.*

The English aristocracy may seem to be on the verge of decadence, but it is the only real aristocracy left in the world today. It has real political power through the House of Lords and a real social position through the Queen. An aristocracy in a republic is like a chicken whose head has been cut off: it may run about in a lively way, but in fact it is dead. There is nothing to stop a Frenchman, German, or Italian from calling himself the Duke of Carabosse if he wants to, and in fact the Continent abounds with invented titles. But in England the Queen is the fountain of honours and when she bestows a peerage upon a subject she bestows something real and unique.

The great distinction between the English aristocracy and any other has always been that, whereas abroad every other member of a noble family is noble, in England none are noble except the head of the family. In spite of the fact that they enjoy courtesy titles, the sons and daughters of lords are commoners – though not so common as baronets and their wives, who take precedence after honourables. (So, of course, do all knights, except Knights of the Garter, who come after the eldest sons and the daughters of barons, but before the younger sons.) The descendants of younger sons, who, on the Continent, would all be counts or barons, in England have no titles and sit even below knights. Furthermore, the younger sons and daughters of the very richest lords receive, by English custom, but little money from their families, barely enough to live on. The sons are given the same education as their eldest brother and then turned out, as soon as they are grown up, to fend for themselves; the daughters are given no education at all, the general idea being that they must find some man to keep them – which, in fact, they usually do. The rule of primogeniture has kept together the huge fortunes of English lords; it has also formed our class system.

But there is in England no aristocratic class that forms a caste. We have about 950 peers, not all of whom, incidentally, sit in the House of Lords. Irish peers have no seats, though some Irish peers have a subsidiary UK peerage giving a seat; Scottish peers elect sixteen representatives from among themselves. Peeresses in their own right are not, as yet, admitted. Most of the peers share the education, usage, and point of view of a vast upper middle class, but the upper middle class does not, in its turn, merge imperceptibly into the middle class. There is a very definite border line, easily recognizable by hundreds of small but significant landmarks.

When I speak of these matters I am always accused of being a snob, so, to illustrate my point, I propose to quote from Professor Alan Ross of Birmingham University. Professor Ross has written a paper, printed in Helsinki in 1954, for the *Bulletin de la Société Neo-philologique de Helsinki*, on 'Upper-Class English Usage'. Nobody is likely to accuse either this learned man or his Finnish readers of undue snobbishness. The Professor, pointing out that it is solely by their language that the upper classes nowadays are distinguished (since they are neither cleaner, richer, nor better-educated than anybody else), has invented a useful formula: U (for upper class) -speaker versus non-U-speaker. Such exaggeratedly non-U usage as 'serviette' for 'napkin' he calls non-U indicators. Since 'a piece of mathematics or a novel written by a member of the upper class is not likely to differ in any way from one written by a member of another class . . . in writing it is in fact only modes of address, postal addresses and habits of beginning and ending letters that serve to demarcate the class' . . . The names of many houses are themselves non-U; the ideal U-address is PQR where P is a place name, Q a describer, and R the name of a county, as 'Shirwell Hall, Salop'. (Here I find myself in disagreement with Professor Ross – in my view abbreviations such as Salop, Herts, or Glos, are decidedly non-U. Any sign of undue haste, in fact, is apt to be non-U, and I go so far as preferring, except for business letters, not to use air mail.) 'But', adds Professor Ross, 'today few gentlemen can maintain this standard and they often live in houses with non-U names such as Fairmeads or El Nido.' Alas!

He speaks of the U-habit of silence, and perhaps does not make as much of it as he might. Silence is the only possible U-response to many embarrassing modern situations: the ejaculation of 'cheers' before drinking, for example, or 'it was so nice seeing you', after saying good-bye. In silence, too, one must endure the use of the Christian name by comparative strangers and the horror of being introduced by Christian and surname without any prefix. This unspeakable usage sometimes occurs in letters – Dear XX – which, in silence, are quickly torn up, by me.

After discoursing at some length on pronunciation, the professor goes on to vocabulary and gives various examples of U and non-U usage.

Cycle is non-U against U *bike*.

Dinner: U-speakers eat *luncheon* in the middle of the day and *dinner* in the evening. Non-U-speakers (also U-children and U-dogs) have their *dinner* in the middle of the day.

Greens is non-U for U *vegetables*.

Home: non-U – 'they have a lovely *home*'; U – 'they've a very nice *house*.'

Ill: 'I was *ill* on the boat' is non-U against U *sick*.

Mental: non-U for U *mad*.

Note paper: non-U for U *writing paper*.

Toilet paper: non-U for U *lavatory paper*.

Wealthy: non-U for U *rich*.

To these I would add:

Sweet: non-U for U *pudding*.

Dentures: non-U for U *false teeth*. This, and *glasses* for *spectacles*, almost amount to non-U indicators.

Wire: non-U for U *telegram*.

Phone: a non-U indicator.

(One must add that the issue is sometimes confused by U-speakers using non-U indicators as a joke. Thus Uncle Matthew in *The Pursuit of Love* speaks of his *dentures*.)

Finally Professor Ross poses the question: Can a non-U-speaker become a U-speaker? His conclusion is that an adult can never achieve complete success 'because one word or phrase will suffice to brand an apparent U-speaker as originally non-U (for U-speakers themselves never make mistakes)'. I am not quite sure about this. Usage changes very quickly and I even know undisputed U-speakers who pronounce girl 'gurl', which twenty years ago would have been unthinkable. All the same, it is true that one U-speaker recognizes another U-speaker almost as soon as he opens his mouth, though U-speaker A may deplore certain lapses in the conversation of U-speaker B.

From these U-speakers spring the sensible men of ample means who generally seem to rule our land. When the means of these sensible men become sufficiently ample they can very easily be ennobled, should they wish it, and join the House of Lords. It might therefore be supposed that there is no aristocracy at all in England, merely an upper middle class, some of whom are lords; but, oddly enough, this is not so. A lord does not have to be born to his position and, indeed, can acquire it through political activities, or the sale of such unaristocratic merchandise as beer, but though he may not be a U-speaker he becomes an aristocrat as soon as he receives his title. The Queen turns him from socialist leader, or middle-class businessman, into a nobleman, and his outlook from now on will be the outlook of an aristocrat.

Ancestry has never counted much in England. The English lord knows himself to be such a very genuine article that, when looking for a wife, he can rise above such baubles as seize quartiers. Kind hearts, in his view, are more than coronets, and large tracts of town property more than Norman blood. He marries for love, and is rather inclined to love where money is; he rarely marries in order to improve his coat of arms. (Heiresses have caused the extinction as well as the enrichment of many an English family, since the heiress, who must be an only child if she is to be really rich, often comes of barren or enfeebled stock.) This unconcern for pedigree leads people to suppose that the English lords are a jumped-up lot, and that their families are very seldom 'genuine' and 'old'. One often hears it said, 'No Englishman alive today would be eligible to drive in the carriage of a King of France.' 'Nobody really has Norman blood.' 'The true aristocracy of England was wiped out in the Wars of the Roses.' And so on.

There is some truth in all these statements, but it is not the whole truth. Many of our oldest families have never been ennobled. Some no longer hold peerages. The ancient Scrope family has, in its time, held the baronies of Scrope of Marsham and Scrope of Bolton, the earldoms of Wiltshire and of Sunderland, the sovereignty of the Isle of Man, but the head of the family is now Mr Scrope. If he should be offered a peerage he would no doubt proudly refuse. The only existing families known to descend from knights who came over with William the Conqueror in time to fight at Hastings, the Malets, the Giffards, and the Gresleys, are another case in point. Of the Norman knights who came during William's reign or later, some were never anything but country gentlemen, but some are the direct ancestors of modern peers: St John, Talbot, West, Curzon, Clinton, Grey, Seymour, St Aubyn, Sinclair, Haig, and Hay, for instance. There are 100 peers of England from before the Union (including Prince Charles, as Duke of Cornwall). All of them are descended in the female line from King Edward III, except possibly Lord Byron, though a little research would probably find him an Edward III descent. All peers, except barons, are officially styled 'Cousin' by the Queen; as regards most dukes and earls this is not so much fiction as a distant truth. Only 26 earls have been created in this century and they have all been great men like Lloyd George and Haig. (The Haigs have borne arms and lived at Bemersyde since the twelfth century but had never previously been ennobled.)

The dukes are rather new creations. When James I came to the throne there were no dukes at all, the high traitors Norfolk and Somerset having had their dukedoms attainted. They were both restored in 1660. Between 1660 and 1760, 18 dukedoms were created. On the whole, Englishmen are made dukes as a reward for being rich or royal (4 descend from bastards of Charles II), though dukedoms have sometimes been bestowed for merit. The oldest title is that of earl. Several medieval earldoms still exist. Sixty-five barons hold titles from before 1711. Three hundred and twenty-seven of the present-day peerages were created before 1800, 382 belong to families which have borne arms in the direct male line since before 1485 and which are therefore eligible, as far as birth is concerned, to be Knights of Malta.

*

But whether their families are 'old' or 'new' is of small account – the lords all have one thing in common: they share an aristocratic attitude to life. What is this attitude? The purpose of the aristocrat is to lead, therefore his functions are military and political. There can be no doubt of the military excellence of our noblemen. Two hundred and fourteen peers alive today have been decorated in battle or mentioned in despatches. The families of the premier duke and the premier earl of England hold the George Cross. In politics, including the unglamorous and often boring local politics, they have worked hard for no reward and done their best according to their lights.

The purpose of the aristocrat is most emphatically not to work for money. His ancestors may have worked in order to amass the fortune which he enjoys, though on the whole the vast riches of the English lords come from sources unconnected with honest toil; but he will seldom do the same. His mind is not occupied with money, it turns upon other matters. When money is there he spends it on maintaining himself in his station. When it is no longer there he ceases to spend, he draws in his horns. Even the younger sons of lords seem, in all ages, to have been infected with this point of view: there is nothing so rare as for the scion of a noble house to make a fortune by his own efforts. In the old days they went into professions – the Army, the Navy, diplomacy, and the Church – in which it is impossible to earn more than a living. Those who went to the colonies were administrators, they rarely feathered their nests – the great nabobs were essentially middle-class. Nowadays younger sons go into the City, but I have yet to hear of one making a large fortune; more often they lose in unwise speculations what little capital they happen to own.

All this should not be taken as a sign that our lords are lazy or unenterprising. The point is that, in their view, effort is unrelated to money. Now this view has, to a large extent, communicated itself to the English race and nation with the result that our outlook is totally different from that of our American cousins, who have never had an aristocracy. Americans relate all effort, all work, and all of life itself to the dollar. Their talk is of nothing but dollars. The English seldom sit happily chatting for hours on end about pounds. In England, public business is its own reward, nobody would go into Parliament in order to become rich, neither do riches bring public appointments. Our ambassadors to foreign states are experienced diplomatists, not socially ambitious millionairesses.

This idiosyncratic view of money has its good side and its bad. Let us glance at the case history of Lord Fortinbras. Fortinbras is ruined – we are now in the 1930s. (All English noblemen, according to themselves, are ruined, a fantasy I shall deal with later, but Fortinbras really is.) He is not ruined because of death duties, since his father died when he was a child, before they became so heavy, but because he and his forebears have always regarded their estates with the eyes of sportsmen rather than of cultivators. It is useless for him to plead that the policy of cheap corn has been his downfall; an intelligent landowner has always been able to make money with prize cattle, racehorses, market gardens, timber, and so on. But Fortinbras's woods have been looked after by gamekeepers and not by woodmen, his farms have been let to tenants chosen for their tenderness towards foxes and partridges rather than for their agricultural efficiency. His land is undercapitalized, his cottagers live in conditions no better than those of their Saxon forebears, water and electric light are laid on in his stables but not in the dwellings of his tenantry. He has made various unwise speculations and lost a 'packet' on the Turf. In short, he deserves to be ruined and he is ruined.

Now what does he do? He is young, healthy, and not stupid; his wife, the daughter of another peer, is handsome, bossy, and energetic. She is the kind of woman who, in America, would be running something with enormous efficiency and earning thousands. They have two babies, Dominick and Caroline, and a Nanny. Does it occur to either Lord or Lady Fortinbras to get a job and retrieve the family fortunes? It does not. First of all they sell everything that is not entailed, thus staving off actual want. They shut up most of the rooms in their house, send away the servants (except, of course, Nanny) and get the Dowager Lady Fortinbras and her sister to come and cook, clean, dust, and take trays upstairs to the nursery. Old Lady Fortinbras is quite useful, and Lady Enid is a treasure. The Fortinbrases realize that they are very lucky, and if at heart they wish there were a mother's hall for the two ladies to sit in of an evening, they never say so, even to each other. Fortinbras chops the wood, stokes the boiler, brings in the coal, washes the Morris Cowley, and drives off in it to attend the County Council and sit on the Bench. Lady Fortinbras helps in the house, digs in the border, exercises the Border terriers, and also does a great deal of committee work. They are both on the go from morning to night, but it is a go that does not bring in one penny. Their friends and neighbours all say, 'Aren't the Fortinbrases wonderful?'

Comes the war. They clear the decks by sending Nanny and the children to an American couple, the Karamazovs, whom they once met at St Moritz and who have sent them Christmas cards ever since. Fortinbras goes off with his Territorials and Lady Fortinbras joins the ATS. Their war records are brilliant in the extreme, their energy, courage, and instinct for leadership have at last found an outlet, and in no time at all they both become generals. After the war they are not surprised to find themselves more ruined than ever. The Karamazovs, whose lives for several years have been made purgatory by Dominick, Caroline, and Nanny, especially Nanny, send in a modest bill for the schooling of the young people which Fortinbras has no intention of settling. It would seem unreasonable to pay for one's children to be taught to murder the English language and taught, apparently, nothing else whatever. Dominick, failing to get into Eton, has had to be sent to some dreadful school in Scotland. Besides, what did the Karamazovs do in the war? Nothing, according to Nanny, but flop in and out of a swimming pool. The Karamazovs come to England expecting to be thanked, fêted, and paid, only to find that their friends have left for the Northern Capitals.

Now the Fortinbrases are getting on, over fifty. Dominick having come of age, they have broken the entail and sold everything, very badly, as the house is full of dry rot and the farms are let to tenants who cannot be dislodged. However, a little money does result from the sale. They arrange a mews flat behind Harrods where, generals once again, they will continue to cook and wash up for the rest of their days. They both still sit on endless committees, Fortinbras goes to the House of Lords, they kill themselves with overwork, and have never, except for their Army pay, earned one single penny. 'Aren't the Fortinbrases wonderful?' Well yes, in a way they are.

Now, while the Fortinbrases have the typical aristocratic outlook on money, the state of their finances is by no means typical. Most people, nowadays, take it for granted that the aristocracy is utterly impoverished, a view carefully fostered by the lords themselves. It takes a shooting affray, letting police and reporters into a country house, to remind the ordinary citizen that establishments exist where several men-servants wait on one young woman at dinner. There are still many enormous fortunes in the English aristocracy, into which income tax and death duties have made no appreciable inroads. Arundel, Petworth, Hatfield, Woburn, Hardwick, Blenheim, Haddon, Drumlanrig, Alnwick, Stratfield Saye, Harewood, Knole, Knowsley, Wilton, Holkham, Glamis, Cullen, Cliveden, Highclere, Althorp, Mentmore – all vast houses – are still inhabited by lords who have inherited them, and this little list is a mere fraction of the whole. The treasures such houses contain are stupendous. When the Duke of Buccleuch came to visit the Louvre, the curator, who had been to England and seen the Duke's collection of French furniture, greeted him with the words: 'I apologize for the furniture of the Louvre, M le Duc.'

Another English duke owns a collection of *incunabula* second only to that formerly in the possession of the Kings of Spain, and more Groslier bindings than the Bibliothèque Nationale. A jeweller told me that out of the one hundred finest diamonds in the world, sixty are in English families. One could go on citing such instances indefinitely.

The English, so censorious of those foreigners (the French peasantry for instance) who do not pay their taxes as they should, have themselves brought tax evasion within legal limits to a fine art. Death duties can be avoided altogether if the owner of an estate gives it to his heir and then lives another five years. One agreeable result of this rule is that old lords are cherished as never before. Their heirs, so far from longing to step into their shoes, will do anything to keep them alive. Doctors and blood donors hover near them, they are not allowed to make the smallest effort, or to be worried or upset, and are encouraged to live in soft climates and salubrious spots.

The crippling effects of supertax also can be overcome in various ways by those who own large capital sums. The aristocrat can augment his fortune in many a curious manner, since he is impervious to a sense of shame (all aristocrats are: shame is a bourgeois notion). The lowest peasant of the Danube would stick at letting strangers into his home for 2s. 6d., but our dukes, marquesses, earls, viscounts, and barons not only do this almost incredible thing, they glory in it, they throw themselves into the sad commerce with rapture, and compete as to who among them can draw the greatest crowds. It is the first topic of conversation in noble circles today, the tourists being referred to in terms of sport rather than of cash – a sweepstake on the day's run, or the bag counted after the shoot.

'I get twice as many as Reggie, but Bert does better than me.'

The baiting of the trap is lovingly considered.

'Mummy dresses up in her Coronation robes, they can't resist it.'

'I say, old boy, look out – you don't want to pay entertainment tax.'

'No, no – I've taken counsel's opinion.'

'We've started a pets' cemetery – a quid for a grave, three quid for a stone, and a fiver if Daphne writes a poem for it.'

Of course the fellow countrymen of people who will descend to such methods of raising cash imagine that they must be driven to it by direst need. The fact is they thoroughly enjoy it. Also it has become a matter of policy to appear very poor. The lords are retrenching visibly, and are especially careful to avoid any form of ostentation: for instance, only five of them saw fit to attend the last coronation in their family coaches. Coronets on luggage, motor-cars, and so on, are much less used than formerly. Aristocrats no longer keep up any state in London, where family houses hardly exist now. Here many of them have shown a sad lack of civic responsibility, as we can see by looking at poor London today. At the beginning of this century practically all the residential part of the West End belonged to noblemen and the Crown. A more charming, elegant capital city would have been far to seek. To the Crown – more specifically, I believe, to King George V in person – and to two Dukes, Westminster and Bedford, we owe the fact that London is not yet exactly like Moscow, a conglomeration of dwellings. Other owners cheerfully sold their houses and 'developed' their property without a thought for the visible result. Park Lane, most of Mayfair, the Adelphi, and so on, bear witness to a barbarity which I, for one, cannot forgive.

The lords have never cared very much for London, and are, in this respect, the exact opposite of their French counterparts, who loathe the country. But even where his country house is concerned, the English nobleman, whose forebears were such lovers of beauty, seems to have lost all æsthetic sense, and it is sad to see the havoc he often brings to his abode, both inside and out. His ancestors spent months abroad, buying pictures and statues, which he cheerfully sells in order to spend months abroad. Should one of his guests perceive that a blackened square of canvas in a spare bedroom is a genuine Caravaggio, that picture will appear at Christie's before you can say Jack Robinson, though there is no necessity whatever for such a sale. The Caravaggio buyer planted his estate with avenues and coppices and clumps of cedar trees. The Caravaggio seller fiddles about with herbaceous borders, one of the most hideous conceptions known to man. He never seems to plant anything larger than a flowering prunus, never builds ornamental bridges, or digs lakes, or adds wings to his house. The last nobleman to build a folly on his estate must have been Lord Berners and he was regarded as foolish indeed to do such a thing. The noble eccentric, alas, seems to be dying out. Lord Berners was one, another was the late Duke of Bedford, pacifist, zoologist, and a good man. One of the chapters of his autobiography, I seem to remember, was headed 'Spiders I have Known', and he tells of one spider he knew whose favourite food was roast beef and Yorkshire pudding. The great days of patronage, too, are over, though there are country houses which still shelter some mild literary figure as librarian. The modern nobleman cannot, however, be blamed for no longer patronizing art, music, and letters. Artists, musicians, and writers are today among the very richest members of the community and even an English aristocrat could hardly afford to maintain Mr Somerset Maugham, M. Stravinsky, or M. Picasso as part of his establishment.

Voltaire very truly said that those who own are those who wish to own: this wish seems to have left the English lords. Divest, divest, is the order of the day. The nobleman used to study a map of his estate to see how it could be enlarged, filling out a corner here, extending a horizon there. Nowadays he has no such ambitions; he would much rather sell than buy. The family is not considered as it used to be; the ancestors are no longer revered, indeed they are wilfully forgotten, partly perhaps from a feeling of guilt when all that they so carefully amassed is being so carelessly scattered. The dead are hardly mourned. 'Far the best for him,' the children say, cheerfully (so long, of course, as he has lived the requisite five years). Nobody wears black any more. The younger generation is no longer planned for, and there is a general feeling of 'après nous le déluge'.

*

The instinct of the lords to divest themselves of age-long influence and rights extends to their influence and rights in the Church. Most of them are members of the Church of England; though there are forty-seven Roman Catholics with seats in the House of Lords. On the whole, the lords, in common with most of their fellow countrymen, have always regarded religious observance as a sort of patriotic duty. The Church is the Church of England and must be supported to show that we are not as foreigners are. A friend of mine voiced this attitude during the war: 'Well, you know, I don't do fire-watching or Home Guard and I feel one must do something to help the war, so I always go to Church on Sunday.' I am sure he did not imagine that his prayers would drive back the German hordes; he went as a gesture of social solidarity. Hitherto, the livings of our Church have been the gift of landowners, who have generally chosen downright, muscular Christians of low Church leanings. 'Don't want lace and smells in my Church.' Zeal has always been frowned upon. As it is impossible to remove a parson once he is installed in his living, some of the most ringing rows of all time have been between the Manor and the Vicarage. Now, however, faithful to the spirit of divest, divest, the temporal lords are busily putting their livings at the disposal of their spiritual colleagues, the Bishops. Many people think that this will lead to more lace, more smells, and more un-English zeal in the Church, and indeed greatly alter its character. Incidentally, the marriage customs of the peerage have lately become very lax. One peer in eight has divested himself of his wife, and foreigners notice that there are rather more duchesses than dukes in London society today.

As for the House of Lords which gives the English aristocrat his unique position, Lord Hailsham, himself an unwilling member, says that the majority of peers are voting for its abolition 'with their feet', by simply neglecting their hereditary duties. It must be said that the number of regular attendants has never been very large, and the august chamber has always been characterized by an atmosphere of the dormitory if not of the morgue. This is distressing to an active young fellow like Lord Hailsham but it is nothing new. One of the merits of the Upper House has been to consist of a hard core of politicians reinforced now and then by experts, and only flooded out in times of crisis by all its members. These have hitherto proved not unrepresentative of public opinion. Now, however, it seems that it is hardly possible to get through the work, so small is the attendance.

Does this apparent abdication of the lords in so many different directions mean that the English aristocracy is in full decadence and will soon exist only like the appendix in the human body, a useless and sometimes harmful relic of the past? It would not be safe to assume so. The English lord has been nurtured on the land and is conversant with the cunning ways of the animal kingdom. He has often seen the grouse settle into the heather to rise and be shot at no more. He has noticed that enormous riches are not well looked on in the modern world and that in most countries his genus is extinct. It may be that he who, for a thousand years, has weathered so many a storm, religious, dynastic, and political, is taking cover in order to weather yet one more. It may be that he will succeed. He must, of course, be careful not to overdo the protective colouring. An aristocracy cannot exist as a secret society. Nor must he overdo an appearance of destitution. There is the sad precedent of George Neville, who was deprived of his dukedom (Bedford) by Act of Parliament because 'as is openly known he hath not, nor by inheritance may have, any livelihood to support the name, estate and dignity . . .'

But the English lord is a wily old bird who seldom overdoes anything. It is his enormous strength.

JAMES BALDWIN

Notes of a Native Son

James Baldwin (1924–87) was born in Harlem, where his father was a preacher. As a young man he moved to Paris, but Harlem stayed with him. His first novel, Go Tell It on the Mountain *(1953), was nakedly autobiographical and later fictions were solidly rooted in his New York childhood. But it was as an impassioned civil rights polemicist that Baldwin won international fame in the early 1960s – with* Nobody Knows My Name *(1961) and* The Fire Next Time *(1963). A collection of Baldwin's non-fiction,* The Price of the Ticket, *was published in 1985. 'Notes of a Native Son' was first published by Beacon Press in 1955.*

I

On the twenty-ninth of July, in 1943, my father died. On the same day, a few hours later, his last child was born. Over a month before this, while all our energies were concentrated in waiting for these events, there had been, in Detroit, one of the bloodiest race riots of the century. A few hours after my father's funeral, while he lay in state in the undertaker's chapel, a race riot broke out in Harlem. On the morning of the third of August, we drove my father to the graveyard through a wilderness of smashed plate glass.

The day of my father's funeral had also been my nineteenth birthday. As we drove him to the graveyard, the spoils of injustice, anarchy, discontent, and hatred were all around us. It seemed to me that God himself had devised, to mark my father's end, the most sustained and brutally dissonant of codas. And it seemed to me, too, that the violence which rose all about us as my father left the world had been devised as a corrective for the pride of his eldest son. I had declined to believe in that apocalypse which had been central to my father's vision; very well, life seemed to be saying, here is something that will certainly pass for an apocalypse until the real thing comes along. I had inclined to be

333

contemptuous of my father for the conditions of his life, for the conditions of our lives. When his life had ended I began to wonder about that life and also, in a new way, to be apprehensive about my own.

I had not known my father very well. We had got on badly, partly because we shared, in our different fashions, the vice of stubborn pride. When he was dead I realized that I had hardly ever spoken to him. When he had been dead a long time I began to wish I had. It seems to be typical of life in America, where opportunities, real and fancied, are thicker than anywhere else on the globe, that the second generation has no time to talk to the first. No one, including my father, seems to have known exactly how old he was, but his mother had been born during slavery. He was of the first generation of free men. He, along with thousands of other Negroes, came North after 1919 and I was part of that generation which had never seen the landscape of what Negroes sometimes call the Old Country.

He had been born in New Orleans and had been a quite young man there during the time that Louis Armstrong, a boy, was running errands for the dives and honky-tonks of what was always presented to me as one of the most wicked of cities – to this day, whenever I think of New Orleans, I also helplessly think of Sodom and Gomorrah. My father never mentioned Louis Armstrong, except to forbid us to play his records; but there was a picture of him on our wall for a long time. One of my father's strong-willed female relatives had placed it there and forbade my father to take it down. He never did, but he eventually maneuvered her out of the house and when, some years later, she was in trouble and near death, he refused to do anything to help her.

He was, I think, very handsome. I gather this from photographs and from my own memories of him, dressed in his Sunday best and on his way to preach a sermon somewhere, when I was little. Handsome, proud, and ingrown, 'like a toenail', somebody said. But he looked to me, as I grew older, like pictures I had seen of African tribal chieftains: he really should have been naked, with warpaint on and barbaric mementos, standing among spears. He could be chilling in the pulpit and indescribably cruel in his personal life and he was certainly the most bitter man I have ever met; yet it must be said that there was something else in him, buried in him, which lent him his tremendous power and, even, a rather crushing charm. It had something to do with his blackness, I think – he was very black – with his blackness and his beauty, and with the fact that he knew that he was black but did not know that he was beautiful. He claimed to be proud of his blackness but it had also been the cause of much humiliation and it had fixed bleak boundaries to his life. He was not a young man when we were growing up and he had already suffered many kinds of ruin; in his outrageously demanding and protective way he loved his children, who were black like him and menaced, like him; and all these things sometimes showed in his face when he tried, never to my knowledge with any success, to establish contact with any of us. When he took one of his children on his knee to play, the child always became fretful and began to cry; when he tried to help one of us with our homework the absolutely unabating tension which emanated from him caused our minds and our tongues to become paralyzed, so that he, scarcely knowing why, flew into a rage and the child, not knowing why, was punished. If it ever entered his head to bring a surprise home for his children, it was, almost unfailingly, the wrong surprise and even the big watermelons he often brought home on his back in the summertime led to the most appalling scenes. I do not remember, in all those years, that one of his children was ever glad to see him come home. From what I was able to gather of his early life, it seemed that this inability to establish contact with other people had always marked him and had been one of the things which had driven him out of New Orleans. There was something in him, therefore, groping and tentative, which was never expressed and which was buried with him. One saw it most clearly when he was facing new people and hoping to impress them. But he never did, not for long. We went from church to smaller and more improbable church, he found himself in less and less demand as a minister, and by the time he died none of his friends had come to see him for a long time. He had lived and died in an intolerable bitterness of spirit and it frightened me, as we drove him to the graveyard through those unquiet, ruined streets, to see how powerful and overflowing this bitterness could be and to realize that this bitterness now was mine.

When he died I had been away from home for a little over a year. In that year I had had time to become aware of the meaning of all my father's bitter warnings, had discovered the secret of his proudly pursed lips and rigid carriage: I had discovered the weight of white people in the world. I saw that this had been for my ancestors and now would be for me an awful thing to live with and that the bitterness which had helped to kill my father could also kill me.

He had been ill a long time – in the mind, as we now realized, reliving instances of his fantastic intransigence in the new light of his affliction and endeavoring to feel a sorrow for him which never, quite, came true. We had not known that he was being eaten up by paranoia, and the discovery that his cruelty, to our bodies and our minds, had been one of the symptoms of his illness was not, then, enough to enable us to forgive him. The younger children felt, quite simply, relief that he would not be coming home anymore. My mother's observation that it was he, after all, who had kept them alive all these years meant nothing because the problems of keeping children alive are not real for children. The older children felt, with my father gone, that they could invite their friends to the house without fear that their friends would be insulted or, as had sometimes happened with me, being told that their friends were in league with the devil and intended to rob our family of everything we owned. (I didn't fail to wonder, and it made me hate him, what on earth we owned that anybody else would want.)

His illness was beyond all hope of healing before anyone realized that he was ill. He had always been so strange and had lived, like a prophet, in such unimaginably close communion with the Lord that his long silences which were punctuated by moans and hallelujahs and snatches of old songs while he sat at the living-room window never seemed odd to us. It was not until he refused to eat because, he said, his family was trying to poison him that my mother was forced to accept as a fact what had, until then, been only an unwilling suspicion. When he was committed, it was discovered that he had tuberculosis and, as it turned out, the disease of his mind allowed the disease of his body to destroy him. For the doctors could not force him to eat, either, and, though he was fed intravenously, it was clear from the beginning that there was no hope for him.

In my mind's eye I could see him, sitting at the window, locked up in his terrors; hating and fearing every living soul including his children who had betrayed him, too, by reaching toward the world which had despised him. There were nine of us. I began to wonder what it could have felt like for such a man to have had nine children whom he could barely feed. He used to make little jokes about our poverty, which never, of course, seemed very funny to us; they could not have seemed very funny to him, either, or else our all too feeble response to them would never have caused such rages. He spent great energy and achieved, to our chagrin, no small amount of success in keeping us away from the people who surrounded us, people who had all-night rent parties to which we listened when we should have been sleeping, people who cursed and drank and flashed razor blades on Lenox Avenue. He could not understand why, if they had so much energy to spare, they could not use it to make their lives better. He treated almost everybody on our block with a most uncharitable asperity and neither they, nor, of course, their children were slow to reciprocate.

The only white people who came to our house were welfare workers and bill collectors. It was almost always my mother who dealt with them, for my father's temper, which was at the mercy of his pride, was never to be trusted. It was clear that he felt their very presence in his home to be a violation: this was conveyed by his carriage, almost ludicrously stiff, and by his voice, harsh and vindictively polite. When I was around nine or ten I wrote a play which was directed by a young, white schoolteacher, a woman, who then took an interest in me, and gave me books to read and, in order to corroborate my theatrical bent, decided to take me to see what she somewhat tactlessly referred to as 'real' plays. Theater-going was forbidden in our house, but, with the really cruel intuitiveness of a child, I suspected that the color of this woman's skin would carry the day for me. When, at school, she suggested taking me to the theater, I did not, as I might have done if she had been a Negro, find a way of discouraging her, but agreed that she should pick me up at my house one evening. I then, very cleverly, left all the rest to my mother, who suggested to my father, as I knew she would, that it would not be very nice to let such a kind woman make the trip for nothing. Also, since it was a schoolteacher, I imagine that my mother countered the idea of sin with the idea of 'education', which word, even with my father, carried a kind of bitter weight.

Before the teacher came my father took me aside to ask *why* she was coming, what *interest* she could possibly have in our house, in a boy like me. I said I didn't know but I, too, suggested that it had something to do with education. And I understood that my father was waiting for me to say something – I didn't quite know what; perhaps that I wanted his protection against this teacher and her 'education'. I said none of these things and the teacher came and we went out. It was clear, during the brief interview in our living room, that my father was agreeing very much against his will and that he would have refused permission if he had dared. The fact that he did not dare caused me to despise him: I had no way of knowing that he was facing in that living room a wholly unprecedented and frightening situation.

Later, when my father had been laid off from his job, this woman became very important to us. She was really a very sweet and generous woman and went to a great deal of trouble to be of help to us, particularly during one awful winter. My mother called her by the highest name she knew: she said she was a 'Christian'. My father could scarcely disagree but during the four or five years of our relatively close association he never trusted her and was always trying to surprise in her open, Midwestern face the genuine, cunningly hidden, and hideous motivation. In later years, particularly when it began to be clear that this 'education' of mine was going to lead me to perdition, he became more explicit and warned me that my white friends in high school were not really my friends and that I would see, when I was older, how white people would do anything to keep a Negro down. Some of them could be nice, he admitted, but none of them were to be trusted and most of them were not even nice. The best thing was to have as little to do with them as possible. I did not feel this way and I was certain, in my innocence, that I never would.

But the year which preceded my father's death had made a great change in my life. I had been living in New Jersey, working in defense plants, working and living among southerners, white and black. I knew about the South, of course, and about how southerners treated Negroes and how they expected them to behave, but it had never entered my mind that anyone would look at me and expect *me* to behave that way. I learned in New Jersey that to be a Negro meant, precisely, that one was never looked at but was simply at the mercy of the reflexes the color of one's skin caused in other people. I acted in New Jersey as I had always acted, that is as though I thought a great deal of myself – I had to *act* that way – with results that were, simply, unbelievable. I had scarcely arrived before I had earned the enmity, which was extraordinarily ingenious, of all my superiors and nearly all my co-workers. In the beginning, to make matters worse, I simply did not know what was happening. I did not know what I had done, and I shortly began to wonder what *anyone* could possibly do, to bring about such unanimous, active, and unbearably vocal hostility. I knew about jim crow but I had never experienced it. I went to the same self-service restaurant three times and stood with all the Princeton boys before the counter, waiting for a hamburger and coffee; it was always an extraordinarily long time before anything was set before me; but it was not until the fourth visit that I learned that, in fact, nothing had ever been set before me: I had simply picked something up. Negroes were not served there, I was told, and they had been waiting for me to realize that I was always the only Negro present. Once I was told this, I determined to go there all the time. But now they were ready for me and, though some dreadful scenes were subsequently enacted in that restaurant, I never ate there again.

It was the same story all over New Jersey, in bars, bowling alleys, diners, places to live. I was always being forced to leave, silently, or with mutual imprecations. I very shortly became notorious and children giggled behind me when I passed and their elders whispered or shouted – they really believed that I was mad. And it did begin to work on my mind, of course; I began to be afraid to go anywhere and to compensate for this I went places to which I really should not have gone and where, God knows, I had no desire to be. My reputation in town naturally enhanced my reputation at work and my working day became one long series of acrobatics designed to keep me out of trouble. I cannot say that these acrobatics succeeded. It began to seem that the machinery of the organization I worked for was turning over, day and night, with but one aim: to eject me. I was fired once, and contrived, with the aid of a friend from New York, to get back on the payroll; was fired again, and bounced back again. It took a while to fire me for the third time, but the third time took. There were no loopholes anywhere. There was not even any way of getting back inside the gates.

That year in New Jersey lives in my mind as though it were the year during which, having an unsuspected predilection for it, I first contracted some dread, chronic disease, the unfailing symptom of which is a kind of blind fever, a pounding in the skull and fire in the bowels. Once this disease is contracted, one can never be really carefree again, for the fever, without an instant's warning, can recur at any moment. It can wreck more important things than race relations. There is not a Negro alive who does not have this rage in his blood – one has the choice, merely, of living with it consciously or surrendering to it. As for me, this fever has recurred in me, and does, and will until the day I die.

My last night in New Jersey, a white friend from New York took me to the nearest big town, Trenton, to go to the movies and have a few drinks. As it turned out, he also saved me from, at the very least, a violent whipping. Almost every detail of that night stands out very clearly in my memory. I even remember the name of the movie we saw because its title impressed me as being so patly ironical. It was a movie about the German occupation of France, starring Maureen O'Hara and Charles Laughton and called *This Land Is Mine*. I remember the name of the diner we walked into when the movie ended: it was the 'American Diner'. When we walked in the counterman asked what we wanted and I remember answering with the casual sharpness which had become my habit: 'We want a hamburger and a cup of coffee, what do you think we want?' I do not know why, after a year of such rebuffs, I so completely failed to anticipate his answer, which was, of course, 'We don't serve Negroes here.' This reply failed to discompose me, at least for the moment. I made some sardonic comment about the name of the diner and we walked out into the streets.

This was the time of what was called the 'brownout', when the lights in all American cities were very dim. When we reentered the streets something happened to me which had the force of an optical illusion, or a nightmare. The streets were very crowded and I was facing north. People were moving in every direction but it seemed to me, in that instant, that all of the people I could see, and many more than that, were moving toward me, against me, and that everyone was white. I remember how their faces gleamed. And I felt, like a physical sensation, a click at the nape of my neck as though some interior string connecting my head to my body had been cut. I began to walk. I heard my friend call after me, but I ignored him. Heaven only knows what was going on in his mind, but he had the good sense not to touch me – I don't know what would have happened if he had – and to keep me in sight. I don't know what was going on in my mind, either; I certainly had no conscious plan. I wanted to do something to crush these white faces, which were crushing me. I walked for perhaps a block or two until I came to an enormous, glittering, and fashionable restaurant in which I knew not even the intercession of the Virgin would cause me to be served. I pushed through the doors and took the first vacant seat I saw, at a table for two, and waited.

I do not know how long I waited and I rather wonder, until today, what I could possibly have looked like. Whatever I looked like, I frightened the waitress who shortly appeared, and the moment she appeared all of my fury flowed toward her. I hated her for her white face, and for her great, astounded, frightened eyes. I felt that if she found a black man so frightening I would make her fright worthwhile.

She did not ask me what I wanted, but repeated, as though she had learned it somewhere, 'We don't serve Negroes here.' She did not say it with the blunt, derisive hostility to which I had grown so accustomed, but, rather, with a note of apology in her voice, and fear. This made me colder and more murderous than ever. I felt I had to do something with my hands. I wanted her to come close enough for me to get her neck between my hands.

So I pretended not to have understood her, hoping to draw her closer. And she did step a very short step closer, with her pencil poised incongruously over her pad; and repeated the formula: '. . . don't serve Negroes here.'

Somehow, with the repetition of that phrase, which was already ringing in my head like a thousand bells of a nightmare, I realized that she would never come any closer and that I would have to strike from a distance. There was nothing on the table but an ordinary watermug half full of water, and I picked this up and hurled it with all my strength at her. She ducked and it missed her and shattered against the mirror behind the bar. And, with that sound, my frozen blood abruptly thawed, I returned from wherever I had been, I *saw*, for the first time, the restaurant, the people with their mouths open, already, as it seemed to me, rising as one man, and I realized what I had done, and where I was, and I was frightened. I rose and began running for the door. A round, potbellied man grabbed me by the nape of the neck just as I reached the doors and began to beat me about the face. I kicked him and got loose and ran into the streets. My friend whispered, *'Run!'* and I ran.

My friend stayed outside the restaurant long enough to misdirect my pursuers and the police, who arrived, he told me, at once. I do not know what I said to him when he came to my room that night. I could not have said much. I felt, in the oddest, most awful way, that I had somehow betrayed him. I lived it over and over and over again, the way one relives an automobile accident after it has happened and one finds oneself alone and safe. I could not get over two facts, both equally difficult for the imagination to grasp, and one was that I could have been murdered. But the other was that I had been ready to commit murder. I saw nothing very clearly but I did see this: that my life, my *real* life, was in danger, and not from anything other people might do but from the hatred I carried in my own heart.

II

I had returned home around the second week in June – in great haste because it seemed that my father's death and my mother's confinement were both but a matter of hours. In the case of my mother, it soon became clear that she had simply made a miscalculation. This had always been her tendency and I don't believe that a single one of us arrived in the world, or has since arrived anywhere else, on time. But none of us dawdled so intolerably about the business of being born as did my baby sister. We sometimes amused ourselves, during those endless, stifling weeks, by picturing the baby sitting within in the safe, warm dark, bitterly regretting the necessity of becoming a part of our chaos and stubbornly putting it off as long as possible. I understood her perfectly and congratulated her on showing such good sense so soon. Death, however, sat as purposefully at my father's bedside as life stirred within my mother's womb and it was harder to understand why he so lingered in that long shadow. It seemed that he had bent, and for a long time, too, all of his energies toward dying. Now death was ready for him but my father held back.

All of Harlem, indeed, seemed to be infected by waiting. I had never before known it to be so violently still. Racial tensions throughout this country were exacerbated during the early years of the war, partly because the labor market brought together hundreds of thousands of ill-prepared people and partly because Negro soldiers, regardless of where they were born, received their military training in the South. What happened in defense plants and army camps had repercussions, naturally, in every Negro ghetto. The situation in Harlem had grown bad enough for clergymen, policemen, educators, politicians, and social workers to assert in one breath that there was no 'crime wave' and to offer, in the very next breath, suggestions as to how to combat it. These suggestions always seemed to involve playgrounds, despite the fact that racial skirmishes were occurring in the playgrounds, too. Playground or not, crime wave or not, the Harlem police force had been augmented in March, and the unrest grew – perhaps, in fact, partly as a result of the ghetto's instinctive hatred of policemen. Perhaps the most revealing news item, out of the steady parade of reports of muggings, stabbings, shootings, assaults, gang wars, and accusations of police brutality, is the item concerning six Negro girls who set upon a white girl in the subway because, as they all too accurately put it, she was stepping on their toes. Indeed she was, all over the nation.

I had never before been so aware of policemen, on foot, on horseback, on corners, everywhere, always two by two. Nor had I ever been so aware of small knots of people. They were on stoops and on corners and in doorways, and what was striking about them, I think, was that they did not seem to be talking. Never, when I passed these groups, did the usual sound of a curse or a laugh ring out and neither did there seem to be any hum of gossip. There was certainly, on the other hand, occurring between them communication extraordinarily intense. Another thing that was striking was the unexpected diversity of the people who made up these groups. Usually, for example, one would see a group of sharpies standing on the street corner, jiving the passing chicks; or a group of older men, usually, for some reason, in the vicinity of a barber shop, discussing baseball scores, or the numbers, or making rather chilling observations about women they had known. Women, in a general way, tended to be seen less often together – unless they were church women, or very young girls, or prostitutes met together for an unprofessional instant. But that summer I saw the strangest combinations: large, respectable, churchly matrons standing on the stoops or the corners with their hair tied up, together with a girl in sleazy satin whose face bore the marks of gin and the razor, or heavy-set, abrupt, no-nonsense older men, in company with the most disreputable and fanatical 'race' men, or these same 'race' men with the sharpies, or these sharpies with the churchly women. Seventh Day Adventists and Methodists and Spiritualists seemed to be hobnobbing with Holy-rollers and they were all, alike, entangled with the most flagrant disbelievers; something heavy in their stance seemed to indicate that they had all, incredibly, seen a common vision, and on each face there seemed to be the same strange, bitter shadow.

The churchly women and the matter-of-fact, no-nonsense men had children in the Army. The sleazy girls they talked to had lovers there, the sharpies and the 'race' men had friends and brothers there. It would have demanded an unquestioning patriotism, happily as uncommon in this country as it is undesirable, for these people not to have been disturbed by the bitter letters they received, by the newspaper stories they read, not to have been enraged by the posters, then to be found all over New York, which described the Japanese as 'yellow-bellied Japs'. It was only the 'race' men, to be sure, who spoke ceaselessly of being revenged – how this vengeance was to be exacted was not clear – for the indignities and dangers suffered by Negro boys in uniform; but everybody felt a directionless, hopeless bitterness, as well as that panic which can scarcely be suppressed when one knows that a human being one loves is beyond one's reach, and in danger. This helplessness and this gnawing uneasiness does something, at length, to even the toughest mind. Perhaps the best way to sum all this up is to say that the people I knew felt, mainly, a peculiar kind of relief when they knew that their boys were being shipped out of the South, to do battle overseas. It was, perhaps, like feeling that the most dangerous part of a dangerous journey had been passed and that now, even if death should come, it would come with honor and without the complicity of their countrymen. Such a death would be, in short, a fact with which one could hope to live.

It was on the twenty-eighth of July, which I believe was a Wednesday, that I visited my father for the first time during his illness and for the last time in his life. The moment I saw him I knew why I had put off this visit so long. I had told my mother that I did not want to see him because I hated him. But this was not true. It was only that I *had* hated him and I wanted to hold on to this hatred. I did not want to look on him as a ruin: it was not a ruin I had hated. I imagine that one of the reasons people cling to their hates so stubbornly is because they sense, once hate is gone, that they will be forced to deal with pain.

We traveled out to him, his older sister and myself, to what seemed to be the very end of a very Long Island. It was hot and dusty and we wrangled, my aunt and I, all the way out, over the fact that I had recently begun to smoke and, as she said, to give myself airs. But I knew that she wrangled with me because she could not bear to face the fact of her brother's dying. Neither could I endure the reality of her despair, her unstated bafflement as to what had happened to her brother's life, and her own. So we wrangled and I smoked and from time to time she fell into a heavy reverie. Covertly, I watched her face, which was the face of an old woman; it had fallen in, the eyes were sunken and lightless; soon she would be dying, too.

In my childhood – it had not been so long ago – I had thought her beautiful. She had been quick-witted and quick-moving and very generous with all the children and each of her visits had been an event. At one time one of my brothers and myself had thought of running away to live with her. Now she could no longer produce out of her handbag some unexpected and yet familiar delight. She made me feel pity and revulsion and fear. It was awful to realize that she no longer caused me to feel affection. The closer we came to the hospital the more querulous she became and at the same time, naturally, grew more dependent on me. Between pity and guilt and fear I began to feel that there was another me trapped in my skull like a jack-in-the-box who might escape my control at any moment and fill the air with screaming.

She began to cry the moment we entered the room and she saw him lying there, all shriveled and still, like a little black monkey. The great, gleaming apparatus which fed him and would have compelled him to be still even if he had been able to move brought to mind, not beneficence, but torture; the tubes entering his arm made me think of pictures I had seen when a child, of Gulliver, tied down by the pygmies on that island. My aunt wept and wept, there was a whistling sound in my father's throat; nothing was said; he could not speak. I wanted to take his hand, to say something. But I do not know what I could have said, even if he could have heard me. He was not really in that room with us, he had at last really embarked on his journey; and though my aunt told me that he said he was going to meet Jesus, I did not hear anything except that whistling in his throat. The doctor came back and we left, into that unbearable train again, and home. In the morning came the telegram saying that he was dead. Then the house was suddenly full of relatives, friends, hysteria, and confusion and I quickly left my mother and the children to the care of those impressive women, who, in Negro communities at least, automatically appear at times of bereavement armed with lotions, proverbs, and patience, and an ability to cook. I went downtown. By the time I returned, later the same day, my mother had been carried to the hospital and the baby had been born.

III

For my father's funeral I had nothing black to wear and this posed a nagging problem all day long. It was one of those problems, simple, or impossible of solution, to which the mind insanely clings in order to avoid the mind's real trouble. I spent most of that day at the downtown apartment of a girl I knew, celebrating my birthday with whisky and wondering what to wear that night. When planning a birthday celebration one naturally does not expect that it will be up against competition from a funeral and this girl had anticipated taking me out that night, for a big dinner and a nightclub afterwards. Sometime during the course of that long day we decided that we would go out anyway, when my father's funeral service was over. I imagine I decided it, since, as the funeral hour approached, it became clearer and clearer to me that I would not know what to do with myself when it was over. The girl, stifling her very lively concern as to the possible effects of the whisky on one of my father's chief mourners, concentrated on being conciliatory and practically helpful. She found a black shirt for me somewhere and ironed it and, dressed in the darkest pants and jacket I owned, and slightly drunk, I made my way to my father's funeral.

The chapel was full, but not packed, and very quiet. There were, mainly, my father's relatives, and his children, and here and there I saw faces I had not seen since childhood, the faces of my father's one-time friends. They were very dark and solemn now, seeming somehow to suggest that they had known all along that something like this would happen. Chief among the mourners was my aunt, who had quarreled with my father all his life; by which I do not mean to suggest that her mourning was insincere or that she had not loved him. I suppose that she was one of the few people in the world who had, and their incessant quarreling proved precisely the strength of the tie that bound them. The only other person in the world, as far as I knew, whose relationship to my father rivaled my aunt's in depth was my mother, who was not there.

It seemed to me, of course, that it was a very long funeral. But it was, if anything, a rather shorter funeral than most, nor, since there were no overwhelming, uncontrollable expressions of grief, could it be called – if I dare to use the word – successful. The minister who preached my father's funeral sermon was one of the few my father had still been seeing as he neared his end. He presented to us in his sermon a man whom none of us had ever seen – a man thoughtful, patient, and forbearing, a Christian inspiration to all who knew him, and a model for his children. And no doubt the children, in their disturbed and guilty state, were almost ready to believe this; he had been remote enough to be anything and, anyway, the shock of the incontrovertible, that it was really our father lying up there in that casket, prepared the mind for anything. His sister moaned and this grief-stricken moaning was taken as corroboration. The other faces held a dark, noncommittal thoughtfulness. This was not the man they had known, but they had scarcely expected to be confronted with *him*; this was, in a sense deeper than questions of fact, the man they had not known, and the man they had not known may have been the real one. The real man, whoever he had been, had suffered and now he was dead: this was all that was sure and all that mattered now. Every man in the chapel hoped that when his hour came he, too, would be eulogized, which is to say forgiven, and that all of his lapses, greeds, errors, and strayings from the truth would be invested with coherence and looked upon with charity. This was perhaps the last thing human beings could give each other and it was what they demanded, after all, of the Lord. Only the Lord saw the midnight tears, only He was present when one of His children, moaning and wringing hands, paced up and down the room. When one slapped one's child in anger the recoil in the heart reverberated through heaven and became part of the pain of the universe. And when the children were hungry and sullen and distrustful and one watched them, daily, growing wilder, and further away, and running headlong into danger, it was the Lord who knew what the charged heart endured as the strap was laid to the backside; the Lord alone who knew what one would have said if one had had, like the Lord, the gift of the living word. It was the Lord who knew of the impossibility every parent in that room faced: how to prepare the child for the day when the child would be despised and how to *create* in the child – by what means? – a stronger antidote to this poison than one had found for oneself. The avenues, side streets, bars, billiard halls, hospitals, police stations, and even the playgrounds of Harlem – not to mention the houses of correction, the jails, and the morgue – testified to the potency of the poison while remaining silent as to the efficacy of whatever antidote, irresistibly raising the question of whether or not such an antidote existed; raising, which was worse, the question of whether or not an antidote was desirable; perhaps poison should be fought with poison. With these several schisms in the mind and with more terrors in the heart than could be named, it was better not to judge the man who had gone down under an impossible burden. It was better to remember: *Thou knowest this man's fall; but thou knowest not his wrassling.*

While the preacher talked and I watched the children – years of changing their diapers, scrubbing them, slapping them, taking them to school, and scolding them had had the perhaps inevitable result of making me love them, though I am not sure I knew this then – my mind was busily breaking out with a rash of disconnected impressions. Snatches of popular songs, indecent jokes, bits of books I had read, movie sequences, faces, voices, political issues – I thought I was going mad; all these impressions suspended, as it were, in the solution of the faint nausea produced in me by the heat and liquor. For a moment I had the impression that my alcoholic breath, inefficiently disguised with chewing gum, filled the entire chapel. Then someone began singing one of my father's favorite songs and, abruptly, I was with him, sitting on his knee, in the hot, enormous, crowded church which was the first church we attended. It was the Abyssinian Baptist Church on 138th Street. We had not gone there long. With this image, a host of others came. I had forgotten, in the rage of my growing up, how proud my father had been of me when I was little. Apparently, I had had a voice and my father had liked to show me off before the members of the church. I had forgotten what he had looked like when he was pleased but now I remembered that he had always been grinning with pleasure when my solos ended. I even remembered certain expressions on his face when he teased my mother – had he loved her? I would never know. And when had it all begun to change? For now it seemed that he had not always been cruel. I remembered being taken for a haircut and scraping my knee on the footrest of the barber's chair and I remembered my father's face as he soothed my crying and applied the stinging iodine. Then I remembered our fights, fights which had been of the worst possible kind because my technique had been silence.

I remembered the one time in all our life together when we had really spoken to each other.

It was on a Sunday and it must have been shortly before I left home. We were walking, just the two of us, in our usual silence, to or from church. I was in high school and had been doing a lot of writing and I was, at about this time, the editor of the high school magazine. But I had also been a Young Minister and had been preaching from the pulpit. Lately, I had been taking fewer engagements and preached as rarely as possible. It was said in the church, quite truthfully, that I was 'cooling off.'

My father asked me abruptly, 'You'd rather write than preach, wouldn't you?'

I was astonished at his question – because it was a real question. I answered, 'Yes.'

That was all we said. It was awful to remember that that was all we had ever said.

The casket now was opened and the mourners were being led up the aisle to look for the last time on the deceased. The assumption was that the family was too overcome with grief to be allowed to make this journey alone and I watched while my aunt was led to the casket and, muffled in black, and shaking, led back to her seat. I disapproved of forcing the children to look on their dead father, considering that the shock of his death, or, more truthfully, the shock of death as a reality, was already a little more than a child could bear, but my judgment in this matter had been overruled and there they were, bewildered and frightened and very small, being led, one by one, to the casket. But there is also something very gallant about children at such moments. It has something to do with their silence and gravity and with the fact that one cannot help them. Their legs, somehow, seem *exposed*, so that it is at once incredible and terribly clear that their legs are all they have to hold them up.

I had not wanted to go to the casket myself and I certainly had not wished to be led there, but there was no way of avoiding either of these forms. One of the deacons led me up and I looked on my father's face. I cannot say that it looked like him at all. His blackness had been equivocated by powder and there was no suggestion in that casket of what his power had or could have been. He was simply an old man dead, and it was hard to believe that he had ever given anyone either joy or pain. Yet, his life filled that room. Further up the avenue his wife was holding his newborn child. Life and death so close together, and love and hatred, and right and wrong, said something to me which I did not want to hear concerning man, concerning the life of man.

After the funeral, while I was downtown desperately celebrating my birthday, a Negro soldier, in the lobby of the Hotel Braddock, got into a fight with a white policeman over a Negro girl. Negro girls, white policemen, in or out of uniform, and Negro males – in or out of uniform – were part of the furniture of the lobby of the Hotel Braddock and this was certainly not the first time such an incident had occurred. It was destined, however, to receive an unprecedented publicity, for the fight between the policeman and the soldier ended with the shooting of the soldier. Rumor, flowing immediately to the streets outside, stated that the soldier had been shot in the back, an instantaneous and revealing invention, and that the soldier had died protecting a Negro woman. The facts were somewhat different – for example, the soldier had not been shot in the back, and was not dead, and the girl seems to have been as dubious a symbol of womanhood as her white counterpart in Georgia usually is, but no one was interested in the facts. They preferred the invention because this invention expressed and corroborated their hates and fears so perfectly. It is just as well to remember that people are always doing this. Perhaps many of those legends, including Christianity, to which the world clings began their conquest of the world with just some such concerted surrender to distortion. The effect, in Harlem, of this particular legend was like the effect of a lit match in a tin of gasoline. The mob gathered before the doors of the Hotel Braddock simply began to swell and to spread in every direction, and Harlem exploded.

The mob did not cross the ghetto lines. It would have been easy, for example, to have gone over Morningside Park on the west side or to have crossed the Grand Central railroad tracks at 125th Street on the east side, to wreak havoc in white neighborhoods. The mob seems to have been mainly interested in something more potent and real than the white face, that is, in white power, and the principal damage done during the riot of the summer of 1943 was to white business establishments in Harlem. It might have been a far bloodier story, of course, if, at the hour the riot began, these establishments had still been open. From the Hotel Braddock the mob fanned out, east and west along 125th Street, and for the entire length of Lenox, Seventh, and Eighth Avenues. Along each of these avenues, and along each major side street – 116th, 125th, 135th, and so on – bars, stores, pawnshops, restaurants, even little luncheonettes had been smashed open and entered and looted – looted, it might be added, with more haste than efficiency. The shelves really looked as though a bomb had struck them. Cans of beans and soup and dog food, along with toilet paper, corn flakes, sardines and milk tumbled every which way, and abandoned cash registers and cases of beer leaned crazily out of the splintered windows and were strewn along the avenues. Sheets, blankets, and clothing of every description formed a kind of path, as though people had dropped them while running. I truly had not realized that Harlem *had* so many stores until I saw them all smashed open; the first time the word *wealth* ever entered my mind in relation to Harlem was when I saw it scattered in the streets. But one's first, incongruous impression of plenty was countered immediately by an impression of waste. None of this was doing anybody any good. It would have been better to have left the plate glass as it had been and the goods lying in the stores.

It would have been better, but it would also have been intolerable, for Harlem had needed something to smash. To smash something is the ghetto's chronic need. Most of the time it is the members of the ghetto who smash each other, and themselves. But as long as the ghetto walls are standing there will always come a moment when these outlets do not work. That summer, for example, it was not enough to get into a fight on Lenox Avenue, or curse out one's cronies in the barber shops. If ever, indeed, the violence which fills Harlem's churches, pool halls, and bars erupts outward in a more direct fashion, Harlem and its citizens are likely to vanish in an apocalyptic flood. That this is not likely to happen is due to a great many reasons, most hidden and powerful among them the Negro's real relation to the white American. This relation prohibits, simply, anything as uncomplicated and satisfactory as pure hatred. In order really to hate white people, one has to blot so much out of the mind – and the heart – that this hatred itself becomes an exhausting and self-destructive pose. But this does not mean, on the other hand, that love comes easily: the white world is too powerful, too complacent, too ready with gratuitous humiliation, and, above all, too ignorant and too innocent for that. One is absolutely forced to make perpetual qualifications and one's own reactions are always canceling each other out. It is this, really, which has driven so many people mad, both white and black. One is always in the position of having to decide between amputation and gangrene. Amputation is swift but time may prove that the amputation was not necessary – or one may delay the amputation too long. Gangrene is slow, but it is impossible to be sure that one is reading one's symptoms right. The idea of going through life as a cripple is more than one can bear, and equally unbearable is the risk of swelling up slowly, in agony, with poison. And the trouble, finally, is that the risks are real even if the choices do not exist.

'But as for me and my house,' my father had said, 'we will serve the Lord.' I wondered, as we drove him to his resting place, what this line had meant for him. I had heard him preach it many times. I had preached it once myself, proudly giving it an interpretation different from my father's. Now the whole thing came back to me, as though my father and I were on our way to Sunday school and I were memorizing the golden text: *And if it seem evil unto you to serve the Lord, choose you this day whom you will serve; whether the gods which your fathers served that were on the other side of the flood, or the gods of the Amorites, in whose land ye dwell: but as for me and my house, we will serve the Lord.* I suspected in these familiar lines a meaning which had never been there for me before. All of my father's texts and songs, which I had decided were meaningless, were arranged before me at his death like empty bottles, waiting to hold the meaning which life would give them for me. This was his legacy: nothing is ever escaped. That bleakly memorable morning I hated the unbelievable streets and the Negroes and whites who had, equally, made them that way. But I knew that it was folly, as my father would have said, this bitterness was folly. It was necessary to hold on to the things that mattered. The dead man mattered, the new life mattered; blackness and whiteness did not matter; to believe that they did was to acquiesce in one's own destruction. Hatred, which could destroy so much, never failed to destroy the man who hated and this was an immutable law.

It began to seem that one would have to hold in the mind forever two ideas which seemed to be in opposition. The first idea was acceptance, the acceptance, totally without rancor, of life as it is, and men as they are: in the light of this idea, it goes without saying that injustice is a commonplace. But this did not mean that one could be complacent, for the second idea was of equal power: that one must never, in one's own life, accept these injustices as commonplace but must fight them with all one's strength. This fight begins, however, in the heart and it now had been laid to my charge to keep my own heart free of hatred and despair. This intimation made my heart heavy and, now that my father was irrecoverable, I wished that he had been beside me so that I could have searched his face for the answers which only the future would give me now.

NORMAN MAILER

The White Negro

SUPERFICIAL REFLECTIONS ON THE HIPSTER

Norman Mailer (b. 1923) was once praised by Robert Lowell as 'the best journalist in America', but Mailer could not be sure that Lowell meant to praise him. In his own view, he was first of all a novelist. Lowell's instinct was correct, though. Mailer's most telling achievements as a writer have been in the field of deeply personalized non-fiction. The Armies of the Night (1968) and The Executioner's Song (1979) are two of Mailer's most celebrated 'true-life novels' but, for many of his admirers, it is in the essay form that he has been shown at his most crankily compelling. 'The White Negro' was collected in Mailer's Advertisements for Myself (1959).

Our search for the rebels of the generation led us to the hipster. The hipster is an *enfant terrible* turned inside out. In character with his time, he is trying to get back at the conformists by lying low ... You can't interview a hipster because his main goal is to keep out of a society which, he thinks, is trying to make everyone over in its own image. He takes marijuana because it supplies him with experiences that can't be shared with 'squares'. He may affect a broad-brimmed hat or a zoot suit, but usually he prefers to skulk unmarked. The hipster may be a jazz musician; he is rarely an artist, almost never a writer. He may earn his living as a petty criminal, a hobo, a carnival roustabout or a free-lance moving man in Greenwich Village, but some hipsters have found a safe refuge in the upper income brackets as television comics or movie actors. (The later James Dean, for one, was a hipster hero.) ... It is tempting to describe the hipster in psychiatric terms as infantile, but the style of his infantilism is a sign of the times. He does not try to enforce his will on others, Napoleon-fashion, but contents himself with a magical omnipotence never disproved because never tested ... As the only extreme nonconformist of his generation, he exercises a powerful if underground appeal for conformists, through newspaper accounts of his delinquencies, his structureless jazz, and his emotive grunt words.   'Born 1930: The Unlost Generation' by Caroline Bird
Harper's Bazaar, 1957

Probably, we will never be able to determine the psychic havoc of the concentration camps and the atom bomb upon the unconscious mind of almost everyone alive in these years. For the first time in civilized history, perhaps for the first time in all of history, we have been forced to live with the suppressed knowledge that the smallest facets of our personality or the most minor projection of our ideas, or indeed the absence of ideas and the absence of personality, could mean equally well that we might still be doomed to die as a cipher in some vast statistical operation in which our teeth would be counted, and our hair would be saved, but our death itself would be unknown, unhonoured, and unremarked, a death which could not follow with dignity as a possible consequence to serious actions we had chosen, but rather a death by *deus ex machina* in a gas chamber or a radioactive city; and so if in the midst of civilization – that civilization founded upon the Faustian urge to dominate nature by mastering time, mastering the links of social cause and effect – in the middle of an economic civilization founded upon the confidence that time could indeed be subjected to our will, our psyche was subjected itself to the intolerable anxiety that death being causeless, life was causeless as well, and time deprived of cause and effect had come to a stop.

The Second World War presented a mirror to the human condition which blinded anyone who looked into it. For if tens of millions were killed in concentration camps out of the inexorable agonies and contractions of super-states founded upon the always insoluble contradictions of injustice, one was then obliged also to see that no matter how crippled and perverted an image of man was the society he had created, it was nonetheless his creation, his collective creation (at least his collective creation from the past) and, if society was so murderous, then who could ignore the most hideous of questions about his own nature?

Worse. One could hardly maintain the courage to be individual, to speak with one's own voice, for the years in which one could complacently accept oneself as part of an élite by being a radical were forever gone. A man knew that when he dissented, he gave a note upon his life which could be called in any year of overt crisis. No wonder then that these have been the years of conformity and depression. A stench of fear has come out of every pore of American life, and we suffer from a collective failure of nerve. The only courage, with rare exceptions, that we have been witness to, has been the isolated courage of isolated people.

II

It is on this bleak scene that a phenomenon has appeared: the American existentialist – the hipster, the man who knows that if our collective condition is to live with instant death by atomic war, relatively quick death by the State as *l'univers concentrationnaire*, or with a slow death by conformity with every creative and rebellious instinct stifled (at what damage to the mind and the heart and the liver and the nerves no research foundation for cancer will discover in a hurry), if the fate of twentieth-century man is to live with death from adolescence to premature senescence, why then the only life-giving answer is to accept the terms of death, to live with death as immediate danger, to divorce oneself from society, to exist without roots, to set out on that uncharted journey into the rebellious imperatives of the self. In short, whether the life is criminal or not, the decision is to encourage the psychopath in oneself, to explore that domain of experience where security is boredom and therefore sickness, and one exists in the present, in that enormous present which is without past or future, memory or planned intention, the life where a man must go until he is beat, where he must gamble with his energies through all those small or large crises of courage and unforeseen situations which beset his day, where he must be with it or doomed not to swing. The unstated essence of Hip, its psychopathic brilliance, quivers with the knowledge that new kinds of victories increase one's power for new kinds of perception; and defeats, the wrong kind of defeats, attack the body and imprison one's energy until one is jailed in the prison air of other people's habits, other people's defeats, boredom, quiet desperation, and muted icy self-destroying rage. One is Hip or one is Square (the alternative which each new generation coming into American life is beginning to feel), one is a rebel or one conforms, one is a frontiersman in the Wild West of American night life, or else a Square cell, trapped in the totalitarian tissues of American society, doomed willy-nilly to conform if one is to succeed.

A totalitarian society makes enormous demands on the courage of men, and a partially totalitarian society makes even greater demands, for the general anxiety is greater. Indeed if one is to be a man, almost any kind of unconventional action often takes disproportionate courage. So it is no accident that the source of Hip is the Negro for he has been living on the margin between totalitarianism and democracy for two centuries. But the presence of Hip as a working philosophy in the sub-worlds of American life is probably due to jazz, and its knifelike entrance into culture, its subtle but so penetrating influence on an avant-garde generation – that post-war generation of adventurers who (some consciously, some by osmosis) had absorbed the lessons of disillusionment and disgust of the twenties, the depression, and the war. Sharing a collective disbelief in the words of men who had too much money and controlled too many things, they knew almost as powerful a disbelief in the socially monolithic ideas of the single mate, the solid family and the respectable love life. If the intellectual antecedents of this generation can be traced to such separate influences as D. H. Lawrence, Henry Miller, and Wilhelm Reich, the viable philosophy of Hemingway fits most of their facts: in a bad world, as he was to say over and over again (while taking time out from his parvenu snobbery and dedicated gourmandize), in a bad world there is no love nor mercy nor charity nor justice unless a man can keep his courage, and this indeed fitted some of the facts. What fitted the need of the adventurer even more precisely was Hemingway's categorical imperative that what made him feel good became therefore The Good.

So no wonder that in certain cities of America, in New York of course, and New Orleans, in Chicago and San Francisco and Los Angeles, in such American cities as Paris and Mexico, DF, this particular part of a generation was attracted to what the Negro had to offer. In such places as Greenwich Village, a *ménage-à-trois* was completed – the bohemian and the juvenile delinquent came face-to-face with the Negro, and the hipster was a fact in American life. If marijuana was the wedding ring, the child was the language of Hip for its argot gave expression to abstract states of feeling which all could share, at least all who were Hip. And in this wedding of the white and the black it was the Negro who brought the cultural dowry. Any Negro who wishes to live must live with danger from his first day, and no experience can ever be casual to him, no Negro can saunter down a street with any real certainty that violence will not visit him on his walk. The cameos of security for the average white: mother and the home, job and the family, are not even a mockery to millions of Negroes; they are impossible. The Negro has the simplest of alternatives: live a life of constant humility or ever-threatening danger. In such a pass, where paranoia is as vital to survival as blood, the Negro had stayed alive and begun to grow by following the need of his body where he could. Knowing in the cells of his existence that life was war, nothing but war, the Negro (all exceptions admitted) could rarely afford the sophisticated inhibitions of civilization, and so he kept for his survival the art of the primitive, he lived in the enormous present, he subsisted for his Saturday night kicks, relinquishing the pleasures of the mind for the more obligatory pleasures of the body, and in his music he gave voice to the character and quality of his existence, to his rage and the infinite variations of joy, lust, languor, growl, cramp, pinch, scream and despair of his orgasm. For jazz is orgasm, it is the music of orgasm, good orgasm and bad, and so it spoke across a nation, it had the communication of art even where it was watered, perverted, corrupted, and almost killed, it spoke in no matter what laundered popular way of instantaneous existential states to which some whites could respond, it was indeed a communication by art because it said, 'I feel this, and now you do too.'

So there was a new breed of adventurers, urban adventurers who drifted out at night looking for action with a black man's code to fit their facts. The hipster had absorbed the existentialist synopses of the Negro, and for practical purposes could be considered a white Negro.

To be an existentialist, one must be able to feel oneself – one must know one's desires, one's rages, one's anguish, one must be aware of the character of one's frustration and know what would satisfy it. The overcivilized man can be an existentialist only if it is chic, and deserts it quickly for the next chic. To be a real existentialist (Sartre admittedly to the contrary) one must be religious, one must have one's sense of the 'purpose' – whatever the purpose may be – but a life which is directed by one's faith in the necessity of action is a life committed to the notion that the substratum of existence is the search, the end meaningful but mysterious; it is impossible to live such a life unless one's emotions provide their profound conviction. Only the French, alienated beyond alienation from their unconscious, could welcome an existential philosophy without ever feeling it at all; indeed only a Frenchman by declaring that the unconscious did not exist could then proceed to explore the delicate involutions of consciousness, the microscopically sensuous and all but ineffable *frissons* of mental becoming, in order finally to create the theology of atheism and so submit that in a world of absurdities the existential absurdity is most coherent.

In the dialogue between the atheist and the mystic, the atheist is on the side of life, rational life, undialectical life – since he conceives of death as emptiness, he can, no matter how weary or despairing, wish for nothing but more life; his pride is that he does not transpose his weakness and spiritual fatigue into a romantic longing for death, for such appreciation of death is then all too capable of being elaborated by his imagination into a universe of meaningful structure and moral orchestration.

Yet this masculine argument can mean very little for the mystic. The mystic can accept the atheist's description of his weakness, he can agree that his mysticism was a response to despair. And yet . . . and yet his argument is that he, the mystic, is the one finally who has chosen to live with death, and so death is his experience and not the atheist's, and the atheist by eschewing the limitless dimensions of profound despair has rendered himself incapable to judge the experience. The real argument which the mystic must always advance is the very intensity of his private vision – his argument depends from the vision precisely because what was felt in the vision is so extraordinary that no rational argument, no hypotheses of 'oceanic feelings' and certainly no sceptical reductions can explain away what has become for him the reality more real than the reality of closely reasoned logic. His inner experience of the possibilities within death is his logic. So, too, for the existentialist. And the psychopath. And the saint and the bullfighter and the lover. The common denominator for all of them is their burning consciousness of the present, exactly that incandescent consciousness which the possibilities within death have opened for them. There is a depth of desperation to the condition which enables one to remain in life only by engaging death, but the reward is their knowledge that what is happening at each instant of the electric present is good or bad for them, good or bad for their cause, their love, their action, their need.

It is this knowledge which provides the curious community of feeling in the world of the hipster, a muted cool religious revival to be sure, but the element which is exciting, disturbing, nightmarish perhaps, is that incompatibles have come to bed, the inner life and the violent life, the orgy and the dream of love, the desire to murder and the desire to create, a dialectical conception of existence with a lust for power, a dark, romantic, and yet undeniably dynamic view of existence for it sees every man and woman as moving individually through each moment of life forward into growth or backward into death.

It may be fruitful to consider the hipster a philosophical psychopath, a man interested not only in the dangerous imperatives of his psychopathy but in codifying, at least for himself, the suppositions on which his inner universe is constructed. By this premise the hipster is a psychopath, and yet not a psychopath but the negation of the psychopath, for he possesses the narcissistic detachment of the philosopher, that absorption in the recessive nuances of one's own motive which is so alien to the unreasoning drive of the psychopath. In this country where new millions of psychopaths are developed each year, stamped with the mint of our contradictory popular culture (where sex is sin and yet sex is paradise), it is as if there has been room already for the development of the antithetical psychopath who extrapolates from his own condition, from the inner certainty that his rebellion is just, a radical vision of the universe which thus separates him from the general ignorance, reactionary prejudice, and self-doubt of the more conventional psychopath. Having converted his unconscious experience into much conscious knowledge, the hipster has shifted the focus of his desire from immediate gratification toward that wider passion for future power which is the mark of civilized man. Yet with an irreducible difference. For Hip is the sophistication of the wise primitive in a giant jungle, and so its appeal is still beyond the civilized man. If there are ten million Americans who are more or less psychopathic (and the figure is most modest), there are probably not more than one hundred thousand men and women who consciously see themselves as hipsters, but their importance is that they are an élite with the potential ruthlessness of an élite, and a language most adolescents can understand instinctively, for the hipster's intense view of existence matches their experience and their desire to rebel.

Before one can say more about the hipster, there is obviously much to be said about the psychic state of the psychopath – or, clinically, the psychopathic personality. Now, for reasons which may be more curious than the similarity of the words, even many people with a psychoanalytical orientation often confuse the psychopath with the psychotic. Yet the terms are polar. The psychotic is legally insane, the psychopath is not; the psychotic is almost always incapable of discharging in physical acts the rage of his frustration, while the psychopath at his extreme is virtually as incapable of restraining his violence. The psychotic lives in so misty a world that what is happening at each moment of his life is not very real to him whereas the psychopath seldom knows any reality greater than the face, the voice, the being of the particular people among whom he may find himself at any moment. Sheldon and Eleanor Glueck describe him as follows:

The psychopath ... can be distinguished from the person sliding into or clambering out of a 'true psychotic' state by the long tough persistence of his anti-social attitude and behaviour and the absence of hallucinations, delusions, manic flight of ideas, confusion, disorientation, and other dramatic signs of psychosis.

The late Robert Lindner, one of the few experts on the subject, in his book *Rebel Without a Cause – The Hypnoanalysis of a Criminal Psychopath* presented part of his definition in this way:

... the psychopath is a rebel without a cause, an agitator without a slogan, a revolutionary without a programme: in other words, his rebelliousness is aimed to achieve goals satisfactory to himself alone; he is incapable of exertions for the sake of others. All his efforts, hidden under no matter what disguise, represent investments designed to satisfy his immediate wishes and desires ... The psychopath, like the child, cannot delay the pleasures of gratification; and this trait is one of his underlying, universal characteristics. He cannot wait upon erotic gratification which convention demands should be preceded by the chase before the kill: he must rape. He cannot wait upon the development of prestige in society: his egoistic ambitions lead him to leap into headlines by daring performances. Like a red thread the predominance of this mechanism for immediate satisfaction runs through the history of every psychopath. It explains not only his behaviour but also the violent nature of his acts.

Yet even Lindner, who was the most imaginative and most sympathetic of the psycho-analysts who have studied the psychopathic personality, was not ready to project himself into the essential sympathy – which is that the psychopath may indeed be the perverted and dangerous front-runner of a new kind of personality which could become the central expression of human nature before the twentieth century is over. For the psychopath is better adapted to dominate those mutually contradictory inhibitions upon violence and love which civilization has exacted of us, and if it be remembered that not every psychopath is an extreme case, and that the condition of psychopathy is present in a host of people including many politicians, professional soldiers, newspaper columnists, entertainers, artists, jazz musicians, call-girls, promiscuous homosexuals and half the executives of Hollywood, television, and advertising, it can be seen that there are aspects of psychopathy which already exert considerable cultural influence.

What characterizes almost every psychopath and part-psychopath is that they are trying to create a new nervous system for themselves. Generally we are obliged to act with a nervous system which has been formed from infancy, and which carries in the style of its circuits the very contradictions of our parents and our early milieu. Therefore, we are obliged, most of us, to meet the tempo of the present and the future with reflexes and rhythms which come from the past. It is not only the 'dead weight of the institutions of the past' but indeed the inefficient and often antiquated nervous circuits of the past which strangle our potentiality for responding to new possibilities which might be exciting for our individual growth.

Through most of modern history, 'sublimation' was possible: at the expense of expressing only a small portion of oneself, that small portion could be expressed intensely. But sublimation depends on a reasonable tempo to history. If the collective life of a generation has moved too quickly, the 'past' by which particular men and women of that generation may function is not, let us say, thirty years old, but relatively a hundred or two hundred years old. And so the nervous system is overstressed beyond the possibility of such compromises as sublimation, especially since the stable middle-class values so prerequisite to sublimation have been virtually destroyed in our time, at least as nourishing values free of confusion or doubt. In such a crisis of accelerated historical tempo and deteriorated values, neurosis tends to be replaced by psychopathy, and the success of psycho-analysis (which even ten years ago gave promise of becoming a direct major force) diminishes because of its inbuilt and characteristic incapacity to handle patients more complex, more experienced, or more adventurous than the analyst himself. In practice, psycho-analysis has by now become all too often no more than a psychic blood-letting. The patient is not so much changed as aged, and the infantile fantasies which he is encouraged to express are condemned to exhaust themselves against the analyst's non-responsive reactions. The result for all too many patients is a diminution, a 'tranquillizing' of their most interesting qualities and vices. The patient is indeed not so much altered as worn out – less bad, less good, less bright, less willful, less destructive, less creative. He is thus able to conform to that contradictory and unbearable society which first created his neurosis. He can conform to what he loathes because he no longer has the passion to feel loathing so intensely.

The psychopath is notoriously difficult to analyse because the fundamental decision of his nature is to try to live the infantile fantasy, and in this decision (given the dreary alternative of psycho-analysis) there may be a certain instinctive wisdom. For there is a dialectic to changing one's nature, the dialectic which underlies all psycho-analytic method: it is the knowledge that if one is to change one's habits, one must go back to the source of their creation, and so the psychopath exploring backward along the road of the homosexual, the orgiast, the drug-addict, the rapist, the robber and the murderer seeks to find those violent parallels to the violent and often hopeless contradictions he knew as an infant and as a child. For if he has the courage to meet the parallel situation at the moment when he is ready, then he has a chance to act as he has never acted before, and in satisfying the frustration – if he can succeed – he may then pass by symbolic substitute through the locks of incest. In thus giving expression to the buried infant in himself, he can lessen the tension of those infantile desires and so free himself to remake a bit of his nervous system. Like the neurotic he is looking for the opportunity to grow up a second time, but the psychopath knows instinctively that to express a forbidden impulse actively is far more beneficial to him than merely to confess the desire in the safety of a doctor's room. The psychopath is ordinately ambitious, too ambitious ever to trade his warped brilliant conception of his possible victories in life for the grim if peaceful attrition of the analyst's couch. So his associational journey into the past is lived out in the theatre of the present, and he exists for those charged situations where his senses are so alive that he can be aware actively (as the analysand is aware passively) of what his habits are, and how he can change them. The strength of the psychopath is that he knows (where most of us can only guess) what is good for him and what is bad for him at exactly those instants when an old crippling habit has become so attacked by experience that the potentiality exists to change it, to replace a negative and empty fear with an outward action, even if – and here I obey the logic of the extreme psychopath – even if the fear is of himself, and the action is to murder. The psychopath murders – if he has the courage – out of the necessity to purge his violence, for if he cannot empty his hatred then he cannot love, his being is frozen with implacable self-hatred for his cowardice. (It can of course be suggested that it takes little courage for two strong eighteen-year-old hoodlums, let us say, to beat in the brains of a candy-store keeper, and indeed the act – even by the logic of the psychopath – is not likely to prove very therapeutic, for the victim is not an immediate equal. Still, courage of a sort is necessary, for one murders not only a weak fifty-year-old man but an institution as well, one violates private property, one enters into a new relation with the police and introduces a dangerous element into one's life. The hoodlum is therefore daring the unknown, and so no matter how brutal the act, it is not altogether cowardly.)

At bottom, the drama of the psychopath is that he seeks love. Not love as the search for a mate, but love as the search for an orgasm more apocalyptic than the one which preceded it. Orgasm is his therapy – he knows at the seed of his being that good orgasm opens his possibilities and bad orgasm imprisons him. But in this search, the psychopath becomes an embodiment of the extreme contradictions of the society which formed his character, and the apocalyptic orgasm often remains as remote as the Holy Grail, for there are clusters and nests and ambushes of violence in his own necessities and in the imperatives and retaliations of the men and women among whom he lives his life, so that even as he drains his hatred in one act or another, so the conditions of his life create it anew in him until the drama of his movements bears a sardonic resemblance to the frog who climbed a few feet in the well only to drop back again.

Yet there is this to be said for the search after the good orgasm: when one lives in a civilized world, and still can enjoy none of the cultural nectar of such a world because the paradoxes on which civilization is built demand that there remain a cultureless and alienated bottom of exploitable human material, then the logic of becoming a sexual outlaw (if one's psychological roots are bedded in the bottom) is that one has at least a running competitive chance to be physically healthy so long as one stays alive. It is therefore no accident that psychopathy is most prevalent with the Negro. Hated from outside and therefore hating himself, the Negro was forced into the position of exploring all those moral wildernesses of civilized life which the Square automatically condemns as delinquent or evil or immature or morbid or self-destructive or corrupt. (Actually the terms have equal weight. Depending on the telescope of the cultural clique from which the Square surveys the universe, 'evil' or 'immature' are equally strong terms of condemnation.) But the Negro, not being privileged to gratify his self-esteem with the heady satisfaction of categorical condemnation, chose to move instead in that other direction where all situations are equally valid, and in the worst of perversion, promiscuity, pimpery, drug addiction, rape, razor-slash, bottle-break, what-have-you, the Negro discovered and elaborated a morality of the bottom, an ethical differentiation between the good and the bad in every human activity from the go-getter pimp (as opposed to the lazy one) to the relatively dependable pusher or prostitute. Add to this, the cunning of their language, the abstract ambiguous alternatives in which from the danger of their oppression they learned to speak ('Well, now, man, like I'm looking for a cat to turn me on . . .'), add even more the profound sensitivity of the Negro jazzman who was the cultural mentor of a people, and it is not too difficult to believe that the language of Hip which evolved was an artful language, tested and shaped by an intense experience and therefore different in kind from white slang, as different as the special obscenity of the soldier, which in its emphasis upon 'ass' as the soul and 'shit' as circumstance, was able to express the existential states of the enlisted man. What makes Hip a special language is that it cannot really be taught – if one shares none of the experiences of elation and exhaustion which it is equipped to describe, then it seems merely arch or vulgar or irritating. It is a pictorial language, but pictorial like non-objective art, imbued with the dialectic of small but intense change, a language for the microcosm, in this case, man, for it takes the immediate experiences of any passing man and magnifies the dynamic of his movements, not specifically but abstractly so that he is seen more as a vector in a network of forces than as a static character in a crystallized field. (Which latter is the practical view of the snob.) For example, there is real difficulty in trying to find a Hip substitute for 'stubborn'. The best possibility I can come up with is: 'That cat will never come off his groove, dad.' But groove implies movement, narrow movement but motion nonetheless. There is really no way to describe someone who does not move at all. Even a creep does move – if at a pace exasperatingly more slow than the pace of the cool cats.

IV

Like children, hipsters are fighting for the sweet, and their language is a set of subtle indications of their success or failure in the competition for pleasure. Unstated but obvious is the social sense that there is not nearly enough sweet for everyone. And so the sweet goes only to the victor, the best, the most, the man who knows the most about how to find his energy and how not to lose it. The emphasis is on energy because the psychopath and the hipster are nothing without it since they do not have the protection of a position or a class to rely on when they have overextended themselves. So the language of Hip is a language of energy, how it is found, how it is lost.

But let us see. I have jotted down perhaps a dozen words, the Hip perhaps most in use and most likely to last with the minimum of variation. The words are man, go, put down, make, beat, cool, swing, with it, crazy, dig, flip, creep, hip, square. They serve a variety of purposes and the nuance of the voice uses the nuance of the situation to convey the subtle contextual difference. If the hipster moves through his life on a constant search with glimpses of Mecca in many a turn of his experience (Mecca being the apocalyptic orgasm) and if everyone in the civilized world is at least in some small degree a sexual cripple, the hipster lives with the knowledge of how he is sexually crippled and where he is sexually alive, and the faces of experience which life presents to him each day are engaged, dismissed or avoided as his need directs and his lifemanship makes possible. For life is a contest between people in which the victor generally recuperates quickly and the loser takes long to mend, a perpetual competition of colliding explorers in which one must grow or else pay more for remaining the same (pay in sickness, or depression, or anguish for the lost opportunity), but pay or grow.

Therefore one finds words like go, and make it and with it, and swing: 'Go' with its sense that after hours or days or months or years of monotony, boredom, and depression one has finally had one's chance, one has amassed enough energy to meet an exciting opportunity with all one's present talents for the flip (up or down) and so one is ready to go, ready to gamble. Movement is always to be preferred to inaction. In motion a man has a chance, his body is warm, his instincts are quick, and when the crisis comes, whether of love or violence, he can make it, he can win, he can release a little more energy for himself since he hates himself a little less, he can make a little better nervous system, make it a little more possible to go again, to go faster next time and so make more and thus find more people with whom he can swing. For to swing is to communicate, is to convey the rhythms of one's own being to a lover, a friend, or an audience, and – equally necessary – be able to feel the rhythms of their response. To swing with the rhythms of another is to enrich oneself – the conception of the learning process as dug by Hip is that one cannot really learn until one contains within oneself the implicit rhythm of the subject or the person. As an example, I remember once hearing a Negro friend have an intellectual discussion at a party for half an hour with a white girl who was a few years out of college. The Negro literally could not read or write, but he had an extraordinary ear and a fine sense of mimicry. So as the girl spoke, he would detect the particular formal uncertainties in her argument, and in a pleasant (if slightly Southern) English accent, he would respond to one or another facet of her doubts. When she would finish what she felt was a particularly well-articulated idea, he would smile privately and say, 'Other-direction . . . do you really believe in that?'

'Well . . . No,' the girl would stammer, 'now that you get down to it, there is something disgusting about it to me,' and she would be off again for five more minutes.

Of course the Negro was not learning anything about the merits and demerits of the argument, but he was learning a great deal about a type of girl he had never met before, and that was what he wanted. Being unable to read or write, he could hardly be interested in ideas nearly as much as in lifemanship, and so he eschewed any attempt to obey the precision or lack of precision in the girl's language, and instead sensed her character (and the values of her social type) by swinging with the nuances of her voice.

So to swing is to be able to learn, and by learning take a step towards making it, towards creating. What is to be created is not nearly so important as the hipster's belief that when he really makes it, he will be able to turn his hand to anything, even to self-discipline. What he must do before that is find his courage at the moment of violence, or equally make it in the act of love, find a little more between his woman and himself, or indeed between his mate and himself (since many hipsters are bisexual), but paramount, imperative, is the necessity to make it because in making it, one is making the new habit, unearthing the new talent which the old frustration denied.

Whereas if you goof (the ugliest word in Hip), if you lapse back into being a frightened stupid child, or if you flip, if you lose your control, reveal the buried weaker more feminine part of your nature, then it is more difficult to swing the next time, your ear is less alive, your bad and energy-wasting habits are further confirmed, you are further away from being with it. But to be with it is to have grace, is to be closer to the secrets of that inner unconscious life which will nourish you if you can hear it, for you are then nearer to that God which every hipster believes is located in the senses of his body, that trapped, mutilated and nonetheless megalomaniacal God who is It, who is energy, life, sex, force, the Yogi's *prana*, the Reichian's orgone, Lawrence's 'blood', Hemingway's 'good', the Shavian life force; 'It'; God; not the God of the churches but the unachievable whisper of mystery within the sex, the paradise of limitless energy and perception just beyond the next wave of the next orgasm.

To which a cool cat might reply, 'Crazy, man!'

Because, after all, what I have offered above is an hypothesis, no more, and there is not the hipster alive who is not absorbed in his own tumultuous hypotheses. Mine is interesting, mine is way out (on the avenue of the mystery along the road to 'It') but still I am just one cat in a world of cool cats, and everything interesting is crazy, or at least so the Squares who do not know how to swing would say.

(And yet crazy is also the self-protective irony of the hipster. Living with questions and not with answers, he is so different in his isolation and in the far reach of his imagination from almost everyone with whom he deals in the outer world of the Square, and meets generally so much enmity, competition, and hatred in the world of Hip, that his isolation is always in danger of turning upon itself, and leaving him indeed just that, crazy.)

If, however, you agree with my hypothesis, if you as a cat are way out too, and we are in the same groove (the universe now being glimpsed as a series of ever-extending radii from the centre), why then you say simply, 'I dig', because neither knowledge nor imagination comes easily, it is buried in the pain of one's forgotten experience, and so one must work to find it, one must occasionally exhaust oneself by digging into the self in order to perceive the outside. And indeed it is essential to dig the most, for if you do not dig you lose your superiority over the Square, and so you are less likely to be cool (to be in control of a situation because you have swung where the Square has not, or because you have allowed to come to consciousnesss a pain, a guilt, a shame or a desire which the other has not had the courage to face). To be cool is to be equipped, and if you are equipped it is more difficult for the next cat who comes along to put you down. And of course one can hardly afford to be put down too often, or one is beat, one has lost one's confidence, one has lost one's will, one is impotent in the world of action and so closer to the demeaning flip of becoming a queer, or indeed closer to dying, and therefore it is even more difficult to recover enough energy to try to make it again, because once a cat is beat he has nothing to give, and no one is interested any longer in making it with him. This is the terror of the hipster – to be beat – because once the sweet of sex has deserted him, he still cannot give up the search. It is not granted to the hipster to grow old gracefully – he has been captured too early by the oldest dream of power, the old fountain of Ponce de León, the fountain of youth where the gold is in the orgasm.

To be beat is therefore a flip, it is a situation beyond one's experience, impossible to anticipate – which indeed in the circular vocabulary of Hip is still another meaning for flip, but then I have given just a few of the connotations of these words. Like most primitive vocabularies each word is a prime symbol and serves a dozen or a hundred functions of communication in the instinctive dialectic through which the hipster perceives his experience, that dialectic of the instantaneous differentials of existence in which one is forever moving forward into more or retreating into less.

V

It is impossible to conceive a new philosophy until one creates a new language, but a new popular language (while it must implicitly contain a new philosophy) does not necessarily present its philosophy overtly. It can be asked then what really is unique in the life-view of Hip which raises its argot above the passing verbal whimsies of the bohemian or the lumpenproletariat.

The answer would be in the psychopathic element of Hip which has almost no interest in viewing human nature, or better, in judging human nature, from a set of standards conceived *a priori* to the experience, standards inherited from the past. Since Hip sees every answer as posing immediately a new alternative, a new question, its emphasis is on complexity rather than simplicity (such complexity that its language without the illumination of the voice and the articulation of the face and body remains hopelessly incommunicative). Given its emphasis on complexity, Hip abdicates from any conventional moral responsibility because it would argue that the results of our actions are unforeseeable, and so we cannot know if we do good or bad, we cannot even know (in the Joycean sense of the good and the bad) whether we have given energy to another, and indeed if we could, there would still be no idea of what ultimately the other would do with it.

Therefore, men are not seen as good or bad (that they are good-and-bad is taken for granted) but rather each man is glimpsed as a collection of possibilities, some more possible than others (the view of character implicit in Hip) and some humans are considered more capable than others of reaching more possibilities within themselves in less time, provided, and this is the dynamic, provided the particular character can swing at the right time. And here arises the sense of context which differentiates Hip from a Square view of character. Hip sees the context as generally dominating the man, dominating him because his character is less significant than the context in which he must function. Since it is arbitrarily five times more demanding of one's energy to accomplish even an inconsequential action in an unfavourable context than a favourable one, man is then not only his character but his context, since the success or failure of an action in a given context reacts upon the character and therefore affects what the character will be in the next context. What dominates both character and context is the energy available at the moment of intense context.

Character being thus seen as perpetually ambivalent and dynamic enters then into an absolute relativity where there are no truths other than the isolated truths of what each observer feels at each instant of his existence. To take a perhaps unjustified metaphysical extrapolation, it is as if the universe which has usually existed conceptually as a Fact (even if the Fact were Berkeley's God) but a Fact which it was the aim of all science and philosophy to reveal, becomes instead a changing reality whose laws are remade at each instant by everything living, but most particularly man, man raised to a neo-medieval summit where the truth is not what one has felt yesterday or what one expects to feel tomorrow but rather truth is no more nor less than what one feels at each instant in the perpetual climax of the present.

What is consequent therefore is the divorce of man from his values, the liberation of the self from the Super-Ego of society. The only Hip morality (but of course it is an ever-present morality) is to do what one feels whenever and wherever it is possible, and – this is how the war of the Hip and the Square begins – to be engaged in one primal battle: to open the limits of the possible for oneself, for oneself alone, because that is one's need. Yet in widening the arena of the possible, one widens it reciprocally for others as well, so that the nihilistic fulfilment of each man's desire contains its antithesis of human co-operation.

If the ethic reduces to Know Thyself and Be Thyself, what makes it radically different from Socratic moderation with its stern conservative respect for the experience of the past is that the Hip ethic is immodera-tion, childlike in its adoration of the present (and indeed to respect the past means that one must also respect such ugly consequences of the past as the collective murders of the State). It is this adoration of the present which contains the affirmation of Hip, because its ultimate logic surpasses even the unforgettable solution of the Marquis de Sade to sex, private property, and the family, that all men and women have absolute but temporary rights over the bodies of all other men and women – the nihilism of Hip proposes as its final tendency that every social restraint and category be removed, and the affirmation implicit in the proposal is that man would then prove to be more creative than murderous and so would not destroy himself. Which is exactly what separates Hip from the authoritarian philosophies which now appeal to the conservative and liberal temper – what haunts the middle of the twentieth century is that faith in man has been lost, and the appeal of authority has been that it would restrain us from ourselves. Hip, which would return us to ourselves, at no matter what price in individual violence, is the affirmation of the barbarian, for it requires a primitive passion about human nature to believe that individual acts of violence are always to be preferred to the collective violence of the State; it takes literal faith in the creative possibilities of the human being to envisage acts of violence as the catharsis which prepares growth.

Whether the hipster's desire for absolute sexual freedom contains any genuinely radical conception of a different world is of course another matter, and it is possible, since the hipster lives with his hatred, that many of them are the material for an élite of storm troopers ready to follow the first truly magnetic leader whose view of mass murder is phrased in a language which reaches their emotions. But given the desperation of his condition as a psychic outlaw, the hipster is equally a candidate for the most reactionary and most radical of movements, and so it is just as possible that many hipsters will come – if the crisis deepens – to a radical comprehension of the horror of society, for even as the radical has had his incommunicable dissent confirmed in his experience by precisely the frustration, the denied opportunities, and the bitter years which his ideas have cost him, so the sexual adventurer deflected from his goal by the implacable animosity of a society constructed to deny the sexual radical as well, may yet come to an equally bitter comprehension of the slow relentless inhumanity of the conservative power which controls him from without and from within. And in being so controlled, denied, and starved into the attrition of conformity, indeed the hipster may come to see that his condition is no more than an exaggeration of the human condition, and if he would be free, then everyone must be free. Yes, this is possible too, for the heart of Hip is its emphasis upon courage at the moment of crisis, and it is pleasant to think that courage contains within itself (as the explanation of its existence) some glimpse of the necessity of life to become more than it has been.

It is obviously not very possible to speculate with sharp focus on the future of the hipster. Certain possibilities must be evident, however, and the most central is that the organic growth of Hip depends on whether the Negro emerges as a dominating force in American life. Since the Negro knows more about the ugliness and danger of life than the white, it is probable that if the Negro can win his equality, he will possess a potential superiority, a superiority so feared that the fear itself has become the underground drama of domestic politics. Like all conservative political fear it is the fear of unforeseeable consequences, for the Negro's equality would tear a profound shift into the psychology, the sexuality, and the moral imagination of every white alive.

With this possible emergence of the Negro, Hip may erupt as a psychically armed rebellion whose sexual impetus may rebound against the antisexual foundation of every organized power in America, and bring into the air such animosities, antipathies, and new conflicts of interest that the mean empty hypocrisies of mass conformity will no longer work. A time of violence, new hysteria, confusion and rebellion will then be likely to replace the time of conformity. At that time, if the liberal should prove realistic in his belief that there is peaceful room for every tendency in American life, then Hip would end by being absorbed as a colourful figure in the tapestry. But if this is not the reality, and the economic, the social, the psychological, and finally the moral crises accompanying the rise of the Negro should prove insupportable, then a time is coming when every political guidepost will be gone, and millions of liberals will be faced with political dilemmas they have so far succeeded in evading, and with a view of human nature they do not wish to accept. To take the desegregation of the schools in the South as an example, it is quite likely that the reactionary sees the reality more closely than the liberal when he argues that the deeper issue is not desegregation but miscegenation. (As a radical I am of course facing in the opposite direction from the White Citizens' Councils – obviously I believe it is the absolute human right of the Negro to mate with the white, and matings there will undoubtedly be, for there will be Negro high school boys brave enough to chance their lives.) But for the average liberal whose mind has been dulled by the committee-ish cant of the professional liberal, miscegenation is not an issue because he has been told that the Negro does not desire it. So, when it comes, miscegenation will be a terror, comparable perhaps to the derangement of the American Communists when the icons to Stalin came tumbling down. The average American Communist held to the myth of Stalin for reasons which had little to do with the political evidence and everything to do with their psychic necessities. In this sense it is equally a psychic necessity for the liberal to believe that the Negro and even the reactionary Southern white are eventually and fundamentally people like himself, capable of becoming good liberals too if only they can be reached by good liberal reason. What the liberal cannot bear to admit is the hatred beneath the skin of a society so unjust that the amount of collective violence buried in the people is perhaps incapable of being contained, and therefore if one wants a better world one does well not to hold one's breath, for a worse world is bound to come first, and the dilemma may well be this: given such hatred, it must either vent itself nihilistically or become turned into the cold murderous liquidations of the totalitarian state.

VI

No matter what its horrors the twentieth century is a vastly exciting century for its tendency is to reduce all of life to its ultimate alternatives. One can well wonder if the last war of them all will be between the blacks and the whites, or between the women and the men, or between the beautiful and ugly, the pillagers and managers, or the rebels and the regulators. Which of course is carrying speculation beyond the point where speculation is still serious, and yet despair at the monotony and bleakness of the future has become so engrained in the radical temper that the radical is in danger of abdicating from all imagination. What a man feels is the impulse for his creative effort, and if an alien but nonetheless passionate instinct about the meaning of life has come so unexpectedly from a virtually illiterate people, come out of the most intense conditions of exploitation, cruelty, violence, frustration, and lust, and yet has succeeded as an instinct in keeping this tortured people alive, then it is perhaps possible that the Negro holds more of the tail of the expanding elephant of truth than the radical, and if this is so, the radical humanist could do worse than to brood upon the phenomenon. For if a revolutionary time should come again, there would be a crucial difference if someone had already delineated a neo-Marxian calculus aimed at comprehending every circuit and process of society from ukase to kiss as the communications of human energy – a calculus capable of translating the economic relations of man into his psychological relations and then back again, his productive relations thereby embracing his sexual relations as well, until the crises of capitalism in the twentieth century would yet be understood as the unconscious adaptations of a society to solve its economic imbalance at the expense of a new mass psychological imbalance. It is almost beyond the imagination to conceive of a work in which the drama of human energy is engaged, and a theory of its social currents and dissipations, its imprisonments, expressions, and tragic wastes is fitted into some gigantic synthesis of human action where the body of Marxist thought, and particularly the epic grandeur of *Das Kapital* (that first of the major *psychologies* to approach the mystery of social cruelty so simply and practically as to say that we are a collective body of humans whose life-energy is wasted, displaced, and procedurally stolen as it passes from one of us to another) – where particularly the epic grandeur of *Das Kapital* would find its place in an even more God-like view of human justice and injustice, in some more excruciating vision of those intimate and institutional processes which lead to our creations and disasters, our growth, our attrition, and our rebellion.

ARTHUR KOESTLER

Return Trip to Nirvana

Arthur Koestler (1905–83) was born in Budapest and educated in Vienna. His first book, a memoir of his Spanish Civil War experience, was written in German, as was Darkness at Noon, *Koestler's fictionalized attack on totalitarian dictatorships. In the 1940s he began publishing in English. Koestler wrote chiefly on politics but in his later years (he committed suicide in 1983) he developed a near-obsessive interest in the 'paranormal'. His 'Return Trip to Nirvana' can be read as an early document in the history of Anglo–American 'drug culture'. When published in the* Sunday Telegraph *in 1967, it bore the gloss: 'mythical hallucinations induced by drugs are arousing controversy in America. After taking a mushroom drug used in Mexico, the author challenges Aldous Huxley's defence of the cult.'*

A few weeks ago I received a letter dated from Divinity Avenue, Cambridge, Massachusetts. That symbolic address refers to the Center for Research in Personality of Harvard University. The writer was a friend, an American psychiatrist working in that Department.*

Dear K . . . ,

Things are happening here which I think will interest you. The big, new, hot issue these days in many American circles is DRUGS. Have you been tuned in on the noise?

I stumbled on the scene in the most holy manner. Spent last summer in Mexico. Anthropologist friend arrived one weekend with a bag of mushrooms bought from a witch. Magic mushrooms. I had never heard of them, but being a good host joined the crowd who ate them. Wow! Learned more in six hours than in past sixteen years. Visual transformations. Gone the perceptual machinery which clutters up our view of reality. Intuitive transformations. Gone the mental machinery which slices the world up into

---

* The friend in question was Dr Timothy Leary who, a few years later, was to attain world-wide notoriety as the leader of the LSD cult.

abstractions and concepts. Emotional transformations. Gone the emotional machinery that causes us to load life with our own ambitions and petty desires.

Came back to USA and have spent last six months pursuing these matters. Working with Aldous Huxley, Alan Watts [noted authority on Zen Buddhism], Allen Ginsberg the poet. We believe that the synthetics of the cactus peyote (mescalin) and the mushrooms (psilocybin) offer possibilities for expanding consciousness, changing perceptions, removing abstractions.

For the person who is prepared, they provide a soul-wrenching mystical experience. Remember your enlightenments in the Franco prison? Very similar to what we are producing. We have had cases of housewives who have never heard of Zen, experiencing *satori* [mystic enlightenment] and describing it . . .

We are offering the experience to distinguished creative people. Artists, poets, writers, scholars. We've learned a tremendous amount by listening to them . . .

We are also trying to build this experience in a holy and serious way into university curricula . . . If you are interested I'll send some mushrooms over to you . . . I'd like to hear about your reaction . . .

Shortly afterwards, I went to the States, to participate in a Symposium at the University of California Medical Center in San Francisco. One of the main subjects of the Symposium was 'The Influence of Drugs on the Individual'. But this was not much of a coincidence, as, at the present moment, a surprising number of Americans, from Brass to Beat, seem to have, for different reasons, drugs on the brain: the Brass because they are worried about brain-washing and space-flight training; the Beat because drugs provide a rocket-powered escape from reality; the Organisation Men because tranquillisers are more effective than the homely aspirins and fruit salts of yore; the medical profession because some of the new drugs promise a revolution, by 'chemical surgery', in the treatment of mental disease; and the spiritually frustrated on all levels of society because drugs promise a kind of do-it-yourself approach to Salvation. Thus there is a confluence of motives, and an inflation in academic drug-research projects, financed on a lavish scale by Government agencies, universities and foundations.

On the way from San Francisco to my friend at Harvard, I stayed for a few days at the University of Michigan at Ann Arbor. I had been invited there for quite different reasons, but on the first morning of my stay the subject of the magic mushroom cropped up. The psychiatrist in charge of the mushroom was an Englishman of the quiet, gentle, un-American kind. Based on his own experiences – he had taken it on several occasions – and on experiments with ten test-subjects, he ventured the tentative opinion that, compared to the fashionable wonder-drugs mescalin and lysergic acid, the effect of the mushroom was relatively harmless and entirely on the pleasant, euphoric side.

It is well known that the mental attitude, the mood in which one enters the gates of mushroomland, plays a decisive part in determining the nature of the experience. Since Dr P. was such a pleasant person and the atmosphere of his clinic appealed to me, I volunteered as a guinea pig – though I felt a little guilty towards my enthusiastic friend in Harvard. We fixed the date of the experiment, and I was told not to make any appointments on that day until the evening, as I would remain under the influence of the drug for about six hours.

Just before awakening on the morning of the appointed day, I had a dream which is relevant to what follows. I saw standing before me a large earthenware jar; in it squatted a man, with only his head visible over the rim of the jar; the colour of his face was a yellowish brown, he seemed in great pain, but had a resigned look; a dispassionate voice explained to me that this was St Michael undergoing martyrdom; and that presently he was to be lifted out and put into another jar to be boiled alive in oil. I woke up with a faint nausea, and at once connected the dream with an experience on the previous day. In one of the laboratories for experimental psychology, I had seen a monkey's head – its body was hidden behind an enclosure so that the head alone was visible. An electric plug had been inserted into the creature's skull, and a wire led from it to the ceiling. The plugged head was perfectly, unnaturally still (the body was immobilised in a restraining jacket); only the eyes, old as Methuselah's, turned in their sockets to follow the visitors' movements, quietly, resignedly.

I hasten to reassure the reader that, as far as human knowledge goes, the monkeys in these experiments do not suffer pain. The plug is connected to electrodes which are inserted into the brain under anaesthesia, and once placed, cause neither pain nor discomfort: the purpose of the experiment does not concern us here. I had read about it before; nevertheless, the sight of that sad little head, with the electric plug sticking out of its fur, filled me with an unreasoning horror; hence the dream about St Michael's martyrdom. Thus I faced the mushrooms in a depressed state of 'floating anxiety', as the psychiatrists say.

The mushroom comes synthesised, in the shape of little pink pills; they look harmless and taste bitter. I swallowed nine of them (18 milligrams of psilocybin), which is a fairsized dose for a person of my weight. They were supposed to start acting after thirty minutes, and reach their maximum effect after about an hour.

However, for nearly an hour nothing at all happened. I was chatting with Dr P. and one of his assistants, first in his office, then in a room which had a comfortable couch in it and a tape recorder; after a while I was left alone in the room, but Dr P. looked in from time to time. I lay down on the couch, and soon began to experience the kind of phenomena which have been repeatedly described by people who experimented with mescalin. When I closed my eyes I saw luminous, moving patterns of great beauty, which was highly enjoyable; then the patterns changed into planaria – a kind of flatworm which I had watched under the microscope the previous day in another laboratory; but the worms had a tendency to change into dragons, which was less enjoyable, so I walked out of the show simply by opening my eyes. Then I tried it again, this time directing the beam of the table-lamp, which had a strong bulb, straight at my closed eyelids, and the effect was quite spectacular – rather like the explosive paintings of schizophrenics, or Walt Disney's *Fantasia*. A flaming eddy, the funnel of a tornado, appeared over my head, drawing me upward; with a little auto-suggestion and self-dramatisation I could have called it a vision of myself as the prophet Elijah being taken to Heaven by a whirlwind. But I felt that this was buying one's visions on the cheap ('Carter's little mushrooms are the best, mystic experience guaranteed or money refunded'); so I again walked out of the show by forcing my eyes to open. It was as simple as that, and I congratulated myself on my sober self-control, a rational mind not to be fooled by little pills.

By now, however, even with open eyes, the room looked different. The colours had become not only more luminous and brilliant, but different in quality from any colour previously seen; they were located outside the normally visible spectrum, and to refer to them one would have to invent new words – so I shall say that the walls were breen, the curtains were darsh, and the sky outside emerdine. Also, one of the walls had acquired a concave bend like the inside of a barrel, the plaster statue of the Venus of Milo had acquired a grin, and the straight dado-line was now curved, which struck me as an exceedingly clever joke. But all this was quite unlike the wobbling world of drunkenness, for the transformed room was plunged into an underwater silence, where the faint hum of the tape recorder became obtrusively loud, and the almost imperceptible undulations of the curtains became the Ballet of the Flowing Folds (the undulations were caused by warm air ascending from the central-heating body). A narrow strip of the revolving spool of the tape recorder caught the gleam of the lamp every few seconds; this faint, intermittent spark, unnoticed before, observed out of the corner of the eye on the visual periphery became the revolving beam of a miniature lighthouse. This lowering of the sensory threshold and simultaneous heightening of the intensity and emotional significance of perceptions is one of the basic phenomena of the mushroom universe. The intermittent light-signal from the slowly revolving spool became important, meaningful and mysterious; it had some secret message. Afterwards I remembered, with sympathetic understanding, the fantasies of paranoiacs about hidden electric machines planted by their enemies to produce evil Rays and Influences.

The signalling tape recorder was the first symptom of a chemically induced state of insanity. The full effect came on with insidious smoothness and suddenness. Dr P. came into the room, and a minute or two later I saw the light – and realised what a fool I had been to let myself be trapped by his cunning machinations. For during that minute or two he had undergone an unbelievable transformation.

It started with the colour of his face, which had become a sickly yellowish brown – the colour of the monkey with the electric plug. He stood in a corner of the room with his back to the green wall, and as I stared at him his face split into two, like a cell dividing. It oscillated for a while, then reunited into a single face, and by this time the transformation was complete. A small scar on the Doctor's neck, which I had not noticed before, was gaping wide, trying to ingest the flesh of the chin; one ear had shrunk, the other had grown by several inches, and the face became a smirking, evil phantasm. Then it changed again, into a different kind of Hogarthian vision, and these transformations went on for what I took to be several minutes.

All this time the doctor's body remained unchanged, the hallucinations were confined to the space from the neck upward; and they were strongly two-dimensional, like faces cut out of cardboard. The phenomenon was always strongest in that corner of the room where it had first occurred, and faded into less offensive distorting-mirror effects when we moved elsewhere, although the lighting of the room was uniform. The same happened when other members of the staff joined us later. One of them, the jovial Dr F., was transformed into a vision so terrifying – a Mongol with a broken neck hanging from an invisible gallows – that I thought I was going to be sick; yet I could not stop myself staring at him. We stood face to face in the 'evil corner', and with my pupils dilated by the drug I must have looked unpleasant, for he asked in an embarrassed voice: 'Why are you staring at me so?' In the end I said: 'For God's sake let's snap out of it', and we moved into another part of the room, where the effect became much weaker.

As the last remark indicates, I was still in control of my outward behaviour, and this remained true throughout the whole three or four hours of the experience. But at the same time I had completely lost control over my perception of the world. I made repeated efforts 'to walk out of the show' as I had been able to do during the first stages on the couch, but I was powerless against the delusions. I kept repeating to myself: 'But these are nice, friendly people, they are your friends'; and so on. It had no effect whatsoever on the spontaneous and inexorable visual transformations. At one stage, these spread from the faces of others to my own right hand which shrivelled into a cripple's, and to the metal bars of the table lamp, which were transformed into the claws of a predatory bird. Then I asked for a mirror to be brought in, expecting to see a picture of Dorian Gray. Strangely enough, there was no change in my own face.

After an hour or two (one's inner clock goes completely haywire under the drug), the effect began to wear off. They gave me a sedative, and after a suitable interval took me back to the hotel, where I had a meal with one of the doctors in the public dining-room. The world was normal again, except for a minute or two when the doctor's head, for the last time, went through two or three rapid mutations across the dining-table. These, however, were no longer frightening, but rather like a brilliant actor's impersonations of various character-types in quick succession – all of which, I felt with deep conviction, were different aspects of the doctor's personality. This conviction of possessing the gift of second sight, of being able not only to 'read' but to *see* a person's hidden character as if it were projected on a screen, is another typical symptom in certain forms of schizophrenia. I had faint recurrent whiffs of it for quite a while. The faces of friends or of strangers in the train would for a moment become unreal, like projections of a magic lantern, and at the same time revealing their innermost secret – but I never managed to express or define just what had been revealed. This was the only after-effect of the experience that I am aware of. It lasted for about a week.

When the mind is split into separate layers, some of which function more or less normally, while others are deranged, one exists in a world of paradox. At certain moments I thought that I had been lured into a trap, that the malign faces surrounding me were somehow connected with the Gestapo or the GPU, and it was a comfort to know that the room was on the ground floor so that if it came to the worst I could bolt through the window. I always managed to snap out of it after a moment or two, persuading myself that all this was a delusion; but the *visual* delusions persisted independently of my better knowledge, and against these I was helpless. The horror of the experience lies not so much in the apparitions themselves, but in the moments of panicky suspicion that the condition might become irreversible.

And that suspicion is not entirely unfounded. One member of a medical research team whom I met, inadvertently took an overdose of the pills with the result that he suffered from intermittent delusions of persecution for a period of two months. I know of two other people who experimented under insufficient medical supervision and had to be hospitalised for varying periods. These, however, are exceptions. I have mentioned before that all of Dr P.'s previous subjects had positive, euphoric experiences; I 'broke the series', as he ruefully remarked over post-mortem drinks on the next day. The same is true of the majority of the Harvard team's subjects. The reasons why I had been so unlucky are related to the monkey and the subsequent dream; they were the wrong kind of preparation. If one adds to this the burden of past experiences as a political prisoner, of past preoccupations with brain-washing, torture and the extraction of confessions, it will seem evident that I was a rather unfortunate choice for a guinea pig – except perhaps to demonstrate what mushroomland *can* do to the wrong kind of guinea pig. The phantom faces were equally obvious projections of a deep-seated resentment against being 'trapped' in a situation which carried symbolic echoes of the relation between prisoner and inquisitor, monkey and experimenter, persecutor and victim. Poor Dr P. and his nice colleagues had to endure what they would call a 'negative transference', and serve as projection screens for the lantern slides of the past, stored in the mental underground. I suspect that a sizeable minority of people who try for a chemical lift to Heaven, will find themselves landed in the other place. This may be due to character or accident – the wrong time or setting for the experiment bringing the wrong type of lantern slides out of storage; and no experimental psychiatrist, however skilled, can exercise complete control over all the variables in the situation, nor guarantee the result.

I do not want to exaggerate the small risks involved in properly supervised experiments for legitimate research purposes; and I also believe that every clinical psychiatrist could derive immense benefits from a few experiments in chemically induced temporary psychosis, enabling him to see life through his patients' eyes. But I disagree with the enthusiasts' belief that mescalin or psilocybin, even when taken under the most favourable conditions, will provide artists, writers or aspiring mystics with new insights, or revelations, of a transcendental nature.

I profoundly admire Aldous Huxley, both for his philosophy and uncompromising sincerity. But I disagree with his advocacy of 'the chemical opening of doors into the Other World', and with his belief that drugs can procure 'what Catholic theologians call a gratuitous grace'.* Chemically induced hallucinations, delusions and raptures may be frightening or wonderfully gratifying; in either case they are in the nature of confidence tricks played on one's own nervous system.

I have before me a file, compiled by the Harvard research team, containing the productions of various writers and scholars while under the influence of one of the drugs, or shortly afterwards. The first, by a well-known novelist, starts:

Mainly I felt like a floating Khan on a magic carpet with my interesting lieutenants and gods . . . some ancient feeling about old geheuls in the grass, and temples, exactly also like the sensations I got drunk on pulque floating in the Xochimilco gardens . . .

* *The Doors of Perception*, London, 1954.

The second, by an aspiring writer, starts:

Dear . . . Experiences with Psilocybin in me have been very tastey & eatable & when the effects come on, wham, I am in the middle of this ever grower larger and larger cosmos of vibrating hums of wishes & desires & mistroy plays as in Shaskerpiere, about to enter the stage & speack in the play. Somehow these pills make the soul more real . . . [The spelling is a semi-conscious mannerism often induced by the drug.]

The third is the beginning of a poem, also by a well-known writer, called *Lysergic Acid (God seen thru Imagination)*:

It is a multiple million eyed monster | it is in all its elephants and selves | it hummeth in the electric typewriter | it is electricity connected to itself, if it hath wires | it is a vast Spiderweb | and I am on the last millionth infinite tentacle of the spiderweb . . .

Some of the reports in the file, written after the experience, are in a more sober vein, but not a single item contains anything of artistic merit or of theoretical value; and the drug-induced productions were all far beneath the writers' normal standards (Huxley's report was not in the file). While working on the material I was reminded of a story George Orwell once told me (I do not recall whether he published it): a friend of his, while living in the Far East, smoked several pipes of opium every night, and every night a single phrase rang in his ear, which contained the whole secret of the universe; but in his euphoria he could not be bothered to write it down and by the morning it was gone. One night he managed to jot down the magic phrase after all, and in the morning he read: 'The banana is big, but its skin is even bigger.'

I had a similar revelation when I took the mushroom the second time, under more happy and relaxed conditions. This was in the apartment of my Harvard friend from whose letter I have quoted, and there were six of us in a convivial atmosphere, after dinner and wine. All of us took various amounts of the pill, and this time I took a little more (either 22 or 24 mg, for I lost count). Again there were delusions: the room expanded and contracted in the most extraordinary manner, like an accordion played slowly; but the faces around me changed only slightly and in a pleasant manner, becoming more beautiful. Then came the Moment of Truth: a piece of chamber music played on a tape recorder. I had never heard music played like that before, I suddenly *understood* the very essence of music, the secret of its magic; the harmony of the spheres was revealed to me ... Unfortunately, I was unable to tell the next day whether it had been a symphony or a quintet or a trio, and whether by Mendelssohn or Bach. I may just as well have listened to Liberace. It had nothing to do with genuine appreciation of music; my soul was steeped in cosmic schmalz. I sobered up, though, when a fellow mushroom-eater – an American writer whom I otherwise rather liked – began to declaim about Cosmic Awareness, Expanding Consciousness, Zen Enlightenment, and so forth. This struck me as downright obscene, more so than four-letter words. This pressure-cooker mysticism seemed the ultimate profanation. But my exaggerated reaction was no doubt also mushroom-conditioned, so I went to bed.

In *Heaven and Hell*, defending the mescalin ecstasy against the reproach of artificiality, Huxley, the most highly respected exponent of the cult, argues that 'in one way or another, all our experiences are chemically conditioned'; and that the great mystics of the past also 'worked systematically to modify their body chemistry ... starving themselves into low blood sugar and a vitamin deficiency. They sang interminable psalms, thus increasing the amount of carbon dioxide in the lungs and the bloodstream, or, if they were orientals, they did breathing exercises to accomplish the same purpose.' There is, of course, a certain amount of truth in this on a purely physiological level, but the conclusions which Huxley draws, and the advice he tenders to modern man in search of a soul, are all the more distressing: 'Knowing as he does ... what are the chemical conditions of transcendental experience, the aspiring mystic should turn for technical help to the specialists in pharmacology, in bio-chemistry, in physiology and neurology ...'

I would like to answer this with a parable. In the beloved Austrian mountains of my school-days, it took us about five to six hours to climb a 7000-foot peak. Today, many of them can be reached in a few minutes by cable-car, or ski-lift, or even by motorcar. Yet you still see thousands of schoolboys, middle-aged couples and elderly men puffing and panting up the steep path, groaning under the load of their knapsacks. When they arrive at the alpine refuge near the summit, streaming with sweat, they shout for their traditional reward – a glass of schnapps and a plate of hot pea-soup. And then they look at the view – and then there is only a man and a mountain and a sky.

My point is not the virtue of sweat and toil. My point is that, although the view is the same, their vision is different from those who arrive by motorcar.

GORE VIDAL

The Holy Family

Gore Vidal was born in 1925, the grandson of a US senator, and he has made much of his historical access to the inner circles of American power-making. Indeed, power is one of Vidal's recurring preoccupations: be it power in Washington, or ancient Rome, or Hollywood. His novels include Julian *(1964),* Washington DC *(1967),* Hollywood *(1990) and – most famously –* Myra Breckenridge *(1968). In more than one of his essays and memoirs, Vidal has spoken candidly of his acquaintance with the Kennedys (see* Palimpsest: A Memoir, *published in 1995). 'The Holy Family' first appeared in* Esquire *in April 1967 and was reprinted in Vidal's* Collected Essays *(1974).*

From the beginning of the Republic, Americans have enjoyed accusing the first magistrate of kingly ambition. Sometimes seriously but more often derisively, the president is denounced as a would-be king, subverting the Constitution for personal ends. From General Washington to the present incumbent, the wielder of power has usually been regarded with suspicion, a disagreeable but not unhealthy state of affairs for both governor and governed. Few presidents, however, have been accused of wanting to establish family dynasties, if only because most presidents have found it impossible to select a successor of any sort, much less promote a relative. Each of the Adamses and the Harrisons reigned at an interval of not less than a political generation from the other, while the two Roosevelts were close neither in blood nor in politics. But now something new is happening in the Republic, and as the Chinese say, we are living 'in interesting times'.

In 1960, with the election of the thirty-fifth President, the famous ambition of Joseph P. Kennedy seemed at last fulfilled. He himself had come a long way from obscurity to great wealth and prominence; now his eldest surviving son, according to primogeniture, had gone the full distance and become president. It was a triumph for the patriarch. It was also a splendid moment for at least half the nation. What doubts

387

one may have had about the Kennedys were obscured by the charm and intelligence of John F. Kennedy. He appeared to be beautifully on to himself; he was also on to us; there is even evidence that he was on to the family, too. As a result, there were few intellectuals in 1960 who were not beguiled by the spectacle of a President who seemed always to be standing at a certain remove from himself, watching with amusement his own performance. He was an ironist in a profession where the prize usually goes to the apparent cornball. With such a man as chief of state, all things were possible. He would 'get America moving again'.

But then mysteriously the thing went wrong. Despite fine rhetoric and wise commentary, despite the glamor of his presence, we did not move, and if historians are correct when they tell us that presidents are 'made' in their first eighteen months in office, then one can assume that the Kennedy administration would never have fulfilled our hopes, much less his own. Kennedy was of course ill-fated from the beginning. The Bay of Pigs used up much of his credit in the bank of public opinion, while his attempts at social legislation were resolutely blocked by a more than usually obstructive Congress. In foreign affairs he was overwhelmed by the masterful Khrushchev and not until the Cuban missile crisis did he achieve tactical parity with that sly gambler. His administration's one achievement was the test-ban treaty, an encouraging footnote to the cold war.

Yet today Kennedy dead has infinitely more force than Kennedy living. Though his administration was not a success, he himself has become an exemplar of political excellence. Part of this phenomenon is attributable to the race's need for heroes, even in deflationary times. But mostly the legend is the deliberate creation of the Kennedy family and its clients. Wanting to regain power, it is now necessary to show that once upon a time there was indeed a Camelot beside the Potomac, a golden age forever lost unless a second Kennedy should become the President. And so, to insure the restoration of that lovely time, the past must be transformed, dull facts transcended, and the dead hero extolled in films, through memorials, and in the pages of books.

The most notorious of the books has been William Manchester's *The Death of a President*. Hoping to stop Jim Bishop from writing one of his ghoulish *The Day They Shot* sagas, the Kennedys decided to 'hire' Mr Manchester to write their version of what happened at Dallas.

Unfortunately, they have never understood that treason is the natural business of clerks. Mr Manchester's use of Mrs Kennedy's taped recollections did not please the family. The famous comedy of errors that ensued not only insured the book's success but also made current certain intimate details which the family preferred for the electorate not to know, such as the President's selection of Mrs Kennedy's dress on that last day in order, as he put it, 'to show up those cheap Texas broads', a remark not calculated to give pleasure to the clients of Neiman-Marcus. Also, the family's irrational dislike of President Johnson came through all too plainly, creating an unexpected amount of sympathy for that least sympathetic of magistrates. Aware of what was at stake, Mrs Kennedy tried to alter a book which neither she nor her brothers-in-law had read. Not since Mary Todd Lincoln has a president's widow been so fiercely engaged with legend if not history.

But then, legend-making is necessary to the Kennedy future. As a result, most of the recent books about the late president are not so much political in approach as religious. There is the ritual beginning of the book which is the end: the death at Dallas. Then the witness goes back in time to the moment when he first met the Kennedys. He finds them strenuous but fun. Along with riotous good times, there is the constant question: How are we to elect Jack President? This sort of talk was in the open after 1956, but as long ago as 1943, according to The Pleasure of His Company, Paul B. Fay Jr made a bet that one day Jack would be JFK.

From the beginning the godhead shone for those who had the eyes to see. The witness then gives us his synoptic version of the making of the President. Once again we visit cold Wisconsin and dangerous West Virginia (can a young Catholic war hero defeat a Protestant accused of being a draft dodger in a poor mining state where primary votes are bought and sold?). From triumph to triumph the hero proceeds to the convention at Los Angeles, where the god is recognized. The only shadow upon that perfect day is cast, significantly, by Lyndon B. Johnson. Like Lucifer he challenged the god at the convention, and was struck down only to be raised again as son of morning. The deal to make Johnson Vice-President still causes violent argument among the new theologians. Pierre Salinger in With Kennedy quotes JFK as observing glumly, 'The whole story will never be known, and it's just as well that it won't be.' Then the campaign itself. The great television debates

(Quemoy and Matsu) in which Nixon's obvious lack of class, as classy Jack duly noted, did him in – barely. The narrowness of the electoral victory was swiftly erased by the splendor of the inaugural ('It all began in the cold'. Arthur M. Schlesinger Jr, *A Thousand Days*). From this point on, the thousand days unfold in familiar sequence and, though details differ from gospel to gospel, the story already possesses the quality of a passion play: disaster at Cuba One, triumph at Cuba Two; the eloquent speeches; the fine pageantry; and always the crowds and the glory, ending at Dallas.

With Lucifer now rampant upon the heights, the surviving Kennedys are again at work to regain the lost paradise, which means that books must be written not only about the new incarnation of the Kennedy godhead but the old. For it is the dead hero's magic that makes legitimate the family's pretensions. As an Osiris-Adonis-Christ figure, JFK is already the subject of a cult that may persist, through the machinery of publicity, long after all memory of his administration has been absorbed by the golden myth now being created in a thousand books to the single end of maintaining in power our extraordinary holy family.

The most recent batch of books about JFK, though hagiographies, at times cannot help but illuminate the three themes which dominate any telling of the sacred story: money, image-making, family. That is the trinity without which nothing. Mr Salinger, the late President's press secretary, is necessarily concerned with the second theme, though he touches on the other two. Paul B. Fay Jr (a wartime buddy of JFK and Under Secretary of the Navy) is interesting on every count, and since he seems not to know what he is saying, his book is the least calculated and the most lifelike of the ones so far published. Other books at hand are Richard J. Whalen's *The Founding Father* (particularly good on money and family) and Evelyn Lincoln's *My Twelve Years with John F. Kennedy*, which in its simple way tells us a good deal about those who are drawn to the Kennedys.

While on the clerical staff of a Georgia Congressman, Mrs Lincoln decided in 1952 that she wanted to work for 'someone in Congress who seemed to have what it takes to be President'; after a careful canvass, she picked the Representative from the Massachusetts Eleventh District. Like the other witnesses under review, she never says *why* she wants to work for a future president; it is taken for granted that anyone would, an interesting commentary on all the witnesses from Schlesinger (whose

A Thousand Days is the best political novel since *Coningsby*) to Theodore Sorensen's dour *Kennedy*. Needless to say, in all the books there
is not only love and awe for the fallen hero who was, in most cases,
the witness's single claim to public attention, but there are also a
remarkable number of tributes to the holy family. From Jacqueline
(Isis-Aphrodite-Madonna) to Bobby (Ares and perhaps Christ-to-be)
the Kennedys appear at the very least as demigods, larger than life.
Bobby's hard-working staff seldom complained, as Mr Salinger put it,
'because we all knew that Bob was working just a little harder than we
were.' For the same reason 'we could accept without complaint [JFK's]
bristling temper, his cold sarcasm, and his demands for always higher
standards of excellence because we knew he was driving himself harder
than he was driving us – despite great and persistent physical pain and
personal tragedy.' Mrs Lincoln surprisingly finds the late President
'humble' – doubtless since the popular wisdom requires all great men
to be humble. She refers often to his 'deep low voice' [*sic*], 'his proud
head held high, his eyes fixed firmly on the goals – sometimes seemingly
impossible goals – he set for himself and all those around him'. Mr
Schlesinger's moving threnody at the close of *his* gospel makes it plain
that we will not see JFK's like again, at least not until the administration
of Kennedy II.

Of the lot, only Mr Fay seems not to be writing a book with an eye
to holding office in the next Kennedy administration. He is garrulous
and indiscreet (the Kennedys are still displeased with his memoirs even
though thousands of words were cut from the manuscript on the narrow
theological ground that since certain things he witnessed fail to enhance
the image, they must be apocryphal). On the subject of the Kennedys
and money, Mr Fay tells a most revealing story. In December 1959
the family was assembled at Palm Beach; someone mentioned money
'causing Mr [Joseph] Kennedy to plunge in, fire blazing from his eyes.
"I don't know what is going to happen to this family when I die," Mr
Kennedy said. "There is no one in the entire family, except Joan and
Teddy, who is living within their means. No one appears to have the
slightest concern for how much they spend."' The tirade ended with
a Kennedy sister running from the room in tears, her extravagance
condemned in open family session. Characteristically, Jack deflected
the progenitor's wrath with the comment that the only 'solution is to
have Dad work harder'. A story which contradicts, incidentally, Mr

Salinger's pious 'Despite his great wealth and his generosity in contributing all of his salaries as Congressman, Senator and President to charities, the President was not a man to waste pennies.'

But for all the founding father's grumbling, the children's attitude toward money – like so much else – is pretty much what he wanted it to be. It is now a familiar part of the sacred story of how Zeus made each of the nine Olympians individually wealthy, creating trust funds which now total some ten million dollars per god or goddess. Also at the disposal of the celestials is the great fortune itself, estimated at a hundred, two hundred, three hundred, or whatever hundred millions of dollars, administered from an office on Park Avenue, to which the Kennedys send their bills, for we are told in *The Founding Father*, 'the childhood habit of dependence persisted in adult life. As grown men and women the younger Kennedys still look to their father's staff of accountants to keep track of their expenditures and see to their personal finances.' There are, of course, obvious limitations to not understanding the role of money in the lives of the majority. The late President was aware of this limitation and he was forever asking his working friends how much money they made. On occasion, he was at a disadvantage because he did not understand the trader's mentality. He missed the point to Khrushchev at Vienna and took offense at what, after all, was simply the boorishness of the marketplace. His father, an old hand in Hollywood, would have understood better the mogul's bluffing.

It will probably never be known how much money Joe Kennedy has spent for the political promotion of his sons. At the moment, an estimated million dollars a year is being spent on Bobby's behalf, and this sum can be matched year after year until 1972, and longer. Needless to say, the sons are sensitive to the charge that their elections are bought. As JFK said of his 1952 election to the Senate, 'People say "Kennedy bought the election. Kennedy could never have been elected if his father hadn't been a millionaire." Well, it wasn't the Kennedy name and the Kennedy money that won that election. I beat Lodge because I hustled for three years' (quoted in *The Founding Father*). But of course without the Kennedy name and the Kennedy money, he would not even have been a contender. Not only was a vast amount of money spent for his election in the usual ways, but a great deal was spent in not so usual ways. For instance, according to Richard J. Whalen, right after the pro-Lodge Boston *Post* unexpectedly endorsed Jack Kennedy for the Senate, Joe Kennedy loaned the paper's publisher $500,000.

But the most expensive legitimate item in today's politics is the making of the image. Highly paid technicians are able to determine with alarming accuracy just what sort of characteristics the public desires at any given moment in a national figure, and with adroit handling a personable candidate can be made to seem whatever the zeitgeist demands. The Kennedys are not of course responsible for applying to politics the techniques of advertising (the two have always gone hand in hand), but of contemporary politicians (the Rockefellers excepted) the Kennedys alone possess the money to maintain one of the most remarkable self-publicizing machines in the history of advertising, a machine which for a time had the resources of the Federal government at its disposal.

It is in describing the activities of a chief press officer at the White House that Mr Salinger is most interesting. A talented image maker, he was responsible, among other things, for the televised press conferences in which the President was seen at his best, responding to simple questions with careful and often charming answers. That these press conferences were not very informative was hardly the fault of Mr Salinger or the President. If it is true that the medium is the message and television is the coolest of all media and to be cool is desirable, then the televised thirty-fifth President was positively glacial in his effectiveness. He was a natural for this time and place, largely because of his obsession with the appearance of things. In fact, much of his political timidity was the result of a quite uncanny ability to sense how others would respond to what he said or did, and if he foresaw a negative response, he was apt to avoid action altogether. There were times, however, when his superb sense of occasion led him astray. In the course of a speech to the Cuban refugees in Miami, he was so overwhelmed by the drama of the situation that he practically launched on the spot a second invasion of that beleaguered island. Yet generally he was cool. He enjoyed the game of pleasing others, which is the actor's art.

He was also aware that vanity is perhaps the strongest of human emotions, particularly the closer one comes to the top of the slippery pole. Mrs Kennedy once told me that the last thing Mrs Eisenhower had done before leaving the White House was to hang a portrait of herself in the entrance hall. The first thing Mrs Kennedy had done on moving in was to put the portrait in the basement, on aesthetic, not political grounds. Overhearing this, the President told an usher to restore the painting to its original place. 'The Eisenhowers are coming to lunch tomorrow,' he explained patiently to his wife, 'and that's the first thing she'll look for.' Mrs Lincoln records that before the new Cabinet met, the President and Bobby were about to enter the Cabinet room when the President 'said to his brother, "Why don't you go through the other door?" The President waited until the Attorney General entered the Cabinet room from the hall door, and then he walked into the room from my office.'

In its relaxed way Mr Fay's book illuminates the actual man much better than the other books if only because he was a friend to the President, and not just an employee. He is particularly interesting on the early days when Jack could discuss openly the uses to which he was being put by his father's ambition. Early in 1945 the future President told Mr Fay how much he envied Fay his postwar life in sunny California while 'I'll be back here with Dad trying to parlay a lost PT boat and a bad back into a political advantage. I tell you, Dad is ready right now and can't understand why Johnny boy isn't "all engines full ahead".' Yet the exploitation of son by father had begun long before the war. In 1940 a thesis written by Jack at Harvard was published under the title *Why England Slept*, with a foreword by longtime, balding, family friend Henry Luce. The book became a best seller and (Richard J. Whalen tells us) as Joe wrote at the time in a letter to his son, 'You would be surprised how a book that really makes the grade with high-class people stands you in good stead for years to come.'

Joe was right of course and bookmaking is now an important part of the holy family's home industry. As Mrs Lincoln observed, when JFK's collection of political sketches 'won the Pulitzer prize for biography in 1957, the Senator's prominence as a scholar and statesman grew. As his book continued to be a best seller, he climbed higher upon public-opinion polls and moved into a leading position among Presidential possibilities for 1960.' Later Bobby would 'write' a book about how he almost nailed Jimmy Hoffa; and so great was the impact of this work that many people had the impression that Bobby had indeed put an end to the career of that turbulent figure.

Most interesting of all the myth-making was the creation of Jack the war hero. John Hersey first described for *The New Yorker* how Jack's Navy boat was wrecked after colliding with a Japanese ship; in the course of a long swim, the young skipper saved the life of a crewman, an admirable thing to do. Later they were all rescued. Since the officer who survived was Ambassador Kennedy's son, the story was deliberately told and retold as an example of heroism unequaled in war's history. Through constant repetition the simple facts of the story merged into a blurred impression that somehow at some point a unique act of heroism had been committed by Jack Kennedy. The last telling of the story was a film starring Cliff Robertson as JFK (the President had wanted Warren Beatty for the part, but the producer thought Beatty's image was 'too mixed up').

So the image was created early: the high-class book that made the grade; the much-publicized heroism at war; the election to the House of Representatives in 1946. From that point on, the publicity was constant and though the Congressman's record of service was unimpressive, he himself was photogenic and appealing. Then came the Senate, the marriage, the illnesses, the second high-class book, and the rest is history. But though it was Joe Kennedy who paid the bills and to a certain extent managed the politics, the recipient of all this attention was meanwhile developing into a shrewd psychologist. Mr Fay quotes a letter written him by the new Senator in 1953. The tone is jocular (part of the charm of Mr Fay's book is that it captures as no one else has the preppish side to JFK's character; he was droll, particularly about himself, in a splendid W. C. Fields way): 'I gave everything a good deal of thought. I am getting married this fall. This means the end of a promising political career, as it has been based up to now almost completely on the old sex appeal.' After a few more sentences in this vein the groom-to-be comes straight to the point. 'Let me know the general reaction to this in the Bay area.' He did indeed want to know, like a romantic film star, what effect marriage would have on his career. But then most of his life was governed, as Mrs Lincoln wrote of the year 1959, 'by the public-opinion polls. We were not unlike the people who check their horoscope each day before venturing out.' And when they did venture out, it was always to create an illusion. As Mrs Lincoln remarks in her guileless way: after Senator Kennedy returned to Washington from a four-week tour of Europe, 'It was obvious that his stature as a Senator had grown, for he came back as an authority on the current situation in Poland.'

It is not to denigrate the late President or the writers of his gospel that neither he nor they ever seemed at all concerned by the bland phoniness of so much of what he did and said. Of course politicians have been pretty much the same since the beginning of history, and part of the game is creating illusion. In fact, the late President himself shortly after Cuba One summed up what might very well have been not only his political philosophy but that of the age in which we live. When asked whether or not the Soviet's placement of missiles in Cuba would have actually shifted the balance of world power, he indicated that he thought not. 'But it would have politically changed the balance of power. It would have appeared to, and appearances contribute to reality.'

From the beginning, the holy family has tried to make itself appear to be what it thinks people want rather than what the realities of any situation might require. Since Bobby is thought by some to be ruthless, he must therefore be photographed as often as possible with children, smiling and happy and athletic, in every way a boy's ideal man. Politically, he must *seem* to be at odds with the present administration without ever actually taking any important position that President Johnson does not already hold. Bobby's Vietnamese war dance was particularly illustrative of the technique. A step to the Left (let's talk to the Viet Cong), followed by two steps to the Right, simultaneously giving 'the beards' – as he calls them – the sense that he is for peace in Vietnam while maintaining his brother's war policy. Characteristically, the world at large believes that if JFK were alive there would be no war in Vietnam. The myth-makers have obscured the fact that it was JFK who began our active participation in the war when, in 1961, he added to the six hundred American observers the first of a gradual buildup of American troops, which reached twenty thousand at the time of his assassination. And there is no evidence that he would not have persisted in that war, for, as he said to a friend shortly before he died, 'I have to go all the way with this one.' He could not suffer a second Cuba and hope to maintain the appearance of Defender of the Free World at the ballot box in 1964.

The authors of the latest Kennedy books are usually at their most interesting when they write about themselves. They are cautious, of course (except for the jaunty Mr Fay), and most are thinking ahead to Kennedy II. Yet despite a hope of future preferment, Mr Salinger's self-portrait is a most curious one. He veers between a coarse unawareness of what it was all about (he never, for instance, expresses an opinion of the war in Vietnam), and a solemn bogusness that is most putting off. Like an after-dinner speaker, he characterizes everyone ('Clark Clifford, the brilliant Washington lawyer'); he pays heavy tribute to his office staff; he praises Rusk and the State Department, remarking that 'JFK had more effective liaison with the State Department than any President in history,' which would have come as news to the late President. Firmly Mr Salinger puts Arthur Schlesinger Jr in his place, saying that he himself never heard the President express a lack of confidence in Rusk. Mr Salinger also remarks that though Schlesinger was 'a strong friend' of the President (something Mr Salinger, incidentally, was not), 'JFK occasionally was impatient with their [Schlesinger's memoranda] length and frequency.' Mrs Lincoln also weighs in on the subject of the historian-in-residence. Apparently JFK's 'relationship with Schlesinger was never that close. He admired Schlesinger's brilliant mind, his enormous store of information . . . but Schlesinger was never more than an ally and assistant.'

It is a tribute to Kennedy's gift for compartmentalizing the people in his life that none knew to what extent he saw the others. Mr Fay was an after-hours buddy. Mrs Lincoln was the girl in the office. Mr Salinger was a technician and not a part of the President's social or private or even, as Mr Salinger himself admits, political life. Contrasting his role with that of James Hagerty, Mr Salinger writes, 'My only policy duties were in the information field. While Jim had a voice in deciding what the administration would do, I was responsible only for presenting that decision to the public in a way and at a time that would generate the best possible reception.' His book is valuable only when he discusses the relations between press and government. And of course when he writes about himself. His 1964 campaign for the Senate is nicely told and it is good to know that he lost because he came out firmly for fair housing on the ground that 'morally I had no choice – not after sweating out Birmingham and Oxford with John F. Kennedy.' This is splendid but it might have made his present book more interesting had he told us something about that crucial period of sweating out. Although he devotes a chapter to telling how he did not take a fifty-mile hike, he never discusses Birmingham, Oxford, or the black revolution.

All in all, his book is pretty much what one might expect of a PR man. He papers over personalities with the reflexive and usually inaccurate phrase (Eisenhower and Kennedy 'had deep respect for each other'; Mrs Kennedy has 'a keen understanding of the problems which beset mankind'). Yet for all his gift at creating images for others, Mr Salinger seems not to have found his own. Uneasily he plays at being US Senator, fat boy at court, thoughtful emissary to Khrushchev. Lately there has been a report in the press that he is contemplating writing a novel. If he does, Harold Robbins may be in the sort of danger that George Murphy never was. The evidence at hand shows that he has the gift. Describing his divorce from 'Nancy, my wife of eight years', Mr Salinger manages in a few lines to say everything: 'An extremely artistic woman, she was determined to live a quieter life in which she could pursue her skills as a ceramicist. And we both knew that I could not be happy unless I was on the move. It was this difference in philosophies, not a lack of respect, that led to our decision to obtain a divorce. But a vacation in Palm Springs, as Frank Sinatra's guest, did much to revive my spirits.'

Mr Fay emerges as very much his own man, and it is apparent that he amused the President at a level which was more that of a playmate escorting the actress Angie Dickinson to the Inaugural than as serious companion to the prince. Unlike the other witnesses, Mr Fay has no pretensions about himself. He tells how 'the President then began showing us the new paintings on the wall. "Those two are Renoirs and that's a Cézanne," he told us. Knowing next to nothing about painters or paintings, I asked, "Who are they?" The President's response was predictable, "My God, if you ask a question like that, do it in a whisper or wait till we get outside. We're trying to give this administration a semblance of class."' The President saw the joke; he also saw the image which must at all times be projected. Parenthetically, a majority of the recorded anecdotes about Kennedy involve keeping up appearances; he was compulsively given to emphasizing, often with great charm, the division between how things must be made to seem, as opposed to the way they are. This division is noticeable, even in the censored version of Mr Manchester's *The Death of a President*. The author records that when Kennedy spoke at Houston's coliseum, Jack Valenti, crouched below the lectern, was able to observe the extraordinary tremor of the President's hands, and the artful way in which he managed to conceal them from the audience. This tension between the serene appearance and that taut reality add to the poignancy of the true legend, so unlike the Parson Weems version Mrs Kennedy would like the world to accept.

Money, image, family: the three are extraordinarily intertwined. The origin of the Kennedy sense of family is the holy land of Ireland, priest-ridden, superstitious, clannish. While most of the West in the nineteenth century was industrialized and urbanized, Ireland remained a famine-ridden agrarian country, in thrall to politicians, homegrown and British, priest and lay. In 1848 the first Kennedy set up shop in Boston, where the Irish were exploited and patronized by the Wasps; not unnaturally, the Irish grew bitter and vengeful and finally asserted themselves at the ballot box. But the old resentment remained as late as Joe Kennedy's generation and with it flourished a powerful sense that the family is the only unit that could withstand the enemy, as long as each member remained loyal to the others, 'regarding life as a joint venture between one generation and the next'. In *The Fruitful Bough*, a privately printed cluster of tributes to the Elder Kennedy (collected by Edward M. Kennedy), we are told, in Bobby's words, that to Joe Kennedy 'the most important thing . . . was the advancement of his children . . . except for his influence and encouragement, my brother Jack might not have run for the Senate in 1952.' (So much for JFK's comment that it was his own 'hustling' that got him Lodge's seat.)

The father is of course a far more interesting figure than any of his sons if only because his will to impose himself upon a society which he felt had snubbed him has been in the most extraordinary way fulfilled. He drove his sons to 'win, win, win'. But never at any point did he pause to ask himself or them just what it was they were supposed to win. He taught them to regard life as a game of Monopoly (a family favorite): you put up as many hotels as you can on Ventnor Avenue and win. Consequently, some of the failure of his son's administration can be ascribed to the family philosophy. All his life Jack Kennedy was driven by his father and then by himself to be first in politics, which meant to be the President. But once that goal had been achieved, he had no future, no place else to go. This absence of any sense of the whole emerged in the famous exchange between him and James Reston, who asked the newly elected President what his philosophy was, what vision did he have of the good life. Mr Reston got a blank stare for answer. Kennedy apologists are quick to use this exchange as proof of their man's essentially pragmatic nature ('pragmatic' was a favorite word of the era, even though its political meaning is opportunist). As they saw it: give the President a specific problem and he will solve it through intelligence and expertise. A 'philosophy' was simply of no use to a man of action. For a time, actual philosophers were charmed by the thought of an intelligent young empiricist fashioning a New Frontier.

Not until the second year of his administration did it become plain that Kennedy was not about to do much of anything. Since his concern was so much with the appearance of things, he was at his worst when confronted with those issues where a moral commitment might have informed his political response not only with passion but with shrewdness. Had he challenged the Congress in the Truman manner on such bills as Medicare and Civil Rights, he might at least have inspired the country, if not the Congress, to follow his lead. But he was reluctant to rock the boat, and it is significant that he often quoted Hotspur on summoning spirits from the deep: any man can summon, but will the spirits come? JFK never found out; he would not take the chance. His excuse in private for his lack of force, particularly in dealing with the Congress, was the narrow electoral victory of 1960. The second term, he declared, would be the one in which all things might be accomplished. With a solid majority behind him, he could work wonders. But knowing his character, it is doubtful that the second term would have been much more useful than the first. After all, he would have been constitutionally a lame duck president, interested in holding the franchise for his brother. The family, finally, was his only commitment and it colored all his deeds and judgment.

In 1960, after listening to him denounce Eleanor Roosevelt at some length, I asked him why he thought she was so much opposed to his candidacy. The answer was quick: 'She hated my father and she can't stand it that his children turned out so much better than hers.' I was startled at how little he understood Mrs Roosevelt, who, to be fair, did not at all understand him, though at the end she was won by his personal charm. Yet it was significant that he could not take seriously any of her political objections to him (e.g. his attitude to McCarthyism); he merely assumed that she, like himself, was essentially concerned with family and, envying the father, would want to thwart the son. He was, finally, very much his father's son even though, as all the witnesses are at pains to remind us, he did not share that magnate's political philosophy – which goes without saying, since anyone who did could not be elected to anything except possibly the Chamber of Commerce. But the Founding Father's confidence in his own wisdom ('I know more about Europe than anybody else in this country,' he said in 1940, 'because I've been closer to it longer') and the assumption that he alone knew the absolute inside story about everything is a trait inherited by the sons, particularly Bobby, whose principal objection to the 'talking liberals' is that they never know what's really going on, as he in his privileged place does but may not tell. The Kennedy children have always observed our world from the heights.

The distinguished jurist Francis Morrissey tells in *The Fruitful Bough* a most revealing story of life upon Olympus. 'During the Lodge campaign, the Ambassador told [Jack and me] clearly that the campaign ... would be the toughest fight he could think of, but there was no question that Lodge would be beaten, and if that should come to pass Jack would be nominated and elected President ... In that clear and commanding voice of his he said to Jack, "I will work out the plans to elect you President. It will not be any more difficult for you to be elected President than it will be to win the Lodge fight ... you will need to get about twenty key men in the country to get the nomination for it is these men who will control the convention ..."'

One of the most fascinating aspects of politician-watching is trying to determine to what extent any politician believes what he says. Most of course never do, regarding public statements as necessary noises to soothe the electorate or deflect the wrath of the passionate, who are forever mucking things up for the man who wants decently and normally to rise. Yet there are cases of politicians who have swayed themselves by their own speeches. Take a man of conservative disposition and force him to give liberal speeches for a few years in order to be elected and he will, often as not, come to believe himself. There is evidence that JFK often spellbound himself. Bobby is something else again. Andrew Kopkind in the *New Republic* once described Bobby's career as a series of 'happenings': the McCarthy friend and fellow traveler of one year emerges as an intense New York liberal in another, and between these two happenings there is no thread at all to give a clue as to what the man actually thinks or who he really is. That consistency which liberals so furiously demanded of the hapless Nixon need not apply to any Kennedy.

After all, as the recent gospels point out, JFK himself was slow to become a liberal, to the extent he ever was (in our society no working politician can be radical). As JFK said to James MacGregor Burns, 'Some people have their liberalism "made" by the time they reach their late twenties. I didn't. I was caught in crosscurrents and eddies. It was only later that I got into the stream of things.' His comment made liberalism sound rather like something run up by a tailor, a necessary garment which he regrets that he never had time in his youth to be fitted for. Elsewhere (in William Manchester's *Portrait of a President*) he explains those 'currents and eddies'. Of his somewhat reactionary career in the House of Representatives he said, 'I'd just come out of my father's house at the time, and these were the things I knew.' It is of course a truism that character is formed in one's father's house. Ideas may change but the attitude toward others does not. A father who teaches his sons that the only thing that matters is to be first, not second, not third, is obviously (should his example be followed) going to be rewarded with energetic sons. Yet it is hardly surprising that to date one cannot determine where the junior Senator from New York stands on such a straightforward issue (morally if not politically) as the American adventure in Vietnam. Differing with the President as to which cities ought to be bombed in the North does not constitute an alternative policy. His sophisticated liberal admirers, however, do not seem in the least distressed by his lack of a position; instead they delight in the *uses* to which he has put the war in Vietnam in order to embarrass the usurper in the White House.

The cold-blooded jauntiness of the Kennedys in politics has a remark-able appeal for those who also want to rise and who find annoying – to the extent they are aware of it at all – the moral sense. Also, the success of the three Kennedy brothers nicely makes hash of the old American belief that by working hard and being good one will deserve (and if fortunate, receive) promotion. A mediocre Representative, an absentee Senator, through wealth and family connections, becomes the President while his youngest brother inherits the Senate seat. Now Bobby is about to become RFK because he is Bobby. It is as if the United States had suddenly reverted to the eighteenth century, when the politics of many states were family affairs. In those days, if one wanted a political career in New York one had best be born a Livingston, a Clinton, or a Schuyler; failing that, one must marry into the family, as Alexander Hamilton did, or go to work for them. In a way, the whole Kennedy episode is a fascinating throwback to an earlier phase of civilization. Because the Irish maintained the ancient village sense of the family longer than most places in the West and to the extent that the sons of Joe Kennedy reflect those values and prejudices, they are an anachronism in an urbanized non-family-minded society. Yet the fact that they are so plainly not of this time makes them fascinating; their family story is a glamorous continuing soap opera whose appeal few can resist, including the liberals, who, though they may suspect that the Kennedys are not with them at heart, believe that the two boys are educable. At this very moment beside the river Charles a thousand Aristotles dream of their young Alexanders, and the coming heady conquest of the earth.

Meanwhile, the source of the holy family's power is the legend of the dead brother, who did not much resemble the hero of the books under review. Yet the myth that JFK was a philosopher-king will continue as long as the Kennedys remain in politics. And much of the power they exert over the national imagination is a direct result of the ghastliness of what happened at Dallas. But though the world's grief and shock were genuine, they were not entirely for JFK himself. The death of a young leader necessarily strikes an atavistic chord. For thousands of years the man-god was sacrificed to ensure with blood the harvest, and there is always an element of ecstasy as well as awe in our collective grief. Also, Jack Kennedy was a television star, more seen by most people than their friends or relatives. His death in public was all the more stunning because he was not an abstraction called The President, but a man the people thought they knew. At the risk of *lèse-divinité*, however, the assassination of President Nixon at, let us say, Cambridge by what at first was thought to be a member of the ADA but later turned out to be a dotty Bircher would have occasioned quite as much national horror, mourning, and even hagiography. But in time the terrible deed would have been forgotten, for there are no Nixon heirs.

Beyond what one thinks of the Kennedys themselves, there remains the large question: What sort of men ought we to be governed by in the coming years? With the high cost of politics and image-making, it is plain that only the very wealthy or those allied with the very wealthy can afford the top prizes. And among the rich, only those who are able to please the people on television are Presidential. With the decline of the religions, the moral sense has become confused, to say the least, and intellectual or political commitments that go beyond the merely expedient are regarded with cheerful contempt not only by the great operators themselves but also by their admirers and, perhaps, by the electorate itself. Also, to be fair, politicians working within a system like ours can never be much more than what the system will allow. Hypocrisy and self-deception are the traditional characteristics of the middle class in any place and time, and the United States today is the paradigmatic middle-class society. Therefore we can hardly blame our political gamesmen for being, literally, representative. Any public man has every right to try and trick us, not only for his own good but, if he is honorable, for ours as well. However, if he himself is not aware of what he is doing or to what end he is playing the game, then to entrust him with the first magistracy of what may be the last empire on earth is to endanger us all. One does not necessarily demand of our leaders passion (Hitler supplied the age with quite enough for this century) or reforming zeal (Mao Tse-tung is incomparable), but one does insist that they possess a sense of community larger than simply personal power for its own sake, being first because it's fun. Finally, in an age of supercommunications, one must have a clear sense of the way things are, as opposed to the way they have been made to seem. Since the politics of the Kennedys are so often the work of publicists, it is necessary to keep trying to find out just who they are and what they really mean. If only because should *they* be confused as to the realities of Cuba, say, or Vietnam, then the world's end is at hand.

At one time in the United States, the popular wisdom maintained that there was no better work for a man to do than to set in motion some idea whose time had not yet arrived, even at the risk of becoming as unpopular as those politicians JFK so much admired in print and so little emulated in life. It may well be that it is now impossible for such men to rise to the top in our present system. If so, this is a tragedy. Meanwhile, in their unimaginative fierce way, the Kennedys continue to play successfully the game as they found it. They create illusions and call them facts, and between what they are said to be and what they are falls the shadow of all the useful words not spoken, of all the actual deeds not done. But if it is true that in a rough way nations deserve the leadership they get, then a frivolous and apathetic electorate combined with a vain and greedy intellectual establishment will most certainly restore to power the illusion-making Kennedys. Holy family and bedazzled nation, in their faults at least, are well matched. In any case, the age of the commune in which we have lived since the time of Jackson is drawing to a close and if historical analogies are at all relevant, the rise of the *signori* is about to begin, and we may soon find ourselves enjoying a strange new era in which all our lives and dreams are presided over by smiling, interchangeable, initialed gods.

ELIZABETH HARDWICK

The Oswald Family

Elizabeth Hardwick was born in 1916 in Kentucky and has published several novels – most notably, Sleepless Nights *(1979). For some years she was married to the poet Robert Lowell. Hardwick is best known as a literary essayist: for* Partisan Review *in the 1940s and 1950s and, since 1963, for the* New York Review of Books *which, in that year, she helped to found. Her essay collections include* A View of My Own *(1962),* Seduction and Betrayal *(1974) and* Bartleby in Manhattan *(1983), which includes 'The Oswald Family'.*

The Warren Report appears, as if it were the last chorus of a tragedy by Euripides: 'Many things the gods achieve beyond our judgement. What we thought is not confirmed, what we thought not, the gods contrive. And so it happens in this story.' In the fading light, the Report sums up: 'Out of these and many other factors which may have molded the character of Lee Harvey Oswald there emerged a man capable of assassinating President Kennedy.'

From the shades of their anxious, detested obscurity, the calamity brought forth to view some of the most disquieting people we have ever encountered. We are given lives and desires we would not willingly have confronted, and we have seen a sort of nakedness we were not eager to acknowledge.

Oswald: There is about him a special invisibility, a peculiar opacity. Those few persons who remain in doubt about his guilt are perhaps reinforced by the impenetrability of this disturbing figure. He does not seem equal in mania or in tenacity of Idea to the catastrophic deed. He had made the most dramatic and awful effort at self-definition but even so he remains buried, unyielding. He is pale, rancorous, with a special sullen yearning whose dimensions are impossible to measure. Odd words occur to those who remember him: he is all smirks and mutterings, silences and unsociable shrugs. We see him nearly always in some mood of strained, self-conscious chagrin. Not laughter or joking; only sulky refusals or arguments.

Oswald is a ghostly anachronism in a cast of characters completely caught up in the lusts of the 1960s. How hard it is to believe he was born in 1939, that he had just barely turned twenty-four when he died. Most of all he is a Depression figure; unemployment, despair, scarcity follow him about. The tone of his aspirations, the very notes of his formulations ring out dimly from another decade. He says he thinks of his mother and brother only as 'workers'. The boom, the Eisenhower era, do not seem to have touched him. The arguments of the Thirties interest him much more deeply than Civil Rights, that great cause of his generation. He is hostile to society but the beatnik 'revolt', centering as it does on personal relations, has nothing to say to him. His sensibility is metallic, he walks about, borne down by the iron of his backward-looking temperament. He arises as if from a troubled sleep of a decade or two. He lived in Texas, an open highway, and could not drive a car. Only his interest in Cuba connects him with the present, and even there, as always, we find obfuscation, peculiarity, invisibility.

In many ways, Oswald's early years are the most easily understood because they come to us through our seers who foretell the future and interpret the past: the social workers and psychiatrists. Oswald with their help takes shape; he is like many another whose biography we read in the daily press. He is fatherless, underprivileged, neglected. His circumstances were bleak, especially during the New York period when he and his mother seemed to have been friendless, isolated, and confused. The seers are quick to put the blame on the mother. She is self-concerned, neglectful.

Oswald's hopes for himself are intellectual rather than practical. He is not concerned with acquiring skills or a trade but rather with an effort to solve his problems by ideas. The striking aspect of this is Oswald's paralysis with words. The 'Historic Diary' published in *Life* magazine is just barely on the border of literacy. Books are taken out from libraries, but there is every evidence that Oswald was incapable of systematic, careful reading about Communism or anything else. When he applied for admission to the Albert Schweitzer School in Switzerland he gave as his favorite authors, Jack London, Charles Darwin, and Norman Vincent Peale. The incongruity of the list points to his ignorance of all three. Yet it is pretension, the projection of his ambitions and hopes in ideological terms that stay in one's mind as a puzzle. He seems a good deal like those *lumpen* intellectuals of the early Thirties in Germany and Austria, empty, ignorant, rootless men, without any gifts or skills but still with a certain conceit that made them want to make from the negative of their personalities some sort of programmatic certainty. There is nothing in Oswald's letters or in his papers that shows any comprehension of radical polemics. His interest in Communism and the Soviet Union is of the sketchiest kind. 'I am a Marxist, but not a Leninist–Marxist,' he says, whatever that may mean. His pathetic 'Historic Diary' is completely free of generalizing power or political observation. He seems to know nothing about Russia; his discomforts there are not intellectual or moral but mundane, day to day.

Just as he listed Darwin and Norman Vincent Peale, so he holds up in his fascinating photograph – that profoundly interesting self-portrait he has left to posterity – two guns and two newspapers, the Communist *Daily Worker* and the Trotskyist *Militant*. There he stands in the midst of his iconography, his composition of himself surrounded by his weapons and his emblems of Idea.

Along with his ignorance, his failure with words, Oswald does not seem to have had any general capabilities. His tragic achievements – including the sure marksmanship that killed President Kennedy – can be explained only as accidental, statistical. He was fired from his job in a photographic shop, but he had learned just enough to forge, by tricks of photography, a Selective Service card for his alias, A. Hidell.

So far as we can tell, it was not so much laziness that made Oswald such a poor worker as a lack of capability and no doubt the same impatience and shallowness that appear in his intellectual efforts. His nature is secretive, but if the Report is telling us all it knows his secretiveness is more disabling than efficient. (Insofar as any detective-story aspects of the case still remain after the Warren Report, the most mysterious questions about Oswald's activities are the visit to Mexico, his letter to the Soviet Embassy in Washington, and the awful choice of President Kennedy as his victim.) He made the extreme commitment when he asked for Soviet citizenship, but he could not carry this to completion. Even his most daring decision, before he began to shoot, could not give form to his formlessness. He tried Russia for a while and then changed his mind.

Oswald seemed to feel his defection could be erased, when it suited him, washed off with a sponge. No doubt he felt this because he had been so little changed by it. Indeed he was soon back where he had started. In a letter to Governor Connolly he gives a startling indication of the way his mind worked. The letter was written from Russia, protesting the change of his Marine discharge from honorable to dishonorable. He speaks of himself and his situation as though they belonged to someone else. He calls himself 'a case', and then makes the impenetrable suggestion: 'this person [himself] had gone to the Soviet Union to reside for a short time (much in the same way E. Hemingway resided in Paris).' In some sense Oswald, even after he returned, wanted to be 'this person' who had been to the Soviet Union. But of course he stopped short of Soviet citizenship and even residence and came back home with nothing accomplished except that a Russian girl had married him.

We are told that he was arrogant, but he could make little use of this because in the end there was always the problem of his great ignorance. His arrogance was only a part of his striking puritanism. The positives he might have built upon were really negatives: he did not care, apparently, for luxury or possessions and his indifference to these is another way in which he was out of touch with the 1960s. He spent a good deal of his slim earnings paying back the State Department and a loan from his brother. These were genuine acts of sacrifice and planning, a little unexpected in a drifter like Oswald and again more like the poor man of the Thirties than the giddy installment buyer of today. No matter from what angle we view him, Oswald remains narrow and shrunken. And we are not surprised when, upon the release of the Report, sex makes an entrance into his drama. We are told he was a poor performer there, too.

Above all, Oswald was a pre-television spirit. Perhaps only a person somehow immunized to TV by the iron of his nature *could* actually kill Kennedy. The President and his wife were magical beings, spectacularly favored, and engraved like a tattoo on a national psyche because of their position and their natural pre-eminence as television personalities. By assassinating President Kennedy, the embodiment of the 1960s at its most attractive, Oswald suddenly cast light upon the Sixties at its most distressing.

Out of the darkness there appeared Marina Oswald, a revelation we can hardly interpret. But who can doubt the coming 'pop' Americanization of Russia after he has studied this young girl from Minsk? History, or events, exposed her to us in a series of frames: first, shabby, reserved, a proletarian with a tooth missing in front; in the end, on the day the Report was made public, a 'famous' person, with eyelids darkened over in 'Cleopatra' fashion, hair teased high, the gap in the smile filled, a people's capitalist, a success. From the nettle, danger, Marina had deftly plucked the flower, safety. Adaptability so accomplished is perhaps singular. She is like some convert, freshly lifted up; she knows us better than we know ourselves. Marina seems to have been born for the American Southwest. But what an unpropitious coupling with Oswald – the boring, disintegrating zealot. This young woman, as current as today's weather, must have been fortified in her decision by the whisperings of destiny. She herself gave voice to the whisperings when she said somewhere that she would not have married Oswald if he hadn't been an American. In him, she seems to have seen her chance to live in fact what she was in spirit. And no sooner was she in America than she apparently began to feel about Oswald much as those contemporaries of his in high school had felt – a complete distaste for the 'loner', the turtle-like Oswald who didn't 'mix', and who 'kept to himself'. And Marina, modern girl, demanded her right to sexual satisfaction, we are told; it was what she had expected, like a washing machine.

Marina Oswald has not only shown a readiness to tell the truth about her husband, but a talent for the exploitation of sub-plots. Hardly a week passes without some bit in the tabloids. She busies herself and divides with her helpers the profits of recollection. One of the most interesting actions of Marina's – equal to Oswald's sudden inspiration of his likeness to Hemingway – was her invitation to a television crew to cover the baptism of her daughter, Rachel. Father, what shall I do to be saved? The television baptism is one of those instinctive transcendental unions with the over-soul. But, indeed, what other course was left? Rejection, indignation, a bleak, Russian, lower-depths suffering would otherwise have been the lot of the Soviet wife of a presidential assassin. Marina salivates when the bells ring; the country is reassured. Her story must mean something. How to decipher the code? A news account carries her further: a collaborating writer resigned from her employ saying, 'I quit because Marina has come to believe she is as important as the President of the United States.'

Oswald's mother comes to us in the most desolating light. One can only pity her. About her, too, there is the hint of Queen for a Day, the hand waving outside the television studio in the early morning, the testimonial to percentages gained by judicious purchase; but if her son is somehow pre-television, she is, for all her readiness, a television failure and comes off as a villain. The psychiatric chorus had damned her in any case: aggressive, self-centered, neglectful, ineffectual. 'We warn you, Clytemnestra, Orestes will return from exile. You will die by the hand of your son.'

Mrs Oswald tends to mount a defense at just the moment a prudent person would withdraw or acquiesce. She defended her son against the doctors and social workers and she refused 'treatment'. Now, after his 'conviction' as the assassin of President Kennedy she, previously neglectful as we have been told, stands almost alone in her insistence upon his innocence. But she sees her son, not as a young man like others and likewise free of guilt, but as a counterintelligence agent, a historical personage – by which she means, no doubt, a 'celebrity'. Her son has jumped out of the mass of the looking into the company of the looked at. And call her as they will The Terrible Mother, the catastrophe, still she too has her story, the Marguerite Oswald story. She has the great disposition to 'appear', so common in this case. She realized that it was her turn now to rise up from the audience.

Jack Ruby and his sister, Eva, held a sort of instant wake as they sat sobbing before the television set at the time of President Kennedy's death. In his book, *Dallas Justice*, Melvin Belli tells us that Ruby, turning away from his usual struggle to diet, rushed out and bought ten dollars' worth of kosher delicatessen food. 'We cried but we ate,' he said. Ruby, like Oswald, had had a miserable youth, observed and recorded by the angels of the state. He had been in foster homes, and was the damaged son of damaged parents. But he is the opposite of Oswald. Ruby cannot keep out of the way. He is hyperactive, chaotic, talkative. He spends and he owes; he is stingy here and prodigal there: he is sentimental and sadistic. In a rage he nearly beats to death a troublesome visitor to his nightclub, but he cries easily. He seems to be held together by bravado and there are no brakes on his feelings. One doctor spoke of Ruby as 'in love' with Kennedy. The ravening lust for publicity *would* make Ruby 'love' those to whom publicity was a natural result of function and position. And Ruby's identification is nearly complete. He is drawn by the magnet of his hunger. There is the 'Commie rat', Oswald, and here is the ferocious patriot, Ruby. The confrontation is too lucky for Ruby to resist. In truth he did it, as he humbly said, 'for Jackie and the children', and what folly it was for Belli to ignore this truth in favor of electroencephalograms, fugue states, blackouts and the 'psychomotor pool', as the prosecution called his experts. With an appalling trust, Ruby actually believed in cops and famous people, in news reporters and network men. With all his ardor, he rushed in to fill the hole and murdered Oswald. Doing away with the Commie rat was his tribute to the cops, the reporters, the TV gods and the beloved Kennedys. Even after he was given a death sentence he could think of himself only as a celebrated person, a figure in a wax museum. 'Burn my clothes,' he begged his lawyer, fearful lest they be put upon his eternal waxen image.

The Warren Report tells a sordid story of greeds too fierce to measure. The greatly favored and the greatly crippled suffer out their destinies. You feel they have been together on the stage for a long time. It was only that the light had not shone in the dingy corners before. There these impatient people, longing for immortality, were waiting to tell us something.

TOM WOLFE

These Radical Chic Evenings

Tom Wolfe was born in Virginia in 1931 and is often praised for having initiated the so-called 'New Journalism' – a somewhat baggy, catch-all genre defined in the reference books as 'blending literary technique with journalistic fact'. Key New Journalism texts include Mailer's The Armies of the Night *and Truman Capote's* In Cold Blood. *Wolfe's own most famous book-length contribution is* The Right Stuff *(1979), on the American space programme. As a novelist, Wolfe scored a huge critical and commercial success with* Bonfire of the Vanities *(1987). In 1998 he published a second novel, called* A Man in Full. *His essay on 'Radical Chic' appeared in one of his several essay collections,* Radical Chic and Mau-mauing the Flak Catchers *(1970).*

At 2 or 3 or 4 am, somewhere along in there, on August 25 1966, his forty-eighth birthday, in fact, Leonard Bernstein woke up in the dark in a state of wild alarm. That had happened before. It was one of the forms his insomnia took. So he did the usual. He got up and walked around a bit. He felt groggy. Suddenly he had a vision, an inspiration. He could see himself, Leonard Bernstein, the *egregio maestro*, walking out on stage in white tie and tails in front of a full orchestra. On one side of the conductor's podium is a piano. On the other is a chair with a guitar leaning against it. He sits in the chair and picks up the guitar. A guitar! One of those halfwitted instruments, like the accordion, that are made for the Learn-To-Play-in-Eight-Days E-Z-Diagram 110-IQ fourteen-year-olds of Levittown! But there's a reason. He has an anti-war message to deliver to this great starched white-throated audience in the symphony hall. He announces to them: 'I love.' Just that. The effect is mortifying. All at once a Negro rises up from out of the curve of the grand piano and starts saying things like, 'The audience is curiously embarrassed.' Lenny tries to start again, plays some quick numbers on the piano, says, 'I love. *Amo ergo sum*.' The Negro rises again and says, 'The audience thinks he ought to get up and walk out. The audience thinks, "I am ashamed even to nudge my neighbor."' Finally, Lenny gets off a heartfelt anti-war speech and exits.

For a moment, sitting there alone in his home in the small hours of the morning, Lenny thought it might just work and he jotted the idea down. Think of the headlines: BERNSTEIN ELECTRIFIES CONCERT AUDIENCE WITH ANTI-WAR APPEAL. But then his enthusiasm collapsed. He lost heart. Who the hell was this Negro rising up from the piano and informing the world what an ass Leonard Bernstein was making of himself? It didn't make sense, this superego Negro by the concert grand.

Mmmmmmmmmmmmmmmmm. These are nice. Little Roquefort cheese morsels rolled in crushed nuts. Very tasty. Very subtle. It's the way the dry sackiness of the nuts tiptoes up against the dour savor of the cheese that is so nice, so subtle. Wonder what the Black Panthers eat here on the hors d'oeuvre trail? Do the Panthers like little Roquefort cheese morsels rolled in crushed nuts this way, and asparagus tips in mayonnaise dabs, and *meatballs petites au Coq Hardi*, all of which are at this very moment being offered to them on gadrooned silver platters by maids in black uniforms with hand-ironed white aprons . . . The butler will bring them their drinks . . . Deny it if you wish to, but such are the *pensées métaphysiques* that rush through one's head on these Radical Chic evenings just now in New York. For example, does that huge Black Panther there in the hallway, the one shaking hands with Felicia Bernstein herself, the one with the black leather coat and the dark glasses and the absolutely unbelievable Afro, Fuzzy-Wuzzy-scale, in fact – is he, a Black Panther, going on to pick up a Roquefort cheese morsel rolled in crushed nuts from off the tray, from a maid in uniform, and just pop it down the gullet without so much as missing a beat of Felicia's perfect Mary Astor voice . . .

Felicia is remarkable. She is beautiful, with that rare burnished beauty that lasts through the years. Her hair is pale blond and set just so. She has a voice that is 'theatrical', to use a term from her youth. She greets the Black Panthers with the same bend of the wrist, the same tilt of the head, the same perfect Mary Astor voice with which she greets people like Jason, John and D. D., Adolph, Betty, Gian-Carlo, Schuyler, and Goddard, during those *après*-concert suppers she and Lenny are so famous for. What evenings! She lights the candles over the dining-room table, and in the Gotham gloaming the little tremulous tips of flame are reflected in the mirrored surface of the table, a bottomless blackness with a thousand stars, and it is that moment that Lenny loves. There seem to be a thousand stars above and a thousand stars below, a room full of stars, a penthouse duplex full of stars, a Manhattan tower full of stars, with marvelous people drifting through the heavens, Jason Robards, John and D. D. Ryan, Gian-Carlo Menotti, Schuyler Chapin, Goddard Lieberson, Mike Nichols, Lillian Hellman, Larry Rivers, Aaron Copland, Richard Avedon, Milton and Amy Greene, Lukas Foss, Jennie Tourel, Samuel Barber, Jerome Robbins, Steve Sondheim, Adolph and Phyllis Green, Betty Comden, and the Patrick O'Neals . . .

. . . and now, in the season of Radical Chic, the Black Panthers. That huge Panther there, the one Felicia is smiling her tango smile at, is Robert Bay, who just forty-one hours ago was arrested in an altercation with the police, supposedly over a .38-caliber revolver that someone had, in a parked car in Queens at Northern Boulevard and 104th Street or some such unbelievable place, and taken to jail on a most unusual charge called 'criminal facilitation'. And now he is out on bail and walking into Leonard and Felicia Bernstein's thirteen-room penthouse duplex on Park Avenue. Harassment & Hassles, Guns & Pigs, Jail & Bail – they're *real*, these Black Panthers. The very idea of them, these real revolutionaries, who actually put their lives on the line, runs through Lenny's duplex like a rogue hormone. Everyone casts a glance, or stares, or tries a smile, and then sizes up the house for the somehow delicious counterpoint . . . Deny it if you want to! but one *does* end up making such sweet furtive comparisons in this season of Radical Chic . . . There's Otto Preminger in the library and Jean vanden Heuvel in the hall, and Peter and Cheray Duchin in the living room, and Frank and Domna Stanton, Gail Lumet, Sheldon Harnick, Cynthia Phipps, Burton Lane, Mrs August Heckscher, Roger Wilkins, Barbara Walters, Bob Silvers, Mrs Richard Avedon, Mrs Arthur Penn, Julie Belafonte, Harold Taylor, and scores more, including Charlotte Curtis, women's news editor of the *New York Times*, America's foremost chronicler of Society, a lean woman in black, with her notebook out, standing near Felicia and big Robert Bay, and talking to Cheray Duchin.

Cheray tells her: 'I've never met a Panther – this is a first for me!' . . . never dreaming that within forty-eight hours her words will be on the desk of the President of the United States . . .

This is a first for me. But she is not alone in her thrill as the Black Panthers come trucking on in, into Lenny's house, Robert Bay, Don Cox the Panthers' Field Marshal from Oakland, Henry Miller the Harlem Panther defense captain, the Panther women – Christ, if the Panthers don't know how to get it all together, as they say, the tight pants, the tight black turtlenecks, the leather coats, Cuban shades, Afros. But real Afros, not the ones that have been shaped and trimmed like a topiary hedge and sprayed until they have a sheen like acrylic wall-to-wall – but like funky, natural, scraggly . . . wild . . .

These are no civil-rights Negroes *wearing gray suits three sizes too big—*

—no more interminable Urban League banquets in hotel ballrooms where they try to alternate the blacks and whites around the tables as if they were stringing Arapaho beads—

—*these are* real men!

Shoot-outs, revolutions, pictures in *Life* magazine of policemen grabbing Black Panthers like they were Vietcong – somehow it all runs together in the head with the whole thing of how *beautiful* they are. *Sharp as a blade*. The Panther women – there are three or four of them on hand, wives of the Panther 21 defendants, and they are so lean, *so lithe*, as they say, with tight pants and Yoruba-style headdresses, almost like turbans, as if they'd stepped out of the pages of *Vogue*, although no doubt *Vogue* got it from them. All at once every woman in the room knows exactly what Amanda Burden meant when she said she was now anti-fashion because 'the sophistication of the baby blacks made me rethink my attitudes.' God knows the Panther women don't spent thirty minutes in front of the mirror in the morning shoring up their eye holes with contact lenses, eyeliner, eye shadow, eyebrow pencil, occipital rim brush, false eyelashes, mascara, Shadow-Ban for undereye and Eterna Creme for the corners . . . And here they are, right in front of you, trucking on into the Bernsteins' Chinese yellow duplex, amid the sconces, silver bowls full of white and lavender anemones, and uniformed servants serving drinks and Roquefort cheese morsels rolled in crushed nuts—

But it's all right. They're *white* servants, not Claude and Maude, but white South Americans. Lenny and Felicia are geniuses. After a while, it all comes down to servants. They are the cutting edge in Radical Chic. Obviously, if you are giving a party for the Black Panthers, as Lenny and Felicia are this evening, or as Sidney and Gail Lumet did last week, or as John Simon of Random House and Richard Baron, the publisher, did before that; or for the Chicago Eight, such as the party Jean vanden Heuvel gave; or for the grape workers or Bernadette Devlin, such as the parties Andrew Stein gave; or for the Young Lords, such as the party Ellie Guggenheimer is giving next week in *her* Park Avenue duplex; or for the Indians or the SDS or the GI coffee shops or even for the Friends of the Earth – well, then, obviously you can't have a Negro butler and maid, Claude and Maude, in uniform, circulating through the living room, the library, and the main hall serving drinks and canapés. Plenty of people have tried to think it out. They try to picture the Panthers or whoever walking in bristling with electric hair and Cuban shades and leather pieces and the rest of it, and they try to picture Claude and Maude with the black uniforms coming up and saying, 'Would you care for a drink, sir?' They close their eyes and try to picture it *some way*, but there *is* no way. One simply cannot see that moment. So the current wave of Radical Chic has touched off the most desperate search for white servants. Carter and Amanda Burden have white servants. Sidney Lumet and his wife Gail, who is Lena Horne's daughter, have three white servants, including a Scottish nurse. Everybody has white servants. And Lenny and Felicia – they had it worked out before Radical Chic even started. Felicia grew up in Chile. Her father, Roy Elwood Cohn, an engineer from San Francisco, worked for the American Smelting and Refining Co. in Santiago. As Felicia Montealegre (her mother's maiden name), she became an actress in New York and won the *Motion Picture Daily* critics' award as the best new television actress of 1949. Anyway, they have a house staff of three white South American servants, including a Chilean cook, plus Lenny's English chauffeur and dresser, who is also white, of course. Can one comprehend how perfect that is, given ... the times? Well, many of their friends can, and they ring up the Bernsteins and ask them to get South American servants for them, and the Bernsteins are so generous about it, so obliging, that people refer to them, good-naturedly and gratefully, as 'the Spic and Span Employment Agency', with an easygoing ethnic humor, of course.

The only other thing to do is what Ellie Guggenheimer is doing next week with her party for the Young Lords in her duplex on Park Avenue at 89th Street, just ten blocks up from Lenny and Felicia. She is giving her party on a Sunday, which is the day off for the maid and the cleaning woman. 'Two friends of mine' – she confides on the telephone – 'two friends of mine who happen to be . . . not white – that's what I hate about the times we live in, the *terms* – well, they've agreed to be butler and maid . . . and I'm going to be a maid myself!'

Just at this point some well-meaning soul is going to say, Why not do without servants altogether if the matter creates such unbearable tension and one truly believes in equality? Well, even to raise the question is to reveal the most fundamental ignorance of life in the great co-ops and townhouses of the East Side in the age of Radical Chic. Why, my God! servants are not a mere convenience, they're an absolute psychological necessity. Once one is into that life, truly into it, with the morning workout on the velvet swings at Kounovsky's and the late mornings on the telephone, and lunch at the Running Footman, which is now regarded as really better than La Grenouille, Lutèce, Lafayette, La Caravelle, and the rest of the general Frog Pond, less ostentatious, more of the David Hicks feeling, less of the Parish–Hadley look, and then – well, then, the idea of not having servants is unthinkable. But even that does not say it all. It makes it sound like a matter of convenience, when actually it is a sheer and fundamental matter of *having servants*. Does one comprehend?

God, what a flood of taboo thoughts runs through one's head at these Radical Chic events . . . But it's delicious. It is as if one's nerve endings were on red alert to the most intimate nuances of status. Deny it if you want to! Nevertheless, it runs through every soul here. It is the matter of the marvelous contradictions on all sides. It is like the delicious shudder you get when you try to force the prongs of two horseshoe magnets together . . . *them* and *us* . . .

For example, one's own servants, although white, are generally no problem. A discreet, euphemistic word about what sort of party it is going to be, and they will generally be models of correctness. The euphemisms are not always an easy matter, however. When talking to one's white servants, one doesn't really know whether to refer to blacks as *blacks*, *Negroes*, or *colored people*. When talking to other . . . well, *cultivated* persons, one says *blacks*, of course. It is the only word, currently, that implicitly shows one's awareness of the dignity of the black race. But somehow when you start to say the word to your own white servants, you hesitate. You can't get it out of your throat. Why? *Counter-guilt!* You realize that you are about to utter one of those touchstone words that divide the cultivated from the uncultivated, the attuned from the unattuned, the *hip* from the dreary. As soon as the word comes out of your mouth – you know it before the first vocable pops on your lips – your own servant is going to size you up as one of those *limousine liberals*, or whatever epithet they use, who are busy pouring white soul all over the black movement, and would you do as much for the white lower class, for the domestics of the East Side, for example, fat chance, sahib. Deny it if you want to! but such are the delicious little agonies of Radical Chic. So one settles for *Negro*, with the hope that the great god Culturatus has laid the ledger aside for the moment . . . In any case, if one is able to make that small compromise, one's own servants are no real problem. But the elevator man and the doorman – the death rays they begin projecting, the curt responses, as soon as they see it is going to be one of *those* parties! Of course, they're all from Queens, and so forth, and one has to allow for that. For some reason the elevator men tend to be worse about it than the doormen, even; less sense of *politesse*, perhaps.

Or – what does one wear to these parties for the Panthers or the Young Lords or the grape workers? What does a woman wear? Obviously one does not want to wear something frivolously and pompously expensive, such as a Gerard Pipart party dress. On the other hand one does not want to arrive 'poormouthing it' in some outrageous turtleneck and West Eighth Street bell-jean combination, as if one is 'funky' and of 'the people'. Frankly, Jean vanden Heuvel – that's Jean there in the hallway giving everyone her famous smile, in which her eyes narrow down to f/16 – frankly, Jean tends too much toward the funky fallacy. Jean, who is the daughter of Jules Stein, one of the wealthiest men in the country, is wearing some sort of rust-red snap-around suede skirt, the sort that English working girls pick up on Saturday afternoons in those absolutely *berserk* London boutiques like Bus Stop or Biba, where everything looks chic and yet skimpy and raw and vital. Felicia Bernstein seems to understand the whole thing better. Look at Felicia. She is wearing the simplest little black frock imaginable, with absolutely no ornamentation save for a plain gold necklace. It is perfect. It has dignity without any overt class symbolism.

Lenny? Lenny himself has been in the living room all this time, talking to old friends like the Duchins and the Stantons and the Lanes. Lenny is wearing a black turtleneck, navy blazer, Black Watch plaid trousers and a necklace with a pendant hanging down to his sternum. His tailor comes here to the apartment to take the measurements and do the fittings. Lenny is a short, trim man, and yet he always seems tall. It is his head. He has a noble head, with a face that is at once sensitive and rugged, and a full stand of iron-gray hair, with sideburns, all set off nicely by the Chinese yellow of the room. His success radiates from his eyes and his smile with a charm that illustrates Lord Jersey's adage that 'contrary to what the Methodists tell us, money and success are good for the soul.' Lenny may be fifty-one, but he is still the *Wunderkind* of American music. Everyone says so. He is not only one of the world's outstanding conductors, but a more than competent composer and pianist as well. He is the man who more than any other has broken down the wall between elite music and popular tastes, with *West Side Story* and his children's concerts on television. How natural that he should stand here in his own home radiating the charm and grace that make him an easy host for leaders of the oppressed. How ironic that the next hour should prove so shattering for this *egregio maestro!* How curious that the Negro by the piano should emerge tonight!

A bell rang, a dinner-table bell, by the sound of it, the sort one summons the maid out of the kitchen with, and the party shifted from out of the hall and into the living room. Felicia led the way, Felicia and a small gray man, with gray hair, a gray face, a gray suit, and a pair of Groovy but gray sideburns. A little gray man, in short, who would be popping up at key moments . . . to keep the freight train of history on the track, as it were . . .

Felicia was down at the far end of the living room trying to coax everybody in.

'Lenny!' she said. 'Tell the fringes to come on in!' Lenny was still in the back of the living room, near the hall. 'Fringes!' said Lenny. 'Come on in!'

In the living room most of the furniture, the couches, easy chairs, side tables, side chairs, and so on, had been pushed toward the walls, and thirty or forty folding chairs were set up in the middle of the floor. It was a big, wide room with Chinese yellow walls and white moldings, sconces, pier-glass mirrors, a portrait of Felicia reclining on a summer chaise, and at the far end, where Felicia was standing, a pair of grand pianos. A pair of them; the two pianos were standing back to back, with the tops down and their bellies swooping out. On top of both pianos was a regular flotilla of family photographs in silver frames, the kind of pictures that stand straight up thanks to little velvet- or moiré-covered buttresses in the back, the kind that decorators in New York recommend to give a living room a homelike lived-in touch. 'The million-dollar *chatchka* look,' they call it. In a way it was perfect for Radical Chic. The nice part was that with Lenny it was instinctive; with Felicia, too. The whole place looked as if the inspiration had been to spend a couple of hundred thousand on the interior without looking pretentious, although that is no great sum for a thirteen-room co-op, of course . . . Imagine explaining all that to the Black Panthers. It was another delicious thought . . . The sofas, for example, were covered in the fashionable splashy prints on a white background covering deep downy cushions, in the Bill Baldwin or Margaret Owen tradition – without it looking like Billy or Margaret had been in there fussing about with teapoys and japanned chairs. *Gemütlich.* . . Old Vienna when Grandpa was alive . . . That was the ticket . . .

Once Lenny got 'the fringes' moving in, the room filled up rapidly. It was jammed, in fact. People were sitting on sofas and easy chairs along the sides, as well as on the folding chairs, and were standing in the back, where Lenny was. Otto Preminger was sitting on a sofa down by the pianos, where the speakers were going to stand. The Panther wives were sitting in the first two rows with their Yoruba headdresses on, along with Henry Mitchell and Julie Belafonte, Harry Belafonte's wife. Julie is white, but they all greeted her warmly as 'Sister'. Behind her was sitting Barbara Walters, hostess of the *Today Show* on television, wearing a checked pants suit with a great fluffy fur collar on the coat. Harold Taylor, the former 'Boy President' of Sarah Lawrence, now fifty-five and silver-haired, but still youthful-looking, came walking down toward the front and gave a hug and a big social kiss to Gail Lumet. Robert Bay settled down in the middle of the folding chairs. Jean vanden Heuvel stood in the back and sought to focus . . .

f/16 . . . on the pianos . . . Charlotte Curtis stood beside the door, taking notes.

And then Felicia stood up beside the pianos and said: 'I want to thank you all very, very much for coming. I'm very, very glad to see so many of you here.' Everything was fine. Her voice was rich as a woodwind. She introduced a man named Leon Quat, a lawyer involved in raising funds for the Panther 21, twenty-one Black Panthers who had been arrested on a charge of conspiring to blow up five New York department stores, New Haven Railroad facilities, a police station, and the Bronx Botanical Gardens.

Leon Quat, oddly enough, had the general look of those fifty-two-year-old men who run a combination law office, real estate, and insurance operation on the second floor of a two-story taxpayer out on Queens Boulevard. And yet that wasn't the kind of man Leon Quat really was. He had the sideburns. Quite a pair. They didn't come down just to the intertragic notch, which is that little notch in the lower rim of the ear, and which so many tentative Swingers aim their sideburns toward. No, on top of this complete Queens Boulevard insurance-agent look, he had real sideburns, to the bottom of the lobe, virtual mutton-chops, which somehow have become the mark of the Movement.

Leon Quat rose up smiling: 'We are very grateful to Mrs Bernstein' – only he pronounced it 'steen'.

'STEIN!' – a great smoke-cured voice booming out from the rear of the room! It's Lenny! Leon Quat and the Black Panthers will have a chance to hear from Lenny. That much is sure. He is on the case. Leon Quat must be the only man in the room who does not know about Lenny and the Mental Jotto at 3 am . . . For years, twenty at the least, Lenny has insisted on *-stein* not *-steen*, as if to say, I am not one of those 1921 Jews who try to tone down their Jewishness by watering their names down with a bad soft English pronunciation. Lenny has made such a point of *-stein* not *-steen*, in fact, that some people in this room think at once of the story of how someone approached Larry Rivers, the artist, and said, 'What's this I hear about you and Leonard Bernstein' – *steen*, he pronounced it – 'not speaking to each other any more?' – to which Rivers said, '*STEIN!*'

'We are very grateful . . . for her marvelous hospitality,' says Quat, apparently not wanting to try the name again right away.

Then he beams toward the crowd: 'I assume we are all just an effete clique of snobs and intellectuals in this room . . . I am referring to the words of Vice-President Agnew, of course, who can't be with us today because he is in the South Pacific explaining the Nixon doctrine to the Australians. All vice-presidents suffer from the Avis complex – they're second best, so they try harder, like General Ky or Hubert Humphrey . . .' He keeps waiting for the grins and chuckles after each of these mots, but all the celebrities and culturati are nonplussed. They give him a kind of dumb attention. They came here for the Panthers and Radical Chic, and here is Old Queens Boulevard Real Estate Man with sideburns on telling them Agnew jokes. But Quat is too deep into his weird hole to get out. 'Whatever respect I have had for Lester Maddox, I lost it when I saw Humphrey put his arm around his shoulder . . .' and somehow Quat begins disappearing down a hole bunging Hubert Humphrey with lumps of old Shelley Berman material. Slowly he climbs back out. He starts telling about the oppression of the Panther 21. They have been in jail since February 2 1969, awaiting trial on ludicrous charges such as conspiring to blow up the Bronx Botanical Gardens. Their bail has been a preposterous $100,000 per person, which has in effect denied them the right to bail. They have been kept split up and moved from jail to jail. For all intents and purposes they have been denied the right to confer with their lawyers to prepare a defense. They have been subjected to inhuman treatment in jail – such as the case of Lee Berry, an epileptic, who was snatched out of a hospital bed and thrown in jail and kept in solitary confinement with a light bulb burning over his head night and day. The Panthers who have not been thrown in jail or killed, like Fred Hampton, are being stalked and harassed everywhere they go. 'One of the few higher officials who is still . . . in the clear' – Quat smiles – 'is here today. Don Cox, Field Marshal of the Black Panther Party.'

'Right on,' a voice says to Leon Quat, rather softly. And a tall black man rises from behind one of Lenny's grand pianos . . . *The Negro by the piano* . . .

The Field Marshal of the Black Panther Party has been sitting in a chair between the piano and the wall. He rises up; he has the hard-rock look, all right; he is a big tall man with brown skin and an Afro and a goatee and a black turtleneck much like Lenny's, and he stands up beside the piano, next to Lenny's million-dollar *chatchka* flotilla of family photographs. In fact, there is a certain perfection as the first Black Panther rises within a Park Avenue living room to lay the Panthers' ten-point program on New York Society in the age of Radical Chic. Cox is silhouetted – well, about nineteen feet behind him is a white silk shade with an Empire scallop over one of the windows overlooking Park Avenue. Or maybe it isn't silk, but a Jack Lenor Larsen mercerized cotton, something like that, lustrous but more subtle than silk. The whole image, the white shade and the Negro by the piano silhouetted against it, is framed by a pair of bottle-green velvet curtains, pulled back.

And does it begin now? – but this Cox is a cool number. He doesn't come on with the street epithets and interjections and the rest of the rhetoric and red eyes used for mau-mauing the white liberals, as it is called.

'The Black Panther Party,' he starts off, 'stands for a ten-point program that was handed down in October 1966 by our Minister of Defense, Huey P. Newton . . .' and he starts going through the ten points . . . 'We want an educational system that expresses the true nature of this decadent society' . . . 'We want all black men exempt from military service' . . . 'We want all black men who are in jail to be set free. We want them to be set free because they have not had fair trials. We've been tried by predominantly middle-class, all-white juries' . . . 'And most important of all, we want peace . . . see . . . We want peace, but there can be no peace as long as a society is racist and one part of society engages in systematic oppression of another' . . . 'We want a plebiscite by the United Nations to be held in black communities, so that we can control our own destiny' . . .

Everyone in the room, of course, is drinking in his performance like tiger's milk, for the . . . Soul, as it were. All love the tone of his voice, which is Confidential Hip. And yet his delivery falls into strangely formal patterns. What are these block phrases, such as 'our Minister of Defense, Huey P. Newton.'—

'Some people think that we are racist, because the news media find it useful to create that impression in order to support the power structure, which we have nothing to do with . . . see . . . They like for the Black Panther Party to be made to look like a racist organization, because that camouflages the true class nature of the struggle. But they find it harder and harder to keep up that camouflage and are driven to campaigns of harassment and violence to try to eliminate the Black Panther Party. Here in New York twenty-one members of the Black Panther Party were indicted last April on ridiculous charges of conspiring to blow up department stores and flower gardens. They've had twenty-seven bail hearings since last April . . . see . . .'

—But everyone in here loves the *sees* and the *you knows*. They are so, somehow . . . *black*. . . *so funky*. . . so metrical . . . Without ever bringing it fully into consciousness everyone responds – communes over – the fact that he uses them not for emphasis but for punctuation, metrically, much like the *uhs* favored by High Church Episcopal ministers, as in, 'And bless, uh, these gifts, uh, to Thy use and us to, uh, Thy service'—

'. . . they've had twenty-seven bail hearings since last April . . . see . . . and every time the judge has refused to lower the bail from $100,000 . . . Yet a group of whites accused of actually bombing buildings – they were able to get bail. So that clearly demonstrates the racist nature of the campaign against the Black Panther Party. We don't say "bail" any more, we say "ransom", for such repressive bail can only be called ransom.

'The situation here in New York is very explosive, as you can see, with people stacked up on top of each other. They can hardly deal with them when they're *un*organized, so that when a group comes along like the Black Panthers, they want to eliminate that group by any means . . . see . . . and so that stand has been embraced by J. Edgar Hoover, who feels that we are the greatest threat to the power structure. They try to create the impression that we are engaged in criminal activities. What are these "criminal activities"? We have instituted a breakfast program, to address ourselves to the needs of the community. We feed hungry children every morning before they go to school. So far this program is on a small scale. We're only feeding fifty thousand children nationwide, but the only money we have for this program is donations from the merchants in the neighborhoods. We have a program to establish clinics in the black communities and in other ways also we are addressing ourselves to the needs of the community . . . see . . . So the people know the power structure is lying when they say we are engaged in criminal activities. So the pigs are driven to desperate acts, like the murder of our deputy chairman, Fred Hampton, in his bed . . . see . . . in his sleep . . . But when they got desperate and took off their camouflage and murdered Fred Hampton, in his bed, in his sleep, see, that kind of shook people up, because they saw the tactics of the power structure for what they were . . .

'We relate to a phrase coined by Malcolm X: "By any means necessary" . . . you see . . . "By any means necessary" . . . and by that we mean that we recognize that if you're attacked, you have the right to defend yourself. The pigs, they say the Black Panthers are armed, the Black Panthers have weapons . . . see . . . and therefore they have the right to break in and murder us in our beds. I don't think there's anybody in here who wouldn't defend themselves if somebody came in and attacked them or their families . . . see . . . I don't think there's anybody in here who wouldn't defend themselves if . . .'

—and every woman in the room thinks of her husband . . . with his cocoa-butter jowls and Dior Men's Boutique pajamas . . . ducking into the bathroom and locking the door and turning the shower on, so he can say later that he didn't hear a thing—

'We call them pigs, and rightly so,' says Don Cox, 'because they have the way of making the victim look like the criminal, and the criminal look like the victim. So every Panther must be ready to defend himself. That was handed down by our Minister of Defense Huey P. Newton: Everybody who does not have the means to defend himself in his home, or if he does have the means and he does not defend himself – we expel *that man*. . . see . . . As our Minister of Defense, Huey P. Newton, says, "Any unarmed people are slaves, or are slaves in the real meaning of the word" . . . We recognize that this country is the most oppressive country in the world, maybe in the history of the world. The pigs have the weapons and they are ready to use them on the people, and we recognize this as being very bad. They are ready to commit genocide against those who stand up against them, and we recognize this as being very bad.

'All we want is the good life, the same as you. To live in peace and lead the good life, that's all we want . . . see . . . But right now there's no way we can do that. I want to read something to you:

' "When in the course of human events, it becomes necessary for one people to dissolve the political bands which have connected them with another, and . . ." ' He reads straight through it, every word. ' ". . . and, accordingly, all experience hath shown, that mankind are more disposed to suffer, while evils are sufferable, than to right themselves by abolishing the forms to which they are accustomed. But when a long train of abuses and usurpations, pursuing invariably the same object, evinces a design to reduce them under absolute despotism, it is their right, it is their duty, to throw off such government, and to provide new guards for their future security."

'You know what that's from?' – and he looks out at everyone and hesitates before laying this gasper on them – 'That's from the Declaration of Independence, the American Declaration of Independence. And we will defend ourselves and do like it says ... you know? ... and that's about it.'

The 'that's about it' part seems so casual, so funky, so right, after the rhetoric of what he has been saying. And then he sits down and sinks out of sight behind one of the grand pianos.

The thing is beginning to move. And – hell, yes, the *Reichstag fire!* Another man gets up, a white named Gerald Lefcourt, who is chief counsel for the Panther 21, a young man with thick black hair and the muttonchops of the Movement and that great motor inside of him that young courtroom lawyers ought to have. He lays the Reichstag fire on them. He reviews the Panther case and then he says:

'I believe that this odious situation could be compared to the Reichstag fire attempt' – he's talking about the way the Nazis used the burning of the Reichstag as the pretext for first turning loose the Gestapo and exterminating all political opposition in German – 'and I believe that this trial could also be compared to the Reichstag trial ... in many ways ... and that opened an era that this country could be heading for. That could be the outcome of this case, an era of the Right, and the only thing that can stop it is for people like ourselves to make a noise and make a noise now.'

... and not be Krupps, Junkers, or Good Germans ...

'... We had an opportunity to question the Grand Jury, and we found out some interesting things. They all have net worths averaging $300,000, and they all come from this neighborhood,' says Lefcourt, nodding as if to take in the whole Upper East Side. And suddenly everyone feels, really *feels*, that there are two breeds of mankind in the great co-ops of Park Avenue, the blue-jowled rep-tied Brook Club Junker reactionaries in the surrounding buildings ... and the few *attuned* souls here in Lenny's penthouse. '... They all have annual incomes in the area of $35,000 ... And you're supposed to have a "jury of your peers" . . . They were shocked at the questions we were asking them. They shouldn't have to answer such questions, that was the idea. They all belong to the Grand Jury Association. They're somewhat like a club. They have lunch together once in a while. A lot of them went to school together. They have no more understanding of the Black Panthers than President Nixon.'

The Junkers! Leon Quat says: 'Fascism always begins by persecuting the least powerful and least popular movement. It will be the Panthers today, the students tomorrow – and then . . . the Jews and other troublesome minorities! . . . What price civil liberties! . . . Now let's start this off with the gifts in four figures. Who is ready to make a contribution of a thousand dollars or more?'

All at once – nothing. But the little gray man sitting next to Felicia, the gray man with the sideburns, pops up and hands a piece of paper to Quat and says: 'Mr Clarence Jones asked me to say – he couldn't be here, but he's contributing $7500 to the defense fund.'

'Oh! That's marvelous!' says Felicia.

Then the voice of Lenny from the back of the room: 'as a guest of my wife' – he smiles – 'I'll give my fee for the next performance of *Cavalleria Rusticana*.' Comradely laughter. Applause. 'I *hope* that will be four figures!'

Things are moving again. Otto Preminger speaks up from the sofa down front: 'I geeve a t'ousand dollars!'

Right on. Quat says: 'I can't assure you that it's tax deductible.' He smiles. 'I wish I could, but I can't.' Well, the man looks brighter and brighter every minute. He knows a Radical Chic audience when he sees one. Those words are magic in the age of Radical Chic: it's *not* tax deductible.

The contributions start coming faster, only $250 or $300 at a clip, but faster . . . Sheldon Harnick . . . Bernie and Hilda Fishman . . . Judith Bernstein . . . Mr and Mrs Burton Lane . . .

'I know some of you are caught with your Dow-Jones averages down,' says Quat, 'but come on—'

Quat says, 'We have a $300 contribution from Harry Belafonte!'

'No, no,' says Julie Belafonte.

'I'm sorry,' says Quat, 'it's Julie's private money! I apologize. After all, there's a women's liberation movement sweeping the country, and

I want this marked down as a gift from *Mrs* Belafonte!' Then he says: 'I know you want to get to the question period, but I know there's more gold in this mine. I think we've reached the point where we can pass out the blank checks.'

More contributions . . . $100 from Mrs August Heckscher . . .

'We'll take *anything*!' says Quat. 'We'll take it all!' . . . He's high on the momentum of his fund-raiser voice . . . 'You'll leave here with nothing!'

But finally he wraps it up. A beautiful ash-blond girl with the most perfect Miss Porter's face speaks up. She's wearing a leather and tweed dress. She looks like a Junior Leaguer graduating to the Ungaro Boutique.

'I'd like to ask Mr Cox a question,' she says. Cox is standing up again, by the grand piano. 'Besides the breakfast program,' she says, 'do you have any other community programs, and what are they like?'

Cox starts to tell about a Black Panther program to set up medical clinics in the ghettos, and so on, but soon he is talking about a Panther demand that police be required to live in the community they patrol. 'If you police the community, you must live there . . . see . . . Because if he lives in the community, he's going to think twice before he brutalizes us, because we can deal with him when he comes home at night . . . see . . . We are also working to start liberation schools for black children, and these liberation schools will actually teach them about their environment, because the way they are now taught, they are taught not to see their real environment . . . see . . . They get Donald Duck and Mother Goose and all that lame happy jive . . . you know . . . We'd like to take kids on tours of the white suburbs, like Scarsdale, and like that, and let them see how their oppressors live . . . you know . . . but so far we don't have the money to carry out these programs to meet the real needs of the community. The only money we have is what we get from the merchants in the black community when we ask them for donations, which they *should give*, because they are the exploiters of the black community'—

—and *shee-ut*. What the hell is Cox getting into that for? Quat and the little gray man are ready to spring in at any lonesome split second. For God's sake, Cox, don't open that can of worms. Even in this bunch of upholstered skulls there are people who can figure out just *who* those merchants are, what group, and just how they are *asked* for donations, and we've been free of that little issue all evening, man – don't bring out *that* ball-breaker—

But the moment is saved. Suddenly there is a much more urgent question from the rear: 'Who do you call to give a party? Who do you call to give a party?'

Every head spins around . . . Quite a sight . . . It's a slender blond man who has pushed his way up to the front ranks of the standees. He's wearing a tuxedo. He's wearing black-frame glasses and his blond hair is combed back straight in the Eaton Square manner. He looks like the intense Yale man from out of one of those 1927 Frigidaire ads in the *Saturday Evening Post*, when the way to sell anything was to show Harry Yale in the background, in a tuxedo, with his pageboy-bobbed young lovely, heading off to dinner at the New Haven Lawn Club. The man still has his hand up in the air like the star student of the junior class.

'I won't be able to stay for everything you have to say,' he says, 'but who do you call to give a party?'

In fact, it is Richard Feigen, owner of the Feigen Gallery, 79th near Madison. He arrived on the art scene and the social scene from Chicago three years ago . . . He's been moving up hand over hand ever since . . . like a champion . . . Tonight – the tuxedo – tonight there is a reception at the Museum of Modern Art . . . right on . . . a 'contributing members'' reception, a private viewing not open to mere 'members' . . . But before the museum reception itself, which is at 8.30, there are private dinners . . . right? . . . which are the *real* openings . . . in the homes of great collectors or great climbers or the old Protestant elite, marvelous dinner parties, the real thing, black tie, and these dinners are the only true certification of where one stands in this whole realm of Art & Society . . . The whole game depends on whose home one is invited to before the opening . . . And the game ends as the host gathers everyone up about 8.45 for the trek to the museum itself, and the guests say, almost ritually, 'God! I wish we could see the show from here! It's too delightful! I simply don't want to *move!*' . . . And of course, they mean it! Absolutely! For them, the opening is already over, the hand is played . . . And Richard Feigen, man of the hour, replica 1927 Yale man, black tie and Eaton Square hair, has dropped in, on the way, *en passant*, to the Bernsteins', to take in the other end of the Culture tandem, Radical

Chic . . . and the rightness of it, the exhilaration, seems to sweep through him, and he thrusts his hand into the air, and somehow Radical Chic reaches its highest, purest state in that moment . . . as Richard Feigen, in his tuxedo, breaks in to ask, from the bottom of his heart, 'Who do you call to give a party?'

PHILIP ROTH

My Baseball Years

Philip Roth was born in 1933, in New Jersey, and emerged as a novelist in the early 1960s with Letting Go. *His most famous success, though, came in 1969, with* Portnoy's Complaint, *and this was followed by a series of brilliantly funny novels starring Nathan Zuckerman, a Jewish writer suspected of anti-Semitism by several of his Jewish critics. Roth also wrote* The Great American Novel *(1973), in which his love of baseball features strongly, and in the 1990s he has published some of his most scaldingly powerful work so far:* Sabbath's Theater *(1995),* American Pastoral *(1997) and* I married a Communist *(1998). Reading Myself and Others (1975) is a collection of Roth's essays and it includes 'My Baseball Years'.*

In one of his essays George Orwell writes that, though he was not very good at the game, he had a long, hopeless love affair with cricket until he was sixteen. My relations with baseball were similar. Between the ages of nine and thirteen, I must have put in a forty-hour week during the snowless months over at the neighborhood playfield – softball, hardball, and stickball pick-up games – while simultaneously holding down a full-time job as a pupil at the local grammar school. As I remember it, news of two of the most cataclysmic public events of my childhood – the death of President Roosevelt and the bombing of Hiroshima – reached me while I was out playing ball. My performance was uniformly erratic; generally okay for those easygoing pick-up games, but invariably lacking the calm and the expertise that the naturals displayed in stiff competition. My taste, and my talent, such as it was, was for the flashy, whiz-bang catch rather than the towering fly; running and leaping I loved, all the do-or-die stuff – somehow I lost confidence waiting and waiting for the ball lofted right at me to descend. I could never make the high school team, yet I remember that, in one of the two years I vainly (in both senses of the word) tried out, I did a good enough imitation of a baseball player's *style* to be able to fool (or amuse) the coach right down to the day he cut the last of the dreamers from the squad and gave out the uniforms.

Though my disappointment was keen, my misfortune did not necessitate a change in plans for the future. Playing baseball was not what the Jewish boys of our lower-middle-class neighborhood were expected to do in later life for a living. Had I been cut from the high school itself, *then* there would have been hell to pay in my house, and much confusion and shame in me. As it was, my family took my chagrin in stride and lost no more faith in me than I actually did in myself. They probably would have been shocked if I had made the team.

Maybe I would have been too. Surely it would have put me on a somewhat different footing with this game that I loved with all my heart, not simply for the fun of playing it (fun was secondary, really), but for the mythic and aesthetic dimension that it gave to an American boy's life – particularly to one whose grandparents could hardly speak English. For someone whose roots in America were strong but only inches deep, and who had no experience, such as a Catholic child might, of an awesome hierarchy that was real and felt, baseball was a kind of secular church that reached into every class and region of the nation and bound millions upon millions of us together in common concerns, loyalties, rituals, enthusiasms, and antagonisms. Baseball made me understand what patriotism was about, at its best.

Not that Hitler, the Bataan Death March, the battle for the Solomons, and the Normandy invasion didn't make of me and my contemporaries what may well have been the most patriotic generation of schoolchildren in American history (and the most willingly and successfully propagandized). But the war we entered when I was eight had thrust the country into what seemed to a child – and not only to a child – a struggle to the death between Good and Evil. Fraught with perilous, unthinkable possibilities, it inevitably nourished a patriotism grounded in moral virtue and bloody-minded hate, the patriotism that fixes a bayonet to a Bible. It seems to me that through baseball I was put in touch with a more humane and tender brand of patriotism, lyrical rather than martial or righteous in spirit, and without the reek of saintly zeal, a patriotism that could not so easily be sloganized, or contained in a high-sounding formula to which you had to pledge something vague but all-encompassing called your 'allegiance'.

To sing the National Anthem in the school auditorium every week, even during the worst of the war years, generally left me cold. The enthusiastic lady teacher waved her arms in the air and we obliged with the words: 'See! Light! Proof! Night! There!' But nothing stirred within, strident as we might be – in the end, just another school exercise. It was different, however, on Sundays out at Ruppert Stadium, a green wedge of pasture miraculously walled in among the factories, warehouses, and truck depots of industrial Newark. It would, in fact, have seemed to me an emotional thrill forsaken if, before the Newark Bears took on the hated enemy from across the marshes, the Jersey City Giants, we hadn't first to rise to our feet (my father, my brother, and I – along with our inimical countrymen, the city's Germans, Italians, Irish, Poles, and, out in the Africa of the bleachers, Newark's Negroes) to celebrate the America that had given to this unharmonious mob a game so grand and beautiful.

Just as I first learned the names of the great institutions of higher learning by trafficking in football pools for a neighborhood bookmaker rather than from our high school's college adviser, so my feel for the American landscape came less from what I learned in the classroom about Lewis and Clark than from following the major-league clubs on their road trips and reading about the minor leagues in the back pages of *The Sporting News*. The size of the continent got through to you finally when you had to stay up to 10.30 pm in New Jersey to hear via radio 'ticker-tape' Cardinal pitcher Mort Cooper throw the first strike of the night to Brooklyn short-stop Pee Wee Reese out in 'steamy' Sportsmen's Park in St Louis, Missouri. And however much we might be told by teacher about the stockyards and the Haymarket riot, Chicago only began to exist for me as a real place, and to matter in American history, when I became fearful (as a Dodger fan) of the bat of Phil Cavarretta, first baseman for the Chicago Cubs.

Not until I got to college and was introduced to literature did I find anything with a comparable emotional atmosphere and aesthetic appeal. I don't mean to suggest that it was a simple exchange, one passion for another. Between first discovering the Newark Bears and the Brooklyn Dodgers at seven or eight and first looking into Conrad's *Lord Jim* at age eighteen, I had done some growing up. I am only saying that my discovery of literature, and fiction particularly, and the 'love affair' – to some degree hopeless, but still earnest – that has ensued, derives in part from this childhood infatuation with baseball. Or, more accurately perhaps, baseball – with its lore and legends, its cultural power, its seasonal associations, its native authenticity, its simple rules and transparent strategies, its longueurs and thrills, its spaciousness, its suspensefulness, its heroics, its nuances, its lingo, its 'characters', its peculiarly hypnotic tedium, its mythic transformation of the immediate – was the literature of my boyhood.

Baseball, as played in the big leagues, was something completely outside my own life that could nonetheless move me to ecstasy and to tears; like fiction it could excite the imagination and hold the attention as much with minutiae as with high drama. Mel Ott's cocked leg striding into the ball, Jackie Robinson's pigeon-toed shuffle as he moved out to second base, each was to be as deeply affecting over the years as that night – 'inconceivable', 'inscrutable', as any night Conrad's Marlow might struggle to comprehend – the night that Dodger wild man, Rex Barney (who never lived up to 'our' expectations, who should have been 'our' Koufax), not only went the distance without walking in half a dozen runs, but, of all things, threw a no-hitter. A thrilling mystery, marvelously enriched by the fact that a light rain had fallen during the early evening, and Barney, figuring the game was going to be postponed, had eaten a hot dog just before being told to take the mound.

This detail was passed on to us by Red Barber, the Dodger radio sportscaster of the forties, a respectful, mild Southerner with a subtle rural tanginess to his vocabulary and a soft country-parson tone to his voice. For the adventures of 'dem bums' of Brooklyn – a region then the very symbol of urban wackiness and tumult – to be narrated from Red Barber's highly alien but loving perspective constituted a genuine triumph of what my English professors would later teach me to call 'point of view'. James himself might have admired the implicit cultural ironies and the splendid possibilities for oblique moral and social commentary. And as for the detail about Rex Barney eating his hot dog, it was irresistible, joining as it did the spectacular to the mundane, and furnishing an adolescent boy with a glimpse of an unexpectedly ordinary, even humdrum, side to male heroism.

Of course, in time, neither the flavor and suggestiveness of Red Barber's narration nor 'epiphanies' as resonant with meaning as Rex Barney's pre-game hot dog could continue to satisfy a developing literary appetite; nonetheless, it was just this that helped to sustain me until I was ready to begin to respond to the great inventors of narrative detail and masters of narrative voice and perspective like James, Conrad, Dostoevsky, and Bellow.

PHILIP LARKIN

The Pleasure Principle

Philip Larkin (1922–85) is now generally recognized as Britain's most important post-war poet. Larkin began his career, though, as a novelist – with Jill *(1946) and* A Girl in Winter *(1947) – and it was not until the publication of* The Whitsun Weddings *(1964) that his reputation as a major poet was thoroughly secured. Larkin's* Collected Poems *appeared in 1988, in a posthumous edition edited by Anthony Thwaite, who also edited Larkin's* Letters *(1992). During his lifetime, Larkin published two books of non-fiction prose:* All What Jazz *(1970), a round-up of his jazz reviews from the 1960s, and – in 1983 – an essay collection:* Required Writing: Miscellaneous Pieces 1955–82.

It is sometimes useful to remind ourselves of the simpler aspects of things normally regarded as complicated. Take, for instance, the writing of a poem. It consists of three stages: the first is when a man becomes obsessed with an emotional concept to such a degree that he is compelled to do something about it. What he does is the second stage, namely, construct a verbal device that will reproduce this emotional concept in anyone who cares to read it, anywhere, any time. The third stage is the recurrent situation of people in different times and places setting off the device and re-creating in themselves what the poet felt when he wrote it. The stages are interdependent and all necessary. If there has been no preliminary feeling, the device has nothing to reproduce and the reader will experience nothing. If the second stage has not been well done, the device will not deliver the goods, or will deliver only a few goods to a few people, or will stop delivering them after an absurdly short while. And if there is no third stage, no successful reading, the poem can hardly be said to exist in a practical sense at all.

What a description of this basic tripartite structure shows is that poetry is emotional in nature and theatrical in operation, a skilled recreation of emotion in other people, and that, conversely, a bad poem is one that never succeeds in doing this. All modes of critical derogation are no more than different ways of saying this, whatever literary, philosophical or moral terminology they employ, and it would not be necessary to point out anything so obvious if present-day poetry did not suggest that it had been forgotten. We seem to be producing a new kind of bad poetry, not the old kind that tries to move the reader and fails, but one that does not even try. Repeatedly he is confronted with pieces that cannot be understood without reference beyond their own limits or whose contented insipidity argues that their authors are merely reminding themselves of what they know already, rather than re-creating it for a third party. The reader, in fact, seems no longer present in the poet's mind as he used to be, as someone who must understand and enjoy the finished product if it is to be a success at all; the assumption now is that no one will read it, and wouldn't understand or enjoy it if they did. Why should this be so? It is not sufficient to say that poetry has lost its audience, and so need no longer consider it: lots of people still read and even buy poetry. More accurately, poetry has lost its old audience, and gained a new one. This has been caused by the consequences of a cunning merger between poet, literary critic and academic critic (three classes now notoriously indistinguishable): it is hardly an exaggeration to say that the poet has gained the happy position wherein he can praise his own poetry in the press and explain it in the class-room, and the reader has been bullied into giving up the consumer's power to say 'I don't like this, bring me something different.' Let him now so much as breathe a word about not liking a poem, and he is in the dock before he can say Edwin Arlington Robinson. And the charge is a grave one: flabby sensibility, insufficient or inadequate critical tools, and inability to meet new verbal and emotional situations. Verdict guilty, plus a few riders on the prisoner's mental upbringing, addiction to mass amusements, and enfeebled responses. It is time some of you playboys realized, says the judge, that reading a poem is hard work. Fourteen days in stir. Next case.

The cash customers of poetry, therefore, who used to put down their money in the sure and certain hope of enjoyment as if at a theatre or concert hall, were quick to move elsewhere. Poetry was no longer a pleasure. They have been replaced by a humbler squad, whose aim is not pleasure but self-improvement, and who have uncritically accepted the contention that they cannot appreciate poetry without preliminary investment in the intellectual equipment which, by the merest chance, their tutor happens to have about him. In short, the modern poetic audience, when it is not taking in its own washing, is a *student* audience, pure and simple. At first sight this may not seem a bad thing. The poet has at last a moral ascendancy, and his new clientele not only pay for the poetry but pay to have it explained afterwards. Again, if the poet has only himself to please, he is no longer handicapped by the limitations of his audience. And in any case nobody nowadays believes that a worthwhile artist can rely on anything but his own judgement: public taste is always twenty-five years behind, and picks up a style only when it is exploited by the second-rate. All this is true enough. But at bottom poetry, like all art, is inextricably bound up with giving pleasure, and if a poet loses his pleasure-seeking audience he has lost the only audience worth having, for which the dutiful mob that signs on every September is no substitute. And the effect will be felt throughout his work. He will forget that even if he finds what he has to say interesting, others may not. He will concentrate on moral worth or semantic intricacy. Worst of all, his poems will no longer be born of the tension between what he non-verbally feels and what can be got over in common word-usage to someone who hasn't had his experience or education or travel grant, and once the other end of the rope is dropped what results will not be so much obscure or piffling (though it may be both) as an unrealized, 'undramatized' slackness, because he will have lost the habit of testing what he writes by this particular standard. Hence, no pleasure. Hence, no poetry.

What can be done about this? Who wants anything done about it? Certainly not the poet, who is in the unprecedented position of peddling both his work and the standard by which it is judged. Certainly not the new reader, who, like a partner of some unconsummated marriage, has no idea of anything better. Certainly not the old reader, who has simply replaced one pleasure with another. Only the romantic loiterer who recalls the days when poetry was condemned as sinful might wish things different. But if the medium is in fact to be rescued from among our duties and restored to our pleasures, I can only think that a large-scale revulsion has got to set in against present notions, and that it will have to start with poetry readers asking themselves more frequently whether they do in fact enjoy what they read, and, if not, what the point is of carrying on. And I use 'enjoy' in the commonest of senses, the sense in which we leave a radio on or off. Those interested might like to read

David Daiches's essay 'The New Criticism: Some Qualifications' (in *Literary Essays*, 1956); in the meantime, the following note by Samuel Butler may reawaken a furtive itch for freedom: 'I should like to like Schumann's music better than I do; I dare say I could make myself like it better if I tried; but I do not like having to try to make myself like things; I like things that make me like them at once and no trying at all' (*Notebooks*, 1919).

KINGSLEY AMIS

Why Are You Telling Me All This?

Kingsley Amis (1922–95) won fame in the 1950s with his first book,
Lucky Jim *(1954) and subsequently published a dozen or so gloomily
comic novels, winning the Booker Prize in 1986 for* The Old Devils.
*Amis was knighted in 1990, presumably for his services to literature.
In addition to his fiction, Amis published several volumes of verse and
of prose non-fiction. He also edited numerous anthologies. His* Memoirs
*appeared in 1991. In the early years of his career, Amis was highly
active as a reviewer and literary essayist. In 1970 he published* What
Became of Jane Austen, and Other Questions, *and in 1990 there was*
The Amis Collection: Selected Non-Fiction 1954–1990. *'Why Are You
Telling Me All This?' appeared in* The Spectator *in 1986.*

Reading almost any piece of writing above the emotional level of a
guidebook or a public notice is like listening to someone talking to you
in private, talking to you alone. However well aware you may be that
the words have reached and are continuing to reach countless others,
you feel, in the act of reading, I suggest, like an audience of one, that
is to say in a relation of peculiar intimacy and immediacy, less intense
than when in company with a real person but otherwise very much the
same, and unique in being so.

Accordingly you respond to what you are being told, if it is told well
enough, very much as you would in life, thrilling to the adventures,
chuckling at the funny bits, feeling a touch of the tender emotions when
these are appealed to. This more or less simple correspondence breaks
down when what you are being told consists of a passage of explicit
sexual description, or ESD.

In life, the recounting of sexual confidences by one man to another
(I know there are other possible combinations) is governed by an
unspoken but pretty stringent contract if they are to be admitted at all.
Even in the most favourable circumstances, venturing into physical
detail is in danger of producing discomfort in the hearer. This discomfort

is not really shock, not at any rate the sort that old ladies are supposed to feel at being reminded, or perhaps more fully informed, of the disgusting things people get up to. It is more like embarrassment, born of uneasy speculation about what sort of fellow it can be who is prepared to tell you all this. Whether he does it to boast, to indulge his fancy, to advertise his emancipation from something or other, to shake you out of your bourgeois sedateness, etc, will hardly concern you. Nor will you take the slightest notice of any pretences he may make of increasing the store of human knowledge, affected or half-baked protestations of wonderment at the mystery of it all, or suchlike. Whereas if his theme is the horror or nastiness of it all you will already have left. Very well, let it be shock, but at his telling it, not at whatever he might or might not have done.

Try as he may, the writer of such things is seized by the same trap as his social counterpart. No matter that, by the very act of agreeing to read his tale, you have given him something of the privilege of a close friend, and that the conditions of reading make him at the same time secure from interruption and available for pondering *ad libitum*. Indeed, the fact that he well and truly has your ear only makes it worse of him. A writer has none of the real-life excuses of drunkenness, caprice, boredom. It is his considered judgement that you should be told exactly what he or what's-his-name got up to. No matter either how sincerely he thinks, or would say he thinks, that his intentions are immaculate, how loudly he protests his devotion to art, truth, love, self-understanding, the essential holiness of sex or anything else; the unbreakable connection between literature and life reduces him to the same moral level as the chap you make sure of avoiding in the pub.

It is often said that the sexual act is ludicrous to a detached observer, though opportunities to check this on the ground, so to speak, must be rare. Certainly sex is a subject very well suited for comic treatment, so much so that some accounts of sexual behaviour notoriously attract laughter against that writer's intention, and *Lady Chatterley's Lover* might be a masterpiece of unconscious humour but for the boring non-sexual bits in between. The book also provokes in full measure the irritation that is never far from the reader's mind in such cases, expressible perhaps by the grumble, 'Well, all I can say is if it was me doing it, I wouldn't be doing it like that.'

A full ESD in comic terms, if possible at all, would be a dubious venture; what little I have seen along those lines has indicated that a little goes a long way. But obviously enough the real sight of a copulating couple would to most people not be funny in the least. Most people finding themselves somehow faced with it would, from feelings I need not indicate, get out as fast as they could. A minority would stay; more practically, they would have fixed it up in the first place.

In life, that minority is a small one; among readers, not so small. These readers, voyeurs at one remove, are, of course, purposeful and responsive readers of pornography, obtaining sexual excitement from what purport to be accounts of others' behaviour. Pornography is unlike any other kind of writing. It has no analogy with the social act of talking to someone and its reader has no sense of an author; places, time, individuals and their motives and reactions and whole lives vanish too. In this sense, as in others, it is dehumanising. And it is no respecter of motives. I mean that any detailed account of copulation, however 'purely' intended, is liable to excite sexually those whom it does not revolt, bore or move to laughter. That is in the strict sense the dilemma of the explicit describer. Some writers cheerfully ignore it and may make a lot of money, for instance Harold Robbins, whose *The Storyteller* shows its very Robbins-like 'hero' writing a rape scene in a visibly worked-up state.

Well, if you don't mind your readers seeing you in that light, go ahead and run off all the ESDs you fancy; forget that there are those to whom another fellow's sexual excitement is the least engaging thing in the world. In the present context to infer its presence is to realise that you have crossed the frontiers into pornography-on-purpose. Like many frontiers this one is often hard to draw precisely, but you can tell straight away which side of it you are on.

To argue in this way is not – obviously, I hope – to interdict sex as a literary subject. The special importance of that subject, however, imposes special restraints on those setting out to deal with it. Such restraints are not constricting to a writer of any care or skill. Quite the contrary: the tension between the need to make matters clear enough and the need to do so tactfully can be turned to artistic account, like the poetic tension between metre and natural speech. In *Jude the Obscure* it is not just that Hardy succeeds in telling us all we need to know about Jude and Arabella, and Jude and Sue, without ever taking us into the bedroom; the manner of his success is part of the literary success of the novel. In Henry Newbolt's poem, 'The Viking's Song', a less familiar example, we hear how the raider's first forays were not welcome to the recipient territory. But, approaching the shore now,

> Where once but watch-fires burned
> I see thy beacon shine,
> And know the land hath learned
> Desire that welcomes mine.

Nothing could be clearer, or less explicit; and again, the poem would not just be less good if Newbolt had said, 'Darling, when I first started to . . .' etc, it would not exist at all.

The ESD-merchant's greatest disservice is not that of offending briefly and effaceably against good taste and good sense too, though he or she asks to be reminded that at a time when anything may be published there is a particular duty to be responsible. It is that the very nature of the enterprise reinforces the assumption that physical sex is the important part or the most interesting or only interesting part of sex. Life and a great deal of literature teach the importance and interest of those moments and days and whole relationships which are deeply sexual, but in which nobody even looks like touching anybody. Of course, the trouble with that sort of thing is that it can be quite difficult to write about. Breasts and buttocks are child's play.

JOAN DIDION

Goodbye to All That

Joan Didion was born in 1934, and most of her fiction is set in her native California, or in Central America. Her first novel, Play It As It Lays, *was published in 1970; her most recent,* The Last Thing He Wanted, *in 1997. Over the years her deadly, deadpan manner has not noticeably softened. Joan Didion has also written screenplays – with her husband, John Gregory Dunne (who is also a distinguished essayist) – but she is probably most often praised for her non-fiction. 'Goodbye to All That' was first collected in Didion's* Slouching Towards Bethlehem *(1968).*

> How many miles to Babylon?
> Three score miles and ten –
> Can I get there by candlelight?
> Yes, and back again –
> If your feet are nimble and light
> You can get there by candlelight.

It is easy to see the beginnings of things, and harder to see the ends. I can remember now, with a clarity that makes the nerves in the back of my neck constrict, when New York began for me, but I cannot lay my finger upon the moment it ended, can never cut through the ambiguities and second starts and broken resolves to the exact place on the page where the heroine is no longer as optimistic as she once was. When I first saw New York I was twenty, and it was summertime, and I got off a DC-7 at the old Idlewild temporary terminal in a new dress which had seemed very smart in Sacramento but seemed less smart already, even in the old Idlewild temporary terminal, and the warm air smelled of mildew and some instinct, programmed by all the movies I had ever seen and all the songs I had ever heard sung and all the stories I had ever read about New York, informed me that it would never be quite the same again. In fact it never was. Some time later there was a song on all the jukeboxes on the upper East Side that went 'but where is the schoolgirl who used to be me,' and if it was late enough at night I used to wonder that. I know now that almost everyone wonders something like that, sooner or later and no matter what he or she is doing, but one of the mixed blessings of being twenty and twenty-one and even twenty-three is the conviction that nothing like this, all evidence to the contrary notwithstanding, has ever happened to anyone before.

Of course it might have been some other city, had circumstances been different and the time been different and had I been different, might have been Paris or Chicago or even San Francisco, but because I am talking about myself I am talking here about New York. That first night I opened my window on the bus into town and watched for the skyline, but all I could see were the wastes of Queens and the big signs that said MIDTOWN TUNNEL THIS LANE and then a flood of summer rain (even that seemed remarkable and exotic, for I had come out of the West where there was no summer rain), and for the next three days I sat wrapped in blankets in a hotel room air-conditioned to 35°F and tried to get over a bad cold and a high fever. It did not occur to me to call a doctor, because I knew none, and although it did occur to me to call the desk and ask that the air-conditioner be turned off, I never called, because I did not know how much to tip whoever might come – was anyone ever so young? I am here to tell you that someone was. All I could do during those three days was talk long-distance to the boy I already knew I would never marry in the spring. I would stay in New York, I told him, just six months, and I could see the Brooklyn Bridge from my window. As it turned out the bridge was the Triborough, and I stayed eight years.

In retrospect it seems to me that those days before I knew the names of all the bridges were happier than the ones that came later, but perhaps you will see that as we go along. Part of what I want to tell you is what it is like to be young in New York, how six months can become eight years with the deceptive ease of a film dissolve, for that is how those years appear to me now, in a long sequence of sentimental dissolves and old-fashioned trick shots – the Seagram Building fountains dissolve into snowflakes, I enter a revolving door at twenty and come out a good deal older, and on a different street. But most particularly I want to explain to you, and in the process perhaps to myself, why I no longer live in New York. It is often said that New York is a city for only the very rich and the very poor. It is less often said that New York is also, at least for those of us who came there from somewhere else, a city for only the very young.

I remember once, one cold bright December evening in New York, suggesting to a friend who complained of having been around too long that he come with me to a party where there would be, I assured him with the bright resourcefulness of twenty-three, 'new faces'. He laughed literally until he choked, and I had to roll down the taxi window and hit him on the back. 'New faces,' he said finally, 'don't tell me about *new faces*.' It seemed that the last time he had gone to a party where he had been promised 'new faces', there had been fifteen people in the room, and he had already slept with five of the women and owed money to all but two of the men. I laughed with him, but the first snow had just begun to fall and the big Christmas trees glittered yellow and white as far as I could see up Park Avenue and I had a new dress and it would be a long while before I would come to understand the particular moral of the story.

It would be a long while because, quite simply, I was in love with New York. I do not mean 'love' in any colloquial way, I mean that I was in love with the city, the way you love the first person who ever touches you and never love anyone quite that way again. I remember walking across Sixty-second Street one twilight that first spring, or the second spring, they were all alike for a while. I was late to meet someone but I stopped at Lexington Avenue and bought a peach and stood on the corner eating it and knew that I had come out of the West and reached the mirage. I could taste the peach and feel the soft air blowing from a subway grating on my legs and I could smell lilac and garbage and expensive perfume and I knew that it would cost something sooner or later – because I did not belong there, did not come from there – but when you are twenty-two or twenty-three, you figure that later you will have a high emotional balance, and be able to pay whatever it costs. I still believed in possibilities then, still had the sense, so peculiar to New York, that something extraordinary would happen any minute, any day, any month. I was making only $65 or $70 a week then ('Put yourself in Hattie Carnegie's hands,' I was advised without the slightest trace of irony by an editor of the magazine for which I worked), so little money that some weeks I had to charge food at Bloomingdale's gourmet shop in order to eat, a fact which went unmentioned in the letters I wrote to California. I never told my father that I needed money because then he would have sent it, and I would never know if I could do it by myself. At that time making a living seemed a game to me, with arbitrary but quite inflexible rules. And except on a certain kind of winter evening – six-thirty in the Seventies, say, already dark and bitter with a wind off the river, when I would be walking very fast toward a bus and would look in the bright windows of brownstones and see cooks working in clean kitchens and imagine women lighting candles on the floor above and beautiful children being bathed on the floor above that – except on nights like those, I never felt poor; I had the feeling that if I needed money I could always get it. I could write a syndicated column for teenagers under the name 'Debbi Lynn' or I could smuggle gold into India or I could become a $100 call girl, and none of it would matter.

Nothing was irrevocable; everything was within reach. Just around every corner lay something curious and interesting, something I had never before seen or done or known about. I could go to a party and meet someone who called himself Mr Emotional Appeal and ran The Emotional Appeal Institute or Tina Onassis Blandford or a Florida cracker who was then a regular on what he called 'the Big C, the Southampton–El Morocco circuit' ('I'm well-connected on the Big C, honey,' he would tell me over collard greens on his vast borrowed terrace), or the widow of the celery king of the Harlem market or a piano salesman from Bonne Terre, Missouri, or someone who had already made and lost two fortunes in Midland, Texas. I could make promises to myself and to other people and there would be all the time in the world to keep them. I could stay up all night and make mistakes, and none of it would count.

You see I was in a curious position in New York: it never occurred to me that I was living a real life there. In my imagination I was always there for just another few months, just until Christmas or Easter or the first warm day in May. For that reason I was most comfortable in the company of Southerners. They seemed to be in New York as I was, on some indefinitely extended leave from wherever they belonged, disinclined to consider the future, temporary exiles who always knew when the flights left for New Orleans or Memphis or Richmond or, in my case, California. Someone who lives always with a plane schedule in the drawer lives on a slightly different calendar. Christmas, for example, was a difficult season. Other people could take it in stride, going to Stowe or going abroad or going for the day to their mothers' places in Connecticut; those of us who believed that we lived somewhere else would spend it making and cancelling airline reservations, waiting for weatherbound flights as if for the last plane out of Lisbon in 1940, and finally comforting one another, those of us who were left, with the oranges and mementos and smoked-oyster stuffings of childhood, gathering close, colonials in a far country.

Which is precisely what we were. I am not sure that it is possible for anyone brought up in the East to appreciate entirely what New York, the idea of New York, means to those of us who came out of the West and the South. To an Eastern child, particularly a child who has always had an uncle on Wall Street and who has spent several hundred Saturdays first at FAO Schwarz and being fitted for shoes at Best's and then waiting under the Biltmore clock and dancing to Lester Lanin, New York is just a city, albeit *the* city, a plausible place for people to live. But to those of us who came from places where no one had heard of Lester Lanin and Grand Central Station was a Saturday radio program, where Wall Street and Fifth Avenue and Madison Avenue were not places at all but abstractions ('Money', and 'High Fashion', and 'The Hucksters'), New York was no mere city. It was instead an infinitely romantic notion, the mysterious nexus of all love and money and power, the shining and perishable dream itself. To think of 'living' there was to reduce the miraculous to the mundane; one does not 'live' at Xanadu.

In fact it was difficult in the extreme for me to understand those young women for whom New York was not simply an ephemeral Estoril but a real place, girls who bought toasters and installed new cabinets in their apartments and committed themselves to some reasonable future. I never bought any furniture in New York. For a year or so I lived in other people's apartments; after that I lived in the Nineties in an apartment furnished entirely with things taken from storage by a friend whose wife had moved away. And when I left the apartment in the Nineties (that was when I was leaving everything, when it was all breaking up) I left everything in it, even my winter clothes and the map of Sacramento County I had hung on the bedroom wall to remind me who I was, and I moved into a monastic four-room floor-through on Seventy-fifth Street. 'Monastic' is perhaps misleading here, implying some chic severity; until after I was married and my husband moved some furniture in, there was nothing at all in those four rooms except a cheap double mattress and box springs, ordered by telephone the day I decided to move, and two French garden chairs lent me by a friend who imported them. (It strikes me now that the people I knew in New York all had curious and self-defeating sidelines. They imported garden chairs which did not sell very well at Hammacher Schlemmer or they tried to market hair straighteners in Harlem or they ghosted exposés of Murder Incorporated for Sunday supplements. I think that perhaps none of us was very serious, *engagé* only about our most private lives.)

All I ever did to that apartment was hang fifty yards of yellow theatrical silk across the bedroom windows, because I had some idea that the gold light would make me feel better, but I did not bother to weight the curtains correctly and all that summer the long panels of transparent golden silk would blow out the windows and get tangled and drenched in the afternoon thunderstorms. That was the year, my twenty-eighth, when I was discovering that not all of the promises would be kept, that some things are in fact irrevocable and that it had counted after all, every evasion and every procrastination, every mistake, every word, all of it.

That is what it was all about, wasn't it? Promises? Now when New York comes back to me it comes in hallucinatory flashes, so clinically detailed that I sometimes wish that memory would effect the distortion with which it is commonly credited. For a lot of the time I was in New York I used a perfume called *Fleurs de Rocaille*, and then *L'Air du Temps*, and now the slightest trace of either can short-circuit my connections for the rest of the day. Nor can I smell Henri Bendel jasmine soap without falling back into the past, or the particular mixture of spices used for boiling crabs. There were barrels of crab boil in a Czech place in the Eighties where I once shopped. Smells, of course, are notorious memory stimuli, but there are other things which affect me the same way. Blue-and-white striped sheets. Vermouth cassis. Some faded nightgowns which were new in 1959 or 1960, and some chiffon scarves I bought about the same time.

I suppose that a lot of us who have been young in New York have the same scenes on our home screens. I remember sitting in a lot of apartments with a slight headache about five o'clock in the morning. I had a friend who could not sleep, and he knew a few other people who had the same trouble, and we would watch the sky lighten and have a last drink with no ice and then go home in the early morning light, when the streets were clean and wet (had it rained in the night? we never knew) and the few cruising taxis still had their headlights on and the only color was the red and green of traffic signals. The White Rose bars opened very early in the morning; I recall waiting in one of them to watch an astronaut go into space, waiting so long that at the moment it actually happened I had my eyes not on the television screen but on a cockroach on the tile floor. I liked the bleak branches above Washington Square at dawn, and the monochromatic flatness of Second Avenue, the fire escapes and the grilled storefronts peculiar and empty in their perspective.

It is relatively hard to fight at six-thirty or seven in the morning without any sleep, which was perhaps one reason we stayed up all night, and it seemed to me a pleasant time of day. The windows were shuttered in that apartment in the Nineties and I could sleep a few hours and then go to work. I could work then on two or three hours' sleep and a container of coffee from Chock Full O' Nuts. I liked going to work, liked the soothing and satisfactory rhythm of getting out a magazine, liked the orderly progression of four-color closings and two-color closings and black-and-white closings and then The Product, no abstraction but something which looked effortlessly glossy and could be picked up on a newsstand and weighed in the hand. I liked all the minutiae of proofs and layouts, liked working late on the nights the magazine went to press, sitting and reading *Variety* and waiting for the copy desk to call. From my office I could look across town to the weather signal on the Mutual of New York Building and the lights that alternately spelled out TIME and LIFE above Rockefeller Plaza; that pleased me obscurely, and so did walking uptown in the mauve eight o'clocks of early summer evenings and looking at things, Lowestoft tureens in Fifty-seventh Street windows, people in evening clothes trying to get taxis, the trees just coming into full leaf, the lambent air, all the sweet promises of money and summer.

Some years passed, but I still did not lose that sense of wonder about New York. I began to cherish the loneliness of it, the sense that at any given time no one need know where I was or what I was doing. I liked walking, from the East River over to the Hudson and back on brisk days, down around the Village on warm days. A friend would leave me the key to her apartment in the West Village when she was out of town, and sometimes I would just move down there, because by that time the telephone was beginning to bother me (the canker, you see, was already in the rose) and not many people had that number. I remember one day when someone who did have the West Village number came to pick me up for lunch there, and we both had hangovers, and I cut my finger opening him a beer and burst into tears, and we walked to a Spanish restaurant and drank Bloody Marys and *gazpacho* until we felt better. I was not then guilt-ridden about spending afternoons that way, because I still had all the afternoons in the world.

And even that late in the game I still liked going to parties, all parties, bad parties, Saturday-afternoon parties given by recently married couples who lived in Stuyvesant Town, West Side parties given by unpublished or failed writers who served cheap red wine and talked about going to Guadalajara, Village parties where all the guests worked for advertising agencies and voted for Reform Democrats, press parties at Sardi's, the worst kinds of parties. You will have perceived by now that I was not one to profit by the experience of others, that it was a very long time indeed before I stopped believing in new faces and began to understand the lesson in that story, which was that it is distinctly possible to stay too long at the Fair.

I could not tell you when I began to understand that. All I know is that it was very bad when I was twenty-eight. Everything that was said to me I seemed to have heard before, and I could no longer listen. I could no longer sit in little bars near Grand Central and listen to someone complaining of his wife's inability to cope with the help while he missed another train to Connecticut. I no longer had any interest in hearing about the advances other people had received from their publishers, about plays which were having second-act trouble in Philadelphia, or about people I would like very much if only I would come out and meet them. I had already met them, always. There were certain parts of the city which I had to avoid. I could not bear upper Madison Avenue on weekday mornings (this was a particularly inconvenient aversion, since I then lived just fifty or sixty feet east of Madison), because I would see women walking .Yorkshire terriers and shopping at Gristede's, and some Veblenesque gorge would rise in my throat. I could not go to Times Square in the afternoon, or to the New York Public Library for any reason whatsoever. One day I could not go into a Schrafft's; the next day it would be Bonwit Teller.

I hurt the people I cared about, and insulted those I did not. I cut myself off from the one person who was closer to me than any other. I cried until I was not even aware when I was crying and when I was not, cried in elevators and in taxis and in Chinese laundries, and when I went to the doctor he said only that I seemed to be depressed, and should see a 'specialist'. He wrote down a psychiatrist's name and address for me, but I did not go.

Instead I got married, which as it turned out was a very good thing to do but badly timed, since I still could not walk on upper Madison Avenue in the mornings and still could not talk to people and still cried in Chinese laundries. I had never before understood what 'despair' meant, and I am not sure that I understand now, but I understood that year. Of course I could not work. I could not even get dinner with any degree of certainty, and I would sit in the apartment on Seventy-fifth Street paralyzed until my husband would call from his office and say gently that I did not have to get dinner, that I could meet him at Michael's Pub or at Toots Shor's or at Sardi's East. And then one morning in April (we had been married in January) he called and told me that he wanted to get out of New York for a while, that he would take a six-month leave of absence, that we would go somewhere.

It was three years ago that he told me that, and we have lived in Los Angeles since. Many of the people we knew in New York think this a curious aberration, and in fact tell us so. There is no possible, no adequate answer to that, and so we give certain stock answers, the answers everyone gives. I talk about how difficult it would be for us to 'afford' to live in New York right now, about how much 'space' we need. All I mean is that I was very young in New York, and that at some point the golden rhythm was broken, and I am not that young any more. The last time I was in New York was in a cold January, and everyone was ill and tired. Many of the people I used to know there had moved to Dallas or had gone on Antabuse or had bought a farm in New Hampshire. We stayed ten days, and then we took an afternoon flight back to Los Angeles, and on the way home from the airport that night I could see the moon on the Pacific and smell jasmine all around and we both knew that there was no longer any point in keeping the apartment we still kept in New York. There were years when I called Los Angeles 'the Coast', but they seem a long time ago.

JOHN UPDIKE

The Bankrupt Man

John Updike was born in Pennsylvania in 1932 and has published many celebrated novels – most notably, perhaps, his cherishable 'Rabbit' tetralogy. Non-Rabbit fictions include Couples *(1968),* Bech: A Book *(1970) and – in 1998 –* Toward the End of Time. *In addition to his fiction, Updike has been a voluminous reviewer of new books – mainly for the* New Yorker, *where he worked as a staff writer in the 1950s. Two large volumes of his non-fiction prose have appeared in recent years:* Odd Jobs *(1991) and* Hugging the Shore *(1993), from which 'The Bankrupt Man' is taken.*

The bankrupt man dances. Perhaps, on other occasions, he sings. Certainly he spends money in restaurants and tips generously. In what sense, then, is he bankrupt?

He has been declared so. He has declared himself so. He returns from the city agitated and pale, complaining of hours spent with the lawyers. Then he pours himself a drink. How does he pay for the liquor inside the drink, if he is bankrupt?

One is too shy to ask. Bankruptcy is a sacred state, a condition beyond conditions, as theologians might say, and attempts to investigate it are necessarily obscene, like spiritualism. One knows only that he has passed into it and lives beyond us, in a condition not ours.

He is dancing at the Chilblains Relief Association Fund Ball. His heels kick high. The mauve spotlight caresses his shoulders, then the gold. His wife's hair glistens like a beehive of tinsel above her bare shoulders and dulcet neck. Where does she get the money, to pay the hairdresser to tease and singe and set her so dazzlingly? We are afraid to ask but cannot tear our eyes from the dancing couple.

The bankrupt man buys himself a motorcycle. He is going to hotdog it all the way to Santa Barbara and back. He has a bankrupt sister in Santa Barbara. Also, there are business details to be cleared up along the way, in Pittsburgh, South Bend, Dodge City, Santa Fe, and Palm

Springs. Being bankrupt is an expansionist process; it generates ever new horizons.

We all want to dance with the bankrupt man's wife. Sexual health swirls from her like meadow mist, she sparkles head to toe, her feet are shod in slippers of crystal with caracul liners. 'How do you manage to keep up ap – ?' We drown our presumptuous question murmurously in her corsage; her breasts billow, violet and gold, about our necktie.

The bankrupt man is elected to high civic office and declines, due to press of business. He can be seen on the streets, rushing everywhere, important-looking papers flying from his hands. He is being sued for astronomical amounts. He wears now only the trendiest clothes – unisex jumpsuits, detachable porcelain collars, coat sleeves that really unbutton. He goes to the same hairdresser as his wife. His children are all fat.

Why do we envy him, the bankrupt man? He has discovered something about America that we should have known all along. He has found the premise that has eluded us. At our interview, his answers are laconic, assured, delivered with a twinkle and well-spaced, conspiratorial, delicious lowerings of his fine baritone.

Q: When did you first know that you were bankrupt?
A: I think from birth I intuited I was headed that way. I didn't cry, like other infants.
Q: Do you see any possibility for yourself of ever being non-bankrupt?
A: The instant bankruptcy is declared, laws on the federal, state, and local levels work in harmony to erode the condition. Some assets are exempted, others are sheltered. In order to maintain bankruptcy, fresh investments must be undertaken, and opportunities seized as they arise. A sharp eye on economic indicators must be kept lest the whole package slip back into the black. Being bankrupt is not a lazy man's game.
Q: Have you any word of advice for those of us who are not bankrupt?
A [*with that twinkle*]: Eat your hearts out.

The interview is concluded. Other appointments press. He and his family must put in a splendid appearance at the Meter Readers' Benefit Picnic. They feed grapes to one another, laughing. The children tumble in the tall grass, in their private-school uniforms. The bankrupt man's wife is beginning to look fat, sunlight dappling her shoulders. Only he maintains a hard edge, a look of bronze. He wins the quoit toss and captains the winning tug-of-war team; the other side, all solvent small-business men in gray suits, falls into the ditch. Magnanimously, he holds down to them a huge helping hand. By acclamation, he is elected to the vestry of all the local Protestant churches and eats the first piece of the Meter Readers' Bicentennial Chocolate Layer Cake.

This galls us. We wish to destroy him, this clown of legerity, who bounces higher and higher off the net of laws that would enmesh us, who weightlessly spiders up the rigging to the dizzying spotlit tip of the tent-space and stands there in a glittering trapeze suit, all white, like the chalk-daubed clown who among the Australian aborigines moves in and out of the sacred ceremonial, mocking it. We spread ugly rumors, we mutter that he is not bankrupt at all, that he is as sound as the pound, as the dollar, that his bankruptcy is a sham. He hears of the rumor and in a note on one-hundred-percent-rag stationery, with embossed letterhead, he challenges us to meet him on West Main Street, by the corner of the Corn Exchange, under the iron statue of Cyrus Shenanigan, the great Civil War profiteer. We accept the challenge. We experience butterflies in the stomach. We go look at our face in the mirror. It is craven and shrivelled, embittered by ungenerous thoughts.

Comes the dawn. Without parked cars, West Main Street seems immensely wide. The bankrupt man's shoulders eclipse the sun. He takes his paces, turns, swiftly reaches down and pulls out the lining of both pants pockets. Verily, they are empty. We fumble at our own, and the rattle of silver is drowned in the triumphant roar of the witnessing mob. We would have been torn limb from limb had not the bankrupt man with characteristic magnanimity extended to us a protective embrace, redolent of cologne and smoking turf and wood violets.

In the locker room, we hear the bankrupt man singing. His baritone strips the tiles from the walls like cascading dominoes. He has just shot a minus sixty-seven, turning the old course record inside out.

He ascends because he transcends. He deals from the bottom of the deck. He builds castles in air. He makes America grow. His interests ramify. He is in close touch with Arabian oil. With Jamaican bauxite. With antarctic refrigeration. He creates employment for squads of lawyers. He gets on his motorcycle. He tugs a thousand creditors in his wake, taking them over horizons they had never dreamt of hitherto.

He proves there is an afterlife.

A. ALVAREZ

Risk

A. Alvarez was born in London in 1929, and is widely regarded as Britain's most influential post-war critic of new poetry. His anthology, The New Poetry *(1963), together with its combative Introduction, still stands as a key document in any account of the development of British verse since the mid-1950s. Alvarez has also published poetry and fiction and several non-literary prose works: on poker, on oil-rigs, on mountaineering, and – well, fair enough – on sleep. His essay 'Risk' was first published in* GQ *magazine in 1992.*

In my early thirties, after my first marriage broke up, I acquired a brief reputation as a wild man: I drove fast cars, played high stakes poker, and spent more time than I could decently afford off in the hills, climbing rocks with the boys. Admittedly, this reputation only applied in the London literary world, where the standards, by any stretch of the imagination, were not high. As far as the hard men on the climbing scene in the 1960s were concerned, I was a minor player. They accepted me because I was a good man to have second on the rope – strong and not prone to nervousness – and also perhaps, because most of them were fugitives from the square world of business, engineering, plumbing, medicine or teaching, and I worked in what they considered an odd, faintly exotic trade. When it came to piss-ups and really hard routes, I wasn't in their league. Even so, the Welsh hills and the Cornish sea-cliffs were the places I was happiest, and where, I felt, my real life was led. Writing was just a way of filling in time between weekends.

A happy second marriage changed all that. Yet even thirty years later, in my sixties, I still tried to get to the rocks any Sunday when the weather was halfway decent, although my stamina and flexibility were sharply diminished, and the cliffs I went to – a little sandstone outcrop called Harrison's Rocks, near Tunbridge Wells – would fit comfortably into the foyer of a modern skyscraper. And whenever I was deprived of my weekly fix by work or rain or my increasingly decrepit body, I suffered withdrawal symptoms: restlessness, irritability, a glum conviction that my week had been spoiled.

Climbing, I mean, is an addictive sport, although what it is that gets you hooked is by no means clear. Some people climb to get away – not 'Because it's there', but 'Because you're here', where 'you' is the job, the town, the wife, the kids, the dog. Others climb because they are turned on by the degree of physical and mental self-control needed to get up a difficult piece of rock in good style, with minimum effort and minimum fuss. The worst climb to prove something, to show they are tougher and stronger and more skilful than they might otherwise appear. The best climb simply for the fun of it, because they like the company, the hills, the curious on-off physical rhythm – blinding effort on the pitches, long period of goofing-off on the belays – and the general anarchy of the climbing world. Most of us probably climb for a mixture of all those reasons. But there is one thing we have in common – the thing, I suspect, that initially turned us on to the game and then kept us coming back to it – the adrenalin rush. Climbing is a risky pastime – if something goes wrong, you may get hurt – and risk produces adrenalin, and the adrenalin high is addictive.

I was sixteen, when I first went to the mountains in North Wales. The trip was organized by my school, and the master in charge was a gung-ho, old-style, spirit-of-the-hills freak – he had been a reserve on a pre-war Everest expedition – whose idea of fun in the hills was to see how fast we could slog up to the summit of Tryfan and back down to the Ogwen Valley. I loathed the boring, remorseless grind as much as I loathed him.

But one day he took us up a rock route on the Idwal Slabs. The hard bit – the crux – was a steep little wall, with what seemed like a good deal of empty air below it, and widely-spaced holds that looked far too small for my clumsy nailed boots. I studied it a long time, convinced that I was going to fall off. Then I strolled up it without any effort at all, as easily as if it had been flat. What I felt, as I pulled onto the ledge at the top, was a surge of pure elation and well-being, the kind of glow and happiness I suppose a drug-addict must get from a fix. I was hooked and all I wanted to do was repeat the experience. But the weather closed in, we went back to the mountain-bashing, and it was not until the end of my first year at Oxford, four years later, that I climbed again. After that, however, I didn't stop, although, as I gained experience, the situations that produced that lovely surge of elation became steadily more improbable.

The elation is heightened by the fact that climbing is a peculiarly uncluttered sport; it depends on the climber, not the equipment. When I began, all that was needed was a rope, boots, carabiners and a few nylon slings to hook around flakes of rock to protect you against a fall. Since then, the safety gear has improved enormously, and the modern hard men are festooned with gear when they hit the rocks: artificial chockstones – called 'nuts' and 'friends' – bags of chalk to improve their grip, and other arcane goodies – sticht plates, nut-keys, descendeurs. Some of them also dress up in glaring Lycra tights and snappy singlets that show off their muscles, although the prevailing style – in Britain, at least – is still government-surplus shabby. Yet no amount of flashy gear will get you up a climb, and the well-being you feel is intensely private and physical. No doubt, every athlete feels the same on his best days, but in climbing that style of contentment is attainable long after you pass your physical prime.

There is also the pleasure of the company you keep in the hills. Climbing, after all, is a maverick sport, and the people who do it consistently are interesting and rather private. Some lead very successful lives, because the kind of drive that will get you up a mountain will also stand you in good stead in a career. But there are many natural anarchists in the climbing world, who have chosen to grub along outside the system in order to be able to make their own timetables and not to answer to any boss. What all of them have in common – the employed and the unemployable – is a taste for black humour and a wicked eye for pretension. Climbing has its phoneys, but they don't have an easy time. It is also a curiously classless activity. What you do away from the rocks simply doesn't count. The group I climbed with regularly at Harrison's Rocks included a freelance computer programmer, a security guard, a municipal gardener, an odd-job man, a business tycoon and a schoolboy. The tycoon and I, being older and less competent than the others, were benignly tolerated.

In recent years, there has been a great leap forward in climbing standards. Routes that were once climbed by artificial means – by hammering pitons into cracks, and hanging *étriers*, miniature nylon ladders, from them – are now climbed free, by simple muscle-power.

This is the result of the introduction of indoor climbing walls, on which the young tigers train every day of the week, whatever the weather. These artificial walls have had much the same effect on climbing as the birth control pill had on sex-life in the 60s: they have made it possible to do what you like, when you like, without fear of the consequences. People who train regularly on climbing walls perform at such a high standard that there are now, in effect, two quite separate types of climbing – with training and without – and a whole category of very hard climbs – Extreme – with more subdivisions than all the old-style grades put together.

Yet the rewards are much the same, whatever standard you climb at. You get to wild, beautiful, lonely places, and the people you go with are mostly funny and irreverent and impervious to pretension. Climbing is also a physical activity of a special, rather intellectual kind. Each pitch is a series of specific local problems: which holds to use, and in which combinations, in order to climb it safely, and with the least expenditure of energy. Every move has to be worked out by a kind of physical strategy in terms of effort, balance and consequences. You have to think with your body, and think clearly, because if you get it wrong there is sometimes a risk of being hurt.

It was that aspect of climbing that I always found peculiarly satisfying – perhaps because I am a professional writer. Camus once remarked – he was talking about Nietzsche – that it is possible to live a life of wild adventure without ever leaving your desk. Maybe. But, most of the time, writing is a sedentary, middle-class occupation, like accountancy or psychoanalysis, though more lonely. For five or six days each week, I sit at my desk and try to get the sentences right. If I make a mistake, I can rewrite it the following day or the next, or catch it in proof. And if I fail to do so, who cares? Who even notices?

On a climb, my concentration is no less, but I am thinking with my body instead of with my addled head; and if I make a mistake, the consequences are immediate, obvious, embarrassing, and possibly painful. For a brief period and on a small scale, I have to be directly responsible for my actions, without evasions, without excuses. In the beautiful, silent, useless world of the mountains, you can achieve a certain clarity, even seriousness of a wayward kind. It seems to me worth a little risk.

*

That, at least, is how I used to justify my addiction to the sport. But maybe I was kidding myself. I realise that the elation I first experienced as a schoolboy on the Idwal Slabs was an adrenalin rush, the great surge of hormone that increases heart activity and muscular action, and generally prepares the body for 'fright, flight or fight'. What had produced it, I think, was not so much the physical effort as the exposure – the sensation of all that free air and empty space below the little wall. Instead of frightening me, the exposure turned me on. (If it doesn't turn you on you will never be a climber, no matter how physically adept you may be, because you will always secretly be scared.) But the real point was, when the elation came I recognised it; I had been there before.

Since then, I have thought a lot about that adrenalin high – I have also spent a good deal of effort recreating it, by one means or another – and I think I now know why it felt familiar. It brought back the first and more or less only memory I have of my early childhood. When I was about twelve months old, I had a major operation to remove a lymphatic growth from my left ankle. I remember nothing about the surgery, of course, but what I do remember, *vividly*, is re-learning to walk. *Re*-learning, because my first steps were presumably taken indoors and very young, whereas the scene I remember takes place at the King Henry's Road entrance to Primrose Hill. I assume I must be two or three years old. My nanny is kneeling a few yards away, beckoning. There is a dangerous stretch of gravel between her and me. 'Come on,' she says. 'There's a good boy.' I start forward unsteadily, half expecting her to move towards me. She doesn't, and I make it all the way on my own. Triumph and elation, the adrenalin rush. I now think I was learning a simple lesson: either I could be a cripple, dependent on other people to wheel me around, or I could become an active, upright, paid-up member of the human race. But in order to do so, I had to take risks.

I was ten the next time I got that high. It happened in the old Finchley Road swimming baths, which have since been demolished. Up until that time, swimming baths were forbidden territory for me. The doctors said the chlorine in the water was bad for the fragile skin on my still troublesome ankle. But then, the doctors said everything was bad for my ankle and, anyway this was 1940, the war was on, and there was no nanny to keep me in line. So when the school went swimming, I went along with them. I splashed around in the shallow end, learning how to swim, but all that really interested me was the high board at the far end of the pool. There was one man using it who knew what he was doing – swallow dives, somersaults, deadman's dives, back flips, the whole bag of tricks – and I couldn't take my eyes off him. It was the most graceful thing I had ever seen.

The school's swimming instructor was an ex-drill sergeant, small and muscle-bound, with tattooed arms. When I asked him to teach me how to dive, he told me to sit on the pool's edge, put my hands above my head and roll forwards, pushing myself off with my feet. I practised that manoeuvre until the hour was up. The next visit, a week later, he got me standing upright and diving off the edge. The instructor was a martinet and every time I surfaced he looked at me with distaste: 'Point your toes!' 'Don't look down, look up!' 'Keep your legs straight!' 'Point your bloody toes, I said!' The next week, I went up onto the high board. It was a fixed board, covered with coconut matting, and its front edge bent slightly downward. It seemed outrageously high as I stood there, trying to work up my courage. Gradually, the echoing voices disappeared and I felt as if I were cocooned in silence. I waved my arms vaguely in the way I'd been taught, tried to look up, not down, and launched myself into space. For a brief moment, I was flying. When I hit the water, I crumpled ignominiously, and my legs were all over the place. The instructor looked at me with contempt and shook his head. But even he could not diminish my elation. That's what they mean by 'free as a bird', I thought.

The London blitz began a couple of months later. For a ten-year-old child, to whom the idea of death is meaningless, the bombs falling nightly, the anti-aircraft guns pounding away on Primrose Hill, the smashed-up houses I explored with my friends and, above all, the brilliant aerial ballet acted out above our heads during the Battle of Britain were sources of endless excitement, not fear. My disorganised parents delayed sending me off to boarding school until 1943, long after the blitz was over. By that time, I was well and truly hooked on the adrenalin high. When I found rock-climbing, I was already an addict looking for a fix.

'Life is impoverished,' Freud wrote, 'it loses in interest, when the highest stake in the game of living, life itself, may not be risked.' Later, when my days as a wild man were over and I had begun to kick my adrenalin habit, risk came to mean different things. Character, for example. I once spent a night out on an overhanging cliff-face, during which it became more or less obvious to me that my companion and I were going to freeze to death. We had taken certain risks (we thought they were calculated; in fact, they were stupid), and then got caught in a snowstorm. When the snow stopped, the temperature plummeted, and there was nothing to do but sit it out on a minuscule ledge – each of us had one buttock on, one buttock off – and hope we would make it through to the morning.

Silence is one of the attractions of the mountains – a total silence you find only above the timber-line, where nothing moves but the wind. But not on this occasion. The lower six hundred feet of the route had been up a steadily overhanging wall; the last thousand feet followed a crack that was partly overhanging and never less than vertical. Because the rock on the summit had been warmer than that of the north face we were on, the snow had melted above and turned the crack into a waterfall. Our bivouac ledge was protected from it by an overhang and, although we tried to stay awake (body temperature drops when you sleep), we kept nodding off, lulled by the sound of falling water.

At some dead point of the night, I woke feeling something was wrong. 'What's up?' I said. To my surprise, I found I was whispering. We sat still, listening. But there was nothing to hear. Finally, my companion said, 'The waterfall's frozen.' He, too, was whispering. It occurred to me that that was how freezing to death would be – numb and sound-less. First the waterfall, then us. It was an idea I could have done without.

I suppose most people are worried about how they will behave under pressure. Certainly, I emerged from that night on the bare mountain with frost-bitten fingers and a greatly increased self-confidence. I no longer felt I had continually to justify myself, apologize and explain, I had learned that I was a survivor, that I didn't fall apart in a crisis, and that was a lesson that stood me in good stead later in other, very different risk situations: bad runs of cards at the poker table, bad runs of luck in my professional life.

At the time, however, the night out was just a part of being young, and being young meant being resilient and fit and lucky enough to get away with it. It also meant what Tom Wolfe called 'pushing the envelope'. When we got back to the hut the next morning, ravenous and swaying with exhaustion, we had reached the far, frayed ends of our tethers. But that, in itself, is something. To discover how much you can take, at what point you will or will not crack, is a useful piece of self-knowledge. Most young people want to test their limits – physically, intellectually, emotionally. Fighter pilot jocks do it one way, budding tycoons do it another, and artists do it another way still when they 'make it new'. It is a means of finding out what life has to offer or what kind of life you are capable of. It is a form of initiation rite. And the fact that it is sometimes deadly serious does not mean that it isn't also pleasurable.

On the contrary, it is the seriousness that makes it pleasurable. As every poker player knows, the best way to bring a dying game back to life is to raise the ante. Risk concentrates the mind, sharpens the senses and, in every way, makes life sweeter by putting it, however briefly, in doubt. The late Jack Straus, one of the world's greatest poker players and highest rollers – he once bet $100,000 on the outcome of a high school basketball game – was a pushover in what he considered 'small games', where the wins and losses were reckoned in four figures or thereabouts; but he was hard to beat in the big games. This was not because he was rich; his gambling habits away from the poker table and his casual generosity kept him permanently strapped. (He used to say, 'If they'd wanted you to hold on to money, they'd have made it with handles on.') It was because he wasn't interested: 'I wouldn't pay a ten-year old kid a dime an hour to sit in a low-stakes game and wait for the nuts,' he once told me. 'If there's no risk in losing, there's no high in winning. I have only a limited amount of time on this earth, and I want to live every second of it. That's why I'm willing to play anyone in the world for any amount. It doesn't matter who they are. Once they have a hundred or two thousand dollars' worth of chips in front of them, they all look the same to me. They look like dragons, and I want to slay them.' It was typical of Straus that, when he won the World Series of Poker, in 1982, he got less pleasure from the $520,000 prize money than from the fact that, on the first day, he had been down to his last $500, and had bluffed and outsmarted his way back from the dead. Like Hemingway, Straus's favourite proverb was, 'Better one day as a lion than a hundred years as a lamb.'

Risk activities – at the poker table, in the mountains, under the water, in the air, in caves – are all examples of what Jeremy Bentham called 'deep play'. And because Bentham was the father of utilitarianism, he profoundly disapproved of the concept. In deep play, he thought, the stakes are so high that it is irrational for anyone to engage in it at all, since the marginal utility of what you stand to win is grossly outweighed by the disutility of what you stand to lose. Straus, when he gambled, was willing to bet all he had – and no one can wager more than that. When my companion and I spent our cold night out, the gain was the dubious satisfaction of having climbed a difficult route in difficult conditions; what we stood to lose was our toes or our fingers or even our lives. Yet, however deep the play was, it was still play, and pleasure doesn't necessarily cease when things go wrong. On that occasion, I was particularly lucky because I was with Mo Anthoine, a brilliant climber and a marvellously funny, anarchic man, who seemed indestructible until brain cancer ambushed him a few years ago. While we perched on our ledge, waiting for the big chill, Mo behaved as if everything was perfectly normal. He kept the one-liners coming and the tone light. We swopped jokes, recited limericks, sang songs. In retrospect, it may have been the coldest night I have ever sat through, but I have spent far gloomier ones warm in bed with the wrong woman.

You burn out, of course, as you get older. I gave up diving early because my sinuses couldn't take it, sports cars went when the kids came, and, although I went on climbing until I was sixty-three, I made sure, latterly, that I was always on a top rope. I loved the exercise, but if I fell off the most I stood to lose was face. The poker games have got bigger, but you can blame that on inflation. I console myself with the thought that it was great while it lasted.

Not long ago, however, a friend took me flying in his old Tiger Moth biplane – a trim, elegant machine, with two open cockpits, one behind the other. To sit with your head in the open air, while the plane spins and rolls and loops and pirouettes, is the ultimate form of play. In every sense, it is a freedom from gravity – from the earth's heavy pull and from the responsibilities of everyday routine. Total freedom and also total happiness. Forget highboard diving, sports cars, poker, even climbing. None of them ever produced the pure rush of adrenalin – heart pounding, blood coursing sweetly through the veins – that I felt the first time I looped the loop in the Tiger Moth. At last, I truly understood what they meant by 'free as a bird'. Thank God, I thought, the bad old habits are still in place.

JONATHAN RABAN

Living on Capital

Jonathan Raban was born in Norfolk in 1942 and began his career as a literary academic. In the 1970s, with his Arabia Through the Looking Glass *(1979), he established a reputation as a highly original travel writer, a reputation consolidated – indeed, amplified – by later books, mostly set in America–* Old Glory *(1981) and* Hunting Mr Heartbreak *(1990) – or out at sea:* Coasting *(1986). Raban has published one novel,* Foreign Land *(1985), and a collection of essays,* For Love and Money *(1987), in which 'Living on Capital' appears. The essay was first published in 1977.*

I suppose that everyone is really the father of their own family. We make them up, these private sanctuaries, prisons and sunny utopias. Visiting other people's families, I've always found it hard to square what I've seen with the legend as it was told to me in the car on the way. The characters are always much bigger or smaller, nicer or nastier, than they ought to be. It's like seeing a play performed by a weekly rep working from the wrong text. One's own legend is doubly distrustable. One has all the ruthless impartiality of a critic writing up a show in which he has been both casting director and one of the stars. Legend it must be, not accountancy or gritty realism; and like all genesis myths, its garden, its rib and its fruit of the tree are symbols. When it comes to his own family, no one can afford to be a fundamentalist.

Once upon a time, before the idea of 'family' ever took hold, there was just my mother and I. We lived in a sweet cocoon, and it was much like having an idyllic extramarital affair. My father was away 'in the war': he was a photograph on the mantelpiece; he was the morning post; he was part of the one o'clock news on the wireless. He was not so much my father as the complaisant husband of the woman I lived with – and I dreaded his return. Meanwhile, we made hay while the sun shone. I had contracted a wasting disease called coeliac, and I was fed, like a privileged lover, on specially imported bananas and boiled brains. We learned to read together, so that I could spell out paragraphs from *The Times* before my third birthday. We stoved in the bottoms of eggshells, so that witches wouldn't be able to use them as boats. We saved up our petrol rations, and drove to my grandmother's house in Sheringham. My mother's Ford Eight, AUP 595, had been bought in 1939 with money she'd earned writing love stories for women's magazines, and it was the perfect vehicle for conducting a romance. Bowling along Norfolk lanes at a hair-raising thirty, with the windows down and the smell of pollen, leather and motor oil in my nose, I felt that this was the life. I meant to keep on as I had started; riding in the front seat with kisses and confessions, and the Ribena bottle conveniently near the top of the hamper.

I was a bag of bones. But I had already acquired the manner of a practised gigolo. My illness gave me the right to constant attention. With my forehead in my mother's hands, I was sick until my throat bled. When I wasn't being sick, I was being loquacious. Since my mother had only me to talk to, I'd picked up an impressive vocabulary which I was perpetually airing and adding to. Too weak to play with other children – whom I regarded from a distance as rough, untutored creatures – I looked to grown-ups for the concern and admiration that were clearly my due. I feared the mockery of the few children who were allowed ('No rough games, mind!') to enter my bone-china world. My one friend was the doctor's son, who'd been crippled with polio and went about in a steel frame that was almost as big as himself. When I was three, my mother told me that children like him and me would go on scholarships to nice schools, but that the village children would all go to knocky-down schools like the one up the road. I saw myself and my mother sailing out in my scholar ship, its sail filling with the offshore wind on the beach at Sheringham, its prow headed into a romantic sunset, away from the line of jeering, unkempt children on the shore.

I hadn't reckoned with my father. I had once made my mother cry, when I had enquired whether he was likely to be killed by Germans; and I was often puzzled by the depth of her engrossment when a new batch of letters arrived from North Africa, then Italy, then Palestine. Curiously, I have no memory at all of my father coming back on leave. He must have blended into the other occasional visitors – many of them in uniform – to our house. Was he the man who took us both out to lunch one Sunday at a Fakenham hotel, where I remember the stringy rhubarb and a fit of sickness in the lavatory? I'm not sure.

At any rate, he was a complete stranger when he turned up late one morning, carrying a khaki kitbag across Hempton Green – the moment at which family life began for me. My first impression of him was of an unprepossessing roughness. The photo on the mantelpiece showed a junior officer so boyish he looked too young to shave. My father's jowl was the colour and texture of emery paper. His demob suit, too, seemed to have been woven out of corn-stubble. When my mother and he embraced, right there in the open on the green, I was mortified. I studied the faded white lettering on his bag: Major J. P. C. P. Raban R. A. By what right did this tall soldier in his ill-fitting civilian suit horn in on our household? The question took me several years to even begin to answer.

My father must have been a bit shaken too. His spindly, solemn son can hardly have been the beamish three-year-old he might have looked forward to. He was obviously unused to children anyway, and had had no practice at dealing with precocious little invalids who cried when he spoke to them. He brought with him the affectedly hearty manners of the mess, and tried to make friends with me rather as he might have jollied along a particularly green subaltern. On the afternoon of his arrival, he carried me by my feet and suspended me over the water-butt in the back garden. As I hung, screaming, over this black soup of mosquito larvae, my mother rushed out of the house to my defence.

'Only a game,' said my father. 'We were just having a game.' But I knew otherwise. This terrifying Visigoth, fresh from the slaughter, had tried to murder me before we'd even reached teatime. I ran bleating to my mother, begging her to send this awful man back to the war where he so clearly belonged. My father's fears were also confirmed: unless something pretty firm in the way of paternal influence was applied here and now, I was going to turn out a first-rate milksop, an insufferable little wet.

My father's feelings about 'wets' may have been streaked with anxieties of his own. Before the war, he had been a shy young man who had scraped through School Certificate at a minor public school. From there he had gone to a teachers' training college, and had done a probationary year of teaching (at which he had not been a success) before enlisting in the Territorial Army. In the army, he blossomed. He was rapidly promoted. He got married. He found himself suddenly a figure of some considerable poise and authority. When the war ended, he had hoped to transfer to the Regular Army but had been discouraged from doing so. By the time we met, he was 27, already at the end of a career he had been able to shine at. He had, along with his forced officer-style jocularity, a kind of preternatural gravity; he had learned to carry his own manliness with the air of an acolyte bearing an incense-boat. My father in his twenties was a profoundly responsible young man who had grown up late and then too quickly. He was stiff, avuncular and harsh by turns. I think that he felt my namby-pamby nature obscurely threatened his own manhood, and he set about toughening me up.

I was frightened of him. I was afraid of his irritable, headachey silences; afraid of his sudden gusts of good humour; afraid of his inscrutable, untouchable air; and afraid, most of all, of his summary beatings, which were administered court-martial fashion in his study. A toy left overnight in the path of the car got me a spanking; so did being unable to remember whether I had said 'thank you' to my hostess after a four-year-old's birthday party. He introduced me to a new cold world of duties and punishments – a vastly complicated, unforgiving place in which the best one could hope for was to pass without comment. Perhaps my father had cause to believe that the world really was like this, and was simply doing his best to rescue me from the fool's paradise unwittingly created for me by my mother. I felt then that he was just jealous of my intimacy with her, and was taking his revenge.

For weeks after the war he hung about the house and garden. He clacked out letters to potential employers on my mother's old portable Olivetti. He practised golf swings. He rambled round and round the birdbath in his demob suit. He made gunnery calculations on his slide rule. I played gooseberry – a sullen child lurking in passageways, resentfully spying on my parents. I felt cuckolded, and showed it. When my father eventually found a job, as the local area secretary of TocH, his work took him out of the house most evenings: when he drove off to Wisbech and Peterborough and King's Lynn, I would try to seduce my mother back to the old days of our affair. We listened to *Dick Barton* on the wireless over cocoa, and then I would launch into an avalanche of bright talk, hoping to buy back her attention and distract her from the clock. I felt her joy at having my father home, and I think I did sense her distress at my conspicuous failure to share it. I also felt a twinge or two of shame at our snugness. From my father, I was beginning to learn that my behaviour was distinctly unmanly, and these cocoon-evenings were clouded with guilt. When my father said, as he did several times a week, 'You are going to have to learn to stand up for yourself, old boy,' I shrank from the idea but knew it to be unarguably right.

But my father and I grew grim with the responsibilities that had been placed on our shoulders. I think we both felt helpless. He had inherited a role in life which he could only conceive in the most old-fashioned terms: he had to become a Victorian husband and father, a pillar of the family, the heir to the fading Raban fortunes. I had inherited *him*. And we both chafed under the weight of these legacies, both of us too weak to carry them off with any style. He bullied me, and he in turn was bullied by the family dead. If I feared him, he had Furies of his own – the ancestors and elderly relations who had set him standards by which he could do nothing except fail.

My father was not an eldest son, nor was his father. It must have been just his seriousness, his air of being the sort of young man who could take responsibility, his obvious dutifulness towards his own father, that marked him out. Whatever it was, it seemed that every dotty uncle and crusty great aunt had named him as an executor of their wills. Whenever anyone in the family died, my father got busy with auctioneers and lawyers; and our house began to fill with heirlooms. Vans arrived with furniture and pictures and papers in tin boxes. Things went 'into store', then had to be brought out because it cost too much to keep them in the repository. We were swamped by my father's ancestors.

They looked down on us disapprovingly from every wall. In vast, bad, oxidized oil portraits, in pencil-and-wash sketches, in delicate miniatures, in silhouettes, they glared dyspeptically from their frames. There was the Recorder of Bombay. There was General Sir Edward. There was Cousin Emma at her writing desk. There were countless Indian Army colonels and mean-mouthed clerics. There were General Sir Edward's military honours mounted on velvet in a glass case. On top of the wireless stood the family coat of arms (a raven, a boar's head, some battlements and a motto that I don't remember). They were joyless, oppressive trophies. They represented a hundred-and-something years of dim middle-class slogging through the ranks of the army and the church. The faces of these ancestors were like their furniture – stolid, graceless but well-made in that provincial English fashion which equates worth with bulk. There was no fun in them, and only the barest modicum of intelligence. They looked like people who had found the going hard, but had come through by sticking to the principles that had been drummed into them at boarding school.

We revered them, these implacable household gods. We tiptoed around their hideous furniture: '*Don't* play on the games table; it's an *an*tique—'; we ate our fish fingers with their crested forks; we obediently tidied our own lives into the few humble corners that were left behind by the importunate family dead. My father bought books on genealogy (*How to Trace Your Family Tree* by L. G. Pine), and buried himself in index cards and the 1928 edition of *Burke's Landed Gentry*. Summer holidays turned into sustained bouts of ancestor-worship of a kind that might have been more appropriate to a pious Chinese than to an English middle-class family on its uppers. In a Bradford Jowett van (my mother's Ford had been sold, and I now rode second class, in the back) we trailed through Somerset, hunting for churchyards where remote cousins were supposed to have been buried. My father scraped the lichen off tombstones with a kitchen knife, while I looked for slow worms under fallen slates. On wet days, he took himself off to the record offices in Taunton and Exeter, where he ploughed through parish registers, checking births, marriages and deaths in eighteenth-century villages. 'We come', he said, 'from yeoman stock. Good yeoman stock.'

Then there were the living to visit. Most seemed to be elderly women living with a 'companion', and they stretched, like a row of hill forts, across southern England from Sussex to Devon. Each holiday, my father appeared to discover a new great aunt. Their houses were thatched, and smelled of must and dog. The ladies themselves were mannish, always up to something in the garden with a hoe and trug. The few men were immobilized, wrapped up in rugs, and talked in fluting falsetto voices. My grandfather, Harry Priaulx Raban (grown-ups called him 'HP'), had retired from his parish in Worcestershire to a Hampshire cottage where, on his good days, he used to celebrate an Anglo-Catholic mass of his own devising in a little room that he'd turned into an alfresco shrine. I sometimes acted as his server on these occasions, piping the responses to his piped versicles. A plain crucifix hung above the improvised altar, surrounded by framed photographs of Edwardian boys at Clifton College. At Prime and Compline and Communion, my grandfather paid homage to his own past in a way that had come to seem to me perfectly natural – for anyone in our family.

My father was barely thirty, yet we lived almost exclusively in the company of the old and the dead. Sometimes his old regimental friends would call, and there was a steady stream of youngish clergymen and colleagues from TocH; these contemporaries brought a boisterous, irresponsible air into the house, a hint of fun which seemed alien to it. Its proper visitors were aunts and elderly cousins – people who nodded at the portraits on the walls and left their sticks in the rack by the front door. In private with my mother, my father had a lightness I have not done justice to. He liked *Punch*, and told stories, and spent a lot of time in the garage tinkering with the car: there was a boyishness about him which was always being forcibly squashed. The lugubrious solemnity was practised as a duty. He behaved as if it was incumbent on him to appear older, stuffier, more deferential than he really was. The silly world of gaiety and feeling was my mother's province, and I think my father felt a stab of guilt every time he entered it. It was *not manly*, not quite worthy of a serious Raban. So he overcompensated, with a surfeit of aunts and ancestors, and made his amends by constructing a vast family tree which he kept rolled up in a cardboard tube. Each year, new lines appeared; forgotten cousins many times removed were resurrected; our yeoman stock inched steadily back through the Georges and into the reigns of Queen Anne and Charles II.

I was five, then six, when my younger brothers were born. These additions to the tree struck me as needless. With ancestors like ours, who needed children? But I had been cuckolded before, and had learned to live with infidelity. Our household was already bulging with family, and my brothers simply added to the clutter. Though my own status was eroded. My mother constantly mixed up our names, and the two leaking babies and I got rechristened, for convenience's sake, as 'the boys', a title that made me cringe with humiliation. I hated their swaddled plumpness, their milky smell, and felt that their babyhood somehow defeated what little progress I had made in the direction of manliness. Lined up with them on the back seat of the Bradford van, surrounded by their cardigans, their leggings, their bootees, their plastic chamber pots and teated bottles, I used to daydream myself into a state of haughty solitude. I acquired a habitual manner of grossly injured dignity.

If I have a single image of family life, it is of a meal table. There is a high chair in the picture, dirty bibs, spilt apple purée, food chaotically laid out in saucepans, a squeal, a smack, my father's suffering brow creased with migraine, my mother's harassed face ('Oh, *Blow!*'), and the line 'William's made a smell' spoken by my younger brother through his adenoids. And over all this, the ancestors glower from their frames and the crested silver mocks from the tabletop. It isn't just the noise, the mess, the intrusive intimacies; it is that hopeless collision between the idea of Family as expounded by my father and the facts of family as we lived them out. We had ideas that were far beyond our means.

At this time my father must have been earning about £600 a year. Like most other lower-middle-class households, we were overcrowded, we had to make do on a shoestring budget and we had neither the money, the time nor the space for the dignities and civilities that my father craved. 'We are', he reminded us, 'a family of *gentlemen*.' Was my teacher at school, I asked, a gentleman? No. A nice man, certainly, but not quite a gentleman. Was Mr Banham up the road a gentleman? No: Mr Banham was in trade. People in trade were not gentlemen: gentlemanliness, it was explained, had nothing to do with money; it was a matter of caste, taste and breeding – and we were gentlemen. This distinction caused me a great deal of anxiety. The few friends I made never turned out to be gentlemen. Some were 'almost'; most were 'not quite'. Their fathers were often much better paid than mine, their accents (to my ears) just as clear. My mother was always keen to stretch the point and allow all sorts and conditions of men into our privileged class; but my father was a stickler for accuracy and knew a parvenu when he saw one. Consequently I was ashamed of my friends, though my mother always welcomed them, at least into the garden if not into the house. They didn't have ancestors and family trees like ours, and I half-despised and half-envied them their undistinguished ordinariness. Once or twice I was unwise enough to let on that I was marked by a secret distinction invisible to the eye – and the consequences tended to support my parents' conviction that the state system of education was barbarous and fit only for young hooligans. I was, predictably (especially since I started to get asthma the moment I stopped having coeliac), a thoroughly unpopular child. At primary school, I started to keep a score of the number of days I had lasted without crying in the playground. It stayed at zero, and I gave it up. But I always believed that I was bullied because I was 'special'. That too happened to you because you were a gentleman.

There was another family on our horizon. Uncle Peter – my mother's brother – lived on the suburban outskirts of Birmingham, and we saw him twice or three times a year. I was his godson, and after I was seven or eight I was occasionally allowed to stay at his house. For me, he was pure legend. Balding, affable, blasé, he would drop in out of the blue in a Jaguar car, smelling of soap and aftershave. Like my mother, Uncle Peter had been brought up by my grandmother in Switzerland, in the last days of servants; but somehow he had managed to escape being a gentleman. He'd taken a degree in engineering at Birmingham University, and during the war had served in the RNVR. If Macmillan had wanted a symbol of postwar meritocratic affluence in the age of You've-Never-Had-It-So-Good, he might well have chosen Uncle Peter, with his car, his sailing boat, his first-in-the-road TV set and his centrally heated suburban villa. Uncle Peter had real class – with a flat a – but he was entirely innocent of the suffocating class snobbery which ruled our roost.

Staying at Uncle Peter's was like being admitted to Eden. There was no smell of guilt in the air, no piety to a lost past. Where we had ancestors, he had Peter Scott bird-paintings and framed photos of ocean racing yachts on his walls. Where we had shelves of family books (sermons, Baker's *Sport in Bengal*, *The Royal Kalendar*, first editions of Jane Austen, a Victorian *Encyclopedia Britannica*), Uncle Peter had copies of the *National Geographic* magazine, *Reader's Digest* condensed books and greenback Penguins. I had often been enchanted by the bright theatre of an illuminated department store window at dusk – the impossibly soft rugs, the virgin upholstery of the three-piece suite, the bottles and glasses set ready on gleaming coffee tables, the glow of steel standing lamps . . . a room designed for immaculate people without memories or consciences. The inside of Uncle Peter's house was like one of those windows come to life. It was my Brideshead. I was dazzled by its easy, expensive philistinism; dazzled, too, by my girl cousins with their bicycles and tennis rackets and the casual, bantering way in which they talked to their parents.

On Sunday morning, no one went to church. I half expected a thunderbolt to strike us down for our audacity, but in Uncle Peter's family church was for weddings, funerals, baptisms and Christmas. Instead, we sat out on the breakfast patio, sunbathing. Uncle Peter stretched himself out on a scarlet barcalounger, put on dark glasses, and settled into his *Sunday Express*. I was nearly delirious. I hadn't realized that it was possible to break so many taboos at once, and Uncle Peter was breaking them all without so much as a flicker of acknowledgement that he was doing anything out of the ordinary. I also felt ashamed. I was so much grubbier, more awkward, more screwed-up than these strange people with their Californian ease and negligent freedom; like any trespasser in Eden, I was always expecting to be given the boot.

Given his belief in stock and blood-lines, it would have been hard for my father to be too openly critical of Uncle Peter. My mother's family (doctors and Shetland crofters) was, of course, not quite up to Raban standards, but Uncle Peter was still definitely a gentleman. So my father limited himself to a few warning shots delivered from a safe distance. 'Don't suppose he gets more than 15 to the gallon out of *that car*.' 'Can't think what he must be paying for moorings for *that boat*.'

'He's always going abroad to conferences,' said my mother.

'One conference, dear. One conference that we actually *know* of.'

To me, he was spoken of as '*your* Uncle Peter', which gave me a certain pride of possession, as I happily took responsibility for the 3.8 Jag, the decanter of Scotch and *that boat*. At Christmas and on my birthday he sent postal orders, and I was briefly *nouveau riche*, happily about to squander the money on status symbols on my own account, like fixed-spool fishing reels and lacquered cork floats. 'You'd better put *that* in your post office savings. Hadn't you, old boy?' So Uncle Peter was laid up where neither moth nor rust corrupted. I loathed my savings-book. When, years later, I first heard the phrase 'The Protestant Ethic', I knew exactly what it meant: it was my father's lectures on the subject of my post-office savings account.

'It's all very well, old boy, your wanting to throw your money down the drain in inessentials now. But when it comes to the time, what are you going to do about the Big Things, eh? Now, that money you've got in the post office; that *grows*. Sixpence in the pound mounts up, you know. Suppose . . . suppose, in, say, three or four years you want a bicycle. Where do you imagine that bicycle is going to come from? I'm afraid, old boy, that bicycles do not grow on trees.'

But in Selly Oak I had ridden in the Jag, and skipped church on Sunday, and a splinter of doubt had lodged in my mind. There were, I now knew, places in the world where bicycles did grow on trees.

When it was announced ('Daddy has had a calling') that my father was going to seek ordination, I lay on the floor and howled with laughter. I can't remember why – it certainly wasn't in any spirit of satire. I think it may have been straightforward nervous hysteria in the face of the fact that my father was on such intimate terms with God. The question had been put to Him, and He had made His position clear. It all sounded a bit like having an interview with one's bank manager. But I was awed and proud. We were high Anglicans – so high that we could almost rub noses with the Romans. The priest, in his purple and gold vestments, was a figure of glorious authority. He was attended by boys swinging incense. He chanted services in plainsong. High in the pulpit, his surplice billowing round him, he exercised a mystique of a kind that, say, a politician could not hope to match. Had my father said that he was going to stand for parliament, I would have been impressed; when he said he was going to be a priest, I was awestruck. I grew intensely vain on the strength of his vocation. I was not only a gentleman; I was about to be the son of a priest. When bullied in the playground, I now thought of myself as a holy martyr, and my brows touched heaven. 'Daddy's vocation' had singled him out from the ruck of common men, just as I expected soon to be singled out myself. I waited for my calling, and pitied my persecutors. At night, I had vivid fantasies in which God and I were entwined in a passionate embrace. By day, I spent my time staring out of the classroom window in a fog of distraction. I was not a clever child. My distinction was a secret between myself, my ancestors and God.

My father was thirty-three – a year younger than I am now – when he became a theological student. For the first time in my life, I realized that he was not actually as old as he had always seemed. We took a rented house on the outskirts of Bognor, and my father bicycled the six miles between there and his college in Chichester, staying in the house only at weekends. He wore a college scarf and went about in cycle clips; he played for the college cricket team and swotted up his notes. Now that he was more often away from the family than inside it, he lost his irritable hauteur, and I began to lose my fear of him. On Saturday afternoons, my mother brought my brothers and me to support his team from the boundary, where we were the centre of a group of pious, hearty young men with the arms of their white sweaters tied round their necks. At college, I think my father must have recaptured some of the ease that he'd felt in his wartime regiment. Most of the other students were younger than him, and he was like an easygoing adjutant among subalterns. I sensed – again for the first time – that he was proud of his family, and we were proud of him.

For those two years we were 'living on capital' – an ominous phrase which meant, in effect, that my parents were blueing their post-office savings; and this hectic, once-in-a-lifetime gesture seemed to liberate and frighten them in equal parts. They went on a spree of economies, putting one gallon of petrol at a time in the car and buying everything in quantities so small that my mother appeared to be going shopping round the clock. They also hatched what was as far as I was concerned their greatest folly. They decided to scrape their last pennies together and send me to public school.

For once, I was happy at school. At Rose Green Primary I had made some friends (no gentlemen, but with my father now a student we were turning into daring bohemians). With private coaching, I muddled, a little improbably, through the eleven-plus, and had a place waiting for me at the grammar school in Chichester. But my parents were expecting to move house at least twice within the next three years, and at ten I had already attended four different schools (a dame, a prep and two primaries). That was the rational side. The irrational side was all to do with ancestors, gentility and manliness.

'Take this business of your asthma, old boy. It's all psychosomatic, you know. Psychosomatic. Know what psychosomatic means? In the head. It's all in the head. It means you bring it on yourself. Public school will clear that one up in no time.'

The brochure arrived. My father had been at King's in the 1930s, and we pored over the blotchy photos of rugger pitches and the cathedral green. My father showed a new, alarming levity; we were boys together

as he pitched into a slightly mad peroration about the joys of doing
'The Classics' and taught me the basic rules of rugger on the drawing
room carpet.

'Pass the ball behind you – like this. Always pass the ball behind,
never in front.'

His own fondest memory of King's had to do with being put into a
laundry basket and having his arm broken. Somehow as my father told
it it came out as pure pleasure. Every Sunday we checked over the
public school rugby results where they were listed in small print at the
back of the *Sunday Times*. When King's won, there was a celebratory
air around the breakfast table; when they lost we were downcast too.
My mother had some Cash's name-tapes made up: J. M. H. P. RABAN
SCHOOL HOUSE. In the evenings, she sewed them into piles of socks,
pants, shirts and towels, checking each item against the matron's printed
list.

When we made our annual trek from aunt to aunt, I basked in the
phrase, repeated like a litany, 'Ah – Jonathan's off to public school,
you know.' God, I was special. Suddenly elevated out of 'the boys', I
towered with distinction. I could barely speak to my old friends at Rose
Green – common little boys who played soccer and went on Sundays,
if they went at all, to nonconformist churches.

At my confirmation service, the Bishop of Chichester preached on a
text from Paul's Epistle to the Ephesians:

> I therefore, the prisoner of the Lord, beseech you
> that ye walk worthy of the vocation wherewith ye are called.

No one that year was walking more worthily than me. Already I was
nursing my own calling and talking regularly to God. I walked in
imaginary vestments, a halo of distinction faintly glowing round my
person.

As my father pointed out, sending me to public school was going to
mean sacrifices – enormous sacrifices. My mother was not going to be
able to buy clothes; my brothers would have to live in hand-me-downs;
with the price of tobacco as it was, my father was going to have to
think seriously about giving up his pipe. This did frighten me. Despite
the fact that I was living in an ever-inflating bubble of persecuted
egotism, it did break in on me that the probable result of all this sacrifice
was going to be that I was going to let everybody down. At nights, I

strained to see myself sprinting away from the scrum towards the touch-line to score the winning try for School House; but the picture would never quite come right. When my father talked about the famous 'house spirit', I was troubled by a stubborn image of myself skulking grubbily, shame-faced, on the fringe of things. I had always been the last to be picked for any side. Would public school really change that? I tried fervently to believe so but some germ of realism made me doubt it. Certainly I felt singled out for peculiar honours, but my vocation was for something priestly and solitary; it wasn't for team games. I was scared by the other children whom I now affected to despise – and the prospect of living in a whole houseful of my contemporaries was frightening. I was beginning to suspect that I had my limits, and my faith in miracles was shaky. But with General Sir Edward and his cronies on one side, and the hand-me-downs and shiny skirts on the other, I went off to King's, teased by the notion that it was I who was the sacrifice.

One memory of being miserable at boarding school is much like another – and none are quite believable. I went when I was eleven; I left when I was sixteen; and I spent an unhealthy proportion of that five years wishing that I was dead. The usual story. For the holidays, I came home to beat my puzzled younger brothers black and blue. I was their monitor; they were my fags. So I was able to share with my family some of the benefits of going to public school.

Our family life seemed full of anomalies and bad fits. There was the problem of my father's age – one moment he was boyish, the next testily patriarchal. There was the mismatch between our actual circumstances and our secret splendour. There was the constant conflict between the superior Victorian family to which we were supposed to belong and the squally muddle of our everyday life. We were short on education, short on money, short on manners; and the shorter we got, the taller grew our inward esteem. In the Anglican Church, and in the succession of clergy-houses that we moved to, we found a kind of objective correlative for our private family paradoxes.

In the 1950s, the Church of England had not changed all that much since George Herbert was a parish priest. It hadn't yet been hit by 'existential theology' or the decadent tomfoolery of the Charismatic Movement. It still stood firm on Parson's Freehold and the idea that the priest was third in line to the squire and the doctor. Even on urban housing estates, where churches were plonked down in the middle to be vandalized before they'd had a chance to be consecrated, the vicar was expected to behave as he would in an agricultural village. The Church was smiled on by the housing authorities presumably because it was felt that it might introduce a cheery, villagey note of 'community' into these godforsaken places. Put a beaming cleric in dog-collar and cassock in Churchill Crescent or Keynes Road, and you are halfway to creating another Tiddlepuddle Magna. In one sense, the clergyman was expressly hired to be an anomaly. Like our family, the Church had a grand past but was down on its luck. Like our family, it was succoured by a sense of its own inner virtue and stature in the face of utter indifference from 90 per cent of the rest of the world. Like my own, its public face was one of superior injured dignity.

My father was given the curacy of a council estate just outside Winchester, and we turned into a parsonage family. To begin with, the ancestors were moved into a council house, disdainfully slumming it in the cramped lounge-diner. They had probably known worse. Long-suffering, ox-like men, their schools, like mine, had prepared them for temporary quarters and outposts of Empire. The Weeke Estate was much like an Indian hill station, with hard rations, lousy architecture and nothing to speak of in the way of society. It was no accident that the one author whose works we possessed in their entirety, in the uniform Swastika edition, was Kipling.

The parsonage was an island. People came to it when they wanted *rites de passage* – to be baptized, married and buried. Or they were in distress: tramps with tall stories on the look-out for a soft touch; pregnant girls, dragged there by grave, ashamed parents; middle-aged women who cried easily; and lots of shadowy people, talking in low confessional voices beyond the closed door of my father's study. When they came to the house, their manners were formal; often they had put on best suits for the occasion. What is it that people want from a priest? Understanding, surely, but not ease or intimacy. Most of all, I suspect, they feel that only a priest can clothe a bitter private hurt or mess with the gravity and dignity that they would like it to deserve.

My father seemed cold and inhibited towards me as if he found our biological connection an embarrassment. But to his parishioners he was able to show a sympathy, even a warmth, that perhaps depended on the formal distance which lay between him and them. In mufti, he was often stiff and blundering. In the uniform of his cassock and his office, he was gentle and considerate. The very things that might have marked him as a misfit outside the priesthood enabled him to be a good priest. I've known a number of people who have told me how much they have admired him, been grateful to him, and thought of him as a consummately good man.

At that time, though, for me he was pure Jekyll and Hyde. I thought of him as a hypocritical actor. Offstage, he seemed to be perpetually irritable, perpetually swallowing aspirins, never to be disturbed. His study – a chaos of papers under a blue pall of St Bruno Rough Cut tobacco smoke – was a place I was summoned to, for a long series of awkward, sometimes tearful, occasionally violent interviews. Once I tried to knock him down, and in my memory he collapses in an amazed heap among the parish magazines, narrowly avoiding cracking his skull on the duplicating machine. But that is probably an Oedipal fantasy. What really happened, I'm afraid, is that the amazement was on my face, and that the collapse too was mine – into weeping apologies. Usually, though, these confrontations followed a pattern as cold and stereotyped as a chess gambit. I stood; my father sat, shuffling papers, filling his pipe. While he stared beyond me out of the window, he would talk with tired logic about my misdemeanours (terrible school reports, insolence, laziness in the house, rumours of girls). The final line was always the same.

'I'm afraid that the trouble with you ... old boy ... is that you appear to have no thought for anyone except yourself.'

Long, long pause. Sound of pipe dottle bubbling in a stem. A faint groan from my father. A muttered monosyllable from me.

'What did you say?'

'Sorry.'

'Sorry – *what*?'

'Sorry ... *Daddy*.'

Another pause, while my father gazes sadly out over a landscape of sandpiles, stray dogs and upturned tricycles.

'I do wish you'd make *some* sort of an effort.'

I did see his point. The sacrifices that were being made on my behalf were all too visible. My father's clothes had been worn to a bluebottle sheen. His shoes gaped. And I was at public school. Worse, I knew that

I was wrong, perhaps even evil, when I accused him of hypocrisy. Here he was, wearing himself through on my behalf, and driving himself to nervous exhaustion in the parish; what right had I to ask even more of a man who was clearly two-thirds of the way to being a living saint? It was further evidence – as if I needed any more – of my own selfishness. With the help of a Penguin book on psychology I diagnosed myself as a psychopath.

The parsonage became a refuge for a number of people who, as social casualties go, were the walking wounded. Most had been left stranded – as we had – in the wrong age or the wrong class. Schoolmistresses, social workers, district nurses, they attached themselves to the fringe of the family, dropping in unannounced with small presents and staying on into the night talking with my father. The closest, most persistent ones were made honorary aunts, and they liked to busy themselves in the house, clucking over my brothers, 'helping' my mother, and making strained conversation with me, until my father, his cassock flapping round his heels, came home from his rounds.

'Hello, dear!' Having spotted the parked Morris Minors round the corner, he had the cheeriness of someone walking through the French windows in a drawing-room comedy. He always discovered the lurking aunts with delighted surprise. 'Ah, Elspeth!' And Miss Stockbridge, or Miss Winnall, or Miss Crawley, glandularly mountainous in tweeds, would produce a tiny, astonished little Bo-Beep voice – 'Oh, hel*lo*, Peter!' – as if their meeting was a stroke of wild coincidence. From my room upstairs, I would hear my father's 'Hmmn . . . hmmn . . . yes . . . yes . . . yes . . . *Oh*, dear. Ah. ha-ha,' while the high, put-upon frequency of the adoptive aunt was lost to all except my father and the neighbourhood dogs.

Much later, when they'd gone, I'd hear my mother's voice. 'Oh, poor old Elspeth – the *poor* soul!' And my father would answer, 'I'm afraid the trouble with *that* one . . .'

The social worker's dealings with his client do have some formal limits. But with a clergyman, nothing is out of bounds. People came to my father for reassurances of a kind no doctor or psychiatrist could offer. This meant that everyone who arrived at the parsonage – even those who came in the guise of my parents' friends – presented themselves as crocks and casualties. The ones who came and came again had things wrong with them that were far too vague to ever cure. They were spiritual things – weaknesses and discontents for which the doctrine of the Resurrection was the only answer. My father had put himself in the position of Miss Lonelyhearts, but he had more pride and less saving cynicism than the columnist in Nathanael West's novel; and his view of this world to which he'd opened our door was one of compassionate condescension.

'We in the parsonage . . .' 'In the parsonage family . . .' 'As a son of the parsonage . . .' My father's lectures nearly always started out with one or other of these riders. We were expected to be exemplary. Our standards of moral and social decorum – unlike those of the natives among whom we'd been posted – were supposed to be beyond either criticism or pity. Another favourite was 'More people know Tom Fool than Tom Fool knows', and I went about the council estate aware that it was full of spies behind curtains. One slip from me, and my father's standing in his parish could come a cropper. On the estate as on the rugger field, I was always letting our side down. At twelve and thirteen, up to no particular good with boys of my own age from the youth club, I sometimes came face to face with my father on his rounds, and pretended not to see him. He misinterpreted these gestures, and thought I was trying to 'cut' him. I wasn't. I was simply ashamed to be caught fraternizing with the children of his problem families – boys who, as he pointed out, had not had my advantages, and whose obvious shortcomings deserved compassion, not uncritical collusion.

On the far fringes of the parish, where the houses stood back from the road behind trees and rhododendrons, the gentry lived. Like the ancestors, they were retired colonels and commanders, admirals and generals. Their children went to boarding schools. Their houses smelled of flowers, dry sherry and wax polish. They weren't problem families; and we visited them shyly when bidden, like poor cousins, trying as best we could to tiptoe through their loud gravel. It usually took fifteen minutes for me to find myself out on the back lawn with their daughter, where we would both stand awkwardly scuffing our heels and smiling fiendishly.

'Do you play tennis?'

'No.'

'Oh what a pity. When Henry's here, we play a lot of tennis. But Henry's at Dartmouth, you know.'

'Oh, dear.'

'Mummy said she thought you might play tennis.'

'I'm sorry.'

'Oh – not to worry!'

Desperation. With an hour to kill, we would inspect abandoned tree-houses like a pair of undertakers visiting a cemetery on their day off.

'I say, you didn't hear a bell, did you?'

'I don't think so.'

'I could have sworn . . . I suppose Mrs Hawkins must be late with tea. Awfully boring for you, I'm afraid.'

'Oh, no! No, no, no!'

'Are you in YF?'

'Er . . . I don't think so.'

'Ah, there's the bell. Good-oh.'

Then, quite suddenly in the middle of the 1950s, a lot of bells began to ring. The first one I remember hearing was Frankie Lymon singing 'I'm not a juvenile delinquent', which went to the top of the hit parade sometime in 1955, I think. Bill Haley and his Comets made their first British tour, and in Worcester, where I was at school, there was hardly a seat left intact after *Rock Around The Clock* was shown at the Gaumont. I read *Look Back In Anger*, Joyce's *Portrait of the Artist*, and Anouilh's *Antigone*, and somehow managed to muddle them together into a single work of which I was the hero. There was the Chris Barber band and the Beaulieu Jazz Festival. There was CND, which for me meant the triumphant end of the CCF. All at once it was possible to think of oneself as a member of a generation and not as a member of a family; and the generation provided me with new standards that were even more liberated than Uncle Peter's. It seemed that over-night my minuses had all changed to pluses. The generation loathed my ancestors even more than I did; it despised team games; its heroes were sulky, sickly solitaries like Juliette Greco in her death-mask phase. At sixteen, I discovered that the inchoate mess of my relations with my father had been all the time, unknown to me, a key battle in the coming revolution. And I was on the winning side. It was like having my dream of scoring the winning try in the house match come true. We continued to have rows – about my wearing a CND badge at family meals, about bringing *that* rag into *this* house (the *New Statesman* into the vicarage), about girls ('Not really the kind of girl you'd wish to introduce to Mummy, is she?'), about the width of my trouser-bottoms (18 was permissible, but 16 was 'teddy boy'). But I too now wore an expression of distant superiority through these wrangles. An outsider looking in might have seen us as a pair of quarrelling mirror-images – two glazed faces speaking in the accents of the same old school.

I was much too absorbed in the enthralling process of my own adolescence to notice that bells had begun to ring for my father too. Something happened. Perhaps it came about on his parish rounds, as he found himself drawn in to the tangle of other people's lives, unable, finally, to maintain his distance. Perhaps it had to do with the difficulties he found himself in when he skirmished with the local worthies who regarded the church as an extension of their own drawing rooms. Perhaps he just strayed one day from under the oppressive shadow of the family past and found the air clearer and the going easier. At any rate, he changed. The first thing to go was his Anglo-Catholicism, which he dropped in favour of a kind of basic, ecumenical Christianity. Sometime in the 1960s, he slipped out of his ancestral family toryism and became a Labour voter. He exchanged his living in a Hampshire village for a vast parish of tower blocks in Southampton. His passion for ancestor-hunting turned into a scholarly interest in social history. On holiday one year, he grew a beard. It was as if a row of buttons on a tight waistcoat had suddenly given way.

I have written about him as if he was dead – the Oedipal fantasy again. But when we see each other now, I find it hard to detect more than shadows of the man I remember as my father. The ancestors are still hanging on the walls of his vicarage, but they have the air of inherited lumber now, and have lost their power to hex. We talk easily. We both think of ourselves as victims of our upbringing – and beneficiaries of it too. The solitariness of his priesthood and my writing is a shared legacy: we have each had to learn how to be alone in society in the practice of our odd, anomalous crafts. A little more than ten years ago, we both suddenly realized that we were chips off the same family block – and I think that the discovery surprised him as much as it did me. When I showed my father this piece in galley proof, he said: 'What you've written here is really a confession on my behalf.'

It is certainly a confession on mine. Looking at the other man, it occurs to me that he may have been a wilful invention of my own. Did

I conceive him on the green when I was three as a jealous, defensive fiction? And did I let this fiction die only when I was old enough to leave the family and do without a father to be afraid of?

Perhaps. I don't know. 'There's some *slight* exaggeration – I hope,' my father said, handing me back my galley sheets. I'm afraid so.

KARL MILLER

Are You Distraining Me?

Karl Miller, born in 1931, is probably best known as an influential editor. Over the years, he has served with high distinction as literary editor of The Spectator *and the* New Statesman, *as editor of the* Listener *and as founder/editor of the* London Review of Books. *From 1974 to 1992 he was Lord Northcliffe Professor of Modern English Literature at University College London. His books include* Cockburn's Millennium *(1975),* Authors *(1989), and two volumes of autobiographical memoir,* Rebecca's Vest *(1993) and* Dark Horses *(1998). His essay, 'Are You Distraining Me?', first appeared in 1976 and its preoccupation with dual personality was developed in Miller's much-praised 1985 book,* Doubles.

The jazz musician Sandy Brown died in 1975. I was a friend of his for many years, but I never knew that he was half-Hindu, or that there were two of him, in the persons of Sandy Brown and Alistair Babb. These persons he identifies and names in an autobiography which is due to be published, and I had to wait until I read that work before I made the discoveries I'm referring to. I want to show that they are substantially the same discovery. It is an interesting discovery, to my mind, and I hope it will become clear why I also say that it will remain an interesting discovery even if some of his statements are discovered to be a put-on on Sandy's part, and fictional.

We both went to the Royal High School of Edinburgh, he being slightly older and already a notorious Mephistophelean playground presence before I got to the Temple of Theseus. Built in the 1820s as a further monument lavished on the city's Classical New Town, the school was a copy of the Athenian edifice of that name. It has recently, and disgracefully, been stripped of the schoolboys for whom it was built, and is soon to house the unSandyish devolved deliberations of the Scottish Assembly. Its glooms, colonnades and fine proportions were not inhospitable: an impressive building, but pre-Victorian in the sense that it was scaled to accommodate human behaviour rather than to overwhelm or sneer at it. Ankle-breaking steep staircases – not very accommodating, I admit – seemed to descend into a nineteenth century where martinet Classics masters equipped their students to be public-spirited Scottish Whigs and to fight for and draft the Reform Bill. In the classrooms were roaring fires, large enough for suttee or the stake. I remember the hearth of Room Three, with one boy inadvertently toasting a standing penis which had slipped out of his shorts in the heat of the moment – as if to poke the past, or salute the embers and old flames of the Athens of the North.

The boys wore elegant black jackets and caps, which displayed the school badge, a white castle, and a motto on a scroll: *Musis respublica floret*. A civic place, the High School, now civically betrayed. But Sandy would have nothing to do with these sables and insignia. He wore what I remember as a yellow bow-tie, and what he remembered as a brown velvet bow-tie: whatever it was, it hung out, and fell about, in a very mocking way. He was bald, and bold, and bad. And he was a jazz musician. At the Royal High, 'musical' was a word which described those who belonged to the choir and orchestra, which performed to applause in spotless white on the platforms of concert halls, and were drilled and fretted over by a red-haired elderly Englishman (the name, Mellalieu, was euphony itself, and comprised, he said, all the vowels used in vocal music). In that world, Sandy was an outcast, and on occasion an outlaw – as he had already recognized himself to be in the world of Willowbrae Avenue, the district where he lived with his mother. Sandy was late for school, comical, hostile, friendly, formidable. I was a swot, less late for school, and we could not be pally. But I was keenly conscious of him, and would watch him, and perhaps I had already glimpsed that it was Sandy, rather than the swots and concert artistes, who was in touch with the muses. And in the playground there were others like him in that respect. The Royal High helped to make the British jazz of the forties and fifties the best in Europe, and yet at the school itself it was an extra-curricular activity – rated low and dirty by the authorities. Education is a wonderful thing.

For a number of years after we left school we met only once or twice, in the thick of jazz-band balls, where I was a fish out of water and he was Moby Dick, blowing his clarinet. Then, in London, we became pals. For some six years I edited the *Listener*, and he used to write about jazz in that journal, leading, meanwhile, two lives – that of a jazz musician and that of an acoustician-architect. In the second capacity he worked as a BBC employee, before quitting to start his own firm, and as a BBC employee he may be said to have found his only rival for awkwardness and intransigence in the straight musician Hans Keller. His jazz pieces would often tax the Corporation with a failure to take jazz seriously and treat it decently, and with a policy which led to the destruction of important tapes. His pieces were full of character and invention: full, too, of knots and congestions, and not the easiest copy in the world to edit. But they bore the stamp of the talent, style and wit which never failed him, and of that excellent pride of his. It was very like him to answer as he did when he was asked, in a BBC Television interview recorded in his last days, whether he'd prefer to be, if he had to choose, an architect or the world's best jazz clarinettist. Sandy said: 'You must excuse my arrogance, but do you really suppose that I'm not?' His pieces were the pieces of the man who made that reply.

An outsider might wonder whether the combativeness of his articles, the insistent claims made on behalf of the musicians he felt closest to, were affected by the resentments of a jazz musician whose standing, and hearing, had been attacked by the explosive arrival, in the sixties, of pop music and the groups – of all that jazz which was not his jazz. This gave him trouble, but did not make him bitter, though the acoustician in him counted the decibels of the new sounds, and the cost in eardrums. I'm sure he never doubted that his own music had kept its virtue. There were later times when an evening of that music among his friends was like a gathering of brave spirits, a blessed remnant, surrounded by their fit audience though few. But they came to play, not to complain or commiserate, and I did not notice any of the rancour which you get with writers who feel cheated of celebrity.

I was curious to read his posthumous autobiography, and I think it a remarkable document, a convincing picture of an artist's life, of the pleasures and pains, fantasies and phantasmagorias, which the practice of an art brings with it, and on which it ensues. I also discovered that the autobiography had a special interest for me, and it may be worth explaining what that interest is.

Not long ago I published a book called *Cockburn's Millennium*. The Cockburn in question was an Edinburgh man, and a High School man, and the book is an account of his life and times. Henry Cockburn was a Whig historian and lawyer who helped to draft the Scottish Reform Bill of 1832, and who wrote beautiful autobiographies, of which his *Memorials* is the best-known. In the course of the book I discussed the theme of double identity as it is manifested in the Gothic or Romantic literature which appeared in Britain, Germany and elsewhere during Cockburn's lifetime. Scotsmen have been thought to have been more than usually exercised by the theme, and have been responsible for some of the most compelling treatments of the theme, such as Hogg's *Confessions of a Justified Sinner* and Stevenson's *The Strange Case of Dr Jekyll and Mr Hyde*. I didn't want it to be supposed that Cockburn was some kind of split personality or Gothic personage, or a subscriber to the Gothic account of human nature, which increasingly insisted on its essential duality. But he could employ the Gothic vocabulary of duality, and could do so in order to describe his own behaviour. Furthermore, his tastes were both classical and romantic, as became the inhabitant of a town that was two towns, offering the rival attractions of a surviving medieval enclave and a Neoclassical utopia. He was in certain respects a divided man, whose divisions could appear to re-enact, and also to precede, the quarrel with his father over politics which took place in his youth.

It struck me as reasonable, therefore, to ask whether he might have been influenced by whatever compulsions of the period gave rise to the distinctive Scottish preoccupation with double lives and second selves. These possibilities were studied with frequent reference to hitherto unpublished writings by Cockburn which were included in the book – above all, the poems which he wrote in private. Critics who suggested that he had been wickedly Gothicized, and who suggested, in effect, that the standing interpretation of his career as that of a hard-headed Whig lawyer who relaxed by writing classical commentaries and civic gossip needed to be reaffirmed, were inclined to ignore the manuscript writings, together with the sensitivity to new outlooks, and the evidence of divided loyalties, which these and other writings of his embody.

It was an effort to get the arguments and affinities satisfactorily sorted out. I wanted to present a picture of Cockburn's experience which would make him look like a human being, and which would keep its distance from the sensationalism of the early, and the latterday, Gothic literary modes: I didn't want him looking like some precursor of that tribe of gentlemen, real and imaginary, who stole through the twilights of the Victorian Babylon, and who were conceived of in terms of their shameful secrets, and of their willingness to confess such secrets.

For every person who is excited by the talk of double and divided selves which has never ceased since Cockburn's time, there are two who will hard-headedly assert that such things are just a fashion or fad, a convenient high-flown way for writers to talk about certain of the ordinary human difficulties and recourses – to talk, for instance, about role-playing and hypocrisy. Scholarship knows for a fact that doubles are a dream. While I was writing the book, I used to wonder what it might be like to feel divided, to feel that it wasn't nonsense to say that you had more than one self. John Stonehouse has claimed that an established personality was supplanted by another, and in Gothic style, in order to lead a new life, he pretended that he had died. But then many might be suspicious of these claims. I had known what it was to experience contradictory desires, but the self I was conscious of – for all that I could be conscious of it – had always appeared the same: without imagining that I was ever likely to be mistaken for James Callaghan, I had always felt myself sole and undivided – *e pluribus unum*, like the United States of America. And yet it seemed conceivable that you didn't have to be subject to chemically-induced hallucinations, or clinically mad, in order to be beside yourself, in order to consign part of your pleasures and ambitions to a separate self which could be experienced as something other than a hypothesis, as something other than romantic hyperbole.

In the course of the book, a scheme was worked out for the attitudes and compulsions which might have helped to shape the response to the idea of duality during Cockburn's lifetime. The scheme laid stress on repressive religion and authoritarian parenthood; on rebellious conduct in relation to family codes, and to the customs of the country as these were enjoined within the family; on the doubting, double or contradictory character which such conduct could assume; on the interest in orphans which is evident in the literature of the first half of the nineteenth century, and on the role of the self-constituted orphan which certain mutineers could adopt. The role of the self-constituted orphan could be enacted by a second self, and could therefore form part of a 'double life' (I am using this last expression in a sense broader than the one which is now colloquial, and which makes it mean very little more than 'delinquency'). The recourse to fantasies of duality and bereavement could sometimes seem to be related to a son's quarrel with his father, and could also seem to include elements of the Oedipal experience predicated by Freud.

By these and other features of the scheme I was worried at the time. But I feel less bashful about them now, and I am bound to say that Sandy's memoir has enabled me to take heart. Here is a man who was both a real and imaginary orphan. Here is a double life, confessed – as has rarely happened – in terms of autobiography rather than fiction. Here, we might hope, are duality's very words.

Confessions, fantasies and affectations of duality are largely restricted to the literature of the subject. But the literature of the subject may well have promoted a disposition to feel split, to affect to feel split, and to behave in Gothic ways. It may well have encouraged Mr Stonehouse to inform the House of Commons, on 21 October last year, that a 'parallel personality took over, separate and apart from the original man'. And it may equally well have encouraged the psychiatrist referred to in that statement to instruct Stonehouse to use this language, to speak of his 'psychiatric suicide'. The arrival of this parallel personality, we are to think, caused him to simulate a drowning in Miami, and to disappear. While writing the book, I had classed this as a Gothic act: then, late in the day, I came across a manuscript letter of Cockburn's in which an Edinburgh youth, oppressed by the feats expected of him at the school Cockburn helped to found, Edinburgh Academy, feigned a drowning in the Danube, and disappeared. Seized by 'a sudden Germanizing of the noddle', supposed Cockburn. Was Stonehouse's noddle Germanized at any point? Whether or not he was ever impressed by a reading of E. T. A. Hoffman, Hogg, Stevenson and company, it is hard to suppose him unaffected by the impact of the Gothic tradition, by the correspondence between its doctrine of duality and the ordinary understanding of tensions and dilemmas which appear to have persisted in the society, and by the translation of that doctrine into the doctrines of some of our current psychologies. And I believe that the same could be said of Sandy Brown, alias Alistair Babb.

Stonehouse's 'Confessions', entitled *Death of an Idealist*, are by no means forthcoming about this aspect of the affair, among others. The book has in common with the overcharged public record of his breakdown that it does not allow one to guess how far he has controlled, and how far he has been controlled by, his impersonations and performances. As I write, he is in court facing criminal charges, and the prosecuting counsel has been speaking in such a way as to persuade people that the psychiatric explanation of his pretended drowning, the talk about a new self or leaf, was really an alibi of a kind for the conduct he is charged with. I doubt whether the question of his sincerity will be settled by the verdict of the court, any more than it was settled by his autobiography. Literature has pronounced, and we needn't flatly disbelieve, that indictable offences are highly compatible with some kind of first-hand experience of duality, while also being compatible, of course, with elaborate excuses. And if we do decide that Stonehouse's account is fictional, it would be as well to remember that fiction can be interesting and instructive.

Death of an Idealist is very much a politicians' book, as we can see when, during his troubles, Stonehouse feels the truth of the saying: 'I can deal with my enemies but heaven save me from my friends.' Cockburn once wrote: 'Enemies are easily managed, but wrong-headed friends are the very devil.' This statement is linked, in the book, to the quarrel with his kindred, but it is also the kind of thing that politicians say, and think. As well as idealists. It is worth adding that those who share an interest in duality – or an involvement in politics – need not be very like one another, any more than duality has to lead to larceny. Cockburn's 'wrong-headed friends are the very devil' is like a précis of those Gothic tales where such friends were a way of talking about someone's capacity to prove his own worst enemy, in the days when heaven and hell were thought to care about plights of that sort. Cockburn has accidentally described what happens in Hogg's *Confessions*.

I don't remember whether Sandy ever spoke to me about the nineteenth-century fictions of duality, but he needn't have read them in order to have been aware that double lives of one kind or another were especially Scottish. He was once friendly, in a special sort of way, with the Scotsman who is duality's leading authority in the modern world, and who is known for his polemical concern with the self-protective powers which duality can bring to bear in relation to the family and with the sufferings to which it may be a response: this is R. D. Laing. How far Sandy's autobiography derives from an influential literature, how far it copies the fictions it may be thought to corroborate, is unclear. But it is likely that it owes something to Laing, who owes something to Scotland. At any rate, it is plain from the autobiography that an intelligent and in some respects hard-headed man could feel himself to be double – to the extent of enlisting the old confessional metaphor of the second self in order to evoke his experience and account for it. In order to make sense of what had become of him, lying in a hospital bed at the end of his days, with, perhaps, a consequent freedom to pick and choose his metaphors, he chose to be someone with two selves at least, the second of which, roughly speaking, was an orphan.

These memoirs of his could not readily be broken down to form an item in the *Dictionary of National Biography*. A few early episodes are dwelt on to the complete exclusion of a very great deal. It is as if they were the matrix from which issued almost everything of importance that he ever was, though this would have to be called a false impression: the memoirs are family-free, for instance, as far as his wife and children are concerned, which was certainly not true of his life. They open with a meditation on colours which have obsessed him, and this serves to introduce a strain of phantasmagoria. For the purposes of his autobiography, family is parents. His upbringing in India is sketched: there are words about a father – of whom Sandy may have been very much the son – who cuts himself off from the Raj by marrying a woman who was coloured. As the offspring of a mixed marriage; Sandy suffers an ostracism and orphaning of his own. Then he is bereaved by his father's death, which shook and distressed him, launching, amid his fantasies, like a ship of death, the yellow submarine of a coffin. Masturbation and girls put those fantasies to brisk work. He breaks a leg, and evokes operations at the Edinburgh Royal Infirmary (the odysseys of those born in that city will often be a royal road).

The operations are traumatic, conveying the sense of an agony of birth mingled with one of bereavement. The acid, threatening colours of before recur as the colours of birth, the brightest imaginable, with the wave-machine at Portobello Pool delivering an additional element of threat. Out of all this travail – born, bereaved, cast out and of doubtful caste, operated on, threatened, sobbing, ejaculating – emerges an orphan lad, a fellow who is two fellows, as Stevenson expressed it: Alistair Babb and Sandy Brown, his real name scarcely less apt than his pseudonym. If the first of these two fellows, whose name is Americanized at times as Al Babb, took that name from the well-known oriental Ali Baba, this might indicate that the early sufferings gave birth to the clarinettist whose career another self went on to manage. But I'd prefer to be tentative about the principle which governed the separation of his two selves, which governed his self-administered Siamesing (Cockburn's word, and Stonehouse's), and about the 'ligature' which bound these selves together. This strange operation, in which the Royal Infirmary played its involuntary part, cannot be said to be carefully explained in Sandy's Memorials, though it is made to seem vividly authentic. The invented name, incidentally, may allude, not only to Ali Baba, but to the word 'alibi'.

Those people who knew Sandy-Alistair might object that he wasn't *like* an orphan: no one could have been less plaintive. I agree. The orphan was, as it were, internal, historical. He was not like any Victorian orphan of the storm, on the wrong side of the window-pane in his nightie, while the thunder pealed loud and long. In point of appearance, he was not unlike some fierce sailor – say, Captain Haddock of the Tintin books. In point of style, a style in which that broken leg had not been forgotten, he was much more like a Captain Hook than a Peter Pan, as much Captain Ahab as the white whale. Or, to return to the *dramatis personae* of Gothic duality, he was more of a princely tempter than any of the outcasts tempted by such princes, though he was occasionally tempted and occasionally fell.

It was like him to tempt me to give up playing football, on grounds of old age: he told me at lunch, over the escalope Milanese, that when he'd come to watch me play, as he'd stealthily done the previous weekend, he'd found that I was past it. You don't say that lightly even to a Sunday footballer. The untouchable was uttering the unspeakable. The untouchable didn't seem to mind that Rodney Marsh of Queen's Park Rangers was quite old. Sandy rightly admired the brilliance of Marsh's individualism, his eccentric or orphan style.

He was both of each pair of opposites or opponents that could be detected in him. Such were his united states. Nevertheless (Muriel Spark once observed that this is *the* Edinburgh word, pronounced 'niverthelace'), the orphan in him seems to have mattered, and his autobiography sets out to say so – to expose the self that might not have been taken for granted, that might not even have been detected, and wasn't by me, amid the activities of the outlaw. We have his word for it that his behaviour incorporated the fears of an outcast, bewildered by the country to which he had come to be cast away for a further term, a country which threatened him, and was to threaten his music.

On the face of it, his double life was that of a romantic, hairy jazzman, off to Ronnie Scott's or rattling in his van to places like Craigellachie, who was also a business executive with his auditoria in Iboland. But there was more to it than that: it seems to have amounted to a complex of double, or to several, lives. Just as a new leaf may turn out to proliferate in fresh identities, duality is easily seen now as multiplicity. And to see it as that is to wonder who can be free of it – to wonder who isn't *e pluribus*, who isn't the polity of multifarious denizens which Stevenson predicated. It would not be surprising if in recent years, when the subject has often been wondered about, and when Marilyn Monroe was able to declare that there were 700 Arthur Millers, the single life has looked meagre and insufficient.

Sandy was dual or plural to the extent that he could call himself by two names, and could behave as a victim who was also an outlaw or pirate. In other words, there was an isolation in him, never outgrown, which accompanied his being masterful, ambitious. Here we have what is probably the least superficial aspect of his double life, though it does not do much to correct or qualify what we have been accustomed to think of outlaws or pirates. His autobiography, as I've said, may provide duality's very words. These words could well be taken to mean that his two or several selves were hypothetical or figurative, and they do not allow one to know for certain whether he considered himself more divided than most people are. At the same time, they suggest that the hypothesis was believed, and experienced, that it could be experienced with the force of hallucination, and that it was best described in the language of hallucination.

Among the symptoms of his condition was the way he had of making you feel both liked and disliked, of attacking his friends with ironies. In my own case, memories of school may have sharpened his ironies, and fetched him to the touchline. He could see in me the swot who played second fiddle in the raucous royal, high school orchestra. This enabled him to discover that I couldn't play football.

I mentioned Edinburgh words a moment ago, and Sandy's autobiography is eloquent about the part played by language in his life. In India and afterwards, his father's isolation and death were referred to by the family in embarrassed words which seemed to be surrounded by invisible inverted commas, and in Edinburgh at large, words were used in a distinctive way which could also invite inverted commas. Edinburgh has two languages – Scots and posh English. A lot of the first survived in Sandy till the end of his life – the voice rather than the vocabulary. This situation is no impediment to the double life, but it causes quaintness, and a precarious aplomb. Double-tongued schoolboys have a tendency to be a bit pedantic and scholarly, and are drawn to jargon and the higher gibberish in a manner that may be less common among one-tongued Southerners, as Cockburn called them, of the same age.

On one occasion in Sandy's youth, the manager of Edinburgh's West End Cafe, where jazz was played, refused to let him in after closing-time. Out in the cold, Sandy enquired: 'Are you distraining me?' The last brown-and-cream tram – with its little lurching alternative spiral staircases at either end, like the two parts of a double life – had long gone to Joppa or Corstorphine. There he was, lost in the dark and stormy night of Shandwick Place and Prince's Street, frowned at by Binn's department store, cast out by the Caledonian Station: there was Caledonia's orphan, whose word for his own plight, 'distraining', was a practical, legal word signifying bankruptcy and the surrender of worldly goods, a word of doubtful application here, you could say, and yet the *mot juste*. When I read it in his memoirs, that word brought back Edinburgh and Midlothian to me as nothing else could have done. Having hurt my leg at my village school, I told the teachers, with the air of a James Callaghan: 'I collidded with another boy.' The teachers laughed at the mispronunciation, and I was aware that there were two sorts of word. Scots words could be low and bad, apparently, and big English words could be dangerous: from both sorts, schoolboys stood distrained, or strained.

Words mattered to Sandy because he was a wit. Humour was his element, almost as much as music. His wit discharged itself, not so much in repartee and epigram, as in stories and fantasies, and in the letters he wrote, which were seldom grave. Once he was showing his mother-in-law the sights of London. They were travelling by bus, and the bus was making its way along Fleet Street. 'And this', said Sandy of a recently excavated temple, 'is where they found the Roman remains.' Round-eyed, in the accents of Edinburgh, his mother-in-law cried: 'Terrible!' Or rather: 'Tairrible!' Once, when he'd come to visit me at the *Listener*, he asked permission to leave with the commissionaire the monstrous Martian sky-blue crash-helmet which he sometimes wore. Sorry, it was more than the commissionaire's job was worth. Sandy explained to me that this man belonged to a class with which jazz musicians were familiar, and for which they had a name. Like many another janitor, custodian and sky-high official, he was a Job's Worth.

Sandy, single-mindedly, was the opposite of a Job's Worth, and he was seldom sorry. He liked to play with words. His blue bonnet or helmet buzzed with verbal bees, with coinages and christenings. There were words for the disease that killed him: malignant hypertension. It sounds like a grim name, and could be a name for what happens to artists – to jazzmen, whose lives tend to be short. He used to point out that, after 40, he was living on borrowed time, statistically speaking. But he did not speak statistically when he gave news of his illness. He spoke humorously. And I was too stupidly self-absorbed at the time to take in that he was done for. He died a Roman death. He wouldn't go into intensive care after a heart attack, and waited at home instead with a glass of whisky – watching a Scotland–England rugby game, in which Scotland could have triumphed and didn't, suffering one of its fiascos or Floddens – for its successor, which did not keep him waiting very long.

In the last two years or so, three of my dearest friends have died in middle age. The others were the critic Marius Bewley and Tony White. All three were of divided nationality: Tony was literally half-French, Marius spiritually Anglo-American. Marius died in the loathing of Nixon's America, but his great wit could signal how much he enjoyed some other Americas, to the point of patriotism. As for Sandy, he was half-Hindu and an Anglo-Indian who was also an intensely Scottish Anglo-Scot. It might have been said of Tony what the boxing Brando, whom he resembled, said in *On the Waterfront*: 'I could have been a contender.' By this I mean that he had it in him to be a very good actor, and in fact proved himself one in his early days at Cambridge. But he gave it up, and devoted himself to football, to friendship, to solitude, to reading, writing, working as a builder, and to building himself a house in the wilds of Ireland. When he broke his leg colliding on the football field, the junior hospital doctors were on strike, so that he was discharged from hospital straight away after the leg was set, and he had a great deal of trouble getting attention from hospitals when complications came: no doubt it was more than their jobs were worth. A blood clot produced an embolism. I'm told that he would have died anyway – even if these doctors and hospital officials had behaved like human beings. Some people would say that it was wrong for a grown man to go on playing football and caring about it, and painfully ridiculous to die of it: that it could only have made sense, this zeal, if he had been signed by Queen's Park Rangers. Well, I think he felt that it was better to play football than to do what most of his contemporaries were doing, and I am not exaggerating when I say that he would have thought it rich, and a rich joke, to die like this.

Each of the three died before his time, at a time when this had begun to seem like quite a good idea, and their deaths have made their friends feel like orphans. I loved them very much, and am glad of the chance to write in their praise. It might have been advisable to talk less about duality in doing so: an unreal world, and a subject on which it is hard to trust your perceptions. Equally, the experience of the colliding and distrained, in their infirmary of broken legs and divided selves, can often seem like an unreal world, though it is one of which few people are ignorant. Niverthelace, I can trust what I felt about these men, and I hoped that this would help me to write about Sandy's Confessions, in which two lives, or nine, are darkly revealed.

JOHN CAREY

Down With Dons

John Carey was born in 1934, and is Professor of English Literature at Oxford. He is, in other words, a most successful don. Carey has published several critical books – on Dickens, Thackeray and Donne – and he is chief book critic for the London Sunday Times. *His essay 'Down With Dons' first appeared in 1975 and is reprinted in* Original Copy *(1987), a collection of Carey's essays and reviews.*

From the viewpoint of non-dons, probably the most obnoxious thing about dons is their uppishness. Of course, many dons are quite tolerable people. But if you ask a layman to imagine a don the idea will come into his head of something with a loud, affected voice, airing its knowledge, and as anyone who has lived much among dons will testify, this picture has a fair degree of accuracy. The reasons are not far to seek. For one thing, knowledge – and, in the main, useless knowledge – is the don's *raison d'être*. For another, he spends his working life in the company of young people who, though highly gifted, can be counted on to know less than he does. Such conditions might warp the humblest after a while, and dons are seldom humble even in their early years. Overgrown schoolboy professors, they are likely to acquire, from parents and pedagogues, a high opinion of their own abilities. By the time they are fully fledged this sense of their intellectual superiority will have gone very deep and, because of the snob-value attached to learning and the older universities, it will almost certainly issue in a sense of social superiority as well. Modern young dons sometimes feel guilty on this score, and break out in jeans, sweat-shirts and other casual wear, in the forlorn hope that they will be taken for persons of the working class. However, the very deliberateness of their disguise is an earnest of their real aloofness.

Anyone wishing for a whiff of the more old-world, unashamed brand of donnish uppishness could scarcely do better than thumb through *Maurice Bowra* (Duckworth, £3.25), a sheaf of tributes which, besides giving a complete anatomical rundown of Sir Maurice from his 'curiously twisted navel' to his private parts (resembling, Francis King bafflingly reports, 'Delphi in microcosm'), casts some telling light on the social assumptions of its contributors and subject. The editor is Hugh Lloyd-Jones, Regius Professor of Greek at Oxford. His is a name that sticks in my mind because of a contribution he made, two or three years back, to some correspondence in *The Times* about dons' pay. It was at a time when the miners or the power-workers or some other vital body were having one of their strikes, and an English tutor at University College called Peter Bayley wrote in suggesting that, by comparison with such people, dons were perhaps paid too much. Professor Lloyd-Jones replied that, if Bayley thought that, he could never have done any worthwhile teaching or research. The discourtesy of this retort was, I suppose, calculated: a reminder of professorial eminence. But what struck me as weird was that Professor Lloyd-Jones should apparently have no inkling that, as against a miner or a power-worker, his own contribution to the community was of uncommonly little consequence, and that what he deemed worthwhile teaching or research would impress most of the people whose taxes went towards paying his salary as a frivolous hobby. Humility, it seemed to me, was the only becoming attitude for academics in the debate about pay, since their avocations, and their maintenance at the public expense are, if they don't happen to be nuclear physicists or doctors, notoriously difficult to justify. How these aspects of the matter could have escaped Professor Lloyd-Jones puzzled me for a goodish while. In the end I attributed it to the insulating effect of donnish uppishness. Years of self-esteem had, as it were, blinded the Professor to his true economic value.

Bumptiousness and insolence are the quite natural outcome of such a condition, and the Bowra volume has some excellent examples of both. When holidaying abroad, we are told, Sir Maurice would size up other tourists and, though they were perfect strangers to him, 'pronounce with shameless clarity on their social origins: "English LMC"'. We learn, too, of his behaviour at a Greek play to which he was taken:

He drew attention, shortly after the rise of the curtain, to the knees of the Chorus, and engaged those on either side in such brisk conversation that a cold message was delivered to me during the interval to keep him quiet or get out.

Behind such conduct can be detected the unhesitating donnish assumption that the comfort and pleasure of ordinary people are of no account when set against the need to advertise one's superiority.

Don-fanciers love this rudeness, of course, and suck up to those who dole it out. The kind of people who work as secretaries and dogsbodies in the various Faculties, for instance, can often be heard relating, with many a titter, the latest offensive outburst of Professor This or Dr That. Dons' children, too, are likely to admire and imitate their parents' ways, and this can make them peculiarly detestable. A good many Oxford (and, I suppose, Cambridge) citizens must have bitter memories that would bear this out, but an experience of my own will serve as an illustration of the general truth. For a while I lived opposite a don's family. The father, a philosopher, was a shambling, abstracted figure, whom one would glimpse from time to time perambulating the neighbourhood, leering at the milkbottles left on doorsteps and talking to himself. If he had any contact with the outside world, or any control over his numerous children, it certainly wasn't apparent. To make matters worse, the mother was a don too, and the house was regularly left in the children's sole charge. The result was bedlam. The din of recorded music resounded from the place at all hours, and it never seemed to occur to anyone to shut a window or moderate the volume. One summer afternoon, when I was doggedly trying to mark a batch of A-level papers, my patience gave out, and I crossed the street to protest. As usual, every gaping window blared: it was like knocking at the door of a reverberating three-storey transistor set. Not surprisingly I had to pound away at the knocker for a good while before anyone heard. Eventually a teenage girl, one of the daughters, answered, and – with the familiar upsetting mixture of outrage and humiliation that one feels on such occasions – I asked if she would mind playing the music a little more quietly. The girl gave a supercilious smile. 'Oh,' she said, 'it's no good your complaining about that. The whole street got up a petition about us once, but it didn't have any effect.' And with that she shut the door.

I withdrew, trembling with impotent rage, and quite unfit, needless to say, to mark any more scripts that day, even if the row across the street had abated – which it didn't. For a while after that I got into the way of asking after this girl whenever I was talking to anyone who knew the family, in hopes that I would hear she had been run over or otherwise incapacitated. Unfortunately she never was, so far as I know. But it was through one of these conversations that I came to hear of another of her escapades. My interlocutor on this occasion was a Professor of Moral Philosophy, and he explained that the girl had caused considerable consternation at her school because she had discovered how to manufacture (using clay, All Bran and other ingredients) a compound which closely resembled human excrement, and had left quantities of this in little heaps around the classrooms. How they found out it was her, I don't know, but apparently they did. My informant was immensely tickled by the affair, and shook with laughter when relating the discomfiture it had caused to the school staff.

In a moral philosopher that might seem a surprising reaction to such foulmindedness. But in fact he was illustrating another common donnish attribute, namely, contempt for authority, particularly the authority of those whom, like schoolteachers or policemen, the don feels to be in a lowly position compared to himself. Dons' children are notoriously arrogant at school, and it's hardly to be wondered at since they find that their elders, like my moral philosopher, greet their misdemeanours with asinine hilarity. The donnish cult of liberty extends further than this, of course. One frequently encounters letters in the press, for instance, with strings of academic signatories, gravely informing some foreign government that the way it deals with its refractory minorities does not tally with donnish notions of freedom. No doubt those who put their names to these documents get a pleasurable feeling of importance, but in fact a don is about as well placed to start clamouring for liberty as a budgerigar. Like the bird, he lives in a highly artificial, protected environment, in which all his wants are catered for. Any appreciable degree of liberty conceded to his fellow beings would quickly put an end to his existence. For it cannot be supposed that the ignorant, philistine majority would go on supporting the universities financially if it had freedom of choice in the matter, since it receives no benefit from these institutions, or none that it could be brought to appreciate, beyond, I suppose, the annual Oxford and Cambridge Boat Race, and even that is less popular than it used to be.

In the Bowra volume much hearty commendation is given to Sir

Maurice's lifelong sympathy with those who 'desired to resist authority', and his support for 'all libertarian causes'. In his youth, one gathers, the causes he mostly spoke out in favour of were buggery and masturbation, though he also encouraged:

open snobbishness, success worship, personal vendettas, unprovoked malice, disloyalty to friends, reading other people's letters (if not lying about, to be sought in unlocked drawers) – the whole bag of tricks of what most people think and feel and often act on, yet are themselves ashamed of admitting they do and feel and think.

The commentator on human nature here is Anthony Powell. He does not record whether smearing ersatz excrement on school furniture would count as 'unprovoked malice' and therefore as a libertarian cause in the Bowra code. However, it seems much on a par with the rest.

But though Sir Maurice continued, apparently, to decry authority long after youth had passed, he himself represented authority for the greater part of his life. He became a Fellow of Wadham in 1922, Warden in 1938, and Vice-Chancellor of Oxford in 1951, and he was an inveterate university politician, adept at imposing his will on committees and at bulldozing himself and his protégés into positions of power. One need go to no hostile account to discover this domineering side to his nature, for his friends who contribute to the memorial volume are effusive about it. For a man so constituted, supporting 'libertarian causes' would plainly entail constant and self-deluding doublethink. Not that Sir Maurice was, in that respect, an untypical don. Dons are inalienably responsible for the government of the colleges and the university, so when they indulge in anti-authoritarian polemics it always involves a lie.

Regrettably undergraduates cannot be counted on to realize this. In their trusting way, they believe that dons are perfectly sincere when they prate of revolution and liberty. It is a misunderstanding that can lead to painful disappointment, for the young tend to carry their beliefs into action, and they then find that the dons, who had seemed such pals, have suddenly turned nasty. Bowra, it appears, was in his early days one of those dons who curry favour by hobnobbing with the undergraduates, and Anthony Powell tells of an occasion on which the conviviality wore thin.

I remember the unexpectedness of a sudden reminder of his own professional status, sense of what was academically correct, when, after a noisy dinner-party at Wadham, someone (not myself) wandering round Bowra's sitting-room suddenly asked:

'Why, Maurice, what are these?'

Bowra jumped up as if dynamited.

'Put those down at once. They're Schools papers. No, indeed . . .'A moment later he was locking away in a drawer the candidates' answers to their examination, laughing, but, for a second, he had been angry. The astonishment I felt at the time in this (very justifiable) call to order shows how skilfully Bowra normally handled his parties of young men.

Quite so. And his skill consisted in concealing from them the truth, which was that his comfortable job depended on keeping them under. Young Powell's astonishment was, surely, quite reasonable. For had not the libertarian Bowra positively recommended the reading of other people's private papers?

The chagrin and surprise undergraduates feel when they come up against reality in this way was recently demonstrated, on a larger scale, at the trial of 18 students before the Oxford University Disciplinary Court. They were accused (and eventually found guilty) of having staged a sit-in at the University Registry. In fact they had been ejected from the building, after a short occupation, by irate Registry staff, who got in through a window. This brush with ordinary, hard-working citizens, who wanted to get on with their jobs, was in itself a disillusioning experience for youngsters intent upon organized idleness, and elicited howls of protest from the undergraduate press. But worse was to follow. Brought to trial, the defendants at first treated the court-room as an arena for libertarian high-jinks, volubly aided by their friends who packed the public gallery. The proceedings were adjourned in uproar. But the court was then reconvened in a smaller room; the revolutionary claque was excluded; and the trial went ahead. Defendants who continued to rant and sermonize and interrupt were first warned, then asked to leave, then, after they had refused, forcibly removed.

As it happened, I was on duty as an usher, so I had a ringside seat. The undergraduates linked arms to form a tight bunch against one wall. The barristers and solicitors, clutching armfuls of papers, huddled against another wall to avoid the mêlée. Eventually a squad of specially conscripted university police, decked out in ill-fitting bowler hats for the occasion, marched in, methodically dragged each offender from his clinging companions, and carried him, kicking and shouting, from the room. There was, I suppose, little violence – much less, say, than you could see on the rugby fields round the university any afternoon of the week. But in the elegantly panelled court-room the panting and scuffling and the bellows of rage from the undergraduates seemed crude and debasing. The defendants who remained behind were stunned. It had plainly never dawned on them that the university would actually enforce discipline. Several wept. I remember particularly a graduate student, who must have been in his early 20s, and whom no one had laid a finger on, blubbing tempestuously in the middle of the court-room. Nor could the students be blamed for this reaction. They had been led astray by their upbringing – by the unquestioning approval of liberty which modern education encourages from nursery school on, as well as by the revolutionary attitudinising of a few leftist dons who, it should be noted, did not appear before the court to take any part of the blame, but retained their lucrative posts after the undergraduates they had beguiled had been sent down.

Bowra, of course, had died a couple of years before any of this took place. One can be pretty sure that he would have felt nothing but regret at the recurrent sit-ins, protest-marches and other diversions by means of which students who have no academic motivation try to justify being at university. However, the support for 'all libertarian causes' celebrated by his obituarists exemplifies, as I have suggested, a widespread donnish cast of mind which inevitably provokes student indiscipline. His response to what he saw of undergraduate militancy was tolerant and lacking in foresight.

When, in 1968, some undergraduates wanted to have their objections to the proctorial system heard by the Privy Council, Bowra was the first to give them public support, and in answer to the objection 'Why should they?' answered simply 'Because they are entitled to and because they want to'.

To anyone less filled with the notion of the special importance of Oxford and its doings, it might surely have occurred to enquire why these already highly privileged youngsters should be 'entitled' to occupy eminent public men with their little upsets, any more than the pupils at any polytechnic or training college or kindergarten throughout the land. Bowra's assumption here partly reflects the Oxford of his youth, adorned with gilded sprigs from the foremost families who would naturally deem it their right to be heard before the highest tribunal. But it also represents a grandiose and typically donnish sense of the university's place in the scheme of things. This, incidentally, is something dons share with militant students, who invariably believe that their grouses are of national importance. In placards and graffiti around Oxford the disciplinary court was referred to as a 'show trial', and the defendants were labelled 'The Oxford Eighteen', as if they were at least on a level with the Tolpuddle Martyrs.

The relative insignificance of Oxford, and of universities in general, Bowra, like most dons, did not care to think about. Anthony Powell tells of how, in his undergraduate days, he once confessed to Bowra, then a rising star in the Oxford firmament, his own impatience with the university, how little he liked being there, and how he longed to get it over and go down. Bowra was so put out that it took 35 years for their relationship to recover. Jobs within the university, and who got them, mattered terribly to him. He fought and intrigued, on and off committees, to get his candidates in. He revelled in the bickering and gossip that surrounded contested elections to academic posts: they brought drama to his life, exercised his quick brain, and gratified his malicious sense of humour. 'To anyone outside a university,' Lord Annan condoningly remarks, 'the frenzy which elections and appointments produce seems petty and absurd.' To some inside, too, one would hope. The kind of scholar who is absorbed enough in learning and teaching to reckon every hour spent on administration and committees wasted may, it is true, leave the field clear for the hardened business-fixers, and is to that extent a liability. Still, he is and must be the life-blood of any university worth the name. He will have something larger and more permanent in view than inter-departmental wrangling or the pursuit of his career, and will consequently be exempt from the degradations attendant on ambition. Bowra's craving for honours, on the other hand, was voracious. When E. R. Dodds, rather than himself, succeeded Gilbert Murray as Regius Professor of Greek, he was bitterly disappointed and, it appears, purposely made things difficult for the new professor. Small-mindedness isn't something one easily associates with Bowra, but it is hard to see his reaction here as the outcome of anything else, and the species of small-mindedness involved is persistently if not uniquely nurtured by universities.

From the academic angle, of course, the chief danger is that the don who bothers himself with administration will get so tied up in it that he will have no time for the subject he's supposed to be studying. The disastrous improvement in modern techniques of photocopying and duplication has greatly added to this peril. Bushels of paper nowadays debouch from university and college offices every week and, as a result of the cry for 'participation', even the undergraduates have been sucked into the papery maelstrom. Some of them sit on committees almost full-time, and the busybodies in their ranks are agitating for sabbatical years, during which they will not have to study at all, but may devote themselves undistracted to needless circulars and memoranda. They will then be indistinguishable from the administrative dons. Even when administration doesn't oust learning (and it didn't in Bowra's case), there's a likelihood that the don who becomes attached to the idea of the university, as distinct from the culture which the university exists to serve, will apprehend that culture in a form which is processed and ordered for university consumption. What were originally great endeavours of the human spirit, the offspring of passion and inspiration, will decline for him into the material of lectures and syllabuses, of examinations and career-furthering books. The flat, pedestrian feel of much of Bowra's writing about Greek literature, which is rather harped on by contributors to this volume, may be relevant here. So may the awful donnishness of jokes on the subject of art and literature. Traipsing round galleries and churches abroad, he would award points to the paintings on show. When you had totted up 50, you were entitled to a drink. Another game was classing the poets, as if in the Final Honours School: 'Goethe', we are told, 'notably failed to get a First: "No: the Higher Bogus", "Maurice, we've forgotten Eliot." "Aegrotat."' And so on.

If this carries a warning for present-day dons, the social set-up at Oxford in Bowra's era may seem too remote to have much relevance. Most undergraduates came from public schools. Often they had been friends at prep school or Eton or Winchester before they came up. It was a tiny, ingrown world. The public-school atmosphere of the memorial volume is appropriately heavy, several contributors debating, as if it were a matter of genuine concern, whether Bowra's explosive mode of speech should be traced to Winchester, via New College, or to his own old school, Cheltenham. As a matter of fact one is probably over-optimistic if one assumes that all this is a thing of the past. The public-school element in the Oxford and Cambridge intake has never dropped much below a half, and is bound to increase over the next few years. This is because the Socialist policy of converting the country's non-fee-paying grammar schools into massive comprehensives, in which the clever and the cretinous are jumbled together, means, in effect, that the non-public-school university entrance candidate will receive less individual attention from the teaching staff than formerly. The more crackbrained type of educational theorist will actually defend this, arguing that teachers should devote their time to the dullards, whose need is greater. But the result is that a candidate whose parents haven't the cash to pay public-school fees is no longer able to compete with his intensively coached public-school counterpart. Thus a policy which was, in concept, egalitarian, is now in the process of turning the older universities back into public-school enclaves, as they were before the First World War. As the dons are, by and large, recruited from among the undergraduates, they too will revert to being exclusively public school before very long. This seems a pity, because the influx of gram-mar-school dons into Oxford common rooms over the last 20 years or so has brought a good deal of sense to the place, and they usually turn out to be uninfected by the donnish follies and foibles I've been outlining. However, the Oxford of the future will not contain them.

Presumably because of the preponderance of public-school boys, there was a fair amount of dandified sodomy around in Bowra's Oxford, and one gathers that he was a participant. Lord Annan says that he regarded sex as something 'to be luxuriously indulged with either boys or girls', and Isaiah Berlin connects his love of pleasure, 'uninhibited by a Manichean sense of guilt', with his enthusiasm for Mediterranean culture. But his homosexuality seems to have been furtive and saddening rather than blithely Hellenic. He was terrified of blackmail. One of his friends, Adrian Bishop, had lost his job in an oil company because of his homosexual escapades, and Bowra dreaded similar exposure. When Gide came to Oxford to collect his honorary degree, he refused to put him up in the Warden's Lodgings for fear of scandal. To commemorate Bishop, he wrote a homosexual parody of the *Waste Land* entitled *Old*

Croaker, enough of which is printed here to show that he, like Forster, had only to touch on this topic for his literary sense to desert him. He wasn't, of course, at all like the popular notion of the donnish fairy queen. On the contrary, he was robustly masculine, and seems to have coveted a stable heterosexual relationship. He dallied with the idea of marriage more than once. 'Buggers can't be choosers,' he retorted, when someone deplored the plainness of a girl he was wooing. But he never married, and his aloneness was recurrently a misery. When a woman friend referred to him in his hearing as a 'carefree bachelor', he flared up: 'Never, *never*, use that term of me again.' He loved children, and the thought of him having to make do with kindness to other people's is not a happy one.

It seems arguable that his homosexuality did not satisfy the deeper demands of his nature, and maybe it should be regarded as something foisted on him by his education rather than an inherent trait. The Oxford he grew up in was unrelievedly male, so the undergraduates, especially the outgoing and social ones, almost inevitably drifted into flirtations with members of their own sex. In these conditions it was hard to learn how to get on, or off, with girls, and Bowra didn't. He never developed much instinct for what they were thinking or feeling, a friend recalls. His bitterest jokes seem to have been about love and marriage. Given all this, it's rather staggering to consider that, half a century later, most of Oxford's colleges are still single-sex, and many dons are determined to keep them that way. Their reasons, when you bother to enquire, never boil down to anything but the obtusest male prejudice. However, they are aided by the fact that the women's colleges also oppose co-education, fearing that mixed colleges, though they would give girls a fairer chance of getting to Oxford, might have an adverse effect on their own class-lists – an ordering of priorities which shows that women, in an emergency, can be just as donnish as men.

Perhaps Bowra's profound interest in eating and drinking was a kind of compensation for the lack of sexual satisfaction in his life. His hospitality was 'gargantuan', we learn, 'his digestion and head ironclad'. The friends who commemorate him plainly regard these as entirely fitting attributes for the successful academic. Indeed *The Times* obituary recorded, as if it were one of his signal achievements, that he had 'greatly raised the standard of hospitality' shown to honorands at Oxford. But to an impartial observer it may perhaps admit of question whether scholarship necessarily entails passing large quantities of rich food and fermented liquor through the gut. True, it is a traditional part of Oxford life. But even Oxford's traditions need reconsideration from time to time, and with Britain rapidly dwindling into a small, unimportant, hungry nation, it seems unlikely that corporate gluttony will flourish in its universities for much longer. Nor need its disappearance be greatly lamented. The spectacle of a bevy of dons reeling away from one of their mammoth tuck-ins is distinctly unappealing, and would be even if there were no such thing as famine in the world. Nevertheless one may be sure that dons will hotly defend their right to swill and guzzle. Their feelings of social superiority, earlier referred to, unfailingly come into play when this issue is raised, and I have known quite young dons seriously contend that college feasts should not be discontinued because, if they were, they would have nowhere to entertain their grand friends. The question is not a minor one but reflects on the way in which university shapes the personality, and therefore on the justification for having universities at all. If it can be shown that the effect of higher education is to stimulate greed and self-indulgence, the public, whose money keeps universities open, may be excused for feeling that these attributes could be picked up more cheaply elsewhere.

Reading about Bowra and his Oxford teaches you, of course, not only what to avoid but also what to imitate, or try to. His positive qualities were immense. Above all, the breadth of his learning offers a challenge and a reproach to modern dons with their increasingly narrow specializations. He had travelled across Russia as a schoolboy, before the revolution, and this gave him a lifelong interest in Russian poetry. He also read French, German, Italian, Spanish, Greek and Chinese. World literature to him was not a set of linguistic cupboards, mostly closed, but a warm and welcoming ocean in which he splashed about freely. He spanned time as well as space. From Homer, Pindar and Sophocles his love and knowledge extended to Yeats, Valéry, Rilke, George, Blok, Cavafy, Apollinaire, Mayakovsky and Lorca. Pasternak, Quasimodo, Neruda and Seferis were his personal friends. Set against these riches, the burrowings of the typical modern researcher shrivel into absurdity. The things that pass for education in graduate departments –

hunting for subjects sufficiently devoid of interest not to have been researched before, manufacturing unneeded theses on unreadable authors – would have filled Bowra with horror and disbelief. He characterized the graduate student as a dinosaur, sinking into a bog under the weight of his erudition.

Another aspect of his approach to literature which looks pretty healthy in retrospect was his indifference to the Cambridge emphasis on 'evaluation' which was all the rage in the thirties. Encouraging youths scarcely out of short trousers to deliver judgment on the masterpieces of the past was not at all what he went in for. He made his pupils aware of literature as a wealth they had still to inherit, rather than as a terrain of fallen idols and soured hopes into which it would be foolish to venture.

The range of his reading challenged your own provinciality and sloth. In the post-war years he was always suggesting that one should read poets whom the new orthodoxy had dismissed as negligible or harmful – Tennyson, Swinburne and Kipling . . . He was a traveller forever suggesting that if only you would journey further some new and life-enhancing experience was yours for the asking.

He enlarged the imagination of his undergraduates, too, by becoming a legend long before his death. Like all legends, he was partly make-believe. People added to him bits and pieces from their own fancy, so that by the end he was not so much a man as a joint fictional venture. This is plain enough from the memorial volume, for we encounter there several different Bowras, according to the writer. He is variously likened to Yeats, Hardy, Swift, the *Royal Sovereign*, one of Napoleon's marshals, and the Heracles of the metope at Olympia. Cyril Connolly's Bowra 'rode high above academic honours' – quite unlike the envious careerist other contributors knew. There is disagreement, too, about his eyes. To Connolly they were '*gli occhi onesti e tardi*, eyes of a platoon commander in the First World War'. Lord Annan remembers them as 'pig's eyes', while for Susan Gardiner it was their 'passion and piercing intensity' that impressed. A passionate pig? Even the story about Bowra and Gide, which one would have imagined was readily verifiable, exists in two versions: the second, also printed here, has it that it was the Vice-Chancellor, not Bowra, who refused to entertain Gide at Oxford, and that Gide was looked after by Bowra and Enid Starkie instead. Far from mattering, the contradictions are proof of Bowra's success. Whatever else may seem obsolete about him, he inspired others to creativity, which is any teacher's most important job.

MARTIN AMIS

Phantom of the Opera:
the Republicans in 1988

Martin Amis was born in Oxford in 1949 and is the son of Kingsley Amis. Best known for his several influential novels – in particular, see Money *(1984) and* London Fields *(1989) – Amis has also worked as a literary journalist and editor. His collections of non-fiction prose include* The Moronic Inferno *(1980) and* Visiting Mrs Nabokov *(1993). 'Phantom of the Opera: the Republicans in 1988' was first published in* Esquire *in 1988 and was collected in* Visiting Mrs Nabokov.

The Republican Convention is history now, and history didn't look too good down in New Orleans, sapped and battered by eight years of Ronald Reagan. Before I develop that thought, though, I feel it's high time I said a few words about my family. I have a wife and two little boys. Over here to cover the Convention, I happened to miss them very much. Why, just before I left, my three-year-old gazed up at me with those big blue eyes of his and said I was the best daddy in the whole world. My wife and I love our boys. And they love us. Okay?

On closing night it looked like a day-care centre up there on the podium, with the three junior Quayles and Bush's great troupe of grandchildren. They all romped and cuddled among the balloons and spangled confetti. (And what do balloons remind you of? How tall are the people you know who like balloons?) Candidates can't keep their hands off the little ones when they're in public, perhaps because it's the only time they ever see them. The Quayles' first task the next morning, I heard, was to hire someone to mind the kids for three months. This childish spectacle at the Superdome provided a new twist on a familiar image: here were politicians kissing their own babies.

Earlier that evening I was in the Media Lounge eating complimentary popcorn and watching the TV monitor. One half of the screen was occupied by a white-haired lady wearing four tiers of pearls and an expression of wry indulgence: the other half showed schoolchildren in slow motion, raising their hands to teacher.

A journalist came up behind me and said, 'What's this?'

'It's an ad for Barbara Bush.'

'Jesus Christ, what's going *on* around here?'

Where has he been? Reagan's is a style-setting administration, and there has been trickle-down. Nowadays, when Chris Evert gets a regular boyfriend, the first thing she does is make an ad about it. On *The Dating Game* the dude will report that his new friend is 'open' and 'communicative' – 'and I admire those skills'. Who is the role model of the nascent media-coaching industry? Forces are working on the American self. Thirty-five-year-olds have spent half their adult lives in the Reagan Era. This has gone on long enough.

'George Bush,' Barbara confided to the camera, and to the cameramen and lighting men and sound men and media consultants who were crouched around her at the time, was 'as strong, decent, and caring as America herself'. She had loved 'this extraordinarily special man', she went on, 'from the moment I laid eyes on him'. Early in the election year the Vice-President had decided that the time was right to tell the public about the death of his first daughter. Now here was Barbara with her side of it, revealing how George's strength ('He held me in his arms') had eventually sustained her. It all seemed to shore up the claim of the Texas delegation which hailed George Bush as 'the best father in America'.

Of course, you feel a bit of a brute going on about all this stuff. But journalists *are* brutalised by modern Conventions – by these four-day ads for the Party. 'This isn't a very interesting Convention so far. It is so well run that there aren't even any lost kids.' That was John Steinbeck in 1956. Dressed in eye-hurting orange blazers, Uncle Sam suits, and baseball outfits, the pink elephants of the GOP talk about shopping and eating and how the Giants did against the Dodgers. At this corporate outing there was no danger of any politics coming your way, though there was always the possibility of scandal. In fact the media was in for a nice surprise: it would soon be propitiated by the blood of J. Danforth Quayle. But until that story broke – and Quayle broke with it – we took our cue from the piety on display and lapsed into a mood of ghoulish cynicism.

First you inspect the concourse leading to the burger-shaped Superdome and all the conventional Convention junk, with its air of commercial

passion and improvisational verve. GO Pork Rinds – They're Repub-
lickin' Good. A blizzard of T-shirts and badges and bumper stickers.
Don't Du-Ca-Ca on the USA. At one table someone is hawking Oliver
North videos. Across the way are life-size cutouts of Reagan and Bush,
and beyond them, an outsize mannequin of Reagan as Rambo (or
'Ronbo', as the British tabloids have it): the seventy-seven-year-old sex
object is stripped to the waist, a cartridge belt athwart his slabbed chest,
and with a giant weapon in his fists. Ronbo is eight feet tall. The slogans
and buzz-phrases cruelly harp on the stature gap. Beware of Greeks
Wearing Lifts. His Only Platform Is Down in His Shoes. Where oh
where is the Democrat with Reagan's inches, his Grecian hair, his
Mitchum chest?

Next, one was obliged to traipse around the fringe meetings in a
wistful search for repulsive policies. Although I was sad to have missed
Phyllis Schlafly's Eagle Forum reception, which featured Robert Bork
and Jeane Kirkpatrick ('It was great,' said one journalist, 'Jeane was
nuts.'), I reposed considerable hope in Pat Robertson, the one-time TV
pastor and tithe mogul. Might Pat talk about Armageddon and Rapture?
Might he denounce credit cards for harbouring the Mark of the Beast?
Might he heal my jet lag?

At the hotel a phalanx of news-parched media was pressing at the
doors of the Robertson reception. No entry until 6, said one of Pat's
people, because 'everybody in there has waited a year and a half' to
hobnob with the great man. '*Please* don't turn this into a press conference.' The media was as good as its word. There was no press conference.
Instead, Robertson was instantly engulfed by a squirming centipede of
mikes and camera tackle; he emerged fifteen minutes later, with an
almost audible pop, and was dragged off through a side door by his
bodyguard. Still newsless, the newspeople took a few disgusted sips of
French cider and trooped off to the Superdome to cover Ronnie Night.

I lingered among the believers, with their fine hair, their thick skins,
and their low blink-rates. Many of the women were still shivering from
the post-Pat frisson. Their man hadn't won, but they had the feeling
that the GOP was gathering him – and them – into its bosom. Clearly
Pat hadn't told them what he must know to be the case: that he's
finished. The next night, true, he would get his prime-time speech
(largely ignored by the cameras) and would thrill the faithful, and the
media, with his talk of 'disease carriers' who place the healthy 'at great

risk'. But Pat's had it: his valedictory press conference was an ill-attended freak show. He'll just have to go back to his old job, serving God with his miracle-service TV spot and stiffing the fuddled and elderly out of their rent cheques and disability allowances.

Pat Robertson at a national convention, equipped with delegates, certainly remains a terrible sight. He is a charlatan of Chaucerian dimensions. To Bush, if not to Reagan, the evangelicals were probably never much more than a useful joke, to be kept happy with promises that can't possibly get past the Senate (like the guff about recriminalising abortion). Anyway, the video vicarage is now in tatters. Yet another institution in Reagan's dream city comes crashing to the ground – and the National Security Council, and Wall Street, and the Attorney General's office, and the Pentagon. Is it over?

Ronnie Night. First the motorcade and its enthralling expression of personal power: half a six-lane city boulevard sealed off and lined with blinkers and excited cops. Four motor-bikes in formation, sirens idling, then six more, then two police cars, then four limousines, then four staff cars (two containing security men, two containing Nancy's helpers and dressers). As soon as the backwash has settled, the cops unplug the bursting sidestreets, and the normal gridlock resumes. No wonder the President looks so young and cheerful: eight years without any traffic.

The time to study Reagan was before he mounted the stage – when he and Nancy took their preliminary seats in the lower gallery. During the imperial entrance, the Reagan face had been divided laterally, the eyes expressing mock alarm, the mouth unqualified gamesomeness. As he settled, a mound of cameras sticklebricked itself into being a few inches from his nose. Reagan jovially waved a hand at the teetering media, as if to say, 'Will you look at all these guys?' Then his smile instantly vanished as he fell into an imitation of a serious man listening to a serious speech. Was it imagination, or did I detect, beneath his mask, the dull throb of astonishment that such modest abilities (plus a few gut instincts) had ushered in, not just a Governorship, not just a Presidency, but an American Era? Apart from that, he looks, he looks . . .

What *does* he look like? He looks like a gorgeous old opera-phantom shot full of novocaine. *Esquire*'s caricaturist Steve Brodner is a longtime student of the Reagan face: 'Ten years ago the face told you a lot about the man. Now that's all gone.' The furtive overlay above the eyes and the wattled dissolution of the jaw have been replaced by clarity and definition. It used to be said that by a certain age a man had the face that he deserved. Nowadays, he has the face he can afford – or the face his handlers decide to go with. One of Dickens's hypocrites has a facial paralysis that gives him a profile of noble immobility; this is the side he presents to his clients, while the hidden half snickers and gloats. With the modern American politician, we must imagine the face *beneath* the face, smarting and flickering with the impostures, the compromises, and the fathomless boredom of public life. Erected by surgeon and makeup man, the face is now the picture window to the soul.

Maureen was there, but Reagan hasn't got any children, or grand-children, that he can plausibly wheel out and love up. So he goes another way: he loves up Nancy. Reagan has never made any secret of his thralldom to Nancy's talents. With his hints of turbulent nights behind the clipped hedges of Brookline, Dukakis has evidently taken yet another arrow from Reagan's quiver: husbandly romancing has voter appeal. Bush is obviously in a corner on this one with Barbara, who will make TV ads but draws the line at dyeing her hair. Besides, as Bush says with a kind of shrug, it's been forty-three years.

This Convention project of loving up Nancy had begun at a lunch in her honour, where Reagan asked, 'What can you say about someone who gives your life meaning? You can say that you love that person, and treasure her.' On Ronnie Night, Tom Selleck was Reagan's surrogate on the stage; he spoke of cancer surgery, the war against drugs, and that day when 'an assassin nearly took away what she loved most in this life'. After Nancy's little address, we got the ad for Ronnie. You know the one: a fifteen-minute collage of newsclips, Bud and Marlboro commercials, and exquisitely lit home movies. So. An actor, then an actress, then an ad; and then another actor – Reagan, with the Speech.

All morning the hall had rung with the words of ardent glozers and fiery mediocrities, chosen for their sex or their skin colour or their extremes of youth and age. Punctuated by the tinny clunk of the gavel, the clichés of the peanut-faced orators laboured towards you at the speed of sound, chased by the PA echo . . . Reagan got up there, and, after one blooper ('Facts are stupid things' – the crowd winced so fondly, so protectively!), a few jokes, several boasts, and a lot of statistics, shared with his countrymen the gift of the trust in a dream of a vision whose brilliant light in a shining moment showed a sweet day of extra love for a special person between the great oceans. 'Here,' he exhaustedly concluded, 'it's a sunrise every day.'

That last revelation can't have been news even in Middle America, which seems to have been in flames all summer. With the Drought, with 50 per cent of all counties declared disaster areas, with the unbreathable city air (not to mention the thirty-foot scum line on the beaches of the North-East), Americans knew all about 'our sunlit new day'. No need to tell *them* 'to keep alive the fire'. Reagan's speech was an apotheosis of a kind: the rhetoric of arcadian green, polluted by reality. Nobody liked it much, even on the floor. Yet the momentum of expectation was so far entrained that the performance somehow passed off as a triumph. This *had* to be the night of rich catharsis, when Reagan's image began its slow wipe, leaving Bush to hurl his first grapple hook across the stature gap.

At lunchtime on the second day the lead local news story was about Convention-related traffic jams. In uniform desperation the media was turning its gaze on the city itself, and duly noting the inevitable contrast between Republicans and New Orleans.

It's true. There is a big difference. Republicans are rich and sober. New Orleans is poor and drunk – and Democrat. Indeed, the city has an air of almost Caribbean laxity. Over Sunday breakfast on my first morning in the French Quarter ('the Quarter'), I watched a teenage girl lurch out of a bar with a beer bottle swinging from her hand. She walked as if she had just come down from Vermont, on horseback; past Big Daddy's Topless and Bottomless Tabletop Dancing she meandered; then she sat on the sidewalk outside a club unceremoniously called the Orgy. No one stared, in forgiving New Orleans. But if I'd had a video camera with me, I could have made a good ad for abortion. In the Quarter, everybody knows about the alternative to *choice*. The alternative to legal abortion is illegal abortion. Just more free enterprise.

There is a little voodoo store a couple of blocks further up Bourbon Street. In the front room there is a tub full of coloured ribbons: 'MOJO'S FOR – LOVE (red and black) stop CONFUSSION (yellow and BLACK) FOR a good health (different colors and stripy BLACK) COURTCASE (BLACK and BLACK)'. In the back room there is a rectangular chest covered in masks and pinecones: 'Pleas do not touch this COFFIN – DANGER – BE WARE of FREDDIES COFFIN!! PS shit HAPPENing'. The store looked far from prosperous. The potency of voodoo, one fears, is definitely on the wane – except in the realm of economics and, perhaps, in that of prophecy. For George Bush was due in town that day. Soon we would hear the sinister creak of Freddie's coffin lid. And shit would be happening.

Like many of the media I began the day by morbidly attending a brunch thrown by the National Rifle Association, with fingers crossed for a few atrocities from the lips of Charlton Heston and Arnold Schwarzenegger. Resplendently present at the bar, Schwarzenegger no-showed on the podium (as he would later monotonously no-show at the Mississippian, Tennessean, and South Carolinian caucus meetings). In the matinée gloom of the curtainless ballroom, Heston was bland and depressingly centrist; we took what solace we could from the opening blasphemies of a local chaplain ('And now a word to our Sponsor. Heavenly Father . . .') and from Phil Gramm's tribute to capital punishment: 'If they hurt other people we want them put in jail, and if they kill other people we want them put to death.' Hearing this, a couple of elegant young ladies at my table joined in the fierce applause; the palms of their right hands sought their throats in flustered affirmation. Civilised girls. But this isn't civilised. Still, gas chambers and gunslinging aren't news at the end of the Reagan Era. Furloughs are news. The media bitterly decamped to Spanish Plaza to wait for Bush.

Vintage aircraft buzzed the shopping mall, two deejays jabbered into microphones, a fat tug befouled the Mississippi with dyed fountains of red and white and blue, gay protesters took their positions – and into this scene of contemporary pageantry the candidate stepped from the riverboat *Natchez*. . . Some minutes later there was this frenzied little blond guy waving his arms around and hollering into the mike, and doing pretty well considering he looked about nine years old. Watching him give his cheek a thorough and astonished wipe after a kiss from Barbara, you might have thought that here was another tearaway Bush grandson. But no: here were three bad decisions (manner, timing, substance) all rolled into one. Here was Dan Quayle.

The TV crews are the Germans of the media. Here they come (watch out), lugging their bazookas and ack-ack launchers, sweating, swearing, and not smiling. They are all elbow and kneecap and have the gracelessness of undisputed muscle. They stand in ranks on crates and platforms, like firing squads. As they focus, their upper lips drag to the left in dead Presley grins. 'They got Channel 56 from Jacksonville, Texas, in here,' said one crewman at the first Bush–Quayle press conference. 'That's how Mickey Mouse it's getting.' I peered through the wires and webbing, the jeans and chinos. When the ticket came on to the stage the cameras phutted like a great flock taking to the air. And there was Quayle, confident, plump-faced, handsome, and stupid, all set to go get 'em.

The process that began in those first few minutes would develop into the detailed recycling of a political being, much of it on prime time. The media chomped him up and pooped him out again. And the contraption that is now being buckled on to a horse and sent out on the campaign trail is no longer the 'Dan Quayle' to whom Dan Quayle so often, and so robotically, refers. He is a hurried creation of the Bush people: the prepped preppy, wired up for a narrow repertoire of frowns and whoops, wired up for limited damage. Facing his first question about Paula Parkinson (the Washington lobbyist he was alleged to have taken on a golfing trip), Quayle made a gesture of erasure with his hand, said 'No' when he meant 'Yes' and looked like the kind of man who would want to beat you up if you swore in front of his wife. You don't come on to the media like that. Then the bombshell: Quayle – the identikit, join-the-dots militarist – had given Vietnam a miss, staying at home and serving with the National Guard. By the next morning there were rumours that Quayle would be dumped from the ticket. Out of the loop for decades, the media was calling, in effect, for a second ballot. The media wasn't just a crowd, busy dispensing free TV. The media was saying that it was a *player*.

Even before the story broke, one remarkable fact had surfaced: here we had yet another major American politician who was quite at sea in the English language, utterly confounded by the simplest declarative sentence. Minutes after the press conference, Bush was blooding his young warrior at the California caucus meeting. Before long, Bush found himself standing there with a look of respectful concentration on his face as Quayle hammered out: 'The question today is whether we are going forward, or past to the back.' Even this miserable commonplace was too much for him. Indeed, the only sentence Quayle seemed really comfortable with was 'Let's go get 'em!' The following night he managed twenty minutes of monosyllabic jingoism on the podium, but a day later, in Huntington, Indiana, his syntax was crazily unspooling all over the courthouse steps. 'The Reserve forces is nothing to say is unpatriotic . . . By serving in Guard somehow is not patriotic, I really do not subscribe to that . . . And a goal cannot be really a no-win situation.'

Quayle was chosen, supposedly, to help ease Bush's passage to the centre, a position he tried to occupy in his 'soft' acceptance speech, with its Whitmanesque intonations and nudges of moral suasion. Four days later we got a glimpse of the contortions Bush must now attempt, when he addressed the VFW in Chicago and sounded like Spiro Agnew: '[Dan Quayle] did not burn his draft card and he *damned sure* didn't burn the American flag!' No other Veep candidate, no other politician, can ever have won such savage praise for not burning the American flag. Bush chose Quayle, I think, because he responded to and took pleasure in his youth, unaware of the slowly dawning reality that *all* baby boomers are unelectable, by definition (none of us is clean: we've all smoked joints, had sex, worn bell-bottoms, gone to the toilet, and so on). Perhaps Quayle is the fanatically right-wing son that Bush never had. More probably, the young man answered to the young man in Bush, to the frisky kiddishness that remains his central implausibility. By golly. Zip-a-dee-doo-dah. Deep doo-doo. Who does *that* sound like?

One night in New Orleans I fell in with some representatives of the pollster and media-consultant community, people who had worked with Bush, or with 'Poppy', as they call him. ('We think Poppy is a regular guy. Mainly because he says *fuck* a lot.') Here, all values are expedient and professionalised, and politics – fascinatingly – is discussed in strictly apolitical terms. I conflate their voices:

'On Spanish Plaza, Quayle looked like he just did a gram of coke. But they only jerked him off the streets of the Quarter an hour before, and that's what power feels like: you're thinking what you were yesterday, what you might be tomorrow. Their first job then was to calm him down. To calm his ass *down*.

'I think everyone's surprised that he seems so vapid. I mean, we're talking Bob Forehead. There's got to be more there. The Bush people are taking shit now but they're smart guys – they must know that Quayle has moves we ain't seen. Hey. What do you get if you cross a chicken and a hawk?'

'I don't know.'

'You get a quayle. If he's going to help the ticket he's got to bond with his generation. That's the whole idea, right? He's *got* to express more ambivalence about the war. Maybe you'd want to do that with paid media later on, where you can control everything. It could all help Bush. It could release a lot of emotion, as opposed to canned emotion, and the challenge then is to steer that energy in your direction.

'Right now America is button-punching. If Bush looks like everybody's first husband, then Dukakis is looking like a great first date. The point is, Bush has better guys. Someone like Bob Teeter really earns his money when you're three days from a race and the tracking says you're seven points down and wondering whether to go with an attack spot or just keep with the positive stuff. Like Bush–Dole in New Hampshire. Anyone can do the numbers. It's the analysis. It's like on the *Vincennes*. Hey. How do you tell the difference between an Airbus and an F-14?'

'I don't know.'

'Exactly. You don't know either.'

At this point we were joined by a young woman from a news network who had spent the day in fruitless search of a Vietnam veteran willing to denounce Dan Quayle. Later, I heard about one of the more recent techniques in market research. You put sixty or seventy people in front of a videotaped stump speech and hand out dials (marked 1–100) on which the audience plots its undulating level of approval. This information goes into a computer. And out comes a tracking graph that gives you an emotional commentary on the speech. Further equipment is available to measure physical responses.

I left with an image of the American electorate, fitted with heartbeat monitor, peter meter, and armpit humidor dial, and pegged out in the political-science lab of the future.

Not that it appears to matter, but in a sense George Bush is everything that Ronald Reagan only seems to be: war hero, sports star, self-reliant achiever, family man. If George is the best father in America, then Ronnie is the worst (he is also, for instance, a war wimp who lied about his record – to Yitzhak Shamir). Yet Reagan has made it all new: the frictionless illusion of a distinguished life is now far catchier than the effortful reality. The only serious omission in Bush's résumé is thirty years in acting school.

Here are three well-placed comments on the Republican nominee. '[Bush's negatives] are not venal negatives, they're warts negatives.' 'We have a perception problem on some compassion issues.' 'The guy's got no biceps, no tattoos – he's not up to it.' It is evident from his career, and from his autobiography, that Bush has always been prepared to do anything, or anything legal, to get the next job. What the 'anything' is in 1988, apart from the usual low blows of a tight race, is a lot of vulgar bull about family (which is ironic, since Barbara Bush must be one of the few remaining housewives in America). After Reagan, though, the messenger is the message, and this messenger tends to pratfall on the steps to the throne. Poor George, with his warts negatives, his compassion-issues perception problem, and his lack of biceps – and of anchors and songbirds and the bruised names of love . . .

Do we get the feeling that the language has taken a beating over the past eight years? It has been an era of euphemism, during which taxes have become revenue enhancements, accountability has demoted itself to deniability, and the lie has turned into the blooper. Reagan bequeaths an economy so unrecognisably deformed that nobody can get a stethoscope close to its chest. He bequeaths the Debt: just as crucially, he bequeaths an atmosphere in which no politician dares discuss it.

Deep, autonomous, imperishable, Reagan's popularity remains the key to everything, including the election. What *is* this woozy affinity between the American people and a *Bonanza* fan who turns in at 10 pm? Either it is all very simple or it is all very complicated. To adapt the writer Clive James on the singer Barry Manilow: everybody you know despises Reagan, but everyone you don't know thinks he's great. When they see Reagan frowning at his cue cards – instead of wanting less, they want more.

For a decade Reagan has impersonated, with an unguessable degree of sincerity, the kind of American we hear a lot about at election time, if at no other: pious, wise, caring, industrious, independent, and above all *average*. The clear truth that this average American is a vain and shifty prodigal is not something that average Americans are raring to face up to. But then it goes still deeper.

In New Orleans the amplifiers sweltered with that special theme: American exceptionalism. Reagan understands that Americans are 'special' (my candidate for the worst word in the current lexicon). They are special – because they really think they're special. Never content just to be, America is also obliged to *mean*; America signifies, hence its constant and riveting vulnerability to illusion. In elevating Reagan – the average American who was special enough to land the best job in the free world – Americans elevate themselves. So perhaps the Era can be viewed as a narcissistic episode: a time when every American was President. Or not every American. Just every American that we don't know.

CHRISTOPHER HITCHENS

On Not Knowing the Half of It:
My Jewish Self

Christopher Hitchens was born in 1947 and has worked for several papers as a waspishly elegant political and literary journalist, mostly in America – where he now lives. He currently writes a regular column for Vanity Fair. *His books include* Prepared for the Worst *(1988) and* Blood, Class and Nostalgia: Anglo-American Ironies *(1990). His essay 'On Not Knowing the Half of It: My Jewish Self' was first published in the New York magazine* Grand Street *and is reprinted in* Performance and Reality: Essays from Grand Street *(1989).*

HOMAGE TO TELEGRAPHIST JACOBS

In the early days of the December that my father was to die, my younger brother brought me the news that I was a Jew. I was then a transplanted Englishman in America, married, with one son and, though unconsoled by any religion, a nonbelieving member of two Christian churches. On hearing the tidings, I was pleased to find that I was pleased.

One of the things about being English, born and bred, is the blessed lack of introspection that it can confer. An interest in genealogy is an admitted national quirk, but where this is not merely snobbish or mercenary, it indulges our splendid and unique privilege of traceable, stable continuity. Englishmen do not have much time for *angst* about their 'roots', or much of an inclination to the identity crisis. My paternal grandfather had a favorite joke, about a Wessex tenant in dispute with his squire. 'I hope you realize,' says the squire, 'that my ancestors came with William the Conqueror.' 'Yes,' returns the yeoman. 'We were waiting for you.' It was from this millennial loam that, as far as I knew, I had sprung. I had long since lapsed my interest in family history as being unlikely to prove any connection to title or fortune. For something to say, I would occasionally dilate on the pure Cornish origins of the name Hitchens, which had once been explained to me by A. L. Rowse in the course of a stuporous dinner at Oxford. The Celtic strain seemed worth mentioning, as representing a sort of romantic, insurgent leaven in the Anglo-Saxon lump. But having married a Greek (accepting confirmation in the Orthodox Church with about as much emotion as I had declined it in the Anglican one) and left England, I never expected any but routine news from the family quarter.

My brother's account was simple but very surprising. Our mother had died tragically and young in 1973, but her mother still lived, enjoying a very spry tenth decade. When my brother had married, he had taken his wife to be presented to her. The old lady had later complimented him on his choice, adding rather alarmingly, 'She's Jewish, isn't she?' Peter, who had not said as much, agreed rather guardedly that this was so. 'Well,' said the woman we had known all our lives as 'Dodo', 'I've got something to tell you. So are you.'

My initial reaction, apart from pleasure and interest, was the faint but definite feeling that I had somehow known all along. Well used to being taken for English wherever I went, I had once or twice been addressed in Hebrew by older women in Jerusalem (where, presumably, people are looking for, or perhaps noticing, other characteristics). And, though some of my worst political enemies were Jewish, in America it seemed that almost all my best personal friends were. This kind of speculation could, I knew, be misleading to the point of treachery, but there it was. Then, most provoking and beguiling of all, there was the dream. Nothing bores me more than dream stories, so I had kept this one to myself. But it was the only one that counted as recurrent and I had also experienced it as a waking fantasy. In this reverie, I am aboard a ship. A small group is on the other side of the deck, huddled in talk but in some way noticing myself. After a while a member of the group crosses the deck. He explains that he and his fellows are one short of a quorum for prayer. Will I make up the number for a *minyan*? Smiling generously, and swallowing my secular convictions in a likable and tolerant manner, I agree to make up the number and stroll across the deck.

I hesitate to include this rather narcissistic recollection, but an account of my reactions would be incomplete without it, and I had had the dream recently enough to tell my brother about it. He went on to tell me that our grandmother had enjoined us to silence. We were not to tell our father who, we knew, was extremely unwell. He had not known that he had a Jewish wife, any more than we had known we had a

Jewish mother. It would not be fair to tell him, at the close of his life, that he had been kept in the dark. I felt confident that he would not have minded learning the family secret, but it was not a secret I had long to keep. My father died a matter of weeks after I learned it myself.

The day after his funeral, which was held in wintry splendor at the D-day Chapel overlooking our native Portsmouth, whence he had often set sail to do the King's enemies a bit of no good, I took a train to see my grandmother. I suppose that in childhood I had noticed her slightly exotic looks, but when she opened the door to me I was struck very immediately by my amazing want of perception. Did she look Jewish? She most certainly did. Had I ever noticed it? If so, it must have been a very subliminal recognition. And in England, at any rate in the *milieu* in which I had been brought up, Jew-consciousness had not been a major social or personal consideration.

We had family grief to discuss, and I was uncertain how to raise the other matter that was uppermost in my mind. She relieved me of the necessity. We were discussing my father's last illness and she inquired his doctor's name. 'Dr Livingstone,' I replied. 'Oh, a Jewish doctor,' she said. (I had thought Livingstone a quintessentially English or Scots name, but I've found since that it's a favorite of the assimilated.) At once, we were in the midst of a topic that was so familiar to her and so new and strange to me. Where, for a start, were we *from*?

Breslau. The home of B. Traven and the site of a notorious camp during the *Endlossung*. Now transferred to Poland and renamed Wroclaw. A certain Mr Blumenthal had quit this place of ill omen in the late nineteenth century and settled in the English Midlands. In Leicester, he had fathered thirteen children and raised them in a scrupulously orthodox fashion. In 1893 one of his daughters had married Lionel Levin, of Liverpool. My maternal grandmother, Dorothy Levin, had been born three years later.

It appeared that my great-grandparents had removed to Oxford, where they and their successors pursued the professions of dentistry and millinery. Having spent years of my life in that town as schoolboy and undergraduate and resident, I can readily imagine its smugness and frigidity in the early part of the century. Easy to visualize the retarding influence of the Rotary Club, and perhaps Freemasonry and the golf club, on the aspirations of the Jewish dentist or hatter. By the time of the Kaiser, the Levins had become Lynn and the Blumenthals Dale. But

I was glad to learn that, while they sought to assimilate, they did not renounce. Of a Friday evening, with drawn curtains, they would produce the menorah. The children were brought up to be unobtrusively observant. How, then, could such a seemingly innocuous and familiar tale come to me as a secret? A secret which, if it were not for the chance of my grandmother outliving both my parents, I might never have learned?

Dodo told me the occluded history of my family. 'Oxford,' she said, materializing my suspicions, 'was a very bad place to be Jewish in those days.' She herself had kept all the Jewish feasts and fasts, but I was slightly relieved to find that, aged ninety-two, she was staunchly proof against the claims of religion. 'Have any of your friends ever mentioned Passover to you?' she inquired touchingly. I was able to say yes to that, and to show some knowledge of Yom Kippur and Chanukkah, too. This seemed to please her, though she did add that as a girl she had fasted on Yom Kippur chiefly to stay thin.

The moment had arrived to ask why this moment had arrived. Why had I had to bury my father to get this far? On the mantelpiece was a photograph of my mother, looking more beautiful than ever, though not as beautiful as in the photograph I possessed, which showed her in the uniform of the Royal Navy, in which she had met my father. I had been interrogating this photograph. It showed a young, blond woman who could have been English or (my fancy when a child) French. Neither in profile nor in curls did it disclose what Gentiles are commonly supposed to 'notice'.

'Your mother didn't much want to be a Jew,' said Dodo, 'and I didn't think your father's family would have liked the idea. So we just decided to keep it to ourselves.' I had to contend with a sudden access of hitherto buried memories. Had my father shown the least sign of any prejudice? Emphatically not; he had been nostalgic for Empire and bleakly severe about the consequences of losing it, but he had never said anything ugly. He had been a stout patriot, but not a flag-waver, and would have found racism (I find I can't quite add 'and chauvinism') to be an affront to the intelligence. His lifetime of naval service had taken him to Palestine in the 1930s (and had involved him in helping to put down a revolt in my wife's neighboring country of Cyprus in 1932), but he never droned on about lesser breeds as some of his friends had done in my hearing when the gin bottle was getting low. If he had ever sneered at anyone, it had been Nasser (one of our few quarrels).

But I could recall a bizarre lecture from my paternal grandfather. It was delivered as a sort of grand remonstrance when I joined the Labour Party in the mid-1960s. '*Labour*,' my working-class ancestor had said with biting scorn, 'just look at them. Silverman, Mendelson, Driberg, Mikardo . . .' and he had told off the names of the leading leftists of the party at that period. At the time, I had wondered if he was objecting to *German* names (that *had* been a continuous theme of my upbringing) and only later acquired enough grounding in the tones of the British Right to realize what he had meant. Imagining the first meeting between him and my maternal grandmother, as they discussed the betrothal, I could see that she might not have been paranoid in believing her hereditary apprehensions to be realized.

And then came another thought, unbidden. Oxford may have been a tough place to be a Jew, but in the European scale it did not rank with Mannheim or Salonika. Yet my parents had been married in April 1945, the month before the final liberation of Germany. It was the moment when the world first became generally aware of the Final Solution. How galling it must have been, in that month, to keep watch over one's emotions, and to subsume the thought of the Breslau camp in the purely patriotic rejoicing at the defeat of the archenemy.

'Well, you know,' said Dodo, 'we've never been liked. Look at how the press treats the Israelites. They don't like us. I know I shouldn't say it, but I think it's because they're jealous.' The 'they' here clearly meant more than the press. I sat through it feeling rather reticent. In January of 1988 the long-delayed revolt in Gaza had electrified Fleet Street, more because some ambitious Thatcherite junior minister had got himself caught up in it than for any reason of principle. The following Sunday, I knew, the *Observer* was to publish a review of *Blaming the Victims*, a collection of essays edited by Edward Said and myself. This book argued correctly that the bias was mostly the other way; even if, as Edward had once put it so finely in a public dialogue with Salman Rushdie, this was partly because the Palestinians were 'the victims of the victims'. I didn't know how to engage with my grandmother's quite differently stated conviction. But when I offered that the state she called 'Israelite' had been soliciting trouble by its treatment of the Palestinians, she didn't demur. She just reiterated her view that this wasn't always the real reason for the dislike they – 'we' – attracted.

Well, I knew *that* already. The Harold Abrahams character in

Chariots of Fire says rather acutely of English anti-Semitism that 'you catch it on the edge of a remark'. Whether or not this is more maddening than a direct insult I could not say from experience, but early in life I learned to distrust those who said, 'Fine old Anglo-Saxon name' when, say, a Mr Rubinstein had been mentioned. 'Lots of time to spare on Sundays' was another thoughtless, irritating standby. This was not exactly *Der Sturmer*, but I began to ask myself: had I ever let any of it go by? Had I ever helped it on its way with a smart remark? Had I ever told a joke that a Jew would not have told? (Plenty of latitude there, but everybody 'knows' where it stops.) In this mood I bid farewell to my grandmother and, leaving her at her gate, rather awkwardly said, '*Shalom.*' She replied, '*Shalom, Shalom,*' as cheerfully and readily as if it had been our greeting and parting since my infancy. I turned and trudged off to the station in the light, continuous rain that was also my birthright.

Enough of this, I suddenly thought. A hidden Jewish parentage was not exactly the moral equivalent of Anne Frank, after all. Anti-Jewish propaganda was the common enemy of humanity, and one had always regarded it as such; as much by instinct as by education. To claim a personal interest in opposing it seemed, especially at this late stage, a distinct cheapening of the commitment. As the makers of Levy's rye bread had once so famously said, 'You don't have to be Jewish.' You don't have to be Jewish to find a personal enemy in the Jew-baiter. You don't have to be a Palestinian to take a principled position on the West Bank. So what's new? By a celebrated and practiced flick of the lever, your enemies can transfer you from the 'anti' column to the 'self-hating'. A big deal it isn't.

Well, then, why had my first reaction to the news been one of pleasure? Examining my responses and looking for a trigger, I turned back to *Daniel Deronda*, which I had thought when I first read it to be a novel superior even to *Middlemarch*:

'Then I *am* a Jew?' Deronda burst out with a deep-voiced energy that made his mother shrink a little backward against her cushions ... 'I am glad of it,' said Deronda, impetuously, in the veiled voice of passion.

This didn't at all meet my case. It was far too overwrought. For one thing, I had never had the opportunity to question my mother. For another, I had not (absent the teasing of the dream) had Deronda's premonitions. My moment in the Jerusalem bookshop, accosted by a matronly woman, did not compare with his *rencontre* in the Frankfort synagogue. On the other hand, the response of Deronda's mother did seem to hit a chord:

'Why do you say you are glad? You are an English gentleman. I secured you that.'

Another memory. I am sitting on the stairs in my pajamas, monitoring a parental dispute. The subject is myself, the place is on the edge of Dartmoor and the year must be 1956 or so, because the topic is my future education. My father is arguing reasonably that private schooling is too expensive. My mother, in tones that I can still recall, is saying that money can be found. 'If there is going to be an upper class in this country,' she says forcefully, 'then Christopher is going to be in it.' My ideas about the ruling class are drawn from Arthurian legend at this point, but I like the sound of her reasoning. In any case, I yearn for boarding school and the adventure of quitting home. She must have had her way, as she customarily did, because a few months later I was outfitted for prep school and spent the next decade or so among playing fields, psalms, honors boards and the rest of it. I thus became the first Hitchens ever to go to a 'public' school; to have what is still called (because it applies to about one per cent of the population) a 'conventional' education, and to go to Oxford.

Until very recently, I had thought of this parental sacrifice – I was ever aware that the costs were debilitating to the family budget – as the special certificate of social mobility. My father had come from a poor area of Portsmouth, was raised as a Baptist, and had made his way by dint of scholarships and the chance provided by the Navy. My mother – well, now I saw why questions about her background had been quieted by solemn references to Dodo's early bereavement. And now I wish I could ask my mother – was all this effort expended, not just to make me a gentleman, but to make me an Englishman? An odd question to be asking myself, at my age, in a new country where most of my friends thought of me as 'a Brit'. But an attractive reflection, too, when I thought of the Jewish majority among my circle, and the special place of the Jews in the internationalist tradition I most admired. It counted as plus and minus that I had not had to sacrifice anything to join up. No struggle or formative drama, true, but no bullying at school, no taunting, not the least temptation to dissemble or to wish otherwise. In its review at the time, *The Tablet* (what a name!) had complained of *Daniel Deronda* that George Eliot committed 'a literary error when she makes Deronda abandon, on learning the fact of his Jewish birth, all that a modern English education weaves of Christianity and the results of Christianity into an English gentleman's life'. Nobody would now speak with such presumption and certainty about 'the results of Christianity', but insofar as this abandonment would not be an act of supererogation on my part, it was by now impossible in any case. In other words, the discovery came to me like a gift. Like Jonathan Miller in his famous writhe in *Beyond the Fringe*, I could choose to be 'not a Jew, but Jew-*ish*'.

Or could it be that easy? I had two further visitations of memory to cogitate. At the age of about five, when the family lived in Scotland, I had heard my mother use the term 'anti-Semitism'. As with one or two other words in very early life, as soon as I heard this one I immediately, in some indefinable way, *knew what it meant*. I also knew that it was one of those cold, sibilant, sinister-sounding words, innately repugnant in its implications. I had always found anti-Jewish sentiment to be disgusting, in the same way as all such prejudices, but also in a different way, and somehow more so. To hear some ignorant person denouncing Pakistani or Jamaican immigrants to Britain was one thing – there would be foulmouth complaints about cooking smells, about body odors and occasionally about sexual habits. This was the sort of plebeian bigotry that one had to learn to combat, in early days as an apprentice canvasser, as a sort of Tory secret weapon in the ranks of the Labour vote. But anti-Semitic propaganda was something else. More rarely encountered, it was a sort of theory; both pseudo and anti-intellectual. It partook of a little learning about blood, soil, money, conspiracy. It had a fetidly religious and furtively superstitious feel to it. (Nobody accuses the blacks of trying to take over international finance, if only because the racists don't believe them capable of mounting the conspiracy.) When I came across Yevtushenko's poem *Babi Yar* at the age of sixteen, I realized that he had seized the essence of the horror I felt; the backwardness and cunning that could be mobilized. I memorized the poem for a public reading that my school organized for the Venice in Peril Fund, and can remember some lines even now without taking down the Peter Levi translation:

> No Jewish blood runs among my blood
> But I am as bitterly and as hardly hated
> By every anti-Semite
> As if I were a Jew.

That seemed to me a fine ambition, even if easily affected at a civilized English boys' school. I know that it was at about that time that I noticed, in my early efforts at leftist propaganda, that among the few reliable allies in a fairly self-satisfied school were the boys with what I gradually understood were Jewish names. There was occasional nudging and smirking in chapel when we sang the line 'Ye seeds of Israel's chosen race' in the anthem *Crown Him*. What did it mean, *chosen*? Could it be serious? I hadn't then read *Daniel Deronda*, but would have shared his stiff and correct attitude (antedating his discovery) that:

Of learned and accomplished Jews he took it for granted that they had dropped their religion, and wished to be merged in the people of their native lands. Scorn flung at a Jew as such would have roused all his sympathy in grief of inheritance; but the indiscriminate scorn of a race will often strike a specimen who has well-earned it on his own account . . .

Oh, I was fair-minded all right. But strict fair-mindedness would suggest the conclusion that it didn't *matter* who was Jewish. And to say that it didn't matter seemed rather point-missing.

The second memory was more tormenting. Shortly before her death, and in what was to be our last telephone conversation, my mother had suddenly announced that she wanted to move to Israel. This came to me as a complete surprise. (My grandmother, when I told her fifteen years later, was likewise unprepared for the revelation.) Now I ransacked that last exchange for any significance it might retrospectively possess. Having separated from my father and approaching middle life, my mother was urgently seeking to make up for time lost and spoke of all manner of fresh starts. Her praise for Israel was of the sort – 'It's a new country. It's young. They work hard. They made the desert bloom' – that one read in the Gentile as well as the Jewish press. The year was 1973 and the time was just after the Yom Kippur war, and in trying to moderate her enthusiasm I spoke of the precariousness of the situation. This was slightly dishonest of me, because I didn't doubt Israel's ability to outfight its neighbors. But I suspected that any mention of the Palestinians would be a pointless expense of breath. Besides, I wasn't entirely sure myself how I stood on that question.

In June 1967 I had sympathized instinctively with the Jewish state, though I remember noting with interest and foreboding a report from Paris, which said that triumphalist demonstrators on the Champs Elysées had honked their car horns – *Isra-el vain-cra!* – to the same beat as the OAS *Algé-rie Fran-çaise!* My evolution since then had been like thousands of other radicals; misery at the rise of the Israeli Right and enhanced appreciation of the plight of the Palestinians, whether in exile or under occupation. Several visits to the region meant that I had met the Palestinians and seen conclusively through those who had argued that they did not 'really' exist. By the time that I moved to the United States, the Left and even the liberals were thrown on the defensive. In America at least, a major part of the ideological cement for the Reagan–Thatcher epoch was being laid on by the neo-conservative school, which was heavily influenced by the Middle East debate and which did not scruple to accuse its critics of anti-Semitism. My baptism of fire with this group came with the Timerman affair, which has been unjustly forgotten in the record of those years.

Even though Jacobo Timerman had been incarcerated and tortured *as a Jew*, his Argentine fascist tormentors were nonetheless felt, by the Reagan administration and by the pre-Falklands Thatcherites, to be fundamentally on our side. (This in spite of the horridly warm relations between the Buenos Aires junta and the Soviet Union.) They did not count, in the new *Kulturkampf*, as a tyranny within the meaning of the act. As a result, Jacobo Timerman had to be defamed.

He was accused of making up his story. He was reviled, in an attack that presaged a later hot favorite term, of covert sympathy for 'terrorism' in Argentina. He was arraigned for making life harder, by his denunciation, for Argentina's peaceable Jewish community. (This charge was given a specially ironic tone by the accusation, made in parallel, that he had overstated the extent of anti-Semitism in that country.) Although some of this slander came from the Francoist Right, who were later to appear in their true colors under the banner of General Singlaub and Colonel North, the bulk of the calumny was provided by neoconservative Jewish columnists and publications. I shall never forget Irving Kristol telling a dinner table at the Lehrman Institute that he did not believe Timerman had been tortured in the first place.

I was very much affected by Timerman's book *Prisoner Without a Name, Cell Without a Number*, partly because I had once spent a few rather terrifying days in Buenos Aires, trying to get news of him while he was *incommunicado*. Not even the most pessimistic person had appreciated quite what he was actually going through. As I read the account of his torture, at the hands of the people who were later picked by Reagan and Casey to begin the training of the *contras*, I was struck by one page in particular. An ideologue of the junta is speaking:

Argentina has three main enemies: Karl Marx, because he tried to destroy the Christian concept of society; Sigmund Freud, because he tried to destroy the Christian concept of the family; and Albert Einstein, because he tried to destroy the Christian concept of time and space.

Here was the foe in plain view. As that pure Austrian Ernst Fischer puts it so pungently in his memoir, *An Opposing Man*: 'The degree of a society's culture can be measured against its attitude towards the Jews. All forms of anti-Semitism are evidence of a reversion to barbarism. Any system which persecutes the Jews, on whatever pretext, has forfeited all right to be regarded as progressive.'

Here were all my adopted godfathers in plain view as well; the three great anchors of the modern, revolutionary intelligence. It was for this reason that, on the few occasions on which I had been asked if I was Jewish, I had been sad to say no, and even perhaps slightly jealous. On the other hand, when in early 1988 I told an editor friend my news, her response was sweet but rather shocking. 'That should make your life easier,' she said. 'Jewish people are *allowed* to criticize Israel.' I felt a surge of annoyance. Was that the use I was supposed to make of it? And did that response, typical as I was to find it, suggest the level to which the debate had fallen? It seemed to me that since the Middle East was becoming nuclearized, and since the United States was a principal armorer and paymaster, it was more in the nature of a civic responsibility to take a critical interest. If Zionism was going to try to exploit Gentile reticence in the post-Holocaust era, it might do so successfully for a time. But it would never be able to negate the tradition of reason and skepticism inaugurated by the real Jewish founding fathers. And one had not acquired that tradition by means of the genes.

As I was preparing for my father's funeral, and readying a short address I planned to give to the mourners, I scanned through a wartime novel in which he had featured as a character. Warren Tute was an author of *The Cruel Sea* school, and had acquired a certain following by his meticulous depiction of life in the Royal Navy. His best known book, *The Cruiser*, had my father in the character of Lieutenant Hale. I didn't find anything in the narrative that would be appropriate for my eulogy. But I did find an internal monologue, conducted by the Master-at-Arms as he mentally reviewed the ship's complement of HMS *Antigone*. The Master-at-Arms dealt in stereotypes:

He knew that Stoker First Class Danny Evans would be likely to celebrate his draft by going on the beer for a week in Tonypandy and then spending the next three months in the Second Class for Leave. He knew that Blacksmith First Class Rogers would try and smuggle service provisions ashore for his mother and that Telegraphist Jacobs was a sea lawyer who kept a copy of Karl Marx in his kitbag.

Good old Telegraphist Jacobs! I could see him now, huddled defensively in his radio shack. Probably teased a bit for his bookishness ('a copy' of Marx, indeed); perhaps called 'Four Eyes' for his glasses and accused of 'swallowing the dictionary' if he ever employed a long word. On shore leave at colonial ports, sticking up for the natives while his hearty shipmates rolled the taxi drivers and the whores. Perhaps enduring a certain amount of ragging at church parade or 'divisions' (though perhaps not; the British lower deck is if anything overly respectful of 'a man's religion'). Resorted to by his comrades in the mess when there was a dispute over King's Regulations or the pay slips. Indefinitely relegated when promotion was discussed – a Captain Jacobs RN would have been more surprising than an Admiral Rickover. In those terrible days of war and blockade, where the air is full of bombast about fighting the Hun, or just fighting, Telegraphist Jacobs argues hoarsely that the enemy is fascism. Probably he has rattled a tin for Spain; collected bandages in the East End for the boys of the International Brigade (whose first British volunteers were two Jewish garment workers).

When the wireless begins to use the weird and frightening new term 'total war', Telegraphist Jacobs already knows what it means. The rest of the time, he overhears the word 'troublemaker' and privately considers it to be no insult.

My father never knew that he had a potential Telegraphist Jacobs for a son, but he hardly ever complained at what he did get, and I salute him for that. I also think with pleasure and pride of him and Jacobs, their vessel battered by the Atlantic and the Third Reich, as they sailed through six years of hell together to total victory. Commander Hitchens, I know, would never have turned a Nelson eye to any bullying. They were, much as the navy dislikes the expression, in the same boat.

As I believe is common with elder sons, I feel more and more deprived, as the days pass, by the thought of conversations that never took place and now never will. In this case, having had the Joycean experience of finding myself an orphan and a Jew more or less simultaneously, I had at least the consolation of curiosity and interest. A week or so after returning from the funeral in England, I telephoned the only rabbi I knew personally and asked for a meeting. Rabbi Robert Goldburg is a most learned and dignified man, who had once invited me to address his Reform congregation in New Haven. He had married Arthur Miller to Marilyn Monroe (converting the latter to Judaism), but resisted the temptation to go on about it too much. After some initial banter about my disclosure ('Aren't you ashamed? Did you see Rabin saying to *break their bones*?') he appointed a time and place. I wanted to ask him what I had been missing.

It may be a bit early to say what I learned from our discussion. The course of reading that was suggested is one I have not yet completed. No frontal challenge to my atheism was presented, though I was counseled to re-examine the 'crude, Robert Ingersoll, nineteenth-century' profession of unbelief. Ever since Maimonides wrote of the Messiah that 'he may tarry', Judaism seems to have rubbed along with a relaxed attitude to the personal savior question, and a frankly skeptical one about questions of wish-thinking such as the afterlife. A. J. Ayer once pointed out that Voltaire was anti-Semitic because he blamed the Jews for Christianity, 'and I'm very much afraid to say that he was quite right. It *is* a Jewish heresy.' When I had first heard him say that, I thought he might be being flippant. But as I talked more with Rabbi Goldburg, I thought that Judaism might turn out to be the most ethically sophisticated tributary of humanism. Einstein, who was urged on me as an alternative to Ingersoll, had allowed himself to speak of 'The Old One', despite refusing allegiance to the god of Moses. He had also said that the old one 'does not play dice with the universe'. Certainly it was from Jews like him that I had learned to hate the humans who thought themselves fit to roll the dice at any time.

Rabbi Goldburg's congregation is well-to-do, and when I visited them as a speaker I had been very impressed by the apparent contrast between their life style, for want of a better term, and their attitudes. I say 'apparent contrast' because it is of course merely philistine to assume that people 'vote their pocketbook' all the time, or that such voting behavior is hard-headed realism instead of the fatuity it so often is. The well-known Jewish pseudo intellectual who had so sweetly observed that American Jews have the income profile of Episcopalians and the voting habits of Puerto Ricans was an example of Reaganism, of what Saul Bellow once called 'the mental rabble of the wised-up world'.

Anyway, what struck me when I addressed this highly educated and professional group was the same as what had struck me when I had once talked to a gathering of Armenians in a leafy suburb in California. They did not scoff or recoil, even when they might disagree, as I droned on about the iniquity and brutality, the greed and myopia that marked Reagan's low tide. They did not rise to suggest that the truth lay somewhere in between, or that moderation was the essential virtue, or that politics was the art of the possible. They seemed to lack that overlay of Panglossian emollience that had descended over the media and the Congress and, it sometimes seemed, over every damn thing. Over drinks afterwards I suddenly thought: Of course. These people already know. They aren't to be fooled by bubbles of prosperity and surges of good feeling. *They know the worst can happen.* It may not be in the genes, but it's in the collective memory and in many individual ones too.

Was this perhaps why I had sometimes 'felt' Jewish? As I look back over possible premonitions, echoes from early life, promptings of memory, I have to suspect my own motives. I am uneasy because to think in this way is, in Kipling's frightening phrase, 'to think with the blood'. Jews may think with the blood if they choose: it must be difficult not to do so. But they – we – must also hope that thinking with the blood does not become general. This irony, too, must help impart and keep alive a sense of preparedness for the worst.

Under the Nuremberg laws, I would have been counted a Blumenthal of Breslau and the denial of that will stop with me. Under the Law of Return I can supposedly redeem myself by moving into the Jerusalem home from which my friend Edward Said has been evicted. We must be able to do better than that. We still live in the pre-history of the human race, where no tribalism can be much better than another and where humanism and internationalism, so much derided and betrayed, need an unsentimental and decisive restatement.

JULIAN BARNES

Mrs Thatcher Remembers

Julian Barnes was born in 1946. His several acclaimed novels include
Flaubert's Parrot *(1984) and* A History of the World in 10½ Chapters
(1989). His most recent novel, England, England, *appeared in 1998. For
some years during the 1990s Barnes wrote a regular column for the*
New Yorker *and in 1995 these columns were collected as* Letters from
London. *'Mrs Thatcher Remembers' was one of these 'letters' and first
appeared in the* New Yorker *in November 1993.*

A few years ago an elderly friend of mine was being examined in a
British hospital for possible brain damage. A psychiatrist catechized
her patronizingly. 'Can you tell me what day of the week it is?' 'That's
not important to me,' came the cagey reply. 'Well, can you tell me what
season of the year it is?' 'Of course I can.' The doctor plodded on to
his next tester. 'And can you tell me who is the Prime Minister?'
'Everyone knows *that*,' my friend answered, half triumphant, half
derisive. 'It's Thatch.'

Everyone did indeed know, for more than eleven long years, that it
was Thatch. No other Prime Minister in my lifetime had been always
there to the extent that Margaret Thatcher was, in terms not just of
longevity but also of intensity. She trained herself to sleep only four
hours a night, and most mornings the nation awoke to a parade-ground
snarl, to the news that it was an 'orrible shower, and the instruction to
double round the barracks again in full pack or else. Those who met
her in private confirmed that she was just as powerful an eyeballer as
on the parade ground. The poet Philip Larkin wrote of the moment
when 'I got the blue flash', going on to moan appreciatively to another
correspondent, 'What a blade of steel!' Alan Clark, a minor Tory
minister and rakehell nob diarist, treasured a moment when 'her blue
eyes flashed' and 'I got a full dose of personality compulsion, something
of the *Führer Kontakt*.' (He also noted her 'very small feet and attractive
– not bony – ankles in the 1940 style'.) Even President Mitterrand,

whom one might expect to be immune on both national and political grounds, can be heard succumbing to La Thatch in Jacques Attali's *Verbatim.* 'The eyes of Stalin, the voice of Marilyn Monroe,' he muses in tranced paradox.

When she came to the Tory leadership in 1975 it seemed as if she might be a brief and token phenomenon. She was of the Tory right, and British politics had for years shuffled between governments of the Tory left and the Labour right: little bits of tax-lowering and denationalization on the one hand, little bits of tax-raising and re-nationalization on the other. Worse, she was a woman: though both major parties had pachyderm prejudices against the species, it had always been assumed that the officially progressive Labour Party was the more likely party to put a woman at its head. Tory women, it was known, preferred men; and so did Tory men. Finally, there was Mrs Thatcher's apparent suburban Englishness: it was confidently asserted that she would get no votes north of the Watford Gap (a motorway service area in the South Midlands). So her first election victory was put down to the temporary weakness of the Labour Party; her second to the knock-on effect of the Falklands War, her third to renewed Opposition-fissuring. That she was deprived of the chance of winning a fourth was due not to the Labour Party, still less to the Tory faithful in the country at large, but to a disgruntled Parliamentary Party which decided (and only by a whisker) that she had passed her vote-by date.

Those who opposed her, who felt each day of her rule as a sort of political migraine, tended to make two fundamental miscalculations. The first was to treat her as some kind of political weirdo. This was understandable, since she was a Tory ideologue, and when had the Conservatives last been a party of ideology, of inflexible programmes, of Holy Grail beliefs? What took years to sink in was the nasty truth that Mrs Thatcher represented and successfully appealed to a strong and politically disregarded form of Englishness. To the liberal, the snobbish, the metropolitan, the cosmopolitan, she displayed a parochial, small-shopkeeper mentality, puritanical and Poujadiste, self-interested and xenophobic, half sceptred-isle nostalgia and half count-your-change bookkeeping. But to those who supported her she was a plain speaker, a clear and visionary thinker who embodied no-nonsense, stand-on-your-own-two-feet virtue, a patriot who saw that we had been living on borrowed time and borrowed money for far too long. If socialism's the Atlantic alliance as the relationship of wise old Greece (Britain, in case you were wondering) to vigorous young Rome. For a while, at least, during Reagan's sleepy-senior-citizen act, Thatcher could pose as the dynamic ideas-merchant.

'Personally dominant, supremely self-confident, infuriatingly stubborn', Mrs Thatcher 'held a strange mixture of broad views and narrow prejudices.' This is the summing up not of some vexed Labourite but of the normally unctuous Kenneth Baker, one of her Party chairmen. (Baker was once tipped for the succession, and his oiliness provoked the comment 'I have seen the future and it smirks'.) She made up her mind, kept to it, spoke it, and repeated it verbatim for as long as necessary. In *The Downing Street Years* she dismisses the hapless John Nott, Defence Minister during the Falklands War, with the neutering line 'His vice was second thoughts.' None of them for Maggie. Larkin was once invited to a dinner party at the house of the historian Hugh Thomas, and recorded her combative and unself-questioning manner: 'Watching her was like watching a top-class tennis-player; no "Uh-huh, well, what do other people think about that", just bang back over the net.' Since the other guests included Isaiah Berlin, V. S. Naipaul, Tom Stoppard, Mario Vargas Llosa, J. H. Plumb, V. S. Pritchett, Anthony Powell, Stephen Spender, Anthony Quinton, and A. Alvarez, this was quite tony company to play tennis in. But then Mrs Thatcher was no more snob-struck by 'vain intellectuals', as she characterizes the breed in her book, than by Tory toffs. There was an early move in her premiership to present her as a PM who liked a workout on the ideas mat with a few top brains – the historian Paul Johnson was one such scrimmager – but it does not seem to have lasted long. Certainly none of the above names even makes it into the index of *The Downing Street Years*: you can have 'Berlin disco bomb' but not 'Berlin, Isaiah'.

Indeed, the subject of the arts occupies a whole two pages here, and one of those is spent describing Mrs Thatcher's heroic but thwarted attempt to bring the Thyssen art collection to Britain. ('It was not only a great treasure but a good investment,' she typically notes.) Where other prime ministers – however truly or hypocritically – like to maintain that the arts are at least a decoration, if not actually an additive, to life, with Mrs Thatcher they do not enter the equation: if you have that sort of spare time, you aren't doing your job as PM. She remembers Macmillan telling a group of young MPs that 'prime ministers (not having a department of their own) have plenty of spare time for reading. He recommended Disraeli and Trollope. I have sometimes wondered if he was joking.' He almost certainly wasn't, and it's significant that John Major, who has gone back to the Macmillan 'easy-listening' style of premiership, also claims Trollope as his favourite writer – indeed, is a member of the Trollope Society. (The fact that the novelist was scathing about politicians, and especially about Tories, doesn't seem to bother modern Conservatives.) Mrs Thatcher, by contrast, cites as her favourite reading 'thrillers by Frederick Forsyth and John le Carré'. This is probably just as well. The sight of Mrs Thatcher pretending to like art would not be for the squeamish.

Far better is her unfeigned response on the occasion when Kingsley Amis presented her at No. 10 with an autographed copy of his novel *Russian Hide-and-Seek*. 'What's it about?' she asked him. 'Well,' he explained, 'in a way it's about a future Britain under Russian occupation.' 'Huh!' she cried. 'Can't you do any better than that? Get yourself another crystal ball!' This put-down ('unfair and unanswerable', Amis noted) failed to decrease the novelist's devotion to the Prime Minister. In his memoirs he calls her 'one of the best-looking women I had ever met' and adds this recherché compliment to her allure: 'This quality is so extreme that, allied to her well-known photogenic quality, it can trap me for split seconds into thinking I am looking at a science-fiction illustration of some time ago showing the beautiful girl who has become President of the Solar Federation in the year 2200.' More routinely, Amis admits that Mrs Thatcher has replaced the Queen as the woman he dreams about most; once, she even drew him close and murmured lovingly, 'You've got such an *interesting* face.' Well, she may make his dreams, but, no, he doesn't make her index, either. Nor, for that matter, does the name of a British subject sentenced to death by a foreign power during her premiership. You would think this might have caused some offence to the notions of British sovereignty, honour and independence that bray out like trumpet cadenzas from these pages; but apparently not. Bad luck, Citizen Rushdie.

Those high concepts are, by contrast, regularly invoked when it comes to one of the central events of Mrs Thatcher's premiership: the Falklands War of 1982. Her account of it has a novel clarity: history with little nuance or complication, whether political or moral. The Argentine invasion of the islands was completely unforeseeable (she set